SANDWICH

A Cape Cod Town

About the Seals:

The double seal, shown on the back cover of this book, was used in Sandwich, Kent, England from the Middle Ages to impress both sides of a lump of wax attached by a ribbon to an official document. It shows a royal British Lion and a ship entering a harbor. Sandwich was historically a ferry point to the continent; the title Earl of Sandwich was conferred by Charles II in 1662 with a special role to escort his future Queen and other royal visitors to England.

The later Sandwich seal, shown below and for impression on paper itself, showed half the ship and half the lion. All Massachusetts towns were required to establish a town seal by 1900 and the design shown on the front cover of this book, was proposed by Miss Melanie Elisabeth Norton, daughter of Colonel Charles L. Norton, and soon to be wife of Jonathan Leonard. She drew American eagles in place of the British lions. The Latin inscription means "Haven after many a shipwreck."

SANDWICH

A Cape Cod Town

by R. A. Lovell, Jr.

Another plantation was begun (and called Sandwich) about fifteen miles beyond Plimouth, towards Cape Cod, by many families, which removed from Sagus otherwise Lynn.

—John Winthrop, *History of New England, Vol. 1 p. 253.*

If no other lover of the things of old will undertake to set in order the annals of Sandwich, the publick may well expect the favour from the historian of Plimouth. The possession of the faculty is evidence of the call to such a work

—James Savage, editor of Winthrop's *History, 1825.*

Published by the
Town of Sandwich, Massachusetts
2019

Cover photo credit (top): Boardwalk: Original photo by Kathleen Coggeshall

Cover photo credit (bottom): Postcard depicting Main Street circa, 1908: Town of Sandwich Archives Collection

Interior Layout & Cover Design: K.R. Conway, Wicked Whale Publishing

DEDICATION

The 5th printing is dedicated to the Friends of the Sandwich Town Archives and its members. This book would not be available without their tireless efforts to incorporate Russell's edits in the newest edition and their work to gain public support and funding for its republication.

Second Printing 1987

Third Printing 1996

Fourth Printing: 2015

Fifth Printing: 2019

LCCCN 84-052758

974.492
L94
Lovell, (Russell) A Jr., 1918-2018
Sandwich, A Cape Cod Town. Sandwich Archives and
Historical Center, 1984. 2nd printing 1987. 3rd printing 1996, 4th printing 2015
photographs, maps.
I. Title. 1. Sandwich, Mass. - History.
2. Bourne, Mass. - History
LC: 84-052758

ISBN: 978-0-9967023-0-0

Design and Production

Wicked Whale Publishing

P.O. Box 264

Sagamore Beach, MA 02562-9998

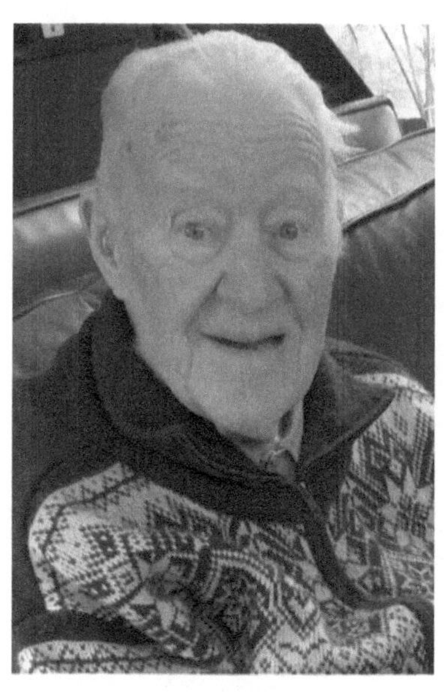

ABOUT THE AUTHOR

The author of this book, Russell A. Lovell, Jr., passed away at his home in Sandwich on the evening of December 31, 2018, two weeks after the celebration of his 100th birthday. Mr. Lovell left us with a legacy of dedicated study and passion for the unique history of Sandwich. Mr. Lovell moved to Sandwich in 1970 and was quickly drawn into the study of Town's distinct past. He worked with the Sandwich Historical Society Glass Museum, Sandwich Historical Commission, Archives and Historical Center Committee, and the Thornton W. Burgess Society to gather the knowledge and expertise to compile and publish this book. While serving as the Town Archivist he devoted his energy and time to the painstaking task of research and preservation. In 1984, the culmination of his tireless efforts resulted in the publication of "*Sandwich, A Cape Cod Town*" which has been cherished by many in our community and beyond throughout the years. He was publicly bestowed with the title "*Town Historian Emeritus*" by Town Clerk, Taylor D. White, during the signing ceremony of the 4th printing of this book in March 2016. He will truly be missed but never forgotten.

FOREWORD TO THE THIRD EDITION

It is with great pleasure that we present a further edition of "Sandwich A Cape Cod Town." The first issue in 1985 was of 2,500 copies, and included the names of advance subscribers. The second edition in 1987 of 1,000 copies was enriched by 47 pages of "Notes on Sources" reflecting the extent of research involved.

New information about Sandwich since the original publication includes the following items:

1. The second wife of founder Edmund Freeman was Elizabeth Raymen or Raymond, whose marriage is shown in Cowfold Sussex Parish records August 10,1632. This is the Elizabeth who rests with Edmund under the unique "Saddle & Pillion" grave markers in Sandwich.

2. A Boston lawyer named Thomas Lechford in the period 1638-1641 kept accurate notes of his cases, deeds, wills and other transactions. These were published as "Notebook Kept by Thomas Lechford Esq" in 1885 and again in 1988. The text of a deed from Thomas Dexter Senior to his son Thomas Dexter of a grist mill and lands in Sandwich is dated October 24,1638, showing that our grist mill was already in existence by that date.

3. Plymouth Colony Records have numerous references to a Thomas Boreman, Burman, Bordman etc. from 1633 on, who was of Sandwich in 1637 and who appears on our Meadowlands list of 1640 and our Arms list of 1643. Descendants of the Thomas Bowerman who married in Barnstable and founded a large family in Falmouth prefer to believe that their ancestor was the carpenter who rebuilt the Plymouth fort in 1635. However, a careful analysis of references shows two separate careers:

   a. *Thomas Boardman* was in Plymouth 1633 from London, repaired the fort in 1635, in Sandwich 1638 with wife Luce, on our Meadowlands list 1640, Arms list 1643, took the Oath of Fidelity 1644, removed to Yarmouth by 1648, active there on committees, married secondly in 1678 Elizabeth Rider Cole, died 1689, widow alive 1693, no record of his earlier children as residents in this County.

   b. *Thomas Bowerman* came to Sandwich from Saugus, removed to Barnstable by 1639, married Hannah Annable March 3,1644/5, active in West Barnstable to death in 1663. Had property in Middleboro and Falmouth. His son Thomas Jr. married Mary Harper of Sandwich and lived in Falmouth from 1690, a member of the Friends Meeting, numerous descendants.

4. The term "Incorporation" of the five early Cape Cod towns was given by historian Frederick Freeman as follows:

   Sandwich Yarmouth & Barnstable 1639

Nauset 1646 (later Eastham)

Sucanesset 1686 (later Falmouth)

However, the charter or patent for Plymouth Colony did not include the word "incorporate" or refer to the right to establish new town government, so that this "incorporation" of towns is an invention by Freeman without authority or meaning, even though the dates of "incorporation" appear on town seals in civic programs and local histories. What these dates signify is the acceptance of deputies from the towns to Plymouth quarterly court meetings, instead of the general requirement that all free men attend.

Towns in Plymouth Colony were simply clusters of population where local control came only very slowly, in contrast to Mass Bay Colony where town governments had strong powers and grew rapidly.

5. With the sole exception of Thomas Tupper, the "Ten Men of Saugus" who founded Sandwich do not come off well as participants in early town government, and in the case of the marshlands allocation show themselves as distinctly indifferent to the interests of their fellow townsmen. To the original 60 families here, access to the salt marshes was critically important for salt hay, since upland hayfields had not been cleared. However, the Ten Men declared themselves owners of all the marsh along the shores near their farms, forcing the other families to go much further to marsh along the barrier beaches. This unfair allocation was protested strongly in spring 1638, but was not finally settled until 1640 when the Ten Men got half their original allocation and had to take the other halves at remote points. The real town leaders who carried this out were Richard Bourne, John Vincent, George Allen, Robert Bodfish and Joseph Holway.

6. Reverend Stephen Bachiler was born in 1561 and must have been one of the oldest people in New England. He brought with him from England a number of Wing, Sanborn and other relatives in 1632, who stayed with him in several removes around Mass. Bay where he attempted to preach. Governor Winthrop knew him well but objected to his theology. This Rev. Bachiler and a small group of hardy supporters walked to Cape Cod in the fall of 1637 and started a settlement at what is now the boundary between Barnstable and Yarmouth, apparently without formal sanction from Plymouth Colony. Lacking support for new supplies and settlers, the Bachiler party walked back north in the spring of 1638 after what must have been a winter of great hardship. We feel it is logical that widow Deborah Wing and her four sons were part of this group, and that they remained in Sandwich in early 1638. Their home was at present 8 Morse Rd. In 1647 Deborah and her son John and friend John Dillingham removed to Yarmouth, then in 1657 relocated again to what is now Brewster. Plymouth Colony objected to their settling so far from town government, but they persisted and both Wing and Dillingham founded large families. Both Deborah and her father died in their 100th year.

7. Daniel Wing Senior of Sandwich, had a daughter Lydia who was a most remarkable rebel against the conventional life style in her family and town. She returned to Sandwich about 1677 at age 30 with two small sons born in Rhode Island, and lived with these boys in a primitive hovel previously used by Indian women tending to summer crops on open planting fields. This was unheard of, and furthermore, the land had not been granted to her or to anyone. (This field where she settled is now the park around the Military Museum at Heritage Plantation of Sandwich). Her living here was a matter of deep embarrassment to her father and to the Quaker community, who gave her gifts of shoes, com, wool and cash, and would have found her a proper house, but she refused to move. Her story continues to her death at about 57, a rebel to the end.

8. Another extraordinary Sandwich woman was Bathsheba Ruggles born in the Newcomb Tavern on Grove St. in 1746. Her parents brought her to Hardwick in 1753 where she grew up in the stormy but glamorous home of Brigadier Timothy Ruggles. She married one Joshua Spooner of Middleboro and settled in Brookfield where she had four children. Obviously of unbalanced mind, she plotted and carried out the death of her husband with the aid of three ex-soldiers. This crime, the trial of the four in Worcester, and the execution of the four by hanging in Worcester July 2, 1778 was of sensational interest at the time and ever since. Her minister, Rev. Maccarty of Worcester, and her brother-in-law, Dr. John Green, as well as several midwives, urged that her execution be delayed until after the birth of her child, as she was five months pregnant. Nevertheless she was hung, possibly out of an irrational fear and hostility toward her father who had become a leading Tory. Now a new piece of evidence has emerged—that the State official, John Avery Jr., who signed her death warrant was closely related to the victim, Joshua Spooner, and was able to retaliate in a most illegal and inhumane way.

9. Nathaniel Freeman Jr. of Sandwich was a Harvard graduate in 1787 and classmate of future President John Quincy Adams. He was elected to Congress and was clearly headed for a public career. However, he died in Sandwich in 1800 of tuberculosis, and chose in his last months of pain and frustration to use alcohol. This tragic case was discussed by the minister, Rev. Jonathan Burr, with the visiting Yale President Timothy Dwight, and found its way into Dwight's volume "Travels in New England" that a number of Sandwich residents were "debased by the use of ardent spirits". There is no evidence that our town was any different in this respect from other New England towns, and in fact support for temperance is repeatedly found here.

10. A flat stone with rough inscribed letters was seen in the 1880's by Nathan Bourne Hartford of the town of Bourne, when he was a boy. The stone was located in an Indian home overlooking Great Herring Pond in Bournedale. Hartford and his friend Percival Hall Lombard organized the excavation of the site of the Aptucxet Trading Post (built 1627) in the

1920's and the erection here of a replacement building as a unique historical center for the Bourne Historical Society. The inscribed stone was relocated here in the 1930's and much publicized as of possible Runic (Viking) origin, or even of Punic (Phoenician) origin, and experts made readings of its possible meaning in both languages. However, serious study of many inscribed stones in the USA leads to the conclusion that no Runic stone or Viking presence has been proven in the whole USA, and no Phoenician presence anywhere in North or South America. Hence the Aptucxet stone must be regarded as an Indian petroglyph, but still of great interest.

The Sandwich Archives and Historical Center at 145 Main St. Sandwich, Mass 02563 will be responsible for the distribution of this Third Edition of "Sandwich A Cape Cod Town" through local outlets and by mail across the country. Shortly we can expect the publication of "Vital Records of Sandwich Mass to 1885" by the New England Historic Genealogical Society, which will stimulate new interest in Sandwich history and families. The Archives has prepared a list of page-by-page corrections and additions to the text of the book "Sandwich A Cape Cod Town" which will be available for sale at nominal cost, and readers are urged to obtain this. The Archives has also a stock of 47-page copies of the "Notes on Sources" which should be of value to those who own only the first edition.

RAL

INTRODUCTION

Tourists abound in Sandwich village, photographing the spire of the Wren church, feeding the waterfowl, watching the miller, wandering through the shining galleries of the Glass Museum, the beautiful grounds of Heritage Plantation, and the charming Burgess Museums. Questions are constantly asked, not only by the daily visitors, but by prospective settlers who buy old houses or new ones as Sandwich grows swiftly in size. There are also many questions arising from the national interest in genealogy-where did my Sandwich ancestors live? What did they do? Where are they buried?

Books or pamphlets have not been available to answer many of these questions. Some visitors have obtained help at the Sandwich Public Library or at the Sandwich Archives Center, but wide gaps in written source material persist. In the Barnstable County histories of Frederick Freeman, Simeon Deyo and Charles Swift are Sandwich chapters, but these nineteenth century works are dated and do not readily answer modern questions. Detailed source material is available in Plymouth Colony Records, in early newspapers, in our Town Meeting Records and in family genealogies, but this sort of material is hard to find and even harder to interpret. At the opposite end of the information spectrum is the weekly to annual tourist literature endlessly repeating cliches and generalities.

The themes of Sandwich history which are of the greatest public interest, indeed of national significance, are probably five—the instant acceptance of the first Quaker visitors here and start of meetings in 1658; the early efforts to teach and convert Indians resulting in the formation of Mashpee Reservation; the growth and spread of many American families from here; the making of Sandwich glass; and the origin of the Thornton W. Burgess wildlife and conservation message. Since the establishment of the Sandwich Archives and Historical Center in 1977, systematic studies have been made which have shed new light on all these themes, and have evolved important new understandings of other parts of Sandwich history. These include the position of the town founder, Edmund Freeman, in the town and Colony; the severe land allocation problems of the early town; the location of the houses of the families in 1667; the lands and activities of the Bourne family in Mashpee; the issuance of the common lands in sheep pasture, twenty-acre lots and woodlots; the life here and later of Timothy Ruggles; the presence here of two groups of Acadians; the role of Nathaniel Freeman before, during and after the Revolution; events in the forty-year period of the Benjamin Percival diary; the building of the Wren church; the settlement of the borders of Sandwich and of Mashpee, the way in which Town Neck was lost to public ownership; the unique story of the breakup, reassembly and second breakup of the Freeman Farm; and the analysis of the growth and decline of the early Sandwich families. This new historical material richly deserves public attention and invites further reflection and study. In the Archives Center work a number of common assumptions about Sandwich have been found to be mistaken, such as the early dates on the Hoxie, Tupper, Skiff and Dillingham houses; the Cotton house as part of the Daniel Webster Inn; the first meetinghouse as a log cabin; the death of Marshal Barlow in the snow at Christopher's Hollow; and that the floor of the Town Hall was sloping to prevent dancing at the request of the Quakers.

For clarity in reading the earlier chapters of this book, we wish to insert here a note on the double-year dates used. Up to and including the year 1752, in the period from January 1 through March 24, the year is properly defined by a double number as 1699/1700 or 1751/2. The reason is that both a religious year beginning March 25 (the Annunciation, or conception of Christ) and a calendar year beginning January 1 were recognized, some scribes using one system and some the other. Only the use of both years makes it perfectly clear, the lower number being the religious year, the second and higher number the calendar year. From March 25 on the two were the same. Among those who used the religious year, William Bradford wrote in *Of Plimoth Plantation* — "and being now come to the 25th of March, I shall begin the year 1621." After 1752 only the calendar year was officially used.

Our interest in writing this book has been to bring to the people of Sandwich and to our cousins and friends around this country a clear and straightforward account of what happened in Sandwich over its long existence. The initial text became far too long and we have been forced to prune greatly what we would wish to relate, and have also dropped much appendix material (lists of officials, ministers, veterans, etc.) and have even reluctantly dropped the lengthy footnotes and source references for each chapter. These references and supplementary materials of course remain available and we invite questions from those who wish to pursue one or another chapter or period.

This book is chronological within subject clusters. There are eight chapters on the 1600s, seven on the 1700s, twelve on the eventful 1800s and eight on the present century. There are three chapters devoted entirely to Indians, which may be unexpected. Readers looking for details of the period since 1950 may be disappointed. Abundant material indeed is available in the daily pages of the *Cape Cod Standard Times,* in other newspapers, in the Selectmen's correspondence, and in other files of town business. However, time and space for this book became increasingly restrictive and we have had to leave the recent period of intense change and rapid growth for later perspective. We have made use of oral histories, both taped and verbally recorded, for our twentieth century chapters. The papers written by members of the Historical Society earlier in this century were found to preserve much of the oral traditions, but to lack documentation and detail in many cases. These gaps have been filled by studies of Town Meeting Records, of family assemblages from vital records, of cemetery records, and in systematic surveys of houses and buildings. Because of this wealth of background, we urge and hope that the town will permit publication of these further elements of Sandwich history:

Vital Records to 1884 when the Town divided.

Town Meeting Records through 1792 (the first three volumes).

Inventories of historic assets in buildings, sites and cemeteries.

The Percival Diary, 1777-1817, a Sandwich treasure.

The list of those who have contributed to this history personally through documents, photographs and information is long. At the Sandwich Historical Society Doris Kershaw, Gordon Swan and Martha Hassell were extremely helpful. In the Nye, Tupper and Wing Family Associations, Rosanna Cullity, Dr. Eleanor Tupper Bierkoe and Ruth Sisson respectively have been unfailingly interested and generous. In locating the original Percival Diary we must all be grateful to Seaver R. Harlow and his cousin, Esther C. O'Brien. Others who have helped greatly include Robert L. Armstrong, Ray Barlow, Elizabeth Beale, Amelia Bingham, Martha Blake, Virginia Wing Blake, Donald Bourne, Charles Burke, Mildred Cahoon, Anna Caron, Peter Cook, Letitia Coppi, Norma Crosby, Shirley Cross, Carolyn Crowell, Eunice Dickinson and her sister Annie D. Williamson, David Douglas, Warner Eldredge, Beth Ellis, Robert H. Ellis, William J. Ellis, Robert Farson, Clara N. Field, William E. Foster, Ella Freeman, Stanley Freeman, Bertrand French, Alice Gibbs, Howard Goodwin, Reverend Harry Gordon, Clarence Haines, Benjamin S. Harrison, Ellen Holway, Channing Hoxie, Harold and Margaret Hutcheson, Lombard Jones, Joan Kaiser, Roberta Lawrence, Helen Mooney, Joan Morrow, Mabel Morrow, Mary Haines Morrow, Mildred Nickerson, Blake Norris, Henry Perry, Frances W. Pope, J. Louis Roberti, Mary Leonard Shaw, Martha Gibbs Sigl, Donald R. Small, Dr. Dirk Struik, Nina Sutton, John Tassinari, Col. Ronald Thomas, J. Albert Torrey, Eugene Williams and Clare Morse Wing.

In the actual assemblage of this book many more thanks are in order. Barbara Gill has overseen the proofreading, the pruning, and organized the photographs and maps. Caroline Kardell provided informative contacts with learned societies, plus organization and bibliography. Jane Morrow Mercier performed feats of typing from microfilm and other sources which now seem legendary. After her, Leona Koslowsky, Dorothy O'Connor and Kathleen Pond have made the text a reality. Bruce Stanford helped with town funds at a critical point and Mrs. Edna Petitjean gave us a most necessary and welcome hand in how to improve wording, how to punctuate and how to capitalize. Some six hundred friends of Sandwich history showed their confidence and support by ordering and paying for their copies of the book well in advance. To them go our gratitude and appreciation; their names are listed in the later pages as a permanent record.

Lastly the author wishes to express to the voters of the town his appreciation of the privilege and honor it has been to be allowed to work for the town in the recent years of restricted budgets and competing claims. The town's history is a rich and extraordinary one in which all can take pride. The errors and omissions in this reading will all be mine.

R. A. Lovell, Jr., Sandwich, Mass., July 1984.

CONTENTS

THE SPIRIT OF NEW ENGLAND

This picture was taken by Asa S. Wing Jr. and appeared as the Frontispiece in the July 1941 issue of the Magazine Antiques. The editors valued its attractive composition, clear photography and the purity of its New England scene, with the white church, the tall elms, the colonial house, the millpond and horse-drawn wagon. The photograph was taken in the mid-1930s when two telegraph poles were present but the overhead wires had not become obtrusive. The wagon driver was Wallace Howes. The church at this time had not been restored and was used only for two summer services a year, with other Federated services at the Unitarian Church nearby. The Dunbar house still had its original portico, later replaced by a broken pediment and lights design on the facade of the house.

CHAPTER 1

SETTLING SANDWICH

One is struck by the number of voyages made from Northern Europe to the New England region after the abandonment of the Greenland settlement, but before the *Mayflower*. Fishermen came annually, probably in large numbers, but left few traces. Spain was granted the whole North American coast by a Papal Edict of 1493, but England and France ignored this claim. For England, John Cabot explored the northern coasts for England in 1495 and 1496, and others in 1502. For France, Verrazzano explored the coast in 1524, Cartier in 1534 to 1540 and Champlain in 1603. Sir Walter Raleigh attempted a settlement in Virginia in 1587. In 1602 Bartholomew Gosnold was the first to leave a detailed description of the Cape Cod area, landing at Cuttyhunk and on the south coast, as well as Provincetown. Gosnold aided in the later settlement at Jamestown in 1607 and died there. In 1606 formal patents were issued to the London Company for settlements in "Virginia" (south of latitude 41°), and to the Plymouth Company for settlements north of 38°. There were several attempts to settle Maine between 1607 and 1617. Captain John Smith coined the term "New England" in his 1614 map and named the harbor of New Plymouth. His map called the Sandwich area "Chawam Barwick." The Dutch, too, had explored this coast and called the Sandwich area "Chawam Boswijk." The word Chawam is strongly suggestive of our Shawme.

There were also early voyages here by traders, both French and English, some of whom were unscrupulous with the Indians, killing or enslaving those who came aboard, which of course meant problems for the next visitors to that area. A French vessel was wrecked off the outer Cape in 1616 and all but three of the crew were killed by the Nausets in retribution for previous abuses. These three were enslaved and of these, two were passed up Cape "for sport." The one who remained, a blond man, was spared and allowed by Sachem Aspinet to marry, and is said to have warned Aspinet of the coming power of the whites. His grave, including the body of his child, was accidentally uncovered by the Pilgrims in 1620 at Truro. In 1619 Captain Thomas Dermer visited New England, which he had seen as a lieutenant of John Smith's in 1614; he now brought back the Indian Squanto from Europe, who had been abducted in 1614 by the infamous Thomas Hunt. Dermer learned of the two French captives and is said to have recovered them at what is now called Monument Neck on Buzzards Bay, just south of the Manomet River. Dermer called this place Frenchman's Point. He took the two Frenchmen to Virginia, and in the spring of 1620 returned to Cape Cod and visited New Plymouth. (His account of New Plymouth, dated June 30, 1620, finally came into William Bradford's hands.) Dermer was attacked by Indians at Chatham and again at Martha's Vineyard and escaped, but died of his wounds in Virginia.

The Sandwich Area before 1637

In January 1622/3, Gov. Bradford came to Sachem Caunacum in the Manomet River area to buy corn for the Colony. He would then have seen for himself the geographic feature that made the Sandwich area unique as a bridge between Massachusetts Bay on the north and Buzzards Bay on the south. The overland distance between the bays was eight miles, but to an Indian in a canoe, only one half mile was portage. One could paddle up the Scusset River to its headwaters, walk over the saddle to the Manomet River (at present Bournedale) and float down to the other bay. The Pilgrims took good advantage of this situation in 1627 when they built a small vessel and a trading post on Monument Neck for trading with the Indians and with the Dutch at Manhattan. Bradford says:

> "That they might ye better take all convenient opportunities to follow their trade, both to maintaine themselves, and to disingage them of those great sumes which they stood charged with and bound for, they resolved to build a smale pinass at Manamet, a place 20 miles from ye plantation, standing on ye sea to ye southward of them unto which, by an other creeke on this side, they could cary their goods, within 4 or 5 miles, and then transport them over land to their vessell, and so avoyd the compasing of Cap-Codd, and those deangerous shoulds and so make any vioage to ye southward in much shorter time, and with farr less danger. Also for ye safeties of their vessell & goods, they builte a house their, and kept some servants, who also planted corne, and reared some swine, and were allways ready to goe out with ye barke when ther was occasion. All which tooke good effecte, and turned to their profite."

This was the scene then for the celebrated visit to Plymouth by the Secretary of the Dutch Governor General at Manhattan, Isaac de Rasieres. In October 1627, the secretary came to the Aptuxcet Trading Post in his vessel, the *Nassau,* and asked that the Pilgrims send a vessel down the coast to Scusset to meet him. This visit was historic for its accurate description of Plymouth of that day and for de Rasieres' introducing the Pilgrims to the use of wampum as a medium of trade with the Indians. Secretary de Rasieres referred to Frenchman's Point, showing that he too knew of Dermer's paper.

Another early event in the Sandwich area is the wreck of a small vessel from Boston in January 1631/2. This is described by Goodwin as follows:

> "Richard Garrett, a shoemaker at Boston, sailed for Plymouth, with his daughter and four men. Near the Gurnet a storm struck them, their stone killock broke in pieces, and after several hours their boat stranded on the Cape. Landing, they found no fuel. Two men started on foot for Plymouth, and seven miles along met two

squaws whose husbands were close at hand. Next day one of the Indians went forward with them; but one of the whites died at the Manomet trading-house, and the other on reaching Plymouth. In the meantime the second Indian husband had gone back to the boat, where, building a wigwam over the four sufferers and making a fire, he carefully nursed them. Garrett soon dying, the Indian with his tomahawk chopped in the frozen ground a grave eighteen inches deep, and to protect the body from wolves brought wood and made a pile over the spot. Bradford had by this time sent a relief boat from Plymouth, but yet another man died on the spot from gangrene. The only survivors, the Garrett girl and Henry Harwood, 'a godly young man' from Boston were taken to Plymouth."

We suggest that the wreck was in the Scorton Beach area, and that the seven-mile walk brought the two men to the present Bournedale sector where there was an Indian village, and where the Indians showed such compassion. Goodwin adds that these Indians would have been "well rewarded as Bradford was very scrupulous in such cases."

The trading post was unroofed and wrecked by the great hurricane of August 15, 1635, and was not rebuilt. The site however was well known to the Sandwich settlers who were later granted land there, Thomas Burgess and his son-in-law Ezra Perry. The site was excavated and described in the 1850's and completely rebuilt in 1930 as an historic attraction, now known as the Aptucxet Trading Post.

The Ten Men of Saugus

The first information of the settling of Sandwich is in an item in the Plymouth Colony Records dated April 3, 1637 reading as follows:

> "It is also agreed by the Court that those tenn men of Saugust, viz Edmond Freeman, Henry Feake, Thomas Dexter, Edward Dillingham, William Wood, John Carman, Richard Chadwell, William Almey, Thomas Tupper & George Knott shall have liberty to view a place to sitt down & have sufficient lands for three score famylies, upon the conditions propounded to them by the Governor and Mr. Winslowe."

The Lynn historian, Alonzo Lewis, wrote of the migration down to Cape Cod:

> "This year (1637) a large number of people removed from Lynn and commenced a new settlement at Sandwich. The grant of the town was made on the third of April by the Colony of Plymouth. . .Thomas Dexter did not remove, but the rest of the above named went with forty six other men from Lynn."

Saugus Plantation, from which most of the sixty founding families of Sandwich had moved, was first settled in 1629 and occupied a huge stretch of land between Charlestown and Salem. With the development of Salem and Boston, following the massive influx of settlers in 1630, Saugus became a well-travelled area and increased rapidly in population. Its name was changed to Lynn late in 1637. The original area of Saugus Plantation now comprises the eight cities and towns of Lynn, Lynnfield, Nahant, Reading, North Reading, Wakefield, Saugus and Swampscott.

What of the departure of so large a group from Saugus? It was a unique event as far as Plymouth Colony was concerned, to receive a whole new plantation of nearly sixty families. In 1637 Governor Winthrop was deeply concerned with the Pequod War, and had just seen a large group depart to form a new Colony at New Haven. The assistant Governor, William Coddington, had just left to join the exiled Roger Williams in Rhode Island. Mary Dyer and Anne Hutchinson had had ominous irregular births. Anne Hutchinson and her followers would soon be expelled. These were all traumatic events, while the orderly departure of a group from Saugus was not seen as a problem or an unlucky matter. The influx of new people from England continued to increase; from Saugus many had already gone up into Essex County and New Hampshire to settle there. Alonzo Lewis of Lynn noted for 1640:

> "In the short space of ten years from its settlement we have seen six other towns deriving their origin from Lynn: yet the place continued to abound with inhabitants, and this year beheld the commencement of the seventh."

This was to be Southampton, Long Island. Lewis also notes that a few from Lynn also moved to Yarmouth and to Barnstable on Cape Cod.

Those Who Went to Sandwich

The impetus for founding the new town on Cape Cod originated from a dedicated and persuasive leader, Edmund Freeman of Pulborough, Sussex. He arrived in October 1635 on the ship *Abigail* with his wife Elizabeth and their four children Edmund, John, Alice and Elizabeth. Freeman was a person of some prestige being the brother-in-law of Mr. John Beauchamp of London, an investor in Colonial ventures who had a stake in Plymouth Colony.

The English origins of Edmund Freeman are better known than those of many early settlers in New England. He owned property in Pulborough, Sussex, where he married his first wife Bennett Hodsoll, and had six children. Two died young, and Bennett herself died in 1630. Edmund then married a woman named Elizabeth whose identity has long been sought by his descendants and by genealogists. She has been called Gurney, Gravely, Perry and Bennett, but we believe now that her name was Elizabeth Raymen or Raymond as shown in her marriage to Edmund Freeman August 10, 1632 at Shipley Sussex. As we saw above, Edmund, Elizabeth, and four youngsters, Alice 17, Edmund Jr. 15, Elizabeth 12 and John 8 embarked on the *Abigail* in 1635. Another unrelated Freeman group was on the same ship, which has caused confusion as to their possible relation to the Edmund Freemans. Later, in Sandwich, a fifth child, Mary Freeman, was in the family, but her birth is not recorded. She may have been born in Massachusetts to Edmund and Elizabeth, or may have been adopted here.

There were over two hundred passengers on the ship with the Freemans, some of high distinction, including Reverend Hugh Peter, Sir Henry Vane, John Winthrop, Jr. and Reverend John Wilson. There were a few cases of smallpox on the *Abigail* and a wealthy man named Dennis Geere died shortly after arrival. His will was preserved in English records and provided bequests to Thomas Tupper, Benjamin Nye, Thomas Landers and Thomas Greenfield, all doubtless fellow passengers. Edmund Freeman was a witness to the Geere will. Another passenger was William Almy, returning with his family. These persons (Tupper, Nye, Landers, Greenfield and Almy) all became part of the group that moved with Freeman (or soon after) to Sandwich. Others already in Saugus included the following persons who were referred to in the Massachusetts Bay Colony records as follows:

Richard Chadwell, Shipwright, released of debts by Thomas Mayhew of Medford in 1635.

Thomas Dexter was punched by Captain Endicott, 1631, and recovered £10 damages. He claimed to have bought the whole of Nahant from a Sachem named Poquanum, called Black Will, in exchange for a suit of clothes in 1630. A Nineteenth Century lithograph of this famous transaction has been widely copied, and we present it here as well. Black Will, however, sold his "rights" to Nahant to others as well, but Dexter's claim gained great notoriety as he, his son, and even his grandchildren tried to get it validated in Court. Dexter was one of the founders of the Saugus Iron Works and contracted to supply flux rock for the furnace. He seems to have come to Sandwich early and built the grist mill which bears his name, but then returned to his large farm and busy operation in Lynn.

Edward Dillingham, accounts with Richard Saltonstall in 1636.

John Carman, received money from an estate in 1631.

POQUANUM selling NAHANT
to Thomas Dexter, for a suit of Clothes.

1630.

Lithographed for the History of Lynn

This nineteenth century drawing from Lewis' History of Lynn is without foundation as to Dexter's appearance but the sale doubtless did occur. However Chief Poquanum (Black Will) also sold rights to Nahant to others and Dexter could not establish his title. This scene appears on the Nahant Town Seal.

William Wood, at a General Court 1635/6. (William Wood was an early Town Clerk in Sandwich, and is specifically identified by the Lynn historian Alonzo Lewis both as the author of *New England's Prospect* and as the person who removed to Sandwich. William Wood spent several years in early Saugus, then returned to London and published his book in 1634. Wood's book found a ready sale in England and went through two more editions. It contains a clear description of life in the New World, especially that of the Indians. A definitive new edition of this book was edited by Professor Alden T. Vaughan in 1977. Dr. Vaughan is not convinced that the author, who returned to Saugus in 1635, is indeed the William Wood who came to Sandwich.)

Henry Feake, goldsmith, admitted a free man 1632 in Bay Colony.

Reverend William Leveridge, allowed in 1635 to transport corn out of the Bay Colony.

Widow Deborah Bachiler Wing, arrived in Saugus 1632 with four sons in the party with her father Reverend Stephen Bachiler.

Settlers from Plymouth

Mr. Freeman must have decided on founding his town in Plymouth Colony, but there has been no record so far found as to his reasons or procedures. He and Mr. Leveridge established a brief residence in Plymouth, or adjoining Duxbury, and there were joined by thirteen others who ultimately came to Sandwich. Some of these thirteen had also been in Saugus earlier, others were Plymouth residents: William Bassett, Jr., James Skiff, Richard Bourne, John Vincent, Thomas Armitage, Thomas Burgess, Thomas Butler, George Slawson, John Dingley, John Fish, William Harlow, Henry Sanders, Joseph Winsor. Of the above group, Vincent, Burgess and Butler were neighbors of the Bassetts at Duxbury, and may have encouraged him to join the new group at Sandwich. The authorities at Plymouth were well aware of the small size and slow growth of their Colony compared to Massachusetts Bay Colony, and regarded the formation of new towns like Sandwich or Taunton with ready approval when they drew new settlers away from Massachusetts Bay Colony or from England. The above persons were not of early Plymouth families, with the sole exception being Bassett, son of William Bassett of the *Fortune.*

The First Use of the Name Sandwich

Our town was settled in 1637, and the earliest use of the name Sandwich is found in the actual writings of the time at the end of that year. The first reference seems to be in John Winthrop's *History of New England* in which he writes:

> "Another plantation was begun (and called Sandwich) about fifteen miles beyond Plimouth, towards Cape Cod, by many families, which removed from Sagus, otherwise Lynn."

This page is marked 1637, and the reference to Lynn probably dates it as after

November 20th when in Massachusetts Bay Records we read "Saugust is called Lin."

There are references to Sandwich in standard works (Goodwin's *Pilgrim Republic* and Bradford's *History of Plimoth Plantation)* which seem to refer to Sandwich as existing at an earlier date, such as Bradford's trip here in Jan. 1622/3 to buy corn from the Indians, and the wreck of a ship here in 1635. However, the original sources refer to places with Indian names—Manomet in the year 1623 and Scusset Beach in 1635 in the above examples, places that later became part of Sandwich.

The first use of "Sandwich" in Plymouth Colony Records refers to a court trial in Plymouth on January 2, 1637/8:

> "Michaell Turner complaineth against John Davis in an action upon the case to the damnage of £20 for not delivering his goods he hired his boate to carry from Weymouth to Sandwich. The jury found for the defendant, and awarded him fifty shillings damnage and charges of the Court, because the complaintant should have set up a pole with a white cloth on the topp, whereby the harboures mouth might be discovered unto them."

This failure to deliver Turner's goods to Sandwich obviously happened several weeks or even months before the trial, so that it occurred during the calendar year 1637. It shows that a settlement was going on, that coastal trade was in operation, and that Sandwich had a harbor, the mouth of which was all but invisible from the sea.

Though the original grant of April 3, 1637 does not mention the word Sandwich, the same grant is referred to twice again in Plymouth Colony Records. Early in 1648 Bradford formally turned over the initial area he had bought from the Indians to Edmund Freeman and his associates, using these words:

> "Whereas about tenn yeares past the within named William Bradford Governor and the Rest of his parteners within written being of the old Companie have Purchased the Towne of Sandwidge of the Indians and paied to them for the said purchase the vallew of sixteene pound nineteen shillings in Comodities. . ."

The Government at Plymouth formally confirmed to each town in the Colony its right to its lands in 1685 and the Act on Sandwich states:

> "a certayn tract of lands was by William Bradford and his Associates assembled in Court the 3rd of April one thousand six hundred thirty and seven granted unto Mr. Edmund Freeman, Henery Feake, Thomas Dexter and other of their Asociates to erect a plantation or town in this Government and to receive in more inhabitants to them according to order and duly to dispose of said lands to such as were or should be orderly admitted to them into said township which was afterwards called Sanditch."

The South part of Nevv-England, as it is Planted this yeare, 1634.

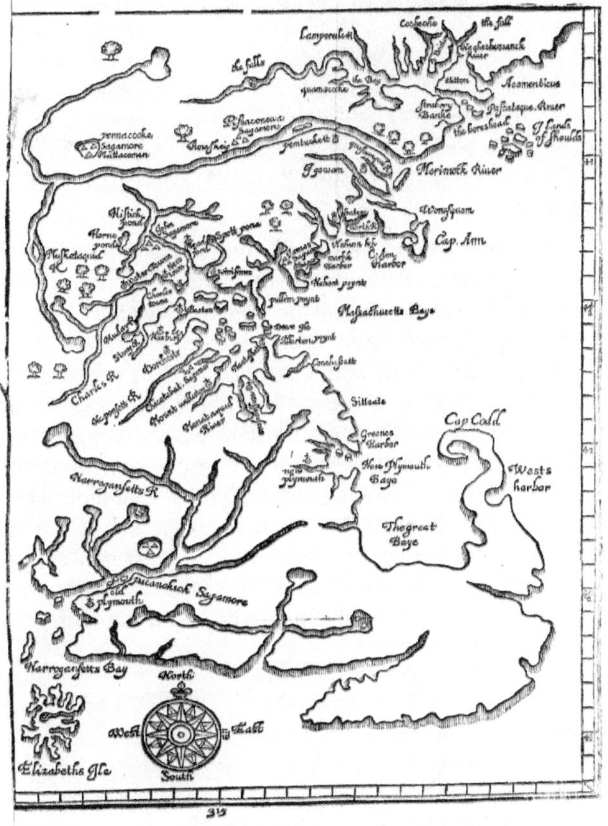

This map of New England appeared in William Wood's book New England's Prospect. It is likely that the author was one of the Ten Men of Saugus woo founded Sandwich. Reproduced by courtesy of Houghton Library, Harvard University.

The Humphrey Connection

John Humphrey, an Assistant Governor of the Massachusetts Bay Colony, came from a substantial Dorset family and early on associated himself with John Winthrop and others, who with the Earl of Lincoln in Boston, Lincolnshire, formed the nucleus around which the Massachusetts Bay Colony was created. Humphrey, who had two children by a previous marriage, married

Lady Susan, the daughter of Thomas Clinton, Earl of Lincoln. His colleague, Isaac Johnson, married her sister Lady Arbella. The Humphreys had a residence in Sandwich, Kent, which was then one of the embarkation points for the New World. They did not join the exodus of the great fleet of 1630 but remained in London and Kent organizing supplies and finance for New England. They finally came to Boston in 1634, and Humphrey was assigned lands in the Saugus area as Assistant Governor for this sector of the Colony. He and Lady Susan had at least five children.

He was an ambitious man and is said to have aspired to a colony of his own. Late in 1641 he and Lady Susan departed for England, leaving all their children here with his eldest daughter Ann who had married William Palmes. They never returned, and Humphrey died in 1661, reportedly losing all his capital in various ventures.

Why is Humphrey important to our Sandwich story? He was the magistrate at Saugus when the big group of nearly fifty families left for Cape Cod in 1637, and must have approved the venture. Furthermore, he is the only person of authority whom we have been able to identify who had a strong connection with Sandwich, Kent, and who was also in a position to suggest a name for the new town. None of the sixty early families here came from old Sandwich. Nevertheless, there were similarities which would have occurred to one who knew both areas—flat marshes, a shallow harbor, a wide bay running northeast/southwest. In Kent, one portion of their channel was even called Buzzer's Reach or Buzzer's Belly. This has a strong sound of our Buzzards Bay. Even more, the Aptucxet Trading Post, and its proven Dutch connection, would have reminded anyone who knew Kent of the large population of Dutch and Flemish refugees in Sandwich and their long-standing trade with Holland.

It is possible that one day a document will be found suggesting how our town really got its name. Until then we feel the strongest case is that suggested here through John Humphrey.

The Settlers of 1637 to 1640's

The names of the first settlers here are listed in accordance with their length of stay in the new settlement:

Long-term Settlers

George Allen	John Fish	Edward Perry
William Bassett Jr.	Nathaniel Fish	Ezra Perry
Anthony Besse	Edmund Freeman	James Skiff
Robert Bodfish	Edmund Freeman Jr.	Thomas Tupper
Richard Bourne	Joseph Holway	Daniel Wing

Thomas Burgess
Thomas Butler
Edward Dillingham
John Jenkins
Thomas Landers
Benjamin Nye
Deborah Wing
Stephen Wing

Settlers Gone Before 1700

John Briggs
George Buitt
Richard Chadwell
Thomas Dexter Jr.
Henry Feake
Jonathan Fish
John Freeman
Peter Gaunt
John Green d. 1660
Richard Kerby
George Knott
William Leveridge
John Newland
William Newland
Michael Turner
John Vincent
Joseph Winsor
Anthony Wright
Nicholas Wright
Peter Wright

Settlers Gone Before 1650

William Almy
Thomas Armitage
John Blakemore
George Bliss
Thomas Boardman
Thomas Bowerman
William Braybrook
John Carman
Thomas Chillingsworth
Edmund Clark
George Cole
Thomas Dexter Sr.
John Dillingham
John Dingley
Henry Ewer
John Friend
Andrew Hallett Jr.
Thomas Hampton
William Harlow
William Hedge
William Hurst
John Joyce
John King
John Miller
Vincent Potter
Henry Saunders
George Slawson
John Stutely
Richard Wade
Thomas Willis
Deborah Wing and son John
Edward Wollaston
William Wood

CHAPTER 2

THE OLD COLONY

In 1630 the population of Plymouth Colony was concentrated in Plymouth and Scituate with about five hundred people. When the large settlement began at Boston in 1630, there was a sudden demand for food, cattle, timber, tar and other supplies. The people at Plymouth obtained land grants in Duxbury, Marshfield and northward where the soil produced better crops than in Plymouth, and enjoyed high prices for their exports to Boston. These two areas became towns in their own right, Duxbury in 1637, and Marshfield in 1640. Scituate received newcomers directly from England and was already considered a town in 1636, becoming the strongest and wealthiest in the Colony. Families from Boston settled Taunton in 1637. At the same time, Sandwich was settled by Saugus families, followed closely by Yarmouth in 1638 and Barnstable in 1639.

The Colony of Plymouth grew rapidly in the decade of the 1630s as a result of the influx from the Bay Colony, with further emigrants from England to Scituate, plus natural increase. With the outbreak of revolution in England in 1641, emigration to New England virtually stopped and the demand for Plymouth goods collapsed, together with prices. By 1643, however, Plymouth Colony's population was estimated at about three thousand persons. In that year a new settlement was founded by seven families who left Plymouth town for the outer Cape at Nauset. This settlement became Eastham. Governor Bradford rued the exodus of these good Plymouth residents, but the old mother town remained the center of government.

Indian Areas

The original settlements at Plymouth, Duxbury and up to the Bay Colony line were in areas from which the Wampanoag Indian population had been wiped out by disease in 1616. These lands were unused and had cleared fields ready to work. Massasoit, the ruling Wampanoag chief, welcomed the Colony in 1621 as affording him some further protection from the large Narraganset tribe to his west. His treaty of peace and friendship with the Pilgrims extended from 1621 to his death in 1661. In time, however, the whites began to spill over into lands occupied, or at least hunted and fished over, by Indians. Taunton and Sandwich required a negotiation between Bradford and Massasoit in 1637 to arrange the general boundaries. Any further negotiation for local land was then to be carried out with nearby resident Indians, but required Plymouth approval.

Plymouth's Lack of Ministers

It was a curious anomaly that the intensely religious and motivated group in Plymouth had no central church or religious leader. Pastor John Robinson had remained in Leyden with the group there and had expected to come, but he died in 1625 and there was no one to take his place. By contrast, the settlers in Boston were well-supplied with highly competent Puritan ministers, including Reverend John Cotton. The influence of its ministers led Massachusetts Bay Colony to become a virtual theocracy.

Plymouth Colony insisted that each new town should obtain a minister before it could be organized. This was to be accomplished by the emigration of new ministers from England, or by finding ones not advantageously settled in the Bay Colony. Reverend William Leveridge was among the latter group and was willing to make a change when Edmund Freeman asked him to join his group of Sandwich settlers.

Religion became a profound problem for the governors of Plymouth Colony. Despite all efforts of the founding fathers, the young men brought up in New England were not as steeped in religious faith as their forbears, and the town ministers were not well supported. In 1645 a proposal was made to drop the religious requirement for persons to qualify as voters in the Colony elections. This political tolerance was favored in the various towns, but the vote on the proposal was deferred for further study by the Plymouth General Court. It was not raised again.

The Debts of the Colony

There were one hundred and two people on the *Mayflower* planning to stay in the Colony, forty were from Holland and thirty-nine from England, plus eighteen servants and five hired persons. They were supplied by the business group called the Adventurers who financed the effort. The business agents organizing the supplies were Robert Cushman for the Leyden group and Thomas Weston and Christopher Martin for the Adventurers. The arrangement with the Adventurers was that the Colony would work for seven years, export goods to cover costs and stimulate new investments, then render accounts in 1627. Cushman and Weston remained in England to send the next group, while Martin came to Plymouth. Martin died and his accounts were found muddled. The *Mayflower* went back empty in April 1621. Cushman came out on the *Fortune* in November 1621 with twenty-five new people, but they had only some clothing, little spare food, no tools, no items for trading with the Indians, nor even bedding for the winter. The ship was loaded with furs and clapboards, and agent Cushman went back to try again to raise funds for what was needed in Plymouth.

The problems of the Pilgrims arising from their weak financial position and lack of powerful patrons in England were deeply discouraging. With no prestige and only a weak Patent granted by the Council for New England in 1621, they were judged purely as a business risk. The agent Thomas Weston could raise money only for trips to make a quick profit, so he sent three ships here to fish and to deliver passengers to Virginia. In 1623 Cushman managed to send over two vessels, the *Anne* and *Little James,* with ninety-three people (doubling the size of the Colony). Again, there was no new cloth, no tools, nor trade goods due to the parsimony of the Adventurers in the absence of exports from the Colony. Bradford reported that some of the Colony were now half naked. The *Anne* was sent back loaded, this time with the competent Edward Winslow. In spite of the opposition of Weston, he managed to bring back some supplies and clothing, livestock, a carpenter and a salt maker. He sailed again in 1624/1625 and brought back more livestock. The Adventurers preferred to send out vessels to fish rather than to supply the colony. A return cargo of furs was seized by pirates and lost, and their agent and supporter, Cushman, died of plague in 1625.

The New Agreement

The Pilgrims sent a new representative, Isaac Allerton, to England in late 1626 to negotiate the results of the first seven years. He brought back a new mortgage agreement to repay £1800 in debt and interest in nine annual payments of £200. This needed the signature of many persons as guarantors, since the Colony itself had no legal standing or capital value. A total of twenty-seven men, called the Purchasers, signed the commitment, and to meet the annual payments agreed to put the foreign trade of the Colony into the hands of eight Undertakers who would organize the gathering of exports, and arrange for needed imports and supplies. The Undertakers were to receive a fee for these services in goods from each member of the Colony. Aggressive steps to raise production were taken, such as assigning twenty acres of land to each settler in outright ownership, allocating livestock, setting up trading posts at Manomet and in Maine, and on the Connecticut River. These moves were successful. The eight Undertakers were Bradford, Winslow, Brewster, Allerton, Standish, Howland and Alden of the *Mayflower,* and Thomas Prence of the *Fortune.*

Allerton's Duplicity

Allerton aroused suspicion by borrowing double what he was authorized to get in import goods, at high interest, and claimed that much was brought in for his own account. He continued to do this but the Undertakers managed to make the annual payments and the Colony took on more vitality, receiving the last Leyden people and other new settlers by 1630. However, Allerton and the treasurer of the Adventurers, James Sherley, began to play a crooked game, using the Plymouth assets and funds to finance trading voyages. Any profits from these ventures were for themselves, while losses were charged to the Plymouth account. The Undertakers in Plymouth woke up to this and discharged Allerton as their agent, but the pattern was set and Plymouth found it had no legal or political power to force Sherley and the other Adventurers to render accounts. Edward Winslow went to England in 1634 to try to straighten out these matters. He arranged sales and answered charges against the Colony convincingly, but was the victim of an incredible plot in which he was jailed by Archbishop Laud for the alleged religious beliefs in the Colony. He was held for seventeen weeks while business opportunities were lost and heavy expenses incurred to obtain his release.

So cunning was Sherley that even after this disaster, Winslow urged that more furs be sent to Sherley in 1636. Reluctantly the Colony sent them but still got no settlement. Sherley was then "discharged" in late 1636, meaning that he should incur no more charges and would be sent no more cargo until the accounts of the 1627 mortgage and all the subsequent charges and payments had been accounted for. By Plymouth accounts the furs shipped between 1631 and 1636 should have amply repaid all debts and charges. We can imagine Plymouth's dismay when the other remaining investors, Andrews and Beauchamp, claimed that Sherley had given them nothing and that they too could not force an accounting from him. Their debts were still outstanding and would have to be paid in total.

The Last Three Adventurers

Some payments were then made to Andrews and Beauchamp but Winslow dared not go again to London for fear of being imprisoned. In this impasse Plymouth sought the aid of the Massachusetts Bay Colony, which could be helpful but only if its own interests were also advanced. Three senior Massachusetts Bay representatives went to England in 1641 and sent back a proposal by Sherley to settle all the Plymouth accounts for £1200, of which £500 was to go to Andrews, £400 to Beauchamp and £300 to Sherley. The only snag was that Beauchamp and Andrews must send their full releases in advance. Sherley suggested that the releases would come, and that final payment arrangements be negotiated in Plymouth by persons there who also knew the Adventurers well—John Atwood, William Collier (a former Adventurer) and Edmund Freeman. This team aided the original Undertakers to make an inventory of all the trading goods, trading posts, vessels, assets, and amounts due to the Colony on the trading account, which came to £1400. This amount was later found to be greatly inflated because it valued goods and property at the pre-1641 high prices. The Undertakers decided to sell off all these assets, split the proceeds among themselves and pay off the £1200. All parties involved knew the £1200 claim was wildly inflated with such charges as extra interest, trading losses not concerning the Pilgrims, and other paper losses. Samuel Eliot Morison says flatly that the Boston representatives agreed to the amount because £900 of it would be payable in Boston.

Andrews gravely wrote to Edmund Freeman (Beauchamp's agent and brother-in-law) to the effect that Beauchamp "will not show any account, and Sherley a very unfair and unjust one. And both of them discouraged me from sending the partners (the Plymouth Undertakers) my account." He said that Mr. Beauchamp was not due more than £150 and Sherley nothing. However he said when he gets his own £150 he will return the land in Scituate and give up all claims on the Patent. As it turned out, Andrews finally got £544 in Boston, while Sherley settled for £150 in England. Beauchamp wanted his full £400 in Boston, but his release was incorrectly worded so that this debt hung on for years.

Finally, in 1646, five of the Undertakers pledged real estate in Plymouth to raise part of this sum—Bradford a large farm, Standish and Alden three hundred acres apiece, Prence and Winslow a house each. These pledges are recorded in full in Plymouth Colony Records, and each is made to Freeman. It is not clear exactly how these pledges were cashed, but the record shows that in 1648 the Pilgrims were at last free of debt. The record also indicates that Freeman was an Assistant Governor from 1640 through June 1646, but that he was dropped and never served again. His role in collecting Beauchamp's debt may well have been a factor in this abrupt change of status.

Early Colony Government

The government of 1623 consisted of a governor. who also served as the secretary and treasurer, and one assistant governor. The first new office created was that of Constable. He was to be elected to aid the government and his duties included warning the public of meetings, serving warrants, noting breaches of the peace, carrying offenders to court, keeping the roads and pound, collecting rates and fines, sealing weights and measures, and announcing marriage intentions. Entries began January 1, 1632/3 in that portion of the original volumes of Plymouth Colony Records called "Court Orders", which record the actions of the Governor and his council, which had grown to seven assistants.

The Changes of 1636

By 1636 the spread of towns and growth of population brought about a comprehensive review of the structure of Colony government and its laws and principles. The new government provided:

1. Elections to be held annually in March at a general meeting in Plymouth. Candidates must be freemen.
2. Laws would be voted by the freemen only and no laws passed except by this general consent.
3. Taxes would be levied on all according to estate.
4. A Grand Jury (called Grand Inquest) would be named to bring in presentments to the Court against individuals or towns seen to be breaking the law.
5. Petit Juries for trials as well as the Grand Juries may include inhabitants of good repute not just freemen.
6. The Governor and two Assistants may decide cases of under 40 shillings value or small offenses.
7. Death penalty for seven crimes; the penalties for other crimes and misdemeanors at discretion of the court.
8. Widow to have one third of her husband's personal estate, and one third of his real estate for her lifetime or until remarried.

These regulations were called the General Fundamentals and amounted to a Bill of Rights, differing significantly from English law. Courts were to be held quarterly for Plymouth Colony in March, June, September and December to hear presentments, applications for freeman status, and other public business. The Court held all executive, legislative and judicial powers, and sat monthly to hear civil suits and to weigh crimes and misdemeanors. The seven assistants who sat on the Court had particular regional duties in the local administration of justice, such as conducting marriages, impaneling coroner's juries, examining offenders and seeing that laws were executed and punishments carried out. Offices of secretary and treasurer were created, whose duties had previously been filled by the Governor. The oath of new arrivals and common residents included declaring loyalty to the King and Government, not acting against the Government, reporting such acts by others to the Assistant, and submitting to good and wholesome laws. There was also a specific oath of allegiance and fidelity to be taken by every adult male, and the Assistants were required to administer it to those who had not yet taken it. This Oath of Fidelity was probably administered in a fairly perfunctory way, except when a resident became a freeman or entered military service.

The Freeman's Oath was like the Oath of Fidelity but included another line that he must advance the growth and good of the Plantation. This meant serving in town or Colony offices, attending Colony elections and supporting both church and state. However, significantly as of this period in the 1630's no reference was made in the laws to ministers or churches. Later in the decade, freemen represented about one in six of the male inhabitants, showing that many who were qualified did not seek the privileges of public service.

The office of Constable was divided in 1636 and a new office of Colony Messenger was created to carry out the will of the Governor and Assistants as directed. This included warning of marriages, sealing measures, laying out of lands, holding prisoners, serving warrants, inflicting sentences. Constables were now named for individual towns with local duties to see that laws were not broken, take up prisoners and witnesses, apprehend suspicious persons, and inform the local Assistant. Even in an orderly community these above offices were ones of stress and could be abused, in which case the Grand Juries were quick to present the incumbents for violations of trust.

Town Government

By 1638 the growth of the Colony was such that it was unrealistic to expect all the freemen to attend the Court in Plymouth every March for voting on elections and new laws. Accordingly, the office of the town deputy was created, with each town to elect two deputies (freemen) to represent it at Court. At the March 1639 Court, the slate of proposed central officers was made up, with approval to be voted in the June Court. In this way if a deputy could not attend he could send in his ballots. Deputies attended each quarterly Court from then on, and it was found highly effective to have new laws and regulations proposed at one Court and then finally accepted or rejected at the next Court, allowing for local discussion. Residents who had taken the Oath of Fidelity were allowed to vote in local elections and town laws. It had already been ruled in 1636 that towns could make local orders not contrary to the general ordinances. In 1639 the towns were again urged to meet and make rules to maintain their neighborhoods. In 1640 it was provided that towns themselves might levy taxes and distrain property to settle amounts due. Grand Juries did not hesitate to present towns for failure to maintain roads, exercise militia, build bridges, or if they should suffer disorderly people to settle. In 1641 towns were required to provide for their own poor. The office of Town Clerk was created in 1646 to record births, deaths and marriages, to register voters, and certify those proposed as freemen. The growth of towns was thus a natural state in the evolution of the Colony, and their governments were encouraged to evolve rapidly to reduce the detail to be carried to Plymouth for action. However the towns were not formally incorporated because the Plymouth Colony charter did not empower the Colony to create town governments, whereas the Mass. Bay Colony could. This meant that much local town business had to be settled in Plymouth, while in Mass. Bay the town governments had broad local powers. Sandwich did not get its first Selectman until 1667.

Good and Wholesome Laws

The earliest laws of the Colony were soon proved inadequate, and so in 1636 a new set of laws was written. The death penalty was to be carried out for seven crimes: treason, witchcraft, murder, arson, rape, sodomy and bestiality. Other cases of the most serious sort, such as theft of ships or munitions, resulted in whipping, branding or banishment. Immoral acts were to be punished at the discretion of the Court. Other matters decided upon were misdemeanors, ("breaking the King's peace") social regulations, commercial regulations, town rights and duties, regulations regarding Indians, regulations on arms, and the many and various types of civil cases.

There were a great many lawsuits in early Plymouth over matters of debt, trespass and slander. The slander cases were usually settled at a small percentage of the damages asked. The litigants were seeking a forum for grievances and therefore settled quickly after being heard. Some individuals were in Court frequently. Others never sued or appeared before the Court.

The Court heard an astonishing variety of cases and disposed of most of them with dispatch. Serious cases were put to one or another Assistant to study and advise. Minor infractions or misdemeanors produced fines or sentences of stocks or whipping, but these were often suspended. Admitting that there was little secret in a small town and little privacy in anyone's life in those days, some of the presentments suggest snooping and harassment rather than concern for order. Many of those presented were repeaters with well-known propensities for fighting, cursing, and drinking.

CHAPTER 3

EARLY DAYS IN SANDWICH

The first settlement at Sandwich was along the borders of the salt marshes and the streams, facing Cape Cod Bay, in a strip about a mile deep and ten miles long. These marshes with their hay crop, their shellfish and wildfowl provided a generous natural resource for immediate use by the new arrivals. Although the Indians had always used this area for hunting and fishing, leaving trails and campsites, none lived here. There were three distinct marsh systems, called Scusset, Shawme and Scorton.

Scusset had as its chief stream Scusset Creek which rose in a boiling spring near the present Sagamore Bridge. These boiling springs were in deep valleys where the surrounding acquifer produced a generous flow of underground water, rising in a spring area at nine hundred to one thousand gallons per minute, so much that they never froze over.

Scusset Marsh had a large clay upland in the middle now called Sagamore Hill (seventy-four feet high) which was connected to the mainland by a low but solid causeway. Scusset Creek turned at this causeway and flowed around the base of Sagamore Hill and out into Cape Cod Bay. The other streams here were Tupper Creek and Bass Creek arising from smaller springs and from steady fresh water seepage from all along the upland.

Shawme Marsh had as its chief stream the Shawme River, arising in a red cedar bog in what is now upper Shawme Pond. Another major stream was Spring Hill River arising in Boiling Springs Pond. The other streams were named Parsonage and Ox-Pasture Creeks. Between Scusset and Shawme Marshes was a large upland extending to the Bay, called Shawme Neck. (The word Shawme, whose meaning has not been found, applied only to the stream, the marsh and the neck, but not to an Indian tribe and not to the Sandwich area in general.)

The Scorton Marsh was the largest of the three systems, with major springs at Lawrence's Hole near present Chase Road, and near the Nye Family House. Between Shawme and Scorton was a large upland, Spring Hill, extending to the Bay. Within Scorton was another large upland Ploughed Neck. Scorton was distinctive because it connected by a narrow stream and strip of marsh over to Barnstable Great Marsh system. This made an island of a large block of upland on the shore, Scorton Neck.

The tidal waters of Cape Cod Bay had a slow counterclockwise motion around this shore, bringing down sediments from the cliffs in Plymouth and distributing them in barrier beaches along the shore of Sandwich and Barnstable.

The recent glacier had completely shaped this peninsula and nearby mainland, leaving tumbled hills to mark the end of the different lobes of ice. The one on the mainland had left the hills from Manomet Point, Plymouth south to Sandwich and Falmouth then out on the Elizabeth Islands. Another lobe had left terminal hills from Sandwich down the Cape to Truro. Two glacial events had shaped the particular topography at Sandwich. Large ponds in South Plymouth had found a drainage channel south at what is now Bournedale, cutting close to the moraine hills and flowing down into Buzzards Bay. Then the melting glacier in Cape Cod Bay had formed a fresh water lake which had found a weak point in the encircling hills and had broken through forming a deep runoff valley which connected to the earlier streambed at Bournedale. At the highest point this valley was only thirty-two feet over final sea level, as compared to hills of two hundred feet on both sides.

When Indians settled this area, they found it was only a one half mile portage from the headwaters of the Scusset Creek over to the other stream (the Manomet River) flowing into Buzzards Bay. Along the upper reaches of the Manomet River and the shore of Herring Pond was an Indian settlement called Comassakumkanet, with Caunacum as Sachem until his death in 1623. According to Chief Red Shell, a twentieth century Indian descendant, Comassakumkanet simply meant "trail going south." The trail headed south on a straight line toward Quisset, and was called the Meganset trail. In addition to its geographic importance the Manomet River was of great value to the settlers because of its annual massive run of alewives which headed upstream to spawn in Great Herring Pond. The Aptucxet Trading Post was established on the Manomet River near the bay, as described in chapter one.

Early Land Grants in Sandwich

As settlers came to Sandwich they were allowed sections of upland to build on and sections of salt marsh for haying. They came on invitation from the "Ten Men of Saugus" who (with possibly a few others) had already claimed all the marshland with convenient access from the upland along what is now Tupper Road, Town Neck, and the town dock area, the central area of the original town. The other settlers were forced to go much greater distances to their sections of the marsh. This resulted in complaints. These were brought to Reverend Leveridge in 1638, and he framed the specific questions to be brought to the General Court for answer. The following summarized exchange from these questions indicates much concerning the relations between the settlers, their leaders, and the Plymouth government:

1. Whether the undertakers have a full gift of the lands at Sandwich or a conditional grant only for settling. . . .

   Answer: For your "undertakers" we prefer "committees" as suiting more properly the relation between them and us (Committees in this sense means persons to whom a trust or charge is given). Their grant is conditional not absolute, being for the ease of the government.

2. Whether such of them as are still at Saugus shall. . . . possess any lands at all in case they come not to inhabit?

   Answer: Negatively, for when they made suit to us it was as a people . . . pretending removal with all possible conveniency (speed).

3. Whether . . to add some others in their stead .. . such as are of the church there or neighbors of good report?

   Answer: Affirmatively. . . such as this government shall approve of.

4. Whether if this power be abused how it may be reformed? (There is no previous reference to "this power" but in context it means the powers of the Committees of Sandwich).

   Answer: As abuses shall arise upon due complaint the Magistrate must do justice as in other cases

5. Whether in particular it be not an abuse of the power in case they should monopolize the chief places of conveniency for lands, woods, meadows etc. to the prejudice of the town in general?

   Answer: Such the case may be, and the damage so great to the whole as not to be suffered; but if the Committees be faithful and able of estate, their pains will require more than ordinary accomodation.

6. Whether two townships etc. (question not completed)

   Answer: We made the grant of the lands to one; neither can there be any other without the allowance of the government; but if the land far off be disposed of for farms to men of estate, we see no cause of dislike.

These were important statements, admitting that the Ten Men may have erred but that they nevertheless deserve "more than ordinary accomodation." As to forming two towns instead of one, it is curious to find this suggested right at the outset of the settlement. At this period the only other nucleus of people was in the Spring Hill area.

The lands in question remained an issue because nine months later on March 5, 1638/9 we read in Plymouth Colony Records:

> "It is ordered by the Court that the meadowlands at Sandwich which were laid forth shall be new divided again, by equal portions according to each man's estate, and some of the townsmen to be joined with the Committees in doing thereof"

The only person singled out as particularly offending was Andrew Hallett who was not one of the Ten Men. Two men were assigned to

> "make report unto the Court that if those proportions which Andrew Hallett hath assumed to himself there shall be so prejudicial to the whole that then some just and equal order may be taken therein to

prevent the evil consequences it may be to the whole plantation."

The Court clearly became irritated with both Committees and the complainers because on September 3, 1639 it directed:

> "Whereas it is very probable that diverse of the Committees of Sandwich have not faithfully discharged that trust reposed in them by receiving into the town diverse persons unfit for Church society. . . and have disposed the greatest part of the lands there already to very few that are in Church society or fit for the same, so that without speedy remedy our chiefest end will be utterly frustrate. . .such of the Committee as are herein faulty to appear at the next Court of Assistants to answer the complaint and in the meantime not to dispose of any more lands there. . .nor make sale or convey any of their lands. . .to any person."

Clearly outside help was needed. Thomas Prence and Captain Standish (the ramrods of discipline) were appointed "to hear and determine all differences and controversies amongst the Committees and inhabitants of Sandwich." The points agreed to at a meeting in Sandwich on October 3, 1639 were:

1. Scorton Neck shall be reserved to the town as a Common for the breeding of their young cattle
2. Shawme Neck to be reserved for a Common to the town.
3. Wood on these Necks shall be free for all provided it be without waste and spoil.
4. As to those not fit for Church society it was ordered that none shall be admitted without consent and approbation of Mr. Leveridge and the Church.
5. Any inhabitants who are disposed to sell their estates and depart the town shall not sell to any person except he be generally approved of by the whole town. (Land was not being sold, only the buildings, fences, and improvements made by the occupant.)
6. For the preventing of discords in the disposal of lands, the Committees shall receive direction from Mr. Prence in all such occasion as shall be needful.

The following April 16, 1640 at a general meeting it was agreed that a new meadowlands authority under Prence should be established with full powers to reallocate the meadows. The members were:

For the Committees	**For the Townsmen**
Edmund Freeman	John Vincent
Henry Feake	Richard Bourne

Edward Dillingham	George Allen
Richard Chadwell	Robert Bodfish
John Carman	Joseph Holway

The principles on which this group were to act were:

1. That those who had meadows between the Scusset and Shawme Rivers should have their portions halved, and equivalent given elsewhere.
2. That a portion of the other meadows not be granted now but held back.
3. That Joshua Pratt of Plymouth lay out the lots approved at sixpence/acre.
4. That certain charges of the Committees for services to the community be paid up by the rest of the inhabitants. If this is done by mowing time, then much of the above reserved meadow is to be issued to all; if not, the Committees may mow the reserved area.
5. That 60 or 80 acres west of the Scorton River remain in reserved status.
6. That meadow granted earlier outside the favored area between Scusset and Shawme Rivers may be kept by original grantees if desired.
7. That these new grants be made perpetual.

This group successfully issued the new grants as follows:

	Average	*% of Marsh*
The Ten Men 4 to 42 acres	16.6 Acres	45%
Next 4 men, 10 to 15 acres	13.0 Acres	14%
Next 13 men, 5 to 7½ acres	6.4 Acres	22%
Last 31 men, 1 to 4 acres	2.2 Acres	19%

More than half the men received a total of only nineteen percent of the meadows said to be proportional to their "estate and quality." Benjamin Nye was listed but given no meadow at this time as he was unmarried. The most interesting allocation was to Thomas Dexter: "twenty-six acres if he come to live here; six acres for his mill."

Thomas Dexter, one of the Ten Men, was awarded six acres for having built a grist mill, but because he returned to his interests in Saugus, he gave up the conditional grant of twenty-six acres. His son, however, was able to claim the six acres here, and to obtain new land in his own right.

The Sandwich lands were distributed according to a formula which required each household to have an adequate homesite near a spring or stream, plus a generous section of upland for a woodlot and for grazing. The precious saltmarsh was allocated according to taxable estate, which at that time did not include the value of the land which had been assigned free, but rather consisted of animals, tools, furniture, cash and other skills and assets brought to the community. This was the measure of a man's "quality."

The Meeting House and William Leveridge

Mr. Leveridge was an English university graduate who like many of his generation opted to come to New England in the 1630's with the Puritan migration. There was a great need here for ministers for each of the new towns that were being settled. He lived briefly in Dover, New Hampshire but was doubtless contacted by Edmund Freeman's group on behalf of the prospective Sandwich settlement. He was in Plymouth or Duxbury in 1637 with the group that included Vincent, Bourne, Slawson, Burgess, Bassett, Armitage, Skiff and Butler, which soon settled in Sandwich. According to Plymouth Colony Records he was proposed as a freeman of the Colony March 7, 1636/7, and on November 7, 1637 there is a reference to Plymouth lands formerly used by "Leverich." Leveridge is said to have been a "Teacher" in Duxbury during his temporary stay here, a paid position in the church allowing preaching but not baptism or administering sacraments. He is described as a man of great piety and meekness. At an early Town Meeting in Sandwich January 7, 1650/1 one of the items of business was "there shall be a levy of five pounds raised for Mr. Leveridge for to pay for covering and parting his house with board which was long since promised to be done for him by the Town." Roofs at this time were of boards and battens rather than thatch or shingle, and the "parting" was doubtless the interior partitions. Leveridge's meekness obviously had not gained him much of a house. Another factor mentioned concerning him is that he was influenced by his colleague Charles Chauncey, a learned minister forced out of England by Archbishop Laud. Chauncey came to Plymouth and was a "Teacher" there in the period 1638-1649, after which he was accepted in Scituate and ordained. Chauncey was said to favor baptism of infants by total immersion, and Communion services held at night by candle light. He could not in Plymouth actually perform these services since he was not ordained there, but Leveridge is said to have agreed with him, and in the religious turbulence of that time this doubtless would have eroded support for Leveridge among many of the Sandwich flock.

The first mention of a meetinghouse in Sandwich is in Plymouth Colony Records September 3, 1639:

"Whereas Joseph Winsor has a lot in the town of 8 pole broad & 12 pole long, or there about, which he purchased of Thomas Chillingsworth, which was Thomas Hamptons, deceased, and that the place is fit for public use, it is ordered that the town shall have it for other use, they giving the said Joseph Winsor as much as the same is worth; and in the mean season the said Winsor to keep his possession thereof until he be provided for elsewhere."

This lot of eight by twelve rods was one hundred ninety-eight feet along Main Street and one hundred thirty-two feet along River Street and had the advantage of being exactly central to the original settlement. The town from the beginning was divided into areas east and west of the Shawme millstream, and the first bridge was over this stream at the head of tidal high water in the marsh, where River Street now crosses. As a final note on this meetinghouse, a drawing was produced in the early twentieth century purporting to show what it may have looked like—a square building with log walls and a thatched hip roof. This drawing was found to be taken from an earlier drawing of the first meetinghouse at Hartford, Connecticut, which had clapboard walls and a shingled roof. These features were then redrawn to the more popular idea of an ancient and venerable building—log walls and thatched roof. In this case these would be completely unhistoric, as there were no log-walled buildings in the Colony and thatch had been forbidden from 1627 because of fire danger.

Early Relations with Plymouth

At the Court held March 6, 1637/8, when Sandwich had been settled about nine months, John Vincent was elected the first Constable, showing that the settlement had acquired substance. Captain Standish and John Alden were requested by the Court to "go to Sanditch and set forth their bounds of the lands granted them." This would be the bounds agreed by Bradford when he cleared the Indian title with the Sachem at Manomet and possibly with Massasoit himself.

After Vincent, the Constable in 1639 was George Allen, who took the Oath of Fidelity just before his oath of office. Allen was among the oldest in the town, at least fifty-seven here as he was over sixty and not included in a 1643 list of those able to bear arms, those between sixteen and sixty. He was an Anabaptist, one of the liberal-to-radical religious minorities, but a strong town supporter and acceptable to the Plymouth Court as sufficiently orthodox and of good repute. He brought a good estate and no less than six sons to the town.

When Sandwich was fully accepted as a Town at the Court of June 1639, the first two deputies were John Vincent and Richard Bourne, persons well known in Plymouth, who were then commencing their long course of public service. The process of settling down and becoming a town was not exactly tranquil. In addition to the meadowlands controversy already mentioned, Plymouth Court at this time gave the town some blunt warnings:

> Many citizens were found "deficient in arms," (including Freeman himself).
>
> Many were warned that their swine should have nose rings as required by law.
>
> The town was presented for allowing unfit persons to settle.

James Skiffe was ordered to carry out Henry Ewer and his wife and goods to the place from which he brought them. This was in 1638, and Ewer was still here for the meadow issue in 1640 when he was allowed one acre, the minimum, but he did disappear after this from the records.

Joseph Winsor and Anthony Besse were presented for disorderly keeping house alone in Sandwich. Both later married and became useful citizens. As single men working to get established at this early date, one wonders what this presentment was supposed to correct?

These cases involved only minor fines or warnings, and must be seen in the light of cautions and reminders that the settlers were being watched. Other new towns were treated similarly.

In 1643 following an Indian alert the four orthodox Colonies in New England formed a loose Confederation to coordinate defense policies and improve communication. Six of the Plymouth towns including Sandwich were encouraged to organize a standing militia company composed of freemen, not servants, who had taken the Oath of Fidelity. They elected their own officers, provided their own arms and trained several times a year. John Ellis became the Lieutenant of the Sandwich troop for a long period. Earlier in 1639 John Blakemore had been appointed simply to exercise the inhabitants in arms. The first military test came in 1645 when five young men from Sandwich joined an expedition against the Narraganset and were away seventeen days. Local militia were promptly "presented" if they failed to train regularly.

In 1640 the three Cape towns were presented by the Grand Jury to enforce their share in building a bridge over the Eel River in the southern part of Plymouth village. A similar bridge over the Jones River north of Plymouth was to be charged to the towns on that side. These bridges seemed never to be adequately built and the long road down to the Cape never properly laid out or maintained. All through the seventeenth century, these projects kept reappearing on the record as fines to the towns for neglect, or requiring committees to make report and as new demands for action by the Towns.

Edmund Freeman Senior, 1590-1682

As the Town's founder there is an abiding interest in Edmund Freeman, his origins, family, purpose in founding the town, and his contribution to the town and colony. We have mentioned that he came first to Saugus in 1635 with his wife and four children. He was doubtless in Plymouth or Duxbury by 1636 as he was at a general meeting of all accepted freemen in Plymouth, March 7, 1636/7 and was appointed to a special inquest on the laws and abuses. There is however no reference to his occupying land in Plymouth or Duxbury as there is for several of the others who came to Sandwich. The historian Thomas Hutchinson in paying tribute to Plymouth Colony lists Edmund Freeman after the *Mayflower* planters and among the later great Assistant Governors (Hatherly, Willett, Thomas and Cudworth) as one of the true founders of the Old Colony. Curiously he omits Collier and Thomas Prence from this list, while including the faithless Allerton. Edmund's descendant Reverend Frederick Freeman writing in the 1850s praises his ancestor but does not summarize what he did, or try to evaluate his contribution.

In the midst of the meadowlands controvesy in 1639 in which the ten proprietors did not come off well, Freeman is found to have gone back to England by himself, a curious abdication but possibly necessitated by family interests in Sussex. The only known result of this trip was that he brought back a consignment of hats to sell, worth £52, and that the merchant in London had to press repeatedly for payment. Freeman was sworn in as an Assistant Governor on June 2, 1640 and continued then to be elected annually through the year beginning June 1645, a total of six terms. Among his local Cape Cod assignments were:

June 1640 - To hear causes in the Cape towns with representatives of Barnstable and Yarmouth

June 1641 - To hear a case at Yarmouth on land bounds.

Sept. 1641 - To see a maid whipt for stealing at Barnstable.

Dec. 1641 - To see Anne Lynceford whipt for adultery at Yarmouth, also her consort Thomas Bray.

March 1641/2 - Other offenders to be whipt at Barnstable. At this Court he himself was presented for lending a gun to an Indian. (Somehow every act was observed and reported to the Court, suggesting a paid informer system.)

Sept. 1642 - One of a special Council of War on Indian matters

June 1644 - To hold Court in the three Cape towns

June 1645 - To take the oaths of elected officials etc.

March 1645/6 - To hear a case at Yarmouth

In 1645 he received John Beauchamp's power of attorney to collect the £400 still due to Beauchamp on the Colony's debts and trade balance, and as we saw in the previous chapter began to take steps to raise this sum through receiving pledges based on real estate and houses owned by the eight original Undertakers. Possibly the stresses produced by this painful procedure are the reason he was not re-elected to the Court in 1646. His descendant Frederick Freeman said the reason was that he was too liberal. There is certainly a good case for this as well.

Late in 1645 an influential settler in Scituate, Captain William Vassal, petitioned the Plymouth Court to legalize the toleration for men of every religious belief who would still "preserve the civil peace and submit unto government." In Plymouth the Court of seven plus the governor was evenly divided, probably Standish, Hatherly, John Browne and Edmund Freeman in favor of toleration, while Governor Bradford, Edward Winslow, Prence and Collier opposed. The older Pilgrims had become more conservative and resented the tendencies of the day put forward by newcomers. The conservative faction obtained a delay for further consideration and the matter was never raised again. Historians agree that this was a turning point for the Colony, after which it began to pass laws requiring Church attendance and penalizing criticism of the ministers or government. It could well be that Edmund Freeman used the Beauchamp collection affair as a plausible basis for not serving further as an assistant, but chose himself not to stand again for Colony office over the toleration issue.

Freeman and William Newland were elected deputies from Sandwich in 1646. Freeman significantly was fined for non-appearance at the March election and law-making session in June. After this the astonishing fact is that in the next thirty-six years of his long life he withdrew himself almost totally from public life. He was elected Constable in 1650, a minor office for one of his background, and even this may be a mistake of Senior for Junior by the scribe or copyist. It is hard indeed from what we know now to account for his total change of attitude shown by his rejection of all official participation in the wracking problems ahead for his own town, his brainchild.

One last official role did remain for Freeman to play at this time, turning over to the town his agreement with Bradford to accept the whole grant back in 1637. The first document is in the Plymouth Colony Court Records July 7, 1646 reading:

> "It is agreed upon and ordered by the Court that when the inhabitants of Sandwich have paid a debt of £17 or £18 owing to the old company, and paid the charge and purchase of their township, . . .that then the Committees or Undertakers shall yield up the lands undisposed of to the town, to be given forth and disposed by such persons as the town shall appoint, and that every inhabitant having lands granted him shall pay proportionately to the said payments."

Governor Bradford's resignation of his rights to Sandwich then followed:

"Whereas about ten years past the within named William Bradford Governor and the rest of his partners within written being of the old company have purchased the town of Sandwidge of the Indians and paid to them for the said purchase the value of sixteen pounds nineteen shillings in commodities; now know ye that I the said William Bradford my self and in behalf of my partners for and in consideration of the sum of £16, 19s to me in hand paid by Edmund Freeman of Sandwidge; I the said William Bradford have assigned sold and set over all my right and title that either myself or my partners have to the said town of Sandwidge by reason of the said purchase: to have and to hold to him the said Edmund Freeman his heirs and assigns for ever, In witness whereof I have set to my hand this 24th of Jan 1647/8."

A group of six of the leading townspeople (excluding any of the original ten Proprietors) was promptly set up February 26, 1647/8 with the purpose "to agitate things betwixt the Committees and the town." This group was composed of George Allen, John Vincent, William Newland, Anthony Wright, Robert Bodfish and Richard Bourne. They agreed with Freeman to satisfy the just demands of the Committees for various charges concerning the foundation of the town. (These charges might represent such items as hiring a ship or horses and carts to transport goods to Sandwich, initial stocks of food and tools.) The town group also agreed to pay Freeman the sum of £17 plus the £16, 19s which he had laid out to Bradford. This transaction was not finally concluded until August 20, 1651 when the same group (less George Allen who had died) gave Freeman as one of the Committees several described parcels of land for his part of charges about founding the town, and for the £17 a ten acre meadow plus £4 cash lent by Freeman, Jr., and another £4 lent by widow Joan Swift. (Cash was scarce in those days.) Freeman then gave a formal statement to Bradford that all his rights and titles as a Proprietor had been turned over to the town itself, excepting only the lands he had been granted personally. Among these he specifically referred to Plymouth Neck and to the lands in Sandwich given his son John Freeman lately removed to Eastham, which were to remain in the family, rather than being surrendered on departure as was the usual case.

The other remaining members of the "Ten Men" also received land grants in recognition of their signing off early costs and special rights as original Proprietors. The Ten Men were:

William Almy - sold his house to Freeman in 1642 and left for Rhode Island, then Long Island.

John Carman - left for Long Island before 1643.

Richard Chadwell - sold his house to Freeman in 1646 mentioning its glass windows; interestingly also sold his past and future rights as an original Proprietor of the town. He did not, however, remove but built another house in Spring Hill where he died childless in 1681. Served occasionally as Highway Surveyor and Assessor.

Thomas Dexter Sr. - never lived in Sandwich after building the grist mill. Settled in West Barnstable from Lynn in 1646, retired to Boston in 1673, died 1677.

Edward Dillingham - remained in Sandwich all his life, served as Deputy once, Assessor three times, kept out of controversy, died 1667.

Henry Feake - only public record one term as Deputy, removed to Long Island 1652.

Edmund Freeman - remained in Sandwich all his life, supported good causes such as rebuilding the mill and meetinghouse, opposed persecution of Quakers, died 1682 the last of the Ten Men.

George Knott - no public record, died 1649; only daughter married Thomas Tobey.

Thomas Tupper - the oldest man we know of in Sandwich (59 in 1637) listed as able to bear arms in 1643 altho then 65; accused of light and lascivious carriage toward the adultress Anne Lynceford but was only admonished; allowed to solemnize marriages in Sandwich as a reputable senior; served the town in many offices; did lay preaching in the town. Died 1676 in his 99th year; lived on Dock Lane.

William Wood - constable 1640, early Town Clerk, no record after 1649.

CHAPTER 4

THE 1667 PROPERTY SURVEY

Plymouth Colony towns were advised to appoint a town clerk in 1646, among whose duties were to record results of town meetings, to write down records of births, deaths, and marriages, to copy deeds and wills, to record imports of duty-taxed items (i.e. munitions, tobacco and spirits) and to record shipments of horses. These vital records, land records and imports were to be passed on to Plymouth. The reporting of information from the towns in process of formation had been the task of the regional assistant governors; then the duty passed to town deputies and constables. The main records of births, deaths, and marriages of the period to 1651, at least for Sandwich, are still the Plymouth Colony Records.

The earliest original records of the town clerk are preserved here in Sandwich in a volume entitled *General Records.* The surviving pages are almost certainly incomplete and contain a mixture of entries not in chronological or subject order. Town meeting records begin January 7, 1650/1, but the entries refer to a ten-pound levy previously made, suggesting strongly that some pages are now lost. In addition the *General Records* includes vital statistics, land grants and agreements, cattle earmarks, horse records, and lists of townsmen. Among the records of births are certain family groups supplied by the families to the town clerk, as the events predate the establishment of the office and even of the town.

We now quote in full the records of town meetings held in the calendar year 1651, with brief comments on background and scope.

Meeting, January 7, 1650/1

> It is agreed upon by the town to pay unto Richard Bourne twenty shillings and his levy for as much as he is rated in the ten pound levy lastly made, in consideration of his labor and the pains that he has taken in business concerning the town, as in selling of lands to satisfy the Committees and the like.

Comment: Lands that had been issued could be sold to other townsmen to raise funds to pay taxes. Other land transactions were made to consolidate holdings, provide for sons and make way for newcomers. Since there was little cash and the lands were poorly bounded, these land transactions had to be made on barters and promises with inadequate records, leading to dispute and arbitration. Bourne was a good detail man and filled a vital role in the fussy administrative work.

In the item cited above he is being paid one Pound (twenty shillings) and forgiven his personal tax in recognition of these skilled services. This was not a trivial award. As to value of money at this time, Mr. Willison in his *Saints and Strangers* published in 1945 suggested that a pound in Plymouth Colony was about fifty dollars in 1945 values. This would be more like one hundred dollars in 1984, and a shilling five dollars.

Meeting January 7, 1650/1

> The five pound levy to complete Mr. Leveridge's house was passed [see chapter 3]. Agreed that this levy shall be made by those four men which were chosen to make the ten pound levy above mentioned, Mr. Vincent, William Newland, Thomas Tupper, Robert Bodfish.

Comment: The order followed at these early town meetings was to consider and vote on a specific project, then agree on a levy for new funds to meet it. A group was then assigned to allocate the levy to the townsmen, and to follow up on both the payments and the completion of the project. Since cash was limited, payments were made in crops when gathered, or in boards, nails, or services. This set up circuits of payments by which the levy would finally be accumulated, and the group responsible for the project reimbursed. At this time the town had no treasurer and no central repository for assets, so that typically for a certain levy one person held the town's available cash, another the town's grain, another some whale oil ready for call. All this took much accounting and patience, and those willing to serve were contributing a great deal of time and effort.

Meeting May 22, 1651

> It is ordered by the town that these four, Goodman Tupper, Goodman Burgess Sr., Nathaniel Willis and William Gifford shall have power to call a town meeting, they seeing occasion for the same, giving the town three days warning, and these meetings thus warned shall be lawful meetings and what neighbors shall stay (away) above an hour after the time appointed shall lose their votes in what is done before they come.
>
> It is ordered that the Constable shall every year give up his accounts to the town at the town meeting, for that year they have been Constables, before they chose another, or else to stand another year Constable.
>
> It is agreed upon by the town that in regard Peter Wright wants land, and upon his request of half a dozen acres of the town that they have manifested themselves likely to be freely willing to give him so much. Moreover the town has freely given also to Nathaniel Willis six acres of land in regard to his great need of land both to build and plant on.

Comment: Early town meetings were held any day except Sunday, and typically at least four times per year. Ten voters represented a quorum. The constable's job was an unpopular one (reporting on lawbreakers, bringing people to Plymouth Court, carrying out sentences) and sooner or later almost everyone had to accept his stint at the unwelcome task. For the illiterate, tallying his accounts for the year must have been one of the hardest parts. The early land grants were in the strip adjacent to the existing homesteads. Everyone's location, experience and capabilities were well understood, and the new grants were a recognition of capacity to use the land or a reward for services to the town.

> ***Meeting June 23, 1651***
>
> It is now agreed upon by the town that the forementioned Peter Wright shall range out his six acres of land above him along by the east side of Mr. Feake's land toward Spring Hill, above the cartway, between Mr. Feake's land and Wolves Hollow.

Comment: This general location in current terms would be south of Route 6A between Chipman Road and Gully Lane. The steep natural valley through which Crowell Road dips was then called Wolves Hollow and is referred to in various deeds and grants.

> ***Meeting November 21, 1651***
>
> It is ordered by the town that these five men, Mr. Vincent, Thomas Tupper, William Newland, Richard Bourne and James Skiff being chosen by the town shall make a levy of six pounds for the payment of the Clerk and the Committees.

Comment: Since the office of town clerk, like that of minister, was a paid position, the funds had to be voted in the town meeting. Cash or the equivalent in goods or services had to be allocated. Other officers were unpaid. Expenses for travel to Plymouth were reimbursed, however.

These items are all that survive of town meeting record for 1651.

Mary Freeman and Edward Perry

Edward and his brother Ezra Perry and three sisters came to Sandwich as teenagers in the early 1640's with an older lady Sarah Perry. These five all married and became strongly identified with the town. Edward's home was out on Old County Road probably in the Talbot's Point area, and he later became the town's leading Quaker, a forceful dedicated literate and conscientious man. In 1653 when criticism of the established church and Colony government was mounting, Perry married Mary Freeman, a young lady in Edmund Freeman's household. The young couple took each other in marriage and declined the services both of Thomas Tupper, who was authorized to conduct marriages in Sandwich, and of the magistrate for this district. Plymouth Court was very stern about this as a bad example in the town and Colony, and fined Perry £5 for his refusal, with a promise of a similar fine every quarter until he conformed. There is no record that he ever did. The Court must have been angered at Edmund Freeman as well for permitting this breach in his own family. The only recorded result is that Thomas Tupper was made a scapegoat and was dismissed from his authority to marry couples in Sandwich. The Edward Perrys had nine children and many famous descendants, including Matthew Calbraith Perry, Oliver Hazard Perry and August Belmont Jr.

Church Criticism

We have mentioned the 1646 petition in Plymouth Court to allow religious toleration which was sidetracked by conservatives in the Court, who were acting quite differently from the government that had practiced compromise and democracy in the 1620s. In retrospect this loss of toleration and cooperation after 1646 marks a significant turning point. Before this, church attendance had not been enforced. Miles Standish came from a Catholic family and had never been a church member. It was not required of freemen to be church members but only of good report and fit for church membership. The first rumblings in Sandwich were in 1651 when the Grand Jury presented the following persons all of Sandwich:

Ralph Allen Senior and his wife
George Allen Junior and his wife
William Allen and Richard Kerby
Peter Gaunt and his wife
Edmund Freeman Senior and his wife
Goodwife Turner and Widow Knott

The charge was "not frequenting the public worship of God, contrary to order made the 6 of June 1651." This order read "if any lazy slothful or profane persons in any of the towns neglect to attend public worship, they shall pay for each offense ten shillings or be publicly whipped." At this same Court Ralph Allen Sr. and Richard Kerby "were summoned to answer for their deriding wild speeches of and concerning God's Word and ordinances." At the next Court these two were fined £5 each to be paid within three months or suffer whipping. The refusal of Edward Perry to allow Tupper or anyone in the Plymouth government to solemnize his marriage was another eloquent protest against the new persecuting spirit of the government.

The Departure of Leveridge

A combination of hostility by a few, lack of moral support by town leaders and church attenders, plus loss of pecuniary support, led Mr. Leveridge to give up his charge in Sandwich in 1654 and remove to Long Island, then being settled by English groups. Others from Sandwich accompanied him or had preceded him there. His "implacable opponents" in Sandwich were said to be William and John Newland, Peter Gaunt, Richard Kerby, Ralph and George Allen. Sandwich was here demonstrating the same sweeping and radical attitude of scorn of church authority which was found in varying degrees in all towns in this Colony. The spread and depth of this unprecedented development must have struck dismay and astonishment into the magistrates and officials of the Colony. The reason for this rejection of the ministers in so many towns must have been very deep seated, rooted in the very nature of the experience of building up these new towns in the wilderness, and it was utterly futile of the government to call those townsmen who turned away from the ministers "lazy, slothful and profane." Indicative of the wide-spread dissent are the following items concerning towns and their ministers.

Plymouth: John Raynor left in 1654 over doctrinal disputes; no minister until John Cotton Jr. 1669

Barnstable: John Lothrop died in 1653; not replaced until Thomas Walley 1663

Yarmouth: John Miller removed 1652 after a sermon against the government; not replaced until Thomas Thornton 1662.

Scituate: Charles Chauncey left 1654 pleading hardship and poverty

Taunton: A long gap between the departure of Nicholas Street and the ordination of George Shove in 1665

Eastham: John Mayo left 1649 after dissensions; his successor Thomas Crosby left when forced to make all his own collections; not replaced until Samuel Treat in 1672.

Sandwich: After the departure of Leveridge in 1654, town was not supplied until 1675 by John Smith; the last town in the Colony to re-install a minister after what Mather called "The Dark Days."

In 1655 Peter Gaunt, Ralph and George Allen were again before the Court for not frequenting public worship. Gaunt stated that he knew no public visible worship. Sarah Kerby uttered "suspicious speeches" against Mr. Bourne and Mr. Freeman and was sentenced to be whipped if this offense was repeated.

As a final note on Mr. Leveridge, it is recorded that the Commissioners of the United Colonies (the channel for expenditure of funds for Indian mission work) approved allowances to Leveridge in 1652 and 1653 to encourage him to learn the Indian language and work among the natives in his area. He is said to have begun these labors in despair of his white congregation, and to have interested two of his most faithful supporters, Tupper and Bourne, in this missionary work. The tradition in Sandwich is that after Leveridge's departure these two, Tupper and Bourne, conducted services of lay teaching and preaching in the meetinghouse. Each had particular supporters and whichever was the more numerous on that Sunday determined who was chosen to carry the service. This may have happened only a few times. However, it is recorded in 1655 town meeting records that a special subscription was raised to build a new place for public meetings, and that the contributors included Newland, Kerby, the Allens, Jenkins, Butler, Johnson and others who later became the most determined Quakers. Furthermore (perhaps even more remarkably), Tupper and Bourne followed Leveridge's lead and interested themselves keenly in the state of Indian affairs near this town, and deepened these early interests into family commitments extending over one hundred years in both cases. Leveridge worked with Indians on Long Island and died there in 1677. After his departure from Sandwich he was accused by the town of giving a gun to an Indian in exchange for commodities, and a £5 fine was laid against him in absentia.

To Build the Mill New Again

After the return of Thomas Dexter Sr. to Lynn, the mill probably remained in control of his family. We find that Thomas Dexter Jr. was the miller when a charge was brought against him for using an improper toll-dish. He was cleared. Thomas Jr. came to Sandwich before 1645 when he was charged with shipping away a horse that was subject to military requisition for the Narraganset campaign. He was henceforward found frequently in town records, as constable 1647, and surveyor of highways 1648. He married Elizabeth Vincent, daughter of John Vincent, in 1648. Apparently the first grist mill became inoperable, as we note from the town meeting records of June 26, 1654:

> "The town has given full power to Mr. Edward Dillingham and Richard Bourne in their behalf to agree with Thomas Dexter to go on to build the mill new again, and what the said Mr. Edward Dillingham and Richard Bourne do promise to the said Thomas Dexter the town has engaged themselves to stand to their agreement."

However no agreement was reached and at a later town meeting, four other men committed themselves to build the mill:

> "The first of March 1654/5 John Ellis, William Swift, William Allen, James Skiff we four men do hereby engage ourselves equally in the building of a mill, to defray and discharge all disbursements about the building of the same and for the present engage ourselves to pay twenty pounds apiece in wheat and beef to be ready to make payment of the same by the last of November next."

Skiff and Swift signed their names, Ellis and Allen their marks. This pledge was to be met by twenty-two townsmen who signed up to repay the four sponsors. It was reported in Frederick Freeman's History that Matthew Allen was to be the new miller. However we find that the item referring to Allen is to allow him to put up a new pound. Dexter seems to have come to terms with the town leaders because the town meeting May 29, 1655 reads:

> "Thomas Dexter does engage himself to build a mill. The town does and has fully engaged themselves by covenant to allow him five pints upon the bushel toll, to build and maintain a mill and the dam and all other things thereunto belonging, and also a miller at his own cost and charge, the time and space of ten year, and grind all their corn that is brought to him to the said mill to be ground without any further demand of them..."

As a final note on the first grist mill, the townsmen did not forget that their agreement with Dexter was for ten years and then could be altered. The town meeting of May 11, 1664 states:

> "The Town has made choice of three men Goodman Chadwell,

Edmund Freeman Thomas Tobey for to agree with Mr. Thomas Dexter Jr. about the grinding of the townsmen's corn for so long time as they shall agree upon. And if these men above mentioned and the said Mr. Thomas Dexter Jr. agree not, then the Town has granted 12 acres of land at the river that comes out of the pond at the head of Benjamin Nye his marsh to any other of the townsmen of Sandwich that will set up a mill—except Mr. Dexter—is agreed upon by the town."

Apparently Mr. Dexter was prickly again about coming to agreement with the committee, because in 1670 we find the town granting the twelve acres to Benjamin Nye "because he did build the mill at the little pond." So the town got its second grist mill, on Old County Road.

Other Town News

There was an annual rush of herring up the Manomet River to spawn in Great Herring Pond. The first mention of herring regulations in town meeting records is:

"March 12, 1651/2 the Town has agreed with Daniel Wing and Michael Blackwell for to catch the fish at Herring Weir for three years for ninepence a thousand for the town, and the town has given them order for to give a time to draw logs to mend the weir, and to pay them in fish the amount not to be above five thousand."

The first mention of support for the poor of the town occurs with the following item:

"June 22d 1652 It is ordered that a lawful meeting upon warrant from the Governor that Goody Bodfish shall have four bushel of wheat of that that is due to the town from George Allen."

Robert Bodfish had died in 1650 leaving widow Bridget with four young children plus a fifth born posthumously. She managed somehow until 1657 when she married a distinguished Barnstable widower Samuel Hinckley Sr., removing to Barnstable with her family. Three of her children remained there and married, but after Hinckley's death in 1663 she returned to Sandwich with son John Bodfish, and both remained the rest of their lives.

The Sandwich militia or train band became active in 1653 when James Skiff was engaged to buy "Pistols Powder Bullets Drum Cutlass and Half Pikes." The next year Mr. Bourne submitted his accounts for shopping in Boston including sea freight on a barrel of powder, two hundred weight of bullets and two hundred weight of lead, and two townsmen were urged to procure a colors set. In 1655 the colors materials were procured—"nine yards of West India stuff"—to be paid for in wheat or butter. Then Lieutenant Ellis the drill master submitted a bill for a drum and freight on the drum from Plymouth, firelocks, muskets, halberd heads, pike, two staffs for the colors and "silk."

Sandwich Population

The original grant to the "Ten Men from Saugus" referred to room enough for three score families. We find there were indeed about sixty families here in the 1637/40 period, whose names were listed at the end of chapter 1. There was a rapid turnover of settlers with some transients coming and going, some valuable new additions arriving, young men marrying, counterbalanced by deaths of the heads of household, and a number of departures as settlers who tried their luck here decided to move elsewhere, During the decade 1640/1650 these initial population factors remained almost exactly in balance, and we are able to list a total of sixty households here in 1650. The changes from 1640 to 1650 are:

Earliest families and independent married men, including the matriarch Deborah Wing.	62
Further arrivals. (See below)	17
Sons forming new households (5 Allens, 2 Freemans, 3 Wings, Burgess, Dexter, Swifts)	14
Total	93
Less deaths of male heads of families	10
Less departures to other towns	27
Balance in 1650	***56***

The arrivals became so much a part of the town that we must list them here: Ralph Allen Senior, William Bassett, Michael Blackwell, John Ellis, Thomas Gibbs, William Gifford, Thomas Greenfield, Benjamin Hammond, John Jenkins, Thomas Johnson, John Newland, Edward and Ezra Perry, John Presbury, Henry Sanderson, William Swift and Thomas Tobey

There were in fact sixty families in 1650 including four households which continued to function with women at the head, namely those of Bridget Bodfish, Katherine Briggs, Martha Knott and Joan Swift.

There were also fifteen transients, probably unmarried, who are mentioned in the records only once. Another category was that of servants and apprentices. Many families employed servants until their period of indenture had been served. They were then free to marry, remove or settle. Richard Handy, Skiff's servant, transferred to Plymouth in 1639, as did Robert Ransom, Dexter's servant, in 1654. Other records mention problems. John Baddo, who was Newland's servant, stole his mare in 1660. In 1655 we find Swift's servant a Welsh girl named Jane Powell, charged with fornication and the subsequent explanation:

"being examined she saith that it was committed with one David

O'Kelley an Irish man servant of Edward Sturgis; she saith she was allured thereunto by him, going for water one evening, hoping to have married him, being she was in a sad and miserable condition by hard service, wanting clothes and living discontentedly; and expressing great sorrow for her evil she was cleared for the present and ordered to go home again."

Jane got off lightly; in fact this story has a wonderfully happy ending in that she and Kelley later married and had a large and successful family in Yarmouth with numerous descendants. She died highly respected in 1711.

Early Land Purchases From Indians

Inevitably Sandwich settlers would wish to push their land holdings outwards. At this early date there was still much unallocated land within the original strip along Cape Cod Bay, owned by the town in general and called the "Commons." Lots were issued regularly as families expanded. The border with Indian lands to the east, south and west was not defined in any record that has survived. The first notice of expansion to the south is in Plymouth Colony Records August 20, 1644:

"George Allen of Sandwich is licensed to cut hay at the ponds beyond Sandwich plains, so he give not the Indians anything for that without approbation of the Bench."

These ponds were probably Peters Pond, Pimlico and Wakeby. This joint use of lands was attempted elsewhere as well. Leveridge had been allowed an Indian field at Manomet "for mowing only." Richard Bourne was allowed to cut hay at Old Field in the Manomet area with the strict understanding that it remained Indian land. The first purchase of new Indian-held land seems to have occurred after this entry in town meeting records:

"May the 13, 1654 the Town have engaged themselves by making choice of these five men Mr. Dillingham, Goodman Bourne, Goodman Tupper, William Newland, Thomas Dexter to frame a petition to the worshipful Court of Plymouth to grant and assist them in purchasing of Manomet with all the properties, to bear them out in all matter of charge and any other thing that shall be needful about the same."

The term "Manomet" or "Monomoyet" strictly meant a burden-carrying place such as a ford or portage. There was a major settlement of Indians along Great Herring Pond and down the banks of the Herring River to the lower valley. The Sachem of Manomet was a person with authority over the Indians in southern Plymouth plus the whole later Sandwich area, also part of West Barnstable and along the western shores of Buzzards Bay down to Woods Hole. Among the whites the word Manomet was taken to refer to the land in the present Canal valley from the herring-catching places west and south to the Pocasset sector comprising the areas of the present villages of Bournedale, Buzzards Bay and Monument. The first white presence here was of course at the Aptuxcet

Trading Post. After 1637 the Sandwich settlers must have joined the Indians at taking herring each spring. As noted above, this herring-catching already involved a weir built of logs that needed replacement by 1652.

In writing of the restoration of the Aptuxcet Trading Post in 1927, Mr. Percival Hall Lombard of Bourne stated that the Plymouth Court had given Thomas Burgess Senior the original trading post site in 1652. We are unable to find a record of this grant to Burgess. An entry in Plymouth Colony Records in May 1655, however, gives Burgess the right to take ten thousand herring per year at his land on the river in addition to his regular share as a citizen. Another reference in July 1655 reads as follows:

> "In reference unto a former engagement unto James Skiffe for his former service, the Court have granted unto him a small parcell or tract of land lying at Mannomett, videlect, a small neck divided into two partes by an inlett of water coming out of the river, directly over against the said Thomas Burgis his land, which was formerly the companies, where they had a trading house, viz all the said necke so divided as abovesaid, with all and singular the appurtenances, privileges, and emunities belonging thereunto, with all the meddow of any kind bordering upon the said necke or lying on the skirts thereof, to have and to hold unto the said James Skiff, he his heires and assignes, forever.
>
> In regard of some straites and hardships upon Richard Bourne and that, in case they shall find any parcells of meadow about Mannomett or other places near, bordering upon Sandwidge that shall not be found to intrench upon lands already granted to any or shall not hinder a plantation, or breed or accation any disturbance amongst the Indians, they have liberty to make use and improve the same for the supply of their wants above expressed."

These grants were sufficiently vague that the "men of Sandwidge" could interpret them almost to suit themselves, so long as the Indians were not disturbed. Only Skiff, as a highly favored person was allowed to buy direct from the Indians for his own account, July 3, 1656:

> "The Court have given liberty unto James Skiff to purchase the land granted to him at Manomet of the Indians there; and in case there shall be a small matter of land more lying next to that already granted him, the Court have granted him liberty to purchase it likewise, and to have it as his own forever to him and his heirs forever."

It is recorded among the accounts of the Sandwich constable William Bassett in May 1657 that he paid out £9 15s for Indian lands. This was for the town account, and these lands would then be available for issue to various townsmen. Later in the year the town voted £4 to buy land at Scorton where Indian rights had been respected and where Barnstable had bought rights on their side of the Sandwich-Barnstable line.

Purchases continued rapidly in the Manomet and Herring River area for the next few years, and spread down the shores of Buzzards Bay, with major purchases in 1659 and 1661 to permit a whole new white settlement called Saconesset in what is now Falmouth. The Indians living along the shore increasingly were pressed into smaller pockets and ultimately into houselots.

The First Property Survey

Land allocation was of the highest importance to all settlers. When the town area was first granted by Plymouth Court, the Ten Men and a representative body of proprietors issued lands to all comers. If a newcomer departed his grant reverted to the town, but if he had built and cleared some land he was allowed to sell both the improvements and the title to the lands given him. Only a few of these early deeds survive but they are important in showing what sort of lands were held in the earliest period. Upon removing to Yarmouth, Andrew Hallett Jr. deeded to Daniel Wing in 1640:

> three acres with dwelling and cowhouse lying between
>
> Slawson's and Newland's land
>
> two acres upland at Scusset for planting
> five acres upland at Spring Hill for planting
> seven and one quarter acres meadow at Pine Neck,
>
> Spring Hill and [probably] Town Neck

We believe this farm is the original Wing Fort property at Spring Hill occupied by Stephen Wing from 1641.

The Plymouth Colony Records recorded the holdings of John Carman, one of the Ten Men. The item indicates the substance of his estate when contrasted with Hallett's. It shows Carman to have:

> fifteen acres house and upland at Scusset
> sixteen acres meadow east of the village
> eight acres meadow off Town Neck near the beach
> ten acres upland probably at Ploughed Neck
> ninety acres woodlot on the plains adjacent to Dexter and Dillingham

There are no records of the original grants to the sixty families, and the bounds of the lots were casual or non-existent. With the rapid turnover of lands due to departures, deaths, new arrivals, and new households formed, with families tending to want to consolidate or swap lands, there was ample occasion for confusion and misunderstandings, with many cases carried to Court. In 1654 the Court ordered that all towns should acquire books and set down the bounds of each man's lands plus sales, divisions, and new grants. These records were to be read and acknowledged at town meeting and if not timely challenged were considered permanent. The town clerks were then supposed to submit copies to Plymouth Court. Since paper was in short supply the minutes of town meetings in Sandwich up to 1658 refer to a very few new grants. This changed in October 1658 when (doubtless at Plymouth urging) a new land regulation was put into effect in Sandwich:

Improved lands (meadow, plowed and fenced lands) were to be valued and became part of the tax base. (Before this, land was free and only buildings, livestock, cash, tools, stores or shares in a boat were taxable.)

Owners were urged to sell off surplus meadow (for marsh hay.)

The town would sell off unallocated meadow with proceeds used for dock work. (Some land of Thomas Tupper's was taken for the dock and an access road.)

A committee of seven were named to record all the lands and bounds.

Charges for the committee's work would be based on onepence per acre for bounded lands (called "ranged out") and fourpence per acre for unbounded lands. (This was a clear incentive for neighbors to register bounds or renew old ones.)

It was an arduous task since a total of two hundred forty-two lots were later described, and even that surviving record is incomplete. The committee selected consisted of the familiar leaders, Edmund Freeman, John Vincent, Edward Dillingham, Richard Bourne, Thomas Burgess, William Newland and Richard Chadwell. Their original book was not preserved, but applicable portions were recopied in 1702 describing the lands owned by the persons here in the year 1667 when the survey was completed. The first entry is January 17, 1658/9 and defines some Ellis property near the Plymouth line and thence proceeded eastward. Generally when the area for a man's residence was reached, then all his lots were described. The date 1667 can be confidently ascribed to this list of properties. Persons who had died or removed by the date (i.e., John Vincent, Edward Dillingham and Richard Kerby) are not on the list, but favored sons (some still unmarried) are included. A new arrival John Jennings who married here in 1667 is not included. The 1667 date is further strengthened by an entry in town meeting records March 16, 1665/6 calling on the surviving members of the committee (i.e., Freeman, Bourne, Chadwell, Newland and Burgess) "for to make an end of bounding men's lands to answer the order of the Court."

The determination of locations of the early residences is of much interest in the history of the town, especially to descendants of the families and as an aid in dating our surviving buildings. Accordingly we have studied the 1667 report carefully to obtain a general synthesis of the lands described. The location is sometimes quite specific as Spring Hill with abutters named plus natural features and roadway directions. If the description of the abutting property is found to match, then confidence in the location is high. The process is an iterative one requiring geography and judicious estimates to form assemblages of the surest sets, then working outwards and cross-checking. We present the tentative results, together with three sketch maps:

Scusset Marsh Area

Edmund Freeman's lands were very extensive and included the whole of Plymouth Neck (also called Freeman's Knob; now Sagamore Hill). His residence was in the area of the Freeman Farm reestablished in the 19th Century. Two houses along the Back Street (Tupper Road) were those of Thomas Burgess and Samuel Briggs. The description of the residences of five families in the Scusset uplands does not permit exact location on the map. John Ellis was clearly the closest to the Plymouth line, and Blackwell was on the road just north of Scusset Creek. Swift, Gibbs and Butler were in between.

Town Neck and the Planting Commons or "Lots"

The map shows this central area of the original town. The Town Neck was fenced for cattle and was used for this purpose until the 20th century. However, the adjacent marsh on the Scusset and Shawme sides was issued to various families for seasonal mowing. There were four residences along the Back Road in the Town Neck area, those of Widow Cecelia Fish, John Jenkins, John Bodfish and his mother Bridget, and Joseph Burgess.

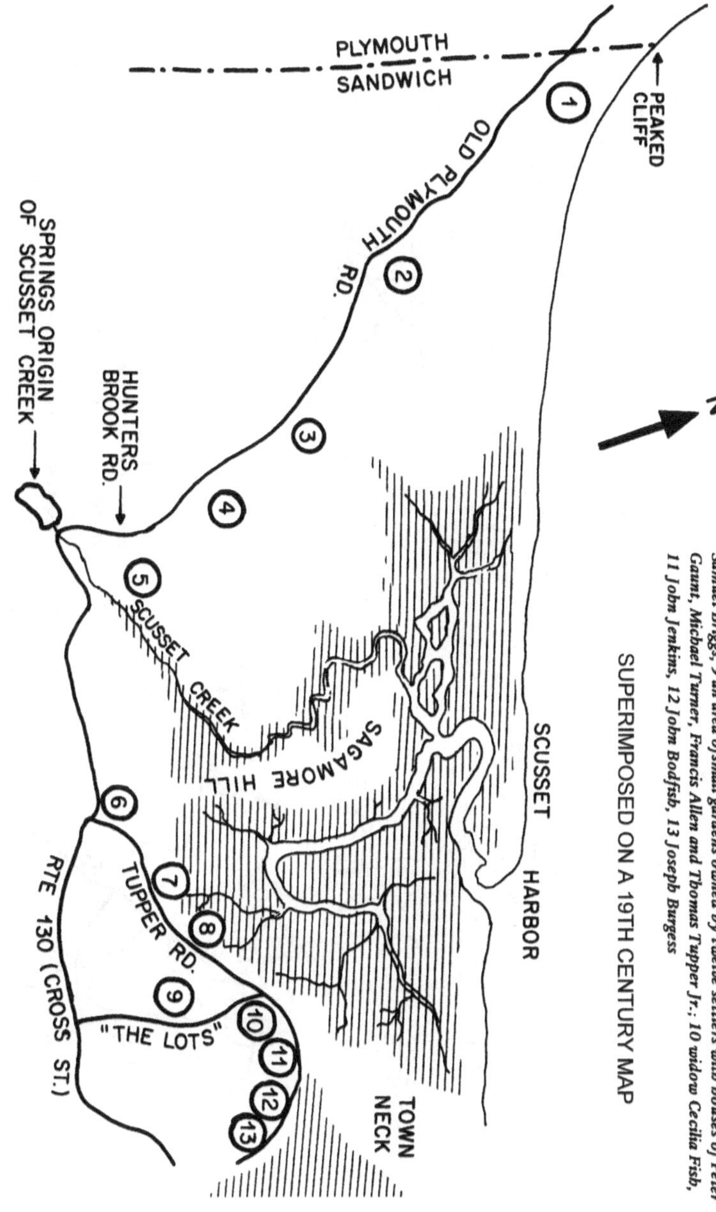

SUPERIMPOSED ON A 19TH CENTURY MAP

Sandwich 1667—Houses in Scusset & Town Neck area

Locations of early settlers are 1 John Ellis, 2 Thomas Butler, 3 Thomas Gibbs, 4 William Swift Jr., 5 Michael Blackwell, 6 Edmund Freeman Sr., 7 Thomas Burgess, 8 Samuel Briggs, 9 an area of small gardens owned by twelve settlers with houses of Peter Gaunt, Michael Turner, Francis Allen and Thomas Tupper Jr.; 10 widow Cecilia Fish, 11 John Jenkins, 12 John Bodfish, 13 Joseph Burgess

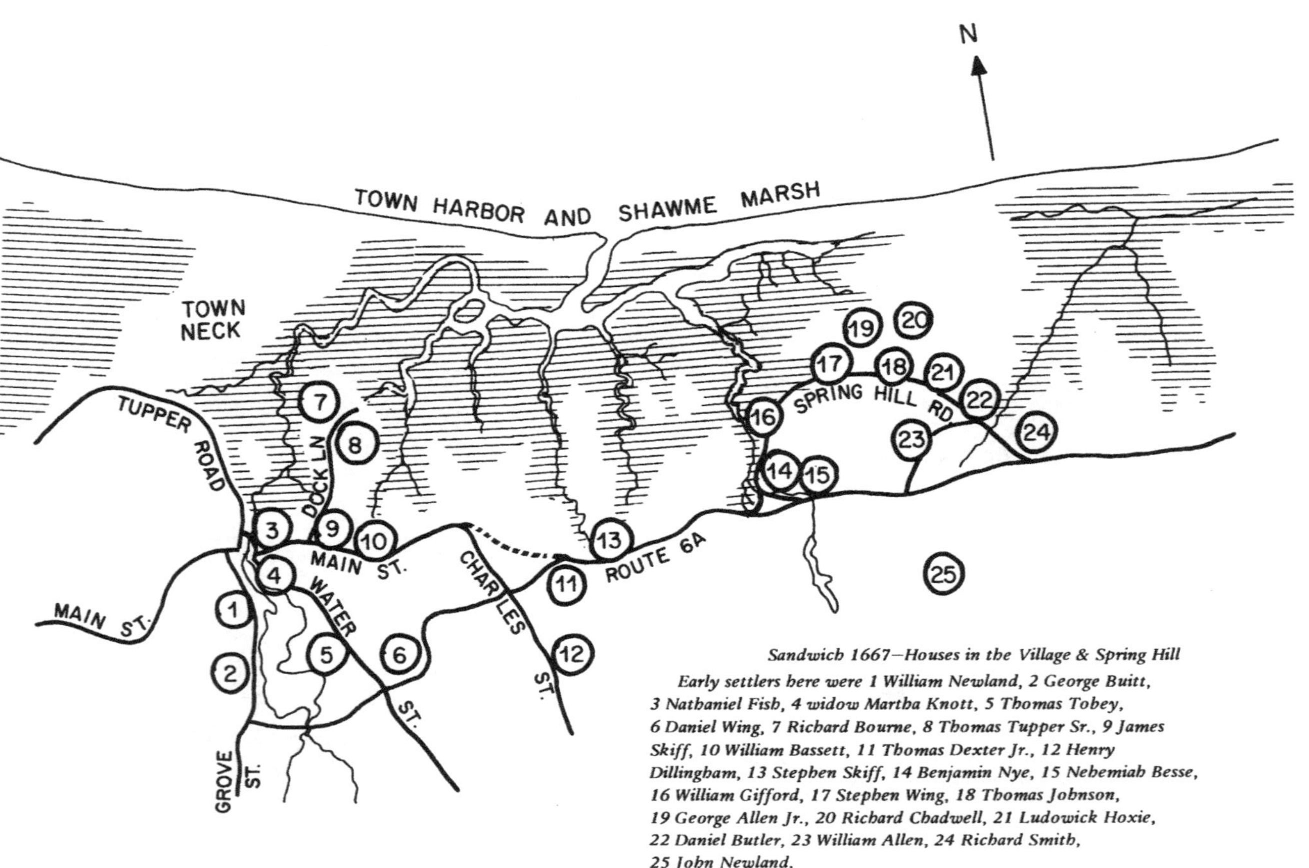

Sandwich 1667—Houses in the Village & Spring Hill

Early settlers here were 1 William Newland, 2 George Buitt, 3 Nathaniel Fish, 4 widow Martha Knott, 5 Thomas Tobey, 6 Daniel Wing, 7 Richard Bourne, 8 Thomas Tupper Sr., 9 James Skiff, 10 William Bassett, 11 Thomas Dexter Jr., 12 Henry Dillingham, 13 Stephen Skiff, 14 Benjamin Nye, 15 Nehemiah Besse, 16 William Gifford, 17 Stephen Wing, 18 Thomas Johnson, 19 George Allen Jr., 20 Richard Chadwell, 21 Ludowick Hoxie, 22 Daniel Butler, 23 William Allen, 24 Richard Smith, 25 John Newland.

A further area of planting settlement is shown on this map, which had been almost completely lost to knowledge, a block of planting fields in three rows each forty rods long running between Cross Street (Old Main Street, at the Dillingham house) across to Town Neck. A depth of four rods on these forty rod strips made an acre, and various acre multiples were laid out to many of the settlers, especially the younger men. This grid can be reestablished with confidence because of the matching abutters. The owners were:

Francis and Jedediah Allen	Samuel Knott (Unmarried)
Peter Gaunt	Samuel Briggs
John Jenkins	Thomas Tupper Jr.
Michael Turner	

Nathaniel Fish and Cecelia widow of John Fish

John Bodfish and his mother Bridget Hinckley

The first reference to these special measured fields seems to be in town meetings records January 22, 1657/8 and reads:

> "If any inhabitant wants land to plant he may have some in the Common for six years and no longer, provided he will be engaged to stack up the roots to make it meet for pasturing and moreover Richard Bourne and James Skiff are appointed by the Town to lay out such land to all persons as have need."

This description seems to allow fields in any location on Town Commons but Skiff owned the large block on Cross Street (Old Main Street) at the base of these measured lots, and the central location once established with access roads seemed to prove popular. By 1666 there were four houses built there, those of Gaunt, Tupper Jr., Francis Allen and Turner. Michael Turner was the senior of this group and his house may well have been there long before the "Lots" were laid out. Six years after the above record, the Town Meeting on January 10, 1663/4 mentions:

> "It is agreed...that James Skiff Sr., shall act...with the rest of the proprietors as they shall conceive to meet and put the divisions of those common meadows to a full issue."

We venture to suggest that these lots became permanent grants. Traces of these early farms could still be seen into the 20th century according to Sandwich historian George Burbank as cellar holes, wells and walls.

Grove Street to Charles Street

The first two houses along Grove Street were those of William Newland and George Buitt. There were no grants between Grove Street and the ponds until the 1680s, except that in 1663 the neck of land opposite William Newland's was taken for a burying ground (Old Town Cemetery). On Water Street the only residences mentioned are those of Widow Knott and of Thomas Tobey. Three other residences are Thomas Dexter's at about the present Crow Farm site, Henry Dillingham's further south on Charles Street and Daniel Wing's on the old Upper Road at what is now 8 Morse Road.

Jarves Street to Ox Pasture Neck

It is a matter of regret that the neck of upland in Shawme Marsh on which the later Jarves Street and glass factories were built does not have an early name to characterize it. This area near the grist mill and meetinghouse, with town dock, was clearly the early town center. Here were the residences of four of the ablest townsmen, Richard Bourne, Thomas Tupper Senior, James Skiff and William Bassett. The location of Nathaniel Fish's house is not clearly stated but since it was taken by the town later as a home for Reverend Roland Cotton it was near the meetinghouse. It is probably the location of Reverend Leveridge's humble house earlier. Tupper's and Bourne's houses are confirmed by later deeds, and the taking of Tupper's land at the foot of the present Harbor Street for the dock is clearly recorded. James Skiff's son Stephen Skiff was married about 1665 and his residence near the foot of present Chipman Road on Route 6A had probably just been built.

Spring Hill

This was the single most populous neighborhood in these early days. Benjamin Nye and Nehemiah Besse were located along the stream arising in Boiling Springs Pond, flowing out into the marsh. Along Spring Hill Road were the houses of William Gifford, Stephen Wing, Thomas Johnson, Ludowick Hoxie, Daniel Butler, and Richard Smith. (This latter was about at the present Agway site.) George Allen Jr. and Richard Chadwell had houses out in the present Countryside area, and bickered with one another repeatedly over roads and bounds. The early lot descriptions refer to a road over the hill which is not obvious on the present topographical map or the property lines. Gifford's land went down to a point on Spring Hill River called Slawson's Stage, although Slawson himself had departed from Sandwich for Stamford, Connecticut about 1641; Slawson's Stage was probably a wharf at the head of the tidewater. William and Priscilla Allen's house was on present Gilman Road. John Newland, brother of William, lived off the main road at a site called "Iron Ore Run." The Cowhouse Meadows east of this Spring Hill area was a branch of Scorton Marsh.

Ploughed Neck

Very nearly all of Ploughed Neck had fallen by grant or purchase to the Freemans. The sons of Edmund Senior (John and Edmund Jr.) had built here, a fact which raises questions as to why they did not build on their father's wide holdings at Scusset. John's house and lands are specified here in 1667 on Ploughed Neck, but he had moved to Eastham in 1650. Edmund Senior had arranged that John's lands should remain in the family. The only others beside Edmund Junior on Ploughed Neck were Thomas Landers and Jedediah Allen.

Landers' holding was about where the present Atwood house stands. The lane past John Freeman's (now Ploughed Neck Road) led over the arm of the marsh to the beach and along to the place where at low tide cattle were forded to and from Scorton Neck summer pasture.

Scorton Neck and Old County Road

This last map shows dwellings from present Hoxie Pond to the Barnstable line. The houses in 1667 were of Henry Sanderson, Edward Perry and Thomas Greenfield; Sanderson's was approximately at Pear Tree Farm, Perry's at the entrance to Talbot's Point and Greenfield's at Phillips' house on Old County Road. Near Jones Lane were Ralph Allen Jr. and Joseph Holway Jr. Further along (at the ancient Cape formerly owned by Harriet M. Taylor) was the home of Robert Harper. A major spring called Lawrence's Hole was located here, mentioned in several lots of this 1658/1666 period and still shown in 1860 as the name of the runoff stream. We venture to suggest this was named for Lawrence Willis, an original Sandwich grantee who aided in sales of Indian land to Barnstable in 1644. The earliest causeway to Scorton Neck was on the present Jones Road, named for Ralph Jones who lived just over the Barnstable line on High Street.

Benjamin Nye was granted land from Little Pond along a stream into Scorton River. In 1670 we have noted that Nye was given a further twelve acres here "because he did build the mill," the town's second grist mill. He probably moved here himself about that date, leaving the Spring Hill house to his eldest son, John.

Confirmations and Surprises

These 1667 location maps are a prime piece of new evidence for town history. They confirm the locations of Ellis, Gibbs, Swift and Blackwell in Scusset; Edmund Freeman Senior at the Freeman Farm site; the Knott family and Thomas Tobey on Water Street; Richard Bourne in the glass factory area; Stephen Skiff near Ox Pasture Neck; Benjamin Nye, William Gifford, Stephen Wing, George Allen, Ludowick Hoxie and William Allen at Spring Hill; Edmund Freeman, Jr., at Ploughed Neck; the Nye lands and residences of Edward Perry, Joseph Holway and Robert Harper on Old County Road. The surprises are equally important:

Thomas Tupper Senior on Dock Lane. The familiar Tupper house on the Back Street (later Tupper Road) seems to have been first occupied by John and Katherine Briggs and their two children. Samuel Briggs married Elizabeth daughter of John Ellis, and about 1682 moved to the new settlement of Rochester with her mother the widow Elizabeth Freeman Ellis. This Briggs house could well date from 1637, and was then taken over by Thomas Tupper Jr., only son of the venerable Thomas Senior who died in 1676. Tupper owned land over to the Lots.

Thomas Burgess' traditional homesite was by the Great Spring just west of Edmund Freeman's home. He was in this home at his death in 1682 and his will mentions "lands" between those of Thomas Tupper and Edmund Freeman where the 1667 house had been.

The four homes along Tupper Road in the Town Neck sector and the four houses upon the later "Lots Lane," (Leveridge Lane) are complete surprises.

The home of Daniel Wing was at the present 8 Morse Road. The earliest grants of lands in the Heritage Plantation area, traditionally associated with Daniel Senior, were made in the 1680s to John Tobey, to Daniel Wing Junior and to John Abbott who had married Daniel Jr.'s sister Lydia Hamilton. The 8 Morse Road house went to Daniel's youngest son Jashub. The house there is still called the Wing Howland house.

The 1667 survey does not mention the earliest homes of Deborah Wing and of Edward Dillingham, both traditionally east of the upper mill pond. Deborah and her son John Wing and young John Dillingham all went to settle in Yarmouth about 1648. All of the area east of the upper pond extending to the lower pond was owned in 1667 by Henry Dillingham, whose home was on Charles Street in the sector then called the Upper Fields.

The location of the homes of William Bassett and James Skiff, Sr. on what is now Main Street in the village area was not previously known. The Bassetts later built homes on River Street and on Main Street west of the mill stream. Skiff had five sons but the only one to remain in Sandwich, Stephen, had already provided for himself further east.

In Spring Hill the Besse, Chadwell, Johnson, Butler, Smith and Newland homes are new discoveries. The Besse house was probably just east of the present "Skiff" house. It is of poignant interest, because here we must assume George Barlow (see chapter 6) married and lived with the widow Jane Besse. In 1664, Plymouth Colony Records note that Nehemiah Besse "is of full age to enter upon the possession and enjoyment of such lands as his father left him" and gave him liberty "to enter upon the full enjoyment and possession of his father's inheritance." As shown in this 1667 survey, Nehemiah then had the Besse home to himself, with Barlow and Jane probably removed over to the Pocasset sector later known as Barlow's Landing.

The completeness of the Freeman ownership of Ploughed Neck comes as a surprise. Edmund Jr. had only one son Edmund III so that it was well into the eighteenth century before sons of Edmund III began to expand out of this fief. Thomas Landers' sons all removed and Jedediah Allen departed to New Jersey about 1678.

Other Houses in 1667

The 1667 properties survey covered only the original settled strip from Scusset through Scorton marshes along the Cape Cod Bay coast. A very few outlying lots do mention Herring River as a bound, but there were no residences there. A check of heads of household in the 1667 period reveals three that were here beyond any doubt, but whose residences, indeed any lands at all, are not mentioned. These missing townsmen were Ezra Perry, George Barlow, and Robert Lawrence plus Richard Handy later. The only explanation that seems possible is that these three already lived along the shores of Buzzards Bay by 1667, and that in these early days of buying Indian lands the committee at Sandwich simply made no attempt to describe the holdings from the Herring River south along the Manomet Valley and down the Buzzards Bay shore to Falmouth. The three omitted names are strongly associated with this area, Ezra Perry on Monument Neck, who obtained the trading post area from his father-in-law Thomas Burgess; George Barlow who about 1664 settled in the sector still called Barlow's Landing; and Robert Lawrence who made his first purchase from Indian Hope alias Pohunna in the Hope Spring area of Cataumet on the Falmouth line about the time of his marriage in 1665.

The only other area in Sandwich granted to the original settlers was up "on the plains," probably off what we now call Route 130 toward Spectacle Pond. There were no houses here and the early large grants to members of the Ten Men (Carman, Dexter, Dillingham, and Freeman) clearly became an undesirable precedent and no more grants were made up here until the general woodlots were issued starting in 1706, when the old grants were not in existence. The first new grant here was of forty or fifty acres to John Tobey in 1681 on the north shore of Peter's Pond where he established a family compound that survived for several generations. This is now the "Oak Grove Yacht Club" or Town property.

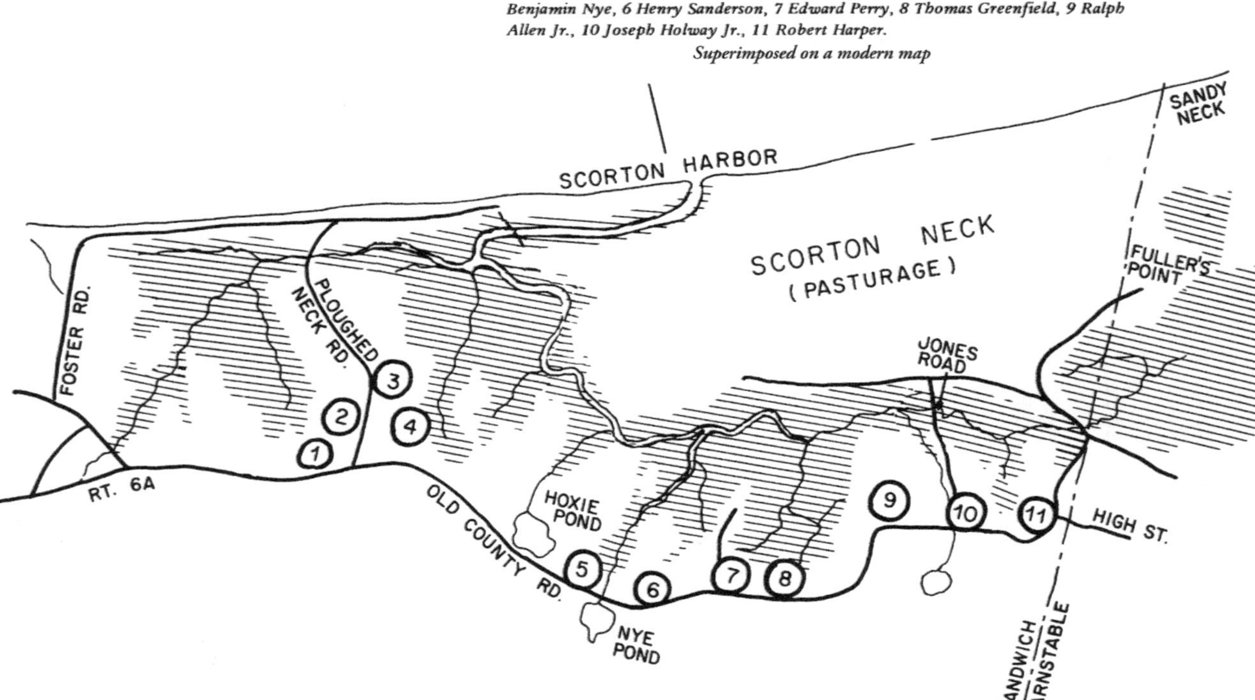

Sandwich 1667—East Sandwich Homes

Locations of early settlers are 1 Thomas Landers, 2 Edmund Freeman Jr., 3 John Freeman (lived Eastham but retained title to house here), 4 Jedediah Allen, 5 mill of Benjamin Nye, 6 Henry Sanderson, 7 Edward Perry, 8 Thomas Greenfield, 9 Ralph Allen Jr., 10 Joseph Holway Jr., 11 Robert Harper.

Superimposed on a modern map

CHAPTER 5

INDIANS

The colonists in New England found a continent of endless forests with a native population having a radically different culture from their own. In the stresses of getting settled, the whites seemed to regard both the forest and the red man as uncomfortable presences to be pushed away. A missionary effort was mounted on Martha's Vineyard, in the Bay Colony and on Cape Cod but was not broadly supported by the white population. After the war of 1675/6 the process of Indian collapse accelerated.

The Wampanoags

From the shores of Narragansett Bay east through the Cape and Islands, the Indians called themselves Pokanoks, the People of the Bays. Their territory was Pokanoket, the ending "-et" generally meaning a place where they did certain things in a certain season of the year. The Pokanoks had shifting borders with other tribes; to the north, the tribe of Massachusets and to the west the Narragansets. Since these two names both represent places, these Indians may have had more specific or internal tribal names. To them, the Pokanok tribes were called Wampanoag, "people of the east." The Massachusets had been badly hurt by the smallpox epidemic of 1616 which wiped out the Pokanok tribe in the Plymouth area called Patuxet. The Narraganset were untouched by that epidemic and were strong at the time of the Pilgrims' arrival. To the west in Connecticut were the Pequods and the Mohegans. To the north in Worcester County were the Nipmucks, and in Maine and New Hampshire the Tarrantines or Abnaki. The leader of the Pokanoks was entitled Massa-sowet or Great Chief, spelled Massasoit by the Pilgrims. His given name was Ousamequin, meaning Yellow Feather. About forty-one when the Pilgrims arrived, he must have achieved his dominant position both by birth and strong mental and physical endowment. His home area at Sowamet (near present Warren, Rhode Island) was chosen so that he could be near his chief enemy, the Narragansets. The other Pokanok leader of status was Corbitant who lived in an area of Rhode Island known as Pocasset. The Pokanoks lived in scattered villages, each with a dominant local leader or sachem. The Manomet group settled around Great Herring Pond. Other Manomet villages spread from Buzzards Bay to Woods Hole, with a number of villages in the Mashpee area. The Mattacheese had settled in the mid-Cape area, the Nauset in the Eastham/Orleans area. The meaning of Nauset is "place of the bend," a name which shows a grasp of Cape geography.

Words and Pronunciation

The local language was Algonquian, and contained some sounds difficult to capture with the English alphabet. In addition the colonists here, even the most educated, were indifferent to the consistent spelling of any words, so that it is difficult now to establish Indian spelling and pronunciation. One of the first rules is that the letter "a" is pronounced as "aw." This sound is very familiar to us today in some terms as Saugus, Nauset, Cataumet and Mohawk. It is less discernible in Massachuset, Narraganset, sachem, Yanno and Pocasset.

Land Use and Outlook

The conventional view is that the wandering natives had no idea of the value of land and sold vast tracts for trinkets. More recent and careful studies conclude that the Indians knew perfectly well what they were doing in selling these tracts. They knew their annual food cycle and their key places and home sites. A critical factor to them was protection from Indian rivals or enemies, rather than from the whites. The Indians sold only woodlands and ocean frontage that they did not value. What they received was of great utility as well as status value. Many land areas were craftily sold twice, once by the sachem and again by a local figure. The land sale process was a unique experience in each area and the seller felt he was ahead in shifting to a new way of life where he did not need his former range. Communication and education were poor so that the cumulative experience was perceived only by a few in authority who found themselves unable to alter the process. In return for their lands the Indians received cloth, metal pots, knives and axes. In addition, they avidly sought guns, vessels, horses and alcohol. The effect of these possessions and temptations was deeply unsettling to tribal life which revolved around conservative elders and medicine men. There was no way to counter the destabilizing forces. The Indians were susceptible to the worst aspects of white culture and fell easy prey to epidemics, alcoholism, debt, gambling and theft. They had no economic base, no way to save, no institutions of support, no bargaining ability, and ultimately little self-respect. Whites exchanged fear of the Indians for contempt. Laws passed to protect and improve the Indian were of little effect.

Early Plymouth Colony Relations

Plymouth had two extraordinary initial advantages in its founding period. The wide stretch of coastline from Scituate to Manomet was free of Indian residents, and Massasoit, the grand sachem, welcomed the white presence as reinforcement against his long-time enemies the Narragansets to his west. Massasoit persuaded a number of his sachems to join him in signing a treaty of amity and mutual support in 1621.

It was Massasoit's continuing support of the Colony government and his high prestige in the Indian world, which were keys to the early stability of the small colony as it survived, and grew. He must have had a remarkable information-gathering system to keep abreast of developments throughout his domain and beyond, and had high intelligence in assessing the logistics of developments of his own tribe and that of the Pilgrims. He had a high regard for Edward Winslow from their first negotiations in the spring of 1621. This special confidence was strengthened in 1623 when Winslow visited the seriously ill Massasoit in Sowamet, Massasoit's home base. Massasoit recovered soon after this visit and, to the superstitious Indian, the cure was a miracle. He warned the Pilgrims of trouble brewing with the Massachuset tribe to the north who planned to wipe out the settlers at Wessaguset. Furthermore, he indicated that his own sachems on Cape Cod might take the opportunity to join in an attack on Plymouth itself. This extraordinary warning was taken seriously and acted on promptly by the Plymouth leaders, and the intrepid Standish, with a force of only eight men, killed seven of the Massachuset leaders at Wessaguset. As a result, the three Cape sachems felt they would be attacked by the invincible Pilgrims and each went into deep hiding. It seems incredible that this reaction of fear and guilt should have led directly to the deaths of all three, namely Caunacum of Manomet, Yanno of Mattacheese and Aspinet of Nauset. Thus the Pilgrims gained a recognition and power far beyond their numbers.

The Indian Squanto, who had a command of English from his unique background of two trips to Europe, is commonly thought of as the kindly benefactor of the new colony. The fact is Massasoit completely distrusted Squanto, who seemed to be playing a power game of his own. Squanto would almost certainly have been removed from power by Massasoit, but he was saved from this disgrace when he died of natural causes in September 1622.

The Indian Hobamock was Massasoit's personal representative to the Pilgrims. Concerning his chief, he told Winslow and Hampden that they would never see his like again among the Indians, continuing, "He is no liar, he was not bloody and cruel like other Indians; in anger and passion he was soon reclaimed, easy to be reconciled toward such as had offended him, ruled by reason in such measure as he would not scorn the advice of mean men; and that he governed his men better with few strokes than others did with many..."

Hobamock lived with Standish until his death in 1623. We learn that in addition to their trading posts in Maine, and at Aptucxet, and on the Connecticut River, the Pilgrims had a trading post at Sowamet in Massasoit's own village. In 1632 a war party of Narraganset came to Sowamet on a sudden raid, but Standish himself happened to be there with a few men. The attack was repulsed, and the Narragansets withdrew when an action with the Pequods was reported on their other border. They did not attack again and Massasoit must have felt that his trust in the Pilgrims was well placed.

Land Sales and Missions

The potential for strains between the Wampanoags and Pilgrims arose with the expansion of Pilgrim towns and the subsequent request for settlement in Indian territories. The areas first sought by the whites were marginal to Massasoit's own main territory: a block at Taunton in the buffer zone with the Massachuset Indians, and the strip at Sandwich on the north shore of the Cape.

The early Pilgrim leaders (Bradford, Winslow and associates) were scrupulous in discussing and paying for these areas before they were settled, which made for orderly arrangements and preserved trust on both sides. The Pilgrims, to their everlasting credit, insisted on this practice and were quick to reprove unauthorized negotiations for land, and settlement in areas where the land had not been purchased. Court records testify to negotiation of grievances on both sides and acceptance of Indian testimony in trials. Land sales, however, continued and spread, and while seeming to provide Indians with income and justice, in fact led all too soon to encirclement and confrontation.

Missionary efforts were begun by Thomas Mayhew Jr. on Martha's Vineyard in 1641. In 1646 Reverend John Eliot of Roxbury began to preach in the Indian language. In Sandwich, William Leveridge was rewarded for studying the Indian language in 1651. Noting this new development, in 1653 Massasoit asked specifically that there should be no proselytizing in this area when allowing a new grant at Swansea very near his own base.

Bay Colony Relations

One of the specific original goals of the Bay Colony was to bring the Indians to religion. The Colony seal shows a native appealing to the Christian world, saying in a long trailing banner, "Come Over and Help Us." In the Boston area, the Indian population was much thinner and more scattered than in Plymouth Colony, and the only chief of status, Chickatawbut, died in a smallpox epidemic in 1633. The Bay Colony's official respect for Indian rights was not so firmly established as in Plymouth Colony.

The Puritan Colony demonstrated its attitude with an attack on the Pequod Indian main encampment in Eastern Connecticut in 1637, when some 700 men, women and children were slaughtered with almost no loss of life in the white force. The horror of this event seems little noted in American history. It was based on reprisal for the Pequod's killing of a white trader. The Narragansets were seen as the next threatening tribe, and when their leader Miantonomo was captured by the Mohegans in 1643, the Bay Colony allowed him to be executed. When the Narragansets seemed to be arming again, a large force of colonists was raised, and although the Narragansets sued immediately for peace, punitive and crushing penalties were assessed. In 1644, the Massachuset Indians submitted themselves and all their lands to the Bay Colony Government without compensation. In exchange, they were awarded small areas for their permanent settlement, but with the specific commitment to accept Christianity and town organization along the lines of white settlements. Reverend John Eliot of Roxbury made these towns his life's work. The first town fully organized was Natick, recognized in 1651, and a number of others followed in the next two decades.

Colonial Expectations for Indians

It was taken for granted that the Indian should make all the adjustments to a radically different way of life, without a lengthy process of cultural bridging.

The whites seemed to have no idea of the effort involved in learning a new language, new laws, new ways of work and social concepts. Only a tiny number of whites made a comparable effort to learn the Indian culture. Reverend John Eliot is described as "disturbed that the Indians were so stupid and senseless that they would not even inquire of the English the road to salvation." In 1650, Plymouth Colony ordered "if upon good experience there shall be a competent number of Indians brought on to civility so as to be capable of a township, upon their request to the General Court they shall have grants of lands for a plantation as the English have." But how were the Indians to be "brought on to civility?" Who were to be their teachers and exemplars? All they were offered were many regressive laws and an incomprehensible religious system that was being mocked even by most whites. The policy against the still independent Indian tribes, the Nipmucks, Mohegans and Narragansets, was savagely repressive. Any "troublesome" Indians who caused damage to a white settler or trader were to be handed over for punishment or could be seized by force. The Indians so seized ("women and children to be sparingly seized unless known to be some way guilty") were to serve the damaged parties (as slaves) "or to be shipped out and exchanged for negroes." The wisest and most experienced man in New England in Indian relations was Reverend Roger Williams, who had been driven from the Bay Colony in 1636 for unorthodoxy, and who dwelt in Rhode Island among the Narraganset with whom he conversed fluently. He is reported to have "thought of embarking on a missionary project but soon dismissed it as presumptuous." He strove to keep the Narragansets neutral as he had in the Pequod War of 1637, and was able to say in 1654 that no member of the tribe had been guilty of taking English blood. He freely admitted, however, that Indians were treacherous and lived in a barbarous and filthy way, and that it was devoutly to be hoped that they could be brought to civility in some degree, and that such civility might even be a leading step toward Christianity. He himself had given up the Puritan fervor with its total intolerance and had become a Seeker, looking for salvation but not condemning others for their courses.

The Society For The Propagation of the Gospel

The astute Edward Winslow had been borrowed from Plymouth and sent to England by the Bay Colony in 1646 on sensitive business. After attacking critics of the Colony's work, he published a tract entitled "The Glorious Progress of the Gospel among the Indians." He made Eliot's early efforts appear vast and fruitful. Those in England who had been to the Colonies and knew the truth kept a diplomatic silence. The United Colonies Commissioners, who handled Indian affairs, were receiving both tribute and fines from various tribes on the order of £300 per year. However, this income did not go to Eliot. Because the Bay Colony was "too poor and struggling to be able to be able to support Eliot's work without English help," Winslow lobbied in the Parliament for an act to permit solicitation of funds from all the churches in England. His efforts succeeded brilliantly, and in 1649 Parliament approved the formation of the Society for the Promoting and Propagating of the Gospel of Jesus Christ in New England. A capital of as much as £16,000 was raised and invested in England, with the interest to come to

America for expenditure under the direction of the Commissioners of the United Colonies. Winslow wished to return to his home and family in Marshfield, but the President of the Corporation in London begged the Commission in New England to get him to stay to further the work of collection and investment. Winslow succeeded so well that he was asked by Cromwell to undertake missions on behalf of the Commonwealth. He died near the West Indies in 1655 without ever returning to Plymouth.

This flow of new money into New England became a fact of great importance. It supported and rewarded Eliot and Daniel Gookin, the official of the Bay Colony government for Indian affairs, as well as other white officials whose work could be related to Indian affairs. It was used to punish and reward those Praying Towns in the process of separating from Indian tradition. It published tracts and catechisms in the Indian language. It built a large new building at Harvard called the Indian College. It bought arms and ammunition for the protection of those bringing the good word to the Nipmucks to the west. All this was created by a brilliant process of propaganda that cost New England nothing. The minister, Hugh Peter, who had been in the Bay Colony for many years is quoted as saying that the mission work "was but a plain cheat and that there was no such thing as a gospel conversion amongst the Indians." Nevertheless, a cynical view of the efforts to convert the Indians in the Bay Colony cannot be sustained when one reads the annual budgets of activities of those involved in the work in the decades of the 1650's and 1660's. It was expensive to take Indian youths of promise from their families and put them up in Roxbury or Cambridge while they were being educated and needed clothing, food, supplies, housing. Those youths who proved themselves were sent on to Harvard where again all expenses had to be met. For example, the following items were included in the budget in 1657:

In clothing for the Indian boys	£30
In corn to Mr. Eliot and his brother	25
To those that diet the Indian boys	12
Salaries of five Indian interpreters and schoolmasters employed by Mr. Eliot	50
The charge of diet of 9 Indian children	85
Their clothing	50
Encouragement for two new Indian towns now to begin	80
Parcel of drugs for sick Indians	10

The only Indian student fully graduated and qualified from Harvard went back to Martha's Vineyard where he died the following year.

Eliot's name now is synonymous with the translation of part of the Bible into the Algonquian language, and its publication for use in Indian churches. This project especially excited new interest and supplies from England included the delivery of a large press, folio paper and an English printer for the work. The project was so glamorous that it justified re-chartering the Society for the Propagation after the restoration of Charles II. The Bible appeared in 1663 and was reprinted in 1685. Copies went to the Praying Towns in the Bay Colony and to Mashpee and Martha's Vineyard, but how much it was used and read by the Indians themselves is questionable. Beautifully bound and clasped presentation copies were struck off and sent to England; one of these was offered for sale in 1979 at £30,000, showing that they still have great curiosity value.

Richard Bourne Finds His Mission

During his successes in London, Winslow had an oil portrait done, making him the only one of the Pilgrims or any of the first generation in Plymouth Colony whose face is now known. In her insightful book, *The Narrow Land,* Elizabeth Reynard pictures Richard Bourne for us:

> "Lawyer trained at the Inn of Court, thickset with iron grey hair...the White Sachem or Little Father, energetic, gentle, with square shoulders thick from wrestling with Lucifer..."

Reynard then goes on to say that Bourne's first act that gained him recognition among the Indians was in 1649 when he went among those suffering from a smallpox epidemic (to which they were sadly prone) and showed himself immune. This gave him some of the magic status that was accorded the poh-wohs or medicine men. As key parts of the Indian cultural pattern, an Indian village could not wholly accept Christianity or a white political structure until the influence of the poh-wohs had been greatly reduced and supplanted. The contest between Bourne and the medicine men must have gone on for years as he gradually attained the use of the language and acquired both acceptance and his inner commitment. His early progress in mission work is shown in the annual budget of Commissioners of the United Colonies:

1657 – Richard Bourne...encouraged to the work

1658 – For pains in teaching the Indians £15

1659 – A teacher of the Indians £20

1660 – For his pains in keeping a constant weekly lecture amongst the Indians £20

1663 – To Mr. Bourne at Sandwich his salary £25

1664 – John Eliot stated "my beloved brother Mr. Bourne is a faithful and prudent laborer and a good man."

1667 – To Mr. Bourne at Sandwich his salary £30.

1672 – To Mr. Richard Bourne £30.
To 3 Indians under Mr. Bourne £15.

In addition to his work with the Indians, Bourne was active in town government. He had already been cited here for his work in settling, allocating and collecting taxes. He served as a deputy in Plymouth, and as selectman. He was appointed to special committees to get difficult things done. Such a committee was created in 1645 to prepare revisions "laws for redress of some present abuses and for preventing of future." He was especially active in arranging purchases of land from the Indians and in bounding both broad grants and individual holdings, work for which he was uniquely qualified. He received a number of lots himself in the Manomet Valley and adjoining areas. One of these grants included the right to take 12,000 herring annually at a place "where Sandwich men take alewives."

Mashpee Lands—Bourne's Control

Beside his home in what later became Jarvesville in Sandwich village, and his extensive lands on the Manomet River, Richard Bourne held certain lands in the Indian-occupied Mashpee area. These lands will be described and traced since they are an essential part of the formation of the Indian reservation and of the Bourne family experience here.

The first reference to Mashpee lands occurs in Plymouth Colony Records in 1654:

"The freemen of Sandwich viz Mr. John Vincent, Thomas Burgess, Thomas Tupper, Richard Bourne and James Skiffe desired some several parcels of land at the places following: viz some land by Marshpee Pond and 10 acres of meadow; some land by Santuit Pond to the value of one hundred acres; a neck of land by Cotuit River to keep cattle; certain meadow lying upon and about a place called Mannamuch Bay."

There is no further reference to this "desired" set of grants. A similar entry occurs in 1660:

"Liberty is granted unto Richard Bourne and Thomas Tupper Senior to look at some land for their accomodation towards the South Sea, and that then a competency will be granted by the Court. The like liberty is granted unto George Barlow, and that those that lay out Richard Bourne's and Thomas Tupper shall also lay out his."

Again there is no further reference confirming that these grants, approved in principle by the Court, were in fact laid out and issued to those named, who were already substantial land owners in Sandwich and in the Manomet/Buzzards Bay sectors. In the normal course of things, as in adjacent Barnstable, a few major grants would have moved white settlement down to Vineyard Sound ("the South Sea") along the major ponds and herring streams, so that Sandwich would have extended all the way from Barnstable Bay to the Sound, with the Indians compressed into a few village areas. This did not in fact happen, and the evidence probably implies that Bourne must have blocked the issuance of these grants because of his increasing commitment to the mission work. There is no further reference to anyone but Richard Bourne owning land in Mashpee. The pattern of the lands finally granted to him is quite clear, and it does not include sectors on Santuit Pond or Cotuit (Santuit) River, as would have occurred if the 1654 proposal had materialized, and if he had then, on his own, bought up all the rights of Vincent, Skiff, Tupper, Burgess and Barlow. Once these competent men had a foothold in a new and valuable area, they would have no reason to sell and every reason to keep title. The fact that Bourne was able diplomatically to block these grants and shortly after to obtain other grants exclusively to himself, is evidence of an extraordinary prestige at Plymouth Court, plus high persuasive powers among his fellow citizens.

Mashpee Lands—Early Bounds

The evidence of Bourne's early vision of an Indian reservation emerges in his skilled work to readjust the fuzzy Barnstable boundary agreed to by Chief Paupmunnock in 1648. The original purchase reads "lands lying and being within the precincts of Barnstable aforesaid faring upon the sea commonly called the South Sea, butting home to Janno his land eastward, and a little beyond a brook called the First Herring Brook westward, and to Nepoyetums and Seaquunks land northward." In 1658 a new agreement was signed in which the western boundary between Barnstable and the Indians was shifted. The language is diplomatic but unmistakable; the Indians regained "all the lands lying to the westward of a northeast line running from the easterly side of the easterly side of the said river, unto the bounds betwixt Sandwich and Barnstable..." This is substantially the same line as still exists today, from the so-called five-mile-post off Asa Meiggs Road, around the easterly side of Santuit Pond "leaving the skirts of good lands to the Indians" then coming in to the middle of Santuit River and down to the Bay. Each side was free to fetch alewives from this river. A note by Thomas Hinckley on this deed confirms that the line was accordingly set, and adds "Richard Bourne of Sandwich being there present." How much study, discussion and negotiation lay behind this concession one must imagine, but it was a rare, almost unique, event for the Indians to regain land once granted away.

Bourne's Lands in Mashpee

Beginning in 1655 Richard Bourne was granted either by Plymouth Colony or by the Mashpee Indians land in several areas:

On Mashpee River just off Mashpee Pond, ten acres straddling the river, originally to use with permission, then half to own, half to use.

A neck of marsh and upland called Manamuchcoy (probably Monomoscoy) in Waquoit Bay, plus adjacent upland called Aunta-Anta.

A homestead and grazing center on present John Ewer Road where he lived when not in his home in Sandwich village.

A five-acre neck in Peters Pond.

A thirty-acre house lot on the east shore of Mashpee Pond.

These land rights also included rights to take 10,000 alewives per year, to cut 10 or 12 loads of marsh hay and rights to cut wood and to graze cattle on lands adjoining his own.

Massasoit Passes

Through the long, eventful years from 1621 Massasoit had kept the letter of his treaty of amity with the Pilgrims. Between Plymouth arms and the peacemaking efforts of Roger Williams in Providence, the Narragansets had been kept from invasion into the Wampanoag country. This peace had kept Massasoit's dignity and honor. In return he had renewed his treaty of amity with the Plymouth Colony in 1639 and signed another with the new power, the Bay Colony. Slowly he gave up lands for settlement in the mainland areas that were his homeland. He seems not to have been interested in the land sales on Cape Cod after 1637. In 1642 we read:

> "Usamequin chose out ten fathom of beads at Mr. Williams and affirmed that he was fully satisfied therewith for his lands at Seekonk, but he stood upon it that he would have a coat more..."

This may be a wistful reference to the time in 1621 when Winslow and his party had visited him at Sowamet and presented him with a splendid red coat trimmed with gold lace. The old chief was especially fond of Winslow, who combined the traits of courage, intuition, statecraft and respect that these gifted leaders shared. News of the death of Winslow in 1655 caused him grief and he sent his two sons, Wamsutta and Metacom, to Plymouth with an official message of condolence. More of the old order passed when Standish died in 1656 and Bradford in 1657. In 1660 when nearing 80, Massasoit felt it was time to abdicate and named his son Wamsutta as his successor. To signal the change of power he sent these two sons to Plymouth in 1660 to receive new English names. Wamsutta was named Alexander, and Metacom, Philip after the famous Macedonian warriors of antiquity. Marking the transition and paying a nice tribute, the Sandwich town meeting for May 18, 1660 included an item reading:

> "The Town has ordered that Richard Bourne shall give out of the Town's stock two coats of trading cloth or one coat of broadcloth...to Usamequin's son."

Massasoit died sometime in the winter of 1660 or early 1661. His death, uneventful at the time, became a profound turning point in the history of the Colony, and in the whole of New England, marking a loss of unity, culture and dignity in the Pokanoks, and a loss of confidence and restraint on the part of the whites toward the Wampanoag leadership. Only a year later, the Plymouth Court ordered Capt. Thomas Willett, an Assistant Governor, "to speak to Wamsutta about his estranging land and not selling it to our colony." In the summer of 1662 a rumor reached Plymouth from Boston that Alexander was plotting with the Narragansets to attack white settlements. He was peremptorily ordered to come to Plymouth to explain, but he delayed, waiting, he said, for Captain Willett, his best friend among the Assistants, to return. The Pilgrims sent an armed force for him and brought him and his party to Plymouth on foot like captives, rather than as the head of a sovereign and respected tribe. Accounts of what then happened vary widely, but he was questioned, released, reappeared with a high fever and soon died. The explanations vary from a) a natural death without any prejudice on either side, b) dying of frustration and impotent rage, or c) deliberately poisoned by the whites. This distressing event led to the accession of his brother Philip as Great Sachem. It also led to further suspicion and failure of communications on both sides. Nevertheless, some land sales continued, and in 1664 John Eliot urged the Plymouth authorities "to give encouragement to John Sassemon who teacheth Philip and his men to read." Sassamon was a Massachuset Indian who had been to Harvard and who was working among the Wampanoags near Middleboro. Massasoit himself had requested that no Christian teaching be carried on among the Indians in his area.

Founding Mashpee

Little has been actually recorded about Bourne's work among the Cape Indians in the 1650's and early 1660's, but it was recognized that it produced results. He must have been an extremely effective teacher in conveying the basics of reading and writing, both in the Indians' own language and in English as well. "Bringing them on to civility," as the phrase went, involved much in explaining the way white society was organized in social relations, earning money, using mechanical devices, and organizing local government. Religious instructions involved many new concepts and much patient repetition to build confidence and acceptance. One wonders how Richard Bourne could have spent so much time with his charges while running his own farm, even with four sons to help, and serving in the town and Colony government. It was an extraordinary performance. His accomplishments are indicated in three formal documents of the years 1665 and 1666. The first document showed a plan for a new way of government administered by the Indians themselves, recognizing the authority of the sachems over their customary areas, but still obviously a change, to operate with Bourne's help and advice. Dated February 7, 1664/5, it reads:

> "Whereas a motion was made to this Court by Richard Bourne in the behalf of those Indians under his instruction, as to their desire of living in some orderly way of government, for the better preventing and redressing of things amiss amongst them by meet and just means, this Court doth therefore, in testimony of their countenancing and incurraging to such a work, do approve of those Indians proposed, viz. Paupmannuck, Keencomsett, Watanamatuck, and Nanquidnumack, Kanoonus, and Mocrust, to have the chief inspection and management thereof, with the help and advice of the said Richard Bourne, as the matter may require; and that one of the aforesaid Indians be by the rest installed to act as a constable amongst them, it being always provided, notwithstanding that what homage accustomed legally due to any superior sachem be not hereby infringed."

A specific reservation for South Sea Indians was proposed in a remarkable testimony of December 11, 1665 in the form of a deed from two Indians of the Mashpee area, Tukonchasun of Santuit and Weepquish of a village called Waskootosse or Waskatasso for the whole Mashpee area, to be held in trust by five other named Indians on behalf of the inhabitants. Part of this document, said to be written in the hand of Bourne himself, reads:

> "We the aforementioned Weepquish and Tukonchasun having right and interest in the forementioned lands of our ancestors and having not formerly sold or given it to any others; do now both of us give all the aforementioned lands from us and ours unto the Indians commonly called the South Sea Indians, and their children forever; and not to be sold or given away from them by anyone without all their consents thereunto, excepting one parcel of meadow and land already sold unto Richard Bourne lying at a place called Manamuchcoy and Aunto-Anto; for which end and purpose for the further security and safety of these lands we leave them in the hands of William Pease, Kanoonus, Ashuwaham, Wonbees and Compocknet to be kept by them for the use and benefit of the South Sea Indians..."

This deed was regarded by the Indians as the real authority for the creation of Mashpee, and was referred to in later years to protest intrusions or revise borders. It stated clearly the principles of joint land ownership by the Indian occupants. Two internal areas were reserved for Bourne. The deed failed, however, to state the authority by which the grant was made, or the value received by them in exchange. Experts read into this act that the two donors represented the traditional non-Christian Indian population, and that the recipients represented the Indians who proposed to live in a delimited area under largely white authority with Christian elements predominating. Such a transfer was not instantaneous but recognized a profound change in Indian society. The two signators do not seem to be known except for this deed. The five recipients included three who were Mashpee residents (Kanoonus, Wonbees and Compocknet), while Pease was from the Falmouth area, and Ashuwaham was of the village of Cotochiese on Oyster Island to the east. The deed was witnessed by three others who all seem to fall on the side of change, namely, Nanquid Numack and Watanamatuck, who had signed the earlier petition for better government, and a literate Indian named Simon, almost certainly Simon Paupmunnock, who became Bourne's successor as preacher. The third document was a deed from Quachetisset of Manomet as senior Sachem for the upper Cape dated November 20, 1666 which formally turned over all his rights and interests in the Mashpee area to the same five Indians named above, thus confirming and reinforcing the previous act. This deed bounded the area beginning at the harbor near Waquoit up to Ashumet Pond, thence named several ponds by Indian names, and down the Koctuit River to Koctuit Bay. The boundary agreed to runs into Popponesset Bay. This deed seems to refer to the next major bay east. The borders given here by Quachetisset may refer to areas to which he felt he had original title rather than Keenkomsit or Yanno, and not the border agreed by Barnstable and

Paupmunnock.

In July 1666, Bourne felt confident enough of the results of teaching the Indians to invite a convocation of ministers, with Governor Thomas Prence and several of the Assistants to assemble in Mashpee. "A good number of the Indians whom Mr. Bourne had been instructing were examined. They gave such an account of their knowledge and belief and of the impression the gospel had made on their hearts; and gave their relations with such affection as was extremely grateful to the pious auditory. The magistrates and ministers convened on the occasion received much satisfaction in what they observed and heard." Nevertheless, this by no means meant that a church of Indian members was accepted at this time. The account of this audition continues: "Such was the strictness of those who conducted the business of the meeting that before they would countenance the advancement of these Indians to church fellowship, they concluded that their confessions should be written, and a copy sent to each church in the Colony for their inspection and approbation if they saw fit, so that if no objections should be offered, they might at a suitable time be permitted and encouraged to enter into church fellowship." This meant a great deal of writing and copying, and Bourne must have known that a personal religious statement, no matter how well motivated, could easily be objected to on grounds of wording or implied beliefs, especially if the auditor were prejudiced against Indians or the creation of an Indian church. The delay was bureaucratic and conservative.

As it turned out, it took four years for the process of "inspection and approbation" to be completed, even though the confessions and relations were said to be "very agreeable to the churches to which they were communicated." The ministers must have been conscious of the fact that there were no Indian churches in all of Plymouth Colony, whereas there were many Praying Towns in the Bay Colony and much mission work on Martha's Vineyard and Nantucket. Bourne had accomplished an extraordinary feat of teaching and personal effort. The great moment of official recognition came on August 17, 1670, when a great convocation of visitors gathered at Briant's Neck, Santuit Pond, for the double service of inaugurating the Indian Church and of ordaining Richard Bourne as its pastor. The ministers included John Eliot Sr., John Cotton Jr. from Plymouth, Indian preachers from Natick and Martha's Vineyard, John Holmes from Duxbury, Thomas Walley from Barnstable, Thomas Thornton from Yarmouth, Samuel Arnold from Marshfield, George Shove from Taunton and Samuel Newman from Rehoboth. Other churches sent senior brethren to this notable ordination, and Governor Prence attended with several of the Magistrates. This large service was held outdoors, reportedly under a spreading oak. There is an Indian reference to the Briant's Neck Church as "an enclosed garden." It would seem necessary to have a building for the year-round teaching and meetings.

ORDINATION OF RICHARD BOURNE-This is an imaginary rendition of the scene of the ordination of Richard Bourne which took place on Briant's Neck in Santuit Pond 1670. Reproduced from the Register of April 1908 by courtesy of the New England Historic Genealogical Society.

Spread of the Mission

Although centered in the Mashpee area villages, Bourne's active teaching and mission work extended widely from southern Plymouth to the Lower Cape, representing a great deal of travel on his part. Much of the work must have been done by educated Indian teachers who worked patiently in the various villages and who would have been able to evaluate the persons with potential for learning to read and to go on to the higher levels of understanding and interest needed to study English, and the ultimate goal—to learn and accept Christianity. Bourne made a report to Daniel Gookin (the official of the Bay Colony for Indian affairs) as to the status of his work here in 1674. Within the immediate Mashpee area, he said were 95 who frequently met together to worship, of whom 24 could read and 10 write. Of these, only two could read English. In the entire area from Plymouth through the Lower Cape there were 497 who attended services, 142 who could read, 72 who could write and nine who could read English. This included persons of both sexes. Bourne, however, lamented the irreligion of many saying they "are very loose in their course to my heart-breaking sorrow."

The Herring Pond Area

The leading Sachem here in the period up to Philip's War was Quachetisset, a traditional Indian who never accepted Christianity but who was a strong supporter of the Plymouth Colony. His signature appears on many deeds of sales of land to the whites, and also on deeds for land sales entirely between Indians, showing that he understood the value of good land titles in the white man's sense. The last deed with his name is dated 1674, strongly suggesting his death at this time. Probably reflecting his passing, the first reference to teaching and mission work here is in 1674, in Richard Bourne's letter to Daniel Gookin, saying that this work was also being done at Comassakumkanit, the chief village in the Herring Pond area. In the spring of 1674/1675 a record appears in Sandwich Town Meeting that permission was given for "a meetinghouse for the Indians to meet in on Lord's Day for this present summer." This meetinghouse was the one built on Burial Hill in Bournedale. There is no further reference to this meetinghouse in Plymouth or Sandwich records, and services may well have been suspended during the war. This meetinghouse, however, is identified by Deyo and others as the one finally removed to Cataumet and used in a new chapel there by Reverend Elisha Tupper.

In view of his great age (he died in 1676 at 98), we doubt that Thomas Tupper Senior was active in the teaching and mission work among Herring Pond Indians. There is no record of support for such a project in the Colony Records as there is for the work of Richard Bourne beginning in 1657. Thomas Tupper, Jr., born in 1638, married Martha Mayhew in 1661 and would have learned of the mission work on Martha's Vineyard, and would have logically been the one to initiate the work here, especially after 1671 when the Cape Indians, including Quachetisset of Herring Pond, signed the testament of fealty to the Colony. Tupper was not ordained, but mastered the Indian language and was able to preach.

The Manomet and Cape Cod Indians

These educational and cultural efforts on Cape Cod quickly became of value politically to the Colony Government in statements of support and loyalty by the Indian population. The efforts also indicated those who clung to their old ways.

After the formation of Mashpee church in 1670, and declarations of loyalty in 1671 by the Indian leaders from Pamet to Herring Pond, the demarcation must have become pointed between this body of friendly Indians and those of the mainland under the direct influence of Chief Sachem Philip. As relations with Philip deteriorated, it was clear that the continued loyalty of the Manomet and "South Sea" Indians was vitally important and that further steps should be taken for their orderly government, particularly to anticipate and relieve controversies and grievances. Assistant Governor Thomas Hinckley of

Barnstable was appointed "to call and keep Court amongst the said Indians at such times and in such places...as he shall think meet...together with the heads or chief of the Indians in the several places to make orders respecting the government of the said Indians...to issue amongst them all civil controversies." Capital cases were still to be heard at Plymouth, and the Indians still had full liberty to appeal to the General Court at Plymouth in any cause. The presence of "grave and sage" Indians was usual when the Court or juries considered serious cases involving Indians. This was probably the only time when real Indian concerns were anxiously sought out to be addressed; usually the process of "bringing them to civility" meant enforcing laws to make them fit the white mold.

Hinckley later stated that he found it much trouble, besides expense, to attend these Courts in Indian lands, but thought his time and pains well spent in endeavoring to bring them to more civility. After the attacks by Philip on white settlements had begun, many Indian leaders of the Cape Cod groups renewed their 1671 covenant of fidelity.

The Worsening of Relations

The stage was set for the Indian conflict. Plymouth's patent ran west to the Blackstone River and down the eastern shore of Narragansett Bay. Sachem Philip had his headquarters on the Mount Hope peninsula. On the Bay shore were the major villages of Pocasset and Sakonnet. These were headed by Squaw-Sachems; at Pocasset by Weetamoe, widow of Wamsutta, and at Sakonnet by Awashonks. White settlements had pressed against the Indian lands; indeed, some individual settlers had been allowed to settle within their confines.

Western Rhode Island was land belonging to the Narraganset, a large tribe that were natural rivals of the Wampanoag. Rev. Roger Williams lived on the west bank of the Blackstone River from 1637 and worked to keep the Narragansets from attacks or actions that would bring down the vengeance of the Bay Colony, or of the Connecticut Colonies. The Rhode Island Colony and the other white groups at Newport and Portsmouth had no army or defense, but remained on good terms with the Narraganset through mutual respect for territories. To the North, the Bay Colony was growing rapidly. Their eastern Indians, the Massachuset, were never numerous and now dwelt exclusively in small Praying Towns where they exercised some self-government. To the west in Worcester County, the Nipmuck seemed tractible and had begun to settle into a few Praying Towns at Grafton and elsewhere, with white towns in other sectors. The Connecticut and New Haven Colonies covered present Connecticut, and up the Connecticut River Valley presently in the state of Massachusetts.

A comparison of the population of the whites and Indians shows that in the Bay Colony there were 22,000 whites, and in Plymouth Colony about 7,500. Taken together, these figures represented more than twice the Indian population of about 12,000. Rhode Island had 4,000 whites and about 3,000 Indians, while Connecticut had 14,000 whites and about the same number of Indians.

Philip, like other Indian leaders, wanted to see his followers enjoy a self-governing and stable life in a secure territory. His father, Massasoit, had allowed whites to settle at Swansea on his own doorstep as early as 1653, and Philip had sold land to the whites after his own accession to power, but increasingly he felt frustration and impotence at their constant encroachment. He freely admitted that the whites had extended him and his father protection from the Narragansets; that they had been fair about each land purchase and in dealing with Indians in their courts. His situation, however, in a shrinking territory was untenable and Plymouth behavior to him, especially after 1672, was increasingly infuriating, treating him with denigration and suspicion. Though his father had been treated as a true potentate and equal, he was now only a subject of the Colony Government. He had nothing of the grasp of affairs that his great father had shown. Plymouth found him surly and insolent, and in their smug confidence that they had always treated Indians fairly, could not imagine his bitterness and rage. Hence Plymouth, and Boston as well, were completely unrealistic in their lack of any military readiness for Indian conflict. They seemed unaware how vulnerable their scattered villages were. Their militias were trained to march in columns and to fire from lines at other stationary lines. The knowledge of Indian warfare that Miles Standish had gained seemed to have been forgotten entirely.

John Sassamon

This key figure was a Massachuset Indian of education who had settled in Wampanoag territory at Nemasket, Middleboro. He knew Alexander and Philip well and had been invited to come to Mount Hope teaching English for various periods. He may have taught Christianity in Nemasket, but was certainly not a minister and was not what he had been called, a "renegade." He was simply a man with a foot in both the Indian and the white world. From personal knowledge, and doubtless from Indian friends, he sensed that Philip would not continue in his uncertainty but would break out in violence. He warned Plymouth of this in the winter of 1674/5, among many such warnings that Plymouth received. Later he was missed and found drowned under the ice in Assawompset Pond near his home. There were no witnesses, but it was suspected at Plymouth that Philip had ordered it, although it could truly have been an accident while he was ice fishing. Much later, one Indian accused another, Tobias, of having caused the crime, but without proof. It was finally learned that the two were enemies and that the accuser owed Tobias money. Tobias was then arrested, and later still, with even less evidence, two more Indians were arrested. They were tried by a white jury, with six safe Indians from Manomet as added jurors. All were called guilty and two were hung immediately, in early June. Their death may well have pushed Philip beyond the brink. After fighting broke out the third suspect was executed by shooting. Sassamon has been accused of being a traitor to Philip in revealing his war plans, but the facts seem clear now that Philip had no plans of any kind to be revealed. He had not stockpiled weapons, clothing, food or canoes. He did not even have any Indian allies except his own Wampanoags, and not all of them by any means. The whites who knew Philip best, Roger Williams and Samuel Gorton in Rhode Island, called him a very nasty and ugly person, completely savage and unpredictable. The term "King" was applied much later.

The War in 1675

Philip's intent was to harass the towns nearest him, taking loot but avoiding conflict. He seems to have felt this would bring Plymouth to a more realistic view and gain himself more respect as a powerful chief, so that his tribe's position could be reestablished with dignity. From the very beginning things got out of hand and out of his control. His warriors seem to have attacked a few houses at Swansea without his knowledge. A substantial white force of ready troops arrived immediately and pushed forward to Mount Hope. Here they halted while the Indians crossed over the bay to Pocasset and broke up into raiding parties with attacks on Dartmouth, Middleboro and Taunton. Meanwhile the white forces at Mount Hope broke up, some Boston men going on to negotiate with the Narragansets, while the Plymouth forces started to dig fortifications at Mount Hope. These troops withdrew as attacks continued elsewhere on outlying farms and settlements. A new force of whites was then formed to back up the main Indian forces at Pocasset. They did not press their advantage at the point of victory when the Indians were without ammunition. The whites stopped at dusk and allowed the Indian forces to melt north during the night so that they could cross the Taunton River and proceed easily northwest up toward the Nipmuck country in Worcester County. The white force was left with only women and children captives. The problem for the whites was divided leadership and a complete lack of intelligence about how to proceed against Indian forces.

The Indian column moving north was burdened with loot and moved slowly. A group of whites from Rehoboth formed to give chase and were joined by two groups of friendly Indians who had arrived via Swansea. One was a force of Mohegans from Connecticut, who had started at the first alarm but had gone to Boston for direction, were sent to Plymouth, then sent to Swansea. The other was a dedicated group of volunteers from the Massachuset Praying Towns. This motley group struck hard and killed some thirty of Philip's men, but stopped when the Mohegans wanted to gather their loot. The Praying Indians proposed to make a fast march around Philip's column and strike it from the front, but the white leaders refused to entrust them with the arms for this attack, lest they should join Philip instead. So this strong force stopped and broke up in confusion, partly because food and supplies had not been organized. Philip went on into the Nipmuck country where he got his first reinforcements. The Nipmuck, although previously quiet, were wildly stimulated by Philip's arrival and commenced attacks on white towns. They were joined by some 200 Indians who had been living in the new Praying Towns in this county, and whose conversion to Christian ways turned out to be skin deep. These terrible attacks started at Mendon, August 14, and spread quickly over the county. White troops were raised but were not prepared for the scouting and backwoods techniques needed, and several columns fell into disastrous ambushes. One troop under Capt. Lothrup at Deerfield was escorting carts of grain but had put their guns in the carts. The men were picking wild grapes when the Indians attacked and scattered them. Ninety men were killed. The towns showed weakness in planning and lack of alertness; some were overrun that needn't have been. The Wampanoag forces kept moving west later in the fall, and Philip reached the area of Albany, New York, where he hoped to raise reinforcements for the spring attacks. The Iroquois tribes in New York State were fierce fighters, but not necessarily his allies. He spent the winter of 1675/6 there.

The Fate of the Narragansets

This strong tribe existed in friendship with its white neighbors in Rhode Island, who had in the past striven to keep it from involvement in war with its Indian neighbors. The white leaders in Connecticut, Plymouth and the Bay Colony now saw them as a major threat if they should throw their full support to Philip. The tribe stood in terrible uncertainty as to what it should do. Plymouth representatives asked it to shelter some non-combatant Wampanoags and they did so. The Bay Colony asked them to attack certain Wampanoags and they did so, killing several and even capturing Weetamoe of Pocasset and many of her village. She was returned unharmed as she promised to follow neutrality. The Bay Company hired some white mercenaries from a privateer who fell on an unsuspecting Narraganset camp and killed 60 Indians. The Narraganset still opted for neutrality and settled for the winter in a strongly fortified winter village at Kingston, Rhode Island with ample stores. The village was probably occupied by 1200 to 1500 persons. The fixed location camp was a magnet for the frustrated United Colonies forces which had shown up so badly against the hit-and-run tactics of Philip and the Nipmucks. A strong force of over 1,000 men was assembled in neutral Rhode Island under General Josiah Winslow of Plymouth, consisting of 315 men from Connecticut, 158 from Plymouth towns and 540 from the Bay Colony. This force was marched south and camped in the open in bitter cold weather overnight at Wickford. Then the next day, December 19, they marched another 15 miles to the Indian camp and commenced their desperate assault against a well fortified and fiercely defended camp. They took heavy casualties but managed to get inside, and the remaining Indian defenders, probably several hundred men, escaped. The white leaders then argued about the camp and its stores and captives of women, children and the injured. Benjamin Church was present as a volunteer, not a line officer, and had been wounded three times. He, and possibly others, argued for staying the night in the warm and comfortable camp where they could take care of their own wounded and defend it against possible later attack. However, Winslow had only one idea and that was to destroy the camp. He deliberately set it on fire and thereby massacred most of the Indian women, children and wounded left behind. Furthermore, the food and stores that the whites themselves now desperately needed were also destroyed. Then came another horror—the march back to their last night's camp, carrying their wounded. It was night, bitter cold, with a heavy snow falling. The casualties of the retreat were about equal to those of the assault. Plymouth lost about 40 men in all, or 25% of its forces, and the other troops about 90 men or 10% of the force. The march took all night and may have been worsened by Indian snipers. The "Great Swamp Fight" was termed a brilliant victory that destroyed the Narraganset power forever, but it was won at a far greater cost than needed, and the massacre of Indians was a permanent shame, comparable to the massacre of the Pequods 40 years before. Capt. John Gorham of Barnstable died of wounds and exposure, and Winslow resigned. Church and his family stayed the winter in the Newport area while he recovered. The surviving Narraganset males scattered, with many going to Maine or Long Island.

The Spring 1676 Attacks

Philip was dealt a sudden and very damaging blow by an attack from the Mohawks in New York State. The attack was initiated by New York authorities, not so much to aid the New England Colonies, but to prevent Philip from bringing in other Indians to his cause. He and his forces moved back to Worcester County where attacks on towns began again by Nipmucks. Philip returned to Plymouth Colony in March. His forces reattacked the previous targets of Swansea, Middleboro, Taunton, Rehoboth and Bridgewater. To the horror of Plymouth authorities, there was an attack on Scituate, (where twenty-three buildings were burned), on outlying portions of Plymouth itself at Halifax and on the village at Eel River (the present Plimoth Plantation). The latter attack was the closest to the Cape and shows the unbelievable unpreparedness of the garrison areas. It was Sunday, March 12, and all the men were at church in Plymouth, leaving the heavy gate of the garrison area open. The Indians rushed in and killed 11 women and children. The strong garrison house, with supplies and valuables, was plundered and burned. At Medfield there was a strong guard but no night watch was kept, and the men were asleep in various houses. Outlying houses were suddenly attacked and half the town was destroyed before a guard could be organized. The Indians melted away without a fight. The worst single Plymouth disaster occurred near Pawtucket, Rhode Island, when a column of 50 whites and 20 Indian allies, under Capt. Pierce of Scituate, was ambushed. From Sandwich, Job Gibbs, M. Blackwell Jr., Stephen Wing Jr., Benjamin Nye Jr. and David Besse were killed. In fact, only one white and eight Indians escaped death. In its desperation, Plymouth decided not to raise further troops but to allow each town to defend itself as best it could. Except for the Cape area, no place seemed to be safe.

Summer 1676

In May, Plymouth's Council of War called on Benjamin Church for advice, and he came to Plymouth from Saconnet by the route that he had followed in 1675, along the coast in a small boat, along the Elizabeth Islands and up to Sandwich, then up the Indian trail from Manomet. He proposed an entirely different sort of military operation, based on about 200 whites and 100 Indians, hand-picked and trained for guerilla fighting. To his astonishment and fury, this proposal was rejected, and he returned to Rhode Island. At about this same time, he visited Awashonks' camp alone, in a stubborn and daring effort to keep her men from joining Philip's forces. He urged her to remove her whole group to the Sandwich area to be away from the fighting. This they finally agreed to do, and in June her son, Peter Awashonks, and two other tribal representatives came to Plymouth Court to offer the tribe's support. They faced hostile and suspicious questions about the tribe's activities during the previous year, and Peter consented to remain as a hostage. Some time during the summer, Awashonks and her supporters came, probably by sea, to Buzzards Bay, and Church joined them for a memorable feast of fish and shellfish on the beach at Onset. A number of warriors were recruited for Church's strike force. He returned to Plymouth to renew his proposals for the fighting, and this time they consented, but with reluctance and conditions. On August 3, he was finally given a Captain's Commission and some discretionary powers.

Benjamin Church's Tactics

Church's method was to form a small strike force of about equal members of whites and Indians, and to train them in woods warfare and scouting. He must have been a man of astonishing strength and personal magnetism to pull this off so quickly and effectively, for such warfare involved exactly trained behavior of these dissimilar soldiers and also wide knowledge of the location of Philip's war parties. They literally hunted down and eliminated each war party in turn, sending most of them into Plymouth as captives. Church's strike forces were more efficient and better organized, certainly better informed, than the war parties that had had little opposition before. Philip must have recognized a new power against him. His only chance of survival, if he had reflected on it, would have been to take his remaining force and retreat to Maine where he could not have been dislodged. Instead, he himself fled to cover in his home area of Mount Hope. No place was safe from Church, however, who closed in on him quietly and launched a dawn attack on August 22. Philip was shot by a Sakonnet. His head was sent to Plymouth where it was mounted on a pole and stood for years. Philip's main forces were with his chief captain, Anawon, who was soon located near Rehoboth. On September 6, Church took Anawon's group of about 60 men in a surprise so complete that they all surrendered, and were sent as captives to Plymouth. In the mopping up that followed, the Squaw Sachem Weetamoe attempted to escape from Pocasset to the north, but in crossing the Taunton River, her raft was overturned and she was drowned.

Results in the Bay Colony

The Nipmucks lost their blood lust during the summer of 1676. They had run out of easy targets, and their numbers had been reduced. They sued for amnesty in August and many captives were brought into Boston where their leaders and those guilty of atrocities were executed. There were horrors on both sides. An encampment of Indian women and children at Hadley had been massacred, and the event made to seem like a victory. Two small groups of Narraganset who had sued for peace were surrounded and butchered.

The war was a disaster for Reverend John Eliot and his emerging Praying Towns. Among those of the Massachusets Indians near Boston, only a few had deserted, and many had volunteered for service with the colonists. They were not trusted on their own, however, and the general population showed its broad hostility against all Indians and even against their white supporters. Most of the Massachuset were required to relocate to Deer Island in Boston Harbor, where they suffered terribly during the winter of 1675/6 from lack of food, shelter and clothing.

Results in Plymouth and Sandwich

In their panic and frustration, Plymouth Court had no sympathy for the refugees and captives that came to Plymouth as soon as military operations began. From the Pocasset confrontation in July 1675 a total of 112 Indian men, women and children were brought to Plymouth. Because a few of the men were said to have been in the fighting, and, in any case, because all were guilty "in that they did not discover that pernicious plot which Philip with others completed against us," they were all condemned to be sold as slaves, most of them to be shipped to the West Indies. Further, a group of 57 refugees from the Dartmouth area came in to Sandwich by boat in August 1675 in a completely submissive way, but were adjudged to be "in the same condition of rebellion as those formerly condemned" and were also sold. These brutal acts against women and children aroused a storm of protest from informed and dedicated persons (i.e. Roger Williams, John Eliot, Thomas Walley of Barnstable) who pointed out that such acts would make those fighting still more desperate and vengeful. Reverend Walley said "we cannot so easily raise armies as send away poor squaws" and pointed out the anger such decisions were provoking among the Cape Indians. Local Indians in the Plymouth area were ordered to Clark's Island for the duration. Some friendly Indians (probably the loyal Manomets who lived in the Manomet Ponds/Break Heart Hill area of South Plymouth) were ordered to Mashpee to live, but this made many settlers fearful of rebellions here.

Among the prisoners at Plymouth were two leaders, Anawon the war-captain and Tuspaquin, brother-in-law of Philip. Church greatly respected these leaders and tried to keep them protected, but during his absence in Boston the public feelings got out of control and the two were executed. The leaders of the attack on the Clark garrison at Eel River were identified and executed, as were others with known responsibility for atrocities. The wife and son of Philip posed a problem, and here again vengeance ruled. They were condemned to servitude and shipped off to the West Indies. Probably others were sold as well, although the records refer only to this couple plus the 160 sold earlier.

The Cape Watch Line

It was decided in January 1675/6 to form a watch line across the narrow belt of land between Buttermilk Bay and Barnstable Bay. This was before the spring hostilities had begun, but already white settlers had been forbidden by Plymouth Court to withdraw from the towns, and all South Sea Indians had been forbidden from coming any closer to Plymouth than Sandwich. The watch line was to be constantly manned by men from the four Cape towns, and it is referred to in Sandwich town meeting records on January 22 that Sandwich representatives Dexter and Swift would meet other towns' representatives at Hallett's in Yarmouth about the scouting at Herring River. Also, in May 1676, men were hired to man the watch line between Wayquonset and the Bay near John Ellis' house. Samuel Sewall visited Sandwich in October 1676. He wrote that Reverend John Smith "showed me also the 3 hills on which the 4 towns kept warders, before which was such an isthmus of about 3 miles and barren plain that scarcely any thing might pass unseen." This passage slot is about 1.2 miles wide from Ellisville down to the White Cliffs area, and if indeed nearly treeless would have made a good area from which to watch. The only hostile person taken here was not caught by the Warders but by Sachem Sepit, son of Quachetisset, who caught a woman sent by Philip to stir up the Cape tribes. Governor Winslow wrote that she should be shot or at least detained.

Sandwich's defense center seems to have been located on Town Neck. Presumably a defensive wall was erected at the narrow entrance to the Neck, among other garrison features. All villages were ordered to have defensive centers built. Possibly this is the origin of the term "Wing Fort" at Spring Hill. Since the Wing house at that time was only small, the term may refer to a palisaded area for a community refuge. The Cape towns invited displaced persons from inland towns badly damaged by Indian attacks to come here temporarily, but all declined with thanks.

Results of the War

Damages of the war with Philip were great—13 towns almost completely destroyed, 50 badly damaged, 600 whites killed, huge debts to be paid by taxes. No aid was ever received from England, but a group of Protestants in Dublin raised £1,000 and sent this over as a gesture. Some funds for the ravaged towns were later raised from sale of Indian lands at Mount Hope and Pocasset. The Bay Colony and Connecticut suffered a hard blow in the number of people killed, in towns damaged and in expenses incurred, but both were strong and recovered quickly. Plymouth, by contrast, was smaller and weaker, and had suffered much more heavily. Some claim that it never fully recovered, and that this contributed to its being absorbed by the new Province of Massachusetts Bay in 1692. Of Massasoit's family, only one daughter survived the war. Her name was Mionie (called Amy) and she was the wife of Tuspaquin. Amy and her son, Benjamin Tuspaquin, lived in the Lakeville area. (A number of Massasoits's descendants survive to this day through Benjamin's offspring.) The Wampanoag were totally crushed and scattered. Only Awashonks kept her group together in the Sakonnet area. Later, small reservations were set up at Dartmouth, Fall River and Lakeville where survivors gathered. Grants of lands in Rochester and areas to the west were made to those whites who had served during the war, or their survivors. Many Indians has been sold as household slaves in the colony, and among these are recorded a sister of John Sassamon, owned by Joseph Burgess of Sandwich. The General Court approved that she be redeemed for £5, one half paid by the Colony for her brother's account and one half by her friends. Some magnificent royal regalia and relics of Massasoit were recovered and held in Plymouth, but then unaccountably were sent as tribute to King Charles in England. When these objects were sought later for possible return for display in Massachusetts, no trace of them could be found.

CHAPTER 6

THE QUAKER DRAMA

In 1623 Governor William Bradford wrote:

> "We may err, and other churches may err, and doubtless do in many circumstances. That honor, therefore, belongs only to the infallible Word of God...and it is too great arrogance for any man or church to think that he or they have so sounded the Word of God to the bottom as precisely to set down the church's discipline without error..."

This is a statement of real humility and tolerance. However, there was a continuing dilution of religious interest as the Colony grew and spread out into new towns, and an unwillingness in the various communities to support such Puritan preachers as happened to become available. Instead of the legal toleration of settlers of all religious beliefs which had been hoped for, Plymouth Court passed a law requiring church attendance and penalizing those who failed to show support. This produced alienation and scorn of the government in many communities.

The Sandwich Scene

As we noted in chapter 3, this alienation was pronounced in Sandwich where there were many families who were not supporters of the established church. Edmund Freeman and others were presented for failing to attend church. The Allen brothers, Newland brothers, Peter Gaunt and Richard Kerby were called the "implacable" opponents of Reverend Leveridge. Ralph Allen and Richard Kerby were fined £5 each, a large sum, "for speaking wild and deriding speeches against God's Word and Ordinances." Sarah Kerby and her sister Jane were in Court for disturbing public worship and abusing the speaker, for which Sarah, a second offender, was whipped. Peter Gaunt affirmed in Court that "he knew no public visible worship." In the face of such unrest, Willliam Bradford in accepting the office of governor in June 1655 stated grimly that, "competent maintenance hath not been afforded to the ministry" and "due course hath not been taken for the suppression of error." Sandwich was certainly one of his targets. Bradford died in 1657 and was succeeded by Thomas Prence, a stern man called "the terror of evil doers."

Quakers in England

George Fox (1624-1691), the son of a weaver, found himself struggling with religious ideas and conflicts. In 1646 he felt he had achieved enlightenment and entrusted himself to begin to preach that "truth is to be found by direct experience of the inner voice of God speaking to the soul." He called this the "Inner Light." His leadership and competence quickly attracted followers whom he was able to hold and organize effectively. He was known to Cromwell who respected him personally but Fox and his followers were imprisoned repeatedly not for specific teaching, but for refusal to swear allegiance, for seeming disrespect in court and for refusal to pay tithes or bear arms. As a sect with no minister, no liturgy and no usual theological system, the Society of Friends seemed to take the resistance to highly formalized Catholic and Anglican church services to an extreme limit. The name Quaker was originally derisive and is said to originate from Fox bidding a magistrate to tremble at the word of the Lord with the judge responding that it was Fox who was the quaker.

Some of Fox's ideas certainly were held in common with other small radical Christian sects which flourished in profusion in England during the Cromwell period. The government under Cromwell supported not only Puritan, but Baptist and Presbyterian preaching; even the Church of England was not seriously disturbed. Fox's skilled speakers were found in all ages and social levels, and his converts rose geometrically for many years. It was decided to send speakers abroad. Several went to the Barbados colony in the West Indies, and from there two women sailed in the *Swallow* for Boston in 1656. These were Anne Austin, an elderly mother of five, and Mary Fisher, a servant, age 22.

Boston 1656

The authorities had heard of the Quakers and were prepared for the arrival of these women as though they came avowing to lead an armed insurrection. They were taken straight to jail without trial, and their books and papers were seized and burned. The Quaker ideals of self-realization and enthusiasm were seen as abhorrent and blasphemous in Boston. Shockingly, the two women were subjected in jail to an obscene search of their bodies for blemishes by which the Devil's agents might have entered. Prison windows were boarded up to prevent contact with the public, and the women were put back on the *Swallow* after five weeks to be returned to Barbados. Their Bibles and personal bedding from the ship were taken by the jailer for his fees. So began the Quaker confrontation.

Two days later, the *Speedwell* docked from London and was found to have on board eight more Quakers, four men and four women:

William Brend	Mary Prince
Thomas Thurston	Sarah Gibbons
Christopher Holder	Mary Weatherhead
John Copeland	Dorothy Waugh

These similarly were jailed and their books seized. They were held eleven weeks before being expelled on the same ship. One who had come with them and worshipped with them was Richard Smith of Long Island, previously of

Plymouth Colony, who had been to England on business. He was returned to Long Island by sea so as not to infect the people. All masters of vessels were advised of a new law requiring £100 fine or imprisonment for bringing in Quakers. All Quakers were to be whipped, imprisoned, held incommunicado, and banished; their books were to be destroyed and their supporters fined. Such a supporter was Nicholas Upsall, an elderly man who was well known as the respectable keeper of the Red Lyon Inn of Dorchester. He had learned of the imprisonment of the two women, and knowing about jail food for the indigent, had kept them supplied which required a bribe of five shillings per week for the keeper. He had done the same for the next eight Quakers. He must have spoken at length with these prisoners to learn their story and some of their beliefs. Upsall then spoke up publicly against their treatment. On the same day as the promulgation of the first anti-Quaker law, October 14, the Court ruled:

> "The Court having considered of the offenses committed by Nicholas Upsall in reproaching of our honored magistrates and speaking against the law made and published against Quakers, judge meet and have determined that the said Upsall for such his offences shall pay as a fine to the country the sum of £20 and also that the said fine being paid, he shall depart out of this jurisdiction within one month and not to return under penalty of imprisonment..."

Upsall in Sandwich 1656/57

Upsall moved south to Plymouth and then seems to have been given a ride to Sandwich by one Tristram Hull of Barnstable, a dealer in horses. Here Upsall found a warm welcome over the winter, and recounted what he had learned in Boston to the intense interest of many in Sandwich. The Court at Plymouth ordered:

"The said Nicholas Upsall, being only licensed by the Court formerly to stay at Sandwich until the extremity of the winter is over, is by special order now warned to depart the government by the first of March next."

Shortly afterwards a "warrant was directed requiring the Constables of Sandwich and Barnstable from one to another to convey Nicholas Upsall to Tristram Hull to be recarried out of the Government." So the old man went to Newport where his adventures were the talk of the day.

Meanwhile in Sandwich, the Court took notice of the fact that Upsall had held meetings frequently at the house of William Allen, and that Richard Kerby and the wife of John Newland were especially involved, "at which meetings they used to inveigh against ministers and magistrates to the dishonor of God and contempt of government." Allen was held in bond of £20 and warned not to hold any meetings at his house "tending to disturbance." Newland was also warned.

The Plymouth Court reacted to the Upsall visit and realizing that in all likelihood more Quakers would arrive from England, issued a mild law that any

Quaker coming by land or sea was to be returned to the place he came from by him that brought him, that he was to be under fine of twenty shillings per week after being found and warned by a magistrate to depart. There were no fines for entertaining Quakers or for attending their meetings, in contrast to the jailings, whippings and fines ordered in Boston. Thus were the first seeds of the Inner Light sown in Sandwich.

The Woodhouse Voyage

The *Woodhouse* was a small vessel built in England by Quaker supporters. She sailed toward New Amsterdam, departing June 3, 1657 under Robert Fowler, Master, carrying eleven Quakers:

Mary Weatherhead	Christopher Holder
Dorothy Waugh	John Copeland
Sarah Gibbons	William Brend
Richard Dowdney	William Robinson
Robert Hodgson	Humphrey Norton
	Mary Clark

Six of these had come to Boston on the *Speedwell* the previous summer. Their return now indicated their determination to make a mark in America. The *Woodhouse* passengers began to preach in Manhattan and Long Island but the Dutch authorities sent the vessel and all the Quakers on to Newport. Holder and Copeland went to Martha's Vineyard which promptly had them moved to the mainland where they were joyfully welcomed at Sandwich. Meetings were arranged by William Newland, their host. A copy of a warrant for their arrest was shown them by a friend Thomas Burgess, Jr. They went on to Plymouth where they were questioned, apparently without invoking hostility, and were then started on their way toward Rhode Island. However, they were soon found again back at Sandwich for further meetings. The Constable William Bassett then rounded them up and brought them before the General Court, which had them escorted fifty miles to Rhode Island.

The authorities in Boston heard immediately of the eleven Quakers from the *Woodhouse* and wrote September 12 urging that Rhode Island, not a member of the United Colonies, "remove those Quakers that have been received and for the future, prohibit their coming amongst you." The spread of the Quakers from Rhode Island which the Commissioners sought to halt was seen as "difficult to the other (Colonies) by means of the intercourse, especially to the places of trade amongst us; which we desire may be safely continued between us." Rhode Island answered, "And as concerning those Quakers (so called) which are now amongst us, we have no law among us whereby to punish any for only declaring by works, etc., their minds and understanding concerning the things and ways of God..."

Two other English Quakers arrived at Newport at this time from the

West Indies, John Rouse the son of a Barbados planter, and William Leddra. The plan was to keep up an assault on Boston, seen as the Lion's Den, by which two would keep arriving to replace two imprisoned or banished. Other regular visits would be made also to Plymouth Colony. Waugh and Gibbons were imprisoned; Brend and Leddra were soon jailed; Holder and Copeland, after their calm visit to Sandwich, were caught in Boston, jailed and whipped.

In addition to the influx from Rhode Island overland, two ladies appeared in Boston by ship, claiming not to be Quaker preachers, but merely arriving back after visits to England. Mary Dyer lived in Rhode Island and was well remembered as the friend of Anne Hutchinson, banished twenty years previously. Anne Burden was come to settle the estate of her deceased husband. However, both were found to be Quaker sympathizers and were promptly jailed. Mrs. Burden was sent back to England but robbed of much of her estate. Mrs. Dyer was held until her husband in Rhode Island could come and pay for her release. All those in Boston jails seem to have been allowed to leave for Rhode Island before the winter, but new harsher laws were enacted in October 1657 against their return.

Meanwhile in Plymouth Colony, Humphrey Norton was taken in October in Sandwich, alone. The name of his host was not recorded. He was escorted all the way to Assonet in the Fall River area and released. Late in the year, Robert Hodgson came on a solitary foray to Plymouth Colony. He held meetings at the Howland brothers' houses in Duxbury and Marshfield, and managed by friendly warnings to escape capture, returning to Rhode Island for the winter. At the October 1657 Court and again in December after the Hodgson escape, Plymouth called in a number of persons involved in the Quaker visits here:

> *William Newland* for his part in the Holder/Copeland visit, was sentenced to find sureties for his good behavior. He was fined twenty shillings for other specific offenses, such as refusing jury duty.
>
> *Ralph Allen, Sr.* for meetings at his house and "unworthy speeches" to the constable (William Bassett) was also sentenced to find sureties. When he and Newland flatly refused to do this, both were jailed and there they remained for five months. This sentence, however, was for their defiance and contempt of court, not for the Quaker entertainment as such.
>
> *Thomas Burgess Jr.* for showing the warrant to Holder and Copeland was admonished and released.
>
> *Henry Sanderson* for refusal to aid the constable in capturing Norton was committed to jail, but apparently released soon.
>
> *Edward Dillingham, Sr.* admonished and released.
>
> *Arthur Rowland* of Marshfield for entertaining Hodgson was required to give bond for future Court appearance. Refusing to do-so, he was

jailed with Allen and Newland and remained there six months. He was fined for abusing the constable. (His brother, John Howland of the *Mayflower* absented himself from the Court when his brother's case was heard.) Also Henry Howland, his son Zoeth and John Howland's son John Jr. were in court over the Hodgson visit.

Hence the evidence is that in 1657 no Quakers were jailed or abused here and in the absence of specific laws against Quaker meetings or entertainment, no townsmen were even fined. However, three were jailed at year's end for stubborn refusal to cooperate with the Court or for abusing the constable.

The Battles of 1658

It was clear from the onslaught of foreign Quakers in the fall of 1657 using Rhode Island as a privileged sanctuary, that more visits could be expected in 1658. The law in the Bay Colony, passed October 14, 1657, provided that anyone concealing or entertaining a Quaker should be fined forty shillings per hour and imprisoned until paid up. Any male foreign Quakers returning after their first visit were to have an ear cut off and on the next visit the other ear. Females returning were to be whipped. Either sex on their fourth visit was to have the tongue bored with a hot iron. Local persons showing support were to be treated similarly.

Plymouth Colony in late 1657 produced its first serious anti-Quaker law, but that was mild compared to Boston's:

> Those entertaining a foreign Quaker were to be fined £5 or be whipped.
>
> Residents seeing a Quaker were to advise the constable or be censured.
>
> The constable was to try to apprehend the visitor and bring him to a Magistrate.
>
> The Magistrate was to jail the visitor and assess the charges of jail and costs of transport out of the Colony.
>
> The Quaker was to engage to leave and not return, or else to stay in jail. There was, however, no provision that foreign Quakers be whipped.
>
> Fines for meetings were forty shillings against the speaker, forty shillings against the house owner and ten shillings per hearer.

Furthermore, the Plymouth Court made a tricky change in an old law to make it apply here. A law of 1651, called Thomas Hinckley's law, had provided for a ten shilling fine for anyone neglecting worship *and* for setting up another church service. This may have arisen from early problems with rival ministers in Barnstable. Now, however, they simply replaced the word *and* by *or,* and pretended no new law had been passed. This made the two sections separate offenses and was very easy to invoke.

The arrivals were not long in coming. Quakers Copeland and Brend were in Court in Plymouth on February 2. The only reference to their activities as Quakers seems to be in Scituate, where they were entertained by a magistrate James Cudworth, who was curious about their views. In Court, Copeland especially attacked John Alden, saying that on his previous appearance here with Holder, Alden's head and knees had trembled. Brend was "found to be a man of a turbulent spirit and forward to abuse men with his tongue." Both were required to depart within forty-eight hours and if found later were to be whipped. They were found again in the Colony February 8 and were accordingly whipped and sent out. At the March 2 Court were issued the first fines for specific Quaker support:

Arthur Howland for permitting meetings, abusing the constable and presenting a critical letter to the Court, fined and continued in jail.

Henry Howland for holding a meeting, fined ten shillings.

Zoeth Howland for criticizing the minister, stocked.

Peter Gaunt, Daniel Wing, Ralph Allen Jr. and William Allen of Sandwich for "tumultuous carriage" at a meeting in Sandwich (probably when Norton was taken). They were admonished only for wearing their hats in Court and were fined a Pound apiece. The others, John Ellis, Steven Wing and Thomas Butler were at the same meeting, but apparently better behaved in Court and were released.

William Newland and Ralph Allen Sr. were released from jail.

Captain James Cudworth of Scituate, an Assistant Governor, was presented because of a letter from Scituate signed by nineteen persons, complaining that he had entertained Quakers in his home. In his defense, Cudworth produced a letter of support from fifty-five persons and stated that he "had entertained some of the Quakers at my house thereby that I might be better acquainted with their principles. I thought it better so to do than with the blind world to censure, condemn, rail at and revile them when they neither saw their persons, nor knew any of their principles; but the Quakers and myself cannot close in diverse things, and so I signified to the Court...that as I was no Quaker, so I would be no persecutor." The Quakers whom Cudworth must have met were Hodgson, Brend and Copeland. The Court relieved him of his command of the militia and the following June pointedly failed to reelect him as Assistant Governor.

Striking hard at the rebellious persons among the townsmen, the Court ruled in early 1658 that these groups would lose their status as freemen:

Quakers or manifest encouragers of them.
Those who speak contemptuously of the Court or laws.
Those judged grossly scandalous as liars or drunkards.
Manifest opposers of the true worship of God.

Those who refuse to do the country service.
Those who refuse to take the oath of fidelity.

Furthermore, it was ordered that a work house adjacent to the jail be erected at Plymouth for those Quakers and others who wandered about with no calling, and idle persons such as rebellious servants and youths.

The resurrection of the oath of fidelity was aimed especially at the new class of Quaker sympathizers. Originally set up in the reorganization of the laws of 1636, it had been widely disregarded. It was now brought into use, and at the June Court, the following persons refused to take the oath on the grounds that it was unlawful on Biblical grounds to take any oath at all:

Robert Harper	Ralph Allen Sr.
Thomas Greenfield	John Allen
Edward Perry	William Allen
Richard Kerby Jr.	George Allen Jr.
Thomas Ewer	Matthew Allen
William Gifford	John Jenkins
Daniel Wing	George Webb

John Newland and Thomas Johnson had also been summoned "but being lame appeared not." George Webb engaged to depart the government in a short time. The others were held liable for the fine. The Sandwich Quaker supporters who were not on this list such as William Newland, Peter Gaunt and others had taken the oath of fidelity much earlier when they served as constable or in military service.

Humphrey Norton appeared in Plymouth on June 1, apparently on a direct challenge to the Court, rather than on any preaching mission. He was accompanied by John Rouse on this trip. Earlier in the year Norton had visited New Haven and had been branded "H" for heretic on one of his hands. He and Rouse were prepared for a stinging attack on the members of the Plymouth Court, especially on Governor Thomas Prence and John Alden. Norton shouted, "Thomas, thou liest!" and "Prence, thou are a malicious man." In a letter left with the Court he continued the invective with "John Alden is to thee like unto a pack-horse upon which thou layest thy beastly bag. Cursed are all they that have a hand therein." The Court suffered two sessions of this before ordering Rouse and Norton to be whipped on June 5. They refused to pay their jailer's fee until June 10, when finally they were allowed to depart.

A Special Marshal George Barlow

Meanwhile the Court's problems kept growing. On June 1 the former constable of Sandwich, William Bassett, had completed his year's service, and was allowed £5 for his many troubles in office. Replacing him as constable of

Sandwich and special marshal for Sandwich, Barnstable and Yarmouth was a newcomer to Plymouth, one George Barlow. Barlow was from the Bay Colony where he had preached at Exeter and at Saco, but had been turned out. He represented himself as a lawyer when he came to Plymouth.

The Court stated:

> "In regard of the more than ordinary occasion that frequently falls out in the town of Sandwich, so as their constable is not able alone to discharge and perform all such things there which respect his office, by reason of many disturbant persons there residing—it is enacted by this Court that there shall be a marshal chosen in the town of Sandwich for to do such services as shall be required of him by the Government... and in case the warrant directed to this marshal of Sandwich for the gathering in of fines, and is driven to make distress, then he shall have power to make choice of one with him; and if the party (the owner of the property) refuse, to prise the said goods so seized on for the country's use, and to have two shillings in the pound for gathering them in…"

A chief marshal (one Samuel Nash) and an under marshal were already in office in Plymouth, but were fully occupied there. This position was originally called messenger in 1633, then was called marshal in 1645. The duties were those of jailer, the administration of punishments, collecting fines and fees. This was a highly stressful, even brutalizing office, and only certain persons would accept such a role, even if well paid. An early incumbent John Holmes was himself frequently before the Court for drunkenness, taking fees for serving warrants, abusing men's names to procure wine and other abuses of office. The arrangement in seizing goods to satisfy a judgement was that the marshal and a representative of the plaintiff would visit the home of the defendant to appraise the goods to be seized. The defendant had the right to choose a representative to aid in valuing the goods, but if he neglected or refused to make a choice, the marshal could name a neutral person on his behalf. The goods to cover the debt and charges were then seized and turned over to the plaintiff, and any excess value was supposed to be returned to the defendant within six days at country pay, that is in corn or other food. Now, however, in 1658 these previous rules were changed so that the marshal and anyone whom he chose could do the selection and the valuation of the goods to be taken, while the delinquent could do little but see his goods or animals carried off. The marshal had power to require aid and assistance of any persons in the execution of his office. The oath of the under marshal of Sandwich, Barnstable and Yarmouth spelled out his right to value and appraise, to gather levy and distrain, and to receive all fees and fines, with ten percent for himself; the oath concluded "and in the town of Sandwich, you shall in all things act as a constable by approaching felons, or other suspicious persons, keeping the peace, serving of warrants or any other public service that of the said constable may be required." Sandwich thereby went abruptly from a democratic town run by its own citizens, to a little police state run by a stranger with wide powers, who turned out to be a nasty and drunken man as well.

Marshal Barlow immediately had a case to work on. William Allen held a Quaker meeting in his house in early June, and Barlow reported to the Court the list of names of those present. On June 5 the Court ordered that all these be fined according to the law (ten shillings each) and Allen forty shillings. It is probably on this sort of evidence, that meetings were now being held in Sandwich by townspeople themselves, without foreign Quakers being necessarily present, that the Society of Friends later claimed that the first regular meetings in North America were held in Sandwich, beginning in 1658. For example, in December 1658 William Newland was fined £19 for thirty-eight meetings at ten shillings each (his wife attending twenty meetings and himself eighteen) which would be consistent with weekly services in the latter half of 1658.

The foreign Quakers' visit most often referred to in connection with Sandwich is the second visit here of Christopher Holder and John Copeland beginning June 20, 1658. Knowing the fines for meeting in private homes, they met in a deep glen ever since known as Christopher's Hollow. However, informers were everywhere, and the two were taken into the marshal's hands on June 23. For some reason this visit was then reported by much later Quaker writers (Bishop, Bowden, and Whitney) as a brutal event, and this version was repeated in the Cape Cod histories of Freeman, Swift and Deyo.

Their version was:

That the Quakers were kept six days under house arrest at Nathaniel Fish's house.

That while there, four Sandwich Friends visited them and were charged as felons, but were released on defense by Fish that the door was open.

That the Sandwich selectmen refused to whip the two Quakers.

That the two were taken to Barnstable where the resident magistrate, Thomas Hinckley, had them tied up near an outhouse and whipped.

That they each received thirty-three lashes with a special three-cord whip brought by Barlow, with tormenting knots on the cords.

That Friends from Sandwich and onlookers from Barnstable cried out in horror at the cruelty of the whippings.

This ugly scenario is then left in the reader's mind as typical of Barlow's methods. However this incident is not mentioned by Goodwin or by recent writers such as Worrall, Newman, or Bacon. The perceptive Amos Otis noted the Barnstable scene but then added "I should not notice this gross scandal if it had not been copied by other historians without comment." He specifically refers to Freeman's History Volume II which had then just been published, and continues "no trustworthy authority can be quoted in its support—its falsity is apparent." We completely agree with Amos Otis in this case, based on the following facts:

The four Sandwich men who visited the Quakers were identically the four in Court the previous March for "tumultuous carriage" representing a most unlikely coincidence if the incidents were separate.

There were no Sandwich selectmen in 1658; even if some administrators here as Bourne, Skiff, Bassett, or others were the ones referred to, they had no power to whip at all. This must be ordered by the Court and administered by a marshal in the presence of a magistrate. There is no reference to this Holder-Copeland visit in Plymouth Colony records, except the one line "William Allen entertained Christopher Holder."

Hinckley was the magistrate responsible for this area, but since the jail was in Plymouth, the marshal would have had no choice but to take the Quakers to Plymouth under existing laws. Even Hinckley could not have ordered a whipping without prior sentence of the full Court.

There was no law at this time that foreign Quakers be whipped simply for visiting or preaching in Plymouth Colony. The only ones whipped were those like Norton and Rouse who offered the Court insufferable insults and contempt.

We conclude that the Barnstable whipping scene and Barlow's dreadful whip were the products of someone's imagination, and regret that it gained currency. The Quaker confrontations were dramatic enough without exaggerations. We feel the visit of Holder and Copeland here nevertheless did occur in June 1658, cementing the regular meeting process and starting the Christopher's Hollow tradition.

The Court voted to have Governor Prence and a few other magistrates hold a special session in Sandwich. This was held on August 27, at Richard Bourne's house. Instead of fact-finding and discussion tending to calm matters, a harsh confrontation occurred with several justices completely losing their temper. As a result, nine converts were disenfranchised on the grounds that they had never technically applied for and been granted townsmen status under regulation of 1639 which stated that none were to be admitted to new towns without consent of the Church and the Court. The nine disenfranchised were Ralph Allen, Sr., Matthew Allen, Thomas Ewer, Thomas Greenfield, John Jenkins, Richard Kerby Jr., Henry Sanderson, Daniel and Stephen Wing. This naturally continued the alienation in the community.

The Court in Plymouth October 2 continued the hard line, fining eleven of the Sandwich Quakers for refusing again to take the oath of fidelity. William Newland was singled out by the marshal on other grounds, and was fined for failing to bring into Court his two daughters who had allegedly abused the marshal. These were teenage girls, daughters of Newland's wife Rose by her previous marriage to Joseph Holway.

Clearly the extraordinary authority given Barlow, or assumed by him, in issuing summons, levying fines and collecting property is evident. Newland soon testified in Court that Barlow broke into his house in the night, and that he suffered much damage. This shows an abrupt transition to a partially lawless state in this period. It was not until June 1661 that the Court finally ruled that no summons could be issued before being entered at the Court, and that all evidence and testimony must be in writing.

The Court ordered that in October 1658 a Day of Humiliation be held throughout the Colony, in view of heavy signs of God's displeasure manifested in "visiting many families with sickness; unreasonableness of the weather and failure of crops; letting loose as a scourge upon us those fretting gangrene-like doctrines and persons commonly called Quakers; the spirit of division and dissension in Church and civil affairs."

CHRISTOPHER'S HOLLOW*-A photograph by Barbara Russell for the Sandwich Historical Commission showing Christopher's Hollow. This deep glen in ancient times was graced with large trees, rocks and a spring and is the place where Christopher Holder preached to Sandwich converts in 1658.*

The laws against the citizens who did not support the government were stiffened. No Quaker was allowed to become a freeman, and all their supporters were to be disenfranchised. Opposers of the laws and of official worship or of military service, as well as the grossly scandalous or debauched were to be disenfranchised. Those who refused the oath of fidelity were to lose their rights to vote or to hold office.

At this unhappy point, another visit of foreign Quakers occurred in Sandwich, John Copeland making his third visit in 1658, and Josiah Cole his first mission to any New England town outside of Newport. Coming here from Martha's Vineyard, Copeland and Cole were entertained by Newland, who was fined December 3. The two were soon apprehended by the marshal and sent out of the Colony by way of Plymouth. At this December 3 Court, it was noted "that frequently diverse of those called Quakers have repaired to Sandwich from other places by sea, coming in at Manomet with a boat." Barlow was urged, upon intelligence of such arrivals, to procure competent help, secure such vessels and apprehend the persons. Also at this Court, James Skiff of Sandwich, one of the most active and competent citizens in town affairs, was summoned for criticizing the law concerning the oath of fidelity.

James Cudworth of Scituate wrote a long letter to his friend John Brown of Plymouth, then temporarily in England. This comprehensive and convincing letter was then printed in England where Cudworth and his Scituate neighbor, Hatherly, were well-known. This was probably one of the first eye-witness accounts to reach England of the persecution of Quakers (outside of Quaker internal letters). He reviewed the course of events in Plymouth and in the Bay Colony, where whippings and three ear-croppings had not worked, and where now those banished were promised death if they returned. He feared that "now Plymouth saddle is on the Bay horse"; that is, that Plymouth Colony would model its laws on those of the Bay Colony. Included were many references to Sandwich:

> "They (the Quakers) have many meetings and many adherents, almost the whole town of Sandwich is adhering towards them.... then all must take the oath of fidelity... if any man refuse, he shall pay five pounds... then out goes the Marshal and fetcheth away their cows... A poor weaver that had seven or eight small children, he himself lame in his body, had but two cows and both taken from him. The Marshal asked him what would he do? He must have his cows. The man said that God gave him them be doubted not, but would still provide for him. To fill up the measure yet more fully, tho to the further emptying of Sandwich men of their outward comforts, the last Court, was pleased to determine fines on Sandwich men for meetings, one hundred fifty pounds whereof William Newland is £24, William Allen £46, the poor weaver £20.. when cruel Barlow, Sandwich Marshal, came to demand the sum.. all the poor man had was not worth £10. What will be the end of such practices the Lord only knows... William Newland was there (Boston) about his occasions

some ten days and they put him in prison twenty-four hours.. but had not proof enough to make him a Quaker, which if they had he should have been whipped; nay, they may not go about their occasions in other towns in our Colony, but warrants lie in ambush to apprehend and bring them before a magistrate to give an account of their business....."

There are some corrections here to note (perhaps inevitable when emotional causes are being pleaded). The lame weaver was Thomas Johnson who had in 1658 but one child, not seven or eight. His net worth however, was indeed low. For the further £10 due, Barlow later had his house and lot attached, valued at £10. The £46 due from William Allen included holding twenty-one meetings in his house at £2 each. Newland's £24 was £19 for thirty-eight meetings and £5 for entertaining Copeland and Cole.

Bay Colony Events, 1658

The assaults of foreign Quakers were not so numerous as in 1657, but were dramatic. Dorothy Waugh and Sarah Gibbons arrived in April and were jailed after attempting to speak in a church. The chief activists were the veterans Christopher Holder, John Copeland, John Rouse and Humphrey Norton, who came to Boston and Salem in July, and were imprisoned until October. Holder, Copeland and Rouse had their right ears cut off, while Norton as a first offender was otherwise tortured but not mutilated. Rouse wrote a letter to Margaret Fell in England (one of Fox's top associates) in which he said "We have two strong places in this land, one at Newport and the other at Sandwich, which the enemy will never get dominion over."

Holder now had a private following. Catherine Scott of Rhode Island, sister of Ann Hutchinson, came to Boston with Mary her eighteen year-old daughter to show support. Catherine was imprisoned and whipped. A dramatic protest was lodged by Mrs. Hored Gardner of Newport, who came to Boston with a nursing baby and a maid. All were imprisoned and the two women whipped.

A small group of partisans of the Bay Colony government petitioned that Quakers should be banished on pain of death, and that if they returned, they should in fact be executed. This petition was reinforced by a similar letter to the four United Colonies Governments by the United Colony Commissioners, who were all of the most hawkish views. The Bay Colony did enact this in October, admitting "notwithstanding all former laws, they have not been deterred."

After their release in Boston, Copeland, Norton and Rouse returned to England to preach and write, while Holder, Robinson, Stephenson and others preached in Virginia and Maryland.

Events in 1659 and 1660

Following the pattern of 1658, the Sandwich converts in 1659 and 1660 continued to be fined for refusing to take the oath of fidelity, and to accumulate other fines for meetings, obstructing the marshal and for entertaining foreign

Quakers. Two sets of foreign Quakers were apprehended here during 1659, and these are of especial interest as they include two who were hung in Boston, Mary Dyer and William Leddra. Peter Pearson and Leddra were apprehended early in 1659 at a meeting in Sandwich and were promptly jailed. Pearson was a new arrival from England via Rhode Island. These two carried Quaker obstructionism to extreme. The only law in Plymouth against foreign Quakers at this time was the one passed in 1657 that they should be jailed until they should engage to depart and not return, paying their jail fees and transport charges. In October 1659 these two were asked if they would engage to leave, and refusing, "were returned to the place whence they came" (jail). In December 1659 the question and results were repeated. At the March 7, 1660 Court, Leddra varied his answer saying in a modern turn of phrase, "It's like if I were at liberty out of prison I might depart in the will of God ere long." To this the Court said "if he would now resolve (the Lord willing) to depart by such a time, he might have his liberty." It was left "that when it should be revealed to him that he might depart, he should send word to the magistrates and he may have his liberty." The record then shows that at last on April 17 Leddra and Pearson, after over a year in jail, engaged to depart and were released.

Plymouth Laws, 1659

In June 1659, the Plymouth Court acknowledged that Quaker books, pamphlets and letters were widely found in the jurisdiction. The marshal and other officials were urged to seize all they could find and bring them to Plymouth. The Court then made three further orders which have an almost wistful note:

> "A proposition be made to the Quakers that such of them as will promise and engage to remove their dwellings out of this government within six months after this present Court and perform it; that no fine be exacted of them as so engage."
>
> "Such as whose estates are so impoverished as they are disabled to remove, they shall have some supply made them out of the treasury to help them."
>
> "Whereas some have desired, and others think it meet to permit some persons to frequent the Quaker meetings to endeavor to reduce them from the error of their ways, the Court considering the promises do permit John Smith of Barnstable, Isaac Robinson, John Chipman and John Cooke of Plymouth or any two of them to attend the said meetings, for the ends aforesaid at any time between this Court and the next October Court."

The Plymouth Court were assuming an incredible persuasive power on the part of their Committee. These four were highly respected individuals. Cooke was Deacon of the church in Plymouth, the others from Barnstable. Isaac Robinson was revered as the son of Reverend John Robinson, the Leyden pastor; Chipman was an Elder of the church in Barnstable and Smith had theological training, later founding a church group of his own in Barnstable. However, after the lightning strikes of new doctrine absorbed from the missionary Quakers and braving the harsh words of Prence and his colleagues on the Court, the converts at Sandwich were not to be changed by gentle urging. It fell to Robinson to present back to the Court the results of the Committee's labors, and they reported in favor of the Quaker position, at least that they not be persecuted. This was not a popular result for the Court, and Robinson was later severely rebuked.

As to removals of families impoverished by the fines, there is no record of any charged to the Colony. The Quakers were already forging their tradition of taking care of their own. Thomas Johnson, the weaver who lost his house, was in fact later found settled in Falmouth. Matthew Allen married and removed to Dartmouth. Robert Harper lost his house and lot in fines, but remained in Sandwich at this time.

In addition to the above new efforts, the laws of the previous October were now exercised, called for disenfranchisement of Quaker supporters, government critics and the grossly scandalous. Four were accordingly sentenced. William Newland and Henry Howland for Quaker support, John Barnes for his frequent and abominable drunkenness and Richard Beare of Marshfield as a debauched person convicted of filthy and obscene practices. What a striking contrast these two pairs of men must have made, one pair dedicated and competent, the other among the dregs of the Colony.

The First Executions

The Puritans of the Bay Colony acted according to their belief that they were the true and only instruments of God's will. They felt that they had incurred the Almighty's displeasure by allowing the Quaker heresy to continue. Their reactions were severe, and the suffering inflicted in Boston continued to be far greater than in Plymouth Colony. Many local supporters were forced to leave the Colony, and others imprisoned for long periods including children. Foreign Quakers seemed to provoke reaction. They returned to be jailed or whipped time after time. Their patience was unlimited. Two, William Robinson and Marmaduke Stephenson, were determined to see if Boston would take their lives. The question was answered on October 27, 1659 when they were hanged and became the first martyrs to their cause.

Mary Dyer and Thomas Greenfield

Paraded before the same scaffold, with expectations of the same fate, was Mary Dyer. She had returned from Newport that fall in spite of her previous banishment. Instead, the authorities took her back to jail and banished her once again to Rhode Island.

Her cause had made Mary Dyer determined, and shortly after this she took the coastal route to Manomet and Sandwich, accompanied by Thomas Greenfield of Sandwich who had visited England and was now returning. The two were promptly seized and brought before the Court which found as follows:

"Whereas Thomas Greenfield coming lately out of England and arriving at Rhode Island came into these parts about the 14th day of November and brought Mary Dyer with him to Plymouth, contrary to an order of Court which prohibits any of those called Quakers to come into this jurisdiction, she, the said Mary Dyer, being one of those so called; and he, the said Greenfield, being examined and required to answer directly whether he had any residence, house or land, at Sandwich, within this government or no, he, refusing to make any answer to that demand, was therefor (after being urged to speak and give answer to the said query) committed to prison according to order, as falling under the account of a foreign Quaker, and at this Court was brought before authority and again examined upon the premises, and refused to make any satisfactory answer; notwithstanding whereas Mr. Edmond Freeman, Senior of Sandwich, appearing in Court and affirming that the said Greenfield had house and land in the liberties of Sandwich, with other concurrent testimony to the same effect, the Court saw reason to release the said Thomas Greenfield, and accordingly he was released, paying his fee, which he refused to do; wherefore the Court was constrained to take other course to satisfy the same out of the estate of the said Greenfield, by warrant directed by the marshal, Barlow, for the same purpose, which said charge of imprisonment amounted to the sum of thirty shillings. And the said Greenfield, for his bringing in or being a conduct to the said Mary Dyer from Rhode Island to Plymouth, was sentenced to pay for her transportation back to Rhode Island the sume of sixteen shillings, and for the fees of Mary Dyer's imprisonment the sum of eleven shillings; which said sums the marshal, Barlow, was by warrant required to levy on the estate of the said Thomas Greenfield, wheresoever he should find it within his liberties."

There is no record that Mary Dyer was questioned by the Plymouth Court. Since she was a "foreign" Quaker, it may be assumed that she paid her fine and continued on her way.

Despite his stubborn refusal to answer the Court's questions, Greenfield was well known to the Court and to Barlow. He had been a Sandwich resident since the Arms List of 1643, had served on the Narraganset campaign in 1645, contributed to a new meetinghouse in 1655, and had been fined in June 1658 for refusing the oath of fidelity. Barlow must have known him especially well from a fracas the previous November over Copeland and Cole's arrest when Greenfield had been fined a Pound for refusing to aid the marshal, and another three Pounds for striking the marshal. In spite of this, Greenfield refused to identify himself and had to be cleared by Edmund Freeman in order to be fined as a resident and allowed to go home. He was, as far as we know, unmarried and lived on Old County Road near Edward Perry, where the marshal would soon come calling to distrain goods.

Robinson and Cudworth

These two highly esteemed citizens had been pillars of the community, but in March 1660 found themselves before the Court for their frank opinions expressed in writing.

> "The Court taking notice of sundry scandals and falsehoods in a letter of Isaac Robinson's, tending greatly to the prejudice of this government, and encouragement of those commonly called Quakers, and thereby liable (according to the law provided in such case) to disenfranchisement, yet we at present forbear the censure until further enquiry be made into things. In reference to Captain James Cudworth, the Court taking notice of his great disaffection to this government and manifest abetting and encouragement of those called Quakers, expressed partly in a letter, owned by himself in the manner of sending it, and in many other carriages of his known to us, and also in a letter strongly conjectured and suspected to be by him sent into England, the which himself hath not yet denied: The promises considered, the Court see cause to bind him over to make a further answer hereunto at the next General Court, to be held in June next; and do therefore require that he put in good security the value of five hundred pounds for the end abovesaid."

In June Robinson was disenfranchised, but then voted back in, while Cudworth was disenfranchised and remained so until the death of Governor Prence in 1672. It has been noted that his bond for appearance at Court, £500, was more than all the currency in circulation in the whole Colony.

The Pursuit of Wenlock

By 1660 many of the first wave of English Quakers had had their battles in New England and had returned to England to write and speak. Others took their places, determined to be heard in the colonies. Wenlock Christoferson had been in Boston jail the previous fall, and now in 1660 was ready for a series of engagements in Plymouth. He made rapid appearances in Scituate, Marshfield, Duxbury and Plymouth in the spring of 1660, but managed to escape capture through the aid of friends. A procession of his hosts, however, was soon before the Plymouth Court, including Ensign Williams of the Scituate militia (who had been one of those succeeding Cudworth in the troop), Henry and Arthur Howland, and John Smith of Plymouth. In August, Wenlock visited Sandwich where his host was William Newland. He was then pursued from house to house by the marshal, who issued summonses right and left for failure to aid him in the capture. Barlow, apparently alone actually caught Wenlock, when Daniel Butler had the temerity to attack the marshal and free Wenlock. For this exploit, Butler earned the distinction of being the only Sandwich convert to be whipped in this Colony. Only one other is known to have been whipped, Robert Harper in Boston. Wenlock was jailed and banished, but in October suddenly reappeared at the Court in defiance of the ban. He obviously sought the Court's rigor with turbulent behavior for which he was laid neck and heels (a painful trussed position) then whipped and finally sent out again. He had earned his spurs.

Mary Dyer's Death, 1660

At this time the Bay Colony Governor John Endicott addressed a long letter to Charles II assuring the King of the loyalty and support of the Colony, craving the continuation of all their civil privileges and saying "We could not live without the public worship of God." As to the Quakers, there was a paragraph of abuse, stating "The Quakers died not because of their other crimes how capital soever, but upon their superadded presumptious and incorrigible contempt of authority... Had they not been restrained so far as appeared, there was too much cause to fear that we ourselves must quickly have died or worse..."

Many years before, Governor Winthrop had called Mary Dyer "a very proper and fair woman, but of a very proud spirit." Now forty-three, she was still called "of a comely and grave countenance" and was determined to offer up her life. She returned to Boston May 21 and was sentenced to die June 1. And so she did, with many expressions of Christian faith, and the greatest composure. An armed guard of 200 were there to prevent intervention. One of the officers of these troops, Edward Wanton, was so moved that he resigned his commission, joined the Friends and became a distinguished member.

The Fines in Plymouth Colony

At the end of 1660 it was again urged that cages by erected for holding prisoners, especially at Sandwich, Duxbury, Marshfield and Scituate. Any inhabitant was now allowed to apprehend foreign Quakers and bring them to a constable or magistrate, and it was noted that "of late time the Quakers have been furnished with horses and thereby they have not only the more speedy passage from place to place to the poisoning of the inhabitants with their cursed tenets, but also thereby have escaped the hands of the officers that might otherwise have apprehended them." Horses were to be seized and forfeited. On a note of humility, the Court ruled that none were to be fined for not coming to the official services. This recognized the continuing wide shortage of ministers and the depth of estrangement from popular support of stated preaching even where it was available.

How much was taken from the Sandwich converts in the period of sustained fining from June 1658 through the end of 1660? A table appeared in Bishop's "New England Judged" which came out in sections in 1660 and 1665, then a condensed version in 1703. This table seems to be the basis for a list of fines and distraints that appear in later histories, presented more as a matter of sorrow and wonder than of proven fact. We have attempted to compare this list with the known fines shown in Plymouth Court Orders and Treasurer's Records, and find some wide discrepancies, which must be due to the fines for attending meetings (ten shillings) or for being host (forty shillings). These fines we venture to suggest were recorded and accumulated by Barlow and may not have been passed on completely to the County Treasurer. For instance, Peter Gaunt had no known fines, but there is a record of the marshal leading off seven cattle to satisfy a £24 claim and his distraints are said in the list to amount to £43. The only meetings fines recorded in Colony-records are £44 against William Allen (host at twenty and attended eight others) and £19 against William Newland and his wife (thirty-eight attendances). We have made a rough estimate of meetings, fines for oaths and other fines for the whole thirty-one months and assembled the following table of possible fines:

Sandwich Quaker Fines June 1658-December 1660

	As estimated by Bishop	Fines in Ply. Col. Rec.	Suggested Total Fines
Edward Perry	£ 90	£ 31	£ 90
William Allen	87	76	126
Ralph Allen, Sr.	68	31	81
Richard Kerby	58	31	76
William Gifford	58	30	75
Matthew Allen	48	30	75
Robert Harper	44	40	85
Peter Gaunt	43		43
William Newland	36	22	77
15 other males plus various wives	147	195	375
Total	679	486	1103

Plymouth Colony Records refer to a total £288 in fines which were prepared but never levied, the Sandwich share of which is in the above suggested total.

The Sandwich Quaker Susan F. Hoxie stated in her paper on the early Sandwich Quakers that upwards of £900 was collected from them which agrees with the above estimates. The figures given by Bishop were assembled hastily in London from various sources, and do not include many names that were fined over the oath or otherwise. Many non-Quakers were also fined for refusing to aid the marshal. These crushing fines were met in part by quiet loans of food, tools, materials and money to support the battered families.

Plymouth Colony: 1661

The last pair of foreign Quakers found in the records here, William Reap and Peter Pearson, were taken in Sandwich in February 1661. Their host was

Peter Gaunt. Reap was a newcomer to the confrontation scene. A total of ten Sandwich converts were accused of tumultuous carriage against the marshal and his aides in securing these "strange Quakers." Here, however, any similarity to previous confrontation ends. The laws of 1657 had been repealed in 1660, and there is no record that Gaunt was fined for entertaining, or his friends for resisting, the marshal, or that Reap and Pearson were even imprisoned. They were questioned at Court as to their intentions, and Reap as a newcomer said that he had come to Sandwich and Barnstable about "merchandising affairs." In spite of his "menacing speeches and proud carriages and expressions, " Reap was allowed to spend the night comfortably at the home of John and Deborah Smith of Plymouth, known Quaker sympathizers. Pearson said that he had come to see his Friends, and uttered "frivolous speeches" to the Court. Although well-remembered for his previous year's stay in Plymouth jail, Pearson was allowed to spend the night at the ordinary, and "on the morrow they took their journey towards Rhode Island." Here was a radical change in the behavior of the Court. The only sufferer at this session was one Joshua Coxhall of Rhode Island who was found to be a Quaker, and had his horse seized by the marshal under the recent horse law. The only explanation possible for the change of attitude would seem to be that word of Quaker protests to Charles II had reached Plymouth, and that it was deemed expedient to remove from the books laws requiring jailing of Quakers. A new law passed in 1661 that the marshal shall seize and whip any foreign Quaker with rods up to fifteen stripes and give him a pass to depart, also that anyone permitting a Quaker meeting shall be fined £15 or be whipped. These seemed to be a harsh escalation of the anti-Quaker laws, but in fact were not tested at all, and represented the same shift in stance as found in the Bay Colony with its cart-and-whip act of the same period, to punish without imprisonment. The new Plymouth laws also went on to admit "there is a constant monthly meeting together of the Quakers from diverse places in great numbers."

The Bay Colony 1661

The ranks of those prepared to enter the Lion's Den of Boston were now greatly reduced. Early in 1661 William Leddra and Wenlock Christoferson made their fateful appearance, both fully prepared as returning after banishment for the sentence of death that awaited them. Governor Endicott insisted on the first sentence and on March 14, after a moving letter of farewell and faith to his friends, Leddra was hung on the Common. Wenlock was to follow, but there was now such a general outcry at these executions that it was delayed, and finally on June 10 he was reprieved and sent out. In all, a group of twenty-eight local Quakers were still in prison in May, and the Court, knowing of impending changes in England, allowed all to be released but with the warning that if found offending again, they would suffer under the new Cart-and-Whip Act. Those released included we believe William Allen of Sandwich and Nicholas Davis of Barnstable.

The notorious Cart-and-Whip Act or Vagabond Quaker Act read in part:

"This Court, being desirous to try all means with as much leniency as

> may consist with our safety to prevent the intrusions of the Quakers who...have not been restrained by the laws already provided, have ordered that every such vagabond Quaker found within any part of the jurisdiction shall...be stripped naked from the middle upwards and tied to a cart's tail and whipped through the town, and from thence immediately conveyed to the constable of the next town towards the borders of our jurisdiction as their warrant shall direct and so from constable to constable..."

This saved imprisonment and much administration.

The first victims of this law were newcomers to Boston, Peter Pearson and his friend, Judah Brown. They were whipped out towards the south via Roxbury and Dedham to the border. Finally in November the King's Missive arrived, addressed to each of the Colonies in New England. The Boston copy was brought by one of its English sponsors, the Salem convert Samuel Shattuck, in a splendid reversal of his role only two years before, when he had been banished. The Missive asked that Quakers in prison be either released or sent to England for trial. The laws in the Colonies against imprisonment and corporal punishment were suspended, but the Quakers were still far from welcome or safe. The Cart-and-Whip Act was reinstated in October 1662, with a limit of only three towns through which a person might be carted.

During the summer of 1661 the Quakers in North America had their first Yearly Meeting at Newport, a large gathering of such strength and enthusiasm that the Puritan authorities must have been impressed.

Barlow's Downfall

We do not know the location of Barlow's house during the period of two and one half years of his persecution of the Quaker group. He had six children by a previous marriage, but there is record only of the youngest two living in Sandwich.

Amos Otis refers to Barlow's children as stealing fruit from the trees of his neighbor Thomas Johnson, but this may have been after Johnson had lost title to the house and was living elsewhere. Johnson had lived just east of Stephen Wing on Spring Hill Road, and if Barlow was near, he would have lived in the present Countryside or Foster Road area. The picture of him and his informers watching for Quaker meetings and foreign visitors, and setting the fines as well as collecting the accumulated charges through distraint of food and property, is an ugly and sad thing. Since he made ten percent of every fine and had only to make periodic returns to Plymouth of his doings, he obviously had a profitable arrangement in his pillage. His victims could and did complain about these irregularities to Plymouth Court.

He took a pair of wheels from Quakers, but had to return them when it was proven that they were on loan. Similarly he had to restore a pair of oxen to Francis Allen taken by mistake. He took a horse of William Newland without notice, and broke into Newland's house in the night causing much damage. Thomas Ewer claimed in Court that Barlow was wearing a coat of Ewer's cloth. He stole Greenfield's corn while the latter was on his trip to England. He took whale oil from John Ellis which he had to return. He was fined only ten shillings for leaving Benjamin Allen in stocks the greater part of the night. He took seven cows from Jenkins and when one later died, he came back and got another live one. There was a similar case with Peter Gaunt, who complained that he should have received the hide of the dead cow.

His divisive effect in the community is shown in a Court trial for libel where a citizen (not a Quaker) forced Jacob Burgess to testify against Newland "or he should not have his daughter to wed."

The Plymouth Court knew perfectly well how traumatic the distraint process was on the victims and how brutal the marshal was in his methods. Bishop reports that Governor Prence said of Barlow "that an honest man would not have, or hardly would, take his place." Thomas Clarke of Plymouth had the courage to rise in Court and say of Barlow "that he is such an one that he is a shame and reproach to all his masters; and that he, the said Barlow, stands convicted and recorded of a lie at Newbury." Nevertheless, he continued in office. The most commonly reported story of Barlow is that he went to William Allen's home, while William was in jail in Boston (probably in the spring of 1661). The house and barn had already been stripped, for William Allen was probably the most heavily fined of any Sandwich Quaker. Taking Priscilla's last cooking pot and bag of meal, he sneered, "Now Priscilla, how will thee cook for thy family and friends, thee has no kettle." To which Priscilla replied in prophetic vein, "George, that God who hears the young ravens when they cry will provide for them, I trust in that God and I verily believe the time will come when thy necessity will be greater than mine."

After 1660, Barlow must have found his income nearly dried up as there were no further fines for refusing the oath, no further broad penalties for holding meetings and no further visits of foreign Quakers to stir up the "tumultuous carriage" on which he throve. It is, therefore, hardly a coincidence that sometime in 1661 he married the widow Jane Besse who lived nearby in Spring Hill. Her husband Anthony had died in 1657, leaving her with two sons and six daughters. Her life may have been hard before, but after Barlow moved in it became a scene of violence.

In October 1661 in Plymouth Colony Records, the sisters Anna, Dorcas and Mary Besse were in Court and placed under heavy bond for future appearance at their trial, for unnatural and cruel carriage towards their father-in-law, George Barlow. These were the eldest sisters, Dorcas about 22, Anna 20 and Mary 16. Anna was in fact already married to Andrew Hallett of Yarmouth and was pregnant. The Court found March 4, 1661/2:

> *"Anna Besse for her cruel and unnatural practice towards her father-in-law George Barlow, in chopping him in the back, notwithstanding the odiousness of her act, the Court,*

considering of some circumstances, namely her ingenious confession, together with her present condition, being with child, and some other particulars, have sentenced her to pay a fine of ten pounds, or to be publicly whipped at some other convenient time when her condition will admit thereof."

Dorcas Besse and Mary Besse, for carriages of like nature towards their father-in-law, though not in so high a degree, were both sentenced to sit in the stocks during the pleasure of the Court; which accordingly was performed. The younger Mary Besse was sharply reproved by the Court, as being by her disobedience the occasioner of the evil above mentioned. Mary Besse this same year married Francis Allen and escaped the house.

George Barlow and his wife were both severely reproved for "their most ungodly living in contention with the other, and admonished to live otherwise." His death occurred between his will of August 1684 and his inventory of October 1684.

Summary of Arrivals in Plymouth Colony

We present below a condensed summary of the various visits of foreign Quakers and their supporters to this Colony:

Nicholas Upsall, December 1656 to March 1657: to Plymouth and wintered in Sandwich
Holder and Copeland, April 1657: to Sandwich and Plymouth from Martha's Vineyard
Norton, October 1657: to Sandwich and Plymouth
Hodgson, December 1657: to Scituate, Marshfield and Duxbury
Brend and Copeland, February 1658: to Plymouth, Scituate, Marshfield, Duxbury
Norton and Rouse, June 1658: Plymouth
Holder and Copeland, June 1658: Sandwich and Plymouth
Copeland and Cole, late 1658: Sandwich and Plymouth from Martha's Vineyard
Leddra and Pearson, April 1659: Sandwich and Plymouth, jailed until April 1660
Dyer and Greenfield, November 1659: to Sandwich by sea and to Plymouth
Wenlock Christoferson, April 1660: to Scituate, Marshfield and Duxbury
Wenlock Christoferson, August 1660: to Sandwich and Plymouth
Wenlock Christoferson, October 1660: to Plymouth
Reap and Pearson, February 1661: to Sandwich and Plymouth

The Early Sandwich Quakers

We also present in condensed form a list of the early Sandwich converts and their families:

Ralph Allen, Sr.: Probably brother of George Sr.; died in Sandwich about 1660;

his son John of Newport was fined here in 1658 and 1662.

William Allen: Son of George Sr.; host of the earliest meetings and with wife Priscilla, one of the leading spirits of the cause

Ralph Allen Jr.: Son of George Sr.; his sons, Benjamin and Joseph were fined here occasionally.

Matthew Allen: Son of George Sr.; active here; his children settled in New Jersey.

Thomas Butler: Often fined, as were his sons Daniel and Obadiah; Daniel was whipped for attacking the marshal and for freeing a foreign Quaker, Wenlock.

Thomas Ewer Jr.: Fined, removed later to Barnstable.

Peter Gaunt: Fined; his children Israel and Lydia were also active.

William Gifford: A lifelong supporter; his second wife Mary Mills endured cart-and-whip in Boston in 1677 before coming to Sandwich.

Robert Harper: Whipped in Boston; married Deborah, sister of Edward Perry; his house and lot were seized here.

John Jenkins: One of the group consistently fined over the oath and meetings.

Thomas Johnson: The lame weaver; his house and lot seized; he resettled in Falmouth, but died in Sandwich at William Allen's home.

Richard Kerby Sr.: Active as were his son, Richard Jr. and daughters Sarah and Jane; Sarah whipped for insolence before the Quaker period.

John Newland: Brother of William; lame, childless, fined with his wife

William Newland: Married Rose (Allen), daughter of George Sr. and widow of Joseph Holway; his Holway stepdaughters attacked the marshal; a leading host of foreign Quakers.

Edward Perry: Educated and diplomatic; became lifelong clerk of the Quaker Meeting here.

Michael Turner: One of the earliest settlers; fined for meetings.

Daniel Wing: Brother of Stephen and of John of Yarmouth, both of whom later became Quakers.

Thomas Greenfield: Unmarried, was a member of the meeting, and escorted Mary Dyer to Sandwich and Plymouth from Newport.

CHAPTER 7

LATER TOWN EVENTS TO 1692

In town meeting records of the 1657-1660 period, there is no reference at all to the Quaker persecutions or to George Barlow. The Quaker group declined public office in this period, putting more of the duties of the town on to a small group who kept things going. As late as 1660 certain persons who were later Quakers were found in the militia, including Daniel Wing, Ludowick Hoxie and Francis Allen. Barlow first appeared in the town record of 1661. William Newland made an unexplained "gift" of land in 1660 to Edmund Freeman Jr. doubtless to repay aid given. Quakers were found in minor town offices such as highway surveyor from 1663, and Edward Perry became a "rater" or assessor of taxes in 1667/8. These evidences of normalization of relations and civic participation say nothing about the earlier edicts of disenfranchisement by Plymouth Colony which seem to have been often ignored. Nevertheless, some tensions remained, possibly caused by perceived differences in grants of new land, a most sensitive subject. Each group had problems of expenses over support of its meetinghouse and services as well as the tremendous strains and taxes brought on by the 1675 and 1676 Indian War; each tended to blame the other for not sharing properly. In 1672, the Court said it would grant new commons to Sandwich settlers, but only to those helpful in the support of the ministry. This kept tension simmering. On March 1, 1674/5, the Court reaffirmed that those who came under the law prohibiting some from voting for officers could not have a grant of marsh. Nevertheless, the town promptly voted April 23, 1675 on a list of persons who had the privileges of the town and this included all the Quakers. Clearly progress in equality was desired and was slowly achieved, but was not easy. The problem of taking the oath of fidelity still remained, and it was wisely seen as a matter of wording. The Friends had to convince the Court of their commitment and engagement of fidelity without the word "oath, " but positions had so hardened that it was difficult to satisfy the conservatives on both sides.

Old Town Burial Ground

In July 1663 the records show "The town has agreed that the little neck of land that lies against William Newland's house shall be appropriated for a burial place for the Town." Newland's house was described in the survey of properties as west of Grove Street so the word "against" here means "opposite." There was an absence on Cape Cod of slate, marble, or other sedimentary stone that could be split flat and carved for a grave marker. These had to be imported from Boston or elsewhere at great expense. Many early burials were marked by horizontal boards of hard wood such as locust supported on posts, but these deteriorated. The earliest markers in Old Town Cemetery are: Thomas Clark, 1683: Thomas Burgess, 1685; Dorothy Burgess, 1687; Ezra Perry, 1689; John Prince, 1689. The Senior Burgesses are said to have imported their slate burial markers from England, but these broke up and were replaced in 1917 by new slates. Ezra Perry was their son-in-law, whose wife Elizabeth (Burgess) was buried here in 1717. Young Prince was the son of Samuel Prince, who came to Sandwich in 1680. His brother, Thomas Prince, became a famous Boston minister.

Town Boundaries

The Town's boundaries with Plymouth, Barnstable and Falmouth have remained remarkably constant since these towns were first settled. The Plymouth line began at Peaked Cliff and ran southwest to a mark on a large rock just west of the outflow of Herring River from Great Herring Pond, thus placing the entire Herring River within Sandwich bounds. From there the line ran across country more westerly to Red River and thence south with the river to Buttermilk Bay and Cohasset Narrows. The Saconesset border began at a place near the Buzzards Bay shore called Hope's Spring, thence easterly to a three-way town marker on the Sandwich road west of Ashumet Pond, with the Indians' lands to the east of the road. The Barnstable line began at a large rock near Ralph Jones' house on present High Street and Howland Lane. From the rock, the line ran northeast through Scorton and Great Marshes, leaving the neck of Fuller's Point in Barnstable and running to a stake at the seaside. From the rock, the line ran southwest five miles to a marked tree just off present Asa Meiggs Road which was a three-way marker with the Indians' lands.

The borders between Mashpee and each of its neighboring towns form a separate subject which will be discussed later in Chapters 12 and 23.

Herring, Whales, Blackbirds, Wolves

The annual flow of herring, especially up the Manomet/Herring River from Buzzards Bay to Great Herring Pond was—and remains—a marvel of nature. Thomas Burgess in the Aptucxet area had an annual grant of 10,000 herring and Richard Bourne with a land-holding further up the stream, an annual allowance of 12,000 herring. The Indians had taken the herring in weirs of brush. The whites found it necessary to control the taking to ensure a fair distribution to both whites and Indians. Each white family received a barrel of herring and each Indian family two barrels.

Whales, blackfish and other oil-bearing mammals occasionally came ashore and were eagerly watched for. The blubber was boiled down in cauldrons on the shore and the oil put up in casks. The finder and work party got shares and the rest was saved to pay town expenses, such as purchase of powder or payment to the minister.

On the opposite score of nature's bounty, men were required to kill blackbirds, probably grackles, at twelve birds per year, or one crow's head per two blackbirds. Bounties were set on wolves because of sheep grazing at large. Wolves remained here until well into the nineteenth century.

Town Officials

The towns were urged to name three or five selectmen from 1662 on, to serve in hearing cases of debt and minor offenses, damage to crops from animals, Indian cases, church attendance, arrival of strangers, and such matters. The first selectmen found in Sandwich records were in 1667, namely Thomas Burgess, James Skiff and Thomas Tupper Senior. The other senior positions were those of deputy to Plymouth Court from 1639, and raters (assessors) from 1651. The same dozen or so early settlers seem to fill all these various positions and must have welcomed able young men of the younger generation. In 1667 Sandwich was allowed to send only one deputy to Plymouth Court instead of two, because of a "scarcity of fit men for public employment." In 1672, a father and son served as selectmen (James and Stephen Skiff) and 1691 brothers Elisha and Shearjashub Bourne. Neighborhood men all had to take turns as local road surveyor, and at least once each head of household had to take the unpopular constable position.

Construction

We have already mentioned the town dock for which the road and land were taken from Thomas Tupper Senior on what was later called Dock Lane in the Jarvesville area. This location was preferred over an alternate route through George Buitt's meadow to another branch of the streams in Shawme Marsh. From later references to Buitt's lands and the fact that a vessel was built and launched off George's Rock Road in 1811, we propose that it was Buitt for whom George's Rock Road was named. The Rock is an erratic located at the edge of the marsh. The dock was finished by John Ellis in 1662, and repaired periodically to 1689 when Samuel Prince was allowed to keep it up.

As to the Dexter Grist Mill in the center of town, an agreement with Thomas Dexter for ten years expired in 1664, and must have been renewed because this mill was in Dexter family hands until 1699. Benjamin Nye built the second grist mill on his stream on Old County Road before 1670, and in 1676 he was allowed to build a fulling mill for processing woolen cloth. The town meeting record states this mill was allowed at Spring Hill but it was clearly built at the Old County Road site.

Thomas Dexter Senior retired to West Barnstable in about 1646 and built a home on top of Scorton Hill. The Scorton Marsh in Sandwich and the Barnstable Great Marshes have a narrow connection through which tidal streams move back and forth as each marsh system reaches high water. The border between Sandwich and Barnstable occurs at this stream, and it is a natural fording place for access from Barnstable to the Fuller property on Scorton Neck as well as to Sandy Neck and the marshes adjacent. Dexter built a causeway at this point connecting Scorton Hill and Scorton Neck. He then sought tolls from the eight Barnstable families who used his causeway for access to marshland off Scorton Neck and Sandy Neck. He had to sue to collect and won his case, but was granted only a one-time sixpence per acre award from those whose lands were affected. This could hardly have paid him for the construction and the court costs.

Town Neck and Scorton Neck

These two necks were of prime importance to the early town as natural calf pastures during the season. Keepers were appointed for each neck. Town Neck was fenced and barred at present Town Neck Road, while access to Scorton was along the East Sandwich Beach from Ploughed Neck and Spring Hill, with the cattle driven across Scorton River at low tide at a "beachy place." There were recurrent problems with the Fullers' use of land on the Sandwich side of the Barnstable line and also with the Indian chief, Sekunk, and his sons Mark and Amos, whose title to Scorton Neck for seasonal residence and fowling was not bought off until the 1680s. A special set of proprietors was agreed on for each Neck in 1678, Scorton run by a set of the residents east of Shawme mill stream, Town Neck by a set from the west. The Jones Road causeway to Scorton Neck was completed by 1667, probably by Joseph Holway Jr. Ultimately, in 1689, Town Neck was assigned to a general group of proprietors to control pasturage and other improvements, while Scorton Neck was issued for farm sites. See maps on pp. 44,48.

Schools

Plymouth Court proposed a school in Plymouth in 1670 to be run in part out of Colony income from fishing off Cape Cod. This seems to have been successful. The first reference to a school in Sandwich is in 1677, when it was approved to secure a schoolmaster to serve in several places, four months in each. James Chadwick was the first schoolmaster. In 1686, James Steward held the position. Payment of £12 per year is recorded.

A Minister at Last

The towns were urged again in 1670 to find and maintain qualified ministers. Suddenly the name John Smith (formerly of Barnstable) appears upon the town records in August 1673:

> "The Town has given unto John Smith ten acres of land for his own proper inheritance forever, provided he come and continue with us to dispense the Word amongst us..."

This was promptly followed in September 1673 by a more specific grant:

> "The Town being met together did appoint and empower Richard Bourne and James Skiff to lay out what lands they shall think necessary and to lay it out near the Town House, some of the land to lie above the House and the rest below the House, and as much of the swamp which lies by the ford as they shall think good for to belong to the House for the use of the Ministry."

We cannot be precise about this description, but believe it covered the area on Water Street (where Smith did in fact build his house, later known as the Hoxie House), plus some further land and marsh nearer the old meetinghouse on its tiny lot at River and Main Street. The "ford", we feel, was the crossing through Mill Creek at the present Town Hall, rather than at River Street where there was a bridge. From then on, references to Smith are frequent. He was in a key position on admission of new townsmen and on readmission of many Quakers, so he was immediately swept into the issue. The problem of the readmission of the disenfranchised hung on for years.

In Plymouth Colony Records, an item is found in June 1675, "Mr. Thomas Dexter and Thomas Tupper are appointed by the Court to gather in the minister's maintenance at Sandwich." At the same Court, "Mr. John Smith, teacher of the Church of Christ at Sandwich" was given right to purchase a tract of Indian land at Pinguin Hole in Cataumet. The term "teacher" refers to a preacher who was not formally ordained. His son John Jr. was fined for not marching with a contingent to the Indian war. The diary of Samuel Sewall records his first visit to Sandwich as a young merchant in October 1676. "Supper at Mr. Smith's, good supper" and the following day "Mr. Smith rode with me and showed me the place which some had thought to cut for to make a passage from the South Sea to the North, said 'twas about a mile and a half between the utmost flowing of the two seas in Herring River and Scusset, the land very low and level, Herring River exceeding pleasant by reason that it runs pretty broad, shallow, of an equal depth, and upon white sand."

Further unexpected light on Smith's early days in Sandwich concerns the small meetinghouse itself. This had been repaired last in 1659 by subscription when the town hoped for a replacement for Mr. Leveridge. With Bourne busy with the Indians and Tupper aging (eighty-two in 1660), the church services were probably infrequent. Visiting ministers included Ichabod Wiswall in 1667 and Thomas Walley in 1671. In 1678 the Quakers carefully recorded that among the complaints against them was one that discouraged funds to repair the Sandwich meetinghouse, which is described as follows:

> "The next particular grievancy lies upon us in the want of a meetinghouse, for this we have already is too little and not capable to repair; those that come to house, some standing without the doors and others sitting and lying without the doors in an unreserved manner in the time of prayer and other public exercise and being asked the reason of their profane acting, the answer is given that there is no room for them in the house, furthermore the house is so bad in great rain that the speaker is not able comfortably to perform his service committed to him, but with the spoiling of his book or clothes and the like is with others present at the same time in so much that many are constrained to abstain from the meeting when it is like to be much rainy, by reason of the uncomfortableness of the place they meet in; though it hath been patched up of labor by 3 or 4 neighbors of their own charge, but yet is as uncomfortable as before."

Possibly as a result of this exposure, the town allowed a voluntary contribution to repair the meetinghouse, and raised funds in corn, silver, nails and shingles for the work. The Quaker source reports that Smith would have been unable to continue but for the hard work of his family. In 1680 the Town voted him £50, with three men named to collect it.

Plymouth Colony and Taxes

There were twelve towns in the Colony in 1666, with the following relative sizes based on property taxes:

Scituate	15.0%
Rehoboth	12.4%
Plymouth & Barnstable each	9.0%
Sandwich, Duxbury & Taunton each	8.3%
Yarmouth & Marshfield each	7.2%
Eastham	6.7%
Dartmouth	5.0%
Sowams (Bristol)	3.6%
Total	100.0%

The value of commodities used to pay taxes in the Colony in 1666 was as follows:

	Stated Value	*Present if £ is $100*
Wheat per bushel	4s. 6d.	$ 22.50
Pork per barrel	£3, 10s.	$ 350.00
Barley per bushel	4s.	$ 20.00
Butter per sizeable firkin	30s.	$ 150.00
Beef per barrel	45s.	$ 225.00
Indian corn per bushel	3s.	$ 15.00
Peas or Rye per bushel	3s. 6d.	$ 17.50
Tar per barrel	9s.	$ 45.00

A live cow was valued at about £3, 15s. or $375.00.

The Town taxes were to be paid in a mix of commodities:

one-third — wheat, or pork, or both

one-third — butter, or barley, or both

one-third — beef, corn, peas, rye or tar

These goods were to be laid down, freight paid, with the treasurer in Boston or Plymouth by the first week in November, which showed that Plymouth regularly exported its produce to the Bay Colony.

Plymouth Colony Weakness

The Colony was growing, but remained economically weak compared to the Bay Colony, or to Rhode Island. It had no deep water ports or strong export cargo. In 1664, the freemen of the whole colony gathered in Plymouth and agreed "that an address shall be made to his Majesty for the further confirmation of our Patent... and for the management and ordering of matters concerning it both for the raising of monies and appointing of men to be employed therein." Another note of the freemen at this meeting was to confirm their right to their old boundary with Rhode Island and Massachusetts. This ran from Saconnet Point along Narraganset Bay shore, past Pocasset and Causumset to the Patucket (Blackstone) River and up the river to the Massachusetts line, then northeast up to Cohasset. There was a need for this request because families from the other colonies had been entering and settling without leave.

The Colony's original charter was outdated and did not provide any power to incorporate new towns, which goes far to explain the way in which new settlements like Sandwich were simply accepted without formal notice, and became part of the Colony. Historians have noted that Plymouth had at least three opportunities to obtain a new Royal Charter during its history, but had somehow failed to get it on each occasion. These were in 1630 when Allerton had been too greedy in asking for a long duty-free period; in 1664 and again in 1680 when its two successive negotiators had died in London. Abruptly events outside the Colony occurred which completely changed the pattern of government.

The Bay Colony charter was declared invalid in 1684 by a Royal Command throwing each of the other Colony charters in question. In response Plymouth did two things: it formed the Colony into three Counties, Barnstable, Plymouth and Bristol, with the principal judicial powers moved to the new county seats; then it undertook a series of confirmatory declarations or deeds from the Colony to each of the towns, confirming their right to the lands within their bounds and the rights of townsmen to the properties which they had been issued by proper authority since the settlement of the town. The Sandwich declaration (its only charter) is dated July 13, 1685 and states:

> "a certain tract of lands was by Mr. William Bradford and his Associates assembled in Court the 3rd April 1637, granted unto Mr. Edmund Freeman, Henry Feak, Thomas Dexter with other of their associates to erect a Plantation or Town in this Government..."

An original copy of the Sandwich grant has not been found in the town clerk's earliest records, and strangely it was not even copied into the Sandwich town meeting records until 1768 when it was entered into Volume Three by the then town clerk Benjamin Fessenden Jr.

There is a gap in Plymouth Colony Records in the period 1686-1688, corresponding to the temporary administration of Governor Andros over all New England in this period. He was sent out by James II, successor to Charles II, and had earlier been Governor of New York after it was taken over from the Dutch, on orders of this same James, then Duke of York. On the accession of William and Mary in 1688, Andros was seized by patriots and sent back to England. There was an interregnum in New England using the previous colonial charter governments to 1692, which ended when Sir William Phipps arrived with authority and staff to form the new Royal Province of Massachusetts Bay. This included most of Plymouth Colony as well as Nantucket, Martha's Vineyard, Maine and even Nova Scotia. Sandwich town meetings continued steadily over the whole period. Taxes in 1686 included a "Country Charge" as well as a "County Charge", and there are references to Petit Juries at Barnstable. In 1687 the Town named Edward Perry as Commissioner, as required by a Warrant from Boston. Otherwise the radical changes at Plymouth and Boston are unnoticed in the town records.

Recovering from the Indian War

The town was assessed stiff fines at the end of 1675 for failing to send enough men to several musters and failing to meet various levies. These fines were largely to be collected from the families of the men who had been called—an unpopular charge and hard to collect. Those given full authority to collect or "to proceed with the delinquents" (meaning make distress on property) were William Swift and George Barlow. How the old marshal must have relished getting back his power to demand payment or make distress! When the war was over a flood of charges must have been levied from Plymouth for troops and supplies, for aid to the wrecked towns, for claims for the dead and injured, as well as local charges for the scouting operation, for troops raised, arms and powder provided. In June 1676 a special committee of four was named (Bourne, Tupper, Skiff and Daniel Wing) "to take an account of what ought justly to be satisfied and ...all the town's debts that appear justly due to be paid." The taxes resulting were not recorded, but were referred to for years after as the Great Rate. The town had to enact special fines for failing to come to town meetings at this time, and also to be stiff about obtaining exact accounts from the persons who had been constables (tax collectors) over this period. In 1679 the constable was authorized to "make distress on all such persons as have not answered all their rates... about the war." In 1680 the Town received a windfall of £28 in silver from its share of sales of former Indian lands at Mount Hope, and this treasure was divided only in proportion to payments received from citizens on the Great War Rate "and no other way."

Purchases of Indian Lands

The Plymouth Court allowed large grants at our Pocasset in 1679 and 1680. Probably with the Court's consent, the town itself commissioned a group of three in 1680 to "buy of the Indians all the undisposed lands that lie between Plymouth, Barnstable and Sucanesset bounds." With their tribal status shaken, it is likely that the Indians who still had extensive holdings of land now began to sell and were reduced soon to the immediate acres around their homes and planting fields. Laws remained on the books giving the Indians full legal rights. Nevertheless after the War, in 1678, three Indians who were found guilty of a theft from Zachariah Allen of Sandwich were sentenced to perpetual slavery to him, to be used or sold as he saw fit. It is doubtful that this sentence would have been imposed before the War; at least there is no record of enslavement for theft.

The Quaker Men's Monthly Meetings, 1672-1693

The principle of a pyramid of meetings, weekly, monthly, quarterly, and annually, had been worked out by George Fox early in his teaching work in England as an efficient method of communication upwards and downwards. He came to America in 1671 and 1672 and came as far north as Newport. However, pressing concerns forced him to return to England from Newport to the undoubted disappointment of his Sandwich followers. There is no detailed record of the meetings for worship and for business in Sandwich which must have taken place between 1658 and 1672, but beginning in June 1672 there is a clear written record. Religious services were held on Sunday mornings and Wednesday evenings, and meetings of men were held the first Friday in each month at 11:00 A.M. Monthly meetings of women Friends are noted in this record as beginning in January 1676/7 on the first Wednesdays.

Meeting Business

The Meeting minutes refer to a contribution or pledge both for specific projects and also to build up standing funds. Expenses were approved such as for purchases, travel expense, road work, books and charity. The minutes refer to prospective marriage of couples in the Society and to reports from committees delegated to look into various problems. Probably the most characteristic feature of these minutes is the ongoing discussion of the status of various members whose words or absence or actions gave uneasiness or concern. This regard for the purity, harmony and religious motivation of the members of the Society was doubtless present from the very beginning of the meetings, but was not in the early public record which reflected only tumultuous behavior, defiance, refusal to swear oaths and other references which seem to indicate extreme turbulence. With the removal of hostile public pressure, and acceptance into the general community, the Quaker group became stable and quiet and were able to concentrate on furthering their faith in their own special patterns. There is evidence of this from the men's Meeting minutes which we will mention very briefly below.

Persons Complained Of

The first meeting June 25, 1672 recorded complaints against three persons: Peter Gaunt, a rebel even before the Quakers came, was now charged with being absent and saying, as he had twenty years before, that he knew no public visible worship; John Ellis the former Lieutenant of the militia, who in old age seemed to show interest in the Quaker movement, now was found absent and stubbornly disinclined to return to make a commitment; Susanna Turner had a child in 1670 and was supported by her brother Isaac; the Friends wanted "to know her status and love to the truth" and whether she would condemn her wicked ways; there is no evidence that she did.

Many persons, in fact nearly everyone in the Meeting except the most saintly, were at one time or another complained of for disorderly speaking or bad carriage toward a neighbor or other minor fault. Some charges were obviously slight, but once recorded had to result in a committee visit and were expected to be resolved by a public confession or letter of self-condemnation. This came very hard from persons who were stubborn, proud, or convinced of their own correctness, and became contests of will which doubtless drove some from the Meeting entirely. The minutes make fascinating reading for these personal insights and human situations.

A Community Within a Community

The Friends had their own meetinghouse, first referred to on September 13, 1672. It was enlarged in 1674 and work continued through 1679. Men's meetings were usually held at William Allen's. They had their own burial place by 1674. A book to record births and marriages was in use by September 1672, and they kept their own records of wills, deeds, lands, mortgages and portions inherited. Road repair for convenience of traveling Friends and visiting speakers was a constant concern, especially when Quarterly Meetings necessitated much travel by whole families to or from Sandwich. After the rebuilding of Dartmouth and the settlement of Rochester, the main road from Newport lay along the line of coastal villages to Sandwich rather than the upper road through Middleboro and Plymouth. This new road involved many stream crossings and the Quakers did not wait for the Colony or the towns to put in the bridges and causeways or fording places. Charity began at home and there are touching references to care of faithful members who had a fire or who had otherwise fallen "low in the outward estate."

Trade and imports are mentioned in connection with the Quakers from the beginning. A network of trade and credit arrangements was set up using their excellent and reliable family networks of communication, and this quickly led to economic security and in some cases, accumulation of real wealth. Quarterly Meetings and wedding celebrations were joyous events, renewing the family ties between the evolving Quaker communities in Yarmouth, Falmouth, Sandwich, Pembroke, Dartmouth and Rhode Island.

The Sandwich Leaders

Edward Perry was the clerk of the Sandwich Men's Meeting, writing not only the minutes, but long letters of pleading to various members whose condition was in deep doubt; also documents on the state of grace in the Sandwich Meeting. He was the spiritual leader of the group here, and became Sandwich's first published author. Pamphlets or tracts by Edward Perry are reported to include "A Warning to New England, " "To the Court of Plymouth, This is the Word of the Lord, " "A Testimony Concerning the Light" and "Concerning True Repentance."

William Newland's role was in negotiations with the Town of Sandwich and the Plymouth Colony government concerning the critical matters of re-establishing voting rights for the disenfranchised, ensuring that Quakers received shares of new land grants or opportunities to purchase lands, and striving to establish abatements on their share of taxes that went to support the established minister. His trips to Plymouth Court about these various sticky matters were numerous and frustrating.

WILLIAM ALLEN HOUSE-The salt-box house built by William and Priscilla Allen about 1672 in Spring Hill, a center of the Sandwich Quaker group. This house was demolished after the death of Alden Allen in 1858. Courtesy of the Sandwich Historical Society.

William and Priscilla Allen were the founders, hosts, and social center of the Sandwich Meeting. They built a new saltbox house at what is now Route 6A in Spring Hill near the twin ponds. This house had a large ell behind it, of two stories. The ground floor had a meeting room where winter services were held, with sleeping rooms for visitors upstairs. Allen held all the Meeting's funds and disbursed for purchases, charity and expenses. Here horses were changed, saddlery repaired, messages came and went, and all paths crossed. In 1672, the Meeting was distressed about the household of the lame weaver, Thomas Johnson, in Falmouth; impoverished and disordered with six children, a seventh born in 1674. The Meeting wanted Johnson and his wife to give up two or three children to be brought up in better conditions, but Mrs. Johnson, not a Quaker, refused. The Meeting brought them a cow and various supplies, and finally in 1680 judged it imperative to remove Johnson to Sandwich where he was lodged at William Allen's. He died in 1683. Another old supporter who became totally dependent was John Newland, whose wife died in 1671 and was childless. He made over his entire property to the Friends' Meeting and lived at Allen's and was still alive at the time of the death of his brother William in 1695. Hence William and Priscilla ran a nursing home as well as guest house.

The Mary Mills Story

In 1675 there was a new law against Quaker meetings in Boston, causing a renewal of deliberate protests. There were carting-and-whipping sentences for those who chose to protest by interrupting public meetings by such symbolic acts as appearing in sackcloth and ashes, or crashing empty bottles in the service. Samuel Sewall records on Sunday, July 8, 1677 at the New South Meetinghouse in Boston "In sermon time there came in a female Quaker in a canvas frock, her hair dishevelled and loose like a periwig, her face as black as ink, led by two other Quakers and two other followed. It occasioned the greatest and most amazing uproar that I ever saw." These ladies were put on trial August 4, 1677 as recorded from Court records in Hallowell's book. They were Margaret Brewster from Barbados, who admitted she came into Mr. Thatcher's Meetinghouse with hair upon her shoulders, ashes upon her head, face colored black, and sackcloth upon her upper garments. After defiant testimony from her, the Judge heard Lydia Wright of Long Island, who said that she had been at peaceful worship with the Friends when interrupted by the constables and told to come instead to public worship; but when she did this, she and her companions were imprisoned until the present Court. Then Mary Miles of Blackpoint, Maine was called, now living in Salem, who admitted her communion with Mrs. Brewster, and said she was willing to go to death if required as some of her Friends and Brethren have done. Barbara Bowers was then called, but both she and Mrs. Brewster said she did not go in with the others. The sentences were passed that Mrs. Brewster was to be stripped to the middle, tied to a cart, drawn through the town and to receive twenty stripes. The other three were also to be tied to the cart, but not stripped. On the Thursday following, August 9, the sentences were executed.

This event is related to Sandwich in that on September 7, 1677 William Allen received back fifty shillings which he had paid in Boston on account of "Margaret Brewster and Lydia Wright and the others that were with them." So Allen at least had been in Boston during the imprisonment and doubtless had witnessed the carting-and-whipping. The real surprise emerges three years later when the Meeting minutes read: "At this meeting Priscilla Allen did manifest herself not willing that Mary Mills should be any longer at her house; the reason she gave to the meeting was that Mary and her (Priscilla's) husband were both set against her." So here we learn that Mary came to Sandwich and stayed with the hospitable Allens, forming an unhappy triangle that finally defeated even Priscilla. Edward Perry and others spoke to Priscilla "and their return was satisfaction to the Meeting." One can only hope that Mary went elsewhere to live, and it must have been a relief to the whole community when in 1683 William Gifford, a widower of 68, abruptly announced his intention to marry Mary Mills, daughter of John Mills of Blackpoint, Maine.

CHAPTER 8

FAMILY SKETCHES

Between 1650 and 1700 Sandwich grew from sixty to a hundred families, each of five to six persons. The changes and growth have been traced in each known family through vital records, and recorded on charts of descent which have been assembled at the Sandwich Town Archives office. The overall changes to 1700 in the families of the town may be summarized as follows:

Families in 1650, including five headed by widows	60
New arrivals from other towns	21
New families formed by sons	108
Total families formed	189
Less deaths of heads of families (42), reduced by four families continuing under widows in 1700	38
Departure of families to other towns	51
Losses	89
Families in 1700, including four headed by widows	100

These brief statistics cover a great deal of human experience, only a small portion of which is known now in personal terms.

Allen

The venerable George Allen, who died here in 1648, had fourteen children by two wives. In addition, a Ralph Allen, Senior, probably George's brother, with eleven children, lived here. The records of these Allens and of several other emigrant Allens in other towns have not yet been disentangled completely by genealogists; some of the intractible features of the problem include their use of the same given names, their frequent removals and the number of guesses made (and put into print) over the years about the Allens.

Ralph was a valiant Quaker who disappeared from the record about 1660, and only his son, Jedediah, had a family in Sandwich. He removed to New Jersey, so that the remaining Allens in Sandwich were of George's line. Three of George's sons had families here, but the record shows many removals to Dartmouth and New Jersey, and the family never again was as large in Sandwich as it had been at first. The memorable home of William and Priscilla, who had no children, went to their nephew, Daniel Allen, and remained in the family about two hundred years.

Barlow

The marshal may have had as many as six children by a previous marriage, and must have brought several here when he arrived in 1658. At least three settled later in Rochester. About 1664 the marshal moved to Pocasset where the region called Barlow's Landing is still associated with the family. Here his sons by Jane (Besse), John and Nathan, brought up families. He remained a turbulent character all his life, but no ill-feelings persisted against his descendants, some of whom even married into Quaker families.

Bassett

William who settled here in 1644 was the son of William Bassett of the *Fortune,* an early settler of Duxbury, then Bridgewater. William Junior held various town offices, but died at only forty-five in 1670. His son, William III was an extremely competent man who became Colonel of Militia, chief Marshal of the County and Register of Probate. Three early Bassett houses survive at 121 and 123 Main Street and 8 River Street.

Besse

Anthony Besse was one of the earliest settlers. He was presented at court in 1639 for "disorderly living along" but the last name of Jane whom he soon married has not yet been learned. They had two sons and six daughters, the last born posthumously, as Anthony died at only forty-eight. He is said to have aided Reverend Leveridge in his early work with the Indians here. The spirit and affection in this family is movingly recalled in his will of 1657:

> To Dorcas my daughter (17) heifers Nubbin, Spark and Young Moose. To Ann (16) heifer Pretty. To Nehemiah, my son (14) heifer Coll; my gun, cutlass and boats. To Nehemiah, and my son David (8), my house and land, clothing and steers Burnett and Raven, equally between them. To Mary (12) heifer Browne. To Jane (10) heifer Daisy. To Elizabeth (5) one ewe lamb. To wife Jane cows Blacking, Moose and Cherry; likewise in case my mother send anything over to me as formerly she hath done, that it be disposed of amongst my family; moreover for the little one my wife goeth with, that my wife give it a portion if God give it life...

We suggest that the Besse house was east of Benjamin Nye's on present Route 6A in Spring Hill, the paternal site inherited by Nehemiah in 1664 when he came of age, and shown in the property survey of 1667. After Jane married Barlow in 1661, she took Elizabeth and the "little one," Rebecca, with her, leaving the six older children in the Besse house. This is suggested in Plymouth Colony Records for 1662 when the cow (Daisy) taken away by Barlow is ordered to be returned to the girl, Jane Besse, under the guidance of the overseers of the estate, Richard Bourne and James Skiff. The younger son David was killed in 1676 in the Indian war. Nehemiah's family removed to Wareham about 1700 and the name became infrequent in Sandwich.

Blackwell

Michael Blackwell was in Sandwich by 1643 and lived by the Scusset River near the present Sagamore Bridge. He was a herring catcher for many years. His two sons each had large families and the name was common here throughout the history of the town.

Bourne

The achievements of Richard Bourne in support of the early town, and especially in creating the reservation of Mashpee and in his missionary work there, place him in the forefront of persons with extraordinary ability in the Colony, indeed, in the whole of New England. Recent writers compare him to Reverend John Eliot, so that his status is still rising as more facts are known. He had three sons by his wife Bathsheba (probably Bathsheba Hallett, although her identity has not been proven). His son Job died in 1677, predeceasing his father, and Job's sons scattered. The second son Elisha inherited the properties in the Herring River and Manomet area, and from him are descended the Bournes in the town of Bourne. The third son, Shearjashub, inherited the lands in Mashpee and in Falmouth. He was the Indian Commissioner and a judge in Barnstable, positions also held by his son Ezra. Shearjashub also had an elder son, Melatiah, who removed from Waquoit to Sandwich village about 1710 and founded a distinguished line here.

Late in life, Richard Bourne married a lively and attractive widow, Ruth Sargent of Barnstable, a widow of Jonathan Winslow of Marshfield. Some of Bourne's correspondence with Ruth survives and makes touching reading. He died in 1682 and left Ruth his Sandwich home in the Jarvesville area. She then married another distinguished older man, Elder John Chipman.

Burgess

Thomas Burgess was one of the earliest settlers and his name is found frequently in the service of the town and in support of the early church. He acquired land in Scusset (Sagamore) and also in the Aptucxet area of the old trading post. His four sons typified the very early spread from Sandwich to occupy land in new towns. Thomas Junior moving to Newport, Rhode Island, John moving to Yarmouth, Joseph going to Rochester; Jacob inherited the family lands in Scusset, just west of the Freeman Farm. Thomas Junior featured in one of the rare divorces of the Colony. After thirteen years of marriage to Elizabeth Bassett, they were divorced and he married Lydia, daughter of Quaker Peter Gaunt, and got a fresh start in Rhode Island.

Chipman

Elder John Chipman and Elder John Smith were both highly respected early settlers at Barnstable. Chipman married Hope Howland, daughter of John Howland of the *Mayflower,* while Smith married Susanna Hinckley, sister of Governor Thomas Hinckley. They were named on the committee to investigate the beliefs of the Sandwich Quakers, and concluded that the sect should not be persecuted, a courageous stand considering the emotion of the time. To the dismay of his church in Barnstable, Elder Chipman resigned his prestigious position and removed to Sandwich shortly after Smith settled here. He was immediately accepted as a townsman. More is known about Chipman's English background than that of most migrants to the New World. He came from the small village of Brinspittal near Dorchester, Dorset. Thomas Chipman, his father, had inherited a valuable mill property as a young man which had been administered and then taken over by a distant relative, Christopher Derby. Thomas had later married, but had never received any capital from Derby. After Thomas' death, his only son, John, at age seventeen emigrated to Plymouth in 1637 under indenture to Richard Derby, son of Christopher. When he was twenty-one, John Chipman made an effort to establish a claim against Christopher Derby, supported by testimony from Ann Hynd, a domestic from the Derby house, who had also come to Plymouth. Again in 1657/8 Chipman made a long deposition of his claim against the Derby estate in England, referring to his sisters Hannah and Tamson and other parties in the case. With the long chain of communication, and the absence of supporters in Dorset, plus the disturbed condition at the end of the Cromwell period, nothing seems to have been done and there is no record that Chipman got any part of his father's property. However, he had a trade in Barnstable as a carpenter, and by public service and hard work earned a highly respected position in the community.

After the death of Hope, his wife, Elder Chipman married Ruth, the widow of Richard Bourne. They lived in the Bourne house in the Jarvesville area, where Ruth was well loved. Rev. Thomas Prince, born here in 1687, described Ruth: "Mrs. Ruth Chipman was a little, lively smart gentlewoman of very good sense and knowledge, of the strictest piety, an excellent spirit of family government, very good skill in the diseases of women and children, very helpful to her neighbors, —a dear intimate friend and mother to my mother; and my mother falling into travail with me, this Mrs. Chipman was the only person, who living just by, occasionally helped me into the world. She survived the Elder and lived and died in great esteem."

Chipman died in Sandwich in 1708 at eighty-eight years and his burial marker survives in Old Town Burying Ground. His youngest son Honorable John Chipman became a distinguished public figure.

Dexter

The figure of Thomas Dexter Sr., is one of the most engaging in our town annals. He was a builder of mills, the iron works, weirs, causeways and farms in old Saugus as well as on Cape Cod. The records indicate that he was contemptuous of government figures, fined for sleeping at meetings, intensely litigious, but constantly used by government on committees to get things done. His children seem to have been born in England and there is no reference to a Mrs. Dexter from the time of his immigration in 1630. His daughters Mary and Frances married and lived in Boston, while his sons Thomas and William settled on Cape Cod, marrying Elizabeth and Sarah Vincent, the daughters of John Vincent of Sandwich. Thomas Jr. ran the Sandwich grist mill, and there is reason to believe from the 1667 property survey that he had a farm in the present Crow Farm area. Later he had a large two-story house in the village on Main Street between the mill and the meetinghouse. He left this house to his son John at his death in 1686, specifying that his wife Elizabeth had permanent rights to the west end. John sold the grist mill to Seth Pope in 1699/1700 and sold his house to Melatiah Bourne in 1710, removing to Rhode Island. Bourne bought the house still guaranteeing Elizabeth Vincent Dexter the west end for her lifetime. She died in 1714, and the house was torn down.

The work team that built the first mill included his sons William and Thomas, Thomas Tupper, Benjamin Nye, John French and John Ellis. In 1673, Thomas Senior retired to the home of his daughter Mary Oliver in Boston, and was buried in the Oliver tomb in King's Chapel in 1677.

Dillingham

Edward Dillingham was one of the "Ten Men of Saugus" who founded the town. His early home is supposed to have been east of the upper millpond, but its site has never been settled. The family in Sandwich is descended from his son Henry who married Hannah Perry and included many Quakers. Henry's brother John removed to the wilds of what is now Brewster in 1648 with his friend John Wing. They founded the branches of the Dillingham and Wing families in that area. Edward died at age seventy-two in the year 1667.

Ellis

Lieutenant John Ellis came to Sandwich early with a son John Junior by a previous marriage. He settled in the Sagamore Highlands area near Plymouth line and became active in town affairs, especially in the militia and in construction projects. He made an excellent marriage to Elizabeth Freeman about 1644 and had a large family, descendants of which remain today in Sandwich and throughout the country. His son Mordecai kept the original house, but its location is not yet known. John's son Matthias (married to Mary Burgess) inherited much of the original Freeman farm. John's other sons left Sandwich for Rochester and Harwich. After the death of Lieutenant John in 1677, his intrepid widow moved to the new settlement of Rochester and became a large landowner in her own right.

Fish

There were three early settlers of Sandwich of this name, almost certainly brothers. John and Nathaniel remained here and their descendants became numerous. Jonathan removed to Long Island in 1654 when many Sandwich families relocated there at the time of Leveridge. The descendants of Jonathan became well known in New York. Nathaniel seems to have lived in the vicinity of the meetinghouse in 1692 when the town voted to buy his house for the use of the new minister, Rowland Cotton.

Freeman

We have mentioned the Freemans frequently in the previous chapters. To summarize briefly, Edmund and his second wife Elizabeth and five children settled in what was then a central location near Scusset Marsh. He became a large landowner, especially here and in the Ploughed Neck area of East Sandwich. He was an Assistant Governor from 1640 through the 1645 term, but then sharply reduced his public offices both in Plymouth Colony and in the town of Sandwich. The two Freeman sons married daughters of Governor Thomas Prence. John Freeman removed to the new settlement at Eastham where Prence lived, and became a town leader and an Assistant Governor himself, founding a large branch of the family there. His sons participated in the settlement of Harwich. Edmund Freeman Jr., resided at Ploughed Neck, but had only one son Edmund III, so that the Sandwich branch remained small until the fourth generation. The original Freeman farm area at Scusset was broken up, the house going to Matthias Ellis, a grandson, who took care of the senior Freemans in their old age. Other portions went to Edward Perry, to Elizabeth Ellis and to John and Edmund Freeman Jr. At the time of the Revolution all this farm area was broken up and sold off, even the "Saddle and Pillion" burial lot of Edmund Senior and Elizabeth. There is a tradition that this knoll (off present Tupper Road) was the site of the first Freeman home which burned, with the replacement house built on the site of the later nineteenth century Freeman farm house. The dignity and poignancy of the Saddle and Pillion burial site makes us regret that the burial places of so many of the founding families, on their own lands, were not permanently marked and are now lost to memory.

Gibbs

The name of the wife of the first Thomas Gibbs (1615-1693) has not been found. Their ancient location was off Old Plymouth Road near the Swifts, Ellises and Butlers, but the exact site is unknown. One son was killed in the Indian War, but three sons married and the family became large and widely dispersed. It is still present in the Sandwich and Bourne area.

Gifford

William Gifford was an early settler at Spring Hill and typifies the rugged progenitive vigor of the founding families. He had five sons, all of whom married, one remaining in Sandwich, one removing to New Jersey and three settling in Falmouth. Many were Quakers. Gifford at sixty-eight married Mary Mills and had two additional sons who had eighteen children between them. The family remained small in Sandwich, through continued out-migration. It is possible that Gifford's lands at Spring Hill were those of first settler, George Slawson, who left here before 1643. Gifford died in 1687 at the age of seventy-two.

Handy

Richard Handy was a later arrival in Sandwich, called a woolcomber, but he apprenticed himself to James Skiff to learn the cooper trade, always a useful skill. He had no recorded lands in the 1667 property survey but settled in Cataumet about the time of his marriage, 1671. His four sons had thirty-five children. Handy is one of the few founders of the town buried at the Old Town Burying Ground.

Holway

Joseph Holway (1605-1647) lived in the Jones Road sector of East Sandwich. He had one son and four daughters by his wife Rose Allen, but died young. The children were brought up by William Newland who married Rose. Joseph Jr. had only one son, Joseph III, and he in turn had only one son, Gideon, who remained in Sandwich. Hence it was not until the fifth generation that the Holways became more numerous in Sandwich. Many were Quakers.

Hoxie

The origin of the founder of the Hoxie family, Ludowick Hoxie, has not yet been established. His family name may have been HAWKES or HAUCKS. He arrived in Sandwich as a young man about 1650 and married in 1666. His sons showed the typical scatter of the period—Joseph and John removed to Rhode Island, Gideon remained in Spring Hill, Hezekiah settled on Spectacle Pond, South Sandwich, while Solomon settled at the former Wing farm on Scorton. Ludowick became a Quaker as did several lines of his descendants. The family remained active in town affairs in all periods.

Landers

Thomas Landers (about 1613-1675) was one of a group who arrived on the *Abigail* in 1635 which included the Freemans, Thomas Tupper, Benjamin Nye and Thomas Greenfield. He did not marry until 1651, after which he had ten children by the energetic and sharp-tongued Jane Kerby. His home in 1667 was adjacent to the Edmund Freeman Jr. lands at Ploughed Neck, which may explain the marriages of three Landers sons to the three Freeman daughters. In later generations this family became numerous in the Cataumet area, in Falmouth and in Rochester.

Lawrence

Robert Lawrence, like Richard Handy, was a later arrival who settled directly at Cataumet near the Falmouth line. He married Sarah Barlow, daughter of the marshal and made purchases of the remains of the Indian-held lands along Buzzards Bay. The family became well-established in Falmouth.

Newland

The figure of William Newland (about 1610-1695) as a town founder and supporter is an attractive one. He was one of the main strengths of the Quaker group in Sandwich. He may have had a previous wife before the widow Rose Allen Holway whom he married in 1648. They had only three daughters, of whom one died young, and one died childless shortly after marriage. Here is a summary of his will dated 1690:

> "my mind and will is that after my decease my body be decently buried by the advice and assistance of my dear friends the People of God called Quakers in their burying place in Sandwich.
>
> I give unto my dear wife Rose Newland the use of all my whole estate of housing, lands and movables... (reserving that listed later), for her natural life.
>
> Unto my son-in-law William Edwards ten shillings. Unto my daughter, Maria Edwards one bed and bolster and bed clothes, sufficient to make to a comfortable lodging.
>
> Unto my brother John Newland thirty acres land at Spring Hill and meadow at Pine Islands and all my wearing clothes for his supply and support. After his decease I do commit the ordering and disposing of it to my overseers for the use and service of the truth we do profess (that is the Quakers).
>
> After my wife's decease, I do give unto my daughter Maria Edwards my housing and lands if she do and shall forsake that violent spirit which hath led her into an violent conversation to the great grief of my heart, and shall not concern herself with any man after the manner of man and wife besides her husband William Edwards during his life; but if my said daughter doth go in such an unclean practice which is to the dishonor of God and of His truth and to the grief of the honest-hearted, and shall concern herself with any man besides her said husband, tending to the bringing forth of children, then this shall make my gift to her what my overseers shall judge meet for her to have of it as they shall see cause, and I do give (the rest) to my granddaughter Elizabeth Edwards...
>
> I do make my wife my executrix and I do desire and appoint my loving friends Edward Perry and my brother-in-law William Allen to be the overseers, they or either of them."

This will remains as touching and sad today as when written. We believe Rose died before he did in 1695, and since Edward Perry died in the spring of 1694/5, it remained for William Allen to carry out the terms. Did Maria change and inherit the house on Grove Street? No one has said, and probably we shall never know.

Nye

Benjamin Nye (1620-after 1704) came to America as a youth on the *Abigail* in 1635, probably with the Tupper family. He came to Sandwich in 1637 with his *Abigail* friends and quickly put down roots. His name is shown in the revised meadowland issue of 1640 but with no amount, probably because he had not yet married and his estate was minimal. However, later that year he married Katherine Tupper, and settled in Spring Hill, where the residence is shown in the 1667 lands survey adjacent to Gifford and Besse. He also had property in East Sandwich on the largest stream flowing into Scorton Marsh, and here he was awarded a further twelve acres because he built a grist mill and also built a second house and fulling mill here. His original house went to eldest son John, and the Old County Road house and mills to son Jonathan. One son removed to Falmouth, but four had families in Sandwich. In spite of many removals to other towns, in the eighteenth century the Nye family was the largest in Sandwich. They were supporters of the established church, and members were found in town government at all periods.

Percival

James Percival (1615-1692) was of the same age as many of the early Sandwich settlers, but had lived in Virginia earlier and only came to Sandwich in 1670. The story of his early life in the south is unknown. He promptly married the widow of William Bassett and had three children. The Percivals removed to the Ashumet Pond area of Falmouth, and their son John moved again to Barnstable. In the eighteenth century certain Percivals returned to Sandwich and will be discussed in a later chapter.

Perry

About 1650 two young brothers and three sisters arrived in Sandwich with an older lady, Sarah Perry, possibly their mother or stepmother. All five married in the period 1651 to 1654. Ezra Perry married Elizabeth Burgess and settled on the Burgess lands in the Manomet River sector, which included the old trading post site. His four sons married and this branch of the family grew rapidly. They were of the conservative group in the town. In contrast was Edward Perry who married Mary Freeman and soon was deeply involved in the Quaker movement. Edward also had a large family, three sons and six daughters. One son remained in Sandwich, Edward Jr., and the other sons removed to Rhode Island. The Edward Perry descendants remained here only in female lines of Wing and Gifford. Both Edward and Ezra Perry had many distinguished descendants.

Pope

This family settled in Sandwich at the very end of the seventeenth century, but is included here because of their special earlier connection in Seth the Trader, which has become part of Sandwich legend. Young Seth (1648-1727) son of Thomas Pope of Plymouth and Dartmouth, came to Sandwich about 1669 as a trader, probably with a backpack containing needles, thread and other portable items. Through some conflict with the selectmen, he was ordered out of town. He left with an irritated promise to come back and buy up the town. He married a daughter of Ezra Perry and became a successful merchant in Dartmouth. True to his promise, he came back to Sandwich in 1699 and bought the Dexter grist mill. He left his eldest son John Pope in charge of the mill. John married a daughter of Elisha Bourne. Their home is now known as the Moody House on Tupper Road. After ten years, John's younger brother Seth Jr. came to Sandwich and married the Bourne sister of John Pope's wife. They started what became the big colonial house at 10 Grove Street and the Popes have lived in this area ever since.

Skiff

James Skiff (about 1610-1685) was one of the hardworking business-like settlers who kept Sandwich going during its early years through continuous public service. His five sons and four daughters all married well, but several removed to Martha's Vineyard and Nantucket. James' son Captain Stephen Skiff (1641-1710) continued his father's tradition of local civic and military duties and became a county magistrate. He had only one son Stephen Jr. who had no children, so that the male line of this notable family lapsed in Sandwich, but many family trees go back to the Skiffs here through female lines. James Skiff Jr. married Elizabeth Neighbor here in 1659, but after eleven childless years he was able to sue for divorce, as Elizabeth had run off to Virginia with another man. James remarried and had six children on Nantucket.

According to the 1667 house survey, James Skiff lived in the central village while Captain Stephen built on what is now Route 6A opposite Chipman Road. The so-called "Skiff House" in Spring Hill has no early connection with the family but was built by a son of John Nye.

Smith

Elder John Smith (about 1614-1716) married Susanna Hinckley of Barnstable and had thirteen children. He attempted to form a separate church in Barnstable in 1662, but an ecclesiastical council ruled against him and he removed, first to Long Island then to New Jersey where he met many Quaker migrants from Sandwich and elsewhere, and bought land. He was back in Sandwich in 1673 where he was personally known, and was invited to reorganize the established church after the long twenty-year gap following the departure of Leveridge. He was able to bridge the different Sandwich factions because he was known to have opposed the persecution of the Quakers. Nothing is known of his religious training in England, and it may well have been slight. Three of his younger sons settled in Sandwich, the others living in Barnstable or New Jersey. His first house was the little saltbox on Water Street which remained in his family to 1857. After retiring from the ministry here in 1689, he lived in a colonial house on Dock Lane near the present Jarves Street, which remained in his family until sold for glass-workers' use in the 1820s.

Many Sandwich families intermarried with the Smiths here. Two grandsons of Elder John, Samuel and Shubael, married Chipman sisters, granddaughters of Elder John Chipman. The historian Frederick Freeman was guilty of a curious error in his *History of Cape Cod* in which he attributed a particular Dorset background to this John Smith. Readers can confirm that this background is identically the same as that described above for John Chipman—father Thomas, sisters Hannah and Tamson, deposition and Derbys and all. A number of genealogists tracing back to this Elder John Smith have been misled by the Freeman text so that this false background has probably been so widely copied that it is now impossible ever to eradicate completely.

Swift

William Swift Senior died here in 1642/3 leaving a single son, William Junior. He, however, had ten children and the family then grew rapidly, both in Sandwich, Falmouth and other centers. The original homesite which burned down was on present Standish Road in North Sagamore. Another early Swift house is still standing at the corner of Old Plymouth Road and Hunters Brook Road, North Sagamore.

Tobey

Thomas Tobey (about 1625-1710) married Martha Knott and inherited her family homestead at what is now 4 Water Street. With seven sons (no daughters) he soon needed more home sites. Son Thomas Junior was killed in the Indian War leaving a posthumous son in Yarmouth. Son John settled north of Peters Pond in a compound that remained in the family for two hundred years. Other sons settled along Water Street and there was extensive resettlement in other towns. There were representatives of the name in Sandwich into the twentieth century.

Tupper

Born in 1578, Thomas Tupper Senior was the oldest man among the early settlers here. He had only two known children, Katherine who married Benjamin Nye, and Thomas Junior who was active in Sandwich. We believe from the 1667 house inventory and references in town meeting records, that Thomas Senior lived near the Town Dock on the Jarvesville neck of land. His son at this time lived in the lotted fields near Town Neck, and we believe soon took over an existing house on Tupper Road since associated with the family. Thomas Senior filled many town positions and was even lay preacher after the departure of Leveridge. He died in 1676. We find no references to Indian missionary work in the Herring Pond area until 1674. This date marked the passing of the conservative old sachem, Quachetisset, who although loyal and helpful to the settlers, had refused all efforts at mission teaching. Hence we feel it was Thomas Tupper Jr. known as Captain Tupper, who proceeded with the missionary effort after the end of the Indian War. He married Martha Mayhew of the famous mission family of Martha's Vineyard. Thomas Jr.'s family included six sons. The

Tupper family never became numerically large in Sandwich, but included many in town offices. The missionizing and education efforts with the Herring Pond and Pocasset Indians extended over three generations of Tuppers.

Wing

The family of the matriarch Deborah (Bachiler) Wing has a special pattern unlike any other in Sandwich. Her husband Reverend John Wing died in 1630 in England, and she accompanied her father Reverend Stephen Bachiler to America in 1632 together with her sister Ann Sanborn (also widowed) and one Bachiler grandson. A third sister Theodate Hussey had already come to America. Reverend Bachiler attempted to preach in several communities in the northern part of the Bay Colony, but was considered too liberal and was harassed by the authorities. Deborah and her four sons came to Sandwich in 1638. Reverend Bachiler returned to England in 1653 and died in 1660 in his hundredth year. One of Deborah's sons also returned to England. The eldest, Daniel, settled (we believe) at his mother's house at 8 Morse Road as shown in the 1667 house survey. His brother Stephen settled at Spring Hill where the house has remained to the present day in Wing family hands. The fourth brother John Wing Jr. in 1648 joined John Dillingham in a bold remove to the unsettled Brewster area, taking his mother Deborah, then about 64, with them. The authorities at Plymouth objected to their settling so far from a town, but Yarmouth soon spread that way. Both founded large families and became Quaker supporters. The matriarch Deborah lived to be nearly a hundred.

In Sandwich, Daniel Wing is always associated with the Heritage area, (which was once thought to be the Andrew Hallett site sold to Daniel in 1640) but town records show that in 1667 this area east of Grove Street was all commons. Daniel Jr. and his sister Lydia Abbott obtained grants here about 1686, starting the holding which under his son Zaccheus Wing became a handsome three-house farm, parts of which were still with the family until 1965. The sons of Daniel Sr. and Stephen formed families on Wings Neck, Scorton, Rochester, Dartmouth, as well as in Spring Hill and the Shawme Pond area, spreading into a family second only to the Nyes in number in eighteenth century Sandwich.

CHAPTER 9

NEW FACES

New arrivals in town are always of interest to the townspeople as bringing new talents and assets; their efforts to settle down, acquire land and establish their presence are followed closely until they are well known and accepted. The arrival of educated persons as ministers, lawyers or teachers is of special impact because of the value of their skills and the weight of their opinions. In the period of this chapter, up to about 1735, Sandwich received a number of important new arrivals who had significant effects on the town or have left records which greatly enrich our knowledge of the town in their time.

Rowland Cotton, Minister of Note

Elder John Smith requested a dismission from his duties in 1688 being then about seventy-four years old. He was asked to remain until the following year, while his replacement was found. A Mr. Jonathan Pierpont of Roxbury, Harvard 1685, was invited and he noted that he was "accompanied by Elder Chipman", one of the only bits of evidence we have that Chipman was actively assisting his old friend Smith in church affairs. Pierpont was inclined to accept a call here because he saw the town needed a new pastor, because the members all admired him, and because "the young men in the place were in danger of being drawn away by the Quakers." He had, however, also received a call to Reading and went there at his father's suggestion. The town's next choice fell on Rowland Cotton, a classmate of Pierpont's at Harvard, who doubtless knew the Sandwich townsmen because he had been brought up in Plymouth. By June 1690 he was admitted a freeman of the town, and was given use of the ministry's lands in September 1690 at Scusset and at Sawpit Neck. More importantly, the town abruptly bought of Nathaniel Fish "the home lot of upland that said Fish now dwells on" and ordered that this lot "together with the skirt of swamp adjoining to it on the westerly side shall lie and remain to the only proper use and behoof of the Reverend Mr. Rowland Cotton and his heirs and assigns forever if he shall continue amongst us... in the work of the Ministry." Nathaniel Fish was about seventy-one at this time. There is no record of the size of his house or his reaction at this taking. From the 1667 survey, we believe this location was near the meetinghouse and probably on or about the present Dan'l Webster Inn site. In 1692 Cotton married a distinguished woman, Elizabeth Saltonstall, widow of the Reverend John Denison of Ipswich (1665-1689) by whom she had had one son before her husband's early death. This child, John Denison, may have been partly brought up by Denison relatives in Ipswich. Cotton was ordained in Sandwich November 28, 1694, with services conducted by Reverend John Cotton (his father), Reverend Ichabod Wiswall of Duxbury, and Reverend Jonathan Russell of Barnstable.

During Cotton's ministry here, the membership of the parish church increased greatly. Cotton was voted £80 per year without collections from Quakers. The Cottons had a large family in Sandwich:

John 1693-1757, Harvard 1710, ordained Newton 1714.
Joanna 1694-1772, married 1719 Rev. John Brown, Haverhill
Elizabeth 1695
Sarah 1696
Nathaniel 1698-1729, Harvard 1717, ordained 1721 Bristol R.I.
Abigail 1699-1732, married 1725 Rev. Shearjashub Bourne, Scituate
Meriel 1700
Roland 1701-1778, Harvard 1719, married 1760 Deborah Mason.
Josiah 1703-1780, Harvard 1722, ordained 1728 Providence R.I.
Ruth 1710, died at 5 weeks.
Ward 1711-1768, Harvard 1729, ordained 1734 Hampton N.H.

Thus all five sons graduated from Harvard and four were ordained in various churches. Two daughters also married ministers. The son Roland became a Colonel of Militia and Representative to the General Court from Woburn, where he lived. He returned to Sandwich in 1753. Cotton and his wife kept up their contacts with friends and relatives in Boston. Judge Samuel Sewall knew them well and refers to them in his visits to Cape Cod, also noting that Cotton preached at Old South Church, Boston in 1709, 1713 and 1717. Sewall rejoiced in the Harvard graduation of 1710 where both of Elizabeth's sons, John Denison and John Cotton, graduated together. John Denison was for several years a teacher at Plymouth, but died young. John Cotton appears frequently in Sewall's diary because he married Mary Gibbs, whose mother became the third wife of Sewall himself. The sons and daughters of Rowland Cotton also appear in Cotton Mather's diary as children of his "kinsman from Sandwich." Rowland Cotton and Cotton Mather were first cousins. There was a scandal in Plymouth in 1697 when the elder John Cotton (1640-1699) was dismissed from his pulpit for adultery. He and his wife Joanna (Rossiter) Cotton removed to Charleston, South Carolina, where he commenced a new Church. There he died in a yellow fever epidemic. His widow returned to Sandwich where she died in 1702.

The Sewall diary records the unexpected death of Reverend Cotton at fifty-five on March 18, 1721/2. The town meeting records state that the town promptly purchased from Madam Cotton her dwelling house and the lands granted personally to Mr. Cotton. She removed to Boston where she died in 1726. In the Burying Ground in Sandwich are four Cotton interrals:

Joanna (Rossiter) widow of Reverend John, Senior

Reverend Rowland. A tablestone ascribed to him has regrettably had its inscribed marble insert panel stolen sometime before 1875

Ruth, daughter of Rowland and Elizabeth, died in infancy

Deborah (Mason) wife of Colonel Roland Cotton, died 1766 aged thirty-six.

Samuel Prince, Merchant

There was money to be made in trade, and each of the coastal towns had packets plying between their area and the consumption centers such as Boston. Sandwich, like Barnstable and Yarmouth, had easy access to the Massachusetts Bay area and the Maine coast, and also to Nantucket, Martha's Vineyard, Rhode Island and Long Island Sound ports. Sandwich had a dock in the Jarvesville area by 1657, another earlier still in Spring Hill (Slawson's Stage) and the first mention of "Sandwich" in 1637 refers to a delivery of goods by sea from Weymouth.

Samuel Prince (1648-1728) came to Sandwich about 1682 from Hull, Massachusetts. He was promptly made a townsman and allowed land "on the commons near the mill" for a house. Frederick Freeman stated that this house was still standing in 1862 and we suggest it was the house on the lakeshore on Grove Street (opposite the 1794 Pope house) which went from Prince to Nathaniel Otis to Nathaniel Freeman. Prince (no relative of former Governor Thomas Prence) accepted town offices and was reimbursed several times for repairing the town dock. He married secondly Mercy Hinckley daughter of Governor Thomas Hinckley.

Though Samuel Prince sold his Sandwich holdings and removed to Rochester in 1710, he had two brilliant sons born in Sandwich, Thomas (1686-1758) and Nathan (1698-1748). Nathan (Harvard 1718) became a teacher and then a missionary and died in the West Indies. Thomas Prince spent time with his Hinckley relatives in Barnstable and as early as age ten began to collect books and manuscripts of all kinds, the start of what became an enormous collection. He graduated from Harvard in 1707 and probably taught school in Sandwich in 1708; at least funds were set aside to be offered to him for teaching here. Among the items he collected from Sandwich were a packet of love letters written to Ruth Winslow by Richard Bourne before their marriage in 1677, and some printed sermons of Reverend John Wing, the husband of the matriarch Deborah Wing. One of his greatest treasures was the manuscript of William Bradford's *Of Plimoth Plantation.* Prince called his collection "The New England Library." He went abroad from 1709 to 1717 to complete his education, and preached for several years to an English church at Coombs, Suffolk. When he finally decided to return to New England, no less than thirty of his parishioners are said to have removed with him. He was ordained at the prestigious Old South Church in Boston in 1718 where he remained until his death forty years later. Further evidence of the astonishing charm of Thomas Prince is found in the diary of Cotton Mather where Mather states:

"By encouraging of Mr. Prince to accept the invitation of the Old

> South Church, I may have a companion with whom I may unite more than any one upon earth in doing service for the Kingdom of God."

Mather preached at Prince's ordination and noted "I will here enter him as one of my relatives, hoping to enjoy a brother in him and a friend more useful than a brother." Cotton Mather was a man of enormous vanity and it is touching to see him welcoming the younger man so quickly and personally, recognizing him as an ally and not a rival. Both were men of vast learning and encyclopedic minds. Mather's *Magnalia,* a historical miscellany, was published in 1702. Prince published in 1736 his *New England's Annals and Chronology,* the first volume in his intended compilation. This book brought his account up to 1630. (Incidentally, several Sandwich families are listed as subscribers in this volume, including Melatiah Bourne, Colonel Roland Cotton and Reverend Benjamin Fessenden. The latter had succeeded Rowland Cotton as minister in Sandwich in 1722, and at Prince's urging, compiled from Sandwich oral and written sources then existing, an account of the Sandwich church history from the days of Leveridge on.) Prince's "New England Library" was given to the Old South Church and stored in a room in the bell tower where the alternate heat and cold would not be what modern archivists prefer. Much worse awaited this invaluable collection during the Revolution, when much of it was stolen or burned.

James Mills, Captain from Maine

In 1978, a Gifford family descendant from Ohio visited Sandwich and casually mentioned that she had an old shipping log and other papers with Gifford family information which had come down in her family. Unwilling to mail originals, she consented to send us photocopies for our study. The hoard included a little leatherbound notebook, missing many pages, which read JAMES MILLS, HIS BOOK 1699, plus a number of 18th century deeds. The Mills book contained references to cargo from Sandwich people for shipment to Boston, and also purchases made in Boston for return to Sandwich. At the back of the book was genealogy of Sylvanus Gifford, son of James and Deborah of Sandwich, and of the family of his son, John Gifford of Lee. This was authentic original historical material, and furthermore it fitted perfectly into material we already had, namely the marriage of Mary Mills of Blackpoint, Maine to William Gifford, and the operations of merchant Samuel Prince. Proofs of the Mary Mills connection were:

> James Mills, unmarried, in his will of October 14, 1720 in Barnstable Probate, named his nephew James Gifford (son of William and Mary), as executor and heir.
>
> The genealogist Savage cites "John Mills, Scarborough (earlier Blackpoint) had John, James, Sarah and Mary who were all charged with neglect of public worship; and Sarah's defence subjected her to stripes."

The connections to Samuel Prince were frequent mention of Prince in the shipping records as "get money from S. Prince" and Prince's own cargo, both from Sandwich and Maine, and of Prince as present in Boston; also a record of early ships registered to Sandwich:

1696 - *Sandwich Flower,* Samuel Prince and Samuel Lawrence, both of
Sandwich.

1701 - *Tryal,* Samuel Prince and Job Randall of Scituate.

1704 - *Adventure,* Samuel Prince of Sandwich.

1705 - *Mayflower,* Ichabod Tupper of Sandwich, part owner.

1711 - *Mary & Abigail,* Nathaniel Otis & Jon Bassett of Sandwich.

1714 - *Hopewell,* Ichabod Tupper and John Trowbridge of Sandwich.

1717 - *Charming Betty,* Nathan Bourne of Sandwich.

With his connections both in Maine and in Sandwich, Mills loaded three or four cargoes of raw materials each year for Boston, selling the materials at dockside and buying items desired by his clients in the country. Prince, as the chief merchant, handled most of the bulk cargo, but the ship's captain could always carry materials for his own account. Items brought to Boston from Sandwich included skins of fox, deer, calf, kid, and raccoon, as well as hides, butter, beeswax, tar, oysters, wheat, pork, barley and corn. Items purchased in the big city for Sandwich people were extremely varied: kettles, lamps, sieve, razor, earthen pots and platters, tools, compasses, hourglasses, silver hairpins, silver buttons, a chafing dish, pewter, sheer cotton, ribbons, silk, chairs, oars, hinges, a grindstone, warming pan, and a tapered cane with ivory head. Foodstuffs ordered included licorice, salad oil, treacle water, loaf sugar, nutmeg, cloves, malt, cheese, and or course, rum. An arithmetic and several Bibles were wanted. Ebenezer Burgess put up fourteen shillings and two silver shoe buckles to pay for his tools. Eliakim Tupper put up eleven shillings to buy a razor and repair his gun at Boston. It was cash in advance unless the client had credit with Mr. Prince.

The cargoes from and to Fairfield, Maine were similar: they put up meat, grain, flax, peas, fat and cheese, and received locks, tools, lampblack, thread, powder, guns, flints, stone jugs and even logwood. This is a splendid detailed record of the times, and a vivid reminder of how much local history has been scattered about this country by Sandwich descendants, much of it now lost or extremely difficult to find except by the happy chance that brought James Mills, Mary Mills and Samuel Prince back together again.

Peter Newcomb, Tavern Keeper

Peter Newcomb (1674-1723) was one of the fifteen children of Lieutenant Andrew Newcomb of Edgartown, Martha's Vineyard. He removed to Sandwich and married Mercy Smith in 1700, granddaughter of Reverend John Smith. He bought a block of land along what is now Main Street west of the millstream, and up to what is now Academy Road, off Grove Street, This land may have belonged earlier to the Turner family, Isaac having removed to Rhode Island in 1689. The land adjoined that bought at the same time by Captain Seth Pope of Dartmouth, including the grist mill and the lands along Grove Street beyond Academy Road formerly Newland's. Newcomb built a substantial two-story house on Grove Street possibly expecting a large family. However, after the birth of his only son William in 1702, there were no more children, and this may have induced him to open his house as Sandwich's first tavern for overnight accomodation of travelers. Before this there were ordinaries, where wine and spirits were sold both by the glass and in bulk, but without rooms for overnight guests.

On his earlier visits to Sandwich, Samuel Sewall had stayed one night each at various homes (i.e., Percival, Dexter, Chipman, Skiff, Smith). In 1706, he was here two nights and attended the Indian meetinghouse at Herring River. He also notes that he saw the harbor, burying-place and mill-pond. In 1714, he and a party left Plymouth for Sandwich including Major Thaxter of Hingham, Captain John Otis of Barnstable (pilot), Mr. Justice Parker of Barnstable and Mr. John Denison, Chaplain. "It did not rain but wet, being an east wind. Got to Newcomb's where we dined. I treated the Barnstable gentlemen. Mr. Cotton came to us and invited Major Thaxter and me to his house." Denison is not mentioned in the invitation to Cotton's house for the evening, as he was the son of Mrs. Cotton by her previous marriage and would be there anyway. At this time he was teaching school in Plymouth and also preaching by invitation. He was a member of Sewall's party with Thaxter, which was en route to Martha's Vineyard on Indian affairs for the Society for the Propagation of the Gospel. "In the evening Mr. Cotton made a short speech of God's mercies in the week past, sung part of the 103rd Psalm, and prayed." On the following day, Sewall, Thaxter and Denison attended Cotton's two sermons at the Sandwich meetinghouse, and Sewall made notes on both in his journal. After the afternoon service, Eldad Tupper Jr. and John Osborne, son of the school teacher, were baptized.

On Monday the party was piloted by William Bassett to Ashumet Pond where they watered their horses at a Fish family home. They reached Falmouth in time for noon dinner, and then sailed over to the Island with their horses. On the return trip the following week, they arrived back in Sandwich by sunset and learned from Madam Cotton that Rowland's aunt Maria, the wife of Reverend Increase Mather, had died in Boston. The following day they rode to Plymouth where the travel party broke up, Sewall paying Denison £2 for his help. Sewall took a coaster, the sloop *Success* for his return to Boston, and typically lists both the cargo of the sloop and what he had for noon dinner on the vessel: pork, peas, New York biscuits and a bottle of wine. His diary provides a fine picture of life on the road.

From the Newcomb Tavern, Peter Newcomb sent his only son William to Harvard, from which he graduated in 1722. His sponsor was Reverend Rowland Cotton who had to educate and prepare his own five sons for Harvard. William's classmates of 1722 were Josiah Cotton, and Joseph Bourne who became a preacher in Mashpee. There is a record that William Newcomb caused a great deal of breakage of glass while at Cambridge, for which Reverend Cotton was initially responsible. William did not enter any of the professions upon his graduation, but owned the Newcomb Tavern after his father's untimely death in 1723. He married well to the only daughter of Judge Melatiah Bourne. He and Bathsheba had eight children before his own early death in 1736 at the age of thirty-four.

Peter Adolph, A Silent Presence

One of the unique themes in Sandwich history is the Peter Adolph story, a man who never knew Sandwich. His grave marker in Old Town Burying Ground tells of his end:

> "Here lyeth ye body of Captain Peter Adolph of New York who dyed by shipwrack in this bay ye 16 of March 1702/3 and was washed on shoar 3 miles below this towne."

The location of the wreck was somewhere along East Sandwich beach or on Scorton Neck. Papers recovered on Captain Adolph's body identified him, and it was doubtless Reverend Cotton who wrote to New York City where the Captain lived and from whence presumably the vessel had been enroute to Boston when wrecked. His widow must have ordered the grave marker, as it is of a stone and by a carver unlike any other in Sandwich. In recent years this carver has been identified as Joseph Lamson of Boston, a well known workman there, but not otherwise represented in southeastern Massachusetts.

Then the widow did an unusual and highly affectionate thing. She sent to Sandwich a bronze bell, possibly thinking that its sound would always be heard where he was buried. The bell has three rows of decorative themes around its shoulder, first a design of cherub faces, flower patterns and an anchor sign. Then there is a line of letters: SI DEUS PRONOBUS QUIS CONTRA NOS 1675. Lastly there is a ring of geometric pattern suggestive of fleur-de-lys. The inscription is from Romans 8:31 and means "If God is for us, who is against us?" The bell is small, weighing about seventy pounds and standing eighteen inches high. It is probably of Dutch origin, but might be German or Belgian. Our one success in researching this bell was with the New York Genealogical and Biographical Society, which provided information on the identity of Captain Adolph and his wife, their children, and even a copy of his will. He was Peter Adolph de Groot, born in Amsterdam in 1655, baptized in New Amsterdam in 1657, son of Pieters and his wife Aechtje (Dirks). His wife was Janeke van Borsum, born 1653 in New Amsterdam, daughter of Egbert and his wife Annetje (Hendriks). They were married in 1678 and had eight children of whom the following four were mentioned in his will:

Adolph, b. 1679 mar. 1703 Rachel Gouderus
Egbert b. 1682
Aechtje b. 1684, mar. 1703 Garret Schuyler
Peter b. 1696, mar. 1717 Rebecca Gouderus

So it was Janeke who sent us the lovely bell. One wonders how it came to be available in New York, since bells are cast to order. Possibly, as happened in Sandwich later, it was used in a small meetinghouse and then was replaced by a larger bell when the building was enlarged. It was placed in the new First Parish Meetinghouse (built 1704) and is first mentioned in town records in August 1707, when selectmen were ordered to "procure some person to open and shut the doors and windows of the meetinghouse and to ring the bell". Later adventures of the bell will be recounted.

Thomas Robie, Talented Graduate

The American Antiquarian Society in Worcester has a portion of a diary kept by one Thomas Robie (1688/9-1729) while teaching school in Sandwich in 1710. The entries are one line a day in a small almanac, and only six months of the diary survives. Thomas Robie was a 1708 Harvard graduate and was teaching here until he should find a church offered to him, or concentrate on one of the other learned professions, medicine or law. Robie is described as a man of varied talents who was competent as an almanac maker, mathematics and astronomy tutor, preacher, physician and Harvard library-keeper. In those days, the Harvard scholar was literally exposed to almost all that was known in the scholarly world of theology, medicine, natural science, law, literature and the classics in Latin, Greek and Hebrew. A dedicated graduate had a very broad education. He and his classmates were among the elite of the province. Mr. Robie easily went from teaching to preaching to working out his almanac for the next year, observed tides and planets, corresponded widely, welcomed travelers and visited around in the homes of the Bournes, Otises, Russells, Princes, Freemans, Cottons, and other educated families.

In this period, Sandwich seems to have had two school teachers, one circulating among the villages and teaching in homes, while the other, called a Grammar Schoolmaster, probably taught the higher grades from a fixed location in the central village. Robie's only note on this is "March 7. I begin to keep school near Pope's." The two Pope houses then were the John Pope house at 110 Tupper Road (Moody House) and the Seth Pope house at 10 Grove Street. His schoolhouse would have been somewhere between. He was on the public payroll, as town meeting of September 26, 1710 reads:

> "The Town by their vote did order the Selectmen to raise by way of rate in such manner as the law directs, the sum of twenty pounds to pay Mr. Thomas Robie our present Schoolmaster, for his service for this present year, and order that it be collected and paid in to him accordingly"

This central school building was doubtless of a very primitive form as the town voted in 1713 to allow certain families "liberty to build a school at their own cost."

Robie lodged at Samuel Prince's home, possibly because he had known Thomas a year ahead of him at Harvard. As we noted, Thomas had taught here for a year after graduation, then took his glamorous trip to Europe and the West Indies, beginning in 1709. Robie noted the arrival and departure of Prince's sloop and others belonging to "Ivory" and to a Captain Trowbridge. Unexpectedly, Prince sold out and removed to Sippican, a part of Rochester which became Wareham. Robie soon went over to Rochester, and after the Princes, saw his friend Timothy Ruggles (Harvard 1707) who had just been ordained at Rochester, and preached for Ruggles. Robie notes the death of a number of persons in Sandwich, most of whom we can identify, but whose deaths did not get registered in the town's vital records. These included:

March 6 - Mr. Pope died (This was Thomas Pope born 1677)
March 18 - William Gifford's child poisoned (Nathan b. 1705)
March 20 - William Gifford's child died
March 25 - William Gifford's child buried
April 21 - Lydia Savory buried, aged 62 (Unknown person)
April 25 - Stephen Wing died, aged 88. (A Quaker, Spring Hill)
April 30 - Goody Johnson died (widow of the lame weaver, Thomas Johnson who had died 1683)
August 29 - Mr. Cotton's child died (Ruth, born July 22)
August 30 - Mr. Cotton's child buried
September 1 - S. Fish's child buried (Seth Jr. born 1709)

Such diaries are a unique window on the world of their day.

Nathaniel Otis, Lawyer and Trader

Among the entries in the Robie diary is one for February 12, 1710: "I received a letter from my father by Mr. N.O." The Robies were from Boston, and Nathaniel Otis was to graduate from Harvard in 1710. His father, Captain John Otis (1657-1727) of Scituate had moved to Barnstable and become a powerful merchant, politician, shipowner and Representative to the General Court; all his four sons graduated from Harvard and continued the family power on Cape Cod. Nathaniel married Abigail Russell late in 1710 and settled promptly in Sandwich. He bought Prince's house on Grove Street, as we read in 1711 town meeting:

> "the Town did give liberty to Nathaniel Otis to set up his warehouse on the Commons, somewhere near to the fence of Peter Newcomb, between his (Otis's) house and the Mill, and to keep it up there not exceeding two years."

The Commons were any land not yet allocated. The "warehouse" on this narrow site must have been a small building, and the two-year limit makes it seem almost temporary. The reason for the location up here on the millpond instead of nearer the town dock on Dock Lane or near the work center at River Street is not completely clear. Otis was both a trader and also a practicing attorney. He became Register of Probate for Barnstable County. He and Abigail had five children, one of whom Martha married Edmund Freeman in 1736, the fifth Edmund Freeman since the founder of the town. Nathaniel Otis died young in 1739 and is chiefly important to us because of his grandchild, Nathaniel

Freeman, born to Edmund and Martha in 1741, who inherited the Grove Street house and returned to Sandwich to occupy it.

Melatiah Bourne, A New Elite

We have referred to Honorable Shearjashub Bourne, son of Richard. He was Representative to the General Court, Indian Commissioner and a large landowner in Sandwich, Mashpee and Falmouth. He died in 1719, leaving his Mashpee and Sandwich lands to his son Ezra, and his Falmouth lands to Melatiah (1674-1742). Melatiah must have been a person of considerable ability as he increased his wealth many-fold. He was selectman of Falmouth for five years from 1701, town clerk 1707 and town treasurer 1708. After this, for some reason, he removed his family to Sandwich in 1710 and purchased a house and land from John Dexter, the former miller. The house, a two-story one built by Thomas Dexter Jr., was located on the millstream between the meetinghouse and the mill, which places it about at the present town comfort station. Melatiah Bourne built a fine new saltbox on the bank across the street on the six acres of orchard and upland bought from Dexter. This six acres must have run from the Dillingham property (present First Church of Christ is on Dillingham land) along Main Street to at least School Street. The new Melatiah Bourne salt-box at 138 Main Street accordingly must be dated about 1711, not the 1692 attributed to it, which is the date of his marriage to Desire Chipman.

MELATIAH BOURNE HOUSE--Salt-box house at 138 Main Street Sandwich built by Melatiah Bourne about 1711, and occupied by his descendants to 1862. Sandwich Historical Commission.

The first reference to Melatiah in town meeting records is in September 1710 when he was authorized by the town to clear and deepen the channel at the town dock and to mend and repair the dock. This clearly indicated that his activities included shipping. The sources of his increasing wealth are not stated, but in his generation, the third from Richard Bourne, were eighteen solvent families with large landholdings and solid connections in all the neighboring towns. These eighteen families were those of Melatiah's brothers, sisters or first cousins. If a related group like this supported one another in trade and credit, the potential for increasing wealth was substantial. Melatiah was a Colonel in the Militia, a justice in the Common Pleas and a Representative to the General Court, ensuring support in many ways.

Benjamin Fessenden, Minister With Opposition

After the death of Cotton in 1722, the town committee in charge of supplying the pulpit called Benjamin Fessenden of Cambridge, a graduate of Harvard 1718. He had been teaching and may have known both Sandwich and the Cottons well. Benjamin's classmate of 1718 was Nathan Prince who had been born in Sandwich. His acceptance in Sandwich was notably swift, and he was ordained September 12, 1722. His initial salary was generous (£90 plus a settlement allowance of £250) and Nathan Prince noted that he would be getting both the Cotton house and a Cotton daughter. He continued his swift acceptance in Sandwich in 1723 with the marriage of his sister Hannah to John Chipman and in his preparing a lengthy account of Sandwich church history for the collections of Reverend Thomas Prince. This history had not been documented before except for scattered references in Plymouth Colony Records and Sandwich town meeting records. He married Rebecca Smith in 1724, and in addition to his pastoral duties engaged in the practice of medicine in the town.

Fessenden kept notes of certain events which were later published by the New England Historic Genealogical Society, including vital records of the town (many not included in the town's own vital record entries), and a list of 135 households in the town population as of 1730. His diary also records the steps by which he built himself a new house in 1729, using the proceeds of the £250 settlement allowance voted to him. Since this house became the Fessenden Tavern in the next generation and finally the Daniel Webster Inn, it is clear that it was different from the Cotton house which doubtless was removed. He names all the persons who worked on the house, some volunteers like his brother Joseph, and parish supporters, others paid as Indian laborers.

With high intelligence, excellent manners and liberal attitude, his future as a minister of prestige should have been assured, but a cloud hung over Fessenden's career. The cloud seems to have come from a child, Ruth Fessenden, born July 11, 1724, probably in Boston or Cambridge. This child was adopted by Benjamin's sister Jane Winship and was married in 1743 to Francis Locke. The Locke Genealogy lists Ruth as Benjamin's daughter, but puts the date of his marriage to Rebecca Smith forward to October 18, 1723, whereas Sandwich Vital Records show it as October 18, 1724. The Locke account of Ruth Fessenden is also followed in the recent (1971) Fessenden genealogy. We only go into this difficulty because of the extraordinary controversy in Sandwich which centered around Fessenden's fitness to serve. As early as October 24, 1724 (the week he married Rebecca Smith) a group of his parishioners pointedly went to Barnstable to receive the sacrament and began to boycott his services. For some reason, the strongest objections were centered in a group of some twenty-five families in the Scusset sector, including Tuppers, Gibbses, Ellises, Swifts, Blackwells and others. Fessenden responded with a "solemn transaction February 23 1725" by which members of the parish were "bound to a united worship." In 1726 a town committee expressed great dissatisfaction at his conduct and called for a Council to meet in November. In 1727 this Council, in its second session, declared him unworthy and disapproved of his preaching until he should repent and remove the scandal from his record. This was followed by a Provincial presentment "for not having a minister settled and qualified according to law." The Scusset group became organized and began to call other ministers to come to preach, including Ward Cotton, youngest son of Rowland. To each of these preachers Benjamin wrote sternly that his church was firmly supported in Sandwich and that he should only preach from the First Parish pulpit. In 1730 a Council firmly found Sandwich to be under sentence of non-communication with neighboring churches until Fessenden should make amends. Beginning in 1731 the dissidents, under Jireh Swift, asked the town meeting to vote on allowing a division into a second Parish with division of assets. The majority of taxpayers refused and supported Fessenden in spite of the censure of all the other seventeen regional churches. The dissidents nevertheless raised funds and built a new meetinghouse in what is now Sagamore Village, just east of the Sagamore Cemetery. The Town refused to relieve them of taxes for support of the First Parish, but a Council in 1733 approved the organization of a new church. In 1734 Fessenden is said to have confessed to a Council, but without the minutes of this and the other Councils, it is impossible to judge. (In partial defense of Mr. Fessenden, it may be suggested that the mother of the child Ruth could not be certain of its father, and that Fessenden had arranged the adoption without certainty that the child was his.) The minority was not satisfied and early in 1735 called Reverend Francis Worcester to Scusset and ordained him on June 18.

The situation was relieved in 1746 only with the early death of Fessenden at forty-five, said to be worn out with his two callings and "his troubles and labors." Reverend Worcester was released shortly after and the Scusset church was given up. The parsonage home was granted to Rebecca Fessenden. Her husband had acquired considerable property and left two educated sons in comfortable circumstances, Benjamin Jr. (Harvard 1746) in Sandwich, and William a physician in Harwich.

School Teachers

The first reference to schools in town meeting records is in 1677 when the town voted to hire a schoolmaster to serve in three places in rotation. The first master of record was James Chadwick for the period 1678-1680, followed by James Stewart. This teacher married about 1689 and was granted land in 1690 and at some point must have shifted to full time farming. James Battersby is of record as being paid from 1699 through 1704 as teacher. These three teachers were not Harvard graduates. Daniel Greenleaf, Harvard 1699, was noted by Fessenden much later as the first grammar school master in Sandwich, probably meaning that in addition to the primary grades (reading, writing and arithmetic) he taught more advanced subjects as English grammar, history, geography and languages. Greenleaf was called to the pulpit in Yarmouth in 1707. Thomas Prince has already been introduced as a Sandwich native who taught for a year in 1708. Beginning in 1710, the town records show the two schoolmasters were paid for several years, representing a great opportunity for the youth of all the villages to get a few months of schooling each year. The central village had some sort of simple building set aside for teaching, whereas in the various villages one of the houses had to serve while the teacher boarded around. Thomas Robie was here in 1710, followed by Joseph Dow in 1711 and 1712. (Freeman quotes his name from town meeting records as James Dorr, but we feel Joseph Dow is the correct reading). The second teacher in this period was a home town product with an unusual background, Samuel Jennings, the son of John Jennings and his wife Ruhamah Turner. Samuel had set out for England at age nineteen to recover some funds due the family, but was captured and impressed into service aboard a British warship. While in Barbados, he determined to get away or die, and swam for a Boston vessel some way off. He was attacked by sharks and badly injured, but was rescued by the Americans and treated by two doctors. One arm had to be amputated and the greater part of one foot. He recovered and returned to New England where he realized that his only livelihood would be in teaching. He secured the required education and began teaching in Sandwich in 1710 at about twenty-five. He married in 1713 and was thereafter found frequently in town service as selectman, clerk, or treasurer. He lived to be eighty years old and often repeated his stories of brutality on the naval vessel and of his rescue from the sharks.

The next teacher of record was Samuel Osborne, a Scot who had been brought up in Ireland and graduated from the University of Dublin. Samuel Osborne (about 1687-1777) was a versatile and learned gentleman of great charm. He came to Sandwich in 1712 from Martha's Vineyard and kept school here until 1718. He was expected to teach four months each in Spring Hill, in the village center, and in Scusset, and even offered Latin and Greek for a modest fee. A smooth and witty speaker, he liked nothing better than challenging a visiting Quaker or minister to debate on any subject. He advocated the extraction and drying of peat for fuel and recommended advanced methods of agriculture and husbandry. While here he married Jedidah Smith (another of the many granddaughters of Reverend John Smith) and had two gifted children. His son John (Harvard 1735) was a poet, mathematician and physician, while his daughter Elizabeth was one of those removing to Nova Scotia where she became a famous midwife as well as a person of beauty, charm and character. (Her grandson John Howard Payne wrote the famous song "Home Sweet Home.") Samuel Osborne became the minister at Eastham from 1718 to 1737, succeeding the great preacher, Samuel Treat of Indian fame. Osborne was finally dismissed from his pulpit as being too liberal, and took his talents to Boston, where he kept a private school until a great age.

The next teacher in Sandwich, John Rogers, was a Scot from Glasgow, but was content to stay in this town where he taught for thirty-six years (1720-1756). During his time the practice was to teach in four to six areas in succession, requiring two years to complete the circuit.

The Commons Are Issued

The main settlements and villages (as indicated in the 1667 house survey) were still near the salt marshes, the bays and the valley of the Manomet/ Herring River. The process of town grants of common land to new families continued, gradually filling in the settled areas. In the western part of the town, purchases from the Indians continued with the remaining Indians becoming more and more confined to house lots and limited woodlands. These official purchases became town land, and could in turn be issued or sold to settlers. Some lands issued earlier were taken back by the town when the parties did not settle (i.e., William Paybody and Josiah Standish of Plymouth). Other early grants on the Plains and in Great Hollow were taken back by the town by purchase or exchange. Each family was strongly conscious of its land holdings and watched for encroachments. The town collectively was well aware of the large area of unoccupied land on the moraines inland and around the ponds, and watched for unauthorized use or settlement. Repeated efforts were made to find and sell off the "strips and skirts" of unowned land between the standing farms. It was only a matter of time before the town would have to face up to the matter of how to allocate the thousands of acres that lay unused in the inland hills and plains.

In 1682 Plymouth Colony issued a reminder to towns that their remaining commons could be issued to the townsmen, and that the townsmen could press for action on this. Still, nothing happened until in 1697 Barnstable started granting woodlots. This may have forced action in Sandwich because in the 1698 town meeting the town agreed that upon proper approval a family could obtain a temporary use of upland commons for six years if the land was fenced and cleared promptly. This may have seemed like a good idea but was immediately abused, and the town for years after had to keep appointing committees to stop unlawful encroachment on the commons. The only persons at this time who had established permanent homes in the upland area were John Tobey north of Peter's Pond, and Hezekiah Hoxie north of Spectacle Pond. Shearjashub Bourne had a home on Mashpee Pond in Indian country, but he was considered a special case because of his Indian duties and was always held to be a Sandwich townsman. Clearly the massive job of dividing some 20,000 acres of woodland among about 100 Sandwich families had to be faced and a program outlined. In 1701 a committee was named which in 1702 produced a list of approved townsmen for land rights, and a general statement on acceptance of further townsmen. (The old term "freemen" with superior rights had been dispensed with.) The plan was to issue the lands in four separate stages:

A set of twenty-acre lots adjoining the home properties and extending up toward the moraine.

Starting from the other direction, a set of forty-acre lots adjoining the Barnstable, Mashpee and Falmouth lines, in the most remote areas, much of it poorly wooded, to be used primarily for sheep pasture as was then being done.

A series of thirty-acre lots of the best woodland, mainly adjoining the twenty-acre series of lots or other properties already owned.

A last division of lots, of whatever size, to divide up all the spaces between the thirty-acre woodlots and the sheep-pasture lands.

This plan was in fact completed, but took a great deal of effort and about twenty years time.

The Twenty-Acre Lots

A list of seventy-five names of eligible townsmen was approved in 1702, including one lot for Rowland Cotton personally and one for the ministry in general. Nine more names were added in 1702/3, eight more in 1705 including several for the collective heirs of worthy deceased family heads. In 1706 five half-shares for newcomers and certain sons were awarded, bringing the total to ninety-four and a half. This supposedly closed the list, and the actual layout and assignment of the lots was largely completed in the years 1705 and 1706. We note about these "twenty-acre lots" that many are easy to locate on the map; the descriptions refer to homesteads or to abutting owners, aiding greatly in locating homes of the period; the lots were laid out directly to the person or parties involved, adjacent to their other holdings, and sometimes were in several pieces tailored to the recipient's convenience; the lots actually total about forty acres each. The phrase "laid out for twenty acres with allowance for barrows" seems to be a generous code set up to reduce friction and complaints. The town meeting agreement was that twenty acres represented the "best land" (all cleared and fertile) and that more land would be granted if the lot was anything less. This gave the surveying party leeway and made for good feeling. The twenty-acre lot survey effort with its generous over-supply of land provided a convenient method of sweeping away old land boundary problems and encroachment situations without embarassment to anyone.

Most of these lots were laid out in about three years but a few were not laid out until many years later. In 1710/11 young William Bassett, Jr. was admitted a townsman and somehow was placed on the twenty-acre lot list, otherwise closed in 1706. His father, Colonel William Bassett, was probably the town's leading citizen at this point. Young Bassett chose for part of his grant a fifteen-acre tract around Monument Swamp, a landmark in what is now the Otis impact area, far from land owned by any family. The lot (40 x 60 rods) was aligned north/south and so stood out clearly when the woodlots were laid out in this area later on in a different alignment. We wish we knew the reason for his choice—possibly to protect an inland marsh which was always a retreat for flowers, birds and wildlife, and quite different from the general woodland of climax forest with grass burnt off annually. This was called the "mainsail lot" because of its shape on the map.

The Sheep Pasture Lots

These lots differ greatly in all respects from the previous twenty-acre series. Records on them are very scanty, and they were laid out as large tracts only, not by individual lot, with the rights-holders expected to organize their collective grazing arrangements on a common basis and not to subdivide the tracts. The first reference to this set of lots is found in town meeting records in March 1705 where it was agreed that the "remote lands" should be laid out into forty-acre rights. Two years later the arrangements were clear enough so that each family was asked to select which one of four areas it wished to belong to. The four were:

1. *Southeast Set* - A roughly square area bounded by Barnstable line, Mashpee line, and the southern halves of Lawrence and Spectacle Ponds. Thirty-six families signed up for shares here, and John Chipman Jr. was allowed a one-half share. There is no record in the woodlot book of the outlines of this tract, but it clearly was in existence before 1715. The early woodlot maps did not survive, with the first known one being traced out by Jesse Boyden in 1848. This shows the southeast sector as divided into exactly thirty-six and one half lots, but how and when these were laid out is as yet unknown. The likelihood is, however, that it was early in the eighteenth century, as by 1750 we find an active community farming in this area, including the Percival, Meiggs, Goodspeed, Jones, Lawrence and Hoxie families. The names of Samuel Hilliard and Edward Dillingham are found as abutters to adjacent woodlots in 1715, suggesting that the whole set was already laid out and issued to the subscribers in severalty.

2. *Peters Pond Set* — Only six families signed up for this area, five Tobeys and John Dillingham. The 1848 woodlot map has no lines suggesting their holdings. The appropriate blank areas on the map are between the Falmouth Road (Route 130), Peters Pond and the Mashpee line, and another area east of Cotuit Road. The east side of Peters Pond was all taken up by Bourne twenty-acre lots.

3. *Snake Pond Set* — This area ran from Snake Pond south to Falmouth and included all the land between Falmouth Road and Turpentine Road. A total of thirty families signed up for this area in 1707. It is not mentioned again in town records until 1714 when the town survey team specified the exact boundaries as a single big tract, and stated that this was for thirty-seven shareholders. The names of the added seven shareholders are unknown. Very shortly after this, the blue-ribbon Awards Committee (described below) decided that Jonathan Fish should have a forty-acre sheep pasture right contiguous to one of the other sets, and this was laid out as the block between Snake Pond and the Falmouth Road, increasing the shares to thirty-eight in this set. It is considered

probable that this area was in fact used as joint pasturage by the thirty-eight shareholders and their descendants for many years. There was no early settlement here as there was in the South Sandwich area. In 1819 a group of descendants of these rights holders in fact petitioned for recognition, and the minutes of their legal meetings have survived in the town records. They requested division of the tract into thirty-eight lots, and this clearly must have been done as the 1848 woodlot map shows the Snake Pond sheep pasture lot tract as divided into thirty-eight separate lots. Number 27 is in two parts, and the Jonathan Fish extra area is easily seen to be number 26.

4. Opening Pond Set - Like the Snake Pond set, this tract of fifteen owners was a single block of land west of Turpentine Road. (The pond itself is a small one near Pocasset Road and Snake Pond Road.) The individual lots were not laid out immediately, as the adjacent woodlots in 1716 are described only as adjoining the tract. Hence it may be that these fifteen lots were not defined until the next century, as were the Snake Pond lots. These sheep pasture lots were called "forty-acre lots" but this tract at 580 x 280 rods would be 1,015 acres or 67 acres per lot.

The First Division of Woodlots

After the twenty-acre lots and the sheep pasture areas had been laid out, the time came to agree on how the woodlots should be divided and assigned. The town agreed on March 5, 1712/13 to divide the remaining commons among the interested townsmen on the 1702 list plus all those admitted since. This had sufficed for the previous issues which were largely to established families and benefited the whole family, particularly in its agricultural activities. The prospective woodlots, however, were different, in that they were not intended for clearing and farming, but were a source of cash income from sale of cordwood indefinitely into the future. Many unmarried adults, craftsmen, and professional people who did not have farms saw the woodlots as an opportunity not to be missed. Hence only a week later another meeting of the proprietors was held at which it was noted "that some persons in said town are aggrieved that they are not accepted and admitted to have interest in said Commons." The meeting must have been a hot one with the two camps emerging, the old proprietors and the "claimers." A new approach clearly was needed, and the meeting agreed on a committee of three distinguished Barnstable men (Colonel John Otis, Lieutenant Ebenezer Lewis and Deacon Samuel Chipman) to hear "the pleas, arguments and allegations" of both sides. Costs of the Committee's work were to be paid equally by both sides. The new voices at this time were partly a reflection of the fact that a number of the town's patriarchs of the first and second generation had recently passed from the scene, and their sons found themselves for the first time with property and prospects of their own.

The Committee allowed things to cool off and then reported the following year that the town should empower an objective (that is, out-of-town) committee to study each family and claimant, and submit a binding list of those who should have rights in the woodlots. This was accepted, and a new committee of five from Plymouth, Barnstable, and Yarmouth was appointed for this task, with "board for horse and man at Peter Newcomb's public house" while they worked here. They brought in their report in May 1714 which stated that thirty more persons should have full rights and sixty-two more should have half rights. This was clearly a victory for the "claimers" party and a dilution of land-holding by senior men in each family. This committee also made a few recommendations to correct what may have been minor inequities in the twenty-acre lot and sheep pasture lot allocations, and strongly recommended that woodlots be set aside for income for the ministry and for the town school. The town, to its credit, accepted this report and promptly started to put it into effect. About one hundred fifty-two lots were needed, and as with the earlier twenty-acre lots, a formula of thirty acres per lot for the best wooded land was adopted, with more land for poorer sections at the discretion of the surveyors. Since these lots generally ran over the moraine, they were hilly, and for fairness they were laid out in long strips so that the terrain was better shared, giving rise to the term "long lots."

The special features of this woodlot issue were that the lots were approximately equal except for location, and that the lots were to be chosen in an order determined by a random drawing of names. The many who had half shares were required to mate up in advance, and if they failed, the matings were done for them before the draw. The surveying work for this important event was painstaking and took nearly a year, during which time a great many purchases and sales of rights or fractions of rights were carried out. Those who had funds bought up rights from those who needed money more than a future wood supply. During the surveying several fractional lots were found to be required by the terrain, and these were granted in town meetings to various persons who had been left out or for other good reasons. It was foreseen immediately that the last ten persons on the list would have poor pickings, and this was solved by laying out three extra lots in scattered locations. The next-to-last five persons would have their choice of any one of these three lots, and could divide it amongst themselves. The last five would have the other two lots to divide up, an ingenious solution.

On the day of the drawing, Deacon Timothy Bourne drew the names from the hat and everyone then knew his order. The sequence was recorded by William Bassett and his son Nathan. The first twenty names then had until 6 P.M. on the second working day to come to Bassett's and register their choices. Then the next twenty had their two days to make their choices. It must have been an absorbed town that watched the selection process for this valuable land.

The Last Division of Woodlots

The first division surveying was completed on June 2, 1716, and the drawing was held immediately. The surveying team was composed of Samuel Jennings and Edmund Freeman for all areas, plus one of the following men, Matthias Ellis, Samuel Perry or John Ellis, for specific areas. This team having worked for over ten months on the First Division, then went back to work July 23 on the second or last division. This set was located in areas between the first division woodlots and the sheep pasture lots. The last division work was completed very speedily in just over two months, reflecting compact lots laid out on a fill-in basis. A total of one hundred fifty-three lots was defined plus one fractional lot. There was no particular size aimed at as a standard for the best land, with the result that these lots are found to vary from only a few acres to one of almost four hundred acres (240 rods square). Size alone was not what was desired, because in the draw held that October, the two biggest lots were taken at the 54th and 101st choices, whereas the first choice was for a small lot near Spectacle Pond.

The release of all this common land to the townsmen was an event of great importance. Our study of each lot has resulted in a new and much improved woodlots map at the Archives Office as a matter of primary record. The initial assignments of all the lots has been summarized in tables. As soon as they were issued, the various lots immediately became subject to resale, exchange, and probate, and changed hands many times. Most were owned in common by many descendants as shown in various wills which passed on a portion of a portion such as a sixth of an undivided third of a woodlot. The lots therefore became a permanent part of the language and working experience of many generations of Sandwich families.

The First Shops

Every settler had a skill that produced cash income or at least goods or services with value for barter, such as the skills of a blacksmith, carpenter, wheelwright, mason, weaver, or cooper. These skills could be practiced on demand or were used to prepare standard goods during the winter months for later sale. Every home had a store or skill of some kind, which was well known to the neighborhood, but retail stores as such did not exist in the villages. Notions and small things might be had of an itinerant like Seth Pope the trader, while imported items or luxury goods had to be ordered from Boston via the packet master.

The first reference to a shop in town meeting records is in 1694 when "the town did give liberty to Job Loring to dig a cellar and set up a shoe-maker's shop in the corner where the land of James Skiff and James Steward join together." Loring was not a Sandwich native and was probably a nephew of Samuel Prince, the merchant. This corner was probably near present Main Street and Jarves Street.

The following year Richard Allen was given an acre in Spring Hill "to set a dwelling house and shop on." His trade was not given. In 1706/7 one Richard Doty of Plymouth was allowed "to set up a shoemaker's shop" near the house of Josiah Swift in the Scusset area. We have already mentioned the "warehouse" which Nathaniel Otis was allowed by the town to set up on Grove Street in 1711. This must have involved goods for resale.

Mills and Public Houses

The town's third grist mill was allowed to Elisha Bourne on Herring River in 1695. There are frequent references after this to requiring the mill to close each spring for six weeks to allow the herring to get up to Herring Pond to spawn.

In 1697 Thomas Smith was allowed to erect a building and "fishing design" beside Scorton Creek. This same Thomas Smith, together with William Bassett of Sandwich and John Otis of Barnstable, was appointed this year by the General Court in Boston "to view a place for a passage to be cut through the land in Sandwich, from Barnstable Bay into Manomet Bay, for vessels to pass through and from the western parts of the country, it being thought by many persons to be very necessary for the preservation of men and estates and that it will be very profitable and useful to the public." This seems to be the first serious proposal to dig the Cape Cod Canal.

In 1699 the town took from Joseph Holway by way of exchange "the way through his land over to Scorton Neck." This is the first reference to the Jones Road causeway over Scorton Marsh leading to Scorton Neck. We have already mentioned the causeway which Thomas Dexter Sr. built earlier over which Route 6A runs at the Sandwich/Barnstable line.

In 1704 a new meetinghouse was erected on the old site at River Street and Main Street. This was a plain boxy building with its side facing Main Street. There was a balcony on the Main Street side with the pulpit opposite. In 1710/11 a west gallery was built, then a turret for the bell was added in 1714 outside the west end on River Street. This is the same building that survived to 1833 although enlarged twice again before then.

In 1717 the town approved several roads as town ways. These included the way up to Richard Handy's in Cataumet, the Falmouth Road from present Forestdale along the Mashpee border past Ashumet Pond, the way to Scorton Harbor (probably present Foster Road to Spring Hill Beach) and the way from Nathan Tobey's above Jashub Wing's house (from above the present old Ansel Tobey house east past the Wing Howland house and on to the Crow Farm). The existing roads in 1717 included the following as through roads:

> Main county road from Plymouth to Barnstable. The route was Old Plymouth Road, Hunters Brook Road, Sandwich Road from Sagamore to Freeman Farm, Tupper Road, River Street, Main Street east, Charles Street, then east to Route 6A through East Sandwich, then Old County Road to the Barnstable line at High Street.
>
> From Hunters Brook Road (under the Sagamore Bridge) to Bournedale and south of the Manomet River along present County Road to the Falmouth line.
>
> From Bournedale along the moraine to Head of the Bay and on toward Wareham and Rochester.

Cross Street from Freeman Farm along present Route 130 to join River Street where there was a bridge over the Mill Creek.

Grove Street and Pocasset Street south to Turpentine Road, joining road from Snake Pond to Pocasset.

Water Street through Great Hollow south to Forestdale area and on to Mashpee and Falmouth Roads.

Cotuit Road east of Peters Pond, Wakeby and Mashpee Ponds leading to Santuit and Cotuit.

Dock Lane, Jarves Street to Town Dock at foot of Harbor Street.

Spring Hill Road.

Nye's Mill Road from present Old Mill Road along portion later renamed Quaker Meetinghouse to Cotuit Road.

Jones Road to Scorton Neck.

Freeman says that in 1717 a dam was built on Tupper Creek in Scusset Marsh to keep out sea water and allow fresh meadows to develop. The remains were still visible in 1860, but would have been destroyed by the Canal. The project is seen in the name "Dike Meadow Creek" on old maps.

Health and the Poor

We have noted that Ruth Chipman, wife of Elder John Chipman, had a special skill with illnesses of women and children. Another nurse of this period was Hannah the second wife of Thomas Tobey Sr. (Hannah Swift Fish 1651-1721). The town paid her twenty-four shillings in 1705 for curing Hannah Cleaves and Elkanah Smith. Mrs. Cleaves was the wife of a newcomer William Cleaves. We note that she must have died later, as he remarried in 1707. The Smith case was especially poignant. Benjamin Smith was the only son of Richard Smith of East Sandwich, an early settler (not related to Reverend John Smith). Elkanah was Benjamin's eldest son, born in 1685 and so was twenty years old when cured by Hannah Tobey. He married soon and had children. Benjamin and his wife had no less than ten other children between 1678 and 1704, of whom none lived to be adults. The town in 1711 agreed to pay to Edward Perry, Jr. of East Sandwich all that which was due to him from Benjamin Smith for making the coffins for Smith's family. Most families at this time in Sandwich were large, with nearly all marrying, so the Smith case may have represented some devastating genetic condition or blood mismatch from which only Elkanah escaped. On a happier note, in Plymouth a Doctor Francis LeBaron was one of the captured crew of a French privateer, and he managed to cure the wife of Goodman Hunter. The town asked permission from Boston to retain LeBaron as a town physician and he settled successfully among the Mayflowers. Mrs. Hunter was the former Rebecca Besse who had married William Hunter at only thirteen to escape the George Barlow household.

There was no class of poor as such at this time. The town had voted in 1706/7, when deciding on townsmen to get their twenty-acre lots, that a block of two hundred acres should be set aside for the poor and for newcomers, but there is no further record that it was laid out or that any land was issued to the poor as such. Those who had had a tragedy might get on-the-spot help from the town, and would live with relatives or friends if unable to work. Some families may have suffered from indolence or alcoholism, but land grants would not have helped them. In 1720 the town agreed to provide a house for Seth Tobey and his wife, who had married in 1719. There must have been special conditions here, as Tobey was a member of a strong family. In 1726 the town voted to build a poorhouse near Mill River. That this was not for lengthy free occupancy is shown by its size, 17' x 13' overall, representing temporary (and spartan) quarters, just the size of the lockup a century later at the same spot.

CHAPTER 10

THE RUGGLES PERIOD

The period of about 1736-1765 we designate the Ruggles period because of the residence here of Timothy Ruggles between 1736 and 1753, one of the best known personages in New England at this time, certainly one of the most dramatic and interesting. The period in Sandwich was marked by much building as the established families grew, intermarried, and prospered. The Cape Breton campaign of 1745, and the French and Indian War started in 1754, involved troops from this county, but we can find no record of those serving from Sandwich, and no mention of these conflicts in town meeting records.

Timothy Ruggles (1711-1795)

There were two weddings on Grove Street, Sandwich in 1736, only a few weeks apart. Martha Otis, not yet nineteen, daughter of Nathaniel Otis, married Edmund Freeman on August 7. Freeman was the fifth in line to bear that name since the founding of the town, and had been graduated from Harvard in the class of 1733, the first Freeman in Sandwich to do so. The other bridegroom was Timothy Ruggles of Rochester, also of the fifth generation of his family in America, Harvard 1732, and of course well known to Freeman. His bride on September 18, was however no dewy eighteen-year-old, but the widow Bathsheba Bourne Newcomb, thirty-two, mother of eight Newcomb children, whose husband William Newcomb had died only that April. Neither cared in the slightest about town gossip. They were married by her father, Judge Melatiah Bourne, probably the richest man in Sandwich. She was the sole owner of the Newcomb Tavern plus two shops, while Ruggles was a successful attorney and Representative to the General Court from Rochester despite his age (twenty-five). Ruggles' practice took him to the three County Courts in this area, Taunton, Plymouth and Barnstable, and he stayed at the Newcomb Tavern when coming to the Cape.

Ruggles and Bathsheba immediately started a family of their own, but he kept his formal residence at Rochester because of his reelection to the General Court from there. In 1739, the unexpected death of Nathaniel Otis in Sandwich created a need for a Sandwich attorney, and thereby cleared Ruggles' way to become a Sandwich resident, which he promptly did. He served as the Sandwich Representative in Boston for six terms during the period he lived here.

BRIGADIER TIMOTHY RUGGLES-Host at the Newcomb Tavern from 1736 to 1753 was Ruggles who had married the widow Bathsheba Newcomb. He had an astonishing career as lawyer, host, military leader, scientific farmer, judge, Representative and leading Tory. He resettled in Nova Scotia. Courtesy Hardwick Museum

The Ruggles Legend

Frederick Freeman devotes a lengthy note to Ruggles in his *History of Cape Cod.* Ruggles is one of those memorable people about whom many stories were told, and of whom we get some physical description. Frederick Freeman says of Ruggles:

> "...from being a guest at the tavern he becomes the landlord. He has married the widow Newcomb... He proves himself indeed a man of vast endowments. Connecting with his law practice the duties of innkeeper, not simply the usual offices of a taverner of olden times are his, but he personally attends both bar and stable—equally expert whether in currying a horse, mixing a cocktail, impressing his guests with the extent of his varied lore, conducting a case in court, or enlightening the wisdom of the legislature by his eloquence. To whatever the versatility of his genius directs itself he is equally *au fait...* Shrewd as a lawyer, quick of apprehension, remarkable for the boldness of his conceptions, of lordly though rude manners, always artful in his addresses to a jury, in fact, singularly sagacious and ingenious, he was eminently qualified..."

The Ruggles family historian writes of him:

> "As a lawyer he was an impressive pleader, his eloquence enhanced by his majestic presence, being above six feet and magnificently proportioned with a noble head... and such had been his success in the early years of his career that his services had been continually in demand in the adjoining counties..."

The Bourne family genealogist quotes other early nineteenth century writers on Ruggles:

> "As a scholar he was much above mediocrity; his reasoning power and legal information placed him among the most able advocates of the day; but his manners were coarse, rough, and offensive; his arguments to a Court were impressive, but in his private conversations he did not so studiously avoid profanity as prudence would have dictated."

> "Timothy Ruggles was well over six feet tall, dark, handsome, with a strong and commanding face. He dressed carefully but not elegantly. He was social, witty, profane, wise about human nature, quick to drop ceremony and convention when they ceased to be of social value. He was a man of few words and never said anything silly. He drank nothing stronger than a small beer, and was almost a vegetarian in a society in which gluttony was one universal excess."

This is the picture of Timothy Ruggles. There are only a few references to life at the Newcomb Tavern. Ivan Sandroff of Worcester, an expert on Ruggles' career, quotes Ruggles as saying "No man should be above his business", and, "He (Ruggles) practiced successfully at two bars, waited at once on the table and stable; umpired at quoit-pitching and foot races." A minister from Middleboro with two companions traveling to Harwich reported that on Monday, February 20, 1748/9 they arrived in Sandwich and stopped at "an inn where there were a company of men drinking and sporting."

NEWCOMB TAVERN-Colonial house at 8 Grove Street built by Peter Newcomb about 1702 and called the Newcomb Tavern until about 1825. It was a center of Sandwich Tories during the Revolutionary period. Sandwich Historical Commission.

The story always quoted about Ruggles occurred in Taunton Court in 1742. In its simplest form, an elderly woman entered the crowded room to be a witness, and was uncertain where to sit. Ruggles conducted her to the bench behind the judge's table. When Justice Lyne entered, he was incensed that anyone should be there, and she pointed to Ruggles as the one who had seated her. He stated innocently "May it please the Court, I thought that the place for an old woman." The authority for the story, Honorable Abraham Holmes of Rochester, born in 1754, knew both Ruggles' father and other witnesses, and is supposed to have told it to Frederick Freeman himself in his own old age.

Ruggles' practice was profitable and he therefore took Province cases where he acted for the Crown at a fixed fee. It was at such cases where his legal opponent was often James Otis of Barnstable, representing private parties. This was Colonel James Otis, Sr. (1702-1778), brother of Nathaniel of Sandwich. They enjoyed sparring and knew one another well. The story is told that Otis came to a tavern where he knew that Ruggles would be putting up, too. He told the tavern keeper that his servant would follow and should immediately be given a glass of rum. When Ruggles came he refused the drink with an oath as he was indeed a teetotaller. The tavern keeper said calmly, "Mr. Otis was right, you are both very tall and very foul-mouthed." Ruggles found a way to get even.

Ruggles and Bathsheba had seven children born in Sandwich. They were Martha (1737), Timothy (1738/9), Mary (1740/1), John (1742), Richard (1743/4), Bathsheba (1745/6), and Elizabeth (1748).

He was appointed excise collector for Barnstable County in 1743. There is no record that he served the town in any other capacity than as a Representative and as moderator at town meetings. His interests were much broader. His first military service is typical. Word reached Sandwich in 1740 that men were being raised in Boston for an action against the Spanish in the West Indies. Ruggles rounded up a company of one hundred at his own expense and marched them to Boston. Ivan Sandroff found the muster role for this company in the State Archives, and learned that the majority were Indians, always available for service and looking for work. Ruggles was commissioned a Captain and paid £400 in expense, but the troop was discharged because of a surplus of recruits. He was thereafter always called "Captain Ruggles" in Sandwich. Sandroff notes that this release was fortunate because most of those embarking lost their lives.

War with France flared in 1745, and a combined British-Provincial army reduced the major French center, Fort Louisburg on Cape Breton Island, Nova Scotia, a brilliant achievement. This fort was later returned to France in the peace treaty, but troubles with the French and their Indian allies continued all along the Canadian border. Through his seat in the General Court, Ruggles was given an extremely important assignment on a committee to visit the upper New York area to plan the building of forts on the western frontier against the French. One of his colleagues was his Harvard classmate Elijah Williams, a gifted military leader.

The Baron of Hardwick

In 1753 Ruggles moved his family to Hardwick, a new town in Worcester County. Bathsheba turned the Newcomb Tavern back to Newcomb hands as William Jr. was now twenty-two, and the other Newcombs were married or grown. All the Newcombs remained in the Cape Cod area. The move to Hardwick was not a quick decision but had doubtless been co-ordinated by many members of the extended Ruggles clan. The key move in the Ruggles group was that of Timothy's uncle, Reverend Benjamin Ruggles of Middleboro, who removed to New Braintree with his eight children. Timothy's aunt Patience and her husband James Robinson settled in Hardwick, as did four Spooner/Ruggles couples from Roxbury and Dartmouth. Of Timothy's brothers and sisters, Benjamin, Joseph, Susanna and Edward all removed to Hardwick with their families, and brother Samuel settled in Barre. As many as twenty-four Ruggles and related households moved to this new area, of whom Timothy was probably the wealthiest and most prestigious. This illustrates the process by which families in the well-populated older seacoast towns would surge out into new areas favorable for settlement.

Timothy and Bathsheba established no ordinary farm in Hardwick. He laid out a deer park and stocked it. He bought imported and local horses of excellent breeds and developed splendid hunting and riding horses. He bought prize bulls and developed a dairy herd. He laid out a large orchard with many fruit varieties. In all these activities, especially the selection of stock, the breeding patterns of his animals and the grafting and propagation of his trees, he displayed the greatest interest and observation in advanced scientific farm practice. He was able to entertain in baronial style, and his home became a magnet for travelers from all over the state. He was elected Representative to the General Court, and by 1756 was also a judge in Worcester, the County seat. These, however, were only a part of his activities.

War had broken out in 1754 with the French on four fronts: Nova Scotia, the Lake Champlain/Lake George sector of New York, the Niagara area and in the Ohio/Western Pennsylvania area. Ruggles raised a regiment from northern Worcester County in 1755, was appointed Colonel and took an honorable part in the attack on Crown Point under Sir William Johnson. This attack failed and Ruggles did not hesitate to criticize British tactics. He showed an instant grasp of terrain and use of troops, and opposed bitterly the British standard methods of marching solid bodies of troops against entrenched enemy positions. There were serious differences between the British officers (who were in charge of the regular troops and the overall effort) and their Provincial allies. The American troops considered themselves fighting for a limited contract period for the officers who had enlisted them, and would fight bravely if well led; the British considered them unreliable and undisciplined.

The next year, 1756, the American forces (all Provincials) won a significant victory at Lake George over the French Baron Diskau. The troops were led by General John Winslow of Plymouth with Ruggles second in command. Ruggles became a Brigadier General in charge of Provincial troops from Massachusetts and Rhode Island. In 1758 the brilliant French General Montcalm repulsed a British attack on Ticonderoga, with heavy British losses. The British had taken Fort Duquesne at Pittsburgh, and Fort Louisburg on Cape Breton, the latter by Lord Amherst and General Wolfe. The following year, Lord Amherst with Ruggles as second in command at last took Fort Ticonderoga. General Wolfe's forces took Quebec, although both he and Montcalm were killed. In 1760 the city of Montreal fell and the fighting subsided.

Ruggles gained wide recognition in this period as a fine officer, completely cool at all times and as a tremendous morale factor among his troops. Many young Americans who fought here later became officers in the American Revolution, and all knew that if Ruggles had chosen the Patriot side he would have been a dominant leader. Another aspect of Ruggles' success in this war is less well known, his natural ability to deal with Indian allies who were extremely valuable as scouts and rangers. Ruggles had an unusual ability to communicate with Indians, treating them courteously and respecting their outlook, which most whites did not. This may have been gained in part through his contacts in Mashpee and Herring Pond, but also must have been innate with him. When serving in the Legislature, he was regularly asked to advise on Indian matters.

After the war, many honors came to Ruggles, a Royal citation, a sinecure position of "Surveyor-General of the Woods" worth £300 per year, a gift of fifteen hundred acres of land in Princeton, Massachusetts called the Potash Farm. He went back to his agricultural pursuits, and established a biennial fair at Hardwick to encourage progress in breeding animals and improving crops. In 1762 he was elected Chief Judge of the Court of Common Pleas in Worcester, and Speaker of the Great and General Court. He was at the peak of an astonishing career. John Adams, the future President, was a young teacher in Worcester at this time, and wrote "Ruggles' grandeur consists in the quickness of his apprehension, steadiness of his attention, the boldness and strength of his thoughts and his expressions, his strict honor, conscious superiority, contempt of meanness..." He was, Adams said, a man of genius and great resolution.

A Removal to Amenia, New York

The removals of the Ruggles families to Worcester County induced a number of other families from Bristol, Plymouth and Barnstable Counties to remove there, including Nyes from Sandwich. The removal of a key family elicited a wave of decisions among those families ready at that time to make such a transfer, but needing a charismatic leader to show the way and lend encouragement in the fateful commitment. These factors are shown also in the case of Judah Swift of Pocasset who married a Falmouth girl and engaged in the business of cutting heavy timber for ships and buildings. He bought the trees on a section of Naushon Island south of Woods Hole, where large hardwoods grew in a deep bowl-shaped valley, presenting a problem to recover. By cutting a spiralling road around and down into this valley he recovered all the timber and realized a profit of three thousand silver dollars on this operation, a large sum in 1769. He took his gains and removed to a new settlement in Amenia, New York, moving his family and possessions by oxcart. A number of Wing and Barlow families from Pocasset joined this successful Swift family in the move to Amenia.

Melatiah Bourne's Will

The passing of the distinguished Judge Melatiah Bourne in 1742 allows us to see the possessions of a Sandwich family of wealth and position. Melatiah had first married Desire, daughter of Elder John Chipman, and had five sons (one deceased) and one daughter. After her death, he married Abigail (Skiff), the widow of Thomas Smith, who had four Smith children. On Bourne's death his property was divided as follows:

Widow Abigail

£75 plus £7½ for a mourning suit

One third of his books of divinity (presumably inherited from his grandfather Richard the missionary.)

Use of one third of his buildings and lands in Sandwich for her lifetime. Also one third of the household utensils and goods except stocks for sale. (He was a gold dealer.)

Services of his negro woman (unnamed) for her lifetime.

(In exchange, Abigail had to release the estate from any claim to a widow's third or rights of dower on the rest of the estate.)

Son Colonel Sylvanus of Barnstable.

£125 plus later payment of £200 from Silas.

All military arms and weapons.

Walking sticks and his watch

Right to purchase a neck of land called Quenamit (believed to be in Mashpee.)

All lands not elsewhere given.

Son John of Falmouth.

Gold shirt buttons

Several lots of land in Falmouth. (He and Sylvanus had already received certain lands by deed.)

Son Shearjashub, minister in Scituate

£100

Black wearing apparel

Son Colonel Silas of Sandwich.

Two thirds of divinity books, household utensils, buildings & lands in Sandwich.

All husbandry tools and utensils.

Tall clock.

Services of negro man, Nero, for one year, after which Nero is to be freed with clothing, bed and chest of possessions.

Daughter Bathsheba (Newcomb) Ruggles.

£25 plus release to her of money she was holding from estate of Wm. Newcomb deceased for her Newcomb children.

Abigail's four Smith children.

£57 on condition of release from other rights.

Favorite grandchildren

£12½ to Dr. Thomas Smith.

Ivory headed cane to Melatiah son of Sylvanus.

Silver shoe buckles to Joseph son of John Bourne

£12½ to each of Bathsheba's seven Newcomb children on reaching 21 or marrying.

First Parish Church.

£2½ (clearly not his favorite charity).

The big saltbox at 138 Main Street soon was entirely in Silas' hands and remained in the family until 1862. This was on the six acres of land bought in 1710 from John Dexter, and, we believe, included a second house built by Silas about 1730 on his marriage, located opposite Dock Lane (Jarves Street).

The Enlarged Meeting House

The beleaguered Reverend Benjamin Fessenden died in 1746; he "rested from his troubles and labors" as his tablet stone in Old Town Burying Ground states. After a prolonged search, Abraham Williams was found and accepted the town's offer, remaining here until his death in 1784. He must have been a healer and peacemaker, as he was able to bring the Scusset group back to the First Parish. Nevertheless, the dissident move in Scusset had touched some sentiments in the growing settlements in Pocasset and Monument for more independence, as shown by a petition from both areas in 1744/5 to be released from payments to the town for schools and the parish charges. This was denied, as was a later appeal from Monument in 1763 to be allowed to operate their own schools.

The First Parish Meetinghouse built in 1704 was about 30 x 36 feet. The town voted in 1756 to have it enlarged by lengthening the building fourteen feet. This brought it to 30 x 50 feet with the long side parallel to Main Street. A balcony on three sides was built, the pulpit was recentered, all new pews were installed and the interior was redecorated. A steeple was added on the old turret, and a new four-hundred-pound bell installed. All this was paid for through an auction of pews, the cost of which was over £20 apiece in the better locations. The committee man, Benjamin Fessenden Jr., reported in 1763 that he had sold the old bell (the Peter Adolph Memorial bell, alas!) to the Barnstable County Courthouse and that he still had a considerable surplus in the building fund. He recommended that the town paint the exterior of the building, which was done. (This is the first reference to paint in the town records.) Horse sheds had been allowed earlier behind the meetinghouse for those coming from a distance, built by the families.

Other Public Projects

The town's fourth grist mill was allowed in 1741/2 to be built on the Spring Hill River by Samuel Wing. At that time the flow was considerably greater than that flowing today. At the same time in 1741/2 the town installed its first passage for herring into Shawme Pond. The Dexter mill would have stopped any spawning runs without a fish ladder. With the new ladder the town then could have introduced a few adult fish from Herring River into the Shawme Pond and if repeated for three years this established a self-perpetuating herring run. In

1759 the town voted to build a bridge over this "waste way" which was at about the present Town Hall location. Herring were an important asset to the town, and each year the town meeting passed new regulations on the fishery, i.e., fines for illegal catching, committees to supervise catching and regulate the auction of surplus fish. After the needs of each family at one barrel apiece and the Indians at two barrels per family the surplus for auction (called "vendue") to the public was in 1765 no less than 400 barrels. These sold at about three shillings per barrel. The fine for illegal catching was nine shillings per barrel. The town bought up some of the land along Herring River to control taking. The surplus funds generated by herring auction were allocated to specific projects or divided to the townsmen with such stipulations as including widows who take care of town orphans but excluding those arrivals who have been warned out. The Herring Pond Indians and even Plymouth citizens near Herring Pond applied via the General Court to share in the surplus funds but were denied.

In 1755 Simeon Dillingham and Thomas Smith Jr. were evidently involved with packet trading, as the town records read that they:

> "have liberty to dig or clear the mud out of the Town Dock and Creek and to build a wharf so as to render it convenient in passing and landing stuffage in scows, they to be paid for wharfage by the persons landing the same until the principal and interest arising for said convenience be repaid them and then the profits of said dock and Wharf to revert to this Town, they to keep an account of their doings upon oath if required by said Town."

The town bought more upland and meadow adjacent to the dock and its approach in 1761. There seems to have been a landing on Old Harbor Creek near the harbor mouth, as in 1767 the town voted to survey a town road and cartway to the Old Harbor. This was laid out through Hoxie and Allen land leading off present Foster Road. A mill was proposed in 1765 between the upper and lower Shawme ponds. A vote on this petition was delayed and then the item seems to have been withdrawn, but the potential mill right at this key spot was recognized as a deed restriction. The mill and dam were finally built here in 1811 by the Wing owners.

Family Census 1750

There were about one hundred families in Sandwich in 1700. This more than doubled to two hundred nine by 1750, as shown in this recapitulation:

Families in 1700	100
New settlers arriving	45
Sons & grandsons forming families	346
Total family formation	491
Less deaths of head of family	139
Less removals to other towns	150
Balance in 1750	202
Actual count in 1750 incl. 7 widows heads of households	209

The census shows vigorous growth of new families from the settled stock. The five largest families (Perry, Nye, Swift, Tobey and Ellis) produced no less than one hundred eleven new families in this period, almost one third of the total. As to removals, there was no favorite relocation area. A few went to new lands in New York, Connecticut, western Massachusetts and Maine, but most went to towns in nearby Bristol and Plymouth counties, with a few moving down Cape or to Falmouth. Most arrivals came from other Cape towns. Those arrivals in this period forming well-known Sandwich branches include James Atkins; Jabez Blossom; Levi Chase; Benjamin Crocker; John Ewer; Joshua Hall; Ebenezer Howland; Shubael, Thomas, Benjamin and Cornelius Jones; Reuben Meiggs; John Percival; Ebenezer and Uriah Weeks. Reverend Fessenden listed one hundred thirty five families in Sandwich in 1730, and we find his list did not include twenty-five Quaker families, also omitting his own and that of schoolmaster John Rogers. The adjusted total of one hundred sixty-two families in 1730 is consistent with 1700/1750 census results and family charts.

Lawful Money and Old Tenor

Town meeting records, wills and deeds of this period all use the term "Old Tenor" and other descriptions of the money used in transactions. Frederick Freeman mentioned the continuing depreciation that afflicted the paper money of this period, and showed that the value of an ounce of silver in 1702 (six shillings ten pence) had risen to three Pounds in paper money in 1749, about a nine-fold depreciation. This was caused by this Province and others issuing Bills of Credit in huge amounts without specie backing. The term "Old Tenor" referred to the depreciated bills of credit and old currency notes in circulation, while "lawful money" was specie or the most recent currency. For example, the will of

Melatiah Bourne in 1742 specified that the cash bequests should all be paid in "lawful money". Only the tiny bequest to the First Parish read "Ten Pounds Old Tenor or fifty shillings lawful money"

This shows a four to one ratio between the amount in the two currencies at that time.

In 1748 Parliament voted a substantial payment to this Province to reimburse expenses incurred in capturing the great French fortress at Louisburg on Cape Breton, which had been carried out almost entirely by New England effort. A new tax of £75,000 was also voted by the General Court. These funds were earmarked to reduce the outstanding bills of credit and set up a silver base for the new currency at a rate of £2.5 or 45 shillings Old Tenor per Spanish milled dollar. (This standard coin was worth eight "pieces of eight", the familiar small coins of pirate legend.) In 1749 the main transfer of this specie was received in Boston amounting to £183,000 in silver and copper coins. The first beneficiary in Sandwich was the new minister, Abraham Williams, who in early 1748/9 had been voted a bonus of one thousand pounds Old Tenor for settling, and an annual salary of four hundred pounds, both convertible now into specie.

CHAPTER 11

THE ACADIAN EXPERIENCE

The expulsion of the French settlers in Nova Scotia known as the Acadians has become one of the great set pieces of American and Canadian history. About ten thousand persons were involved, at least sixty-five hundred of whom were uprooted and scattered along the coast from Massachusetts to the West Indies in the first year of the trauma. Their property was destroyed, families broken up and scenes of the most heartbreaking suffering enacted. The needless cruelty of the action by the British Governor in Nova Scotia was not understood in London for several years, and Governor Lawrence died before an inquiry was organized. Sandwich had a share in this drama due to its key location, and also took a part in the resettling of Nova Scotia by New England families.

Background of the Expulsion

The earliest French settlement was at Port Royal on the protected Annapolis Basin off the Bay of Fundy. The first settlement here was in 1604. The French families elected to develop meadowlands around the Basin and up the valley of the Annapolis River rather than hewing farms out of the forest. They built dikes to keep out the seawater, and floodgates to let out fresh water. Within a year this process produced clean fields for crops. Settlements spread east around the shores of the Minas Basin where the soil was exceedingly fertile. Within a century French settlements in the "Acadia" area included a few in northern Maine, many in what is now New Brunswick and Prince Edward Island, and all around mainland Nova Scotia but excluding Cape Breton Island. This settlement process was far from peaceful. French military leaders outfitted privateers to harass British shipping and fishing operations on the Banks and the New England coast, and encouraged Indian raids on settlements in Maine. Occasionally British and New England forces retaliated by attacking and destroying French settlements. One author estimates that Port Royal with its fort changed hands fourteen times between 1604 and 1713. These hostilities tended to encourage a neutral attitude on the part of the farm population who wanted only to be left alone. When they had a surplus they wanted to be able to take it to Boston. A chronology of events follows:

1710 - British forces took Port Royal and renamed it Annapolis Royal.

1713 - By the Treaty of Utrecht all of Acadia was ceded to the British. The population had one year to either leave or become British subjects.

1718 - The French residents stayed but would not swear allegiance. The British did not want to force them out as they had no settler replacements.

1730 - The population became called "Neutral French" as they were willing to swear not to take up arms against the British. They were largely of peasant stock, poorly educated but deeply religious and of good moral character. Critics called them lazy but the fact is that the fields and orchards and fisheries were so productive that they did not need back-breaking labor to live very comfortably. The French government was putting money into a massive new fort at Louisburg on Cape Breton Island to the east, and the Acadians could hoard specie made selling supplies to the garrison.

1745 - An all-New England force under Sir William Pepperell took Louisburg.

1746 - A great rescue fleet left France to retake Louisburg and rendezvous with a French army from Quebec, possibly to retake all Acadia. However the fleet met disastrous storms and illness, so that only tatters of the force returned to France. The Quebec forces stopped at present Amherst in northern Nova Scotia, while 500 British troops waited at Grand Pre quartered on the population.

1747 - In a surprise February night attack French and Indians dealt a heavy blow to the British at Grand Pre, killing about 100 and capturing or wounding many more. The French forces were driven back but deep suspicions remained over the Acadian position. Liberal British sympathized with them while hostile British regarded them as potential enemies.

1748 - The Treaty of Aix-le-Chapelle returned the Louisburg fort to France in exchange for French properties in India.

1749 - Halifax was founded. Governor Charles Lawrence sought settlers from Britain, Ireland and Protestant Europe but only a few responded to the incentives of land in unsettled areas. European Protestants and Huguenots did settle at Lunenburg on the south coast later.

1754 - French completed a new Fort Beausejour on the New Brunswick line, and the British Fort Lawrence nearby.

1755 - The British planned an attack on Beausejour and took the precaution of disarming Acadians and removing their vessels. The fort fell, but in it were found some 200 Acadians who protested they were impressed into service and were not combatants. This deepened suspicions on both sides. Representatives from Acadian towns came to Halifax to protest but instead were imprisoned. Lawrence decided on mass expulsion but in his letters to London this was read only as an action against those living around Beausejour. Lt. Colonel John Winslow from Plymouth (a descendant of Edward Winslow)was the officer in charge in the Grand Pre area. He called all the male Acadians together and advised them that the whole population would be deported as fast as ships could be procured. The people could keep money, personal and household effects but their lands, estates and animals were forfeit. Parents and small children were generally kept together but larger family groups were deliberately broken up. The vessels were overcrowded and most possessions, tools, dishes, etc. were lost even though essential for living elsewhere. About 1, 923 persons were thus evacuated from the Grand Pre area in September and another 1, 650 similarly from the Port Royal area. These were the largest and most accessible Acadian settlements. The houses and barns were burned and the cattle and sheep left to fend for themselves; all died that winter.

The Dispersion

Six of the first vessels put in to Boston in November for supplies enroute to southern Provinces where one hundred and sixty person were to be left off at Philadelphia, four hundred and thirty-two in Maryland, three hundred and sixty in Virginia, and one hundred twenty-five in South Carolina. Boston authorities were shocked at conditions on board, and ordered that one hundred people should be left in Boston to relieve the overcrowding. Boston may hardly have been aware of the magnitude of the dispersion at this time, and certainly had made no plans to receive and put up the nearly twelve hundred persons who arrived over the next few months. The targets for the East Coast Provinces were said to be:

Massachusetts	1200
Connecticut	700
New York/Pennsylvania	1200
Maryland	500
Virginia/No. Carolina	1000
So. Carolina/Georgia	500
West Indies	500
Total	5600

Barnstable's Share

Records of the Acadians in these first years of the dispersion are scanty and incomplete so that what happened to many individuals is not easy to trace, and even overall numbers in different Provinces are not known with any confidence. These people were considered as prisoners of war, outside of normal town records and were objects of suspicion and uncertainty who spoke little or no English. They were sent in family groups and sets up to twenty for further dispersal by judges and selectmen. They were to be fed and housed and where possible given employment. Their net cost to the towns was to be reported to the General Court for reimbursement, which the Province intended to recover from Nova Scotia. Many of the vouchers submitted by the various towns to the

General Court have been preserved and may be seen in the State Archives. In 1756, Barnstable started providing for a family of eight consisting of Charles Boudreau, his wife and one child; Mary Boudreau, a widow with two children; John Boudreau a bed-ridden invalid about thirty years old and an elderly lady probably mother of one of the parents. A house was rented for them. A typical quarterly bill for food and supplies to Boston amounted to £21.6.6, reduced by labor of Charles as a blacksmith, worth £3. Some quarters show credit for spinning. Donald Trayser observed that they wore wooden shoes and were good at woodcarving. Other towns found the men excellent as axmen and the women at making brooms and baskets. The problems with employment were that the towns already had all the simple skills they needed, and that there were laborers and marginal workers like Indians for whom there were already only very few paying jobs. With their language barrier the French Neutrals must have found life in these Provinces deeply frustrating, and a constant reminder of the dreadful change that had befallen them. In the Barnstable group, the grandmother died in November 1756 and a baby was born in April 1758.

Visitors From South Carolina

The Acadians in Maryland at least had Catholics to pray with. The governor soon complained that "they have eaten us up." Virginia and North Carolina refused to accept the Acadians at all, with the result that about one thousand destined to be sent here were transported to England. Only after the war in 1763 could these be repatriated to France. In South Carolina and Georgia the Acadians were allowed to shift for themselves, with the result that the enterprising started to build or repair small vessels with which to sail north. So swiftly did they do this that on July 1, 1756, Governor Lawrence wrote to Massachusetts that he had learned that some of the Neutrals from the American south had already arrived at Petitcodiac (presently Moncton, New Brunswick) and that more were on the way. Governor Lawrence urged that any arriving from the south be stopped at Massachusetts and held there or his whole effort would be frustrated.

Now Sandwich enters the picture. Captain Elisha Bourne lived on the Manomet River at the head of the tidewater. Bourne was then twenty-three and unmarried. He was astonished on July 20, 1756, to find seven small sailing vessels drawing in. These were one- and two-masted vessels holding a company of no less than ninety-nine Acadians including many women and children. Their leader was a fifty-four-year-old grandfather named Jacques Vigneau, commonly called Jacques Maurice. They had come from Georgia and South Carolina by short stages along the coast, being passed along and encouraged to keep going. Now, however, they were short of supplies, dirty, some sick, and the vessels unready for the long haul around Cape Cod. They had no choice but to put in at Manomet to rest, and hopefully to get help to draw the vessels over to the other Bay. Bourne allowed them to use a campsite and his woodpiles, and began organizing food supplies. He promptly sent word to Colonel James Otis in Barnstable, who ordered that the group be detained awaiting instructions from Boston. On July 23 a letter went off from Boston to Nova Scotia with the unwelcome news; Lieutenant-Governor Phipps stated:

> "I have hereupon ordered their persons and boats to be seized and three or four of them sent to Boston in order to be examined.
>
> "Your Excellency is sensible that a very great number have already been received and supported here, a number much beyond our proportions in case they were to have been distributed among the Colonies by a Rule of that kind and a number much greater than your Excellency originally designed to send here. Norwithstanding this I am fully of opinion that it would be unsafe to suffer them to proceed any further.
>
> "The General Assembly is to set here on the 11th August and as his Majesty's Council apprehended they will be very averse to receive this additional number into the Government, they have therefore desired me to write to your Excellency and ask your further care of these People that they may not remain a burthern upon this province. Phipps."

This group was finally ordered to Boston for dispersal and left on August 5, walking to Sandwich harbor for embarkation with their goods carried on carts. Expenses in Sandwich were carefully recorded for reimbursement. They included:

Soap, a cowhide, 121 feet of boards, 16 gallons of milk, 2 barrels of mackeral, 97 lb salt beef, 195 lbs fresh beef, 50 lbs mutton, pork, a fat sheep, 2½ bushels corn meal, 2½ bushels rye flour, prunes, cheese, turnips, molasses, bread.

Hire of horses and carts to transfer baggage and three of the smaller vessels over land to Cape Cod Bay.

Use of a house the night before departure and eight guards for fear of their moving away in the boats.

Bread and meal put aboard the sloop for women and children.

"Cord wood lay cut which they burned night and day which I can't judge to be less than four cords." (Elisha Bourne's bill)

"To other time I spent in hearing their cries and hungry complaints, riding and sending about to buy provisions, and hindering my own business." (further charges by Bourne)

Sheriff Gorham submitted his own bill to the Province "For transporting 99 French persons Sandwich to Boston £31.7.10."

So the ninety-nine went on to Boston, leaving four vessels here. One wonders whether the Boudreaus in Barnstable were allowed to meet their compatriots. Sheriff John Gorham and his deputy Barnabas Gibbs of Sandwich accompanied the group to Boston, where they were first lodged in Suffolk

County jail. After some delay it was decided to settle twenty in Dartmouth and five in Rochester. Gorham and Gibbs brought these twenty-five back to Sandwich thence on by packet to their new towns. The other seventy-four were to be distributed to ten towns in Bristol County overland from Boston, but the potent Jacques Maurice arranged somehow that his large immediate family of eighteen be kept together and we find them first living in Charlestown. This group from Georgia was all especially identified because its total costs were to be accumulated and charged to Nova Scotia. The other refugees costs in Massachusetts had to be for this Province's own account as a contribution to the war effort, and in view of Nova Scotia's impoverished condition with almost no settlers. The Jacques Maurice party was regarded with extra suspicion by the ultra-vigilant since it had first hand knowledge of American ports and could guide French warships to attack. Because of this "danger to the Provinces, " Charlestown petitioned in September that the Maurice family should be removed inland to Leicester or Spencer. This was done. As of March 30, 1757, Leicester reported that both "James Morris" and his wife were sick and unable to work, and asked that they be relocated. In 1758 they were still at Leicester, seven unable to work and up from eighteen to twenty-one members. They were transferred to Roxbury in December 1758, where Jacques asked for the proceeds from sale of his vessels. He did collect £7. 8. 2 from the sale of the four at Sandwich, auctioned off by Colonel Cotton.

As of March 18, 1758 Nova Scotia was charged £411 for the special group from the south. Other refugee charges by then amounted to over £5300 entirely borne by Massachusetts; by June 1759 the total had risen to over £8500 and the Province decided to seek relief directly from the Crown.

Nova Scotia Seeks Immigrants

In 1758 the fortress at Louisburg was again captured by British and New England troops. This time it was razed, assuring British control of the whole Atlantic area. Having had poor response in its efforts to attract European or British settlers, the Nova Scotia government sent out a proclamation to the New England area advertising free farms, tax relief, and freedom from tithes for support of the Anglican Church. This appeal created interest in many Massachusetts families, especially in Cape Cod and Nantucket where some seamen or soldiers had already been to Nova Scotia and seen the fishing and fertile fields. From 1759 on, New England families began to move to Nova Scotia in substantial numbers. Liverpool was settled by people from Plymouth, Kingston, Eastham and Chatham. So many families left Chatham that the town was greatly reduced. The beautiful Annapolis Valley and Grand Pre areas were settled. The first arrivals at Yarmouth at the west end of Nova Scotia were three from Sandwich who arrived in 1761, Sealed Landers (1722-aft 1767) and wife Thankful (Handy); Ebenezer Ellis (1729-1818) and wife Hannah; Moses Perry (1714-1811) and wife Eleanor (Ellis). These three men were mutual third cousins through Freeman descent, and Ellis and Perry were brothers-in-law. Landers brought with him on the little transport *Pompey Dick* a pair of granite millstones, and built his mill in a narrow valley just north of the harbor. One of these stones has been placed upright with a bronze plaque honoring Sealed Landers as a founder of the town. Other Sandwich families who established important branches in Nova Scotia were the Tuppers, Burgesses and Freemans.

Meanwhile, the capture of Quebec City in 1759 and of Montreal in 1760 ensured a firm British title to all of eastern Canada. More questions continued to be raised in England as to the expulsion of the Neutral French from their settled lands both in terms of its inhumanity, its concealment, the waste of resources in Nova Scotia and the costs and confusion caused in the other Provinces. A full-scale inquiry was ordered in 1760 but Lawrence died before it got underway, a virtual suicide.

The Trahans at Sandwich

In Massachusetts the State Archives and the Journals of the General Court record the flood of bills from the various towns where Acadians were quartered, their petitions for removal or relief, and attendant problems in trying to find them employment and accomodation. In 1760, there was a significant shift of status of the French Neutrals from prisoners of war held at the expense of the Province to temporary residents of the towns where they lived, to be treated like the town's poor at town expense. This caused a widespread relocation to towns which had not had them before. There was much confusion so that a comprehensive census was demanded from each county, from which the new allocations to towns can be found. Barnstable County had gotten off lightly, but now had to put up thirty-seven individuals as follows:

Sandwich Joseph Trahan wife and twin children. (Joseph was a son of John of Eastham)

Falmouth Mary, Joseph and John Trahan, children of Joseph of Sandwich.

Eastham John Trahan wife and two grown children, Charles and Mary.

Truro Peter and John Jr. sons of John Trahan of Eastham.

Barnstable Boudreau family of eight.

Yarmouth John Pellerin, wife and five children.

Harwich Dominick Cloistre wife and four children

Chatham Three persons to be sent from Nantucket (where some 37 neutrals were quartered).

The town must have paid for rent and food for the Trahans for some period but their names do not appear in town meeting records. From modern genealogical records of the Acadian families we learn that Joseph Trahan was born in 1728 and married his wife Anne or Agnes LeBlanc in 1750. The twins were born in 1759 so were very small when they lived here. Possibly the Trahans lived with some Sandwich family and earned enough so that no town charges were required.

The intriguing Trahan visit here seems to have left no traces.

After the Peace Treaty

With the signing of the Treaty of Paris in 1763 all Canada became British with the exception of two small islands south of Newfoundland called Miquelon and St. Pierre. These remain French to this day. They provided a place of settlement for Acadians and also a transshipping center to France. The record of evacuation of the French families from the American provinces is not clear, but obviously most went either to Quebec or to mainland France by various routes. State Archives records contain a list of one thousand nineteen persons at Boston desiring to go to Old France. A list of four hundred ninety-one persons in 1766 petitioned to go to Canada, but the governor there declined to promise support while they got settled. Similarly the Massachusetts governor refused to provide further funds. By 1767 it was estimated that less than one hundred remained in Massachusetts. A group of nine families from Cape Sable (in the Pubnico and Barrington area) had lived in Massachusetts since their removal in 1756, and were allowed to go back to this same area, the only Nova Scotians known to have been directly repatriated in this way. These were Neutral French of a more educated background than the others, having arrived with Charles de la Tour in 1609.

Those Acadians returning to Nova Scotia from New Brunswick and Quebec after 1763 found their old lands in the Minas Basin and Annapolis Valley closed to them, and had to settle in unoccupied lands of poorer soil at the west end of the province, north of Yarmouth. Their descendants are still there today. The patriarch Jacques Vigneau settled at Miquelon Island and many of his grandchildren on the Magdalen Islands in the St. Lawrence River. The Trahans from Cape Cod settled in Napierville south of Montreal.

Nova Scotia's Progress

The New Englanders who removed to Nova Scotia seem to have put down their roots swiftly and worked hard. The New Englanders came as Congregationalists but without ministers or much religious ardor. The new towns later had either Baptist or Methodist churches. As the Revolution loomed, a few more New England families migrated, and during and after the war, a number of Tories or "empire Loyalists" came to settle. The earlier New England stock seemed not to want to become involved, distrusting what they knew of Samuel Adams and John Hancock, and resentful of the occasional American privateer raids on the coast, but still not interested in joining the local British forces either. The new arrivals were heartily welcomed and there was none of the deadly Patriot/Tory division that so scarred life in the American provinces.

In 1785 a Scottish minister Reverend Dr. Andrew Brown came to Nova Scotia and for the first time wrote down the facts of the old French Neutral settlements and their cruel expulsion or imprisonment, with destruction of all their farms and vessels. This he could learn from survivors first hand, particularly the literate group at Cape Sable, and his writings in England after his return brought this matter to the attention of the learned world for the first time. Dr. Brown's material is said to have been the chief source used by Longfellow in his dramatic poem "Evangeline" which became a classic. This one poem did so much to establish and dramatise the Acadian story that in the Grand Pre National Historic Park are both a bust of Longfellow and an heroic statue of Evangeline, whose mere name now symbolizes the whole drama.

CHAPTER 12

PROBLEMS ON THE RESERVATION

The formation of the Mashpee reservation south of Sandwich and the establishment of a successful church there were due mainly to the labor and devotion of the uniquely talented Richard Bourne. The progress of this Indian reservation and eventual town continues to be of direct interest to Sandwich in later periods because of the involvement of the Bourne family in Indian affairs, and the land transactions which determined Mashpee borders with its neighbors.

After the death of Bourne in 1682 a general law on Indian village organization in Plymouth Colony was passed with the familiar purpose "for their better regulating and that they may be brought to live orderly soberly and diligently."

The main features were:

A salaried overseer was to be appointed by the Court in each town where Indians live, "to take oversight and Government of the Indians."

Every tenth Indian was to be appointed by the overseer to "take the inspection care and oversight of his nine men and present their faults and misdemeanors to the overseer." These were called tithingmen.

The overseer and tithingmen shall appoint constables of the Indians who shall attend courts, serve warrants, inflict penalties, attach property.

Every Indian shall pay such rates for his head and estate as the Court shall appoint, to be gathered by the constable.

Once every year the Indians shall be called together to be read all the capital and criminal laws of the Colony that they may know and observe them. Every Indian shall be subject to the laws made for the English and for breach of them shall suffer the same penalty. All Indians for drunkardness shall be severely punished.

No Indians are to travel without a permit.

Indian servants to the English who run away shall be apprehended, whipped and sent home.

The Governor of the Colony is to take care of the preaching of the

> Gospel among them, admitting such Indians to preach as he shall think fit, and to distribute among them what yearly comes from England (funds from the Society for the Propagation).

This policy toward a now defeated and dependent people was not overly punitive but neither did it show any concern for education, for imparting new skills, for providing aids in agriculture or housing or tools by which the Indians could become more a part of the civilization that now surrounded them.

Bourne's Successors

Bourne's religious successor was Simon Popmonnet, the son of venerable Sachem Paupmunnock. Simon preached entirely in the Indian language, but did not enjoy the prestige and authority of his predecessor. Shearjashub Bourne was named the overseer for Mashpee. He had worked closely with his father on Indian affairs and spoke the language. His unusual name (from Isaiah 7:3) means, "A remnant shall remain or survive to carry on the work," and surely provides an interesting coincidence. The historian Frederick Freeman says of him "Shearjashub Bourne Esq. carried on a lucrative trade with the Indians; but in all transactions was noted for integrity. He had great influence with the Mashpees and was highly respected in every community." His tombstone in Old Town Burying Ground reads "He was a virtuous, righteous and merciful man and a great friend to the Indians."

Shearjashub Bourne's Lands

Richard Bourne's will passed all his housing (worth £300) to the widow and children of deceased son Job. Since the Peters Pond house is never referred to again it may have been dismantled and removed. The Sandwich village house was sold by Job's heirs after the death in 1713 of Ruth (Bourne) Chipman. Shearjashub inherited these properties:

Peters Pond neck
Mashpee Pond thirty-acre lot on which he had his home.
Monomoscoy neck and upland
Ten acres on Mashpee River, half to use only, half to own.
Rights to alewives, hay, cutting and grazing.

Two land transactions in 1684 show Shearjashub's central position as overseer. He arranged to build a new meetinghouse at Briant's Neck on Santuit Pond in place of the earlier building there, and in exchange got clear title to the ten acres on Mashpee River. Then he provided a cash advance to the tribe with which they purchased the freedom of their countryman Tom Wampetucke who faced deportation for burglary; in exchange Shearjashub was deeded another neck of land in Waquoit Bay, described as east of Waquoit River, probably referring to Seapit Neck. This was called "a neck of barren land" in 1685.

The Confirmation of Mashpee

Shearjashub and the Indian leaders in Mashpee must have sensed a lack of security in their existing deeds and agreements on land, and decided that more specific legal protection for Mashpee was needed. An important document was signed by Governor Thomas Hinckley and entered in Plymouth Colony Records in 1685. It referred to the December 11, 1665 deed and the November 20, 1666 confirmation quoted in chapter 5, and described the borders of Mashpee as follows:

> "to the westward of Waquoit to a little creek... called Manomoyest, and to the mouth of said Waquoit Harbor to the sea, and from said Manomoyest into the land unto Ashumet Pond and half a mile to the westward of said pond, and so from pond to pond and place to place as is the known northerly bounds thereof. The easterly line runs between Barnstable lands and said Indians in the east leaving the skirts of good land lying next to the eastside of Santuit Pond unto said Indians according to the known and accustomed bounds thereof... and southerly to the sea."

The several pieces of land given to Richard Bourne or to Shearjashub are then described and the document certifies that these plots will be respected. It concludes:

> "The Court on consideration of the premises doth so far confirm said land to the said Indians to be perpetually to them and their children, as that no part of them shall be granted to or purchased by any English whatsoever by the Court's allowance without the consent of all the said Indians."

This basic confirmation is rightly regarded as the full authority for the existence of the reservation from this time on because of the details of the borders and the formal approval of the governor and Court to the protection of the land.

Shearjashub's Further Lands

In 1688 Shearjashub was given a further specific confirmation deed to his Mashpee lands by William Bradford Jr., mentioning the Peters Pond neck, the home lot of thirty acres, the ten acres on Mashpee River, and the two big necks on salt water. However the wording describing these two latter lots is very different from that in the 1685 grant, so as to make the lots or necks impossible to bound. These changes could hardly be a mistake and strongly suggest obfuscation or deception.

In 1694/5 in his first grant obtained through the authority of the new Court at Boston, Shearjashub was given "30 to 40 acres near his home" and "20 or 30 acres upland with skirts of meadow at Waquoit." The word "Mashpee" does not appear in this act and the requirement of prior approval of the tribe may not have been known in Boston. The Mashpee Pond lot was in fact confirmed by the Indians in 1699/1700, (when it already had Ezra Bourne's house on it) plus liberty to cut firewood and graze nearby. In 1718/9 the Indians sold him eight acres just south of his two lots on Mashpee Pond, running between the Pond and South Sandwich Road. On it was the wigwam of old Caleb Popmonnet and a few apple trees, where Caleb was to live for his lifetime.

Mashpee Borders

The earliest definition of the Sandwich/Mashpee border is found in town meeting records of May 1705. In current terms it ran from the Five-Mile stone off Asa Meiggs Road northwest to the present bound at Cotuit Road and John Ewer Road, thence west and slightly south past the shore of Peters Pond to the Sandwich/Falmouth Road (Route 130) thence down the Sandwich/Falmouth Road to the Falmouth line.

The formal definition of the Falmouth/Mashpee border is given by Freeman from Falmouth records of 1725, reading as follows:

> *"Beginning at a creek called Moonomoiest near Wauquoit, and from said Moonomoiest on a straight line about N.W. by N. to a certain tree marked by a heap of stones at the southernmost end of Ashimuit Pond; from thence westerly to a small pine tree now standing near the county road that leads from Sandwich to Falmouth; from thence by the aforesaid road easterly till it meets with the Sandwich line."*

This definition is consistent with the western border of Mashpee described in 1685 as quoted above. Mashpee land accordingly went to the Childs River and included all Waquoit Bay, and also included a triangle west of Ashumet Pond. We have not been able to find any evidence of grants of land to whites in these Waquoit and Ashumet sectors beyond the Bourne grants quoted, but clearly they were settled by whites early. Freeman states without explanation "a large tract on Waquoit Bay was alienated from the Indians about the year 1700 and now belongs to Falmouth."

Decline of Indian Population

The population of Indians at the end of Plymouth Colony was about 214 adults in Mashpee and adjacent places (Falmouth, Scorton Hill, Oyster Harbor); 180 Indians to whom Mr. Thomas Tupper preacheth (Herring Pond, Manomet and Pocasset); 500 elsewhere in Plymouth and Bristol Counties under the general care of John Cotton, and 505 under Reverend Samuel Treat (Yarmouth to Truro). Of the Mashpee Indians, 141 were said to be Praying Indians, or acknowledged Christians. Outside of Mashpee the Indian population continued to decline. Freeman describes how effective Reverend Treat was with Indians, preaching in their language, visiting them in their wigwams and joining in their festivals. However no new reservation on the lower Cape was established, and Freeman states "when brought into contiguity with the English and especially after they had surrendered their lands, they wilted and died!"

Regulations of Massachusetts Bay

After the formation of the Massachusetts Bay Province centered in Boston, the edicts and deeds of the former Plymouth Colony remained in local effect, but a new thrust and attitude evolved in the General Court, and possibly some of the protection that the Mashpees had enjoyed under Governor Hinckley, (who knew them personally) now weakened. A new "Act for the Better Rule and Government of the Indians" was posted from Boston in 1693/4, beginning in the accustomed way "To the intent that the Indians may be forwarded in civility and Christianity, and that drunkenness and other vices be the more effectually suppressed amongst them.." The Governor was impowered to appoint one or more commissioners to have the inspection, care and government of the Indians in their several places and reservations; to have the power of a Justice of the Peace, to hear cases, and to appoint constables and other officers amongst them. Fines and punishments for drunkenness and for supplying drink were the chief offenses provided for in the act, again saying nothing about health, education, employment or protection from exploitation.

A petition by Simon Popmonnet of Mashpee to the General Court in 1700 shows the emerging problem. Indians were encouraged to get into debt through credit purchases or cash fines, and then on collection the rigor of the law permitted binding out children or adults as servants or enforced laborers for long periods. The Indian had nothing of value to sell except his future labor or that of his children. This exploitation was deliberately fostered by the Courts which specified heavy fines rather than imprisonment or corporal punishment, thereby setting up the prisoner for enforced labor. Popmonnet entreated that the English not be allowed to sell to Indians on credit, and that no Indian be made a servant but with the consent of two justices of the peace. Behind the Indians' lack of cash or other assets was his whole background of starting from a simpler culture with few material goods, and his encouragement now to live as the whites did with dishes, tools, cattle, horses, clothing, blankets, all of which had to be bought from the whites. There was little cash income on the plantation except that derived from weaving baskets or selling fish. The only employment outside the plantation readily open to Indians were military service or sailing on packets, whalers or privateers, and these were dangerous and poorly paid. In contacts with the whites, the Indians were made to feel worthless, ignorant and degraded. Of those who left the plantation, few came back. Popmonnet's 1700 petition produced no known change.

It took eighteen years before an act was passed in 1718 providing what Popmonnet had sued for, that the Indians were not allowed to make contracts, bonds or bills unless with the approval of two justices of the peace; and that no indenture as servants be allowed except with approval of two justices of the peace, both to be present at the same time. This law was extended in 1726 to prohibit binding out for servitude of any married Indian, or of a child without the parents' consent; that debts of over forty shillings must be approved by a County Court to be collectible; that Indians may be signed on for two-year voyages of whalers and fishing vessels, or for one-year terms on farms or vessels but only with approval of two justices; that a deposit of £100 must be lodged for safe return of those carried overseas; and that terms of existing indentures beyond one year could be reviewed. The provisions of this new law clearly showed where the abuses were found.

Events in Mashpee

The meetinghouse built in 1684 on Briant's Neck in Santuit Pond proved to be far from central, and in 1717 it was moved to the present meetinghouse site on Route 28. The move was reportedly made by securing the whole building to a solid frame and drawing it on log rollers. The long-time Commissioner Shearjashub Bourne died in 1719 and was replaced by his son Ezra, already a judge and Representative at the General Court. The changes of law in 1718 regarding Indian debts and indenture may possibly be related to this succession. The Indian minister, Simon Popmonnet, died about 1722 after forty years of service, and the question of his successor was an important one. Judge Samuel Sewall (whose own career extended back to the time of Richard Bourne) recommended Joseph Bourne, son of Judge Ezra, freshly graduated from Harvard. Sewall was one of those responsible for disbursement of the income from the Society for the Propagation of the Gospel, and was fully aware of Mashpee problems. Possibly he felt that the father-son combination of Bournes in these two key positions would create new dignity and status in the community. Joseph worked hard on his Algonquian and finally was accepted by the Indian congregation in 1726, being ordained in 1729. Regrettably he never seemed to develop the power and the skill that marked so many of his gifted family. In 1742 he was dismissed by his religious superiors over a civil charge of giving three parishioners a small amount of rum. Frederick Freeman cites a different account, that he was released for "complaining much of the ill-treatment which the Indians received, and of the neglect of the commissioners with regard to his support." The Indian community was determined to preserve and protect their Indian church and language, and immediately accepted and ordained an Indian from Falmouth, Solomon Briant, who had been opposed by unnamed white interests.

The Act of 1746

Mashpee as a reservation and incipient town continued to suffer severely from lack of civic income. There were no taxes since the occupants had so little income, and no Province allowance or other way to meet basic civic expenses such as repair of roads, support of schools and aid to the sick and elderly. The Indians had small gardens but with land owned in common there was no way for entrepreneurs to develop large farms to produce salable crops. Certain Indians cut and sold wood, but had no right to contract with a white man to cut and export wood systematically. In an effort to foster better land-use and develop a real income base for the Indians, a law was passed in 1746 applicable to all Indian plantations in the Province. It provided that three guardians be appointed, near to each plantation, with the power (for a seven year period) to allot land and meadow to each Indian family for their particular improvement, with the remainder of the reservation available to be let out to "suitable persons." The income was to support the sick and elderly, to pay debts of the inhabitants and to be distributed among them "at the discretion of the guardians." Any prior agreements between Indians and outsiders as to wood sales, marsh hay, turpentine or planting were voided.

This act may have been well intended, and the need for community income was indeed desperate, but the guardians' power under the act was despotic, enabling them to favor certain whites and to punish protesting Indians through setting rates, choosing land and distributing income. The opportunities for corruption and exploitation were endless, and could be well concealed in the annual reports. The guardians for Mashpee in this seven-year period were Colonel Sylvanus Bourne, Honorable James Otis and Mr. David Crocker, all of Barnstable. Ezra Bourne was at this time called clerk of the Mashpee proprietors. Sylvanus Bourne was a nephew of Ezra's, son of Ezra's brother Judge Melatiah of Sandwich. He was a member of the Governor's Council and a powerful figure in the Province and county. Both he and Otis benefited from sales to Indians. The effect of the act in Mashpee was predictably a burst of outrage. Twenty-four proprietors addressed a moving petition to the General Court in 1748 over the losses of land and claimed that a reduction of income was being suffered. The State Archives record a stream of petitions to have the guardians removed but the General Court continued to approve their accounts and in 1754 dismissed the petitions and reappointed the guardians for another seven years.

The Indians' claim of reduced net income in this unhappy period is borne out by their enforced consent to sell some of their common land to Ebenezer Thomas in 1755, in order to raise funds to repair their meetinghouse. Once before, in 1743, Solomon Briant had had to appeal to the General Court to sell Indian land in a desperate need for funds. The location of these lost lands is not given, but may have been in either Ashumet or Waquoit sectors which were finally completely alienated. The meetinghouse repairs were inadequate because in 1758 a new meetinghouse was built with funds from the Society for the Propagation. The new meetinghouse was a tribute to Reverend Solomon Briant who had worked hard to keep his community and church together. Now however a new minister was assigned to Mashpee in 1758, a white man, Reverend Gideon Hawley, a Yale graduate of 1749 with Indian experience among the Iroquois in New York and at the Indian school at Stockbridge, Massachusetts. Hawley thought Mashpee a beautiful place, but the Indians appeared to him "abject" compared to the wild free Iroquois. Briant remained as joint pastor preaching in the Indian language while the new minister (although he spoke Algonquian) only preached in English.

REVEREND GIDEON HAWLEY (1726-1807) This sketch in charcoal was executed by his son Gideon Junior. A Connecticut native, Hawley served fifty years in Mashpee at the Congregational Church and initially supported then strongly opposed the status of Mashpee as an independent District and incipient town. Courtesy of Sandwich Historical Society.

Mashpee District

Now a truly extraordinary event occurred. A young schoolteacher named Reuben Cognehew had settled in Mashpee, possibly a Mohican from Connecticut. Seeing the strange form of government control that prevailed in Mashpee, he set out on his own for London and presented the grievances direct to King George III. He must have made an appealing witness because he was given a hearing, and his visit produced instructions from the Crown to Governor Bernard in Boston to look into the matter. The Governor called Cognehew "a very self-important fellow" but did ask the General Court to appoint a committee. This committee reviewed the long record of Indian protests against the guardian system, and received many more of the same in its hearings. Finally in 1763 the General Court passed the act making Mashpee a District, a step in white settlements that usually led to full town status. In Mashpee the initial government apparatus had to be partly white but basic decisions were left to the vote of the accepted proprietors so that the town could really be said to manage its internal affairs. It was to elect five overseers, of whom two must be English; a district clerk and a treasurer both of whom must be English; two wardens and one or more constables. Of great importance was the fact the town could decide what persons would be admitted as inhabitants. The right to vote in town affairs, however, was restricted to proprietors, and to become a proprietor one had to demonstrate birth to a Mashpee mother or father. Land was still held in common although settled families had clearly recognized areas of accepted activity. Only proprietors had vested rights to the commons, and as before, a grant of common land to a non-proprietor had to have both broad proprietor approval and also an act of the General Court showing why it was in the Indians' interest to release part of their commons. Unless married to Indians, whites could not live in Mashpee proper. However, as with Ezra and Joseph Bourne, they could live on the lands legally released to them and could sell or pass on such lands freely. The transition to a new order for Mashpee with its euphoric promise for the future was marked by the deaths in 1764 of both Ezra Bourne, 88, and Colonel Sylvanus Bourne, 70. Ezra, as son and heir of Shearjashub, inherited all the Bourne lands in Mashpee, had spoken the language and was a lifelong Mashpee resident. His role in the long record of suppression of Indian rights in his time is difficult to assess. His nephew Sylvanus was a man of distinguished position in the social, political and economic world in Massachusetts, who had defended the guardian system over the Indians to the last.

There was some increase in Mashpee population after 1763, composed of a varied mix of those who knew of its existence and advantages. There were Indians from other tribes in eastern New England and Long Island. Hutchins lists a few whites who were allowed to settle: a man named MacGregor from Manchester, England; four Hessian soldiers who elected to stay during the Revolution and married Mashpee women; a Mexican and an east Indian from Bombay. The largest new group were free blacks or escaped slaves for whom marriage to Indian women meant a chance for their children to be free. By a historic coincidence, there was a surplus of Indian women and a surplus of black men. The Indian men had to seek employment at sea or in the military or on farms, and many never came back to Mashpee. By contrast, black slaves were drawn as boys and men for labor in the New World. Blacks in Massachusetts had risen steadily from about two hundred in 1676 to over five thousand in 1776. There were doubtless black or mulatto residents accepted in Mashpee well before 1763 as the terms of the 1763 act refer repeatedly to the "Indian and mulatto inhabitants."

Blacks in Sandwich

References to blacks in vital records and in probate records only became common in the 1730s. The earliest mention in Sandwich of a black man is the 1686 sale of Harry, a Negro aged 29 from John Dexter to Jonathan Hallett. Jonathan Tobey sold to Zaccheus Wing in 1735 a mulatto boy Stephen, five. In Old Town Burying Ground is the grave of Jesse, who died in 1737 aged two, son of a servant of Melatiah Bourne. We have noted the two servants of Melatiah Bourne in his will of 1742. Black Jenny was brought up in the family of Elisha Bourne at Manomet. Titus Winchester, the slave of Reverend Williams was born about 1742. The will of Ezra Bourne in 1747 mentioned his Negro servant, Cathron. Newport, the servant of widow Rebecca Fessenden, married one Ruth Kiah in 1749/50. In Plymouth vital records, marriages between blacks are listed as seven in the 1730's, then two or three each decade thereafter. When the new balcony of the Sandwich meetinghouse was built in 1756 it was ordered "that the Committee provide a place aloft for all Negroes, Mulattos and Indians, and that they not be allowed the liberty to set below or on the stairs."

Changes in Mashpee

Accompanying and partly caused by the new population in Mashpee, there was a steady move away from wigwams into frame houses, and a progressive decline of the use of the Algonquian language in favor of English. Earlier there had been the beginning of visiting Indian ministers from Martha's Vineyard and elsewhere which spread the Indian consciousness of their numbers and interests. The arrival of Hawley in 1758 however, signaled the increasing use of English. Solomon Briant became elderly and died in 1775; Freeman says of him that there was finally "some dissatisfaction on the part of the Indians," that he was "not sufficiently prudent in the admission of members" and that he was "rather deficient in economy." The decades of change further weakened traditional Indian culture through the deaths of several respected figures: Isaac Popmet died 1758 at 80, last nominal Chief Sachem; Zephaniah Popmet died 1767 at 90, a man who remembered Richard Bourne; Deacon Zaccheus Popmet died 1770 at 85, a teacher. The deaths of Ezra Bourne in 1764 and of the former Reverend Joseph Bourne in 1767 removed senior whites who were local residents and used the Indian language. These deaths and other changes had the effect of weakening the established Congregational Church in Mashpee as Hawley increasingly isolated himself from the stream of change around him, becoming indifferent to Indians and hostile to blacks and other strangers. He had at first strongly supported the Cognehew effort to secure district status, and enjoyed being one of the commissioners. He came to see the changes it brought as all bad and immoral, and felt that Mashpee must have new and much sterner regulations.

The American Revolution in Mashpee

The Revolution brought an end to the English funds from the Society for Propagation of the Gospel which had been Hawley's chief support. He managed to get an allowance of £100 per year from the Williams Fund at Harvard, and in 1779 got a personal grant of two hundred acres of Mashpee land for his own support. The district also set aside four hundred acres in 1783 to produce income from wood sales to support the meetinghouse. Hawley was allowed to cut wood on this lot. The Mashpee young men joined various American militia units for limited periods with reenlistments, and many joined the Continental Army for long periods. It is probably true that for its size Mashpee contributed more men to the Continental forces than any other town. Except for Army service there were few alternatives. Reverend Hawley later wrote that in 1783 there were seventy widows in Mashpee, and this statement has been repeated by later writers to suggest a terrible war mortality. We find there were thirty-six widows in Mashpee in 1767, and can only find proof of death in service of three or four men. The problem with studying war service of Mashpee men is that they enlisted from many towns and had in many cases adopted white names such as Tobey, Hatch, or Babcock, so that Mashpee identification is uncertain.

The End of the District

Hawley commenced soon to lobby in the legislature for a new law to govern the Mashpees. Possibly his dignified appearance and long record of missionary service was allowed undue credit, and his punitive attitude toward the mixed peoples of Mashpee may have found an overly sympathetic ear in the frustrated Court. While the country had won its independence, the Act of June 12, 1788 put Mashpee back under guardians again as a plantation. The language is hostile, repeating "Indian, Mulatto, and Negro Proprietors" frequently. Three guardians were appointed with sweeping powers to allot land; to lease land out to "suitable" persons; to bring action for ejection against trespassers and illegal entrants; to terminate leases and existing agreements on sale of wood made by the inhabitants; and to approve indentures. The guardians appointed were Reverend Hawley and two Barnstable men, John Percival and Reuben Fish. This act was superceded in January 30, 1789 by a new act providing for a board of overseers of "five discreet and disinterested persons" two from Barnstable County and three from other Counties, with the power to appoint one or more guardians to be the direct supervisors of affairs. A further revision March 4, 1790 enabled the overseers to enforce rental payments from new arrivals and to set up a census of accepted proprietors of Indian descent with power to remove those not approved by the proprietors.

Lands of the Bournes In Or Near Mashpee

A map of Mashpee shows these various areas (below), and a chart of Bourne descent is included here showing the family members for ready identification (end of chapter).

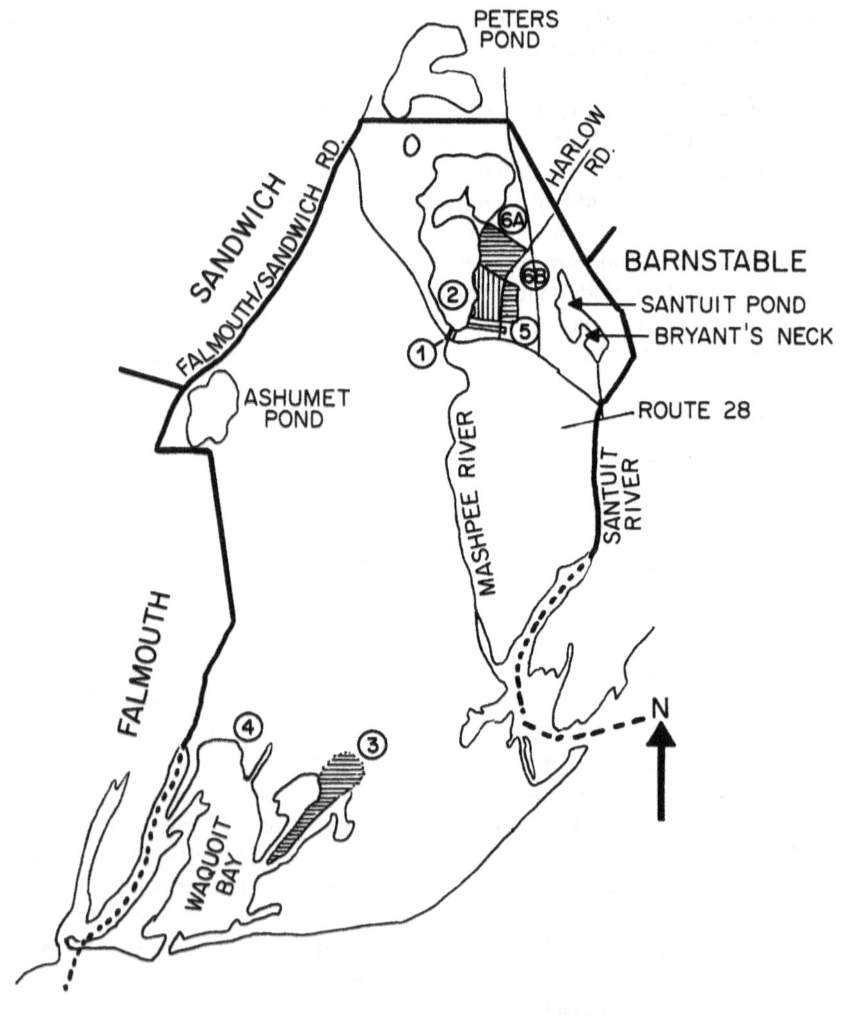

MAP OF BOURNE LANDS IN MASHPEE (previous page) - Reservation boundaries with Falmouth, Sandwich and Barnstable were formally defined in 1685. Before this in 1671/2 the Indians had given Richard Bourne a five acre neck in Peters Pond, then considered as Indian land. Other lands granted by the Indians to Bourne family members of five generations were:

1. *A ten-acre millsite on Mashpee River at Mashpee Pond.*
2. *Two house lots and a lot from Caleb Popmonnet east of Mashpee Pond, about eighty acres in all.*
3. *Peninsula of Monomoscoy and nearby upland called Aunta anta.*
4. *A neck and a lot in the Waquoit area.*
5. *A twelve-acre lot granted to Reverend Joseph Bourne.*
6. *Lands granted to Nathan Bourne in exchange for his giving up family rights to cut hay, take herring, pasture cattle and cut wood on Mashpee commons. This was called "The Bourne Purchase "and comprised (A) a one hundred-ten-acre lot at Great Conaumet and (B) a sixty-five-acre lot adjoining the houselots on Mashpee Pond.*

During long tenure of ownership by Ezra Bourne of the family's Mashpee lands (1714-1764) there is no record of his buying or selling any land in Mashpee. His eldest son Reverend Joseph occupied the house of Shearjashub on the two-house compound after his graduation from Harvard in 1722 and for his lifetime. After his ordination in the Mashpee church, Joseph was given a separate twelve-acre lot in 1730 by the Indians, running between Mashpee Pond and South Sandwich Road. The will of Ezra in 1747 refers to "what he has given Joseph by deeds and other ways," but this is not further explained. In his will, Ezra Bourne left Joseph only the right to continue to occupy the house he lived in. He left his son Samuel of Falmouth his Falmouth lands and the Monomoscoy property. The balance of the Mashpee lands and associated rights, and the Peters Pond land all went to Ezra's son Shearjashub (1713-1781) who lived in Rhode Island, and was then aged fifty-one. This heir enjoyed the family success traits and was a well-to-do manufacturer and judge, not interested in Mashpee. He promptly deeded to his less successful brother Joseph for £5 the house and "about fifty acres surrounded by Indian lands." To the south of it was another thirty acres with the house of Ezra's widow, Martha, who died in 1766. The other Mashpee lands and associated rights were sold to Samuel Bourne of Falmouth, while the Peters Pond neck and twenty-acre lots were sold out of the family.

Samuel Bourne of Falmouth and his son Nathan(1756-1829) shown on the Bourne family chart, are the ones who reassembled all the Bourne properties in Mashpee. Reverend Joseph left his house and lands on Mashpee Pond to his widow. By 1788 young Nathan Bourne had a grist mill on the Mashpee River in the ten-acre lot that had been in the family so long, and within a few years

Nathan also owned the big block of about eighty acres east of Mashpee Pond, the twelve acre lot, the Monomoscoy land and the Waquoit holdings. Nathan's use of these ancient family lands will be taken up again in chapter 23.

Herring Pond Reservation

The creation of Herring Pond Reservation does not seem to be referred to by name in Plymouth Colony Records, but we believe it was in existence by the time of the Province law of 1693/4 referred to earlier.

A second Indian meetinghouse in what was a more convenient location for Indians was built on a knoll facing the south end of Great Herring Pond. Judge Samuel Sewall aided in getting this meetinghouse built as shown in his Letter Book for 1687 and 1688 where he wrote to a carpenter named Edward Milton guaranteeing payment of £30 for the building "not over one-third in money." Its size was 18 x 24 feet. An ancient Indian cemetery is just below on the shore of the pond. Sewall later attended a service in this meetinghouse in 1706 and again mentioned the beautiful Herring River called Pampaspicet by the Indians. Mrs. Keene records in connection with this meetinghouse a curious legend that it became infested with blacksnakes, and that as a result it was removed to a new location east of the pond. Later, an Indian dwelling was built on the meetinghouse site, which continued in occupation until recent years. This site is of especial historical significance because it was under this house in 1933 that a flat stone with rough lettering was found and turned over to the newly rebuilt Aptucxet Trading Post. The lettering was compared to both Punic (Norse) and Punic (Carthage), but seems to have no letters of either type, leaving it a mystery.

At Herring Pond the Plymouth/Sandwich border ran southwest from the Bay to a stone near the mouth of Herring River, then west toward Wareham, and this line ran through Indian territory. The line was never changed substantially from the first settlement of Sandwich, so that the Indian residential area was simply a part either of Sandwich or Plymouth town, but occupied officially by Indians with property rights on a common basis.

By 1707 there were clear lines of demarcation drawn as to what were the Indians' reserved lands. Sandwich appointed three surveyors in 1706/7 "to join with the Indians to run the line between our Town of Sandwich and their bounds." A map of the three portions that comprised the Herring Pond Reservation is reproduced here on page 347. The portions are:

Great Lot (1,997 acres) between the ponds and the Bay, where it was adjacent to the Ellisville neighborhood in South Plymouth.

Meetinghouse Lot (200 acres) north of the Plymouth/Sandwich line in present Cedarville area.

Herring River Lot (266 acres) west of the river and south of the pond with the greater portion in Sandwich including the 1687 meetinghouse site.

From time to time portions of this land were sold to outsiders to raise funds for necessary civic purposes. James Ned in 1745 asked for Province approval to sell, and "Mr. Tupper" (presumably Elisha), was appointed to assist him in the sale. In 1772 Reverend Abraham Williams of Sandwich was authorized by the Court to sell land at Herring Pond in aid of Jabez Wicket, and in 1782 Ephraim Ellis, Missionary, was allowed to sell £100 worth of land to aid the sick.

Thomas Tupper Jr. died in 1706. He was replaced by Josiah Cotton of Plymouth, son of the former Plymouth minister John Cotton. This Josiah, brother of Reverend Roland of Sandwich, was graduated from Harvard in 1698 and later wrote an Indian Grammar. Eldad Tupper, son of Thomas, Jr. was a teacher at Herring Pond but not a preacher. His son Elisha (1707-1787) devoted his life to preaching both here and to Indians at Pocasset. His education and ordination have not been documented, but his reports to the Society for the Propagation of the Gospel, in London, were said to be of great interest as including baptism and marriage records.

Herring Pond Reservation did not share in the change to District status enjoyed by Mashpee between 1763 and 1788, and so experienced less of the turmoil of change brought by the newcomers. The new overseers of Mashpee established in 1788 also were given charge of Herring Pond.

Pocasset Indians

Mashpee for all its problems preserved a wide area of land acknowledged to be exclusively for Indian control, with the borders defined and respected by adjacent towns. Herring Pond represented a stage lower in organization, being of smaller population, with the land considered as being in Plymouth or Sandwich, but with common ownership by the Indians, and its outer boundaries respected by courts. In the Mashpee and Herring Pond reservations, as in others across the state, there were large and small sectors which had been sold off to whites at critical times when funds were desperately needed for projects or simply to establish capital for income to support schools or aid the sick and elderly. The Indian settlement at Pocasset represented a yet simpler stage with Indian families owning scattered lots for houses, gardens and firewood, but entirely within areas of white settlement. Although not taxed, these families had survived a century of shrinkage of their holdings and had few assets or skills. In Pocasset there were eight such families in 1767, all in houses, representing thirty individuals, in a community of possibly fifty English families. Reverend Elisha Tupper preached here as well as at Herring Pond, and is referred to in a petition to the Governor and the General Court by the whites here to become a separate parish with its own meetinghouse. This division into a second parish was allowed by the General Court in 1769 in spite of protests from Sandwich. The Sandwich committee noted scathingly:

> "there being five or six families of Indians living in the northerly part of Falmouth and a few other Indians without any land despersed in Falmouth and Pocassett living as servants chiefly in English families...

> but Mr. Tupper is not, nor ever was, ordained; there being neither English nor Indian Church at Pocassett and but one Indian male member of any church living there and he above sixty years of age, besides, Mr. Tupper who is in his 63rd year. Mr. Tupper having been long in the service, the Commissioners did not choose to cast him off in his old age; and it is likely he will be the last Missionary they will improve at Pocassett, so that they cannot reasonably depend on assistance from that quarter after Mr. Tupper's death."

Mr. Tupper lived until 1787 and the Indians in this part of Sandwich finally removed or died out.

BOURNES INVOLVED IN MASHPEE LANDS

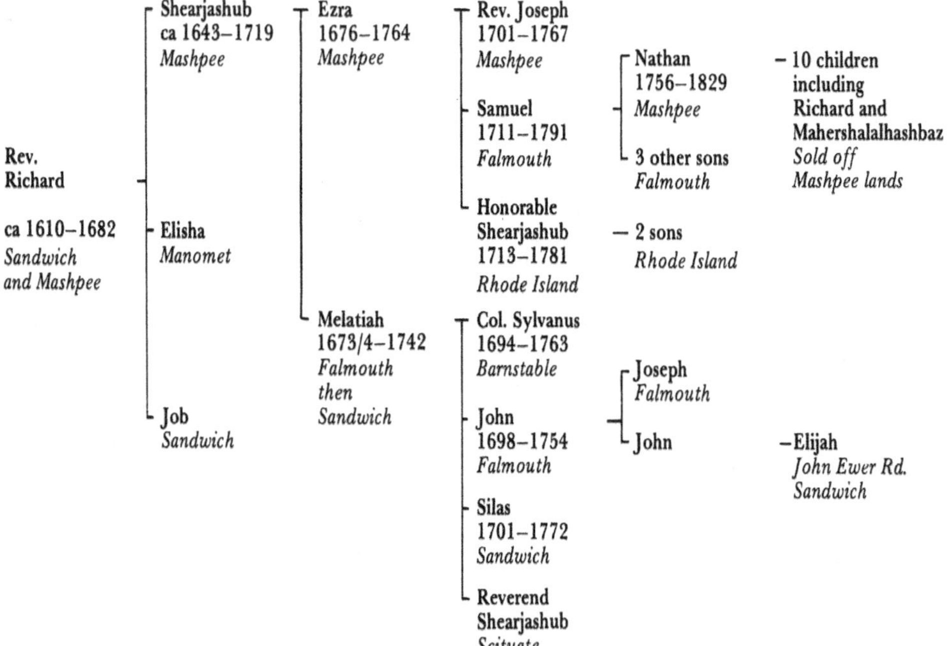

CHAPTER 13

DOCTOR FREEMAN

After the Treaty of Paris in 1763, there was a new realization on both sides of the Atlantic of the vast size and potential of the American and Canadian provinces, so much larger than the British homeland. Britain wanted to keep these huge areas as a source of raw materials and as a market for finished goods, profiting greatly in all aspects of trade, but without formulating any clear idea of what the Americans might wish to do. There was a tendency in Britain to denigrate American will and ability, to consider the colonies in the New World as divided and undisciplined with poor fighting ability (as shown by Provincial troops) and with no overall leadership. They especially felt that Americans should begin to pay something to the Crown in recognition of the vast debts of the recent Seven Years War with France. There was little consideration given to reflect the evolving situation in America, and this bad judgement led swiftly to confrontations which were astonishing and novel to both sides.

The Sugar Act of 1764 and the Stamp Act of 1765 were the first steps in the plan to raise direct revenues in America. New York had the honor of raising the cry of "no taxation without representation." In October 1765 delegates from nine of the thirteen provinces gathered in New York to consider the American position. In the Massachusetts delegation were both James Otis Junior and Timothy Ruggles, representing extremes in the range of positions of leading Americans. Otis was inspired by the vast growth of population and wealth that was sure to come to America and saw relations with the British homeland as an idealized Commonwealth of English nations, mutually reinforcing one another with world-wide powers under the British constitution and the King. Ruggles typified the official position of total support for the existing system with its line of authority from Parliament to the Royal Governors, with their office staffs and local courts, militia and provincial congresses within which he was so soundly established. He felt, therefore, that anything threatening or questioning this establishment was wrong; the present official policies of raising revenue and keeping all manufacturing in Great Britain might be resented, but they should be followed and enforced while negotiating in an orderly way for change. Ruggles attended the conference to meet the leaders from other provinces and to see what they should propose. This Congress passed a set of fourteen declarations on the American position which stated their affection for the Sovereign and their subordination to Parliament, but nevertheless affirmed that they should not be taxed while not represented in the Parliament. They added that the profit from trade with America was the colonies' main contribution to the Crown. They asked repeal of trade controls and the stamp duties, and addressed urgent petitions to the Crown, to the House of Lords and to the House of Commons. Ruggles found that the Congress had gone far beyond what he had expected of it, and refused to sign the documents; he received a severe reprimand from the Massachusetts House of Representatives for his behavior, and was not allowed to read a statement of his reasons into the record. Another who refused to sign, Robert Ogden of New Jersey, was forced to resign from the New Jersey Assembly. Ironically, the petitions to Parliament were not even given a hearing because they were drawn up by an unauthorized assembly.

The ugly part of the Stamp Act controversy was in showing how easy it was to rouse a mob to destroy homes and buildings of the supposed enemies of liberty. The Stamp Act was withdrawn in 1766, but the roots of hostility and suspicion remained to be fanned and enlarged by many succeeding acts of Parliament and of the provincial governors in America.

In 1767 a new trade act placed duties on tea, sugar and many manufactured items imported in large quantity. Reaction to this in Massachusetts was swift and predictable. There were pledges of non-importation in the main ports, and towns inland were all urged to ban the use of the items. The effect of this ban was not as damaging as had been expected on the English merchants, but its effect in the American provinces was a remarkable surge of regional pride and consciousness, and a determination to make locally many of the things previously imported, especially ironware, furniture and fabrics. This increase in local manufacture and encouragement of skills became of great importance in the later conflict, and set the pattern for home-made items for generations to come.

The Governor of Massachusetts Bay dissolved the General Court in 1768, but many of its members met in September, in spite of a considerable military presence in Boston, and prepared a petition to the King. In 1769, James Otis, Junior was attacked by customs agents and dealt such a severe head wound that he never recovered the higher faculties that had enabled him to speak and write so brilliantly on the subject of American rights. The presence of occupying troops in Boston was a constant irritant, and led to the Boston Massacre in 1770. The officer over this British unit was ably defended in court by John Adams. All duties were then withdrawn except for a symbolic three pence a pound on tea, and the troops were kept off the streets, producing a period of relative calm. A number of families from Cape Cod and elsewhere in this period renewed their interest in Nova Scotia as a peaceful place to resettle, and moved there.

Thomas Hutchinson became Governor in 1771, and attempted to force the Legislature to meet outside of Boston, provoking more indignation. Ruggles had continued to be reelected each year as Hardwick Representative, but 1771 was his last year. He had continued stoutly to defend the King's position in debates, and had become with the Olivers and Thomas Hutchinson one of the group totally identified with the Royal authority and hence subjected to constant villification by the masters of propaganda on the Patriot side. One of their master strokes was the creation of Committees of Correspondence in the various towns, to which the literature of protest could be sent, spreading the word and rousing support and interest among those out in the country who might lose enthusiasm without fresh material. The duty on tea continued to be a handy subject of protest, and the Boston Tea Party in late 1773 was a melodramatic event that mocked the Royalists unforgettably. In New York and Philadelphia the tea ships were quietly sent back without confrontation. In retaliation, the Port of Boston was closed in 1774, an act of immense propaganda value. Governor Hutchinson was removed and settled in England, discredited by publication of early letters he had written tending to prejudice Parliament against the American views. Boston became a city under military occupation.

Another development at this critical time was the Quebec Act, restoring French civil law and the Catholic religion in the Province of Quebec. It also added the immense hinterland north of the Ohio from the Appalachians to the Mississippi to British military control from headquarters in Quebec. In practice this meant nothing in the seaboard provinces, but in the propaganda mills of the times it was seen as a horrific threat, and was skillfully exploited to unite the colonies. Beside the Boston Port Bill and the Quebec Act, Parliament in May 1774 passed three new acts completely changing the government of Massachusetts Bay. These provided that the Governor's councillors should not be chosen by the House of Representatives but appointed by the Crown (these were the Mandamus Councillors); Town Meetings were proscribed and the Governor was given the power to appoint and remove judges, and to relocate trials by jury for persons in the government service; Government troops would be quartered at the expense of the population, also Royal sheriffs could appoint jurors rather than drawing their names from jury boxes. The effect of these acts was to transform Massachusetts into a hornets' nest of protest in which British authority in the county seats hung by a thread of loyal judges, sheriffs and militia officers, and was only secure in Boston under total occupation. The Mandamus Councillors found themselves surrounded, and were forced either to flee to Boston or to resign their appointment. Ruggles in Hardwick said goodbye to his family and rode away, never to return to his beautiful estate. Two of his sons accompanied him, and the third remained to try to protect the property, but the house was sacked for papers and weapons, and much damage done. In the various county courts, local crowds stopped the judges and sheriffs from serving in the King's name, and enforced the resignation of militia officers. The House of Representatives, meanwhile, with a heavy Patriot composition took various steps such as organizing Minute Men and Committees of Safety, and assembled military stores at Concord and Worcester. Because of the outburst of national feelings at all these events, a Continental Congress met in September 1774 and again in May 1775. The final events of 1775 and 1776 are too well-known to need more than mention, the attack at Concord and Lexington, the Battle of Bunker Hill, the arrival of Washington in Cambridge and the attack on Quebec.

In August 1775 an important shipment of one hundred barrels of flour arrived at Buzzards Bay from New York. It was carried overland on the portage route by carts, then loaded at Scusset Creek into twenty whaleboats. These were rowed along close to the shore all the way up to Cohasset, then taken by cart to

Washington's camp. Washington immediately recognized the strategic importance of a canal across Cape Cod, and ordered that a survey of the route and costs be made. A Lieutenant Machin completed this plan in 1776 which involved a channel twelve feet deep with two locks. No work was commissioned however.

With the aid of artillery pieces captured from General Burgoyne and dragged from the Hudson overland by General Knox in the winter, Washington was able to force the evacuation of the British from Boston on March 17, 1776. General Howe departed with about eleven hundred people. Part went to Halifax, others to New York which remained in British hands during the entire course of the war. Ruggles settled on Staten Island where he helped organize Loyalist brigades. His sons served with British forces on Long Island and elsewhere.

Doctor Nathaniel Freeman

A chart on an adjacent page shows the descent of Nathaniel in the line of five Edmund Freemans from the founder of Sandwich. Edmund III had invested in land in Mansfield, Connecticut; Edmund IV had removed there in mid-life, and his son Edmund V followed there after a few years of teaching in Dennis. Nathaniel was brought up in Connecticut and read widely under his Harvard-educated father although he did not attend a college. He studied medicine under Doctor Cobb in Tolland, Connecticut and began practicing in Thompson. After marrying he removed to his ancestral home in Sandwich, a highly unusual move in the opposite direction from the usual spread toward new settlements. The reason seems to lie in his strong Otis family connections, shown in the other accompanying chart, the family of his mother, Martha Otis. Nathaniel's biographer, Russell Freeman, stated "He settled in Sandwich with the advice and under the patronage of his maternal great uncle, the distinguished Colonel James Otis... Under his auspices and direction also he went through a regular course of legal reading before the Revolution."

The Sandwich home of Martha's father Nathaniel Otis on Grove Street remained in the family. Colonel James Otis (called James the Juror) was the head of the Otis family's powerful interests in Barnstable including stores, shipping, legal practice, election to the House of Representatives, and various political, judicial and military offices in town and County. This sort of family dynasty needed a succession of gifted and loyal family members in the younger generation. The term "patronage" suggests that Nathaniel was given a substantial incentive to return to Cape Cod and settle, also to read law in preparation for a public career. So he came to Sandwich in early 1765 and practiced medicine plus intensive reading and raising what became a very large family.

NATHANIEL FREEMAN HOUSE-This charming view of about 1884 shows in the center background the home of Dr. Nathaniel Freeman on Grove Street opposite the Pope house. It was a narrow house with an ell, on a high stone foundation, and was torn down about 1895. The men talking are Isaiah Tobey Jones and Charles Chapouil Courtesy of Lombard C. Jones.

Early Years in Sandwich

Nathaniel is first mentioned in Sandwich town meeting records in 1768 when he was elected Moderator. From then on references to him are constant as Moderator, checking selectmen's accounts, distributing the herring profits, and finding the next schoolmaster. He declined direct town administration work as selectman, clerk, or treasurer. The town had been attentive to developments in Boston, building a powder house in Old Town Burying Ground in 1767, and passing the ban of imports of "superfluities" like tea, fabrics and luxuries. When invited to send a representative to the House meeting in Boston in 1768 when it had been banned by the Governor, the town decided forty-two to thirty-three against sending a delegate. The town did agree in 1770 not to import any of the duty-free items until the duty on tea should be lifted. On January 26, 1773 the first Committee of Correspondence for the town was named which included the following eleven persons: Joseph and Stephen Nye, Nathaniel and Simeon Fish, Nathaniel and Seth Freeman, Simeon Dillingham, Moses Swift, Zaccheus Burgess, Mordecai Ellis and Joshua Tobey. This Committee promptly proposed a set of resolves which the town passed:

1. Confirming their rights as outlined in a Boston pamphlet
2. That recent infringements be opposed vigorously

3. That a real threat to the Province's Charter exists.
4. That we will join with other Towns to obtain relief.
5. That our Representative join in a protest to the Crown.
6. That thanks and cooperation be extended to the Boston Committee.
7. That these Resolves be spread upon the record.

This smoothly worded sequence showed that central planning had been done so that the patriot cause was advanced quickly and effectively in receptive towns. Thereafter there were only mild procedural protests from two citizens (Thomas Smith, Jr. and Stephen Chipman). Two Quakers refused to serve on the enlarged Committee of Correspondence, sensing the turn in 1774 towards violence and confrontation. With the Boston Port Bill and Quebec Act and the three anti-Massachusetts Acts of Parliament in early 1774, Sandwich became strongly polarized into Tory and Whig factions. The latter, now a majority, had no difficulty in getting some lengthy parts of the literature of the Committee of Correspondence read into the town meeting records.

The "Body of the People " Event (Monday, September 26, 1774)

This historic episode was carried out so smoothly as to suggest very careful planning in order that the widespread popular indignation should be channeled into constructive acts and not dissipated in random violence or mob action. The idea was to stop the court in Barnstable, also the sheriff's office and militia, from acting in the King's name. This had already been done in Great Barrington and Springfield, and would be done in one way or another in all the county seats across the State. The timetable here was:

A liberty pole for Sandwich was erected, probably near the home of Melatiah Bourne at 138 Main Street who gave the timber. These poles or pollarded trees were supposed to be forty-five feet high, a magic number representing a memorable issue of a liberal newspaper in Britain by John Wilkes against the policies of George III. During the day, men arrived from Rochester, Plymouth, Wareham and Middleboro. A set of resolves had already been drawn up in Rochester. In Sandwich, under Stephen Nye, Moderator, further officers for the next day's march were elected, with Freeman to be leader and speaker.

Tuesday, September 27 (Usual opening day of Court of Common Pleas)

The men stepped out at 6 A.M. at beat of drum in double file. They saluted Chief Justice James Otis, Sr. as they passed his house in West Barnstable, who knew perfectly well what was being done. They arrived at 10 A.M. in front of the court house and joined a large crowd already there from other Cape towns. Freeman was elected moderator, and was described as follows by Abraham Holmes of Rochester, one of those present:

> "Freeman was a fine figure of a man between thirty and forty years of age. (He was 33.) He had a well-made face, a florid countenance, a

bright and dignified eye, a clear and majestic voice, and wore a handsome black lapelled coat, a tied wig as white as snow, a set-up hat with the point a little to the right; in short, had the very appearance of fortitude personified."

DOCTOR NATHANIEL FREEMAN - One of the best known residents of Sandwich, Doctor Freeman was one of the leading Patriots in this county and became a judge, Register and Brigadier General. His correspondence with leading contemporaries was of value to his son Frederick Freeman in writing The History of Cape Cod, where this view appears.

Monday, September 26, 1774

The crowd, estimated at twelve to fifteen hundred, packed about the court house. They voted on regulations and on a committee to draw up general procedures. They also selected a five-man committee to draft an address to the court. The justices were warned to delay their approach, but a deputy sheriff rang the bell and was hauled from the building. The justices, thirteen of them, approached the outer edge of the crowd, and a shouted exchange took place (according to Holmes):

Otis: Gentlemen, what is the purpose for which this vast assemblage is collected here?

Freeman: (from courthouse steps) May it please Your Honor... to prevent the Court from being opened or doing any business...

Otis: Why would you interrupt its proceedings? As is now my duty, I now in His Majesty's name order you to immediately disperse...

Freeman: We thank your Honor for having done your duty; we shall continue to perform ours.

The justices retired. When the formal address was written out it was read to the crowd, approved and given to the court. Tory AB who had threatened to fell the Barnstable liberty pole was seized but denied the fact. Tories CD and EF were accused of writing an address to former Governor Hutchinson and were compelled to sign a statement of apology. The court then answered that hindering the court would not help and that it should continue until the will of the Province Congress and the Continental Congress was known. The crowd refused to accept this. A short declaration was drawn up agreeing not to sit under acts of Parliament. This was approved and signed by all thirteen justices. Tory AB escaped but a draft apology was prepared for him. A committee was named to go to other Cape towns to secure signatures of other justices of the peace and deputies. Committees for each town were named to receive the resignations of all militia officers. Town clerks reported on election of patriotic representatives and rejection of others. The crowd adjourned for the day.

Wednesday, September 28

The Body reassembled at 6 A.M. Justices who had not yet signed did so. The sheriff signed his resignation. An address to Judge Otis was approved urging him to attend a meeting of the House of Representatives at Salem on October 5, and giving him the best wishes of the crowd. This was read to him at his overnight residence and he responded well. Back at the court house the crowd approved patriotic resolutions and adjourned.

Overnight, word reached Barnstable that Tories had cut down the Sandwich liberty pole, and a posse of twenty-two men left immediately to round up the guilty. The Body of the People marched to Sandwich, intercepting an itinerant peddler who sold tea and the interdicted imports. He signed a pledge not to sell such. At Sandwich the Body reassembled near the liberty pole site and learned that the guilty parties had not yet been found. Joseph Otis was elected moderator for this session. The local committee was urged to obtain the resignations of Colonel Roland Cotton and Major Thomas Bourne from the militia. A Tory MN was hauled up and made to sign an apology for insulting statements. An apology or punishment was drafted for the pole-cutters GH, IJ and KL. At this point IJ and KL were produced, who implicated also OP and QR. QR was the informant and was excused. IJ and KL paid £5 each and signed the confession. The Body of the People then broke up with cheers for the Provincial Congress, for Freeman and Otis, for Plymouth and Bristol men, and for the success of the enterprise.

On the following day, September 29, GH was caught, paid the fine and signed the confession. All but one of the militia officers soon signed their resignation as did Edward Bourne a deputy sheriff. One Major UV was a stubborn holdout but on October 15 was hauled to the pole by a large crowd and given no choice but to sign. The three pole-cutters were obliged to help re-erect the liberty pole.

Who Attacked Nabby Freeman?

Frederick Freeman had his father's notes about the Body of the People event, and also notes by Dr. James Thatcher who was a youth of twenty in Barnstable at the time of the event. Freeman's *History of Cape Cod,* Volume I, painted a flattering account of Nathaniel's patriotism and leadership in the event and adds a statement by Thatcher concerning an incident that occurred at Barnstable at the same time. Some vengeful Tories determined to silence a noisy Whig woman who insulted them by her tirades. The account reads:

> "A number of men in disguise entered her chamber in the night, took her from her bed, and after the application of tar and feathers, she was, by a rope fastened around her body, hoisted almost to the top of the pole which had been erected by the Whigs. Her dreadful shrieks soon collected a throng of people; but the poor woman could obtain no other redress than that bestowed by her friends who kindly shaved her head and cleansed it of tar and feathers."

Such an attack on a woman was unheard of, and if true, must have been followed by an intense search for those responsible. Curiously, in those fervently patriotic days, there was no further reference to this ugly incident at all.

A different account of the tarring and feathering was written by Amos Otis of Barnstable in his *Genealogical Notes of Barnstable Families.* According to Otis, Nabby Freeman was an outstanding Tory who kept a small grocery store and continued to sell tea. She had a particular antipathy for Doctor Freeman and others of the radical patriots. Otis's version follows:

> "They were all young men, and acting in the shade of night, perhaps were not recognized in the disguises which they assumed. When they came to the house of Mrs. Freeman she had retired for the

night. They obtained an entrance, took her from her bed to the Green, besmeared her with tar and covered her with feathers. A rail was procured from a fence in the vicinity, across which she was set astride, and either end thereof was placed on the shoulder of a stout youth. She was held in her position by a man who walked at her side, holding her by the hand. When they were tired of the sport, and after they had exacted from her a promise that she would no more meddle in politics, they released her, and the gallant band soon after sneaked homeward."

Amos Otis then goes on to say that a strong party in Sandwich and Barnstable justified this act, and that the venerable old James Otis, Sr. attempted to heal the difficulties and reconcile the parties, particularly a family feud between the Otises and Freemans on one side and the Crocker family on the other. He states that Colonel Otis at a town meeting on May 21, 1776 made what the records call "an apology" but that the town voted not to hear "that part relating to Abigail Freeman and the Crockers' quarrel." We may never know what the old gentleman wanted to explain, or what really happened that night, whether Nabby was hoisted up the pole by Tories or ridden on a rail by Patriots. When Freeman's Volume II appeared in 1862, he added a note in the Barnstable Annals attacking the author of "recent serials purporting to be historical" (Amos Otis) for transposing the facts and parties, by which "the barbarous conduct of the Tories in wreaking vengeance on a respectable female is charged to the opposite party." His indignation still quivers on the page. We tend however to believe Otis, and suggest that there was a broad cover-up of the episode. If Tories had done such a thing, surely they would have been pursued more ardently than they were for simply threatening to chop down a liberty pole. The Barnstable historian Donald Trayser supported the Amos Otis version. Colonel Freeman and Colonel Joseph Otis were later badly snubbed by Barnstable militia, and the Nabby Freeman incident goes far to explain it.

The woman was Abigail Davis of Barnstable, born in 1729 and so forty-five at the time of the attack. She had married David Freeman of Fairfield, Connecticut in 1766 and had returned to Barnstable as a widow. David was a descendant of the Eastham branch of the Freemans. Abigail lived until 1788.

Closing Plymouth Court

On the Tuesday following the Body of the People Event in Barnstable, the County Court in Plymouth was due to sit, and again a large crowd gathered to prevent it. Nathaniel Freeman was there. His son Frederick (quoting an eye-witness to the events) says that the crowd rounded up some known Tories, brought them to the liberty pole and treated them there in a manner painful, dangerous and humiliating. There was a pulley wheel at the top of the pole and each Tory had a rope tied around his waist and was hoisted to the top of the pole. The jolly poem of the day read:

"Then upwards all hands hoisting sail,
They swung him like a keg of ale,

Where looking forth in prospect wide
His Tory errors he espied."

One of those scheduled to be hoisted was an aged and pious Deacon, and the account goes that Doctor Freeman interrupted with a motion "Resolved-that Deacon_________ is a nobody." This was seconded and voted, with the result that the "nobody" was released unharmed.

The Attack on Doctor Freeman

The following evening, Wednesday October 5, Doctor Freeman received a message that a friend needed his attendance. He was suspicious but went out, and in passing the Newcomb Tavern (about one hundred yards from his home) was accosted by three of those who had been caught and fined by the Body of the People the previous week. They demanded he answer for his late conduct in Barnstable and in Plymouth. He walked on and was allowed to pass. On his return, the three again stopped him and said they would compel his attendance in the tavern. Another three rushed out and the six attacked him, probably with sticks of firewood. He did have a sword cane which was smashed, and he was knocked down and badly beaten before friends following him rushed up and saved him. He was borne home bleeding badly with a large head wound which caused a long scar. A crowd gathered very swiftly and there was a strong possibility that those caught would be lynched. Most of the six were secured for a trial which took place on Friday, October 7, at West Barnstable before Judge Otis. Doctor Freeman and all leading patriots were determined in this egregious case to avoid mob action and urged restraint. The families of the accused were said to be greatly distressed at their dishonorable course. They were let off with a total fine of £100 and bonds to insure good behavior.

On the following Monday, October 10, a number of leading citizens, apparently sensing that a great deal of resentment and potentiality for reprisals still existed, had the culprits rearrested and brought to a scaffold under the liberty pole in Sandwich. Here they were forced to sign a letter of confession and repentance drafted by General Goodwin of Plymouth, which seems to have defused the situation.

Further Town Meetings

A town meeting was held Friday, September 30 just after the Body of the People march. Stephen Nye was elected to go to the next meeting of the General Court at Salem on October 5 and received instructions not to consent to any acts of the Mandamus Council, nor to pay for tea as demanded in the Boston Port Bill. He was empowered to join the new Congress of the Province. The Committee on Correspondence had abundant material to report, and the Sandwich meeting approved eleven patriotic resolves supporting the Port of Boston by subscriptions, recommending that a new militia be formed and that a county meeting be held to coordinate town activities; that all peddlers of tea and other imports be suppressed; that a chest of arms with powder and shot be bought.

The October 5 meeting of the General Court at Salem was cancelled by the Governor but the ninety persons already present met as the Provincial Congress and elected John Hancock as its President. They took a number of bold actions such as appointing a new province treasurer to receive public money, providing for a new militia and a corps of Minute Men, and an increase in military stores. On the King's side, Timothy Ruggles caused a paper to be circulated to the "Friends of Government" in every town urging associations to form, denouncing the patriots as "bullies...a mob without order or discipline...easily crushed." By this time and especially in this part of the State after the attack on Dr. Freeman, the population was well polarized and the active Tories found themselves strongly identified and restrained in their potential for public activities.

The town meeting of November 11, 1774 refers to "the several military companies in this town" who were allowed to choose their own officers, assemble their colors, drums, fifes and halberds, hire a drillmaster, and fine delinquents. A sum of £80 was set aside for the military, available from profits of herring sales.

In May 1775 it was voted to establish a watch along the coasts of this town. The committee was to build watch houses at convenient points and man them at two shillings per night. Dr. Freeman and Stephen Nye were chosen as delegates to the next meeting of the Provincial Congress in Watertown May 31. A strong vote was passed, in view of the battles at Concord and Lexington, to consider General Gage and his government as enemies of the country. At this meeting Dr. Freeman was for the first time called Colonel Freeman, noting his recent appointment as Lieutenant Colonel of the First Barnstable Regiment. He and Joseph Nye, Esquire, were chosen as representatives to the Provincial Congress held in Watertown July 19.

After the arrival of General Washington in Cambridge the state quickly went over to a wartime footing. The Sandwich town meeting July 12, 1775:

> "voted that the pay of the watch ordered by the Town cease when the company expected to be stationed in this town on the cost of the United Colonies shall be placed here."

A British raid on Martha's Vineyard and Elizabeth Islands in late May 1775 was reported, when livestock and supplies were taken. Colonel Freeman was constantly employed in 1775 and early 1776 organizing and placing defense companies around the Cape and Islands. He was appointed full Colonel in January, 1776 when a second Militia regiment was raised from Barnstable and Plymouth Counties. Sandwich voted on June 21, 1776 that:

> "should the Honorable Congress of the United Colonies for the safety of those Colonies declare them independent to the Kingdom of Great Britain, we will solemnly engage with our lives and fortunes to support them in the measure."

Ongoing Town Affairs — Pocasset Petition

Reverend Elisha Tupper received approval of the Indian Commissioners to establish a small meetinghouse at Pocasset in 1767. This was moved here from elsewhere and repaired. It was used by whites as well, and probably contributed to the decision to seek full Precinct status. Such status was formally requested in 1769 citing distance to Sandwich Village, Pocasset's population of thirty-one families (about one hundred sixty persons) and its rapid growth. An item in the town warrant about this read POSSET instead of POCASSET and was scornfully voted down. At a later town meeting it was voted that a committee draw up an answer to the petition. The draft was prepared by Major Thomas Bourne of North Sandwich. It was heavily negative and scornful of his fellow townsmen of Pocasset, and said in part:

> "the inhabitants of Pocasset are not now and there is no probability that they ever will be able to perform the duties of a Parish, ...the greatest part of the inhabitants being poor."

In spite of this statement the General Court approved the petition in 1770, with bounds northerly by lands of William and Jonathan Tobey, easterly to the extent of the petitioners' lands in the woods, southerly by Falmouth line, westerly by Buzzards Bay.

Ministry Lands

In 1768 the Quakers of Sandwich, now a large group of about sixty families, petitioned in a persuasive way that they had a right to a share of the lands set aside for the support of the First Parish church. They sought an agreement to share the income from these lands arising from sale of wood and the pasturage of sheep. A committee was appointed to examine the basis for granting the lands and the right of the petitioners. Before a report was brought in, the Pocasset petitioners also asked for a share of the ministry lands being enjoyed by the First Parish. The ministry lands granted in the past were:

A lot of about ten acres listed in the 1667 survey near the original Freeman Farm. This seems to have been sold off but kept its name as the Parsonage Lot.

Scraggy Neck, bought by Thomas Dexter from the Indians in 1667 and allocated to the Parish Church.

One of the twenty-acre lots called Nonesuch, laid out in 1706 somewhere near the present Mid-Cape and Route 130.

A woodlot in the First Division between #69 and #70, near the present junction of Cotuit Road and Route 130.

No report on dividing these lands or their income was brought in, although the subject was raised again in 1785.

Grist Mills

Town approval for the creation of new dams, mills and millponds seems only to have been needed when a herring run was threatened or when an accepted public way had to be changed. Hence, we do not know when certain mills were first set up. In 1776 approval was given to Jesse Barlow "to turn the County Road near his dwelling house so as to accomodate the mill he proposes to erect. He to keep the new road in repair." Sandwich had at one time or another water-powered grist mills in eight locations:

1. Dexter Mill on Shawme Creek in use before 1640, with later fish ladder.
2. Nye's Mill, Old County Road, in use by 1669. In 1769 a town committee was appointed to clear a channel and build the stages so that herring could use this stream and pond. No one was to take herring here until the run was established.
3. Elisha Bourne's mill on Herring River, allowed in 1695 just above the herring-taking house.
4. A mill on Back River attributed by Betsey Keene to John Perry in the 1730s. This is not shown in an 1831 map, but the millpond was preserved.
5. Mill on Spring Hill River allowed to Samuel Wing in 1741/2. This is also not shown in 1831 but was then closed and about to be bought up and converted to a stave mill.
6. Willow Crossing dam and mill on Scusset Creek in Sagamore, called Swift's Mill on an 1825 map. This mill pond is shown on the Machin Canal Survey of 1776, where a "Swivel Bridge" is recommended for the road crossing.
7. Jesse Barlow's mill of 1776 on Pocasset River.
8. A dam and mill on Red Brook in Cataumet is shown on the 1831 map but is not in town meeting records.
9. A grist mill is listed between the Upper and Lower Shawme Ponds in the 1851 sale of the cotton mill.

The Need for Salt

The sale of five to seven hundred barrels of herrings each year at public auction was an important part of the Town's income. These herring were all salted for preservation. The inhabitants of the town at this time could fish for themselves but were required to record their take with the official catcher, and pay for any salt used. Herring were limited to one barrel per family for home consumption. If the catcher's services were used, he could charge one shilling per barrel for green herring and two if dried. The supply of salt became more important as imports fell. Those who bought at auction received a credit if they took unsalted fish, and the town salt thus saved was available to sell to the townspeople for their own use in putting up fish or meat. In 1776 the salt supply became critical and we read in town meeting records:

> "Voted that Mr. Prince Tobey and Mr. John Nye be a Committee to make enquiry how salt may be produced and if on the whole they shall judge it best to procure 100 hogshead on the credit of the town in order to save the alewives that may be taken out of the Herring River the next Spring."

It was recommended by the Continental Congress early in 1776 that steps be taken to encourage the manufacture of salt, and the Massachusetts Legislature recommended to its seaport towns that they use their utmost endeavors to this end. Next, a bounty of three shillings per bushel was offered for all salt made from seawater. The commonest means was boiling down sea water in cauldrons but this required a great deal of wood and labor.

The First Forest Fire

The harsh comments of Thomas Bourne on the petition from Pocasset in 1769 also contain references to the woodlands. He wrote:

> "Their wood by the sale of which they used to make something is grown scarce and remote, and when the wood is off, the land is not fit to improve being cold thin land... the greater part of our land being unfit for improvement except for wood. The settlements are all made by the Sea Shore and round Bays or Ponds — On the northerly part of the town the settlements are about ten miles in length by the Sea — On the southwesterly part the settlements are about nine miles by some large Bays. On the southeasterly part are several villages, by some ponds — A large barren wilderness of small pitch pines and scrub oaks make up the space between the settlements and indeed the centre and far the greater part of the township."

The practice for generations had been to have a large committee "fire the woods" each year as the Indians had done. Usually in April, they burned off the grass and seedlings but did not damage the large standing trees. This kept wide stretches of forest clear of underbrush and encouraged new grass for sheep. The last reference to "firing the woods" was in March 1769 when two were chosen to fire the woods on the north side of the Herring River. This area was largely Indian territory and was still well wooded. Since the grants of the woodlots in 1716 there had been heavy cutting of the most accessible woodlands, with wood exported to the Islands and to cities by packet. Naturally, there were no fire lanes and no reforestation so that what grew amid the dead branches from the forestry operations were pitch pines, brush and scrub oak. A bad fire must have occurred, for the town report of June 16, 1772 requests:

> "a committee to write to Mr. Nye our Representative and give him as particular an account of the damage done by the late terrible fire as

> they are capable of obtaining, and request him to petition the General Court for relief in our Taxes on the account of the loss — not only of our sheep, but on account of the depreciation of the rents of such real estates as have suffered by the fire."

The General Court did in fact appoint three persons to inspect the damage and recommended relief.

Prayer at Public Meetings

The Meetinghouse was used for both religious services and town meetings, and the minister of the official parish church (as opposed to Quakers, Anglicans, and ministers to Indian groups) was supported by taxes. However, there was a sharp division between church services and town meetings, an example of which we find in the minutes of January 26, 1773: "Put to vote whether a Committee be chose to wait on the Reverend Mr. Williams to desire him to open the meeting with prayer. Voted in the affirmative." This was the first reference to prayer in Sandwich town meetings. Possibly the increasing tension of events in Boston produced this result. It was at this meeting that the seven resolves of concern for public safety in Boston were approved. Ephraim Ellis of Herring Pond Reservation was asked to pray in 1774, and Reverend Gideon Hawley of Mashpee once in 1777. Otherwise Reverend Williams was asked to open each new meeting with prayer.

Slavery and Freedom

Without any previous reference to slaves we suddenly find the following item in town meeting records in May 1773:

> "Voted that the present Representative be and hereby is instructed to use his endeavor at the Great and General Court that an Act be passed to prevent the importation of Slaves into this country and that all the children which shall be born of such Africans as are now Slaves among us after said Act shall be freed at 21 years of age."

The local sponsor of this article was not given. The death in the Boston Massacre of Crispus Attucks, who was a fugitive slave, had made him a hero, and in the intense rhetoric of freedom circulating in the provinces, the position of blacks as also having personal rights and aspirations to freedom had to be seen in a new light. A slave in Boston sued for his freedom in 1773, and the court not only freed him but charged his former master court costs and damage. Groups of slaves began to petition their area representatives or the Legislature itself for the identical rights that the patriots were seeking. In the confused times before and during the Revolution, no general legislative action on the rights of Massachusetts blacks was taken, but it was one of the fears of the times that if freedom were not given to slaves, they would join the Loyalists if civil war should come. It is said in Sandwich legend that Reverend Abraham Williams offered his slave Titus Winchester his freedom, but that Titus preferred to wait until Williams' death before becoming free.

FREEMAN BACKGROUND OF NATHANIEL FREEMAN

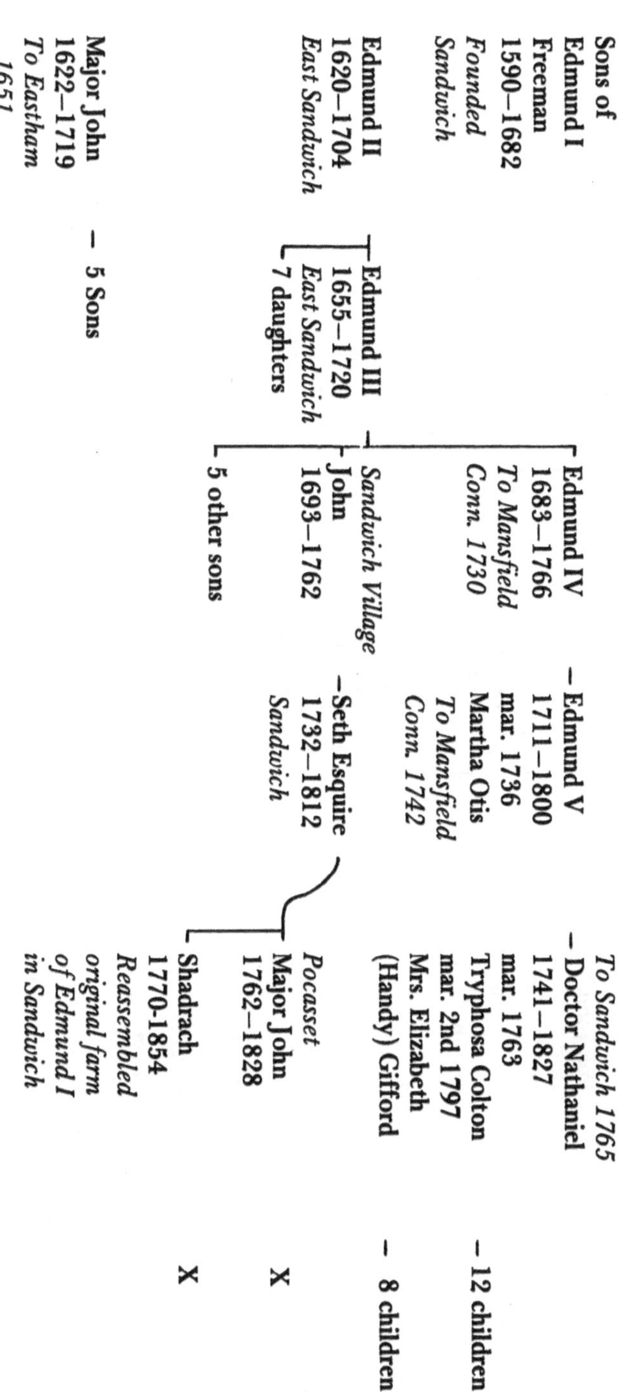
Sons of Edmund I Freeman 1590–1682 Founded Sandwich
Edmund II 1620–1704 East Sandwich
Major John 1622–1719 To Eastham 1651
5 Sons
Edmund III 1655–1720 East Sandwich
7 daughters
Edmund IV 1683–1766 To Mansfield Conn. 1730
Sandwich Village
John 1693–1762
5 other sons
Edmund V 1711–1800 mar. 1736 Martha Otis To Mansfield Conn. 1742
Seth Esquire 1732–1812 Sandwich
To Sandwich 1765
Doctor Nathaniel 1741–1827 mar. 1763 Tryphosa Colton mar. 2nd 1797 Mrs. Elizabeth (Handy) Gifford
Pocasset
Major John 1762–1828
Shadrach 1770-1854 Reassembled original farm of Edmund I in Sandwich
12 children
8 children
X
X

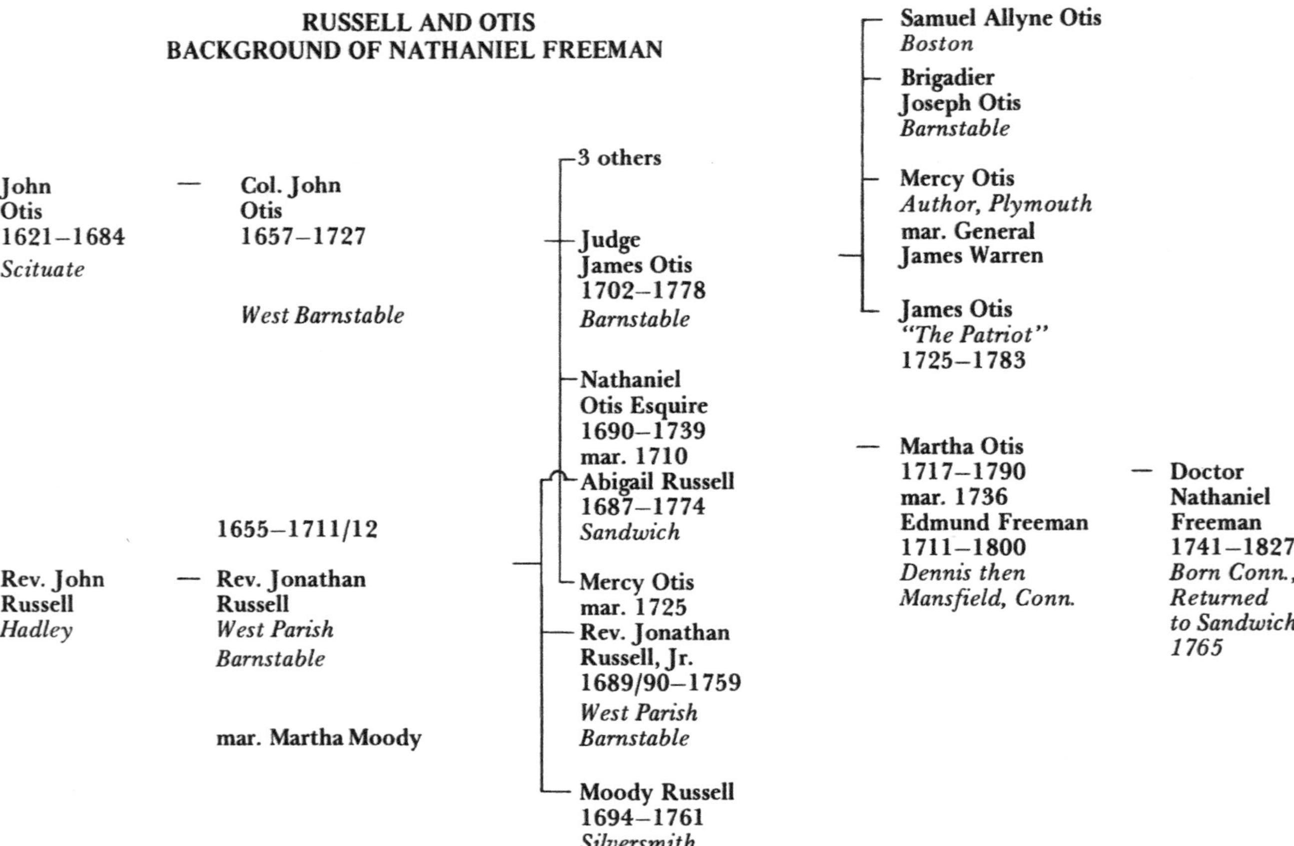
RUSSELL AND OTIS
BACKGROUND OF NATHANIEL FREEMAN
John Otis 1621–1684 Scituate
Col. John Otis 1657–1727 West Barnstable
Rev. John Russell Hadley
1655–1711/12
Rev. Jonathan Russell West Parish Barnstable
mar. Martha Moody
3 others
Judge James Otis 1702–1778 Barnstable
Nathaniel Otis Esquire 1690–1739 mar. 1710 Abigail Russell 1687–1774 Sandwich
Mercy Otis mar. 1725 Rev. Jonathan Russell, Jr. 1689/90–1759 West Parish Barnstable
Moody Russell 1694–1761 Silversmith
Samuel Allyne Otis Boston
Brigadier Joseph Otis Barnstable
Mercy Otis Author, Plymouth mar. General James Warren
James Otis "The Patriot" 1725–1783
Martha Otis 1717–1790 mar. 1736 Edmund Freeman 1711–1800 Dennis then Mansfield, Conn.
Doctor Nathaniel Freeman 1741–1827 Born Conn., Returned to Sandwich 1765

CHAPTER 14

LIFE IN WARTIME

A brief timetable of political and military events is necessary to understand the period of the Revolution in Barnstable County. Such heavy demands were made on all the Cape towns for men, food and clothing that the towns were brought to the point of total inability to supply more. Frederick Freeman's *History of Cape Cod* has great relevancy to this period because he had personal contact with some who lived through the Revolution, and was also the inheritor of a large collection of letters and records accumulated by his father, Nathaniel Freeman.

National Events

With the evacuation of Boston in March 1776 the last British army units left this area, but their navy continued to range along this coast, particularly taking supplies at will from the undefended Elizabeth Islands, Nantucket and Martha's Vineyard. Newport, Rhode Island was occupied by British forces, as were New York City, Savannah, and Charleston. Fighting began in earnest on Long Island, in the New York area and New Jersey, so that the New England contribution thereafter was in men and supplies. The Continental Congress began to function in May 1776 but was profoundly limited by lack of funds through not having any taxing power or foreign support. Currency in Continental dollars was printed, but without specie backing quickly depreciated. The various state representatives were slow to agree on actions, concepts and organization so that the new country had an exceedingly difficult start. In November 1777, Articles of Confederation were accepted establishing the new United States of America, which served as a temporary basis of government until 1789. The British effort to split the colonies by joining forces from Canada and New York ended with the defeat of Burgoyne and capture of his army at Saratoga in October 1777, a watershed event in retrospect and an encouraging one at the time. The thirteen states organized provincial governments, some on the basis of early charters or quick constitutions, others like Massachusetts with elaborate new state constitutions. With major aid from both French troops and naval forces, Lord Cornwallis was cornered at Yorktown and surrendered his seven thousand men in October 1781, ending major military actions. Washington's army however, remained miserably underfed and clothed. Peace negotiations dragged on due to many uncertainties within the new nation as to its borders and its relations to British, French and Spanish interests. Preliminary peace articles were signed at Versailles in November 1782, the Treaty itself September 1783 and Congressional approval January 14, 1784.

Massachusetts Events

General Washington had called for six regiments of seven hundred twenty-eight men each to be raised in Massachusetts for the Continental forces, and later added a seventh. One of these regiments contained two hundred sixty men from Barnstable, enlisted for three years. Only a handful of Sandwich names are on the list, most of the Sandwich quota being reached by hired substitutes from Mashpee and other towns. In addition to the Continental Army, two regiments of militia were organized on the Cape under the overall command of Brigadier Joseph Otis of Barnstable, with Colonel Freeman over one and Colonel Doane the other. These militia units trained regularly but remained at home subject to call for local defense and for service in Rhode Island. The men were paid only when on active duty.

After the departure of Washington for the New York area, the Massachusetts Legislature was the command center for issuing local requisitions for more men for the Continental Army, usually for short periods as three or six months service; also, requisitions for blankets, clothing and food such as meat or equivalent grain. These requisitions were apportioned to the counties and towns on a formula basis by which Barnstable County was one sixteenth of the State and Sandwich one seventh of the County. A census of all males aged sixteen years and older was requested in November 1776, apparently as a gauge of future requisitions.

In these early days certain sea captains from the Cape and elsewhere made desperate runs to the West Indies to get cargoes already paid for or to collect accounts. Many of these vessels were seized but some got back. The Legislature began issuing Letters of Marque authorizing American privateers to take prizes; they may have taken many British vessels, and this too was an extremely risky business. Coastwise packets and fishing vessels rotted at the docks, and in 1779 a complete embargo was declared on all vessels going offshore.

The State Constitution

The Massachusetts Legislature undertook a lengthy process of developing a new state constitution and enlisted the support and input of representatives of the towns at frequent intervals. The Sandwich town meeting recorded the following:

> *Feb. 1778* - Instructed our representative to vote to ratify the overall Articles of Confederation.
>
> *May 1778* - The form of government to be set up in the proposed state constitution was approved in Sandwich 88 to 13. The town at this time sternly urged that Edward Bacon of Barnstable not be seated in the House because he was a known and admitted Tory. (He was in fact expelled but not replaced and the town even re-elected him.)
>
> *Aug. 1779* - A Constitutional Convention was approved but the town

declined to send its own representative.

May 1780 - The draft constitution was available in the town for study to be passed around through the neighborhoods.

Sept. - 1780 First votes in the town for state officers - Governor, Lieutenant Governor and local Senator. In October 1780 the new constitution took effect. It was a brilliant document and served as a model for the later national constitution in 1789. John Adams was one of the architects of the Massachusetts Constitution.

Jan. - 1782 The town agreed that the General Court should urge the new peace commissioners to include in any peace treaty the rights of the United States to offshore fishing.

Dr. Freeman's Many Roles

Doctor Freeman was the Sandwich representative to the Provincial Congress in the stirring days of 1775 and early 1776 from Bunker Hill through the British Evacuation. He is said to have been on the hospitality committee for the arrival of General Washington. He was appointed a Lt. Colonel of Militia in August 1775 and then a full Colonel in January 1776. His long-time sponsor and great-uncle Judge James Otis was still a member of the Governor's Council at this time and was doubtless instrumental in getting Freeman named as Justice of the Peace and Register of Probate for the county in August 1776, and as Justice of the Court of Common Pleas in October 1776. Due to the lawyers and judges serving in Boston or on military assignments, the new county courts met irregularly.

We wish here to bring up the matter of the continuing unpopularity of Freeman and of his cousin Joseph Otis in the town of Barnstable, a most regrettable condition but one which showed the complexity of the times. Amos Otis wrote that Freeman and Joseph Otis were reviewing Barnstable militia troops in their command capacity when a nasty incident occurred in early 1776. The men were ordered to present arms and instead clubbed their muskets, holding them by the barrel with stock over their shoulders. This was a deliberate insult, and Otis, infuriated, shouted, "The Crockers are at the bottom of this!" and commenced fighting with a Crocker officer. Freeman rushed into the tavern nearby and swung his cutlass at a Crocker there, but struck the summer beam in the ceiling. Another Crocker tried to bayonet Freeman. These were all Patriots. This was the scene which old Judge Otis tried later to smooth away at town meeting, where the crowd refused to hear "that part relating to Abigail Freeman and the Crockers' quarrel." Amos Otis added that the Otis/Crocker differences were adjusted and settled, but the differences between Colonel Freeman and the Crockers never. He described Freeman "as talented, opinionated, impetuous and peculiarly infuriating to Tories and those opposed to him, even adding waspishly as a genealogist that the poorest writing and worst spelling in the Probate Records occur during the time he was Register. " It was in this atmosphere of tension that the next incident occurred. Thirteen men of Tory leanings in

Sandwich refused to muster in late 1776 and were apprehended and jailed in Barnstable under war powers. They were then freed from jail by known Tories in Barnstable and went into hiding. Sandwich selectmen, military officers and the Committee of Correspondence indignantly petitioned the General Court on this matter. The Court ordered the county sheriff to apprehend the parties and report back to the Court on his doing and on any opposition he had encountered. Early in 1777, a petition from certain parties in Barnstable went to the General Court complaining against Freeman and Joseph Otis as personally contributing to the "great animosities" and failures to raise troops. A committee of the General Court held hearings for several days in April in Barnstable. These are referred to in the Percival diary as of deep local interest. Official findings have not been located, but Percival said "the parties have compromised affairs."

Freeman was elected Sandwich representative at the House for 1778, 1779 and 1780 when the problems of raising men and supplies from the Cape towns had become acute. He must have acquitted himself well as he was given the honor of heading a state delegation to Army headquarters at West Point in 1779 where he addressed the Massachusetts troops who were ending their three-year hitches, and sought their re-enlistments. He had a campaign chest of £60,000 ($200,000) of which he spent £32,000 on bounties and advances. Upon the reorganization of the State government under the new constitution in 1780, Freeman was confirmed in his military and judicial posts. At this time, there was a desperate shortage of money in the state, and Freeman was given the onerous assignment of pressing the cases against Tory estates, with power to take up and imprison those dangerous to the state and to sell off their property. In other counties there were large Tory estates abandoned which were sold to entrepreneurs who broke them up for sale in smaller pieces.

Brigadier Otis did much good work in the early days of the war but finally became generally unpopular and out-of-touch. He made an unfortunate choice of Brigade-Major in 1780 which outraged the officers in his two militia regiments. Otis was allowed to resign, and in the ensuing reorganization, Freeman was made Brigadier in 1781, and Superintendent of the County.

Militia Activity

The two militia regiments in this county consisted of companies from the various villages, each with an officer corps of captain, two lieutenants, an adjutant and a sergeant. These companies mustered periodically for drill and for carrying on the process of finding new recruits for their own ranks and for obtaining volunteers or draftees to fill the town's quota of men for the Continental Army. Militia membership and musters were unpaid, but travel and per-diem allowances were paid when the militia itself was called out to active duty for brief defense or guard details along the coast. The key officer was the captain of the militia company, who was the chief recruitment agent and the center of identification and loyalty for the company. In Sandwich, Captains Ward Swift and Simeon Fish headed popular companies and served throughout the war. Militia projects were locally led and were manned by men who knew one another and were confident at being near home.

The chief militia events in the Cape area included the following:

Feb. 1776 - A French vessel loaded with molasses and other supplies came ashore on the south coast. This was secured, and although it was suspected that it was headed for Boston, the officers were allowed to sell the cargo locally. A British transport *Friendship* was wrecked at Truro inbound to Boston; General Washington directed that the militia forward all munitions and useful supplies to his camp.

Mar. 1776 - A sloop loaded with evacuees from Boston enroute to Halifax went ashore at Provincetown. This cargo of personal property and families of Tories, some with small pox, posed a serious disposition problem.

Apr. 1776 - British vessels freely visited Martha's Vineyard, Nantucket, and the Elizabeth Islands, seizing supplies. Falmouth asked for a guard of troops for the town.

Sept. 1776 - A detachment was ordered from Cape Cod to proceed to Rhode Island, using sixty whaleboats which were requisitioned in Buzzards Bay by Joseph Nye of Sandwich.

Dec. 1776 - The British occupied Newport. For the next several years militia activity involving Cape Cod troops was undertaken to harass or dislodge the British occupying force, and to guard Providence.

Feb. 1777 - An unsuccessful attack on Aquidneck Island was made. It was noted that the boats were still ready for later use (presumably the sixty whaleboats delivered from Buzzards Bay). The Percival diary records hearing the sound of "great guns at a great distance off" on February 27 and March 6.

August 1777 - An alarm at Truro over a possible invasion. Men and field pieces were ordered to duty.

Oct. 1777 - A large force of 3,000 militia were gathered on the shore near Aquidneck Island, in some secrecy, to effect an invasion and capture of Newport. Benjamin Percival records "20 men drafted for a private (that is undisclosed) expedition out of our company. They marched Oct. 2." As we mentioned earlier, Colonel Freeman was in charge of the Cape brigade. This project was marked by extremely poor planning; the boats were not repaired, supplies not on hand, procedures and training for a serious amphibious project not worked out. The crossing was scheduled and cancelled repeatedly due to weather, and the men in disgust quit in large numbers. The British of course found out about the project and prepared defenses at the ferrying points, and had gunboats ready to cut off the forces that went across. The fiasco was so complete that one of the Brigadiers was court-martialled later. Percival's Diary merely reports on Oct. 31 "the soldiers have returned home without affecting anything. Their object was the taking of Rhode Island." (In those days Aquidneck was called Rhode Island, which had earlier been governed separately from Providence.)

May 1778 - Percival reports "6th to Captain Fish's on an alarm, Falmouth. We returned 8th." Again May 25 "there has been plenty of great guns heard today. We hear the British fleet have burnt Bristol and Warren, R.I."

Sept. 1778 - Joseph Otis spent a week in Falmouth with militia forces, and reported typical enemy action. Fifty sail came from the west and seemed about to attack Falmouth, landing five vessels briefly at Woods Hole. Five American coasters were cornered and captured, one being burned. The militia could only dig in and watch. After the fleet's return westward a few days later, Otis found that they had taken off 9,000 sheep from the Vineyard, 350 cattle, 400 muskets and all the public records and tax money, destroying ships and crops as well. His men were unhappy at not being able to fight, and at the knowledge that they had cut salt hay at home just before the alarm which would be lost before they got back.

October 1778 - The 64-gunner *Somerset* and its squadron stood off Boston, and Percival's diary records Oct. 22 and 24 hearing firing of cannon in that direction.

Nov. 2, 1778 - The *Somerset* grounded at Truro and the exciting word spread rapidly. Militia were ordered to guard prisoners and protect stores and munitions. On Nov. 10 Percival's diary records "Ordered to escort prisoners from Somerset (being marched to Boston). Left home before sunrise. Joined march and got 250 prisoners to Plymouth at dark. Returned same night and got home dawn 11th. About 450 on ship, 30 drowned." The State was very slow to recover the cannon and supplies, and local plunderers stripped the big hulk ultimately of everything.

Dec. 1778 - On Dec. 23 Percival notes "Warned people to training." On Dec. 25, "So cold at training that but fue people met." It was the cold not Christmas that kept the troops at home.

April 1779 - On the 2nd Percival notes "This evening there was an alarm to go to Falmouth, there being a number of vessels seen coming down the Sound." 3rd, "This morning Thomas (his brother) sat out for Falmouth. We plowed this forenoon and afternoon. Hearing heavy cannon towards Falmouth I sat out and got there just after firing ceased. Our people stood it out in a small entrenchment amidst the incessant fire from ten armed vessels manned with Tories. They tried to land with boats but got beat off." 4th, "This morning the vessels came within musket shot of our entrenchment and fired again. We returned the fire, they soon quitted and went to Holmes Hole. They took some boats to Naushon where they killed some cattle and hogs. We hear that we wounded some of them." 5th, "This morning the vessels in Holmes Hole came to sail and proceeded to the eastward towards Nantucket. About noon we were all discharged and came home." 7th, "Before noon alarmed that the shipping from Falmouth were coming again with a reinforcement. After dinner James and I set out. A little before sunset saw the shipping in the Sound. They had been to Nantucket and took several vessels. They set one on fire, we saw the smoke. They made no stop but proceeded up the Sound."

May 1779 - On the 9th, Percival reports: "Silas Goodspeed killed by a musket ball going to Nantucket in an engagement with a Tory privateer." 16th, "A little before dark was alarmed to go to Falmouth. Sat right out in the night, James and Thomas and myself. We got to Falmouth sometime before sunrise." 17th, "Intrenching. The report is they are taking off horses of Naushon. This evening was discharged and got home a little before day. Went and came home afoot."

The Continental Army Service

In the flush of excitement of responding to Washington's early calls for seven regiments from this state (five thousand men) there seems to have been no trouble raising Sandwich's share of about forty-three men. These were for three years' service and those obtained included men from Mashpee. An officer from Charleston, South Carolina was given permission by the General Court to try to raise three hundred seamen here for the defense of South Carolina. This may have drawn off a few Cape men. Later in 1776 an effort was made to raise five thousand men for short duty at Boston and Rhode Island considered as Continental Army service. Sandwich's share was about forty men, but town meeting records only mention ten, because to raise these, £30 had to be borrowed by the town to pay bounties. Hence, by the end of 1776 a number of the more willing Sandwich volunteers were away for three years or saw duty in three-month Continental service. In January 1777, Washington called for fifteen more battalions from this state, amounting to one man in seven of military age. This was a heavy burden because no credit was given for those already absent in the army or on privateers, or unwilling to serve for religious or Tory sentiments. Service in the Continental Army was completely unlike the local militia activities described earlier. In the Continental service, men were assigned to one of the Massachusetts regiments in the field where the officers were unknown, distances great, food poor and morale low. Continental recruits got a certain bonus payment to sign up, then got their wages from the state at the end of their period plus any additional payments guaranteed by the home town, but with inflation the paper currency declined rapidly. Army duty then was strongly resisted, and the few who could tolerate it were hard to find. A major community effort was required to meet this requisition, and by happy chance a page of evidence on the scene in Sandwich at this critical time was preserved at the Sandwich Historical Society. It is a portion of a memorial to the General Court on the problem of raising the men, and shows a town in turmoil:

> "To the Honorable the Council and the Honorable the House of Representatives of the Massachusetts Bay in General Court assembled. The Memorial of the Militia Officers, Selectmen and Committee of Correspondence etc. for the town of Sandwich, humbly sheweth that whereas your Memorialists were directed by a late Act of this Government entitled "An Act for Providing a Reinforcement to the American Army" to enlist by lot or draft our quota part of all the able bodied men from sixteen years old and upwards" etc. and having met with opposition & difficulty thereon we think it our duty to represent to your Honors a true state of facts, and to pray your further directions & interposition thereon.
>
> "Upon our first receiving the Act, we immediately met together, for the purpose of contriving how to procure the men, and after consulting together, considering a number in the Town had done their turns without any bounty, and others had hired hands to do in their room, to do their turns, and as the last men for Rhode Island were raised by draft and generally approved of, and a number of wealthy persons in the Town had refused to do any thing; we judged the most prudent & speedy way to procure the men would be to enlist as many as we could & the rest to draft; especially as we apprehended adding to the establishment of the Court would be attended with evil consequences. Accordingly we divided the men into lots, each lot to procure a man and immediately caused the whole Militia of the town to be warned to appear on the 19th day of December, it being then the 2nd day of December last, and the man lotted be notified therof so that they might be providing their men.
>
> "At the time appointed the Militia came together and your Memorialists endeavoured to enlist the men but failed. In fact we found that some of our best soldiers, who had been in the service, were well disposed, and the most likely to engage again would not turn out till those who had been backward & done nothing & especially those who were open *known Tories* among us had been compelled to march, pay their fines or go to gaol.
>
> "Your Memorialists having then received an explanatory resolve of court were necessitated to make several alterations in the allotment which we accordingly did, and to give the people all the opportunity we could to agree among themselves, and it being now evening we ordered the Militia into the meeting house and acquainted them with the allotments & the reason of it, and notified them that they must procure their men by the then next Wednesday or else we should proceed to drafts. We had been upon this business now several days, and no applications to your Memorialists to call the Town together nor to the Selectmen had been made; nor did we conceive it would be the

most agreeable way to the Town in general for us so to do, although we had frequently heard the Tories were determined to do nothing and some had said they would be damned before they would fight in such a cause—that Howe's proposals were reasonable and we ought to submit etc. But now upon declaring to them the allotment, a disturbance was immediately raised among those called Tories—the committee were call'd Damned Rascals, and told no regard should be paid to their proceedings and were abused and insulted very much—the Tories collected thick round your Memorialists, and bragging of one another that they were *Good Fellows* etc. and stamping with their feet, pounding their fists upon the table, and making all the disturbance they could. This raised the indignation of the Whigs to the highest pitch and had not your Memorialists interposed with their utmost influence & persuasion an affray would have taken place in the meetinghouse, as all the Tories were together and your Memorialists suspect that this opposition of theirs was preconcerted and that they intended to have prevented our doing anything; but with much difficulty we got the people to be quiet especially as it was the night season and an affray would be attended with dangerous consequences, and then the Committee etc. retired to *the house* where they sought to do their business, but were soon alarmed with a report that between 20 and 30 Tories having met at *another house* were drawing up papers & consulting together and that they had abused some of the Whigs that went into the house (although a tavern)—call'd them spies etc. At this the people were enraged & *entered the house;* we were soon informed they were fighting and then thought it our duty as the readiest way to break it up to go and turn those Tories out and disperse them which we did.

"The next day but one, which was that appointed to make the returns from the lots to the Committee, and after the draft was compleatd a Petition was presented to the Selectmen to call a meeting to see if the Town would hire men to supply the places of those ordered to be raised, signed by towards twenty. This made great uneasiness and was supposed, if not done with that view, to have a tendency to retard the business of raising the men. The Selectmen applied to the Memorialists for advice, but we declined giving any advice. A number of the inhabitants being then in the other room were consulted, among whom were several of the signers to the said Petition, and upon consideration of the matter together, it was concluded by the whole for the Selectmen to take the advice of the people who were called in (without your Memorialists). They unanimously advised & consented to withdraw the Petition, and one of the two who presented it withdrew it. After this the Selectmen asked the opinion of your Memorialists who all unanimously judged it the most provident measure. We had compleated our business of drafting and thirteen out of twenty nine of the men were procured but the other lots..."

The selectmen at this time were Joseph Nye, Seth Freeman and Sylvanus Nye. There is no reference in town meeting to expenditures for raising these men, so the twenty-nine needed may have been raised by draft or by funds contributed by the "wealthy persons" who had not helped before. This Memorial also is interesting for its reference to "the house" and to "another house" which were taverns. The first was the public house operated by Benjamin Fessenden, Jr. adjacent to the meetinghouse on Main Street at River Street. The other was the Newcomb Tavern on Grove Street operated by William Newcomb, Jr. where the Tories gathered. The text of the Memorial makes it clear that any Whigs who dared to enter Newcomb's public house were considered spies.

More Men Needed

During the next three years the requisitions for men became an endless series at ever higher cost:

Jan. 1778- £50 raised to hire nine men for eight months.

Sept. 1778 - At a further requisition Brig. Joseph Otis complained to Boston "As the enemy are around and threaten danger here, it is like dragging men from home when their houses are on fire." As a result the latest requisition on this County was lifted.

July 177 - Twelve men for nine months. Three had to be hired by the Quaker community, and the town raised £2550 to pay for the others.

Mar. 1780 - With many of the three-year terms up, many renewals were demanded. Fifteen were needed immediately.

June 1780 - Twenty-four men for six months and forty-three for three months. Sandwich proposed to pay $15 per month to these men in silver, an unheard-of bounty. Their state salary in paper currency was nearly worthless. There is a reference in July to using liquor on muster day to secure enlistments. The town of Barnstable failed to meet this June quota for men, and promptly incurred a large fine from the state. Sandwich asked the General Court to free Sandwich people who owned land in Barnstable from paying taxes resulting from this fine. Clearly things were getting desperate. Part of the Cape's June 1780 levy was cancelled.

Dec. 1780 - Twenty-two men for three years were demanded from Sandwich. This coupled with a huge request for more beef or grain brought Memorials for abatements from several Cape towns as being impossible to meet. A Sandwich committee tried to borrow £660 in silver or gold for bounties, then amounting to sixteen Spanish milled dollars per man per month.

Apr. 1781 - A certain number of the Dec. 1780 men had been raised but many sections of town (called classes) failed to supply men. The Dec. 1780 quota became highly controversial when the town was fined, and attempted to charge this fine to the delinquent classes.

June 1781 - Four men for five months were found, with silver bounties.

Sep. 1781- A requisition for eighteen men for three months was lost in delivery, and the town was fined for failing to meet this draft.

Raising Food and Clothing

In addition to the levies of men for the Continental Army, the towns were asked for supplies for the Continental Army, blankets, clothing and beef. These demands bore very heavily on this county because its normal economy was based on fishing, trade, and maritime employment now defunct. The county produced cloth and food for its own needs but not for export. With many men away, the capacity to produce these supplies was severely limited, and income to pay taxes to support town purchases kept shrinking. Some clothing may have been donated by citizens in the first flush of patriotic fever, but raising these later big quotas came down to finding funds to buy them. The two beef demands in 1780 simply couldn't be met either in cows available for slaughter or in cash that could be borrowed by the town against future taxes. The lower Cape towns rebelled completely against the December beef quota, and later all the Cape towns prepared a petition asking relief in view of their other expenses, impaired incomes and shortage of all materials and animals. Sandwich tried to make a partial payment against the 1780 demands but this offer was rejected. The town then had no choice but to ask for abatement of the levy or accept its fine for non-compliance. The levies included:

Date	*Item*	*County*	*Sandwich*
1775	Blankets	£190.9 worth	a share
1776	Coats, breeches, etc.	"Large amount"	a share
1777	Blankets	160	25
1778	Shirts, shoes and socks	505 sets	55 sets
1779	Shirts, shoes and socks	505 sets	55 sets
1780	Blankets	180	20
1780	Shirts, shoes, socks	353 sets	39 sets
1780	Beef	71, 280 lbs.	11, 120 lbs.

1780	Beef	136, 875 lbs.	21, 253 lbs.
1781	Beef	56, 489 lbs.	8, 000 lbs.
1781	Clothing	238 sets	37 sets
1781	Blankets	119	18

Sandwich Tories

A list of Sandwich Tories has been assembled by the Archives from many sources. Frederick Freeman, whose father was involved so deeply, refused to cite the names of any Tories when writing in the 1850s. It has been estimated that about twenty thousand residents in the Colonies left for British-held areas such as Long Island, New York City, Quebec, Nova Scotia, West Indies or Britain itself. Some of these returned and were accepted back into their communities after 1783. The Sandwich residents who chose to leave probably made their way to Newport, Rhode Island or to the offshore islands where they could find transport to Long Island or New York City. Those imprisoned from Cape Cod were jailed in Boston and were periodically included in exchanges for American prisoners. Sandwich Tories represented the full range of walks of life from laborer through artisans and farmers to the monied gentry. None of the Sandwich Tories were forced to go to Boston in the period before the Evacuation March 17, 1776, and none is found in the lists of the three thousand Americans who applied for pensions or damage claims with the British Government. A brief timetable of events here related to Tories follows:

1774 - Several confirmed enemies of the patriot movement were exposed in the closing of the court and the attack on Doctor Freeman.

1775-1776 - Militia and Continental volunteers were signed up and it became clear that many would have to be forced to serve or to refuse service. The December 1776 Memorial quoted earlier shows the problems when serious efforts were made to draft the unwilling.

1777 - Thirteen were drafted, refused to march and were jailed in Barnstable, where they were released by Tories and escaped. Not knowing their names we do not know how many were caught, fined and returned to Sandwich.

1778 - Six were jailed for trial in February. Those jailed confessed, including "Ruggles' son-in-law" and one in high position (probably Wm. Newcomb Jr. and Melatiah Bourne). Three more were jailed in March and tried. Those still jailed here were released on bond and some took the Oath of Allegiance. The state passed an Act of Banishment listing those who had left, including nineteen from Sandwich.

1779 - Petitions were received from refugees for permission to visit families and to settle affairs; also from families here to be allowed to leave. A petition from Nehemiah Webb in Boston prison for a short visit to Sandwich was approved. The county was ordered to seize property of those banished and sell it; Joseph Nye was to be the agent in Sandwich.

1782 - Permission was given a number of wives and children of men banished and living on Long Island to come to Sandwich to visit relatives.

1783 - It was stated in town meeting that if the estates of two Sandwich women whose husbands had died abroad were to be sold, the women would then become town charges; a decision on sale of these properties was postponed. The peace treaty did not include a national policy or law on refugees, but allowed each state to decide on leniency and restitution or return of confiscated properties. A number did return, and after the exhaustion and confusion of the war period, no animosity was expressed.

Smallpox

This disease was one of the terrors that sprang up periodically in the cities and towns of New England, brought in by travelers on ships. The Indians were especially vulnerable and were repeatedly ravaged. There was a prolonged outbreak in Boston in the 1717-1722 period, when Reverend Cotton Mather and Dr. Zabdiel Boyleston recommended innoculation but found their houses and persons attacked by the superstitious as a result. When smallpox was present in a county seat, as in Barnstable in 1757, court sessions were suspended and all public meetings were closed. A general outbreak of smallpox began in early 1778 in Boston and in many towns. The Percival diary records that a town meeting had been adjourned to February 2, 1778 on account of the disease. Those who had been exposed and recovered were found to be immune, and could act as nurses if sufficiently dedicated. Percival notes that his neighbor in South Sandwich, Samuel Hilliard, seemed to be sick, and he went to West Barnstable to secure the services of James Blossom as a nurse. Fortunately, this case turned out not to be smallpox. Later he notes that Caleb Wing had the disease and died July 1, and that several more in the same house were sick. At the town meeting of February 2, it had been voted that those infected should be removed to the house of John Gibbs which was in the Head-of-the-Bay area near the Plymouth line. The town meeting records:

"The question was put whether the Town will give liberty for such person to be inoculated in the houses of Messrs. John and Silvanus Gibbs as they shall see fit to consent to admit for that purpose under such restrictions and limitations as the Town shall judge most expedient the Small Pox being already in said houses.

Whereas sundry persons belonging to this Town are now infested with the Small Pox, voted that such inhabitants of this town as are already infected by removed to the house of John Gibbs and kept there until

> properly cleansed from infection. And such inhabitants of the Towns who are now in this Town that are infected with said distemper be forthwith removed from this Town—Voted that the Selectmen be directed to take immediate and constant care to see that said house and persons therein are provided with prudent careful nurses and cleansers, that none but such be admitted. That they appoint proper limitations beyond which the persons infected and the attendants shall not pass. That no other person be permitted to go beyond the lines they shall prescribe than such as they shall permit. Also, that they take proper care that the roads are fenced up, the way turned, red flags fixed up and every precaution used to prevent the spread of the infection and to place suitable and sufficient guards to see their regulations are adhered to. If they judge it necessary to see that the cats and dogs in the neighborhood are killed.
>
> Voted, that it is the desire of the Town that each individual use his utmost endeavors that the laws relative to the Small Pox be carried into strict execution."

During the 1778 epidemic, an Indian named Solomon Joseph was also brought to the Gibbs home for treatment.

Inflation

During the Revolution Sandwich's records of taxes and payments were all kept in pounds sterling. This was the currency of issue of Massachusetts state bills in circulation, and of state taxes. Coins in circulation were silver shillings and smaller coins, some gold coins and foreign coins especially the big Spanish milled dollar worth six shillings. Specie was always in short supply. Presumably the specie reserve held by the former Provincial Government in Boston was evacuated with the British forces in March 1776 and lost to the new patriot public treasurer. Public expenses for salaries of soldiers and their clothing and food were great and kept mounting. Probably the chief contributor to inflation was the Continental Congress, which represented an incipient national presence but had no national treasury or powers except what could be extracted from the states. The Congress had no power to tax and without treaties with foreign governments had no ability to borrow. Ultimately, there was recognition from France and Spain but this did not improve the currency backing. The Congress had printed in all some $200 million in Continental Currency to be used to pay soldiers and suppliers, and this is what led the way in devaluation.

Some hints of the paper currency problems are found in town meeting records. On March 13, 1777 the town voted:

> "Whereas there is a considerable sum of money of this and the other States in the hands of the Town Treasurer, which by law is not to be offered in any payments after the first day of December next, therefore, voted that said Treasurer be directed to take such measures as to him shall appear most prudent to get it exchanged or notes for it."

Massachusetts was calling in both old issues of its own currency and especially that of neighboring states in circulation here in exchange for new state issues. In 1779 our constables were still found to be accepting for tax payments "emissions which are taken out of circulation." The Treasurer was authorized to try to exchange it with the state treasury, and to credit the citizens with the equivalent of what the town could realize on the outdated bills. Even worse, the British were found to have damaged the patriot economy by issuing counterfeit bills in large quantity. Repeatedly our constables accepted counterfeits in tax payments, which were turned in by the town to the state treasury, no doubt with fingers crossed. When the state advised the amounts in counterfeits to be made up, the town had no choice but to add this to the next tax, getting a certificate from the constable that the bogus bills had been accepted by him in good faith.

In the first flush of patriotism in 1776, citizens were urged to turn in silver and gold for paper currency, and no doubt some did. There were also urgent appeals for rags to make paper, replacing the imports of good paper now cut off. There were appeals to turn in lead such as in window frames and counterweights, to be used for bullets. Repeatedly, there were appeals to loan funds to the state against state notes, with county officials in charge of the drives. These came on top of town appeals for loans to tide river crises of payments for bounties or to meet state tax deadlines. The Percival diary reports responding to the appeals for loans in periods when he had surplus cash.

Prices in Paper Money

In 1777 and again in 1779 the towns attempted to slow the inflation rate by posting a schedule of prices of common goods and services which citizens should not exceed. The 1777 schedules for Rochester and for Barnstable have been preserved, and are in very close agreement. The schedule in Sandwich in 1779 was written in to town meeting records. The citizens were sternly warned on July 14, 1779:

> "Voted that (nine men) be a Committee for the purpose of seeing that the Resolves of the Convention of Concord be carried into execution and that no person violate the same in this Town, or the prices that may be agreed upon by the foregoing Committee and accepted by the Town and published according to the foregoing vote; and in case they do, to publish their names to the world and report them to this Town that they may be further dealt with as they may think proper."

Therefore the various town committees set the schedule on prices locally. Over a two-year period, prices in paper money increased about twenty fold; what had been shilling numbers now became pounds. The highest inflation was in the local grains, and in imported sugar, molasses and rum. The lowest inflation was in low-value local products such as salt hay (up nine fold), salt itself (up eleven fold), cheese (ten fold) and horse expenses (twelve fold). The surprise is that so much imported material was still quoted, in spite of embargoes and losses. Much of this may have been hoarded and sold sparingly. With the national thirst someone must have been bringing in sugar and rum. Even coffee and chocolate are quoted in 1779. The committee in Sandwich that produced the price guidelines as of August 1779 were hard-headed town leaders who were under no illusions about their ability to stop inflation. They appealed to people's patriotism not to increase prices, and especially to honor the value of paper money by not demanding silver. The town voted as follows on a statement to accompany the posted price guidelines:

> "Whereas trading for silver money has in the opinion of the Town hurt the credit of the currency of this (State) and the United States, any person who has any article to dispose of who refuses to take the currency of this (State) or the United States for such article thereby does an injury to the public–
>
> voted that the Committee choose to take care of such persons as violate the statement above be directed to proceed with such persons as they may know of who demand silver money for such articles as they have to dispose of as they may be directed to do with such as violate the above statement, and that this vote be posted up with the statement."

These leaders set a good example themselves and could use this and other leverage to get the townsmen to sell for paper and keep increases down, but everyone occasionally used silver dollars quietly when some item was badly needed and the other party could be trusted. The hurricane of inflation continued, and very soon even the town had to bargain with silver dollars for the most precious commodity of all—the service of men willing to spend time in the Continental Army.

The number of paper dollars per silver dollar went up from five to one in early 1778, to thirty to one in early 1780, to sixty to one in 1781 at the war's nadir. Town meeting records in 1782 refer specifically to a rate of seventy-five to one in negotiating credit with the state treasurer for a payment made by the town. It became clear that the time of payment was a critical factor in comparing actual value received, for example, in taxes paid by citizens early or late in a collecting period, or bounty paid to soldiers (unless in silver), or town payments to the state treasurer on major installments of state taxes or paid in lieu of beef and clothing. These novel calculations in such trying circumstances must have been extremely difficult for the town treasurer and especially for the town constables who had to extract as many as three separate tax levies from struggling families in a single year. The poorer families got deeply in arrears. Prices escalated particularly in the spring when stocks were down and seed was needed to plant, but slowed in the summer and fall when there was food to sell.

A Collector's Lot is Not a Happy One

The constable's office had become chiefly that of tax collector. It was never a popular job but every year one or two were persuaded to take their turn by the central corps of ongoing town officials. The Revolution, with its swollen expenses and inflation, became a nightmare for the constables. Here is the record of each tax year:

1775 - Two refused but two others accepted.

1776 - The first two named completed their collections.

1777 - Two finally accepted after the first three had refused and paid their fines.

1778 - Two accepted after four refused. An extra bonus of £8 each was granted them over their trouble with the second tax levied. For the first time a board of five assessors was created to aid the selectmen, treasurer and constables in the tax process.

1779 - Two accepted after six refused. An award scale of 1% of collections was set up plus £50. The town this summer was destitute of cash and had to borrow £1,000, and urged the constables to turn in proceeds rapidly to meet urgent demands. In 1780 these two 1779 constables were awarded £57 each for having collected a third levy in one year. In 1782 the 1779 collections were still in arrears and a process against the 1779 constables was voted.

1780 - The office of constable for 1780 was offered at auction but no one bid. The town was divided into six districts and one representative of each was appointed with only one refusal. In 1781 the pay of these constables was considered, and they were allowed 2% of the last levy. Much was found to be uncollected at the end of 1781. In 1782 a committee was formed to start process against the six constables of 1780. The 1780 tax collection problems were compounded by the state fine for failing to raise men. An average cost for men raised was used to assess against the delinquent districts, and a special Resolve was passed by the General Court in 1783 to allow Sandwich to collect this; it was paid off in 1784.

1781 - Two constables agreed to try to collect for £23 each in silver. They were soon in arrears. A process against one was ordered in 1784 but was suspended as nothing would be gained by jailing him.

1782 - Selectmen were unable to find constables at any fee and taxes were not assessed or paid, the first time this had ever happened. Because our state taxes were not paid, the county sheriff was authorized in 1784 to begin distress proceedings. A collector agreed to work for 4½% and enough was raised to pay state taxes and fines.

1783, 1784, 1785 - The selectmen were unable to hire collectors and the town passed no spending appropriations in these years, with no current taxes collected.

JOSEPH NYE ESQUIRE AND STEPHEN NYE – SANDWICH LEADERS IN REVOLUTION

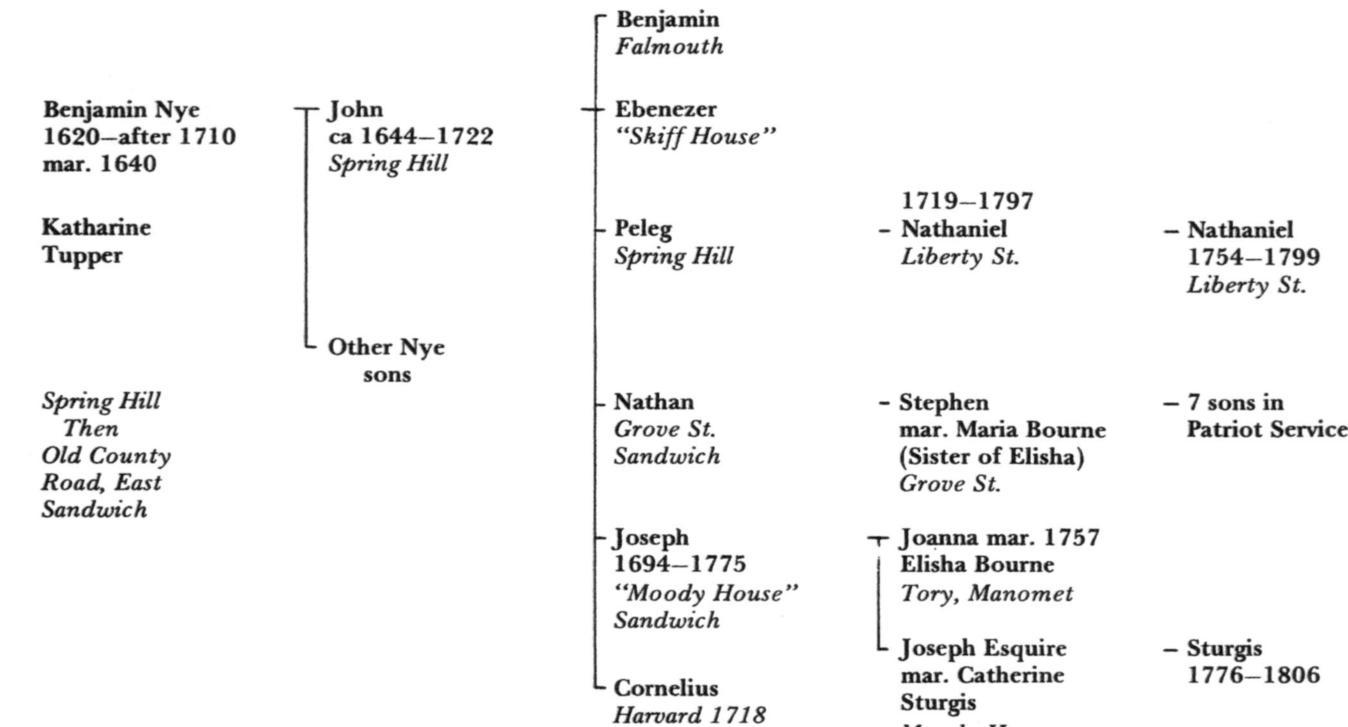

Other Town Events

Silas Tupper continued to serve as schoolmaster throughout the war, rotating through the districts. In 1777 he was paid £95, but thereafter he was only allowed £40, a pittance. In 1784 a proposal was made that one teacher be hired by the town for the village, Spring Hill and Scusset at four months each, and that the other outlying areas have the same cost per person for their own decision on teaching. This was sensible, but nothing could be done without money, and the town was fined for not having any schoolmaster.

The annual herring run was one of the great comforts of the town. In 1777, six hundred barrels were auctioned in addition to all the family use and the allowance of two barrels per family to the Indians. The auction dropped to three hundred fifty barrels in 1778, to three hundred barrels in 1779, and by 1780 the run was so diminished that none could be taken for auction, and only limited amounts were allowed for personal use. Apparently the takings had been excessive for several years, or obstructions had prevented the breeding stock from reaching the pond. This continued for four years, while stocks slowly regained their numbers. In 1784 a small surplus of two hundred barrels was auctioned, some of the first income the town had seen.

In 1781 when tax collections were failing, the tax abatements which had always been given to Reverend Hawley and Reverend Elisha Tupper were suspended. Abatements were given to several of the town's poor and to the families of those who had died in service or of smallpox. The town even claimed a rebate on its state taxes for expenses paid to poor Indians, an item not seen before.

Benjamin Fessenden Jr. had long served as town clerk (1758-1783). As a Harvard man (Class of 1746) he knew perfectly well how to spell "travel" but he continued a private little joke in the town meeting records concerning the town's representatives to the General Court and the various Congresses and Conventions, where they had to complain of the town's problems and bear the burdens of the state. When the town approved their expenses, Fessenden always wrote the entry "travail and attendance." He died in office in the fall of 1783 and was replaced as clerk by his neighbor Melatiah Bourne, Esq. who had recovered the town's confidence after a brief imprisonment for Tory leanings. (The town's most distinguished Tory, Elisha Bourne, reappeared in the town late in 1783 and was promptly allowed to plan a sawmill on Herring River.) The townsmen hated winter town meetings, but two in January 1784 were necessary under the threat of the High Sheriff. They were convened in the cold meetinghouse, then immediately adjourned to the public house of the widow Fessenden where they reconvened in comfort.

Bad as things seemed in Sandwich in 1783, there were others nearby who were ready to join our town. A petition was approved by the town meeting that nine families from the Ellisville sector of South Plymouth should be considered as part of Sandwich. They were much closer to Sandwich than to Plymouth, and may have felt (as the Cataumet group in Sandwich) that they weren't getting much from their own town. Changes of town lines had to be approved by the General Court and this was quashed.

The Dark Day

The Percival diary has a section missing in 1780 so that we are deprived of his account of the Dark Day of May 19. Here is an eyewitness account from a Quaker source entitled *A day I never saw the like before:*

> "The morning opens with thunder and lightnings, on the 19th day of the fifth month called May 1780 the wind at SSW, the sun shined out about 8 o'clock in the morning—about 9 o'clock it began to rain small showers and continuous until about 10 then the rain ceased and the clouds seemed to be gathering together in great thickness and about half past ten there seemed to be a darkness gradually appeared and by eleven it was quite discovered to be something uncommon and by twelve it was so dark that we could not see to read large print in the room, and by dinner time or at one o'clock it was so dark that we could not see to dine, but was obliged to have candles lit as in the evening when the moon shone not very bright, so the darkness continued for about two hours with but little alteration from twelve to two o'clock, at length the darkness began gradually to go off, but left a brassy yellow which was all the time insomuch as silver buckles looked exactly like gold in one's shoes that yellow look continued until about half past three, when it went off pretty suddenly and left the looks of nature much as usual; but in the evening the wind having got to the north or easterly of it perhaps as far as NNE when the smell of sulphur or something like being to the leeward of a swamp that has been burning or a chimney that has been on fire, and a darkness came on in the evening insomuch that we could not see any difference when our eyes were shut fast or when opened—notwithstanding the moon was at its full and that darkness continued until about twelve o'clock at night and then went off, it was to the astonishment and terror of I believe almost every person, for my part I was not without thoughts that the last day had come, for no one that did not see can imagine how gloomy it looked. I leave this a memorandum for future generations to see how it was at that time if the like was ever to be again that they may know it was no more than has been seen before."

The explanation was that there were heavy forest fires to the west, the smoke from which was very dense and then was trapped over this region by a peculiar atmospheric inversion which concentrated the smoke together with a dense cloud cover.

The Farm Life

The wartime in histories and in our town meeting records has few bright spots, but reading the Percival diary of farm life between the Hog Ponds in South Sandwich, one enters a different world. This was the secure life of hard work and plenty of food that kept most of the town sane and stable. This was the life that kept militia men anxious to get home again from their short tours, and made them desperately unwilling to sign up in the Continental service. On the farm the season governed the range of activities and the weather the daily chores. Percival notes for a composite year:

January - To Joseph Lawrence's charcoal pit and loaded up to carry to town tomorrow if it be weather/killing our hogs and cutting up pork/been for the last of our salt hay/Samuel Hilliard has been shoeing our sled/I have been mending shoes.

February - Sowed tobacco seed (in frames).

March - Carting dung and plowing/first robins and blackbirds/pruning our orchard.

April - To town to get plough irons sharpened/sowing oats and clearing a turnip yard/sowing flax

May - Began to harrow for planting/planted 12 acres of corn/Peach trees in bloom/planting potatoes/washed and sheared sheep/turned out 14 sheep in the woods/Appletrees in bloom and very thick.

June - Began to weed corn/turned cattle to the plains (fenced) to pasture/setting out 320 tobacco plants/fired our charcoal pit.

July - Began to hill corn/hoeing tobacco/began to reap rye.

August - Rain catched us with two acres of rye down/pulling flax/mowing oats/pair of oxen killed with the heat/putting flax in water/ground off 2 new scythes.

September - Mowing (salt hay) at Lawrence Hole/carried home a load of hay from Lawrence Hole/winnowed 35 bushels of rye/cutting corn stalks

October - Harvesting beans/bought cattle from the plains and shut up hogs/cribbing corn/gathering winter apples/husking corn and twisting tobacco/pulling up potatoes/got up our sheep—2 missing/bought 12 Greening apple trees, one dollar each/pulled up our Hanover turnips and put them in the ground (sand storage in protected area)/finished husking with assistance of some Indians.

November - Killing a sheep/making hay yard fences/secured our pompions (pumpkins)/Father has been to town with the turnips/calf died last night. I have skinned it/to beach for a load of thatch.

December - Carting split wood/killed our beef cow, 40 lbs. tallow, 465 lbs. meat, hide 58 lbs/work upon the shop chimney/cutting up our

> beef and salting it/School Master Tupper has come today to keep school/a large buck was found dead in Spectacle Pond and frozen in. The ponds are froze to bear.

The Percival Compound

A chart on an adjoining page shows the Percival family. The first in Sandwich was Lt. James who arrived from Virginia, married the widow Mary Rainsford Bassett and had three children. They settled near Ashumet Pond on the main road between Sandwich and Falmouth. Their son John relocated in Barnstable, and his son John moved again to new land in South Sandwich, just south of the two small ponds called the Hog Ponds. Here John and his five sons built up a thriving farm. His four sisters married Peleg Lawrence, Cornelius Jones, Reuben Jones and Benjamin Blossom and lived nearby, these related households forming a supportive neighborhood soon called "Farmersville." Benjamin Percival with a growing family needed a home of his own, and states in his diary in 1782 that he bought his family's old home in Ashumet (which had been sold to the Fish family) knocked it apart June 1 and brought it to South Sandwich where he re-erected it between the Hog Ponds, moving joyfully into "our old or rather new house" on October 9. His brother James built a house just north of the upper pond, so that it became a three-house compound. Brother Thomas lived in the Old County Road/Chase Road area where the South Sandwich men gathered to cut salt hay on their marsh lots in Barnstable Great Marshes and in Scorton Marsh. The three brothers cheerfully set off together to the alarms at Falmouth during the war. By the time the diary opens in January 1777, two of Benjamin's brothers and a sister had already moved to a new plantation area in the Berkshires where a number of Sandwich and Barnstable families had settled.

Hard work around the year was expected but it was shared and food was plentiful. Benjamin, throughout the forty-year period of his diary, notes the progress of the seasons, the joys and tragedies of his neighbors, the rumors of distant events. His expressions are often terse but very expressive:

> *February* - This afternoon we have been to wedding we have had a great wedding.
>
> *Mar.* - Come home from the wedding with some of the weddeners with me. (Weddings were generally held on Thursday and the guests from out of town stayed until the weekend.)
>
> *Jul.* - 50 folks here today a-cherrying.
>
> *Nov.* - A grand husking here this evening 70 or 80 people husked 10 loads.
>
> *Jan.* - (Old Eben Blossom, one of the town's poor, had died at

Gershom Crocker's, and his things were "vendued"). Sylvanus Nye was vendue-master.

Oct. - At Thomas Crocker's (Cotuit) to eat oysters.

Sept. - A number have been here today to eat melons.

There were shopping trips to the Otis general store at West Barnstable:

To Great Marshes for steel - got 2 pounds/to Otis store to get buttons and things/Thomas has been to Great Marshes, got me some paper/got 400 bricks/Mother and Lydia (his wife) to Great Marshes store to get cloaks and riding hoods cut/to Otis's and exchanged some flax for rice and other articles.

There were accidents, illnesses, and suicides:

Dr. Freeman here to my child sick/Thomas to Esquire Marston's to get a tooth out/John Crocker's son 12 had a cart wheel ran over his head which killed him instantly and the same day two young men drowned/Benjamin Nye's son drowned in the mill floom/Josiah Jones scalded in a salt kettle (died in two weeks)/Benjamin Marston's wife hanged herself in a despairing condition sometime past/2 of Joseph Blishes children shot by a lad, one died. Whether done by design is not known.

The Magee Storm

On December 24 and 25, 1778 Percival mentions intense cold. Then on December 26 the diary reads: "Most violent storm I ever knew, snow in entry of house breast deep." On the 25th an American privateer *General Arnold* under Captain James Magee had left Boston but was forced to Plymouth, broke its anchor line and grounded on an outer bar where she was swept by high waves. Rescuers could not reach her for two more days because of the storm and her position. When they finally could get aboard seventy-two men were found dead and thirty-three still alive but badly frozen. Nine more died and of those that survived many required amputation or were permanent invalids. (One from Barnstable, Barnabas Downs, lost both feet but got around on his knees with crutches; he married and had five children.) Many of the crew were from the Cape where the shock was profound. Percival stated "friends of Magee victims from Sandwich and Barnstable went to Plymouth with sheets to lay them out." A mass grave in Plymouth was dug for sixty-six victims, and the other dead were taken by their families. The diary includes a copy of a long poem written to celebrate this tragedy. Percival also notes the widespread damage from the extreme high tides and ice floes brought in from the Bay by the north wind, which "broke Hinckley's bridge and dyke which had kept the tide out of a piece of meadow for a number of years." On January 1, a party of owners surveyed the damages in Great Marshes and found "there was 364 hay stacks come ashore, the highest tide in fifty years." On January 4 and 5 he and his neighbors "help get hay out of the marshes. Got out two stacks which was all we could get to. The ice has broke the staddles to pieces." (Staddles were circles of locust poles on which the stacks were kept above usual high tide until they could be brought ashore.) This was a serious loss of winter and spring food for the cattle, horses and oxen.

The Berkshire Families

In the crisis of raising men and supplies in late 1780, down-Cape towns petitioned for relief setting forth as one factor "the extraordinary diminution of inhabitants" they had experienced. Similarly, Sandwich town meeting records in January 1782, in a petition for relief, cites "the removal of so great a number of their inhabitants." During the period 1771-1790, for which census figures are available, the total population on the Cape remained about stationary but the birth-rate remained high. Obviously, there were many removals which in the stress of war were not well described. Beside the Tory family departures, some families sailed off quietly to Nova Scotia, others to Maine where taxes may have been much less, and in the Percival diary we get a picture of yearly travel to the remote Berkshires, a long trip from inn to inn. The families Percival mentions are ones his community in South Sandwich and West Barnstable all knew, the Chanters, Crockers, Backuses, Goodspeeds, Freemans, Davises, Fullers, Adamses and Percivals. The former Cape people returned every few years for reunions, and relatives here went out to see the new homes and children. Benjamin's father John journeyed to Lee, Lenox and Hartwood in 1777, 1778 and again in 1780, an extraordinary effort, each time in a party with a few more going than coming back. Travel was most commonly in June when the crops were growing, or in November when the harvest was over. (Percival himself made only one trip in 1795.) The Resolves of the State Legislature April 10, 1777 read: "A Committee appointed to repair to Hartwood on Petition of Elisha Freeman." This was Percival's brother-in-law. Hartwood was renamed Washington in 1777.

"A Very Unnatural Murder"

The March 14, 1778 entry in Percival's diary shows how travelers acted to spread interesting news quickly. It reads: "My brother John got here today from Lennox—a very unnatural murder in Brookfield, a woman hired two Russians to kill her husband." Percival and the rest of Sandwich were diverted by this piece of scandal, but would have been astonished to know that the woman in the story was a Sandwich girl, born-Bathsheba Ruggles on February 13, 1745/6 in the Newcomb Tavern. She had been brought up in the glamorous but stormy Ruggles household and had married Joshua Spooner in 1766. Spooner was the son of an English immigrant John Spooner, and was born in 1741.

The facts are, very briefly, that the Spooners lived on a farm in Brookfield and had three living children. He was a trader and opportunist who bought property from the Olivers in Middleboro and five hundred fifty acres from Ruggles himself in 1772. The Spooner marriage was loveless, and she was distraught after the enforced departure of her father, General Timothy Ruggles, in 1774. She welcomed a wounded American army veteran Ezra Ross to the household in 1777, when he was only 17, and early in 1778 found herself pregnant. She determined wildly that Spooner must die, but found Ross unable to carry it off. She hired two British army escapees from Burgoyne's imprisoned forces, Buchanan and Brooks, to do the murder for $1,000. (These men were called Hessians which was garbled to Russians in Sandwich.) They beat and robbed Spooner and dropped him in the well on March 1, fleeing to Worcester with Ross. They were arrested the next day, and Bathsheba the day after. Bathsheba's sister Martha Tufts was charitable enough to bury Spooner.

The trial with its sensational interest posed a problem for the Worcester County Court which had been decimated by the departure of Ruggles and many Tory lawyers and judges. The Governor himself had to organize the trial, and selected four Worcester judges under Judge William Cushing of the State Supreme Court. Lawyer for the state was the famous Robert Treat Paine, the state's Attorney General; for the defense was Levi Lincoln, a brilliant young lawyer, later U.S. Attorney General under Jefferson. The trial was held in Old South Church and ran for sixteen hours, broken only by short recesses. The defense of Bathsheba was insanity as her thinking was extremely irrational. However, as an adultress, a Tory herself and daughter of the dreaded Ruggles, she was doomed. All four were sentenced to hang June 4. Only after the trial did she tell Reverend Maccarty of Old South Church that she was pregnant, and the executions were put off to July 2. Five doctors testified that she was indeed pregnant, and the Governor should then have put off her execution until after the birth. But public opinion was extremely aroused and hostile, and he appointed a pliant jury of twelve women and two men, all midwives, who declared her not pregnant. Late in June Maccarty appealed again desperately, as she was by now five months along. But a third panel of six persons gave a split decision and the great quadruple hanging was on. She was too ill to attend the Execution Sermon, a bitter and courageous denunciation by Maccarty from Deuteronomy 9:13 of the malevolent spirit that took the life of the innocent unborn. The hanging took place before an enormous crowd from all over the state, a unique event. Her sister Mary Green buried her on the Green estate in Worcester, the last woman ever to be hanged for murder in Massachusetts.

PEOPLE IN THE BENJAMIN PERCIVAL DIARY

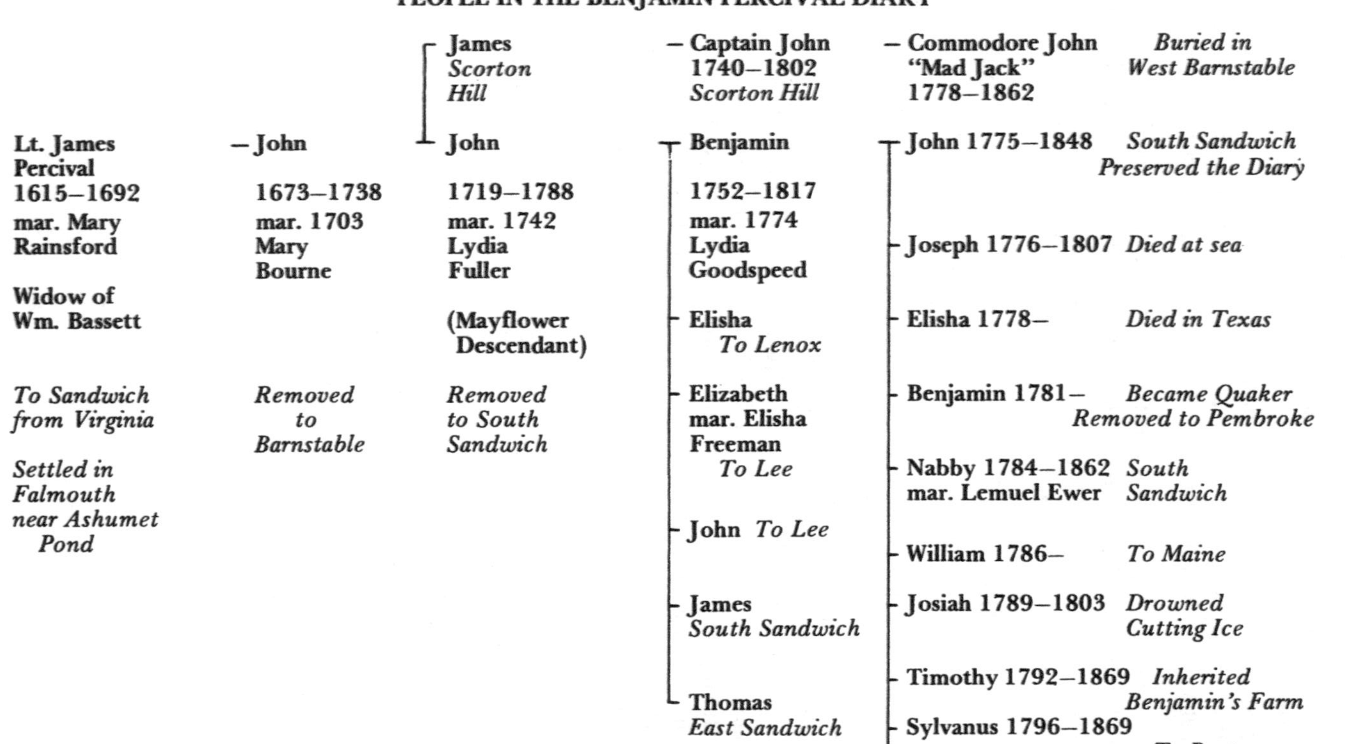
Lt. James Percival
1615–1692
mar. Mary Rainsford
Widow of Wm. Bassett
To Sandwich from Virginia
Settled in Falmouth near Ashumet Pond
John
1673–1738
mar. 1703
Mary Bourne
Removed to Barnstable
James
Scorton Hill
John
1719–1788
mar. 1742
Lydia Fuller
(Mayflower Descendant)
Removed to South Sandwich
Captain John
1740–1802
Scorton Hill
Benjamin
1752–1817
mar. 1774
Lydia Goodspeed
Elisha
To Lenox
Elizabeth
mar. Elisha Freeman
To Lee
John To Lee
James
South Sandwich
Thomas
East Sandwich
Commodore John
"Mad Jack"
1778–1862
Buried in West Barnstable
John 1775–1848
South Sandwich
Preserved the Diary
Joseph 1776–1807
Died at sea
Elisha 1778–
Died in Texas
Benjamin 1781–
Became Quaker
Removed to Pembroke
Nabby 1784–1862
mar. Lemuel Ewer
South Sandwich
William 1786–
To Maine
Josiah 1789–1803
Drowned Cutting Ice
Timothy 1792–1869
Inherited Benjamin's Farm
Sylvanus 1796–1869
To Boston
Harriet 1798–1801

CHAPTER 15

FEDERAL CENSUS

The Federal Census of 1790 was the first of what became decennial events with ever more detailed information. This first one lists only the head of household by name (whether male or female), and the following household composition by numbers:

White males through 15 years old
White males 16 and over
White females all ages
All other free persons (blacks)

There was a category for slaves but none were reported in Massachusetts in 1790. This census does not include those of Indian descent. This first Federal census is of great value in confirming the families that were then present in the town. Population estimates before this were based on tax records, town vital records, genealogical studies, church records and references in town meeting records, but cannot equal the census in precision. The order of names taken by the census-taker in Sandwich was preserved and reflects neighborhood, whereas in some towns the listing was made alphabetical.

Summary of Households to 1790

A chart is included showing the growth of Sandwich households from the founding of the town to 1790. This reflects gains and losses in households in successive periods ending in 1650, 1700, 1750 and 1790. This table deserves study and reflection. It shows the formation of new families through arrival of new settlers and the marriage of local sons. The disappearance of families is then marked by departure to other towns or the death of the head of the family. The Archives has prepared genealogical charts of descent showing these factors in the 17th century and again in the 18th century for all the families, based on town vital records, published genealogies, town meeting records (reflecting start of town activities by new arrivals), wills, deeds and other evidence. While such charts can never be totally complete, they lead to a family composition in 1790 which is consistent with the families found in the Federal Census, so that there were few surprises in persons present or absent. There is evidence for much mobility in all periods. Those arriving came typically from one of the neighboring towns or the Islands. Only a very few came from other States such as James Percival from Virginia, Humphrey Wadey a Quaker from North Carolina and Dr. Freeman from Connecticut. Those removing probably exemplify Cape Cod and other early seaboard towns in supplying families in every generation for the expansion west. The families headed by widows in 1790 represent a big apparent increase over previous periods. The number of widow-households are probably understated in the previous years through ignorance of the actual situation in the various households at the cut-off points 1650, 1700 and 1750. We only counted widows who kept families of young children together or who remarried later and had further families. What is new in the latest period is that six women (some single, some widowed) moved here and settled on their own. Once established, the town about doubled in size every 50 years, and the predominant source of growth was the marriage of local sons. Over the 150 years from 1640 to 1790, Sandwich had grown from 61 to 323 families, and in addition sent out at least 384 families.

SUMMARY OF HOUSEHOLDS TO 1790

	1640/ 1650	*1650/ 1700*	*1700/ 1750*	*1750/ 1790*
Families at start	61	60	100	209
New Arrivals	17	24	45	84
Sons marrying here	15	103	349	363
Total formed	93	187	494	656
Less death of head	11	46	140	205
Less departures	26	45	150	163
Total losses	37	91	290	368
Apparent families	56	96	204	288
Actual census	60	100	209	323
Families headed by widows	4	4	5	35
Estimated persons per family	5	6	6	6.11

The 1820 Federal Census

By 1820 Sandwich had grown to 452 families amounting to 2,484 individuals, a 25% increase in population over 1790. The census was similar to the 1790 one in only having the name of the head of household, but more age analysis was provided. The order of names in the Sandwich record sometimes made a neighborhood record but this was found to be unreliable. Fortunately the Sandwich selectmen over the period 1806-1827 had delegated highway repair authority to elected neighborhood representatives each year, and had made little booklets showing the instructions to each supervisor including the streets he was to work on, the names of the property owners and the amount of tax which was to be collected in cash or worked off at fixed rates by hand labor or rental of teams. Enough of these little highway booklets have survived to define the neighborhood census of 1820 in each district. This is a valuable additional proof of the location of the population, and can be applied back in time to 1790 by use of family charts to confirm the neighborhood structure implicit in the order of the 1790 census listing.

SANDWICH NEIGHBORHOODS AND PEOPLE

	Families		*People*	
	1790	1820	1790	1820
West Town	48	60	307	312
East Town	43	50	219	230
Spring Hill	30	38	160	215
East Sandwich	21	30	139	156
Scorton	18	30	115	139
South Sandwich	29	35	201	239
Snake Pond	16	27	100	176
Subtotal Sandwich	205	270	1,241	1,467
Pocasset	36	54	227	289
Monument	51	75	325	404
Scusset	31	53	188	321
Subt. Bourne	118	182	740	1,017
Blacks unknown location	3	–	10	–
Total Town	326	452	1,991	2,484

The 1790 and 1820 Neighborhoods

The accompanying table shows the town population divided into the respective neighborhoods, with subtotals for the areas which later became Sandwich and Bourne. All sectors show growth, but the Bourne side was growing more rapidly (especially the Scusset area) with the result that the Bourne side increased from about 38% of the town in 1790 to 41% in 1820. Originally the Shawme millstream divided the town almost exactly, but by 1790 the Bourne side plus the West Town sector had become greater than the east side total. As to family size in 1790 the town average of 6.11 persons per family was found commonly throughout all the sectors. However, in 1820 the town average had dropped substantially to 5.5 persons per family, and there was a wider range of sizes in the different parts of the town, from 4.6 in the built-up East Town to 6.8

in rural South Sandwich. Families had fewer children and there were more all-adult households. In 1790 there were ten households of only one person each (eight women and two men) whereas by 1820 the one-person households had risen to 24 (10 women and 14 men). As to women heads of household, there were 41 such families in 1790, and these increased to 53 in 1820.

The Old Surnames

In the 1790 Census some 85 different surnames are found among the population of 323 families. The commonest name was that of Nye with no less than 27 families present in the town, followed by the Wings with 23 families and the Fish family with 22. Beside these three names the next eight most common names were those of Gibbs, Tobey, Ellis, Bourne, Hoxie, Swift, Perry, and Freeman. These 11 family names account for no less than 165 families with 1,034 individuals, amounting to over 50% of the entire town. The Nyes were not only the largest group of families but averaged 7.6 persons in each family against a town average of 6.1 persons per family, so that the 205 Nyes (including servants) comprised 10.3% of the town's entire population.

The next 11 commonest surnames were those of Burgess, Handy, Dillingham, Jones, Allen, Smith, Gifford, Bassett, Blackwell, Ewer and Tupper. These represented 66 families with 390 individuals. The 22 above family names comprised the core of the town's oldest families, and at this point accounted for 71.5% of the town's population.

The rest of the town was in 92 families using 63 different surnames, some of which represented quite recent arrivals while others were of long settled families who had not yet embarked on rapid growth, such as Holway, Pope, Fessenden, Hamblen, and Hall.

In 1820 the Nye family showed its continued robust growth by registering 44 families, up 17 from 1790. Some of the other earliest family groups also showed increases, but the Wings, Handys, Dillinghams, Allens, Smiths, Giffords and Tuppers showed actual declines. The result was that in the 22 early families named above, a growth of only 24 families was registered, so that families of these oldest surnames dropped from 71% of the town in 1790 to 56% in 1820. By contrast over 60 entirely new surnames appeared, and about 80% of the growth of families was in surnames other than that of the earliest families. This does not mean that there was at this point a decline in family size or marriages among the older families, only that with fixed lands the majority of sons preferred to relocate, so that the oldest families provided nearly all the emigrants leaving the town, while more recent families tended to settle in.

New Arrivals

Beside Doctor Freeman, John Percival and Col. Roland Cotton whom we have mentioned, the new arrivals in the 1750/1790 period who made a significant mark in the town included:

Covell and Nathaniel Burgess from Harwich

Rev. Jonathan Burr, new minister replacing Rev. Abraham Williams.

Representatives of the Covell, Faunce, Keene, Crocker, Hamblen and Phinney families.

In the 1790-1820 period, the notable arrivals included Joshua Arey from Harwich, Gideon Batey and Watson Freeman from Boston but originally from Harwich, Paul Crowell from Dennis, John Denson (later called John Trout), Dr. Jonathan Leonard, ministers Ezra Goodwin and David Hunn, and the first representatives of the Battles, Drody, Nightingale, Norris, and Shove families.

Occupations

The 1820 Census included a record of main occupation of the adult males of the household. Only 619 of 697 males of 16 and up responded, showing:

Agriculture	326
Manufacturing	128
Commerce	165

Manufacturing included shipbuilding, milling, salt-making, tanning and iron-working. Commerce must have embraced all other occupations in addition to shop-keeping such as wood-cutting, sailors, fishermen, and the increasing demands of freight and travel services.

Blacks in Sandwich

The 1790 Census listed blacks and mulattos as "All other free persons," and there were no slaves in this State. There were 37 blacks living as servants and workers in various white families, but with no indication of names, age or sex. In addition there were ten living in families of their own but again not named or located. From tax records showing abatements to certain families it is probable that these ten represented three families, namely Cuffie, Sancho and Newport Mye. In 1820 there were only 26 blacks here (20 males, 6 females) of which two (George Cyprus and Sampson Edwards) lived entirely alone, both in Sandwich village, while the other 24 resided with white families.

CHAPTER 16

A NEW START

This chapter describes the close of the careers of three notable men whom we have been following—Doctor Freeman, General Ruggles and Benjamin Percival. Town events over the period 1785 to 1825 are summarized, a period of radical change for the new country and its national government. There was progress in road-building, marine activities, postal service, schools, and local industry. We will devote three chapters to this period—the previous one on population, this on new buildings and the families strongly involved, and then thirdly events in the churches.

Doctor Nathaniel Freeman (1741-1827)

Freeman had twelve children by his first wife, Tryphosa Colton, whom he married before coming to Sandwich. His second son, Nathaniel, Jr. was born here in 1766 and graduated from Harvard in the notable class of 1787. He and his classmate John Quincy Adams were clearly marked for public careers. Nathaniel, Jr. was twice elected to Congress but died of tuberculosis in 1800 at age 34. Another son, Russell, born in 1782, became a distinguished lawyer and was elected to the Legislature and Executive Council. Dr. Freeman married for a second time in 1799 to Elizabeth (Handy), widow of Josiah Gifford, and had eight more children. The eldest was Reverend Frederick born Dec. 1, 1799. He was an historian and inherited his father's property after the death of Elizabeth in 1841. We will outline Frederick's career in a later chapter. Among the other children of Nathaniel, Martha married William Fessenden and became mistress of the Fessenden Tavern, and Sarah married her cousin Shadrach Freeman and aided in the restoration of the Freeman Farm on the original site of the town founder.

Dr. Freeman's public career was long. He was Register of Probate for 47 years, retiring in 1822. He was a Judge of the Common Pleas for 36 years until that court was superceded in 1811 by the Circuit Court. He was a Brigadier of Militia from 1781 to 1793 when he resigned after being passed over twice for the rank of Major General. He was honored by being elected to membership in the Massachusetts Medical Society, Humane Society, Abolition Society, Massachusetts Historical Society and American Antiquarian Society.

He is said to have written a history of the Barnstable County Court in 1801 and it is to be hoped that this document can be traced. He formed a large private library, especially of medical, legal and theological subjects, and penned a lengthy treatise on his religious beliefs, which can be seen at the Sandwich

Historical Society. His home for 62 years in Sandwich was located on Grove St., with grounds extending along the pond to the cemetery. In 1791 he made a proposal to the town regarding this cemetery, noting that it was unfenced, grazed over by animals, and that private efforts to raise funds to fence it had failed. He proposed that he be deeded a triangle of land from the north corner on Grove St., mostly swamp, containing only one square rod fit for burying, stating this corner was useless to the townsmen because it contained the unmarked graves of an Indian and a Spaniard "among whose ashes no white person would ever incline to mix those of his friend." In exchange for this land Freeman undertook to build a stone wall along the road with a framed gate, completed by post and rail fencing. This was approved by the town. We expect accordingly that the area given to Freeman was under the present garage of Mr. Enoch Doble at 19 Grove Street.

Words critical of Doctor Freeman were printed by Amos Otis of Barnstable, probably occasioned by continuing resentment over the Abigail Freeman incident and Crocker quarrels before the Revolution. Otis wrote:

> "These denunciations (by Tories) never affected his reputation as a man or a patriot, but other causes did. He was not a meek man–he would not tolerate the least opposition, consequently made many personal enemies–and among the aged who knew him, few speak in his praise."

Recently the Archives Office in Sandwich was privileged to clear out family papers from the Freeman Farm, and among the documents found was a sensational letter from Major John Freeman of Pocasset to Governor Elbridge Gerry dated Feb. 28, 1811. It protested the proposed inclusion of Dr. Freeman on the new Circuit Court then being formed. It accused Freeman of abusing his position as Register of Probate, claiming that he was guilty of barratry as a Judge, and describing a case involving the author John Freeman in which Nathaniel attempted blackmail of both parties to the settlement of a privateering ship venture under threat of reopening the case. John Freeman minced no words in calling his distinguished cousin "a public criminal, a deceiver of the credulous, an oppressor of the weak, a sycophant to the powerful." It is clear that Nathaniel was not appointed to the new Circuit Court but it is uncertain whether this harsh blast affected the decision.

Brigadier Timothy Ruggles (1711-1795)

Ruggles spent a frustrating six years of the War on Staten Island and then Long Island, aiding in enlisting and recording Loyalists. He was too old for campaigning, and command positions were only given to British officers, but his two sons were in active service. As in the French and Indian War and at Bunker Hill, he could only criticize British tactics. It is said that friends of his persuaded newspapers in New York to refrain from publishing the 1778 news of the trial and execution of his daughter Bathsheba Spooner. However, he had to learn of it, and it darkened and saddened his life. After the defeat at Yorktown he foresaw the evacuation of New York City, so he determined to get an early start and moved to Halifax, Nova Scotia in 1782. Because of his distinguished service in Massachusetts he was given a huge land grant of 10,000 acres, and he applied for a pension and damages from his property losses in Hardwick. He was finally awarded £4,994 on his claim of nearly £20,000 and received a pension of £200/year as a former Mandamus Councillor. The area he chose to settle was at Wilmot in the Annapolis Valley, and his land ran north from the road up over North Mountain, so that it faced south and commanded a splendid view of the valley. Here he got back his old energy and drive—it must have been like starting to build up the Hardwick estate thirty years before. At 72 Ruggles needed help and it is a measure of his personality that he persuaded a young Scottish immigrant, George Stronach, and a settler from Taunton, Mass., Benjamin Fales to work for him, on the promise of grants of 800 acres each after three years. He built a large house facing south, which he called Roseway. Lacking good quarry stone he sent to Boston as soon as shipping was restored in 1784 and obtained a number of dressed blue granite strips from the quarry at Quincy, which he used for steps and foundation facing stones. Under about one quarter of the house was a cellar nine feet deep. He excavated one acre of the best garden to a depth of three feet and removed all rocks and roots. The special feature of this south-facing slope was that it was occasionally cut by deep gulches, locally called vaults, probably from glacial runoff, and Ruggles recognized immediately the value of these vaults as protected sunny places to grow fruit never before attempted in Nova Scotia. He sent for cuttings of his favorite fruits from Hardwick, and these were planted or grafted onto trees set in terraces in the gulches. Soon he had the joy of seeing the apples, peaches, quinces and grapes, the flowers and the exotics and even a number of black walnut trees growing in his new and unique estate at Wilmot. He helped build a new local church now called Pine Grove. His household consisted only of three black servants. Here he entertained in his old open way.

His wife Bathsheba died at Hardwick in 1787 at 84, and their son Timothy promptly removed to Nova Scotia with his children. The General's death came in 1795, also at 84. He had remained active and was showing friends his terraces in the vault when he slipped and opened an old hernia, dying three days later. He was buried at Pine Grove east of the chancel, but no marker was placed. A few miles away, however, in Middleton at the old Anglican Church there, Holy Trinity, there is a memorial to him. His estate was purchased by Lot Phinney (1766-1851) who was the son of Isaac Phinney, a Barnstable emigrant who came to Nova Scotia in 1761. Roseway burned down and a new much smaller house was built squarely on the walls of the cellar portion. The cellar here is nine feet deep.

The Ruggles descendants from three sons and two nephews here include noted public figures in Nova Scotia. Both Stronach and Fales descendants are still to be found in Wilmot.

Benjamin Percival (1752-1817)

The ten children of our diarist are shown on p. 226. Their lives form a typical pattern of the spread and change of the early 19th century. Of the ten, only two sons and a daughter remained in South Sandwich.

Percival was elected a Selectman in 1797 and served thereafter for 19 terms, one of the longest periods of any Sandwich official. He declared his relief in 1816 when at last free of office "it had become a burden." He was Representative at Boston for six terms beginning in 1806, and records the vicissitudes of travel either by packet or stagecoach, and the fun of exploring Boston on foot and dining with colleagues. In 1795 he journeyed to the Berkshires to see his brothers Elisha and John, his sister Elizabeth Freeman, and many friends from Sandwich and Barnstable. The towns of Lee and Lenox were particularly favored by Cape Codders relocating to new lands.

The diary mentions the hurricane of 1815, but it did not do much damage up on the farm. Of more interest is his description of the freak weather of 1816, "the year without a summer" when there were hard frosts every month, and a complete failure of the corn crop. People working outside in July had to wear thick clothes and mittens. The world-wide chill of 1816 was due to an immense volcanic explosion in Celebes, Indonesia.

Benjamin's end came unexpectedly. On Jan. 28, 1817 he noted: "At dinner eating a flat fish I got a bone in my throat, and cannot be got out. I expect it will grow worse the longer it remains there, and I much fear the consequences." He kept working that winter and spring, and does not again mention his health. His last entry was Thursday, April 3: "Fast today (a national day of prayer). Timothy and his mother gone to Meeting. Cloudy." Possibly it was then that his throat became seriously infected. He died April 15 and the diary continued by Timothy April 18: "Father buried yesterday, many people to funeral, he died in the 66th year of his age." Timothy continued entries to April 26 and then stopped. Benjamin Percival was buried in the private cemetery of his friends the Tobeys in their lands north of Peters Pond. His wife Lydia lived to a great age and was buried beside him in 1854. The family burials here also include Harriet and Josiah, Benjamin's children who died young; and John and Lydia, his parents.

Taxes and The Riot Act

When we left this subject in 1785, the Selectmen were seeking to hire constables to collect taxes not only for 1785 but for 1783 and 1784 when no collections had been made. The town was out of funds except for voluntary tax payment by the well-to-do. No spending items were even brought up. The State brought a Court judgment against the town for unpaid 1783 taxes and the town was obliged not only to name special collectors, but to indemnify the Town Assessors who had been fined for holding the State bills without action. The town was also fined for not having a schoolmaster. The two parishes attempted to combine on finding a minister after Williams' death in 1784, but without funds were helpless. The situation without personal or town income reflected a wide paralysis in economic activities in this county and across the whole country. Tempers were very short. Two persons were named to give information against "lawbreakers" and to keep half the fines. No details are found as to the crimes but they were clearly related to hunger and desperation. The Selectmen were found to be drawing expenses and even pay for their duties, but their accounts had not been audited since 1778 and this caused resentment in the tension of the times.

After Shay's Rebellion in 1786 in western Massachusetts, the State officials saw the possibilities of violence everywhere. On Oct. 28, 1786 a State law was passed entitled "Riot Act 1786 Ch 38 An Act to prevent Routs, Riots and tumultuous Assemblies and the evil consequences thereof." This reads in part:

"Whereas the provision already made by law...has been found insufficient: Be it enacted that...if any persons to the number of twelve or more being armed with clubs or other weapons...tumultuously assembled...any constable of the town shall among the rioters or as near to them as he can safely come, command silence...and make proclamation...'I am directed to charge and command and I do accordingly charge and command all persons being here assembled immediately to disperse themselves and peaceably to depart to their habitations or to their lawful business'..."

If the rioters did not disperse in one hour an officer was authorized to command sufficient armed persons and seize them all. Anyone not aiding the officer was to be fined. The rioters were to lose up to all their property, to be imprisoned from six to 12 months, and to be whipped 39 lashes every three months. Any persons who demolished or pulled down any house, shop or barn were to be treated as rioters. This Act was required to be read by the Town Clerk at the Town Meeting in March or April for years afterwards, and the phrase "Read 'em the Riot Act" became part of the language.

Resumption of Money Flow

Town meeting records are not the place to find evidence of how recovery came about, but through the town's ability to resume tax collections and to approve expenditures it is clear that money did begin again to circulate. In 1786 there was an exchange of Continental currency for new notes, and a further official exchange in 1790 when the new Federal Government began to function. State taxes due from 1781 and onwards remained on the town's books as due until formally abated by the State Treasurer, and as late as 1791 there was a vote to choose a new collector to replace Nathaniel Fish, the unlucky collector of 1781, now deceased, to collect arrears remaining in Fish's bills. There was a devaluation on the face amounts of the wartime bonds and bills due from the town so that, for example, we read that Simeon Wing, who lent the town £38 on interest in 1779, is finally to receive a "consolidated" settlement of £2-4-2 in 1789. Other bonds and bills for medical services and support of the poor long past were similarly discounted and settled.

The State granted discounts on the 1781 taxes based on the fact that these taxes could be paid at the time in certificates bought at one third of their nominal value, but that only those with ready money could even buy the certificates. The poor, accordingly, still owed the original full amount, and the town voted to require from them anywhere from one half of the original amount down to nothing at all. Similarly, the 1782 state taxes had been paid at the time at an effective rate of 8s 6d per Pound, so the rest was abated across the board, and the collectors who had paid up for many taxpayers, but had been unable to collect, could now get most of their money back with losses made up by the town. In these ways in 1788 and 1789 the wartime tax burden and outstanding town bills were finally worked off, and the town could actually begin to receive current taxes again and resume normal operations.

In 1789, for the first time in years, the town voted to raise £150 for highway repair, £50 for town operations (principally aid to the poor), and to find a school master. Some tension still showed, particularly over the status of a number of persons from the border areas of Mashpee who had before been allowed as voters in Sandwich but could no longer be, and whether town officers had taken the proper new oath by a certain deadline. Also, when some of the long-sought abatements were finally passed, they were promptly reconsidered and tabled on the grounds that only a small number of voters had approved them at an adjourned meeting, when a matter so important should be voted by the full annual town meeting. Nevertheless the town came back together. One of the helpful notes was the 1788 acceptance of several Tories back into full citizenship and the diplomatic recognition implicit in holding a small adjourned winter town meeting at 6 P.M. in the Newcomb Tavern, rather than in the cold meetinghouse - the first such meeting at Newcomb's since 1757. One wonders whether Doctor Freeman attended.

New Patterns

Many changes began to come about as a result of the new Federal Government and the State Government. In 1788 there was an election for Federal Electors who would choose the first president. Congressmen were also to be elected. From this district Shearjashub Bourne, Esq. was elected, a patrician from Barnstable who had managed to live down the wartime charges against him of trading with the enemy. (He and his father-in-law had shipped whale oil to England.) The State passed a number of new laws relative to town affairs, and these were debated and accepted at various meetings, such as:

Obligation of parents to report births of their children.

Persons licensed to sell spirituous liquors.

Laws respecting binding out the poor.

Laws respecting acceptance of persons as legal residents.

New fair valuation of real estate and assets.

A map of the town showing all borders with dimensions and angles. (The Sandwich plan of 1795 shows a large portion of the central plains area as "Waste Land.")

These laws, and the other activities outlined below, must have given a sense of renewed confidence and progress after long turmoil.

Proposal to Divide the Town

In 1797 a petition was submitted that a second town be divided off including Pocasset, Monument and a strip of settlements along both the southern edge of Plymouth and the northern edge of Falmouth. This petition was considered by a committee who found against it on several counts:

Many in Monument disagreed because they shared a minister with the First Parish.

The new town line would inevitably break up woodlots.

The parsonage lands, herring fishery and other assets would pose division problems.

The town overall accepted the committee's negative report and the project was dropped but not forgotten. The chief petitioner was Seth Perry, a restored Tory, and his proposed name for the new town was *Windsor.* This may have been suggested by Windsor, Ontario, settled by American Loyalists.

Village Center Improvement Association

In 1804 a petition was submitted by a number of leading people in the East and West Town reading as follows:

"We the subscribers being desirous to form an association for the purpose of repairing the Bogs so called in the Centre of the town and making such improvements in the ground as will contribute much to its beauty and ornament, as also to its value and convenience, do hereby ask leave of the town to authorize us in undertaking such improvement and to prohibit the taking off sods etc. therefrom."

This petition was granted but no record has yet been found of resulting activities. New England towns are centered around a crossing of important roads, and typically reserved a piece of central commons as a visual center around which large houses, churches, and town buildings could be placed, with the common reserved for militia drill, band concerts, gardens and monuments. The roads in Sandwich did focus on the grist mill and nearby meetinghouse, but the land enclosed sloped down to a low boggy area along the millstream over which there was only a bridge at River Street and a low bridge below the mill. Buildings did ring this center including the old Bassett house at 8 River Street, the meetinghouse, the Melatiah Bourne house, the gristmill and one or two houses above Tupper Road, but the low land within the ring was not built on after the removal of the Thomas Dexter house opposite Bourne's after 1714. Possibly the Village Center Association had it in mind to enclose the millstream within bunded walls and raise the banks to a higher level which could be made into a central park with trees and gardens. This would have required considerable fill, but if begun might have reserved the area with town approval as a permanent park. This, unfortunately, did not materialize and the area was quickly built on when industrial growth began. The Village Association might also have planned to enclose nearby sections of salt marsh by dikes and reclaim the land as fresh meadow. Projects like this were begun beside Town Neck and in Scorton and Great Marshes.

The Town Poor

The wartime inflation and subsequent depression brought poverty and suffering to a number of families, especially widows, the elderly and those who did not have agricultural resources or close family support. Taxes were forgiven on the estates of war widows, but by 1784 a group of three well-to-do men (Joseph Nye Esq., Seth Freeman Esq. and Doctor Thomas Smith) were urged "to consider of and digest some plan less expensive for the support of such poor persons as are or may become a town charge." Since the town was not passing spending bills it is not stated how the desperately poor were being supported. We suggest that the Selectmen and a few solvent persons were in fact paying taxes voluntarily and that this town income was being spent judiciously on critical welfare cases without formal town action. A committee in 1786 pretended to be surprised that the accounts of the Selectmen had not been audited since 1778, but in the stagnation of all affairs a few people had obviously been keeping things going. The committee said "it is out of our power to examine said accounts without they are disposed for it."

In 1787 a committee brought the town meeting a list of 32 families considered too poor to pay their taxes. The list included many from old families plus some recent arrivals and three black families headed by Newport Mye, Cuffie and Sancho Wilson. However, these families were simply short of cash, not the most destitute. Again in 1788 it was urged that some method less expensive to the Town for supporting the poor be found, referring to persons who had become totally dependent, requiring full maintenance by the town; whose last effects had been auctioned. In view of the large number of new persons found entering the town, about 1790 the Selectmen hastened to notify all arrivals that they should depart the town within 15 days so that they could not automatically claim settlement and possibly town relief. Of the 31 persons warned out in 1790, most came from Barnstable and Plymouth Counties but two came from Rhode Island. Even the new physician, Dr. Jonathan Leonard from Bridgewater, was warned out.

An example of action taken to remove a family that had not established residence and was abusing the town's privileges is provided in letters to the Selectmen in 1803:

"Mr. Nye—Sir there is one Silas Blush in this place with his wife, Cloey, and four or five children who live entirely by Pilfering & stealing he took Ground to till this year where-on he had forty or fifty bushels of corn & two Lazy to Gather it. Sold it all standing & has no other way to Get Corn but by stealing as he will not work. Esq. Bacon told me he would bind him, wife & children out when ever the Town of Sandwich had a mind to send them should have done it before if he had not Gon of. Your hum Svt

John Freeman"

This is the tough John Freeman of Pocasset who wrote the criticism of his cousin Dr. Nathaniel Freeman which we noted earlier. He had to write a second time:

"To the Selectmen of the Town of Sandwich—I hereby enter my complaint to you against Silas Blush as a Toper, he continually pilforing and makes a great disturbance in the neighborhood, therefore pray you would take immediate measures to send him back to his Town of Barnstable where he belongs.

Sandwich Dec. 20, 1803 John Freeman"

This family was returned to Barnstable where presumably Esquire Bacon, one of the Selectmen, could "bind them out." This referred to the practice of selling the services of persons able to work to the highest bidder for a year, the host to feed, clothe and house them and extract services on his own terms. Those unable to work at all would be boarded at various homes as a town expense. Notes found with Benjamin Percival's diary indicate this process. In 1816 a committee reported that it is "for the interest of said town that the poor be put up at vendue as they were last year... under the discretion of the Selectmen." A proposal to hire a house to collect the poor together was voted down in 1815, but finally in 1823 it was voted to buy a small farm "for the town's poor to be supported in" and that a suitable person be appointed "to take the care of the poor house when purchased."

Travel and Shipping

One of the great needs of the new country was for a road network. Overland movement of goods by carts and wagons was extremely slow with ferries at major streams, fords over others, mud and ruts in soft places. The routes were the old connectors between villages, which were sometimes torturously indirect. The Plymouth/Sandwich coastal road was an example — the two towns had been presented at Court since earliest days for failing to keep this road passable. There were long uninhabited sections which both towns found it difficult to pay men to repair, and for which County or State support was non-existent. However, as economic activity began to pick up in the late 1780's, road work was clearly taken in hand as shown by the existence of a stagecoach line between Plymouth and Sandwich about 1790. This connected to a Plymouth/Boston service so that one could start at 5 A.M. at Sandwich three times a week, breakfast at Plymouth, lunch at Scituate and get to Boston sometime in the evening.

Referring to his family's trips to and from the Berkshires, Benjamin Percival noted in 1800 that "wagons and chaises are coming into use for travel." with reference to his family's trips to and from the Berkshires The problem was not the taverns every seven to ten miles along the route, it was the state of the road and the stream crossings, with bridges and ferries too small for large vehicles. In 1813 Sandwich and Plymouth were each fined again for poor roads. The taverns in this sector were Cornish's near Ellisville in South Plymouth, Swift's at West Sandwich, Fessenden's in Sandwich village, Hall's in East Sandwich, Howland's at West Barnstable and so on. Connector lines came to Sandwich from the various Cape towns, so that for most places it was a two-day trip to get to Boston. From the outer Cape, it was much easier and faster to take a packet; old sailors said they had been to China more often than they had been to Boston overland.

Manomet Bridge

The road to Wareham and west led through North Sandwich where one crossed the stream near the herring-catching place. It would save distance from Pocasset and Falmouth to have a bridge over the Manomet River in the area of the present Bourne Bridge (below which the valley widened out into a broad marsh). There had always been a footbridge and ford here but a solid wagon bridge was needed, because of the depth of water at high tide and the presence of ice in winter. Petitions for the bridge were brought in from 1789 on by supporters pointing out benefits to the town and to travelers, but still it was not built. In 1819, and again in 1824, the petitioners were irate enough to sue the town to have the road and bridge put in, but the town simply voted to defend its refusal in Court. It is difficult now to account for this lack of cooperation between the sections of the Town over a relatively minor expense. It may reflect prejudice of a few persons in Sandwich government who were determined to have their way, and it must have contributed to the continued tensions between the western villages and the rest of the town. In this case, Betsey Keene reports in 1824 that the Monument village residents actually built the wooden bridge in question with their own funds.

Marine Activities

One of the first activities to show recovery was the building of small packet ships for coastwise trade. The Hinckley brothers built vessels in West Sandwich itself and somehow got the hulls down the miniscule Scusset River. Later Benjamin Burgess and Abner Ellis got into the sugar trade with Cuba and built larger vessels on Sagamore Hill, the hulls being taken to Boston to complete the fittings. At least one vessel was built at Mill River in Sandwich village, another below Georges Rock Road and others in Scorton River. Many vessels were launched in Buzzards Bay. Together with new wharves, lighters and the cargoes to be moved (firewood, sand and stone) these activities must have been welcome news to many households. Percival mentions in his diary hauling loads of ship timber as far away as Bass River. In 1793 the town appointed a committee to "see what landing places, islands and other public places with the roads leading to the same there are, being the real property of the Town or Proprietors, whether occupied by individuals or still lying common." In 1822 the Town again examined its title to the Dock and Dock Lane in the village, and allowed a new wharf to be built there. Sandwich was considered a port of entry in 1789, under the Barnstable District Collector, and in 1809 foreign vessels were allowed. A lighthouse was built at Wing's Neck in 1849.

There was wide employment of men on coastal packets, whalers, off-shore vessels and fishermen. One ship left Charleston, South Carolina in May 1825 with thirty young men returning to upper Cape Cod towns after winter employment in South Carolina. The ship was never heard from again. Aboard from Sandwich were Charles Bassett, Isaac Bates, Ezra Bourne, Henry and William Crowell, Howland Fish and William Tobey. One of the enterprises particularly employing men from this area in the winter was the extraction of live-oak timber from stands in South Carolina, Georgia and Florida. This was a hard dense timber particularly valued for use in ribs and joints of large ships. It had been in heavy demand in northern shipyards ever since being used for the construction of the *Constitution,* and the other frigates started about 1795. The brothers Elijah and Elisha Swift of Falmouth had entered the live-oak trade in 1818 with a contract to supply it to U.S. Navy Yards. Whaling vessels using live-oak were built at Woods Hole and Wareham.

Whaling

From cutting up whales that happened to come in and beach themselves in the 17th Century, the pursuit of whales had grown to the pursuit of those seen offshore by land-based groups, particularly from Nantucket. By the time of the Revolution this pursuit had become fully organized in vessels prepared for long voyages, and whale men from the Cape and Islands had ventured from the Arctic throughout the Atlantic to Brazil. By 1787 these voyages were again organized and soon continued on to the Pacific and Indian Oceans. John Percival, the son of Benjamin the diarist, shows how Sandwich men entered and stayed with this expanding industry. In July 1794, as a youth of nineteen, he went to Nantucket to join a whaler and was gone for fifteen months around Cape Horn, returning in October 1795. Percival himself had to go to Nantucket in December to secure his son's money from the voyage, over £70. The next summer the young man worked fitting out a vessel in anticipation of shipping out that Fall, only to find that he was not to be given a berth. Fortunately, his father went quickly to "Lawyer Freeman" in Sandwich, then to the Court in Barnstable and got "writs" by which they were able to secure his wages for the summer work. Young John married that year and promptly shipped out for a two-year voyage. His brother Elisha also commenced whaling, apparently preferring the alternate boredom and danger on shipboard to the farm life. Percival notes in 1798 that Simeon Backus got home "having been gone six years and his parents had heard he was dead."

Canal Proposals

Adding to the excitement of the renewal of the packet trade and shipping activities was the prospect that a canal would be cut through between the bays. Each proposal was quickly approved as far as the town land rights were concerned, the first by Thomas P. Batcheller in 1801, the second by Israel Thorndike in 1818. Our Representative in Boston in 1825 was urged to sponsor a resolution of approval to the U.S. Congress to speed a major survey then being carried out.

Postal Service

Regular deliveries of mail between towns probably had their origin with the Committees of Correspondence which wrote so persuasively on the Revolutionary events from 1773. There was a weekly rider bringing and taking mail from Sandwich at least by 1775, using as his drop the residence of Joseph Nye Esq. (the present Moody House on Tupper Road). Earlier the various taverns were centers of communication, and letters were carried between towns by reliable travelers such as lawyers, ministers, Court representatives and packet captains.

With the advent of road-building and scheduled stage coach service, mail deliveries improved greatly and a Federal postal service became a reality. Service from Boston fanned out as roads permitted; to Attleboro in 1789, Worcester and Beverly in 1790, Gloucester in 1792, to Sandwich and Barnstable in 1793, Falmouth in 1795 and Truro in 1798. The pay of the postal riders of $1.00 per day was considered extravagant. The earliest Sandwich post stop is believed to be the home of Nathan Nye, a Selectman, at the corner of what is now Main St. and Dale Terrace. Benjamin Percival mentions the privilege of getting a weekly Boston newspaper in 1794 — he first shared Colonel Abraham Williams' paper by paying the postage. In May 1799 he shared Samuel Fessenden's paper and in October began to share with Nathaniel Freeman. In the 1812/15 wartime period the mails came twice a week, and in 1820 three times a week. In a table of 1831 post offices the following postal agents are found:

West Sandwich - Benjamin Burgess
Sandwich - William H. Fessenden
East Sandwich - Joseph Hall
South Sandwich - Lemuel Ewer
Pocasset - Hercules Weston
Monument - Elisha Perry

Schools

As to the rise of the Sandwich district schools, references in town meeting records and in the Percival diary are not well detailed. In 1788 the town at last hired a grammar school master but only for three months for £10. There were no further town authorizations until 1792 when the town approved £80 for a full-time master with a committee of eight district representatives to decide on how the time of the master was to be allocated between the various districts. If £40 covered this master's salary there was money for building or repair of local buildings. Confirming this we read in the Percival diary that on January 9, 1790 Percival himself "began to keep an evening school I have 15 scholars." Since the town had not voted funds, Percival's stipend must have come from the local parents. The following June, two of his own children "Nabby and Billy went to school for the first time. Nancy Ewer Teacher." This again suggests both a local school building and a local hire of the teacher since there were no town funds voted. In 1793 and each year thereafter there was a budget for a "grammar and other free schools," with the allocation of time of the master first based on tax proportions raised in each district, then from 1797 on by number of children sent to school in each district. The Grammar School was an advanced school kept in the village center, while the other schools were for primary instruction. It is clear that the Hog Pond District had additional teaching locally sponsored, as Percival was again a winter teacher for five weeks in 1795 and six weeks in 1796. He says he had as many as thirty five scholars, an arduous evening schedule for a hard-working farmer. That the schools were locally built and maintained in each district is made clear in his note of April 6, 1814: "A community effort to help underpin the school house." The number of school districts in Sandwich rose from eight to ten in 1804 and to twelve in 1813. A Peters Pond/Wakeby district was created in 1807 where the white parents from adjacent parts of Mashpee could send their children at cost.

Sandwich Academy

About 1797 the First Parish minister here, Jonathan Burr, put up at his own expense a private school building on Water Street. This provided an education at high school and college preparatory level for those youngsters who wanted to go into teaching or one of the professions. The state then offered in 1803 to charter one Academy in each county and to endow it with a half-township of land in Maine, amounting to eighteen square miles. The Academy would be sited in the town which pledged the most money. Sandwich voted to establish a committee to procure subscriptions to establish the county Academy in this town. Because Burr offered his existing school building valued at $500, Sandwich won the Academy location and Burr became headmaster. This Academy was granted its state charter on February 21, 1804, and had a board of eighteen trustees representing Sandwich and eight other County towns. This Academy was highly successful for several years, its teachers being Reverend Elisha Clapp and Miss Bathsheba Whitman. However, after 1808 some religious disagreements in this town became pointed, causing the withdrawal of a number of trustees, who were then replaced by others less representative of a broad range of community interest. The reputation of the Academy as a county-wide school declined, and after 1814 there were periods when it was not even opened at all. However, it continued its existence with the trustees as a small local group retaining the Academy's title to the Maine lands and to the invested endowment funds. Private academies and lyceums were built in other towns of the Cape.

Brickyard

At the seaward end of Town Neck a lens of fine clay suitable for brick-making was discovered, extending under part of the beach. From about 1690 this area had been controlled by the special proprietors' company and fenced for grazing. Accordingly, when a brick kiln was erected here on or close to the beach, the approval of the proprietors was sufficient, without vote of the town. The date of first construction of the kiln has not been established, but may have been after 1790 when construction of houses and mills resumed vigorously.

There is a reference to it in connection with the bombardment of this coast in 1814 by British patrols. The house at 100 Tupper Road, the only brick house in Sandwich, is said to have been built in 1815 of this local brick. In 1819 the town appointed an officer whose title was "Surveyor of Brick." The first deed referring to the brick kiln so far known is dated 1828 when the owners were David Benson and Simeon Leonard. The property was two acres bounded by the shore to the east, private land at the marsh, and by the proprietors' lands.

Saltworks

Salt extraction from sea water during and after the Revolution was necessary because of the interruption of salt imports. It was made by boiling down seawater in big cauldrons, and produced one bushel of sea salt per 350 gallons of seawater. The operation was wasteful of wood and dangerous to the operators, probably because of poor design of the firing arrangements. After the Revolution a highly efficient solar evaporation system was designed in which a windmill pumped seawater to a square wooden tray, which had a sliding roof in case of rain. Evaporation produced a brine from which sodium chloride was finally precipitated, and the brine flowed to a lower tray for further evaporation and precipitation of other salts. These salts were quite pure and could be shoveled, when dry, directly into barrels for shipment. A great deal of pine wood was required, but this became available from Maine, and in the early 1790's salt works were built all over the Cape. There were at least eight in Sandwich, one at Scorton, one at Ploughed Neck, one at Scusset, several on Mashnee Island and Monument Beach. Stephen Sears was given town approval in 1809 to build the one at Scusset, but the others are not mentioned in town meetings. The salt works were vulnerable to storms, especially the great hurricane of 1815, but were quickly repaired and were very efficient with low manpower requirements.

Cotton Mill

With the resumption of foreign trade and imports in the late 1780's, textiles were again brought in, but Americans clearly wanted to build mills of their own. The Embargo on all offshore trade in 1807 was a critical point at which funds usually available for shipbuilding and foreign trade were diverted to local manufacture, and textiles were an attractive market. Wing family members on Grove Street received permission from the town in 1811 to dam up the stream arising from the springs above the Shawme millpond, thereby creating a second millpond eight feet higher than the lower pond. Huge red cedar trees were first removed from the area, leaving submerged stumps visible for years afterwards. By 1813 a small cotton mill was built here. The only description of it, at its sale in 1851, was a building 32 x 42 feet, 3½ stories high, with 500 spindles and 12 power looms, plus a dwelling house. The small size of the stream and its fall (seven feet) may have been limiting factors on the expansion of this mill, inefficient compared to the very large mills elsewhere in the state.

Pocasset Iron Works

A newcomer named Hercules Weston built this plant in 1822. It was originally a blast furnace, for making pig iron out of the spongy bog iron from the swamps. Later it was converted to a foundry for casting finished objects such as stove parts or kettles. Weston's operation was profitable as he soon became one of the town's leading tax payers. The ironworks under various owners was an important employer for this district for much of the 19th century.

Herring River Mills

With its overall drop of about 30 feet from Herring Pond to the Manomet valley, the Herring River in North Sandwich was one of Sandwich's most industrialized spots, at least until steam engines became the chief source of power. There seem to have been three mill sites, the first up near the beginning of the stream at Herring Pond, where in 1717, 1784 and 1792 permission was given by the town to build a sawmill. This seems to have finally been built in 1792, as town meeting records in March 1793 refer to the need for better herring passages" at the place where the Saw Mill now stands." This sawmill should have been an important asset to the town in this period of new growth, but there are no references to it later. Deyo stated in 1890 that its foundation stones could be seen.

The next site is where the present dam still stands in Bournedale above the road to Head-of-the-Bay. This is the site of the original 1695 gristmill, then of a fulling mill for wool and of a nail factory (1821). Later there was an important stave mill here and finally an axe factory. The town had to order these mills shut each spring to allow herring to pass, and to inspect and regulate them frequently.

The lower mill was near the Indian burial hill and just above the herring-catching pond. This was where a major iron works was begun by Elisha Bourne in 1790. It was expanded and rebuilt several times and continued in use through the 19th century.

War of 1812

During this war the British patrolled Massachusetts Bay and Nantucket Sound frequently so that nearly all packet sailings and cargo movements were suspended. Food became short and expensive, and supplies of sugar, molasses and rum became rare. The Percival diary records that one lucky ship from Cuba got to Hyannis and offloaded there. There was great satisfaction on the Cape at helping to cart various goods overland to Boston. He noted October 1, 1814 "300 tons of sugar is carting now." Rates were $5.00 per ton Hyannis to Sandwich, $15.00 per ton Chatham to Sandwich and $20.00 per ton Sandwich to Boston. As in the Revolution there was the rumble of cannon from several directions as engagements or bombardments took place. In June 1814 the town voted to establish a fifteen-man Committee of Safety which was to apply to the Governor to have militia mobilized and stationed to guard the seashores of the town. On September 20 an invasion seemed imminent and the town voted "that the inhabitants of said town will defend their houses and firesides and their families to the last extremity." Burbank reported that the British man-of-war, *Commodore Hardy,* stood offshore and lobbed a few shots into the town; the British officers were said to have mistaken the brick kiln and the stacks of bricks on Town Neck for a fortification, so that they did not come in closer.

There was an attack and shelling at Falmouth where the militia companies raised at Sandwich marched. The commanding officer was Lt. Colonel David Nye of Falmouth, and the Sandwich Companies were raised by Captains Thomas Swift, Seth Hamlin, Obed Butler Nye, and Benjamin Hamlin. The only actual invasion force of British in this area attacked Wareham and burned a cotton factory and several vessels there. The Gifford family in Sandwich has a record that Levi Gifford built a vessel in the marsh off Georges Rock Road and sailed it to Norfolk, Va. in 1811. Finding it too dangerous to try to sail back, he tied up the vessel and returned to Sandwich on foot. After the war he was able to retrieve his ship.

The State of Maine

When the new Province of Massachusetts Bay was established in 1692, not only Plymouth Colony was included but all the District of Maine, an immense area with only a few scattered settlements. This remained under the government of Massachusetts from 1692 to 1820, and a continued effort was made to attract new settlers. During the Revolution a number of Cape Cod families quietly sailed there to escape the endless taxes and conscriptions that prevailed here. A large purchase at Fairfield, Maine was organized in 1781 by Joseph Nye, Esq. of Sandwich, the Revolutionary leader, and by Joseph Dimmick of Falmouth. They obtained a plot of 10,000 acres and divided it into 50 lots of 200 acres each, selling at a silver dollar per acre. The list of purchasers in Sandwich and Falmouth included many Quakers.

The Commonwealth provided grants for veterans of various wars to move to Maine, starting with veterans of King Philip's War and continuing through the Revolution. The grant to the Sandwich Academy shows other efforts by the State to encourage interest and development in Maine. Removals there from Cape Cod were heavy after 1790. The town of New Sandwich (later renamed Wayne) in Kennebec County was settled by many Sandwich families. One celebrated founder of New Sandwich was Benjamin Burgess (1751-1852) who lived to be over 101, and had at his death eleven children, sixty-seven grandchildren, ninety great-grandchildren and ten great-great-grandchildren, all but four or five of whom were then still living. There is hardly a Sandwich family of the older stock which did not send at least a few of its members to Maine. An Act of Congress March 3, 1820 conferred independent statehood on the former District of Maine.

Not all who went to Maine prospered. A letter was received by the Sandwich Selectmen and Overseers of the Poor from their opposite numbers in Fairfield, Maine dated June 4, 1824:

"This is to inform you that Benjamin Dillingham with his wife and

> children have returned from the town of Canaan to this town and are in distress. They have called on this town for support and we have furnished them with the necessities of life and shall continue to relieve them by furnishing them at the expense of the town of Sandwich. You are requested to have them removed from this town as soon as you can make it convenient. They have six children and the seventh not far off, and neither bed nor cloes nor anything to keep them from perishing except what they are furnished with at the expense of the town of Sandwich by the subscribers."

This family must have run into deep misfortunes. Sandwich had supported them in Fairfield for several years, but they were now returned to Sandwich. Benjamin, born in 1785, was one of ten children of his father Benjamin Senior and his wife Desire Tupper who had all removed to Maine. Benjamin Jr. and his wife Polly (Tozier) and one child, Heman, are all found later in the Sandwich almshouse.

Visitors to Sandwich

As transportation improved, travelers began to move about the country and to record their impressions of the towns and villages, taking stock of the people and the unspoiled sights in the new nation. In its position at the gateway to Cape Cod, visitors to this unique peninsula all came through Sandwich. Reverend Dr. Timothy Dwight, President of Yale, made annual trips from New Haven throughout New England and New York State, and published his notes in 1821 as "Travels in New England." He called the Cape Cod people "industrious and orderly" but noted that intemperance was common. He was impressed with the number and quality of the seamen and officers produced here sailing the world over. In general he saw the Cape as an "unpromising tract" but found it furnished the inhabitants "with more comfortable means of support than a stranger would imagine." In Sandwich about 1800 he "lodged at Fessenden's, a very good house," then visited Rev. Burr "a most hospitable and agreeable family, where nothing was omitted which could make our stay pleasant. Mr. Burr has at his own expense built a pretty academy containing at this time a considerable handsome collection of students." He noted however from Burr's testimony that a number of Sandwich inhabitants were "debased by the use of ardent spirits." The aged Rev. Gideon Hawley at Mashpee was a friend of Dwight's father, and his visit to Hawley was a joyous reunion, marred only by the illness of Hawley's son, who died shortly after this visit, of tuberculosis.

As to Burr's testimony about excessive use of spirits in Sandwich, there is no evidence that the town was any different from other towns. The Methodists were starting to preach here at this time and often carried a temperance theme. The keeper of the leading tavern, William Fessenden, was himself a teetotaller but not a temperance crusader. There must have been effective warnings against drink here because at a town meeting in 1819 it was voted "that there shall be no retailer of distilled liquors licensed; and that tavern keepers are not to be approbated unless they desist from mixing and selling to town dwellers." The taverns, in other words, served drinks for transients only and were not drinking places or retailers for local residents. This ban on local sales of liquor was for one year only and was not renewed.

Wendell Davis of Plymouth established a law practice at Sandwich about 1800, continuing until his death in 1830. He was a Representative and State Senator, and contributed to the Massachusetts Historical Society (founded 1792) a series of highly informative essays on the various Cape towns. He said of Sandwich in 1802 that the main village "is embellished with a large and beautiful pond in its center and a fall of water on which are situated a grist mill and fulling mill...round this pond stand the principal houses of the village together with a number of shops." He mentions the meetinghouse and the academy and says of the two public inns that they "are excelled by few if any in the State." He said "the inhabitants in general are substantial livers" and "manifest a fond and steady adherence to the manners employments and modes of living which characterized their fathers." Much of Davis' information about the town's harbors, shipping, agriculture, population and canal site found its way into the later books of Dwight, Kendall, Thoreau and Frederick Freeman. Based on the optimistic estimates of Batcheller in 1801, Davis devoted much space to the prospective canal whose site was defined by the deep glacial cut across the peninsula here, and of the value of the canal to coastwise shipping. Furthermore, Davis saw a vast advantage to the town itself from the construction of the Canal, with hundreds of new dwellings, employment to large numbers, increase in property values, warehouses soon erected on its banks, trade between the southern and northern states facilitated, all calculated to confer immense advantages on the vicinity of such a channel. This exaggerated vision seems to have become part of the town's idea of what the Canal would accomplish, and underlies the instant acceptance of every new survey and proposal until the Canal was finally built.

Articles in the "Collections" of the early Massachusetts Historical Society by Gideon Hawley, Nathaniel Freeman and Wendell Davis doubtless were encouraged by the Society's Secretary Rev. Dr. James Freeman of Truro, minister at King's Chapel, Boston. (This Dr. Freeman was not a descendant of Edmund of Sandwich but of Samuel of Roxbury and Eastham.) His own article on Truro history was greatly valued, and he was clearly an early expert on Cape Cod history.

Hurricane

During the 18th century there had been several late-summer storms which would doubtless be called hurricanes. The memory of the great hurricane of 1635 that stunned the Pilgrims and wrecked Aptucxet, however, had faded, so that it was with shock and disbelief that the people of the Buzzards Bay area felt the full brunt of another major hurricane. This one came Sept. 23, 1815, and pushed salt water up into the Manomet valley to heights never before seen. Witnesses at North Sandwich stated that if the tide had risen another two feet, the waves would have carried over the sill (32 feet over sea level) and gone on over into the Scusset River and Barnstable Bay. Damage to coastal shipping and to salt works was severe, the wreckage carried far inland. The most long-lasting damage was by salt water that killed grass and vegetation; cedar swamps were flooded and the trees died; corn and potatoes rotted and many springs and wells took years to restore. Salt spray was carried for miles inland and defoliated the conifers. Reverend Ezra Shaw Goodwin of the First Parish, Sandwich, had contracted to have firewood cut for sale from Scraggy Neck as part of his pastoral income. His diary for 1815 (to be discussed in the next chapter) reveals that the hurricane carried off 150 cords, a heavy loss of $100 in cutting costs alone.

The Freeman Farm

Under the will of the first Edmund Freeman, his home (near the present Bourne/Sandwich line) and adjacent farm went to his grandson, Matthias Ellis who had taken care of him in old age. Other parts of his wide holdings went to his five children Edmund Jr. of Ploughed Neck, Mary wife of Edward Perry of East Sandwich, John of Eastham and Elizabeth Ellis of Rochester. Each of these four parties, being well established elsewhere, sold off their inheritance around the old home, even including the Saddle and Pillion burial area. About the time of the Revolution, two grandsons of Matthias Ellis owned major portions of the old Freeman area, and both dying about the same time, the various fields, marshes and other lands comprising some twenty-seven lots had to be divided to various heirs. The Probate Court solution to this problem was to divide each parcel in half, no matter how illogical for farm use, producing a patchwork of lots owned by various Ellis, Tupper, Gibbs and other heirs. With the return of economic life and new building in the 1790's, a curious and probably unique development took place here, the re-assembly of a large portion of the Freeman holdings as a working farm by Seth Freeman Esquire's family. He was a Revolutionary War leader, a Selectman for 13 years from 1773, and a member of the Committee of Correspondence; he lived, we believe, on the knoll at present Main Street and Tupper Road. Why and how Seth's family embarked on the re-establishment of the original Freeman Farm is not recorded in any letters or documents so far found, but the stuff of an historical novel is here. The characters at this stage were:

Shadrach Freeman — lived on or near the ancient home site and built a new Georgian-style house about 1795; he and his wife Sarah Freeman (daughter of Nathaniel) had no children but became the hosts and nucleus of the emerging Farm as a family center.

Major John Freeman — served on privateers during the Revolution; married well and settled in Pocasset where he became a large landowner; he was mentioned earlier in this chapter as the one who criticized his cousin Nathaniel so harshly, and had the thriftless Blush family turned out; no children.

Hon. James Freeman — a Representative and State Senator who became High Sheriff of Barnstable County. While on duty enroute to Martha's Vineyard in January 1816 his craft was trapped by ice and he and two colleagues drowned.

Experience — married a glamorous and successful cousin from Harwich Watson Freeman (1762-1813) a young man of an extraordinary war record who had founded an import business in Boston but brought his family up partly in Shadrach's new center in Sandwich; founded the Freeman Cemetery in Sandwich.

SADDLE AND PILLION AT THE FREEMAN FARM - In this view of about 1890 the grave markers of Edmund and Elizabeth Freeman rest on a knoll overlooking the farm buildings in the distance. The main house at left has a large servants' ell. There were two barns and a guest cottage. Bronze plaques were placed on the burial markers in 1910. Freeman Farm Collection, gift of Everard Pratt, Jr., Sandwich Archives.

Deliverance — married a Harwich cousin Gideon Batey who was a half-brother of Watson Freeman's and his business partner; no children; lived near the Farm.

Mary — married Zenas Nye of Sandwich and had a son Seth Freeman Nye (1790-1855) who became a lawyer, Justice and business administrator in Sandwich; worked closely with these Freemans.

All these members of the Seth Freeman family (there were ten in all) made bequests or supported the reestablishment of the Farm as a family center beginning in the early 19th century. This is remarkable because it happened at a time of expansion and rapid change when other early family neighborhoods and farms were going into decline due to relentless removal of the younger generations to work in the cities or the west. It is also noteworthy that the Seth Freemans were from the Sandwich branch while the Watson Freemans were from the Eastham branch so that descendants of both sons of the original Edmund Freeman were represented in re-establishing the family center.

Sandwich in 1831

A newcomer named Jesse Boyden came to Sandwich in the 1820s and became a valuable member of the community. He served as a Selectman from 1829 for 17 years, he was a surveyor, and in Chapter 9 we have referred to his invaluable work in creating the map of the Sandwich woodlots. In 1831 Jesse Boyden produced a map of Sandwich showing the main buildings outside of residences. Except for the glass factory begun in 1825 and its associated store, district school and Catholic Church, the other facilities in the town were as they had been developed over the post-Revolutionary period discussed in this chapter. The map shows fifteen district schools, seven inns (including Hall's on Old County Road, Perry's at Monument, Bourne's at Head of Bay, Gibbs' at North Sandwich and Swift's at West Sandwich) five post offices, eight churches, six grist mills, seven saltworks, four private wharves, one ironworks, two textile mills, a comb factory, two tanneries, a bake shop and thirty-one other shops.

Biggest Taxpayers

On the eve of the expansion due to the glass factory, those paying the largest taxes in Sandwich in 1825 were:

Name	*Real Estate*	*Personal*	*Total Tax*
William Fessenden	8,200	21,000	$82.19
Wendell Davis	1,400	22,000	65.38
Samuel Fessenden	7,500	14,000	59.34
Abraham Wing	18,200	2,000	58.15
Sarah Hoxie	10,700	7,500	50.23
Hercules Weston	11,000	1,600	35.58
Benjamin Burgess	3,300	8,000	31.99
Deming Jarves	10,000	1,000	30.36
William Handy	5,300	3,000	27.30
Rebecca Wing	7,800	1,500	26.47

Personal property included cash, vessels, goods for sale, livestock. In 1825 Jarves was a Sandwich resident with house and barn, a store, 1300 acres of land and stocks in the store. His new glass plant is not included. Two of the richest people in Sandwich were women.

BOSTON,

Plymouth & Sandwich

MAIL STAGE,

CONTINUES TO RUN AS FOLLOWS:

LEAVES Boston every Tuesday, Thursday, and Saturday mornings at 5 o'clock, breakfast at Leonard's, Scituate; dine at Bradford's, Plymouth; and arrive in Sandwich the same evening. Leaves Sandwich every Monday, Wednesday and Friday mornings; breakfast at Bradford's, Plymouth; dine at Leonard's, Scituate, and arrive in Boston the same evening.

Passing through Dorchester, Quincy, Wyemouth, Hingham, Scituate, Hanover, Pembroke, Duxbury, Kingston, Plymouth to Sandwich. *Fare*, from Boston to Scituate, 1 doll. 25 cts. From Boston to Plymouth, 2 dolls. 50 cts. From Boston to Sandwich, 3 dolls. 63 cts.

N. B. Extra Carriages can be obtained of the proprietor's, at Boston and Plymouth, at short notice.— ☞STAGE BOOKS kept at Boyden's Market-square, Boston, and at Fessendon's, Plymouth.

LEONARD & WOODWARD.

BOSTON, *November* 24, 1810.

[Reproduced from a print in possession of the Bostonian Society.]

CHAPTER 17

DRAMA IN THE CHURCHES

When we last referred to the First Parish Meetinghouse in Chapter 10, it had been enlarged in 1756 under Reverend Abraham Williams. A new weathervane was obtained from a distinguished maker of vanes, Shem Drowne, the artist who built the famous grasshopper vane on Faneuil Hall in Boston. The First Parish also received a large pulpit Bible as the gift of Deborah Mason Cotton, wife of Colonel Roland Cotton.

Reverend Jonathan Burr

Following the death of Rev. Williams in 1784, there was a delay in finding a new minister in view of the acute shortage of money. Jonathan Burr was invited in 1786 and installed April 18, 1787. He graduated from Harvard in 1784 so it is probable that he was acquainted with Dr. Jonathan Leonard (HC 1786) and Nathaniel Freeman, Jr. (1787); an excellent teacher and tutor, Burr had written a successful text, "Compendium of English Grammar," that went through several editions and was widely used. His first wife died in 1788 and he married Sarah Smith, daughter of Dr. Thomas Smith, Jr. We believe he lived in "The Lindens" at 23 Water Street (built by Dr. Thomas Smith, Sr.) and that it was Burr who planted the three lindens. The lindens were named Castor, Pollux and Helen. The Burrs had no children but adopted English orphan twins, William and Mary Marston, born in Boston in 1790. Burr built his private academy on Smith family lands near his home in 1797, and resumed teaching. Burr's First Parish area included Monument Village where he preached every sixth Sunday.

The Meetinghouse Enlarged

Burr found that a few of his parishioners joined the new Methodist group starting up in Sandwich, but his own church enjoyed a substantial increase in members so that the First Parish planned an enlargement of the meetinghouse in 1804, the second since it was built in 1704. The building (as lengthened in 1756) was 32 to 36 feet deep by 56 to 60 feet long. It was now deepened by another 12½ feet, through moving the entire north wall with pulpit and pews that much farther north. The front roof and ridge from the bell tower remained in place, so that the back roof slope became flatter. Some of the interior pews were moved forward, and many new box pews were built on the ground floor, as well as in the gallery. The east porch was enlarged and raised to two stories with an enclosed staircase to the gallery level, and a stair to the gallery put into the bell tower so that the two former interior staircases could be removed and that space used for seating. The old vane was rejected and a new vane installed. The carpenter was Jonathan Fish. There is no reference to this enlargement in town meeting minutes because costs were met by resale of the pews.

THE SANDWICH FIRST PARISH MEETINGHOUSE - The sketch at left was done by a scholar from the Academy, and shows the building from Main Street with River Street at left. The tower contains only a bell and short spire. This is the meetinghouse of 1756. Courtesy of The Bayou Bend Collection, The Museum of Fine Arts, Houston.

The sketch at right was done after the addition of the Titus Winchester clock in the tower, with a higher spire. This is the expanded building of 1804. Courtesy of Sandwich Historical Society.

Titus Winchester (1746-1808)

One of Sandwich's historic figures was Titus Winchester who played a unique role in the history of Sandwich. Titus Winchester was a slave in the household of Rev. Abraham Williams. He was offered his freedom but refused, staying with Rev. Williams until his death in 1784. Then, at age 38, he entered one of the only professions open to him, that of steward aboard ocean-going ships, probably out of Salem or Boston. He saved his money and returned to Sandwich in 1806 with his nest egg. In his will in 1807, (written by Wendell Davis), he called himself of Boston but now resident in Sandwich. He left his whole property to the First Parish Church, the interest first to be used to buy a two-faced clock with the works to strike the bell; after the clock was paid for, the interest from his bequest was to be used for church support. Winchester died in 1808, and his executor William Fessenden (one of Burr's chief supporters), had the new clock installed, requiring the raising of the tower and spire. The clock faces were south (toward Main Street) and west (toward River Street). By good fortune, sketches of the meetinghouse and its spire before and after the installation of Winchester's clock have been preserved. The hourly strike was sometimes referred to as the voice of Old Titus. The home of Rev. Williams and Titus Winchester has been preserved. It is the colonial house at the corner of Jarves St. and Route 6A, probably built by or for Rev. Williams in the 1750s. It was occupied by his son, Colonel Abraham Williams, until his death in 1796, after which it was owned by Melatiah Tobey. Titus Winchester's will provided for "a suitable monumental stone with an appropriate inscription thereon." This table stone was erected in Old Town Burying Ground, where it may be seen near the north entrance. In his oration on the history of Sandwich, given in 1889, Reverend N. H. Chamberlain had this to say of Titus Winchester:

> "For the sake of Titus and his race, I trust that longer than that clock's face is black, Sandwich folk will tell their children that the man who gave that clock had a black face, but a life that was very white; that his name was Titus Winchester; and that Christianity, of any honest sort, is forever color blind."

The Church Membership Splits

During the period of the ministry of Jonathan Burr, an historic change took place in Massachusetts concerning the religious beliefs of people of all walks of life. The accepted (Congregational) churches from Colonial times were controlled and financed by all the taxpayers in the Parish area, except those specifically allowed to support a private church, such as the Quakers. The Parish taxpayers approved a new minister and paid him, and could deny him salary and expenses from tax revenues at will. The Parish likewise built or bought parsonages, owned the parsonage lands and other property, and conducted the public affairs of the church. The members of the church itself were a much smaller group, those who professed religion and who controlled internal religious affairs. These Parish churches had no central religious office or controlling authority, but worked well in the long period of homogeneous population and stable traditions. Administrative problems in specific churches were decided by Councils of respected ministers. However, this system was poorly structured to cope with the effects of the rapid expansion of the country after 1790, which brought shifts of population and the arrival of new preachers and ideas from abroad. The result in nearly all Parishes after the Revolution was a rising tide of questioning conventional Calvinistic preaching and the doctrine of the Trinity, and favoring a more liberal religious pattern, later widely accepted as Unitarianism, Methodism and other sects. The practical effect of this slow, but inevitable change of climate, was that in nearly all towns the Parish church was split into two camps which ultimately produced two religious societies, of which one got the existing meetinghouse and Parish property, while the other had to form a new society and build a new church and parsonage. The decision on ownership of the Parish property rested not on the strength of the contending parties within the membership of the parent church, or the inclination of the current minister, but on the voting members of the broad Parish population who still paid the bills through special taxes. In each town this three-level situation had different strengths in its components (church members, minister and Parish voters), which acted to speed or delay the outcome, but ultimately a decision had to be made. Generally, the Parish voters supported the liberal side, which meant that the liberal-leaning religious party in the church got the existing meetinghouse, together with its funds, parsonage, lands and books, while the conservative or Calvinistic group in the church and the Parish had to fund a new church. The current minister would have to be on one side or the other; if old, revered and skilled he might keep the church together, but certainly on his death the will of the Parish majority would prevail, and would decide the school of his successor.

The events in Sandwich, which seemed to many here at the time and later as surprising, unique and traumatic, were quite typical, but with local flavor and drama. Burr knew perfectly well of the religious views on both sides and kept the First Parish strong and unified through the expansion of 1804. His preceptor at the Academy, Elisha Clapp, was a liberal, and as a licensed preacher took the pulpit every sixth Sunday when Burr preached in Monument. Possibly it was this rivalry, or the encouragement of his greatest supporters, William Fessenden and Nathaniel Freeman, that affected him; in any case Burr became pointedly Calvinistic and more dramatic in his sermons and brought in many new worshippers. His liberal opponents were led by Deacons Sylvanus Nye and Lemuel Freeman, both of East Sandwich. Joint committees after 1808 tried to restore balance, but many of the liberals refused attendance and Communion, and the situation became untenable. The liberals were a minority of the church members, and very sensibly called a general Parish meeting in 1811 and obtained a vote of 69 to 64 against Burr, resulting in stopping his future salary and appointing a committee to direct his dismissal. On July 28, 1811 he was prevented from occupying his pulpit by an organized group of outsiders, and could not make himself heard because of outsiders chanting in the gallery. He accordingly marched out with his followers and held service at another place, probably one of the public rooms at Fessenden's. When he left with over 100 followers, the remaining crowd included only eight male members of the church. Another Parish meeting confirmed that Burr's connection to the First Parish Church was dissolved, in spite of representations of supporting Calvinist clergy. In January 1812 the dissident liberal minority obtained a new minister (Ezra Shaw Goodwin), ordained him with their supporting clergy, and kept occupation of the meetinghouse. Burr's followers sued in state Court, but the will of the general Parish citizens determined the Court's findings and the liberals were confirmed in their ownership of the church property, lands, and funds, even though they were a minority of church members.

The Calvinistic Congregational Church.

Burr's followers, led by William Fessenden, formed a new religious society on February 17, 1813, the Calvinistic Congregational Society. They began plans for a new meetinghouse and for $200 bought a tiny piece of land from James Dillingham (who occupied the present Dunbar House), and erected their meetinghouse there. It was like the First Parish nearby, a boxy building, side on to the street, and sized 36 by 52 feet, with a bell tower at the west end. Work went so swiftly that they could hold the dedication on October 20, 1813. The chief speaker was Rev. Dr. Edward Griffen of Park Street Church in Boston, whose church members, together with Old South Church members, contributed a new set of Communion silver vessels. There is no record of the original bell in this new church, whereas the First Parish, by coincidence, received a Revere bell in 1813. This meetinghouse contained a schoolroom where Mr. Burr taught in order to supplement his income. Early in his fateful year of 1811 he had also lost his position at the Sandwich Academy and had resigned as trustee. His enemy in both the school and the church, Mr. Clapp, had returned to Boston in 1810 and became a schoolmaster.

The First Parish Church voted out those church members who had joined Burr. Since the First Parish area covered everyone in Sandwich except the Quakers and the Pocasset Second Parish area, the citizens who now wished to become members of specific private religious societies (and avoid Parish taxes) hastened to go to the Town Clerk and deposit certificates that they had joined other churches. Leaving the First Parish in this way were the names of 159 to the Calvinist church, 46 to the Methodists, 3 to Baptists in Barnstable and 1 to the Quakers. These persons all lost their 1804 investments in the pews in the First Parish Church.

JOHN WARNER BARBER VIEW OF SANDWICH-This is the only view found showing the early Calvinistic chapel on the site of the present First Church of Christ. The smaller buildings in the left foreground are a blacksmith shop, the building that was moved to become the glass museum and lastly the shop that became the Fred Bunker museum. At left rear is the Unitarian Church with Titus Winchester clock and in the distance the two stacks of the glass factory casting their prosperous pall of black smoke. The vertical scale is exaggerated in this drawing of about 1837. Courtesy of Sandwich Public Library from an original book contributed by Lombard C. Jones.

Ezra Shaw Goodwin (1787-1833)

After the severe trials of 1811, the membership of the First Parish began to regain strength. One member had nailed his pew door shut and boarded over the top while Burr remained in the ministry. Reverend Goodwin (Harvard 1807) arrived in 1812 and was ordained in 1813, restoring dignity and integrity to his church society. The Second Parish in Pocasset had petitioned in 1811 that the ministerial lands at Scraggy Neck be turned over to the Second Parish (within which it was located) for support of its ministry, but the town turned this down. A diary kept by Goodwin for the year 1815 has survived and shows how he used Scraggy Neck for sheep-raising and for firewood sales as part of his income. It is a fascinating combination of ministerial duties (preaching and meeting with his church supporters, exchanging pulpits with colleagues, holding marriages and funerals) plus farm work and personal life. For instance in the first week of January:

"Monday Began to instruct F. Dana Leonard and Benjamin Freeman in Latin

"Tuesday Brother Fish dined here (This was Rev. Phineas Fish his Harvard classmate, settled over the Congregational Church at Mashpee).

"Saturday Little cow calved in night.

THE SANDWICH ACADEMY-Sketch by Rebecca Chipman (later Mrs. Newell Hoxie) of the Sandwich Academy where she was first a student then a teacher. The Lombardy poplars in front and at the side of the building were then novel shade trees in vogue. Reverend Jonathan Burr built this as a private school before 1800. Courtesy of Sandwich Historical Society.

"Sunday Preached at home 204:118 (his sermons were numbered and all recorded).

"Monday Merino No. 3 brought a ewe lamb early in the morning."

During the summer he kept his eighty sheep at Scraggy Neck where he went at least weekly, but also used his ministerial lot called Nonesuch at present Route 130 and the Mid-Cape. We believe that Goodwin lived on the hill on Tupper Road opposite River Street. It was later thought that he built and lived in the Brick House, but deeds show otherwise. The diary records the continued tension between his and Burr's churches which prevented his even being seen with Burr or communicating directly with him.

"Friday Feb. 24 Sent an invitation to Mr. Sanford (a young minister studying with Mr. Burr) to supply next Sunday - he said he would but I found many persons exceedingly opposed to his doing it.

"Saturday Feb. 25 Wrote a billet to Mr. S., thanked him for his readiness to supply but excusing him as I am to be at home (due to snowstorm) - invited him to tea next Monday.

"Sunday Apr. 16 Dr. Allyne preached for me all day. Mr. Burr would not let him divide his time between us as he wanted to.

"Tuesday May 16 Returned (from Plymouth in his chaise), brought Mr. Burr as far as Ellis's (tavern in Ellisville) where he took the stage."

The numbers of all his sermons enable us to see Goodwin's careful use of his stock of sermons. As of January 1 he had 202 already written in the years since graduation. During the year he wrote only 40 new sermons (203-242) but had to preach at least 104 plus Thursday lectures, Fasts and Thanksgivings. On a particularly bad Sunday with a small crowd he used two "old sticks" (134 and 135). At the end of the year he concluded his diary with a summary:

"Admitted 4 to the church
Baptized 3, buried 8, married 4 couples.
Experienced much sickness in my own family (a stillborn child).
Met a loss of about $100 by the storm of Sept. 23.
Expended $200.00 on the homestead and paid $150.00 of old debt.
It has been an unprofitable year in regard to the Kingdom of Heaven."

The Methodists

Methodism came to America just before the Revolution but was not presented to rural congregations before about 1790. The gifted preacher Jesse Lee came both to Sandwich Village and to Monument about 1795. He had an eloquent evangelical message, broad appeal and tuneful hymns. The Methodists used attractive lay preachers who, as a team, covered a broad area, providing further variety in the service. Lacking a hall, the Methodists used the First Parish Church, probably on weekday evenings, and also the small Congregational Church at Monument which was only used every sixth Sunday by Rev. Burr. (The membership of this Congregational Church incidentally, stayed with Burr over the 1811 crisis and until his resignation from the Calvinistic pulpit in 1817. The Monument church then secured its own religious society from 1818.) A number of the First Parish Church members tried the Methodist service and joined it as early as 1802, causing some irritation among the Deacons who visited the departed ones and tried to reconvert them. Late in his life, Frederick Freeman wrote a lengthy paper on the history of the church in Sandwich and stated with reference to Methodism in Sandwich in 1804:

> "There were at this time very few in town who assumed the name, and the denomination had no reason to take pride in the social position of all who affected to belong."

Freeman was in physical pain in his last years, but this was still an unchristian thing to say. Among the circuit preachers from 1811 was Levi Nye of Sandwich. The Methodists became an incorporated Society here in 1811 and erected a church building of their own in 1828 on Main Street near Liberty Street.

Separate Methodist congregations were gathered in Scusset and Pocasset, as well as at Monument. The Scusset group raised a church building in 1828, on land given by Nathaniel Swift and using funds advanced by Benjamin Burgess. The ancient church building built in 1732 for the Reverend Worcester group was disassembled and removed to Pocasset about 1807. There had been an Indian church in Pocasset started by Elisha Tupper in 1767 (using timbers from the original Indian chapel built on Burial Hill, Bournedale in 1674/5) which had been joined by the Second Parish Church group allowed to form in 1770. This congregation was not active after the death of Tupper in 1787, but was still in existence as a Parish as we saw from their application to the town for a grant of Scraggy Neck. When Methodist preaching came to Pocasset, this old meetinghouse was enlarged, including the Scusset materials; the Second Parish membership becoming entirely Methodist.

The Hersey Estate

Doctor Abner Hersey of Barnstable (1721-1787) was a physician of great skill whose practice was Cape-wide. It was his custom to ride or drive through each town by a certain route on certain days of the month, whether or not there were any calls, so that all persons needing his services could watch for him to pass. He estimated that his income from his practice was derived as follows from the various towns:

> "7/56 East Barnstable
>
> "6/56 West Yarmouth
>
> "5/56 ea. West Barnstable and South Eastham (Orleans)

"4/56 ea. Sandwich, Falmouth, Yarmouth East (Dennis), Harwich North (Brewster), Chatham and Truro.

"3/56 ea. Harwich South, Eastham and Wellfleet."

His will provided that the income from his farmlands, woodlots and money at interest should be paid annually to the Congregational Churches in the above 13 parishes in accordance with the stated fractions. The Deacons from each church were to meet annually to lease out the farmlands and woodlots for the next year, and to receive and divide the proceeds from the previous year. Dr. Hersey was an extreme eccentric in clothing, but a highly scientific farmer far in advance of his times. His fields were dressed annually with compost and manure so that their yield was extraordinary; and his woodlots carefully managed. After his death however, the 39 deacons simply leased the fields to farmers (who wasted no money on soil care) and allowed cutting on so many acres of woodland that income kept falling and in 29 years the wood was all gone and the income from the farm was so low that it barely met the traveling expenses of the deacons, who had enjoyed tavern fare as an annual treat. The deacons accordingly petitioned the State to break the will and sell off all the assets, to be divided among the 13 churches. This was done and the amount available in 1817 was some $5,600 for the churches, or $100 per share. The Calvinists in Sandwich petitioned for the Sandwich share, but the arbiter was guided by the findings of the Court in 1812, so that the First Parish Church got the $400 cash from the Hersey estate.

THE QUAKER MEETINGHOUSE AT SPRING HILL - This building of 1811 is the third on the same site, the first built in 1672, the second in 1704. Except for electric lights the building is kept in original condition. There is a central movable partition to divide the men's (left) and women's (right) sections for separate meetings. Weekly services are held here in summer. Photo by Sandwich Historical Commission.

Continued Bitterness

The conflict between the two Congregational Churches in Sandwich had become deeply personal, and this continued until about 1880 or after the deaths of everyone who had been an adult at the time of the schism. Burr resigned from the Calvinists in 1817 and was replaced by David L. Hunn. Freeman, in writing of the controversy, said that the First Parish Treasurer (Melatiah Bourne) retained the Treasurer's book of the original church, but that Burr had the record book of church history and minutes of meetings, as well as old papers of Reverend Fessenden and other documents. The First Parish had to sue for repossession of the record book, and knowing that they would be compelled to give it up, the Calvinists made a copy of historic parts after which Hunn gave Goodwin the original volume. According to Freeman, Goodwin turned to the pages on which notes of events after 1811 had been entered by Burr, tore them out and threw them in the fire in front of Hunn. This story may be apocryphal. A comparable but more likely story concerns the Treasurer of the First Parish, Melatiah Bourne, who lived in the family saltbox at 138 Main St. As fate would have it, the new Calvinist meetinghouse was at the very edge of Bourne's land and very close to his house. The story is that he had a small barn near the meetinghouse and made it a point to stir the animals when services were going on. This accordingly became called "The Spite Barn" and entered town legend as such. Later it was moved to a point opposite town hall and became a shop, and later became a part of the Sandwich Historical Society building.

Burr retired to Boston but lived to a great age and came back to Sandwich summers. He died here in 1842 and is buried in Old Town Burying Ground. His home, the Lindens, was sold by the Smith family to Jesse Boyden. It must have been an irritant to Burr to see his Academy building out of repair and in intermittent use. When the First Parish meetinghouse was taken down in 1833 and a new church building erected, the First Parish members met Sundays in the Academy, and this was especially galling to Burr because when he and his followers were lacking a church in 1811 to 1813, he had not been allowed the Academy and met in private homes.

In 1819, the town (in full town meeting) discussed the privileged position of the First Parish Church in retaining the ministerial lands at Nonesuch and Scraggy Neck. It was voted to sell the lands and to divide the proceeds among all the religious societies in the town, thereby ending a long-standing source of dispute, and clearly anticipating the official disestablishment of the Parish system by which only one church enjoyed an income from taxes. The First Parish Church was not called Unitarian during Goodwin's time (to 1833) but thereafter joined the American Unitarian Association.

CHAPTER 18

A GLASS FACTORY

The famous Boston merchant and "Ice King", Frederick Tudor, wrote in 1821: "Sandwich is one of the most pleasant villages in Massachusetts. To persons fond of fishing, sporting or riding it offers greater resources than any other spot in this country." When here, Tudor and his friends always expected the services of Sandwich's unique guide John Trout, who knew the best places for fishing, waterfowl, deer or other game; his real name was John Denson (about 1770-1840). Frederick Freeman states that this guide was so popular that his portrait was hung in the Boston Atheneum. (That may have been so, but it is no longer to be found there.) Other sports who came to Sandwich for relaxation about this time were Daniel Webster and Deming Jarves. Jarves was a dedicated glassmaker, already the General Agent of the New England Glass Company in Cambridge, founded in 1818.

On the death of his father in 1823, Jarves (then 33) inherited $25,000 and had the means to found a new glass factory. After a tour of American glass factories, Jarves decided in 1824 to start his plant at Sandwich because of the extensive forests there and its convenient distance from Boston. In 1824 his agent, Jabez Dame, bought up some 1300 acres of woodlots, also from Nathan Smith, Melatiah Tobey and others, he purchased the proposed site of the factory itself, about six acres near the Town Dock. Jarves probably established a temporary residence in Sandwich itself late in 1824 as the Sandwich Assessors list him as a resident here in 1825 with 1306 acres of land, goods for sale in a store, and a house and barn. Popular legend has it that he urged acceptance of his factory proposal at a town meeting, but if so it must have been privately held as there is no official town record of approving any petition for construction of a glass factory. He was well prepared, as the record reads that ground was broken April 19, 1825 and the first glass objects were actually created July 4. The main building was a wooden one running about east and west, located about opposite present Jarves Street but near the marsh. This building contained a furnace holding eight clay pots for glass, surmounted by a brick chimney. The fuel was dried strips of white pine. There must also have been an annealing oven where new-made glass objects were placed at high heat and gradually moved away for slow cooling. This first factory has been referred to as the Sandwich Manufacturing Co., but again, no official documents seem to bear this name and it was probably simply called the Sandwich Glass Manufactory. About 60 men were involved, housed in new tenements located on Jarves' land, probably the one-story buildings along later Jarves, Harbor and Factory Streets. These homes were a curiosity to the natives as they contained two or four small separate apartments. There is also a reference to a crowded boarding house with four or five beds per room. This may well have been the Rev. John Smith house. The first glass is said to have been cloudy and yellowish because of impurities in the sand, which came from the Town Neck dunes opposite the plant. This could hardly have been a surprise to Mr. Jarves as an experienced glassmaker, and must have been more of a trial run for the furnace and for the eager spectators. Doubtless better silica sand was available as commercial production began immediately. Clean glacial sand deposits were found in the Eel River valley in Plymouth and near Head-of-the-Bay, but neither was as good as that from Morris County, New Jersey, which was probably the main source for Sandwich until the Berkshire deposits were found.

THE GLASS FACTORY IN THE 1830s-The line of buildings at left is on Dock Lane (present Harbor Street) but those at right are not along Factory Street but well east of Factory Street. The tallest chimney is of the so-called X-furnace in the new upper glass house, while the chimney just to its right is the one on the furnace in the original wooden factory. The little building in the foreground is the Catholic chapel erected in 1830 on Jarves Street. The heavy wagon holds firewood Sandwich Archives.

This factory operation probably became stable and promised good success, but being located at a distance from Boston and away from sources of all supplies (except wood) it required extra capital for materials, for supplies, for the employees, and for marketing facilities—in short Jarves needed more working capital. Therefore he had to bring in partners, and accordingly with three others he formed the Boston and Sandwich Glass Co. (hereafter B&S) which was incorporated early in 1826. He sold much of his Sandwich holdings to the new company for $36,625, including the industrial tract, the dwelling houses and other buildings, plus 1,350 acres of woodlots. In exchange he got shares of B&S stock, and became the General Agent of the company, its general manager. The first superintendent of the glass plant was his brother-in-law William Stutson, who established residence in Sandwich at the house now at 7 Jarves Street. Jarves himself lived in town houses in Boston but came to Sandwich at least monthly, staying at Stutson's.

INTERIOR VIEW OF THE B&S-This view shows the same factory from the harbor side. The major stack is in the new upper glass house while the original wooden building and small furnace of 1825 are at left. Firewood and packing barrels are in the foreground. The three small chimneys in front of the upper glass house represent the ovens where lead was produced from litharge. Courtesy Sandwich Historical Society.

The new glass manufactory was not listed in the 1825 tax list. The records for 1825, 1826, and 1831 show much internal change:

Year	*Name*	*Property*	*Value*
1825	D. Jarves, resid.	House & Barn	$ 1, 500
	" "	1306 A land	8, 500
	" "	Stock in a store	1, 000
	Jabez Dame, non-res.	150 A land	1, 200
	" "	Personal	200
1826	D. Jarves, non. res.	½ house & barn	1, 300
	Wm. Stutson, resid.	½ house & barn	1, 300
	"	Personal	1, 000
	J. Dame, non-res.	140 A & personal	1, 200
	B&S	Buildings & store	13, 000

	"	1300 A land	8, 600
	"	Stocks & Machinery	34, 000
1831	D. Jarves non-res.	House	1, 800
	" "	177 A land	1, 200
	" "	8 tenements	3, 300
	Wm. Stutson, resid.	House, land & personal	3, 600
	B&S	Buildings incl. 27 tenements	27, 600
	"	2206 A land	8, 400
	"	vessel & wharf	17, 000
	Jarves & Hall non-res.	10 tenements	2, 500

The large value of glass stocks and other factory contents shown in 1826 appeared again in 1827, then was dropped reflecting no doubt some hard bargaining and evaluation with the town assessors. By 1831 Jarves again had a house, but this we suggest was simply part of his large and varying holdings in the town. He owned rental tenements in his own name and also jointly with another Boston investor. These would be located in the area of the factory but not on the B&S property. By 1831 the B&S, itself, had 27 tenement apartments.

Stutson was factory superintendent until 1848 when he became Resident Agent, reflecting his broader interest in local supplies, real estate, and negotiations with the town. The superintendent for glass making was Theodore Kern. Jarves' other top aide in Sandwich was the Company's clerk and paymaster Charles C. P. Waterman, from Wareham. The glass output of the factory was shipped to Boston where most sales were completed. Since there were no banks in Sandwich the payroll and other local expenses had to be made up in Boston and sent down in cash every two weeks. Stutson and Waterman were Jarves' business partners and personal representatives as well as employees, and were active in establishing local sources for products needed to run and expand the plant, such as bricks, lumber, castings, and barrels. The B&S directors placed a limit on what company funds Jarves could spend at his own discretion, with the result that from the beginning his own funds were involved in local operations, such as leases, purchases and contracts for local supplies and real estate transactions. He moved swiftly to establish and consolidate these operations, relying on local businessmen such as Clark Hoxie. Once well established, a local investment might or might not be sold to the B&S. Here are a few of the early operations illustrating the impact of the plant on the town.

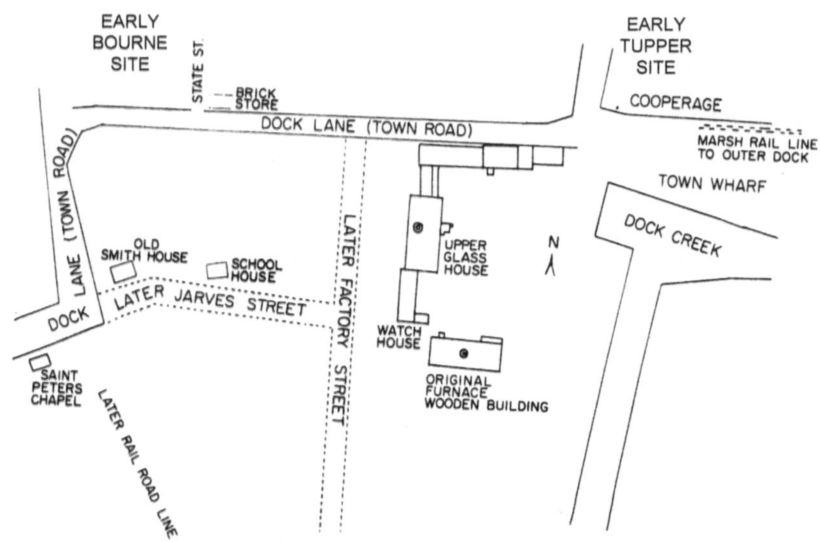

Boston and Sandwich Glass Company about 1835

The Glass Company owned not only the six-acre industrial site but the land in front of the factory where tenements were located, also the brick store at State Street, the cooperage area near the wharf and the marsh railroad line down to the outer dock near the harbor. There were two furnaces for glassmaking, but the line of brick buildings along what was later Factory Street were not yet built. The Catholic Church was erected in 1830.

Company Store

Bringing some sixty city families to new houses in a small section of remote Sandwich village created some novel problems in adjustments and supplies. The stores and amenities available in Cambridge were not instantly available here. The town center and its few stores were close to the mill pond. The B&S immediately built a brick building at the corner of what is now State Street and Harbor Street and stocked it as a general store. The employees were allowed to buy on credit, and probably as a good will gesture townsmen were allowed the same privilege. This caused a rush to the company store and many were slow to pay up. The record books for the first two years are available at the Sandwich Historical Society and make fascinating reading. However the B&S ended the free ride and turned the store over to a contractor who was doubtless more stringent in his collections.

Dock and Harbor Landings

When Jarves came to Sandwich the town owned two marine facilities in the Shawme marsh area. These were the town dock at the end of Dock Lane, and a wharf at a landing area near the Old Harbor Mouth (further east than the present one). Both were ancient features but by no coincidence had recently been improved at no expense to the town. The dock area was a 40-foot wide strip over 350 feet long extending to the navigable portion of Old Dock Creek. The structure there was probably a light planked wharf for offloading "stuffage in scows," and Town meeting records for over a century past refer to repairs and clearing the channel. There was an argument with the Glass Company that a company building was on town owned land, after which the town put in stone bounds to its dock area. The town landing on deeper water was on Old Harbor Creek or Musett Creek, where there was an ancient cartway along the shore and up to Spring Hill. This is also referred to in various early town meeting minutes. Vessels could be tied here and cargo offloaded into barges for landing at shore points at high tide, not only at the Town Dock but up Spring Hill Creek and up Mill Creek to the River Street area. In 1824 Ezra Tobey and Elisha Pope were allowed to build a new wharf here, but not to obstruct passage in and out of the harbor. This was doubtless where packets tied up that did not use the Glass Company wharf.

These modest facilities were clearly not adequate for the volume of goods that began to come and go from the glass factory. In 1831, the Sandwich tax records noted above include a new item "Vessel and wharf $17,000", a very large and sudden increase. The vessel was probably the sloop *Henry Clay* built by Hinckley at West Sandwich. The wharf must have been not only a new wharf built by the B&S in deep water near the harbor mouth but also a marine railway that connected it to the town dock and the factory. This was an expensive and even daring project to speed freight in and out between the factory and the vessels. It took advantage of the fact that a straight line could be drawn from the town dock to deep water without crossing an arm of the winding Dock Creek. The B&S had bought the wharf area as early as 1826 and may well have put in its own pilings and wharf immediately. However, barging in was still necessary until the marine railway was completed. The railway consisted of a trench about 6 feet square dug into the marsh; its sides were lined with planks and it was filled with broken bricks, broken glass, broken pots and ashes. The route crossed five small marsh streams and at each the end of the trench was sealed and the crossing made by heavy timbers. The mix in the trench packed down very solidly, and although flooded at high tide twice a day was a hard foundation for the wooden ties and the narrow gauge tracks. Like the railroad tracks inside the plant, these tracks were only iron strips nailed to wooden rails. Since the roadbed was flat one horse could pull a load of many tons. There was even a car for passengers. The marsh railway was about 1200 feet long and was a bold and novel achievement.

Brickyard

Jarves must have considered the existence of the Town Neck brickyard so near his plant site as a real plus for his enterprise. Bricks were constantly needed, and he or his associates contracted for their production, charging the B&S the Boston price of bricks without freight. Not until 1853 was the B&S directly involved in contracting for the output of the brickyard.

Cohasset Narrows

The B&S received heavy freight at its own dock or "depot" at Cohasset Narrows, such as sand from New Jersey and coal from Virginia. In 1830 the company authorized Jarves "to purchase a new depot, the one at present being too small and not well calculated for their purpose." It is believed that the B&S wharf was in the Narrows and that freight from here was trundled over to Sandwich Village by heavy wagons. This was considered preferable to shipping around the outside of Cape Cod.

Schoolhouse at Jarvesville

By 1830 the inhabitants in the glass factory village (already being called Jarvesville) numbered 371 and constituted an important element in the town. Thirty-six families had applied to the Town in 1828 for status as a school district, which was immediately approved. The school was erected in an open park in front of the factory, as shown in the map of 1849. The Town at this time had a dedicated chairman of the School Committee, Dr. John Harper, who prepared long annual reports on the condition of the district schools. He reported that pupils aged five through fifteen in the Jarvesville District numbered 177 in 1848. The younger children in one room under Mary Hamlen were well behaved, but of 92 children, attendance only averaged 47. Of the 85 older children under Nahum Leonard Jr., the attendance was much worse, about 26 daily. This was the most distressing classroom for the School Committee in the whole town, because parents kept pupils from attending or sent for them to come home while in class. The parents would not visit the school but resented discipline for bad behavior. These unfair conditions caused Leonard to resign, but he was reinstated by the School Committee. The parents of these older children clearly had a low opinion of the value of education and wanted the children at home to run errands or earn money.

Stave Mill at Spring Hill

The local supply operations of Jarves and his Sandwich team are shown to perfection in his prompt establishment of a stave mill to make cheap barrels for shipment of glass. He, Stutson and Clark Hoxie became joint owners of the disused old grist mill at Spring Hill by 1826. They raised the dam to get more power and installed modern saws which were a marvel of efficiency compared to shaping staves by hand as coopers had always done. Two thousand staves and their barrel heads could be turned out by three men in a day. The wood was cheap pine as these barrels were only intended for one-way use to get a light load of glass packed in hay to the nearest sales point. Only two truss hoops were needed.

Other Local Projects

Jarves and Clark Hoxie bought water rights and factory buildings at North Sandwich in 1840 and converted them into a modern foundry and machine shop, the Manomet Iron Co., where castings were made and whole machines were assembled, not only for the glass factory but for other customers. A lumber yard was set up in Jarvesville with a small planing mill operated by that new marvel, a steam engine. This was run by William Stutson's nephew, H. H. Thayer. Local businessmen Isaac K. Chipman and William C. Chipman installed a door, sash and blind woodworking shop in the same building in response to the constant growth of houses and other construction. Jarves even bought a few acres of farmland in an area called Sand Hill and set it aside as a non-sectarian cemetery. Jarves himself sold the lots here at $6.00 each as several deeds testify. It later came to be known as Mount Hope. The earliest markers are those of an infant son of C. C. P. Waterman (buried Oct. 1826) and Sally Stutson, wife of Capt. William Stutson (buried July 1827). Numerous burials of Catholics from the glass factory families came later, but doubtless some of the dead were taken to Boston or Cambridge for burial. Seven Irish were even buried in Old Town Burying Ground. After St. Peter's Cemetery was founded in 1865, most Catholic burials were there.

St. Peters Chapel

The presence of many Catholics in Sandwich from 1825 created a need for a church here, or at least periodic visits by priests. However, the number of priests in Massachusetts was then extremely limited as the only churches in 1830 were at Boston, Salem, Lowell and Charlestown. Bishop Fenwick of Boston bought a small lot on the south side of Jarves Street from Melatiah Tobey on June 26, 1830, and had some prefabricated roof trusses shipped down from Boston. These were assembled into a small building 30' x 40', and the dedication services were held Sept. 19, 1830. The delegation of clergy and singers from Boston came down by packet, but meeting headwinds were badly delayed and only arrived after the scheduled beginning of services. All went well however. The assigned priest, Father Connolly, had to serve groups in Wareham, New Bedford, Rhode Island and elsewhere. The first priest permanently stationed here was Father William Moran in 1850.

The Boston and Sandwich Area

Considering the profound impact that the glass factory had on the town, there is remarkably little reference to it or to Mr. Jarves in town meeting minutes. Events conducted without cost to the town were not brought up unless there was need to seek town approval, and Jarves, Stutson and Waterman showed concern and cooperation when problems emerged. The Selectmen set ten stone bounds to define the town land in the dock area in 1839, then being used intensely. The Selectmen drew the map of the land and its measurements into the town meeting record book, adding the words "they were amicably received by Capt. Stutson who thinks the Glass Company would be willing to assist the town in clearing out the said dock." (Part of this amicability is explained by current town meeting references to finding investments to utilize surplus income.) Dock Lane had run down the line of later Jarves Street to the railroad tracks, then had followed some ancient course to the dock on the marsh. The glass company had immediately built the brick store and the cooper's barn on the north side of present Harbor Street, and a line of their factory buildings, as well as company owned tenements, along the south side of Harbor Street, suggesting strongly (in the absence of town approval to re-route Dock Lane) that, in fact, Dock Lane had already followed a winding course like the present route of Harbor Street, then Church Street and Jarves Street. The Factory Street and Jarves Street sectors east of the tracks were of course all within the B&S land and remained private streets for over a century. Houses began to fill the Jarvesville sector near the factory, and to spread up toward Main Street. In the absence of town planning for new roads, the pattern of roads that emerged was reasonably efficient. A new development came in 1836 when Jarves and others bought the Nathaniel Nye farm of 20 acres which had occupied the area from Liberty Street to the south and east through the wetlands called Ford Creek Swamp. Abruptly, Liberty Street was laid out and further lots became available along that part of Main Street. The "Sandwich That Glass Built" was well along by the 1840s.

Glass Factory in 1849

The Directors of the B&S in the periods of rapid expansion were called on to approve new projects without much description. They were given a visit to the plant at least annually and shown around quickly, but spent a lengthy part of their visit in the comfort of the Central House. They insisted in 1847 on being given a map of the plant and adjacent facilities so that new projects could be better envisioned. This map was finally produced by Jarves in 1849 after current projects were completed and the railroad line installed. The resulting plan of the B&S at that point was extremely useful and widely reproduced both then and later. We show a reduced sketch of it here, together with a suggested layout of the plant about 1835. The heart of the factory was in the furnaces, each holding a ring of clay pots of molten glass. From the description of operations in Ruth Webb Lee's book the following seems to be the sequence of furnaces:

1. The original furnace of 1825 in the wood building. This was enlarged in 1832 and removed together with the whole building in 1848 when the new Lower House was started.

2. The first furnace in the so-called Upper House area; this was called the X house for some reason. This was built in 1828, enlarged in 1831, converted to coal in 1836, enlarged again in 1846, and removed entirely, together with its building, in 1850.

3. The second furnace in the Upper area. This was in a brick 2-story building which for the first time ran along the edge of present Factory Street. It was built in 1841 and, with repairs, remained as one of the main production furnaces throughout the remaining life of the plant. It was dynamited in 1920.

4. The first furnace in the Lower Glass House area was built in 1848 and operated at peak periods. It was demolished in 1907.

5. The third furnace in the Upper House was built in 1850 and replaced the X house. It was in a large two-story brick building

parallel to #3 above, with the two stacks, each about 70' high, on a line about east-west as shown in photographs of the plant. It also was demolished in 1920.

6. The second furnace at the Lower Glass House was erected in 1853 and operated as peaking capacity like #4. The two Lower House stacks were about on a north-south line. It was demolished in 1907.

The map of 1849 shows the new arrangement just completed, with the original furnace gone, the X house and the new Upper House furnace in place along Factory Street and the one Lower House furnace. A new steam boiler and 90' stack had just been built, as had the buildings all along Factory Street. Makers of Sandwich maps of 1857 and later years all relied on this map for the shape of the buildings in the glass factory, whereas in fact, by 1850, the Upper House had a different shape, by 1853 the Lower House was larger and there was also a large new Pothouse. The 1849 map does not show the small furnaces made to hold pots of colored glass, called "monkey pots," which were doubtless in the Upper House area. In general, glass from the Upper House included all that which was intended for cutting, etching or decorating, processes done on the second floors of adjacent buildings. The Lower House furnaces were for intermittent operation to fill large orders at peak periods where the glass was essentially ready for packing as soon as it cooled.

The Glass Output

In view of the extensive writings available about Sandwich glass we will not go into any details here. The arrangement at the Sandwich Glass Museum shows the chronological periods and output by rooms. The earliest glass was blown and molded. By 1827 the use of mechanical presses to create appropriate shapes from the dies in the press and plungers was in use here and was quickly improved by new inventions. After about 1830 Sandwich started to make "lacy" glass using iron molds cut to a very fine sharp pattern, which made the product look like cut glass. The master moldmaker was Hiram Dilloway who made many improvements through invention and innovation. Later in the 1840s, brilliant colors were used in a variety of smooth molded pieces.

Working arrangements at the factory were that glass making went on continuously for four days Monday through Thursday, then stopped. There were either three eight-hour shifts or four six-hour shifts, and the men worked one shift, rested one, then worked again around the clock. During the weekend the fires were kept going in the furnaces and in the annealing ovens. Laboratory staff made up the new batches of clean and colored ingredients which were charged into the pots to be melted and ready by the first shift Monday. Each pot in use was worked by a tightly knit group under the senior glassmaker called the gaffer who did the key steps. Jarves' marvelous achievements were the result of getting the best talent he could find, paying people well, encouraging innovation at all stages, and keeping up relentless attention to detail and maintenance.

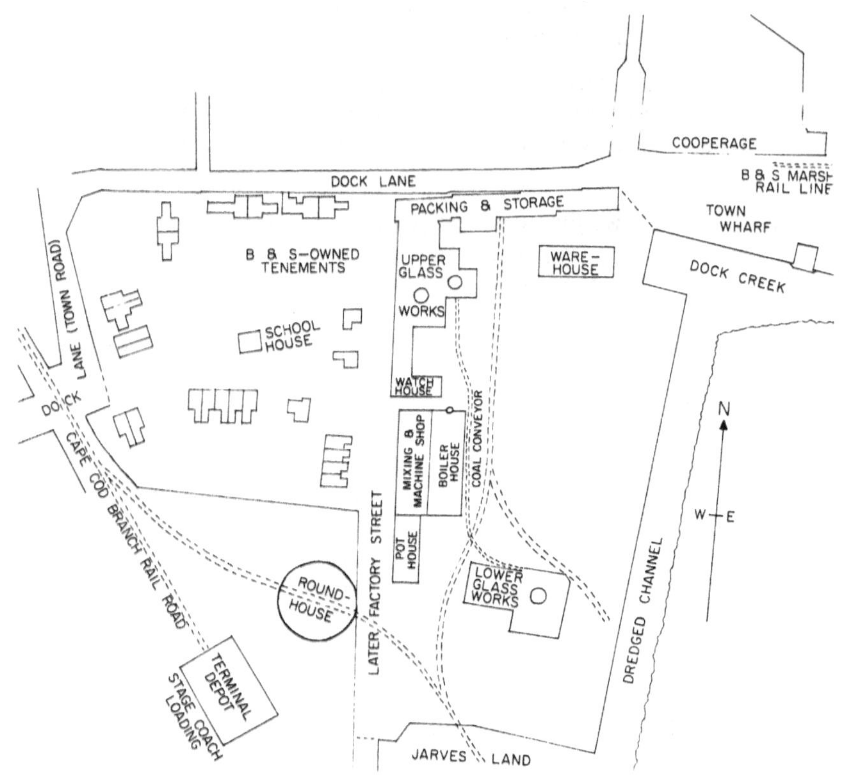

Boston and Sandwich Glass Company in 1849

This plan is based on a drawing of the property prepared by Amos R. Binney of Boston at the request of the directors. It was widely distributed and so remains as the popular idea of the permanent layout of the plant, reproduced on property survey maps and even on the bronze memorial marker on the site. However the plant was in rapid evolution during the 1850s when the six-apartment block was built, the schoolhouse removed, a fenced park installed, an entirely new building built in the upper glass works, a second furnace built at the lower glassworks and a new large pot house built near the channel.

The First Parish Church

On the death of Rev. Goodwin in 1833, the church society (now a private religious society), voted to build a wholly new church building on the site. It was decided to have the tower and entrance on Main Street, but to run the long way of the hall along River Street. Whittemore Peterson of Duxbury, a well-known craftsman, was chosen as builder. His instructions included: size: 65 x 47 feet; arched ceiling; three windows on a side like the windows in the Episcopal Church in Quincy; outside in Gothic style like the Robinson Church in Plymouth;

with pews like the Universalist Church in Quincy. The committee was given the option of including a vestry and utility floor on the ground level, but decided against this. Titus Winchester's two-faced clock was transferred to the new tower which had four points on the corners and a short 16-foot spire. The new minister, Rev. John M. Merrick, arrived in May of 1833 and within a week, by coincidence, the old meetinghouse was pulled down. Jarves bought the frame timbers and is reported to have reused them in one of his factory buildings. He contributed a chandelier to the new church, as he did to all the new churches in Sandwich. This building was ready for dedication October 30, 1833. It had a new 1500 lb. bell.

The Town House or Hall

With its growing population of voters and its improved tax base the town was in good position to build a hall for town meetings. Under State law there was no longer any connection between the town government and any of the religious societies. A vote on building a Town Hall was postponed in 1832 and again in 1833, but once the old meetinghouse was gone the decision was made and a committee promptly went to work. The site was between two shoemaker's shops along the west side of the millstream below the mill. The land here sloped down to the stream and was soft; it was owned by the Newcombs and was donated to the town. The builder selected was Ellis Howland of the Wakeby sector in Mashpee. The building was to be of two stories, with the upper one a hall capable of seating 500 people. The front was later said to resemble the Exchange Building in Boston, but this does not appear as an original directive. The lower level was floored over but not finished otherwise, and the space was available for hire through the selectmen. The foundation must have required a great deal of cut stone, not only for the building but to bridge over the millstream and allow a flat plaza in front of the new building. The ground fill under and around the Hall required 500 tipcarts of gravel, which was supplied by James Faunce who occupied the house at 111 Main Street, now called Uplands. The hill just west of this house gives evidence of such removal.

The upper hall was entered by two winding staircases in the front of the building with separate outer doors from the front porch, so that entry upstairs was not through the lower level. Upstairs the moderator's platform and desk was between the stairwells so that the audience faced north. The floor was laid either sloping or stepped, with the seats permanently secured. It was later said that this was to prevent dancing, but there is no evidence that the building committee ever considered any use of the hall except for public meetings. There was no balcony, but there were two small rooms over the stairwells, one of which was to be "fitted for the accommodation of the Town Clerk's and Selectmen's papers." Mr. Charles H. Freeman was in charge of placing two chimneys, and supplying stoves. There is no mention of who secured the long gray granite slabs for the front steps, almost certainly from Quincy. The building was largely completed by November 1834 and Mr. Howland was released from adding a cupola or dome originally planned. The building cost $4,138.32, and was insured for $3000. The first town meeting held here was on March 16, 1835. The Hall could be obtained at the request of ten citizens at a reasonable charge, but was free if used for town or State affairs. There were outhouses behind the building.

UNITARIAN CHURCH AND BOYDEN BLOCK-Main Street Sandwich before 1880. The Boyden Block is in the foreground with restaurant and shops at left. The taller portion encloses a hall where the Masonic Lodge met. The Boyden stables are at right. The Unitarian Church of 1833 is at the left with the Titus Winchester clock in the tower and original very short spire. The two-faced Winchester clock broke down in 1874. The spire was enlarged and a new four-faced clock was installed higher up. The Boyden Block and stables were destroyed by fire in 1913 including a collection of stagecoaches, a sad loss.

The orderly pace of town affairs is suggested in a vote in 1835 "that the Selectmen meet the first Monday in May in the afternoon at their room in the Town House for the purpose of accomodating all that have business with them, and from that time quarterly through the year."

Other Churches

The Universalists organized a religious society in Sandwich in 1845, and erected a church on Main Street at the corner of Summer Street. The chief supporter of this society was their treasurer, William E. Boyden. The membership declined and the church was closed by 1869 when the empty building was removed to lower Jarves Street to serve as a store and hall.

The Puritan Church was begun in 1847 after Rev. Giles Pease had been dismissed from the Calvinistic Church pulpit in 1846. He took many of his adherents with him, by whom a new Puritan Congregational Church was formed, building a chapel at 10 Jarves Street (now the Belfry Inn). The congregation remained very small however, and Rev. Pease requested permission in 1856 to seek a more remunerative post. Most of the Puritan Church members returned to the Calvinist church. The chapel was used temporarily by the Episcopal group and then became a hardware store.

In spite of the loss of a number of members to the Puritan Church, the Calvinistic Congregational Church remained strong, and under their new minister Rev. Elias Wells, determined to build a new church building on the site of their chapel. The church records in 1847 mention a building committee but do not describe the plans. By good fortune a detailed account appeared in the *Sandwich Observer* for Nov. 18, 1848, reading as follows:

> "The new house is the neatest structure in this county. It was designed by Isaac Melvin, Architect, of Cambridgeport, and built by S. L. James & Co., of Fall River. The body of the house is 54 feet by 46 feet, with 27 foot posts. The tower projection is 18 feet by 28 feet. The spire is 130 feet in height. The interior is finished in very neat style. There are in the main room 62 pews; all of which are in the body of the house, there being an aisle on each side by the wall and a centre one also. The pulpit is of mahogany, built by Samuel H. Allyne of this place, and is a beautiful piece of work. The vestry, under the main part, is about 40 feet by 46 feet, very neatly fitted up with settees; and in the rear of it is the cellar. All the flooring and treads are of hard pine. The house is warmed by furnaces; and lighted by a chandelier, a present as we learn from Deming Jarves, Esq. of Boston. But we are not at home in descriptions of this kind; and we can only say in general, that the house is very thoroughly built of the best materials and after a beautiful plan, and that it is fitted up in as good style as any house in the country. The cost is about $6,000."

Isaac Melvin was a distinguished architect who, early in life, worked with Charles Bulfinch, the designer of the Massachusetts State House and of the U. S. Capitol. Melvin designed a number of public buildings in Cambridge, Boston and elsewhere as well as churches and homes, according to material made available to us by the Cambridge Historical Commission. In particular his large North Ave. Congregational Church built in Cambridge in 1845 had a tall graceful spire with two courses of columns in rings, which is quite similar to the sophisticated design of the Sandwich church. Since Bulfinch and Melvin worked in the classical designs used by Christopher Wren there is reason to call this a "Wren" church, so long as the indirect attribution is understood. This church was completed then during 1848 and has formed a graceful centerpiece of the Sandwich village scene ever since. The former church bell was replaced in 1854 by a much larger bell from the Hooper Company of Boston. A picture appears on page 293.

The Methodist Society was popular in Sandwich and replaced its building on the same site by a much larger church in 1847, dedicated January 7, 1848 in close parallel to the timing of the Calvinists. The architect here was Peleg Mason of Fall River; his building was 60 feet long, 32 feet wide, 34 feet high, and surmounted by a tower and steeple. There was a vestry, study room, and heater in the ground floor rooms. Including the gallery, the seating capacity of the sanctuary was 600. There was a gilded chandelier, the gift of Deming Jarves, Esq. New ministers were assigned here every year or two, providing much variety and interest. There were at this time two well-known glass-makers who were Methodist preachers and evangelizers, Benjamin Haines and Joseph Marsh, both born in England. Their labors at the glass factory prevented their being regularly ordained as full-time ministers over a particular church, but they were fluent and totally dedicated, preaching here occasionally and in the smaller congregations throughout the area. They represented strongly the anti-slavery, anti-liquor, anti-profanity movements of the day but they were not elitist reformers; they lived not on Main Street which they could afford, but with the people in the glass factory village, among their co-workers of all faiths or no faith, setting a vigorous example of what they themselves believed. Everybody got to know a few bars of their favorite Methodist hymns.

Private Schools and District Schools

Hayward's Gazeteer published in 1849 (with data of 1845) lists the following information for this County:

	Sandwich	*Barnstable*	*Falmouth*	*County*
Town Valuation	$788,723	$785,856	$682,998	$4,896,683
Polls	960	1,007	682	8,002
Children 4-16	1,171	1,022	719	9,387
School Monies	10,834	4,319	2,069	32,290
Public Schools	21	20	19	162
Private Schools	22	20	12	110
Academies	1	–	1	5

Such Gazetteer information may be somewhat flawed, but the above comparisons are of much interest. Without the glass factory and its resultant people, houses and stores, Sandwich totals would be far less, probably less than what is shown for Falmouth in all categories. In the matter of public schools, the situation was exceedingly uneven in Sandwich, with 177 children available in the Jarvesville district for a two-room school, 192 children available in the eastern side of the village, again with a two-room school, and 19 district schools of one room each, in the middle of their scattered villages, with an average of 42 children available per school. Some of the district buildings were large and new with big blackboards and windows, where attendance was highly rewarding, but a few were the opposite—ancient, leaky, and sagging, without outhouses, where even a gifted child would have problems. Dr. Harper, the Chairman of the School Committee, stated in 1844 that parents objected to buying so many books for their children because of frequent changes in texts for the public schools, plus the large number of private schools with different texts. This is one of the only references to private schools outside the big well-known ones. Clearly there were many of these little classes in Sandwich, answering a need that could not be met in the public schools for more personalized and specific instruction in less crowded and tumultuous surroundings than a one-room, all-age district school. They were held in fair weather and often rented the public schools or the Academy in the months when not in use. The ads by the teachers are found in the newspapers of the 1840s. Only one in Sandwich of which we are aware was especially built and survives at 3 River Street. This was used by Reverend Asahel Cobb and his daughter Lucia who lived at what is now 141 Main Street. Rev. Cobb had resigned from the Calvinist church in 1842. The famous private schools here included the Sandwich Collegiate Institute opened in March 1845 by Rev. Frederick Freeman, then 46 years old, who had returned from Episcopal pulpits in Plymouth, North Carolina and Maine, and built a large residence and academy building on the hill he called Belle Monte, now the Windswept complex. He had inherited his father's home, library and collections after 1827, and had sold the house to embark on this school venture. His early prospectus describes the Institute as a home for young ladies and gentlemen, all of whom must board there, with a separate chapel for Sunday services and large grounds for recreation. The costs were per 11-week quarter:

Board and basic tuition	$30.00
Special instruction in classics, commerce, navigation or French	3.00
Instruction and use of piano	10.00
Drawing, painting, embroidery	5.00
Art & science of teaching	4.00

Children of clergymen, 15% off. Books and stationery extra.

On July 4, 1845, he held a service of celebration in the chapel at the foot of his drive on Main Street, which was a large enough building to accommodate an organ, all his pupils and staff, plus many guests. The Unitarian Minister Rev. Crafts spoke, as did Dr. John Harper, and the students provided the music. In the evening a large reception was held in the main building, with fireworks at the top of the hill. This must have been the high point of the school's prospects, as it closed in 1849; Rev. Freeman retired to his study to begin the long labor of the *History of Cape Cod.*

Three private schools of much longer duration were located near each other in Spring Hill. Paul Wing's Spring Hill Academy was founded in 1834 and continued until the 1870s. It was held first in his home, which burned in 1851, then in a large 3½-story building which he erected, but which burned in 1862, then in a 2-story building which still survives at 83 Spring Hill Road. This was a day school which accommodated a total of 73 boys and 30 girls in 1841. The most famous pupil was probably Hetty Robinson of New Bedford, a Quaker girl, who became Hetty Green, the Witch of Wall Street. In addition there were two other Quaker schools nearby which were the work of half-sisters Mercy Kelley Wing and Eliza Gould Wing. Mercy, and her husband Joseph Wing, (a brother of Paul Wing) ran the Sandwich Boarding School in two buildings, now 252 and 260 Route 6A in Spring Hill, while Eliza Wing ran the Apple Grove Seminary for girls in the Countryside area. Eliza's husband, Asa Shove Wing, a teacher at both schools, died within a year of their marriage. Illustrations are shown on page 311.

THE CENTRAL HOUSE-General Sabin Smith bought the Fessenden Tavern in 1830 and added the large extension shown at the right in this view, housing dining room and guest rooms. The room reserved for Daniel Webster was the right front on the second floor. The center portion was the Reverend Benjamin Fessenden home of 1729 and the left portion with verandahs was added by Benjamin Junior in the 1750s when the Tavern was established. The Central House under various owners and names kept this form during the rest of the nineteenth century. Sandwich Archives.

The Fessenden Tavern

William Fessenden sold the family tavern to General Sabin Smith in 1830, who very sensibly added a large two-story addition on the east of the old parsonage to provide for the many visitors who now came to Sandwich. The right hand front upstairs bedroom was the one preferred by Daniel Webster; it was served by a dumb waiter.

General Smith called his place Smith's Tavern, and after his death in 1837 the next owners called it the Mansion House. Michael Scott bought it in 1847 and called it the Central House which name was used until 1915 when the Daniel Webster Inn came into being.

The Newcomb Tavern

There is no record of the closing of the Newcomb Tavern. The last guest who spoke of staying at Newcomb's was the arriving B&S paymaster C. C. P. Waterman in 1825. The last host, Lemuel Newcomb, died in 1825 at age 43, leaving a widow and nine children. There was a special problem in this family in that five children were deaf and dumb. Two of the boys later worked at the B&S. They attended the Hartford Asylum for the Deaf and Dumb founded in 1817 and used sign language all their lives.

The Scorton River Crossing

Henry Wing and others living on Scorton Neck petitioned the County Commissioners in 1847 to allow a highway bridge to be built over a navigable stream, the Scorton River, in order to make a direct connection between the County Road at Daniel Fish's house (opposite the present East Sandwich Post Office) and the residences along Scorton Neck, whose only connection to Sandwich was via Jones Road. As in the earlier similar case of the Monument River Bridge, this proposition was objected to by the rest of the town on the grounds of expense, although it would be of great convenience not only to the local people but to travelers up and down the Cape in shortening the County Road. Approval of the Commissioners and the State Legislature was granted over the town's objection and the town lamely agreed to fund it out of surplus revenue. The new crossing was 700 feet long, comprising a low dirt causeway and a timber bridge over the tidal stream. The bridge itself cost only $650, but the new road laid out from Fish's to the Barnstable line came to $3,000, which caused cries of protest at town meeting. When the County began to pick up maintenance costs, the protests died. We have mentioned this item of Sandwich events in the 1840s as an example of information available from the pages of the new weekly newspaper, the *Sandwich Observer.* References to the Scorton bridge and causeway in town meeting records were so scant that a general picture of the events could not be formed.

Early Newspapers

The two early Cape newspapers of which complete runs have been preserved were the *Barnstable Patriot,* published by Sylvanus B. Phinney from 1830, and the *Yarmouth Register,* published by Nathaniel S. Simpkins from 1837. The *Sandwich Observer* was issued by George Phinney in 1845 and continued to 1851. The *Sandwich Mechanic* was issued briefly in 1851, and then in 1852 publication began here of *The Cape Cod Advocate and Nautical Intelligencer* by Benjamin C. Bowman and Matthew Pinkham. These early newspapers contain invaluable current news of local events, and in preparation for this present work we have reviewed the *Yarmouth Register* on microfilm. Through the marvels of computerized newspaper inventories at libraries and historical agencies across the country, a block of five years' issues of the *Sandwich Observer* from 1846 into 1851 was found to be held at the Wisconsin Historical Society. Microfilm of this most valuable series for Sandwich history was studied and has been an essential part of the background for this chapter and the two to follow on railroads and marine activities. Advertisements in these pages trace a line of shops along Jarves Street and Main Street, sprung up to serve a newly affluent community. These newspapers preserve a mass of historical information on what was happening week by week that greatly enriches and explains what otherwise only appears in dry legal language of wills, deeds and records of churches or town meetings.

UNIVERSALIST AND METHODIST CHURCHES-This view of 1869 or earlier is the only one known showing both the Universalist Church at Main and Summer Streets, and beyond it the Methodist Church with its original spire as built in 1847. The Methodist Church spire was replaced by a short square tower. Photograph courtesy of Lombard C. Jones.

Barnstable County Records Fire

Research in Barnstable County history will always be impeded by a massive loss of documentation which occurred in a fire at the Barnstable County Building, October 22, 1827. Details of the fire are given by Trayser in his book

Barnstable: Three Centuries. Destroyed in the fire were 93 large folios of copied deeds, plus a number that were in process of being copied, also three volumes of probate, all but one docket of the civil and criminal court records from 1685, and all the County business records from 1685.

A meeting of Justices, Selectmen and town representatives was held Nov. 9, to try to limit possible "fraudulent and improper practices which may grow out of this calamity, " and to plan a new combined Court and County Building. Citizens were urged to bring in their current deeds to be re-recorded, and this was done at half price. There are, for example, three volumes now at the Registry of Deeds of re-recorded Sandwich deeds, but deeds prior to ownership as of 1827 were not re-recorded.

CHAPTER 19

THE RAILROAD COMES TO SANDWICH

Before the railroad, transport as of about 1840 had advanced immeasurably from the isolation of the 1790s. Shipping between coastal cities and towns by packet was frequent and convenient. Harbors and inland waterways had been greatly improved and lighthouses, bouys and charts were available to improve safety. Where suitable, inland transport by canals was the cheapest means of freight transport. Roads continued to improve in surface and design. Freight to and from inland towns moved by heavy wagons on a regularly scheduled basis. The age of private turnpikes was roughly 1792-1808, when direct new roads were opened up straight across country for rapid travel by coach or wagon but, of course, with tolls for the operator. There were no toll-roads built on the Cape, probably because of the extensive packet network from every Bay point to Boston. This interlocking water and road network was highly organized and working well when the steam locomotive entered the scene, and changed all the factors. To improve its upcountry reach and expand its markets versus New York, the Commonwealth pushed railways strongly.

Southeastern Massachusetts Lines

The sequence of change as it affected Cape Cod began with the Boston/Providence railway, which was completed in 1835. In 1840 a branch from the Boston/Providence line ran from Mansfield through Taunton to New Bedford. At this point the mails and passengers for the Cape were shifted over to New Bedford by rail, then stage to Sandwich, rather than the all-stage route to Plymouth and then to Sandwich. However, in 1845, a rail company called the Old Colony put a new line through from Braintree down to Plymouth. This immediately restored Plymouth as the fastest way to the Cape, and the stage coaches from Sandwich went back to the Plymouth run. New railroad companies throughout Massachusetts now sprang up rapidly to tap the remaining markets for freight and passengers. One group ran a line from Braintree through Bridgewater and Middleboro, then over to Fall River; the following year the New York/Fall River steamboat connection was established, making a boat/train link between Boston and New York which was to become immensely popular and to persist for ninety years.

Cape Cod Branch Railroad

On completion of the Fall River line in 1846, various businessmen, including Clark Hoxie of Sandwich, applied to form a new company called the Cape Cod Branch Railroad (CCBRR) which would run from the Fall River Line at Middleboro through Wareham to Sandwich, a distance of twenty seven miles. This route would serve passengers between the whole Cape and Boston, and would also serve the iron works and other industries at Wareham, and the large and growing glassworks at Sandwich. There was a competing proposal from another group to extend the Old Colony line from Plymouth to Sandwich, but this was not supported locally either in Plymouth or in Sandwich; also rejected was a line from Plympton to Wareham. The State Railway Commission considered these proposals in a quite sophisticated economic study, analyzing cost of construction, volume of freight and passenger business generated. The Middleboro/Sandwich line was approved. The promoters were given two years to complete construction, and immediately started to raise capital in Boston, Fall River, Wareham and Sandwich. They defined the exact route, got their permits and began construction in December 1846.

Simeon Borden was the chief engineer. The route was fairly flat, on glacial outwash plains all the way to the morainal junction at Sandwich, where nature had provided a unique deep valley through the barrier, as though expressly designed for a canal or a railway. There were only three major stream crossings requiring masonry piers: Wareham center, the Cohasset Narrows between Wareham and Sandwich, and over the Manomet River near Monument Village. Minor stream crossings such as over Mill Creek in Sandwich were on timber trestles. The authorization for the line specified that at Wareham center and at Cohasset Narrows, drawbridges had to be provided. The County Commissioners allowed grade crossings everywhere, except at Town Neck where an underpass out to the Neck for cattle was to be built six feet high by fifteen feet wide. A spur of 1½ miles down to the Wareham wharves was included. The most important way stations were at Wareham and Monument, where the buildings were long sheds completely over the track, while the other stations were trackside. At Sandwich the line ended in a fan of tracks in a big barny depot building, 80 feet by 120 feet, which included office, freight station and depot restaurant. Even more impressive was the roundhouse for turning the engine and tender. This had brick walls 100 feet in diameter, and the timber roof was 120 feet high, making it the highest building in Sandwich, except for the tip of the steeple of the Congregational Church at 130 feet. The spur in to the glass factory ran through the roundhouse. Clark Hoxie held the general construction contract for the Sandwich portion. The early stations were reportedly built by Zenas F. Chadwick, a friend of Hoxie's and a later owner of the Central House. There is no reference to the rails for this first section of the line. They were probably the same as for the Sandwich/Hyannis link begun in 1853, for which the contract between CCBRR and the Rensselaer Iron Co. in Troy, New York, still survives. These rails were of a T pattern 56 pounds per yard. The earliest railroads had wooden rails with flat iron strips nailed on top. These strips were 3/8 inch x *2½* inches, and only 12 feet long. They tended to work loose, and if one end snapped up and rode up over the next wheel, the strip would curl up into the car body above with horrid effect. We mention this because in 1896, when the B&S property was being sold, a drawing of the spur into the glass factory specified that the spur inside the yard still had wooden rails.

THE ROUNDHOUSE-The roundhouse, about 1884, as freshly lettered by Henry F. Spurr. Built in 1847 to turn the engine and tender when Sandwich was the railhead, the roundhouse later served as a storehouse, through which the rail spur led into the factory area. The upper glass works chimneys are at left. The roundhoue collapsed in a gale in 1896. Nickerson & Smith Provincetown, photo reproduced courtesy of William Quinn, Orleans.

The contractors hoped to complete the line and start service by January 1, 1848, but the masonry work was only finished in December, so that trains could only operate as far as Wareham for the winter. The grading work during 1847 was said to be held up by a lack of laborers. They were in great demand by other contractors due to a building frenzy in Sandwich that included three churches, dwellings, shops and the glass factory. The causeway across Shawme marsh was of fill laid on the marsh muck, and to the disappointment of the contractor, this section settled badly and had to be relaid. On May 13th, the *Sandwich Observer* reported that a train conveying the Directors, the President of the Senate, and others had gotten to the Scusset station and that rails would shortly be laid for the last two miles. The first mention of this railroad in town meeting records, so momentous for the town, occurred in April when someone complained that the railroad was encroaching on town land at Town Neck. The selectmen reported that a railroad fence did in fact go slightly onto the town's right of way at the road crossing, but that fill from the track embankment had been used for repair of Tupper Road, and that no action need be taken. There was no mention of the fact that the underpass at this crossing, requested by the County, had not been built.

The Grand Opening

A voluntary committee of 20 leading citizens was set up to organize the reception, estimated to involve one thousand persons from out of town. No town money was ever voted. The *Sandwich Observer* pointed out the week before that most citizens were not to be guests at the feast, and one wonders, in the total absence of any police force, how the uninvited were restrained. However, all went splendidly. Tables were set up to fill the entire depot and in fact 1200 were seated. The tables presented a brilliant appearance with fruit dishes and flower vases, all of blue, purple and canary colors, borrowed from the B&S. Flowers and fruit added to the colors. The flowers and plants were provided by Joshua B. Tobey of Wareham and Nahum Stetson of Bridgewater, Directors of the Railroad, and included a number of what must have been real rarities, cactus plants. The word WELCOME was woven with sprigs of cedar onto a large banner of white cloth, and all around the walls of the building were boughs of fragrant cedar. Incredibly, there were even cages of canaries hung along the walls, and a huge tin codfish swung in the air, the work of Josiah Foster of Sandwich.

The day was Friday, May 26, 1848. It was cloudy and as crowds began to gather about noon a heavy shower fell. Just after 1:00 PM the trains approached whistling and the town's bells all began to peal. Even the cars were decorated with evergreens and flowers. The Grand Marshal was Abram Nye, who, with his aides, ushered the guests along the tracks and into the depot where the collation awaited. The toastmaster was Sandwich lawyer Charles B. H. Fessenden who gave a short speech, followed by J. H. W. Paige of New Bedford, President pro-tem of the Board. Flagg's Brass Band played in the background. Others giving addresses were the Lieutenant Governor of the State, Mayor Quincy of Boston, and E. H. Derby, the President of the Old Colony. A comic singer performed, bringing in the names of the railroad directors and speakers into his lyrics. There were many jokes—Boston had heretofore only seen Sandwich through a glass darkly but now face to face—the steam locomotive was a friend to good government but inclined to revolution and always railing—the County should change its name as there would soon be no need for Barns or Stables—the big codfish should be salted down for the next railroad opening on the Cape. The guests were given a little exercise by marching in procession up Jarves Street for a short way, then returning to the cars which left about half past four. The *Sandwich Observer* went to press that same evening for issue on Saturday, and the editor noted that the local committee and others had launched into a post mortem party which was still going on late. He also noted that the Boston people had become very *attached* to the cactus plants and in fact had made off with them. There was no mention of anyone pinching the Sandwich glass. It was one of Sandwich's best days.

There was another smaller party the following Monday, May 29, the day regular service started. About 400 ladies and gentlemen from Rochester and Wareham arrived on the first train about 10 AM on an excursion provided by the railroad. They visited the glass factory and were given a collation of sandwiches, cake and fruit. Afterwards there were speeches, and a singer; a Wareham activist got up a dance, which was so popular that when they were warned to get back on the cars at 3 PM he shouted to the conductor "Go away, Mr. King, your watch is fast. On with the dance." However, Mr. King had his way. The schedule in summer was two trains daily leaving Boston at 7:45 AM and 4:15 PM; leaving Sandwich at 5:45 AM and 3 PM. There was also a daily freight train which had a passenger car attached which only went to Middleboro, where passengers could catch other connections, and the freight was broken up for various destinations. Fare between Boston and Sandwich was $1.50. There were at first no Sunday trains.

The Sandwich Terminal

Although the Sandwich terminal depot was not removed until 1878, no photograph of it has yet been found, whereas the engine roundhouse appears in many views. The station probably had four or five spur tracks, as both passenger and freight trains incoming would need a second track for the engine and tender to pass out and be reversed. There was a "Piazza" from the passenger side where people met the stages arriving from down Cape, with a separate stage line to Snake Pond, Mashpee, South Sandwich and Cotuit. At the Monument station stages left for Pocasset and Falmouth.

There was an abrupt change therefore for the former Fessenden Tavern (and for Swift's Tavern in West Sandwich) where the Plymouth stagecoaches had formerly come in and passengers gotten off to shift over to the next set. The railroad station was now the center of news and travel, where a livery stable was vital for horses and where a restaurant was vital for travelers. Roland Fish was the operator of the Saloon Restaurant in the Sandwich Railroad Depot. He issued a printed broadside on the excellence of his services, a copy of which has most fortunately been preserved at the Sandwich Historical Society. His notice reads:

> "Refreshments and fruits—for the accomodation of travellers, transient visitors and citizens of the town. The Subscriber would take this method to inform his friends and the public that he has taken this stand with the design to bestow unwearied pains in rendering a place worthy of liberal patronage. Passengers going to or from the Cape in the Cars will find this a very convenient place to regale themselves as the Coaches arrive in season to give them opportunity to breakfast before the start of the AM train and to dine before the start of the PM train. Also on return of the trains will find opportunity to get refreshments before taking the coaches for the Cape...The patronage of Gentlemen and Ladies is very respectfully solicited."

There is no reference to alcohol being served in this establishment. The stations on this line were, from Sandwich:

To Scusset (West Sandwich)	2½ miles
Herring River (North Sandwich)	1½ miles

Monument Village	2½ miles
Cohasset Narrows (freight only)	1½ miles
Agawam (corner to Onset)	3 miles
Wareham Center	2 miles

The line stimulated passenger travel by occasional bargain tours to Boston. On Saturday, August 16, 1851, a special train left at 7 AM to visit a show called "Brewer's Splendid Panorama of the Mammoth Cave of Kentucky, Niagara Falls and Western Prairies etc." This was a great bargain at ninety cents round trip, including admission to the show at Boyleston Hall. Many Sandwich people were early shareholders (par value $100), including the importer Benjamin Burgess at twenty shares and several at ten shares—Nathan B. Gibbs, Clark Hoxie, William Stutson, Samuel Fessenden, Henry Wing and Theodore Kern. However, neither Jarves nor the B&S were shareholders, as Jarves wished to keep fully independent of railroad decisions.

The Freight Contracts

Most people could not imagine what the train would do when service began. In 1845, the writer for *Hayward's Gazetteer* commented on the ancient idea of digging a Cape Cod Canal to move goods safely without going around the Cape. However, he noted that the extension of the railroad (then at Plymouth) down through Sandwich to Falmouth would supercede the necessity of the ship canal. All cargo between Boston and the southern ports would go by rail between Boston and Falmouth, and only thereafter by sea. Again, when the Scorton River bridge was proposed in 1847, one of the arguments used against it was that the railroad was then almost at Sandwich and would soon extend down the Cape, making the County Road down Cape unnecessary. Presumably everything and everybody would go by rail. People seeing the long straight rails waited for the first train to come through and said that one would have to look quick or one wouldn't see it all.

None of these vague ideas were of interest to Jarves. The cost and reliability of his critical freight movements were what the railroad was all about, and he wanted to keep his options open to use marine routes as he had in the past. In 1847 he and Clark Hoxie bought up Bourne's Neck (now Taylor's Point) adjacent to the railroad line at Cohasset Narrows so that the B&S could install a substantial wharf and railroad spur for freight both in and out. He had used this area at Cohasset Narrows for years before as an alternative point for bringing in bulk coal, and sand in barrels. This freight had then been brought up to the factory by heavy wagons. With the railroad he set up a clear contract:

Heavy freight Boston to Sandwich (sand)
$1.40 per ton

Lighter freight (glass, straw)

$1.75 per ton

Freight between Cohasset Narrows and the plant
0.50 per ton

Coal and iron by carload reckoned in long tons (2240 lbs.), while sand and packaged articles were reckoned in short tons (2000 lbs.).

All loading and unloading at Sandwich and Cohasset Narrows to be done on B&S premises by B&S labor, in carload lots.

Glass carried at owner's risk.

The B&S in 1850 engaged to run no packet from Sandwich north, and to give the CCBRR all their freight between Boston and Sandwich and between Cohasset Narrows and Sandwich, "provided that the Glass Co. reserves to itself the right to ship by transient vessels from Boston to Sandwich lime, lumber, sand and coal; and from Sandwich to Boston cargoes of glass destined for foreign countries or southern markets south of New York." There was a six-month cancellation clause.

Another Sandwich party deeply affected by the railroad was William E. Boyden, who had run the Plymouth/Sandwich stagecoach since 1822. He and one Witherell promptly formed the Cape Cod Express Company for handling, packing, picking up and delivering local freight, also for moving the mail between post offices and trains. There was a baggage and mail car on each passenger train, and in it Boyden and partner were allowed a "closet" of seventy cubic feet for express packages. Curiously they were not allowed to include boxes of sugar or metal more than 200 pounds each as express. For this Boyden paid $100.00 per month to the railroad. (This William Boyden was not related to the Jesse Boyden of this same period, map maker, surveyor and selectman, who we have mentioned before.)

The CCBRR had freight contracts with each of the manufacturers along the line, including Isaac Keith at West Sandwich, Manomet Iron Co. at North Sandwich, and Howard Perry & Co. at Monument, setting the rates for shipment of coal and iron. In 1852, as the plant expanded, Keith required town approval to put in a spur track, probably for moving gravel from the moraine down to the plant for fill.

Operations and income

The Act incorporating the CCBRR provided the following as Section 8:

> "The Legislature may, after the expiration of four years from the time when said railroad shall be opened for use, from time to time alter or reduce the rate of tolls or other profits upon said railroad, but the said tolls or profits shall not, without the consent of said company, be so reduced as to produce less than 10% per annum, upon the investment of said company."

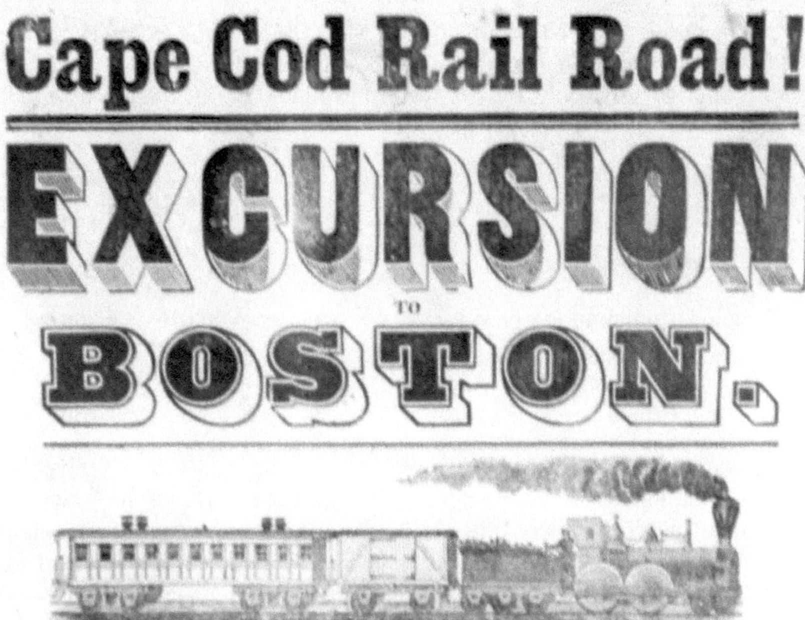

A splendid chance on

SATURDAY, AUGUST 16, 1851,

TO SEE

Brewer's Splendid Panorama!

OF THE

Mammoth Cave of Kentucky, Niagara Falls, and Western Prairies, &c. &c, now Exhibiting at

BOYLSTON HALL!

An extra Train will leave Sandwich at 7 A. M., stopping for Passengers at all the stations on the Cape Cod Road. Exhibition for the party as soon as they arrive in the City.

FARE to Boston and back, including admission to the Panorama, from each Station in Sandwich, 90 cents. From Agawam and all Stations above 80 cents.

RETURNING TRAIN LEAVES BOSTON AT 5 30 P. M.

Of the merits of the above Panorama it is not necessary to speak, suffice it to say that the Artists of Boston pronounce it the best ever exhibited in the city. No one should miss the present opportunity of going to Boston and seeing it.

Vocal and Instrumental Music at the exhibition.

S. BOURNE, Superintendent of Cape Cod Branch Rail Road.

"Times" Steam Cylinder Job Presses—J. H. & F. F. Farwell, Printers, Nos. 3 and 5 State Street, Boston.

A broadside for a bargain round trip to Boston on the Cape Cod Branch Railroad when Sandwich was the railhead. Courtesy of Sandwich Historical Society.

This provision would become effective in May 1852 for the CCBRR, and seems to be designed to ensure that the new railroad did not make excessive profits after the initial period. The only figures readily available are as quoted by Frederick Freeman:

	1849	*1854*
Receipts from passengers	$35,430	$89,130
Receipts from freight	14,970	21,970
Receipts from mail & other	880	4,800
Total	$51,280	$115,900
Running expenses	31,150	59,160
Available for interest, dividends, etc.	20,130	56,740

The cost of building and equipping the line was about $18,000 per mile, said to be less than the cost of any other railroad in the State, and less than half the average cost of all the railroads built there at that time. Hence, the CCBRR should have prospered, with passenger receipts alone covering more than all running expenses. Freight income was not high because of outgoing freight generated was not massive.

The Acorn Confrontation

Possibly the CCBRR directors wanted to improve income generated. Glass had to be their prime target as value of glass produced was now about $350,000 annually, while all other manufacturing in the county amounted to only $196,000 per year, scattered among all the towns, with much shipped off by water or consumed locally. Similarly, although the value of whaling was about $177,000 per year and fishing $400,000 per year in this county, these were diffuse and much was shipped off by sea. Hence, glass constituted a highly valuable and also concentrated source of freight income. This helps to explain one of the classic Sandwich scenes, not documented, but very probably correct in outline. The railroad increased the freight rate on glass, and Jarves in protest said that he would go back to all marine supply and would provide his own vessel for glass shipments. His opposite number, the railroad General Agent Sylvanus Bourne of Wareham, scoffed that the acorn was not yet planted from which would grow the timber for such a vessel. Jarves however was not bluffing and immediately ordered a combination steam and sail vessel which was delivered to Sandwich in 1853. He named it the *Acorn.* By coincidence, the acorn and oak leaf cluster was one of his favorite motifs for decoration.

CONGREGATIONAL CHURCH - An early view of the 1847 Calvinistic Congregational Church building designed by architect Isaac Melvin of Cambridge. This view would have been taken from a window in Town Hall. The stream under the low bridge led to an early herring ladder. There are temporary cables visible here supporting the spire which had been damaged in a gale. Courtesy of Sandwich Historical Society.

Doing economic battle with the railroad was an expensive process for Jarves and the B&S. The old harbor mouth of the Shawme Marsh (like that of the Scusset and Scorton systems) had gradually migrated eastwards and was possibly several hundred yards away from the junction of the main streams (Mill Creek, Dock Creek and Ford Creek). With town permission and enthusiastic cooperation, Jarves got work crews to block up the old mouth of the harbor with brush, stumps and earth, and dig out a new harbor mouth close to his dock. This was done with the aid of ample food and drink supplied by the company. Not only was a new harbor mouth required, but a new dock adjacent to the previous one on Dock Creek, facing onto deeper water. This was called the Acorn Dock. The greater volume of freight to be moved in and out of the plant also seems to have dictated a second track of the marsh railway as is indicated by timbers still visible at the stream crossings and in the bank at the Acorn Dock. Furthermore, and still more amazing, to get small vessels all the way in to the town wharf at the foot of Harbor Street, Jarves had a straight channel dredged along the line of his marsh railway, and the meandering lines of the old Dock Creek blocked up; then about half way out he had a tidal gate built of heavy timbers which could be closed at high tide to hold the waterfront full of water. Part of the reason for this may have been that the new harbor mouth rendered the former town landing at the old harbor mouth inoperative, so that now all vessels must use the outer or inner docks along Dock Creek. Lastly a boardwalk was laid over the marsh beyond the Acorn Dock, carried on a light timber trestle across Mill Creek and over to Town Beach. The remains of this boardwalk were discovered by Miss Carolyn Crowell in 1979. The railroad crossing over Mill Creek was low so that no more barge traffic up Mill Creek was possible.

This was an extraordinary series of construction activities undertaken by Jarves and the B&S. The work was completed about 1854 and enabled the *Acorn* and other vessels to bring all B&S freight in and out of Sandwich harbor. Part of the work may have been necessary, anyway, to improve marine facilities in Sandwich in order to handle the volume of products constantly brought in by sea, as we will show in the next chapter. However, the railroad freight scale came down and soon the *Acorn* remained little used at its dock, but was still a potent symbol.

CHAPTER 20

MARINE MATTERS

After the War of 1812 men in seaside towns returned swiftly to building new vessels or going off to sea. Samuel Eliot Morison reported that from 1815 to 1850, Barnstable County increased its registered tonnage of ships by six-fold. This county did not have water power of a magnitude to attract big industry, and without industries or deep harbors, was slow to attract the railroad or other outside investments. The glass factory, with its early steam power, must be viewed as a unique exception to the rule of this county. (Morison says of the glass factory that it capitalized on Cape sand, which was very careless of him.) The marine interests that sprang back to life along the New England coast included:

Deep Water — To Europe, the Pacific, and the Far East. When gold was discovered in California, this added another great market and encouraged the building of clippers.

Whaling — The search became worldwide and grew until kerosene became common after the Civil War.

Coastwise Freight — Even with the railways, the growth of the country was so rapid that a vast market existed to move lumber, coal, iron, food and textiles up and down the coast. This included sugar from the West Indies, coffee from South America and other long hauls.

Packets — Small fast sloops and schooners connected every seaport town with neighboring cities, and carried light freight and passengers. Service was fast and frequent.

Fishing — Innumerable small vessels from nearly every seaboard town did some fishing, but Provincetown, Boston, Gloucester, and certain ports had large fleets. There were major catches from Georges Bank; some vessels went on the Grand Banks, and others learned seining and trawling.

Vessels built on Cape Cod itself were inadequate to employ the numbers of men brought up to the sea in this county. Lacking shore side jobs, they took to the major ports and entered all the above categories of nautical work with great zeal and natural skill. Young men with a talent for command and some luck soon found themselves running vessels as masters, and could go on to larger vessels and invest their earnings in shares of vessels. These captains, if they survived, could retire in their forties or fifties to a handsome house and put capital into shore side business. Cape towns had an extraordinary number of such captains, either active or retired, creating a dignified part of town with their homes and their aura of travel. This became a main characteristic of the whole Cape Cod legend, to be repeated endlessly ever since. This chapter will highlight a few careers of Sandwich people on the sea in mid-century, and describe the town's role.

Deep Water Sailors

Professor Henry C. Kittredge, in his book, *Shipmasters of Cape Cod,* says "From Sandwich never so prolific of sailors as the rest of the Cape, came Ezra Nye one of the finest of them all...a great figure even among the lordly aristocrats of the transatlantic packet trade." Records for fast runs were what the competing captains coveted. Ezra Nye drove the small liner *Amethyst* from Liverpool to Boston in twenty days. He was given the larger ship *Independence* in 1836 and made the round trip from New York to Liverpool and back in thirty four days, a record unmatched in sail until the arrival of the extreme clippers. He came from Spring Hill, but built two houses in Sandwich village, the Federals at 149 and 152 Main Street. He removed to Newark, and was given a large new ship, the *Henry Clay.* Switching to steam, he was given a side-wheeler, the *Pacific,* and took her from New York to Liverpool in under ten days, the first time this was done by any ship. Distinguished passengers all wanted to sail with Ezra Nye. His finest hour was in 1852 when the *Pacific* came upon a sinking packet, the *Jesse Stephens,* in a gale in mid-Atlantic, and was able to take off all the passengers and crew safely. For this Queen Victoria gave him a medal and a gold chronometer. He retired in 1855 to administrative work in Newark, and turned the *Pacific* over to the celebrated Captain Asa Eldridge of Yarmouth. Alas, in January 1856, the *Pacific* went down somewhere in the North Atlantic.

One of the classics of the sea involves a Sandwich girl, Hannah Rebecca Crowell, who married a distant cousin, Capt. William Howes Burgess of Brewster. At twenty-two he was given command of a new clipper, the *Whirlwind,* and made some fast passages. Hannah accompanied him and kept a journal of great interest, learning incidentally how to calculate the ship's position. She records her husband's drive for speed, his fury at calms and at headwinds, and her inability to stop him from swearing. He was again given a new clipper, the *Challenger,* in 1855, and had the ship's portrait painted by a Chinese artist in Canton. After leaving the Chincha Isles he was taken ill with dysentery and was soon too sick to leave his berth. The nearest doctor was at Valparaiso, twenty-two days away, and with Hannah navigating, the mate sailed the ship. They arrived safely, but the Captain died before they reached port. Hannah made arrangements for his body to be shipped back to West Sandwich, and she took passage home. Burgess was only twenty-seven and she was only twenty-two at this time. A deeply religious person, she gave her favorite brass-clamp Bible to the steward David Graves, a mulatto who had helped her nurse the dying Captain. Graves was steward on the clipper *Ringleader* six years later when it was wrecked on Formosa. An American later found the Bible in the wreckage, and seeing the inscription, had it forwarded to New York whence it finally came back to Mrs. Burgess. She continued her journal and lived serenely for another sixty-one years in West Sandwich, surrounded by the many artifacts she had acquired in the ports of the world. She had the words "I will never marry again" inscribed inside her wedding band, and kept her word, although she is reported to have had fifty-seven proposals. Many of her curios, the Bible and the *Challenger* portrait went to the Sandwich Historical Society at her death in 1917, and are among the most interesting items on display at the Glass Museum.

Another extraordinary story involved Benjamin Franklin Bourne of North Sandwich. In 1850 he was mate on a chartered schooner taking twenty-five adventurers to California from New Bedford. He took a small boat ashore near the Straits of Magellan to obtain food from the native Patagonians, but was captured and barely escaped with his life, being held prisoner for eighty-three days. At length, he heard from them of an island inhabited by whites, whom the Indians wished to capture. They used Bourne as a lure and a white party came close to shore in a whaleboat to investigate. Bourne suddenly broke away and flung himself in the wintry surf and swam for his life, the Indians unable to follow. So he was saved, and finally taken aboard a whaler. He returned to Sandwich in 1852 just three years after leaving, and wrote a book about his adventures entitled *The Captive in Patagonia, or Life among the Giants.*

Whalers

The concentration of whaling in New Bedford and Nantucket is well known, and drew large numbers of Cape Cod men there as sailors and officers, or in work ashore. Jonathan Bourne of Monument became an early investor and shipbuilder in New Bedford, and at one point owned twenty-four whalers, more than any other person. He kept a strong interest in his native town and it is for him that the town of Bourne, created in 1884, was named. There were a few whalers who operated out of two Cape Cod ports, Woods Hole and Provincetown. One, of which we have record, the bark *Ocean,* was owned entirely in Sandwich but was fitted out in Provincetown. The master in 1851 was Capt. Zenas W. Wright of East Sandwich, and the crew of twenty-two officers and men were said to be from Sandwich on this voyage. A personal journal of John J. Harlow of Mashpee (the Wakeby portion that later became Sandwich) shows that he sailed in the *Ocean* in 1852, this time out of Woods Hole under Capt. Joshua Chadwick of Forestdale and an all-Sandwich crew. We have not traced this ship through the repositories of ship's logs and records, but find in a newspaper article of 1862 that she was then sailing out of New Bedford, still Sandwich owned, had completed two successful cruises and departed for a third under Capt. Peleg Cornell, with James M. Chadwick of Sandwich as second mate and eight seamen from Sandwich. Mr. Harlow's log is a fascinating record of whaling in the 1850s and 1860s. He sailed in the bark *Parker Cook* of Provincetown under Capt. John Cook in April 1850 with an all-Sandwich crew whom he named. While off the Azores they landed a whale which struck and upset the boat. The steerer, John Hoxie of Spring Hill, got some turns of rope around his leg and was dragged under. He calmly took out his knife and cut the rope, but the twist about his ankle had all but severed the foot. He was pulled aboard another boat and taken to the ship where the Captain and the cook finished amputating his foot. Then the Captain, who had been among those thrown in the water, went out to get the whale. It was large and fierce, and twice struck the ship violently with its head, but both times on the solid stem of the ship. If it had hit the side of the ship she might well (like the *Essex* of Nantucket) have been sunk. The captain hit the whale three times with an explosive bomb lance and then finally when it slowed, closed in and killed it. Such a whale might indeed have suggested "Moby Dick." After the whale was cut up, the ship bore off to port and landed Mr. Hoxie five days later, where his leg was amputated. He was returned to Cape Cod by the American Consul, and newspaper accounts said he was doing well.

HANNAH REBECCA BURGESS AT HOME - Hannah Rebecca Burgess sitting serenely among some of her collection from her travels around the world with Capt. William Howes Burgess. Some of these items came to the Sandwich Historical Society after her death in 1918. Her home still stands at 1001 Sandwich Road, Sagamore. Courtesy of Sandwich Historical Society.

Other whaling captains from Sandwich (or who at least retired here) of whom we have record include Robert Macy, Edward Nichols, Peleg Nye, David Pierce, Sylvanus Robinson, George W. Bauldry, Nathaniel Burgess, Cyrenus Eldridge, James T. Handy, Nathan Nye and Asaph S. Wicks. Sandwich's best-known whaling captain was Abraham Hoxie of South Sandwich, a whaling master at age twenty-four in 1832 out of New Bedford. He is said to have commanded twelve different vessels, the last of which seems to have been the Schooner *Amelia* of Sandwich. He retired in 1853 at age forty-five and built himself a large house on family property on Spectacle Pond. He probably found this too quiet because in 1857 he bought the ancient Smith family saltbox on the millpond from the estate of Bethia Smith. He lived here until his death in 1888, and the present restored "Hoxie House" at 18 Water Street has made his name a byword on Cape Cod and across the whole country.

The whaler *Abigail* under Capt. Ebenezer F. Nye of Pocasset, was one of six whalers seized by the Southern raider *Shenandoah* in the North Pacific and the Sea of Okhotsk in 1865. All the crews were put aboard one whaler, the *Milo,* to return to San Francisco; the other five whalers were burned. The *Shenandoah* left to cruise along Kamchatka to hunt down other whalers, but Capt. Nye took two open boats and eleven men from the *Milo* and rowed off into the Sea of Okhotsk to find and warn Yankee whalers. He did, in fact, effect the escape of several ships before the return of the raider, and lived to collect a reward from the underwriters of the saved vessels. He also submitted a claim for loss of the *Abigail* of which he was part owner under a war claims procedure. Captain Nye later returned to the Arctic whaling grounds on the *Mount Wollaston;* the vessel was never seen again.

Coasting Trade

The *Hayward Gazetteer* published in 1849 states "Sandwich has no good harbor within the Cape, but navigable accomodations in Buzzards Bay, at which are some shipbuilding, and a number of vessels owned and employed in fishing and coasting." Because the gazetteer books were the only convenient public source of much statistical information, inaccurate statements like this were picked up and repeated by writers and travelers, and became lodged in print permanently. The facts seem to be that more coastwise cargo was brought in to Sandwich than to any other town in the county, and that most of it came in on the Cape Cod Bay side. It wasn't *a good* harbor, but it was a massively used one until after the Civil War when the railway network displaced most coastal freight. The weekly "Marine Intelligence" columns of the *Sandwich Observer* and *Yarmouth Register,* for the period 1846/1849, reflect the arrivals and departures of the coasters:

Schooner *Annabella* - Capt. Gibbs, owned by B&S, 80 tons. Constantly employed moving coal from Philadelphia and sand from Morris River New Jersey, plus a few trips to Maine for lumber. (Some runs were to Cohasset Narrows). She occasionally took glass direct to New York.

Schooner *Samuel Davis* - Capt. J. W. Hoxie, coal from Philadelphia and Richmond, except in winter.

Sloop *Noddle* - Capt. Cummiskey, coal from Boston, except in winter.

Sloop *Susan* - Capt. Swift, coal from Boston and one lumber trip.

Casual vessels from Hallowell, Portland, Gardiner, Bangor and Augusta Maine, with lumber, barrel parts, straw, shingles, potatoes, lime and other cargo—at least weekly from May into December

Casual vessels from Richmond, Philadelphia, Boston, Baltimore and Norfolk to Sandwich (Cape side) with coal or sand, about six a month into November.

In addition there was freight coming regularly into the B&S Cohasset Narrows landing, but the newspaper coverage of the Buzzards Bay shipping was sporadic. However, at least one cargo per week arrived during fair weather. Further than this, outside the B&S operations, a number of vessels came to Pocasset engaged in Southern or local area freight movements, including New Bedford, Nantucket, Wareham, Rhode Island and New York. Our idea of these movements is unfortunately gained in part by reports of marine disasters, without which the voyages would be unknown. The list of Sandwich vessels and Sandwich masters in the various sources of records seems endless, but still, Sandwich was called the least maritime of the Cape Cod towns. A recent study of cargoes shipped out of the one port of Gardiner, Maine in the three and one half year period from 1831 to mid-1834 shows:

To Boston	345	departures
To Sandwich	165	"
To Salem	108	"
To New Bedford	89	"
To Dennis	83	"
To Falmouth	31	"
To 32 other ports	369	"
Total	1190	departures

In this particular period Sandwich received more shipments from Gardiner, Maine than did all other Cape Cod ports combined. The stories of the coasters and their masters and crews are fascinating. Capt. Ezra B. Freeman of East Sandwich had his ups and downs. He lost a vessel under his command; built a house on Ploughed Neck Road, which was struck by lightning in 1860 and destroyed. He escaped death when the chimney fell on the bed where he had been sleeping. He named his new schooner the *Abby Bradford* after his daughter. In 1861 the vessel was captured by the Rebel privateer *Sumter* and towed away. Later, the *Sumter* was captured by the U.S. Navy ship *Powhatan* and the *Abby Bradford* was recovered by a prize crew. Capt. Freeman at forty-seven died from falling into the hold of his ship. By contrast, Capt. Seth Burgess of Monument retired in 1873 at sixty-three having spent over fifty years at sea. He never lost a vessel or even had an accident. His employers in Baltimore were said to be so sure of his judgement that they sometimes did not insure the vessels or cargo entrusted to him. Deyo's *History of Barnstable County,* in its profiles of men of Bourne in 1890, includes the names of David H. Baker, George W. Bacon, Jesse

Barlow, Ellis Blackwell, Pelham Gibbs, Jesse Phinney and Elisha H. Tobey. These were all men who had been masters of coasters in their early years, and lived to come home and build a hotel or start an oyster business or open a store. Seth Burgess and his cousin Nathaniel, the whaler, were among those forming the new town of Bourne.

Packet Service

The Boston packet was not only fast, cheap transportation, it was a social process, an express service and a sporting event. Every town had one and the bigger towns with lots of Boston business like Sandwich had two, one owned by townsmen and one by the B&S. They took some freight but were mainly for passengers. Seating in the cabin was crowded, rather like the press in a stagecoach, and it was impossible to keep out of conversation; people of all social classes joined in democratically. Lots of news and gossip was exchanged. One feature of the trip was a hot dinner served en route, of so generous a size that one wondered how the caterer broke even at twenty-five cents apiece. The packet's time versus its local rival was a matter of wagers, and a losing packet was quickly sold off in favor of a faster sailer. They left on a local tide schedule, and knowing the weather, their return could be accurately predicted. With fair weather they could make three round trips a week. The crew usually protested on religious grounds if the Captain tried to make up time by sailing on Sunday. From 1825 the packets for the town included:

Sloop *Polly* - Roland Gibbs age 19 in 1825)

Sloop *Henry Clay* - George Atkins, sold 1842

Sloop *Sarah* - Calvin Fish

Schooner *Nancy Finlay* - Calvin Fish

Schooner *Cabinet* - Roland Gibbs

Sloop *Osceola 0* Barzillai Sears, sold 1847

Schooner *Wm. G. Eadie* - Stephen Sears

From 1825 the following packets were found for the B&S:

Sloop *Splendid*- Sewall Fessenden

Sloop *Charle* - Charles Nye, sold to Plymouth

Sloop *Sandwich* - Charles Nye

Schooner *Sandwich* - Roland Gibbs

Schooner *Sarah* - George Atkins then Pierce, sold 1849 to Chatham

Propeller *Acorn* - Roland Gibbs, served 1853/1857 then sold to Provincetown

Generally the packets declined after the arrival of the railroad with its better time and reliability. The famous *Acorn* served as the Provincetown/Boston packet for about four years, then was sold to parties in New York in 1862 and reportedly fitted out as a gunboat. After a trip to Havana it was sold again and was probably sunk during the Civil War.

Fishing Vessels

Sandwich apparently only had a few fishing vessels in the offshore cod fleet. The vessels, being small, did not rate an individual listing in Marine columns. The census records do not show where and how a man listed as fisherman was employed. For those that went offshore in small vessels, this was the most dangerous of all the maritime pursuits. Sudden northeast gales in October could catch and decimate the fleet at sea as happened in 1841, 1851, 1854 and 1857. Truro, Wellfleet and other lower Cape towns had a sad number of widows as a result.

Vessels Built in Sandwich

We have listed thirty-one vessels built in Sandwich up to 1864. The largest, the 400-ton *Lysander,* built in 1844 by Burgess & Ellis at Sagamore Hill. Details are available about these vessels for those who wish to study the subject.

Family Effects

As elsewhere on Cape Cod, there was scarcely a family in Sandwich that did not see at least one young man off to sea, and in many families the avocation was almost total. Such families inevitably saw many die in shipwrecks or founderings. Paul Crowell came to West Sandwich from Dennis in 1815 and had a family of eight sons and seven daughters. Of the sons, four went to sea and all were lost. As we have seen, Benjamin Percival lost two out of three sons who went to sea. Israel Tupper, a schoolteacher with five children, moved to Vermont in an attempt to deter his sons from maritime service.

In earlier chapters we have related the town's population to families of the various surnames, and have seen that many of the earliest families began to decline in numbers in the old town by 1820. However, a curious reversal of this trend occurred in Sandwich during the peak of the sailing days among the families most heavily affected by the sea, namely the surnames Gibbs, Ellis, Blackwell, Handy, Barlow, Perry, Phinney, Hoxie, Burgess and Swift. Here is the evidence:

Numbers of Sandwich Families

	Ten families most affected by the sea.	*Ten other old families.*	*Total town families.*
1700	24	38	100
1750	69	73	209
1790	83	11	323

		0	
1820	99	12 8	452
1850	151	91	830
1880	141	66	872

The strongly nautical families peaked in numbers in 1850 and showed only a slight decline in 1880, while some (as Burgess and Swift) even increased in 1880. By comparison, the other ten families, including some of the largest (Nye, Fish, Freeman, Bourne,) declined precipitously after 1820. The total town population of families showed a rapid influx of new families after 1790, rising to a flood after 1825 with the glass factory altering the town's composition radically. Our point here is that the marine interests provided an income which kept new families forming within the particular set of ten old Sandwich surnames listed above, nearly all of whom were in the Scusset / North Sandwich / Monument / Pocasset areas. Even those men engaged in offshore sailing out of Boston, New Bedford and New York could keep their homes and wives in Sandwich. Without the grievous mortality of sons and husbands due to the sea, this growth of local marine families would have been even higher. By comparison, families not so strongly oriented to the sea declined in numbers as sons made their homes elsewhere.

CHAPTER 21

THE 1850s PEAK

The population of Sandwich peaked in the 1850s. It rose from 4,181 persons in the 1850 census to 4,479 in 1860, as new persons came to work in the glass factories and as high levels of marine activity acted to delay the outward migration of many families. The Civil War, like the American Revolution, was a radical event that left the country quite different from what it was before, and Sandwich (with the whole Cape) began a decline in population after 1860 that was to persist for decades. It was down to 3,694 in 1870. So the 1850s have a particular significance for the town as the last of a period of heady growth and a time for enjoyment of what had been accomplished. It is a matter of great regret that our town newspaper of this period, the *Cape Cod Advocate and Nautical Intelligencer,* has survived in only a few scattered issues, and it remains a hope that an extended series of copies will yet be discovered in some attic or storehouse.

The Lure of California

The discovery of gold in California in 1849 was electrifying to the imaginations of all Easterners, but Cape Codders, with their marine connections, had the immediate means for departure at hand, and leave they did. The villages of Pocasset, Monument, and North and West Sandwich provided the greater numbers of those from Sandwich. An early group was called the "Sandwich and Cape Cod Mining & Trading Association", carefully organized as a company with equal contributions, and pledged to share all profits equally; the bylaws said no work would be done on Sundays. Twelve members of this group left New York in November 1849 on the S.S. *Ohio* for Panama. Many ultimately came back, but there is no record of how they fared. The ship *Orion* left Boston in November 1849 with twenty-nine men from Sandwich. Another company was formed which took passage on the *Eugene* with a load of lumber and bricks. Letters began to arrive back home and many were printed in the *Observer* with such news as:

"Gmbling and drinking on the ships and in California is an endless evil; many lose everything.

"Large ships at San Francisco cannot be sailed away for lack of crews and are worthless.

"Firewood is $40. per cord while it is free for the cutting only two miles away.

"Sickness, cost of provisions and poor organization at the camps strip most miners of any gold they find.

"Carpenters get $10 to $16 per day and many Cape Codders turn to this after a brief spell digging.

"Even day laborers and waiters are better off than miners.

"Advice to those at home—don't come.

"Good luck stories are common but always somewhere else."

Levi Nye, the son of the Methodist minister here, reported that he had built the first frame house in Sacramento. Edmund Fish worked at carpentering until his health gave out. He reached Sandwich by way of Panama but died here within a few days of his arrival. The most surprising departure for California was not one of the twenty-year olds but Clark Hoxie, the builder of the Cape Cod Branch Railroad in Sandwich and partner of Jarves in many projects. He became overextended and went into bankruptcy. He stayed in California for many years but returned to Sandwich and is buried in Bay View Cemetery.

Property Map of 1857

The H. F. Walling Company of Boston contacted the various towns in the county and secured approvals and advance payments enabling it to prepare a street map of each town with indications of buildings, and the owner of each. The map of Sandwich appeared in 1857 with information probably from 1856, as a single large sheet with a blowup sector of the crowded village area. This map is a mine of information and has remained of great value ever since. In its usual form it is glued to cloth backing and has colors to denote the 23 school districts. Many of these surviving maps have been varnished and are now darkened or cracked. The clearest example was one printed on heavy white paper without coloring and preserved in the 1876 Centennial Box. This was framed for display at Town Hall, but was apparently stolen as it disappeared soon after, leaving only the frame and glass. This map shows owners, not occupants, so there are many names of renters not given. The chief fault is the wrong location of Sagamore Hill, and distortions in the Scusset area. In addition to the town maps, the Walling firm produced a large map of Barnstable County in 1858, requiring reduction of the type to a very small size. This is of value as a separate map since the type for Sandwich owners is differently arranged from that of the 1857 map, and includes changes and a list of shops.

Town Reports

Having a newspaper press and job printer located on the ground floor of Town Hall was of benefit to history. Dr. Harper's annual report of the School Committee was printed in full in the *Observer,* and also in pamphlet form from 1866. The first reference to the town's financial report is in the town meeting of March 10, 1851 where the town requested that the expenses and income of the year 1850 should be printed up in time for the next meeting April 7, with 300 copies for distribution. The first booklet of town finances that has been located so far is that for the year 1857. The chief headings were State Tax $2,214, County Tax $1,230,Schools $4,000, Poor $1,500, Highways & Bridges $2,500, Emergency Snow Bills $2,471, Salaries & Expenses $2,057. In addition, the town meeting warrants were also printed, and a few broadsides have survived showing programs for musical shows, school programs and other events.

School Districts

As we have mentioned before, the District system in effect through 1862 left much to be desired. Decisions on building maintenance, new construction and controls were in the hands of twenty-three District Committees, and varied widely. Dr. John Harper was a most conscientious School Committee chairman, who visited each school room in the town pointing out the good and bad features of each in his annual reports; however, he had no administrative authority. His Committee sat periodically to examine new candidates for teaching positions but decisions were made by the Districts. The School Committee recommended a list of books for booksellers to stock and parents to buy, but this was all voluntary. A notice by the School Committee in 1855 cites an Act of the State Legislature reading "The School Committee of the several towns and cities shall not allow any child to be admitted to or connected with the Public Schools who has not been duly vaccinated."

The town's most crowded school was #5 in the East Village, with 192 pupils in two rooms, but much absenteeism. We believe the original school was on Main St. at the corner of Liberty St. The parents finally voted to build a new two-story, six-room building in 1849 on what was then renamed School Street. The old schoolhouse and lot were sold.

The Sandwich Academy seems to have been utilized only by teachers on a private basis. The town was well aware that high school level education should be made available, but was uncertain what to do about it. In 1855 it was voted to provide high school teaching in each area every five years. Without later references, we cannot tell how this was to be done, possibly a year in each of the five major sectors in turn.

Town Hall Area

It was voted in 1854 to provide a fireproof room for town papers. This, if built, did not long survive, as the town then voted in 1861 to buy a fireproof safe. When this safe was later sold to the town of Mashpee it was described as weighing 3600 lbs. This must have been on the ground floor, together with the printing plant, Loring's store and a sash window and blind business. In 1860 the town voted to take out the stepped floor and lay a new flat yellow pine floor, with the speaker's table at the south or opposite end. They also voted for new movable seats so that the Hall could be used for other purposes such as dinners and dances. About 1856 a wholly new mill building was built east of the old grist mill, on the site of the former fulling mill. This new mill drew its power from a modern steel turbine wheel installed in 1855 which was both smaller and more powerful than the old wooden mill wheel. Downstairs large blocks of marble were sawn into shapes, which were worked into gravestones, countertops and lamp bases upstairs. The grist mill continued in operation, and near it the shoemaker's shop of Cornelius Eldred.

Street System

For the past sixty years the streets had been maintained by highway agents elected annually from each of twenty-one districts; each was responsible for collecting labor or cash from property owners in his district for road maintenance. With the rise of population and travel, particularly the stagecoaches coming in to the Sandwich railhead, a better system was needed, allowing systematic upgrading of long sections of the main roads. The town report of 1852 describes for the first time the town's highway network and reduced the number of districts from twenty-one to seven.

These were Pocasset 13 miles, Monument 13 miles, Scusset 11, West Village 14, East Village 14, East Sandwich 17, South Sandwich and Scorton 30, total 112 miles. A new Board of Surveyors was established, with authority to allocate the total road budget toward major projects, rather than simply filling potholes and clearing drainage ditches. The practice of planning new roads, laying them out systematically and accepting them as town roads was initiated.

A State Law was adopted permitting sidewalk strips to be taken along designated streets, and laid out, with costs of betterment charged to abutters. In 1860, Jarves Street between Main Street and the railroad tracks, was the first street to be dealt with.

The Railroad Extension

From the beginning of service to Sandwich in 1848, plans were being considered to extend the rail line to Hyannis. Among the prime movers were Nantucket businessmen who wanted fast ferry/train service to the Island. The first route applied for was to West Barnstable, thence diagonally over to West Hyannis and to Lewis Bay. This aroused protests and the route finally approved by the State Commission was the present line through Barnstable Village and Yarmouthport, then sharply southwest along Willow Street and down to the wharf. The name of the former Cape Cod Branch Railroad was changed to Cape Cod Railroad Co. The new company built the extension of 18 miles, the cost of which, again for a fairly level route, was only $18,000 per mile. The construction office at the Sandwich end was a building which is still standing at 163 Route 6A, up on the bank well off the road. This is a 2½ story building (now a residence) of extremely heavy construction to allow for storage of building materials inside. The grounds connect directly to the rails where there was a loading platform at car height.

Several of the contracts for this construction are still preserved in the book of freight contracts mentioned earlier. The iron "chairs" for the rails, the spikes, the masonry work at the street and cattle underpasses, and the rails themselves, 1700 tons, are all described. The line passed close beside the old terminal depot at Sandwich, which remained as a passenger and freight station. The first service to Hyannis on the new line was six years almost to the day from the time service began at Sandwich, May 24, 1854 and connected to the ferry wharf in June 1854. Stagecoaches still met the trains in Sandwich for Forestdale, Mashpee and Waquoit. A new connector line was built from Tremont station in Wareham over to Fairhaven opposite New Bedford so that Cape traffic to and from New Bedford could pass more directly than by the old route from Middleboro down the Fall River Line to Myrick's Junction and then by a third train down to New Bedford.

It was still necessary for passengers for Pocasset, Falmouth, Woods Hole and Martha's Vineyard to take the stagecoach at Monument Station. In retrospect, it seems hard to explain why businessmen in these active towns did not press more vigorously for rail service, having fully as much to gain as did the Nantucket and Hyannis interests. A steam ferry from Woods Hole to Martha's Vineyard was in operation from 1852.

Fire Department

The glass factory had a hand pumping unit for fires and a large central cistern to draw on, but did not allow its unit to leave the factory premises. It was proposed in town meeting in 1845 to purchase a fire engine, but the decision was postponed. In 1849 a private subscription was raised to buy a piece of fire apparatus. For the 1859 parade on the Fourth of July, Engine Company No. 2, marched under Capt. Otis Freeman. At the close of the dinner at the Central House, "The Engine Company was escorted by the Band to the Mill Pond where the engine played for some time." Both Niagara Engine Co. No. 1 under Freeman, and Sandwich Engine Co. No. 2 under Capt. John Hobson, marched in the larger 1860 parade. The organization of these early units was clearly private. It was not until 1869 that a formal town Fire Dept. was approved, and in context it was directed first toward forest fires for which massive response had to be organized quickly.

Town Division 1860

A petition for division of the town appeared in 1860 and surprisingly, this was received amicably and a committee appointed to bring in bounds. These were from a point between North Sandwich and North Scusset, straight south through Succonnesset Pond to the Falmouth line. All of Scusset village was therefore to be in Sandwich. About 30% of the Town's value was in the areas to be set off. Although this proposal had been sent to the Legislature for enactment, 1861 brought hints of national trouble and the project was reconsidered and dropped.

Moving Houses to the Village

New shops opened in Sandwich village and services proliferated. The

Census of 1850 and 1860 show boarders or renters in many houses when all spare rooms were turned to a profit. With houses in the rural areas less used, it was natural that the thrifty owners should move them into the village rather than let them sit empty. There are a number of examples:

The late Lila Peters reported that her grandfather, the carpenter and house mover Gustavus Howland, moved three houses here from Nantucket, including her own half Cape at 199 Main St. and the larger house at 5 Water St.

The Tobey family from north of Peters Pond moved two houses into Sandwich, the Capes at 5 School St. and at 25 Water St. The half-house, formerly on Tupper Road at Route 6A (torn down when the new Cooperative Bank was built), was removed there from the old Dillingham Road "lots" area. The local historian George Burbank claimed that this ancient settlement road (between the Dillingham House on Main St. and Town Neck Road) once had 13 houses on it, but none remained by 1857.

The half-house formerly on Tupper Road at Route 6A (torn down when the new Cooperative Bank was built) was removed there from the old Leveridge Lane “lots” area.

The Capes at 207 Old Main St., 8 Water St. and 22 Grove St. are all on new foundations with evidence of removal here to tiny lots from other original sites. (New foundations were brick or strip granite)

The most remarkable house removal is told in detail in the *Advocate* for May 5, 1860. It concerns the new house built in Gothic Revival style by Capt. Abraham Hoxie on the shore of Spectacle Pond, as described in Chapter 20. Capt. Hoxie sold this house to William Swift, Jr. of Scusset. The house was two stories high with a foundation 27 x 36 feet and could not be knocked apart for moving as were the old post-and-beam Capes. The mover, Gus Howland, assembled 30 yoke of oxen and put this large house on a set of wheels, beginning the torturous task of moving this train (about 300 feet long) down narrow twisting streets with large trees on both sides from South Sandwich down into the village. It took three long days of noise and re-rigging and adjustments, but the house came intact to its final location at 4 Cross St. where it may be seen today.

New Stores and Halls

The Boyden Block was placed on Main Street between the Unitarian Church and the Central House, a long building of several shops and a large meeting hall upstairs. This was built in 1857 by Express Agent William E. Boyden, replacing smaller buildings. It also had a large adjoining livery stable where Boyden kept his old Plymouth stagecoaches. A grand ball was held to celebrate this opening, and the premises were lit by the new gas light. The B&S had installed a gas plant to produce coke and had spare illuminating gas to sell to private customers on certain streets where pipes were laid. This gas supply and its use indoors and out was a source of pride and satisfaction in many shops and homes.

A new Masonic Lodge was formed in Sandwich in 1855 and used the hall at Boyden's for its meetings until Boyden's was destroyed by fire in 1913. This was and remains today the De Witt Clinton Lodge AF&AM. This lodge was later held at the former Methodist Church.

An enterprising young meat dealer, Noble Parker Swift, (brother of William Jr. above) erected a major building in the solid row of shops along Jarves Street in 1859. This building measured 32 feet wide by 40 feet deep with two shops, and had a hall overhead. It was located about where Route 6A now runs. Between fires, rebuilding and changes of ownership the pattern of shops along Jarves St. and along Main Street from Jarves to the Town Hall area was in constant renewal.

Old Town Burying Ground

One of Sandwich's familiar features that appeared at this time was the carefully fitted curved wall in front of the Old Town Burying Ground. This work was done in 1850 by David C. Percival, a civil engineer who built and lived in the house at 6 Water Street. This Percival (a nephew of Benjamin Percival of South Sandwich) was also a skilled mathematician, a craftsman who built violins and cellos, and served the town as Town Clerk and Treasurer. There is no record of town expenditure for this masonry work so it must have been done by subscription. The stone is local glacial mix (rather than the uniform quarry blocks that appeared at this time in foundations of houses in many parts of town) but they were dressed to fit very accurately. Other unusual features of this project are the square end posts of the wall with their big capstones that appear to be made of stucco. These are in fact solid granite, dressed to shape, a fine piece of masonry work. The craftsman was Ebenezer Chamberlain, a mason at the B&S who had embarrassed his family by stealing $400 from a store and spent two years in prison.

John William Jarves (1835-1863)

Of the four sons of Deming Jarves, James J. the eldest lived in Hawaii then Italy; the second son George D. operated a small glass factory in South Boston but died of tuberculosis at age twenty-five; the fourth, Deming Jr. fought in the Civil War and went into other business. Only the third son John W. showed promise as a glass-making successor to his father. At age twenty he married in Sandwich Mary Thayer Waterman, daughter of C.C.P. Waterman of the B&S. The young couple lived in a beautiful new house built for them at 3 Jarves Street designed in Italian Villa style. He worked in the laboratory at the B&S and then from 1859 at the new glass works built in his honor, John W. Jarves and Co. Alas, tuberculosis was no respecter of hopes or famous names. John died in 1863 at twenty-eight, and his and Mary's two children also died soon, surely one of the more poignant episodes in Sandwich history.

PAUL WING SCHOOLS - The upper view shows the large building of the Spring Hill Academy owned and operated by Paul Wing. This building was built in 1851 following the destruction of the previous building. In turn the new building was destroyed by fire in 1862 The lower view shows the later school building with vegetable garden. This building still survives as the residence at 83 Spring Hill Road. Both views courtesy of Virginia Wing Blake

We suggest that it was in honor of this John W. Jarves that Dock Lane was renamed Jarves Street, although the town meeting records do not refer to the change. The first appearance of the name Jarves Street for the portion from Main Street to the railroad tracks appears on the 1857 Wallings property map. Deming Jarves after 1825 only visited Sandwich occasionally on business, whereas John W. Jarves marrying a resident girl in 1855 and making a home here constituted a highly visible and popular representative of the name. Certain shops, however, continued to use the old name Dock Street or Lane for years.

The Episcopal Church

The records of the present St. John's Church state that in 1854 Justice of the Peace Charles Bascom Hall called a meeting in Sandwich to form a new religious society. Among the nine founders was John W. Jarves. An article dated 1900 about his widow says of Jarves "He was a prime mover in the organization of the first Episcopal Society of this place and in the building of the church on Jarves Street, where for several years services were regularly held." Jarves was clerk, treasurer and warden of the new church. The map of 1857 shows the Episcopal Chapel to have been the same as the earlier Puritan Church which disbanded about this time. The formation of this new Episcopal Society seems to have been a painful irritant to Rev. Frederick Freeman, himself an Episcopal minister who since 1844 had conducted Episcopal services in his own chapel on Main St. in the present Windswept area. Freeman said in his History "An unadvised attempt was made this year (1854) by a young clergyman from abroad in transient and hasty visits, to organize a society for the purpose of sustaining the services of the Protestant Episcopal Church; but such as might naturally from their position have been supposed the strongest friends of Episcopacy were neither advising nor consulted in regard to the movement. It soon fell through, as from the manner of its inception was foreseen." The Episcopal group was small, and we must wonder indeed why Rev. Freeman, already here, was so pointedly left out of its fellowship.

New Saint Peter's Church

The Catholics of Sandwich, although numerous, were long restricted to their small chapel beside the railroad, and only enjoyed occasional visits of priests. In 1850 their first resident priest was assigned here, Reverend William Moran, although his area of responsibility extended from Middleboro to Provincetown, plus the Islands. There was a sense of excitement and growth everywhere, and plans were made for a large new church. This was completed in 1854, located at the corner of Willow Street and what was then called James Street. It was a large brick building with beautiful fittings and windows and included a high spire with a bell and clock, surmounted by a ruby glass ball. Since the spire was very high (160 feet) the glass ball could be seen reflecting the light from far at sea and it instantly became a landmark. This church cost $25,000, an extraordinary sum compared to that of the wooden churches of the period. Most unfortunately, the tall spire was vulnerable to the harsh northeast gales that visited this coast, possibly lacking the flexibility of the spires on wooden churches. A storm in January 1857 sent the spire crashing down and damaged the roof. The congregation had to worship in the basement until repairs could be completed. In place of the spire only a square wooden tower was re-erected. The ruby ball idea however was very popular and Burbank reports that these glass balls, blown at the factory, were mounted on flagpoles at various places in the town, the tallest at the corner of Tupper and Main Street where the Nye Family boulder now stands. So far no photograph has been found that shows such a flagpole.

A Picnic for the Bell

The cost of the roof repairs and mortgage on the Catholic Church were a heavy burden, but the congregation was determined to have a new bell for the tower. In August, 1859 the *Cape Cod Advocate* records an event to raise funds for the new bell, toward which $500 had already been subscribed. A picnic was held on a Saturday in a grove on the property of David Foster in Spring Hill. (Foster had come here from Maine in 1832 and married Lydia Gifford; he was very probably a descendant of the early Foster family in Sandwich.) Foster lived at what is now called the Skiff House, and here a procession of some 300 people marched from Jarvesville led by the Sandwich Cornet Band. There were swings in the grove, outdoor games, and a new popular dance called the Copenhagen. The *Advocate* reported "This was but the first attempt of the kind which had been carried into effect by the Catholics of Sandwich." Think, it had been 34 years since the settlement at Jarvesville had begun, and this was the first such event to be held outside the factory village, not the happiest commentary on the American melting pot process. For many at that picnic it may have been their first visit to a beautiful spot only two miles from home. They were not imprisoned in their village; it was just that no one had imagined that such a picnic was possible.

The End of the Chapel

After 1854 the old chapel of 1830, being unused, suffered broken windows, and became an embarrassment to the community. The problem in selling it for removal was in its title. Bishop Fenwick of Boston had bought the land personally from Melatiah Tobey (for $125) and in his will in 1846 had devised the land and chapel to the Catholic Community in Sandwich. This title was excellent for continued occupancy but not for outright sale. Finally Bishop Fenwick's successor Bishop Fitzpatrick in 1855 had to petition the Supreme Judicial Court in Boston for permission to sell the land and building and to reinvest the proceeds in the new Church. This petition was approved so that the sale could be completed. The *Yarmouth Register* reported later that the edifice had been removed to Jarves Street and was being converted into a grocery store by Messrs. Nichols and Sherman. Parts of this store are now incorporated into MacDonald's Sandwich Hardware, and a plaque on the building notes its unique history.

ST. PETER'S ROMAN CATHOLIC CHURCH-This church was completed in 1854 at Willow and Church Streets in the Jarvesville sector. A tall spire was destroyed in 1857 and not replaced. The building walls were damaged in 1898 and the church was torn down in 1900, much of it being re-used in the new Corpus Christi Church on Jarves Street. Courtesy of Sandwich Historical Society.

The Boston and Sandwich Glass Co.

Expansion in this decade (beside the great works in the harbor outlined in Chapter 19) included illuminating gas; a new enlarged brick pothouse near the waterfront and installation of a second furnace at the lower glass house, bringing the number of furnaces to four. In 1850 the company made an immense pressed glass bowl for presentation to Daniel Webster. Of this bowl Jarves wrote "It claims the merit of being much the largest piece of flint glass made by machinery in any part of the world. Two machinists were employed six months in forming the mold. This bowl is the first made in it, and it is called 'the Union Bowl.' The name will not render it less valuable." Webster was always extremely popular in Sandwich and in Mashpee where he came fishing, although less frequently in his later years. He died in Marshfield in 1852. Only one other bowl was ever pressed from this famous mold, and neither seems to have survived.

In January 1859 a steam boiler burst in the power plant killing a worker. With typical speed, the B&S ordered a new unit from the maker in Boston, Harrison Loring, and enlarged the boiler room. A new ninety foot stack, the tallest in the plant, was built partly enclosed in the exterior wall of the building. The boiler provided steam for heating and pumps plus the operation of an engine for rotary power for mechanical work and compressed air.

The public school for this district had stood in the park in front of the upper glass house. In 1851 a new larger two-room schoolhouse was built near Georges Rock Road, allowing the park to be cleared. In 1852 the park was surrounded by a handsome wrought iron fence, with landscaped gardens and a splashing fountain inside.

The Cape Cod Glass Factory

There has been some confusion over the fact that Jarves' new glass factory in Sandwich did business as John W. Jarves & Company until John's death in 1863, but was known from the beginning as the Cape Cod Glass Works. The Sandwich Tax Assessors records throw some light on this, that Deming Jarves owned the factory and land, while John Jarves Co. owned only the machinery and materials. In 1864 Jarves joined his son-in-law H. Frederick Higginson (surviving partner of John W. Jarves & Co.) in deeding the glass factory and its machinery plus certain other assets in North Sandwich and Spring Hill to the Cape Cod Glass Company, to be owned by Jarves and other shareholders.

This new plant was much smaller than the B&S, having only one furnace, but was extremely efficient in layout, had modern facilities for ventilation and safety, and in particular had a new system for preheating coal before adding it to a central location in the furnace, so that combustion was greatly improved and black smoke nearly eliminated. A number of B&S men came to the new plant including Rev. Joseph Marsh and C.C.P. Waterman. About 100 men worked in the new plant. In 1859 a separate building was added for office, shops, power plant, and cutting room, and another smaller building for making clay pots. This new company did not reduce the market or operations of the B&S, so it represented new growth for the town.

We mentioned as part of the harbor work done by the B&S in anticipation of the *Acorn* coming into service that a boardwalk was built from the *Acorn* dock across the marsh and over Mill Creek to the Town Beach. This gave the public access to the beach by way of the marsh railway both for pleasure and for possible rescue work. Later a Lifesaving Service shack was placed here on Town Beach. There is little direct reference to this early boardwalk, but the stumps remain in the creek bed. One William Denson drowned in 1862, and was said by Burbank to have fallen through a hole in the boardwalk. The Sandwich Historical Society has a letter from the B&S to Jarves in 1858 giving him permission to remove planks from the boardwalk for passage of vessels bringing supplies up Mill Creek for construction of the Cape Cod Works. The letter however asked that he replace them for the convenience of the people of Sandwich.

As a further note on harbor changes (as stated in Chapter 19), there was a narrow but solid bridge running from Jarvesville near State Street across the marsh to Town Neck. This bridge was especially for use of a narrow one-horse wagon which brought bricks from the kiln over to Jarvesville. (The location of the bridge for brick carriers was found by Miss Carolyn Crowell through locating the stumps of pilings at low tide.) There was much new brick construction at both glass plants in this period. This bridge is not mentioned in town meeting records. That the public was accustomed to have a bridge short-cut to Town Neck is suggested in a petition to the town in 1883 to have a road built across the marsh at this point. This did not pass.

Money and Taxpayers

A tabulation of town statistics for Barnstable County in 1850 shows that in taxable real estate value Sandwich was second only to Barnstable in the County. The tax rate in 1855 was $2.44 per thousand, down from $3.22 in 1850 due to rapid increases in personal and real estate valuations without equivalent increases in costs of town services. This followed a trend common to the Cape as a whole. The town's biggest taxpayers in 1855 were as follows:

Name	*Property*	*Tax*
Boston & Sandwich Glass Co.	Factory, tenements, vessels, etc.	$611.20
Samuel Fessenden Estate	Funds left in trust	425.28
Manomet Iron Co.	Factory North Sandwich	272.00
Deming Jarves, Boston	Tenements, millrights, stores	221.12
Benjamin Burgess, Boston	Vessels, land, buildings	176.54
Seth F. Nye	Lands, income from practice	146.78
Thomas A. Tobey	Real estate & personal	141.34
Melatiah Bourne	" " "	107.42

The town's tax assessments for real estate and personal property from 1790 through 1860 survive almost completely intact and are housed at the Archives Center as a valuable resource for detailed study of the formation and distribution of wealth throughout the community. Only two of the above eight taxpayers were located principally in the area that became Bourne. In the 1850 listing of towns in this County mentioned above, Sandwich had the second highest total in the category of cash at interest. This note of solvency may have been behind the formation of the Sandwich Savings Bank in 1856. The founders included Deming and John Jarves, two Fessendens and the town's leading merchants and landowners. William Boyden was elected President.

The Isaac Keith Company

Among the town's wealthier citizens in 1855 the name of Isaac Keith did not yet appear, and his flourishing foundry and machine shop at the millpond on Scusset River was called only a shop. However, it was a rapidly growing business of much importance to the town. He continued to use water power from the old Swift's grist mill to run his trip hammers that made such a din in the area pounding iron to make axles, crowbars, steel tools and metal frames for railroad cars. There is good reason to believe he made the cars for the B&S marsh railroad, and dumpcars for the Cape Cod Branch Railroad in 1847 and 1848. He was allowed by the town to build a railroad spur in 1852, and this we suggest was not merely a siding in his plant but a mile or so long track up into the future Canal valley to bring down fill on dump cars to enlarge his plant. He was squeezed between the rail line and the millpond, and could only expand along the track and outwards into the marsh. Soon he acquired a steam engine for mechanical power and the firm grew rapidly during the Civil War.

Seth Freeman Nye (1791-1856)

Blessed with a rugged constitution, retentive memory and administrative ability, Seth Nye began his law and business career in 1815. He became a leading figure in the town, notably as Trial Justice and Justice of the Peace over the eventful period of the expansion of the population due to the glass factory. Three of his account books for court practice, local hearings and business affairs were presented to the Sandwich Historical Society and constitute a remarkable reflection of the times. In his business life he collected debts for out-of-town colleagues; acted as executor for persons dying intestate; cleared up estates and took inventories; acted as administrator of farms or income properties left to widows or minors; wrote letters, wills and deeds; ran a large farming and wood-cutting business for himself, clients and relatives. He had access to vast acreage of woodlots and employed a number of workmen year-round to cut, haul and deliver wood, also hay, stones, manure, and produce, and do farm and maintenance work. He arranged housing for these employees. He took farm produce or goods in exchange for his services and was able to sell anything from coffins to gooseberry bushes. He became one of the richest men in Sandwich. His house, built in 1828, is still a showplace, the beautiful Federal at the corner of Main and Grove Streets. The little flat building down on Grove Street was his law office. Finding that he had three unmarried sisters, he built an addition to his office where they opened a millinery shop. Not many of these early 19th century law-offices survive in New England and Seth Nye's is a treasure.

Seth Nye's Cases

The account book of the civil suits in which Nye took part as a lawyer covers the whole period of his career, 1815-1856. However, the entries only list the parties, date and fees, not the subject of the action and how it was decided. For these we should have to analyze Court records in Barnstable. His cases total 800 in the forty year period, representing a great many trips to Barnstable. The subjects of the suits that he did mention were recovery of debt, property claims, libel and a few divorces.

As a local Trial Justice, Seth Nye held Court in his office whenever cases were brought by the Constable, averaging once a week. The record book that survives covers the period 1850-1856 and lists 225 cases brought before him.

Only rarely did the defendant have an attorney, even when the case was serious. The subject of the action is stated, together with costs and fines, so this makes a full record. The causes included assault and battery 91, violation of liquor laws 28, disturbing the peace 20, larceny 18, pleas to obtain search warrants 13, drunkenness 8, and others including perjury, bastardy, evil disposal, forgery, malicious mischief and injury. The serious cases (perjury, malicious injury, larceny over $100, forgery) resulted in the suspect being bound over to Barnstable Court, pending which he was held in the local lockup if he could not find a bondsman. The cases within Nye's authority were handled speedily. For the guilty there was a fine for the Commonwealth, the amounts of which he held in an escrow account and paid to the County Treasurer quarterly. There were set costs for witnesses and documents plus a charge for his own time which usually ranged from five to eight dollars. In aggravated cases such as attack on a Constable the defendant had to find surety of the peace for six months which meant posting a bond of $100 to $500. The usual assault and battery fine was one dollar—and sometimes only a quarter; these cases involved women both as plaintiffs and defendants. The liquor violations mostly were brought against Michael Scott of the Central House (the only licensee in the village) by ministers, by Stutson or by Joseph Marsh, for such offenses as sales in bulk, to minors, after hours or to known alcoholics. Fines were stiff and Nye could even impose jail terms, but the offenses went on.

SETH FREEMAN NYE'S LAW OFFICE - His office and local court were in the rooms on the right. At left was a millinery shop operated by Seth's sisters, of whom the last (Sabra Nye, 1801-1888) is shown here entering the shop, her bicycle at right. This building became the first Public Library location. Courtesy of Sandwich Historical Society.

Seth Nye once made Robert L. Ripley's "Believe-it-or-not" cartoon for stating that no lawyer could justify a fee of ten dollars. What this probably refers to is his own cost as a Trial Justice in these local cases, and here his record book tends to bear him out. However, where he himself represented a client or an estate he was bound by no such limit.

The Sandwich lockup was a small two-room building on River Street near the millstream. With shingled sides it looked like a shed but the walls were made of solid square beams spiked together so that it was a little fortress for overnight detention.

With his profound knowledge of local families and people, Nye was in a position to help those in difficulties. His will showed that he was owed thousands. An ancient veteran of the Revolutionary War, Joshua Arey, lived up on the moraine in what is now part of Otis Air Base, and Nye's records show that he received Arey's semi-annual pension check of $48 which he cashed for Arey. Nye and his cousin Watson Freeman of Boston, who came to Sandwich regularly, knew those of their relations who were infirm and took steps to protect them. A well-known example was the eccentric who inscribed the boulders up in the Otis target range with the figures called the SAL-N-PRY carvings, not far from Arey's farm; he is said to have been a Nye or a Freeman, but his privacy was preserved by these charitable men.

Town Parades

There was a financial panic in 1857 which slowed the glass factory and indeed induced a wave of cuts in executive salaries in the organization. Shipping and trade began to return in 1858, and the construction of the Cape Cod Glass Works was an optimistic note in the village. In 1859 the town decided to celebrate the Fourth of July noisily, the first such civic celebration on record; before this there had only been school or church picnics with speeches. The program began at dawn with ringing of bells and firing of cannon. At 8 A.M. a parade formed at the Central House—mounted troop, militia troop, Cornet Band, Fire Engine and a youth band of fife and drums. Then there were elaborate floats of trades in action—both glass companies had a furnace smoking, a small pot of glass, and passed out little blown and pressed pieces. A shoemaker was at work, a cooper making barrels and a baker passed out free rolls. The parade returned to the Central House where the Declaration of Independence was read, an oration by Attorney Whittemore given and a dinner served to a select number in the dining room. In the evening the Band played near the Academy and fireworks were shot off from "Fort Hoxie, " the newly occupied home of Capt. Abraham Hoxie who had a saluting cannon on his grounds.

THE SANDWICH LOCKUP-This little two-room building was located at 8 River Street and had thick solid walls for overnight detention of prisoners. Beyond it at the left is the farm on Brady's Island. At right a barn or shop is being moved onto new foundations. The lockup was removed in 1908. Courtesy of Eleanor Spurr.

In 1860 this event was further enlarged, with decorated houses and banners across the main streets while many held open house. The parade was led by a Chief of Police (not mentioned as a town official in the town report) with the Chief Marshal and included three bands, the Sandwich Guards under Captain Chipman, a train of carriages with guests and officials, fire engines and floats of farmers, glass workers, tack makers, coopers, printers, smiths, milliners, boot makers, grocers, stores, cabinet makers and others. After a speech at the Central House the parade broke up but a large number of guests and ticket holders went on to the Town Hall where the first banquet ever held here was served. The carpenters must have worked rapidly to lay the new flat floor approved only in April. The caterer was Mr. Barker the new owner of the Central House, replacing Michael Scott. Frederick Freeman was President-of-the-day and Judge Whittemore toastmaster. No less than thirteen patriotic subjects were proposed and then appropriate responses made by one of those present: to Washington, the Army and Navy, the President, the Ballot Box, the Governor, Cape Cod, the Year 1637 and ending with The Ladies of America. In the evening were not only fireworks but a grand military ball at the Town Hall, again a first for the town. Military excitement was in the air in 1860. The Sandwich Wide-Awakes were demonstrating for Lincoln.

The *Cape Cod Advocate* reported the death in 1860 of Phebe Fuller of Sagamore, aged about 100, widow of a Revolutionary War veteran. With her passing there was only one more pensioner left in Sandwich, and curiously this was another Phebe Fuller.

Temperance Movement

One of the characteristics of this 1850s decade is the determined effort of town leaders, supported by State and local government acts, to control the liquor trade and to reduce intemperance. Town meetings had approved the resolution of the Temperance Society in 1848, approved a by-law controlling sale of intoxicants in 1849 and accepted a committee report on intoxicants in 1850. This established a town liquor agency under strict controls, and forbade private sales by the drink or in bulk except for the bar at the Central House.

In 1852 a State Law, Chapter 322, permitted search and seizure of intoxicants for resale on private premises. This was utilized by the Sandwich Constable repeatedly as seen in the cases brought before Judge Nye. One Theodore Fisher of Sandwich, having been raided and a quantity of liquor removed by the Constable, entered a petition to the Mass. Supreme Judicial Court challenging the constitutionality of the seizure clause of the law on the basis it violated private rights. Chief Justice Lemuel Shaw found the 1852 law in this respect "repugnant to the provisions of the Bill of Rights and the Constitution of the Commonwealth... and must therefore be held unconstitutional and void." This happened in March 1854 and newspapers made much of it.

We are uncertain of the subsequent legislation of seizure, but many persons were certainly arrested on charges of illegal sales here throughout the decade. In 1855 there was a rash of arson, house robberies and threatening letters sent to the selectmen and to leaders in the temperance movement. The town report for 1857 shows how the town liquor agency worked. Jonathan Chipman was town agent and kept careful records. He bought about $550 worth of bottled goods, and sold it for enough to cover his allowance of $120 per year, so the town broke even. He was not allowed to sell to lawbreakers or alcoholics. However supplies could be brought in from towns that were not dry. A shooting death on Christmas 1857 shocked the town, and liquor was clearly a factor. A group on State Street were drinking and playing cards, and threw out a young man who tried to join them. He gathered some friends, who were also inflamed, and they attacked the house with rocks and sticks. A shotgun was fired from the house to warn them off, which unfortunately killed an innocent bystander. The accused was found not guilty.

This disrespect for the law was found in another ugly development of the 1850s. It was a virulent hate campaign against the new waves of immigrants, especially the Irish, as taking jobs of "native" Americans. It produced a political action called the Know-Nothing Party but much of its energies went into hooligan attacks on individuals. In Sandwich Reverend William Moran, a popular priest and fearless leader, was target of at least two attacks on his regular trips between his parishes in Wareham and Sandwich.

Frederick Freeman (1799-1883)

Mr. Freeman received a liberal education and after teaching classes at Newbern Abbey in North Carolina was made principal of the school in 1821. He was licensed to preach in 1823 and from 1824 to 1833 was the minister of the orthodox "Church of the Pilgrimage" in Plymouth, Mass. He then took orders in the Episcopal Church and served a further ten years in Philadelphia and in Maine. It was then reported of him that he became physically disabled for the pulpit, and returning to Sandwich (where his father had left property to him) he opened the Sandwich Collegiate Institute in 1845. This he closed in 1849 and devoted himself to study of the Cape Cod towns and families. He married three times and had 12 children, the last three born in Sandwich in 1845, 1850 and 1856. The first volume of his *History of Cape Cod* appeared in 1858, covering the founding of the area and its history as a whole, plus a detailed chapter on the Reservation of Mashpee. This work was printed for the author on receipt of subscriptions, and the later printings include notes written as late as 1860. Volume II *The Annals of the Thirteen Towns* contains detailed records of the towns and genealogy of certain families. This came out in 1862 and contains names of subscribers to the set. Freeman says in his preface that from about 1812 on his text was brief and confined to a few occurrences of general interest. Charles F. Swift in Deyo's History said in 1890 that Freeman's book "to all time must be the foundation upon which other works of the kind will be based. The difficulties in Mr. Freeman's way were numerous; he had to begin without any considerable previous aid...some of the important epochs were not written up with the fullness and elaboration of the others. But despite these drawbacks, Mr. Freeman's book will always be quoted as the first filial attempt of any Cape Cod man to do appropriate honor to the memory of the pioneers and their successors..." We would agree with this appraisal and recognize the enormous effort required to read the original handwritten town records and vital statistics of all the towns as he did.

The New England Historic Genealogical Society was founded in 1845 as an outgrowth of the Massachusetts Historical Society, especially to recognize and publish genealogical studies and to encourage higher scholastic and procedural standards in presenting genealogical material. Frederick Freeman was a friend and correspondent of the first secretary of this Society, J. Wingate Thornton, and provided materials on Thornton's Cape ancestors, also dedicating the Annals of Yarmouth to him. Thornton in turn, provided flattering notices of the *History of Cape Cod* in the Society's quarterly *Register.* Freeman encouraged other friends to embark on genealogical studies, notably Rev. Dr. Ebenezer Burgess who produced *Descendants of Thomas and Dorothy Burgess of Sandwich* in 1865, and C.C.P. Waterman of Sandwich who assembled much family data for later publication by others.

Freeman's later years in Sandwich were not tranquil. He was sued by a bank in 1866 for a debt of $1, 000 arising from a loan of $650 in 1859, possibly to finance the History. Possibly in reaction, he sued the town of Sandwich in 1866 for $10, 000 arising out of an injury he suffered in an accident on the road between Sandwich and West Sandwich, which was out of repair. He suffered "great bodily pain and distress unfitting him for his business and occupation." This case was finally settled for only $200. Possibly the accident is recalled by Burbank in his reference to Rev. Freeman furiously pursuing a daughter who was eloping in a sleigh, and being forced to stop. In his autobiographical notice in the Freeman Genealogy of 1875, Freeman penned the hope that he might be buried near the Saddle and Pillion with the family ancestor, but this fell on deaf ears and he was buried near his father in Old Town Burying Ground. He was cared for by his wife and daughter in his last years of infirmity, and his passing in 1883 was not specially noted in the town report, while lesser mortals rated a page of respects.

Other Local Writing

Philip Robinson became a Deacon of the West Parish Church Barnstable. As a young man living on Scorton Neck, Robinson wrote a diary for 1851 reminiscent of the Percival Diary in its details of daily life and affectionate recall of people and events.

Reverend Benjamin Haines the Methodist and glass-worker has been mentioned before. A number of his letters and autobiographical notes have been preserved in the family of his brother Edward Haines of Spring Hill, also a glass-worker. Haines describes the immediacy of his religious sense in his day-to-day life, such as the conflict between his love for deer-hunting and his certainty that the Lord did not approve his killing deer. He gave up the sport. Again coming home to State Street late at night from a religious meeting in Spring Hill he was crossing the plank bridge over Ford Creek (present Dewey Avenue) and reflecting on his need to marry again when he got a very clear message from a definite point in the sky that he should marry Sylvinia Bodfish. He immediately proposed and the marriage was a happy one. He was an artist and calligrapher so that his letters and even his records of church services in Forestdale include scroll work, religious symbols, and little rebus pictures.

Lively young people in the Cedarville area of East Sandwich formed a literary group in the late 1840s, and periodically assembled their original writings into a bundle of pages with a printed cover secured by a ribbon. This unique production was called the *Cedarville Gem,* and some twelve Gems have survived, full of arch humor and youthful philosophy, with many poems and essays completely charming.

Thoreau's Visits to Sandwich

Thoreau came twice to Cape Cod with his friend Ellery Channing, in October 1849 and in July 1855, and made two more trips alone in June 1850 and June 1857. His notes on the first three visits were combined and composed as his book *Cape Cod,* published in 1864. His notes on the 1857 visit were printed as an appendix in a 1951 copy of *Cape Cod* edited by Dudley C. Lunt (Bramhall House, N.Y.). The Sandwich portion of *Cape Cod* is from the 1849 and 1850 trips when Sandwich was the railhead. He had with him the Massachusetts

Historical Society *Collections* of 1802 with the articles on the Cape villages by Wendell Davis of Sandwich, and quotes the passages "The inhabitants in general are substantial livers" and that they "manifest a fond and steady adherence to the manners, employments and modes of living which characterized their fathers." After being jammed into the coach and missing lunch he said of the town "Ours was but half a Sandwich at most and that must have fallen on the buttered side some time. I only saw that it was a closely built town for a small one, with glass-works to improve its sand and narrow streets in which we turned round and round till we could not tell which way we were going and the rain came in first on this side and then on that, and I saw that they in the houses were more comfortable than we in the coach." Thoreau's coach would have tried to cross Ford Swamp on present Route 6A, but had to reverse at deepwater and turn back to School Street and out Water Street to the so-called Upper Road that went through Crow Farm to rejoin the present Route 6A. Many writers had called Cape Cod the right arm of Massachusetts, but Thoreau's "bare and bended arm" shows why he was different.

For the 1855 visit he would have gone through by rail to Yarmouth before taking the coach down to Eastham where the beach walk always began. The 1857 excursion was entirely different in that he started walking from Manomet Point in Plymouth south along the beach, then inland at Ellisville where he stayed at Samuel Ellis's house. He talked to an Indian of Herring Pond Plantation, then returned to the strand, and walked to about Sagamore Beach area where he came inland along the road to West Sandwich railroad station, then took the train through to Yarmouthport.

Thoreau has become such a classic in recent years that it is a surprise to see the hostile reaction in the *Yarmouth Register* for Aug. 3, 1855, when an early set of articles about the Cape by Thoreau had appeared in *Putnam*'s *Magazine.* The *Register* said he had no regard for truth and that his portraits of people were caricatures. In fact, these *Putnam's* articles did cut out historical portions of Thoreau's writing, and he cancelled the rest of the publication in *Putnam's.* The book *Cape Cod* did not appear until after his death, and even then the *Register* editor in March 1865, recalling the *Putnam's* articles, abused the book roundly as "the merest of balderdash, " "a great deal in it that isn't true" and "the greater part...isn't worth putting into a book"; "this author discovered a new and curious tribe of aborigines called Cape Codmen, inhabiting the wilds of the County." The following month this editor consented reluctantly to allow a Cambridge book review of *Cape Cod* to be reprinted here; it emphasized his complete originality, his love of nature, and his indifference to towns, to architecture and to much of conventional history. The wonderful words "A man may stand there and put all America behind him" at last reached the newspapers of Cape Cod.

Reporting on Cape Cod

The instinctive reaction against Thoreau's unconventional approach showed that in fact a favored view had emerged of the Cape by this time with such sources and elements as these:

The 1850. *Gazetteer* praises the absence of poverty and social ills; the Cape was an outpost of old purity and manners.

The new Cape Cod Associations of Boston (1851) and of New York (1856) show our deep attachment to home and our eventual return in spite of success elsewhere.

Freeman praised our inns for comfort, recreation and health, not for the mere ostentation and promiscuous crowd at the modern watering places of Nahant or Newport.

The Central House, Sandwich, advertised its unmatched hunting and fishing for sportsmen.

The facts did not always bear out these comfortable pictures, which were based on earlier simpler and idealized times. The Cape was already being exploited and damaged by the recent excesses of population and opportunities for quick profits. Sandwich tried repeatedly to stop illegal and destructive harvesting of oysters. Wildfowl, turtles, lobsters, and deer were gathered in destructive quantities for the city markets. Noting the decline of song birds and wildlife, Freeman has to admit of Sandwich in 1858 "The town once proverbial for its rural pleasantries has been measurably shorn of many of its earlier charms." The worst was in the woodlands—not seen by reporters. Decades of exporting firewood had destroyed all the original open forest, and only certain woodlots were permitted to acquire second and third growth. Meanwhile the open land went to bushes, briars and vines that were swept by uncontrollable fires, and the once beautiful forest had become "a rude and tasteless wilderness." As to the towns and rural villages, there may not have been slums or visible poverty, but neither did the happy reports say anything about the heavy town expenses on the poor and on the almshouse or asylums, or on the way families silently took care of their less fortunate. Farms had been abandoned when the soil gave out without proper replenishment. An omniscient observer would have had much more to say than Thoreau.

CHAPTER 22

THE CIVIL WAR

U.S. Navy Captain John Pope of Sandwich was in command of the Navy Yard at Portsmouth, N.H., in February 1861, when he was ordered to the Mediterranean to take command of the *U.S.S. Richmond,* relieving Captain Duncan H. Ingraham. This was two months before the attack on Fort Sumter in Charleston, but already the division of the U.S. Army and Navy was beginning to take place. Captain Ingraham, a South Carolinian, was returning to the United States to resign his commission. So the long and bloody conflict began.

The First Volunteers

As soon as the news of Fort Sumter arrived, a gathering of citizens in Sandwich took place at Town Hall on Saturday April 20. Theodore Kern, Dr. Leonard and Judge Whittemore led the meeting and a number spoke on patriotic themes. It was agreed that a town meeting should be called "to supply the necessaries of life to the families of those who volunteer." A committee was chosen to confer with the governor on uniforms, and others were appointed to solicit subscriptions for a bounty fund. Captain Charles Chipman of the Sandwich Guards obtained the signatures of fifty volunteers. Four young men of Monument joined a company in formation in Wareham, and one from Sandwich joined a New Bedford unit.

A neighborhood meeting was held at North Sandwich with speeches, illumination, cannons and the Cornet Band. An association called "Soldiers' Volunteer Aid Society" was set up to prepare clothing for the volunteers and to aid their families. Deming Jarves announced that the families of volunteers who lived in any of his tenements or houses should have the premises rent-free during the period of the war. The volunteers legally formed on Monday, May 6, as Company D, Third Regiment of Infantry, Massachusetts Volunteer Militia. A bounty of $20.00 was paid to each, a banner was presented by Major Phinney of Barnstable, and Captain Chipman was given a sword by William Boyden. They left for Boston on May 8, now 76 strong on a three-year enlistment.

That same evening they boarded the steamer *Cambridge* for Fort Monroe, Virginia where they were formally mustered. The *Cambridge* returned to Boston on May 27, bringing back 14 soldiers unable to perform active duties due to physical disabilities, including three from the Sandwich company.

On May 11 a town meeting voted to borrow up to $4,000 to pay benefits to families of volunteers at rates of $2.00 per week for wives, $1.00 for first child and $.50 for each additional child. Volunteers in the Sandwich Company from other towns were included if the other towns did not make such appropriation. The state government then passed regulations about reimbursements to towns for aid to families, with a somewhat lower scale of payments, but the town voted to pay later volunteers at the same scale as the first volunteers, picking up the difference over the state scale.

Northerners in The South

Jefferson Davis issued a proclamation allowing privately owned northern vessels 30 days to depart from southern ports. There was a great deal of trade back and forth to the south in Yankee vessels, Cape Codders being commonly found. Many northerners worked in the south routinely as craftsmen, or teachers. An example is found in an article in the *Yarmouth Register* for June 7, 1861:

> "Arrival from Georgia—The schooner *Hume* of Sandwich, Mass., Capt Thomas G. Nye, arrived here 2d inst., from Satilla River, Georgia, where she was seized on the 25th of April and has since been detained. The *Hume* has been engaged the past winter in carrying rice from the Satilla River to Charleston, S.C. On the 25th of April she was seized by the citizens of Jeffersonton, Camden County, Georgia without pretending any authority for the outrage. Capt Nye was cooly told that he would be permitted to take his departure, but the vessel would be held and appropriated to their own purposes. Capt Nye however, was not disposed thus to relinquish his vessel and persisted in her relinquishment to him, which was finally reluctantly complied with. Finding that they could no longer detain the vessel, she was given up and Capt. Nye sailed thence on the 25th ult. She brings three passengers, Messrs. L. A. Luther and George W. Crandall, carpenters of New London, Conn., who have resided in Georgia, and Miss Frost of East Monmouth, Maine, a teacher who had resided in the South during the last two years.
>
> Capt. Nye represents that the town of Jeffersonton is a small village, comprising a few shanties occupied by a whisky drinking set of bandits!
>
> On Monday and Tuesday last week the *Hume* passed four large steamers heading South, the first two in the direction of Charleston, probably a part of the blockading squadron."

Town Meeting Actions

Calls for more troops came, and a second all-volunteer company departed in August 1862. It was decided to meet a call for nine-months men by draft, and a committee of five recruits were approved by the town to aid the selectmen in carrying out this draft. These men received time and expense money from the town for helping in the onerous work of drafting men for the first time.

The five were Samuel Chipman, George L. Haines, Henry F. Benson, Stillman Wright and Nathaniel C. Hoxie. A total of 74 men were raised in this draft, and they departed. Further enlistments for three years, or the duration, were then encouraged by a bounty of $200 per man. The town voted in April 1863 to pay families of the deceased in accordance with a state schedule. All quotas for war service were met by the town. A list was commenced in June 1863 in the town's Military Book of those "enrolled as a part of the Militia of the Commonwealth." This listcontains 386 names of those then still eligible for service (ages 18-45), some of whom were at sea on whalers or packets, or retired from earlier duty. Further call-ups came in October 1863 and February 1864. At this time re-enlistment efforts began in the field to continue the services of the first waves of three-year men from 1861.

George L. Haines' Letters

George was the son of glassmaker Edward Haines, and worked in the counting room at the B&S. He wrote often of Sandwich news to his older sister, Mary Carr of Buffalo. He was 19 years old in November 1861 when the series starts. His younger brother, J. G. Birney Haines, who went off exulting among the volunteers of May 1861 was at home for a few days. Birney came home again with typhoid fever in June 1862 and died in July at age 18. Edward Haines begged George, now his only son, not to enlist, and George describes his feelings as he sees his best friends go off in the second volunteer group in August 1862. He joined four other Sandwich boys in going around the town to meetings to raise the 74 men needed for the next draft. He did join this time in the nine-months group and wrote from the receiving camp at Readville, Massachusetts in October 1862. He loved camp life, had very good health, liked the officers and expected to be shipped to New Orleans. He was in the Forty-Fifth Regiment, Company D, which bore the Regiment Colors at parades. He loved to hunt, was a good shot, and couldn't wait to get into battle. The Forty-Fifth was sent to duty in Newbern, North Carolina, and in December its first battle was a major one at Kinston with many casualties. He was next to Henry Benson (one of his recruiting team) when Benson was hit through the spine, which later caused his death. He himself had bullets through his metal dipper and his canteen, but escaped without a scratch. Samuel Nye and Frederick Lovell of Sandwich were wounded in this battle. He describes Christmas dinner at camp back in Newbern, chicken stew, boiled sweet potatoes and plum pudding. In January 1863 he was deeply proud to be made Color Corporal of the Regiment, which freed him from daily guard duty but gave him the worst exposure in action. He wrote "Don't worry yourself about me, I shall not be killed." The Colors were rotated to another Company before the next battle. Their camp had small tents and he wrote "I shall be able to live in our pigeon box when I get home." The Regiment remained healthy, there was a river near by for bathing and there were plenty of supplies and drinking water. They came home and were mustered out in July 1863, one of the more fortunate regiments of the war. Back in Sandwich he was struck by the number of marriages going on and expects that he too must "marry somebody the Lord knows who." This George Haines had inherited his uncle

Benjamin's fine penmanship, his skill at sketches and his love of hunting, but not his ardent Methodism. He did in fact marry Sarah Marston whose father and brother worked with him at the B&S.

The Twenty-Ninth Regiment

The largest number of Sandwich troops, as many as 86, were in the Twenty-Ninth Massachusetts Volunteer Infantry, formed in December 1861, including the "Minute Men" volunteers of May 1861. They spent the winter of 1861/2 in Newport News, Virginia, where they were able to witness the battle of the *Monitor* and the *Merrimac.* They saw actions in Virginia and Maryland in 1862 and suffered many casualties at Antietam. In 1863 they were transferred to the western front and fought at Vicksburg, at Jackson, Mississippi, and at Knoxville. In the spring of 1864 those not re-enlisting were transferred to the Thirty-Sixth which returned to Massachusetts and was disbanded. The group of Sandwich men from the Thirty-Sixth returned home on Friday May 27, 1864 and were treated to a royal welcome. All factories, stores, shops, and schools closed so that there was a great crowd at the station and along the parade route to Post Office Square (Jarves and Main Streets) where there was a stand for musicians and speakers. Dr. Leonard was President-of-the Day. His speech was followed by no less than seven other speeches, given by Frederick Freeman, by ministers, lawyers, and county officials. There was a dress parade of the returning men and other veterans present, then a walk to Town Hall where a collation was spread. The hall was decorated with flags and "evergreen mottoes," words made of cedar sprays sewn to long white cloths hung overhead. In the evening the ladies of the town presented a Grand Ball. All this was in honor of the 18 men who returned from the Twenty-Ninth, plus those at home on leave or mustered out who had not been given earlier recognition. We hope that the speeches included the names of those who had re-enlisted (Major Charles Chipman, Lieutenant James Atherton, Sergeant Joseph Madigan, Privates James Ball, Perez Eldridge, David Hoxie, Frederick Lovell) and of the dead (Charles Jones killed in an accident, and Birney Haines, James Heald, Patrick Long, William Woods, all of disease). Of the remaining men from Sandwich who served in the Twenty-Ninth Regiment, six deserted, mostly in Kentucky, four were in hospitals in 1864 and 46 had been transferred to other regiments or discharged for disabilities.

Other Veterans

The Fortieth Regiment of Massachusetts Volunteer Infantry had the second highest number of Sandwich men (51) after the Twenty-Ninth. It served from August 1862 to June 1865 and saw heavy fighting in 1864 at Cold Harbor, Virginia. Three Sandwich men from this regiment were killed and five died of disease. Another regiment with high Sandwich casualties was the Twentieth Regiment, with four killed in battle and one who died of disease. There were Sandwich men in a variety of units; S. Howard Allyne, son of Samuel Allyne of Sandwich was in the west and joined the First California Cavalry. He was killed on patrol duty in Texas. Both James Atherton and Joseph Madigan of Sandwich enlisted in the Twenty-Ninth and were promoted to First Lieutenants through gallantry and competence. Charles I. Gibbs enlisted in the Navy in August 1861 and was warmly welcomed by Captain Pope who said he wished he had a whole scow-load of Cape Codders. Gibbs rose to First Mate of the *U.S.S. Richmond* and was Acting Master when the vessel attacked Vicksburg. He wrote home of two men near him being killed, one of whom was Thomas Flaherty of the B&S. He closed his letter in haste "I am safe and ready for another fight." There were also Sandwich men in the Regular Army and in the Hospital Units.

Major Charles Chipman

This leader of the Sandwich Guards was made the captain of Company D of the Twenty-Ninth when it was organized in late 1861, then promoted to Major, turning over the company to Captain Charles Brady. He was among the many wounded at Antietam and re-enlisted in late 1863 for the duration. He was marked for promotion and was in temporary command of the Fourteenth New York Heavy Artillery at Petersburg, Virginia on August 8, 1864 when a shell exploded nearby, he was killed instantly by shrapnel.

His body was returned to Sandwich for a funeral service at the Unitarian Church where more than 1,000 persons passed by his coffin in respect. He was interred at Freeman Cemetery. The Sandwich Post 132 of the Grand Army of the Republic (GAR) was later named in his honor as the senior officer in the town to die in action.

Lieutenant Ephraim B. Nye

A native of Cataumet, Nye was working in New Bedford when the war started and he joined the Fifth Massachusetts Battery as a private. Within a year he had been promoted to Second Lieutenant and after reenlistment was assigned to the Fourteenth Massachusetts Battery. On March 25, 1865 his unit was in an isolated position in front of Petersburg. Rebels quietly killed the pickets, and it came to hand-to-hand fighting in the battery area. Nye was surrounded and heavily injured in the right leg but when called on to surrender he replied "I never surrender." A rebel then shot him at close range through the heart, and when the battery was retaken he was found stripped of sword, watch, money and all articles. His body was taken to New Bedford for a civic funeral, following which an honor guard brought his casket to Bay View Cemetery, Cataumet. A handsome memorial was later erected, repeating his last words "I never surrender." His name was taken by the Bourne Chapter of the GAR. A Commander of this Chapter, John J. Ryder, later wrote an account *Reminiscences of Three Years Service in the Civil War.* Ryder had trouble being accepted as a volunteer because at 6'2" he weighed only 120 pounds and was thought too weak for service. However, he said he presented too small a target to hit, and outlived most of his comrades.

MAJOR CHARLES CHIPMAN (1830-1864)-Killed at Petersburg, Virginia by shrapnel, Chipman was the senior officer from Sandwich to die in the Civil War. This oil painting was commissioned by the family and now hangs in the Glass Museum Courtesy of Sandwich Historical Society.

The Casualties and Survivors

The names of 40 Sandwich men who died in the war years appear in published regimental records and the *Yarmouth Register.* This is on the order of one in six of those who saw active service. This number must be considered a minimum due to incomplete reports. However, even 40 deaths constitutes a greater total than those from Sandwich known to have been killed in all other wars put together from King Philip's War to the present. This national carnage in the Civil War led to the creation of Memorial Day for honoring the dead of all wars. Most veterans buried here and honored every May 30 died after their active service, and many were from other towns.

The Civil War veterans were numerous and their service records are not always easy to reconstruct. For example, of those who went away May 8, 1861 under Captain Chipman with such high hopes and their $20 bounty, there are six whose records have not been found, but who probably served somewhere. The greatest uncertainty lies in the records of men like Ephraim Nye or Howard Allyne who, although born in Sandwich and intending to return, nevertheless enlisted elsewhere. If they did not write home or if their families here did not make their service known, there is no ready way to trace them.

A remarkable story is told of Stillman Ellis of Sagamore, a sailor who was not a veteran. In April 1865, his ship under Captain Russell Gibbs of Sandwich, was at Washington, DC. unloading marble. When ready to depart, some troops suddenly came aboard looking for John Wilkes Booth who had shot Lincoln. Stillman Ellis bore a strong likeness to Booth, and both he and the captain were roughly seized and were about to be taken away. However, the captain thinking quickly said "Show them your hands, Stillman." The rough hands of a seaman were not those of an actor, and the men were released.

Patrick McGirr had been a constable in Sandwich and we have mentioned his bringing the accused for trial before Judge Seth F. Nye. While in the Ninth Regiment he was run over by a supply wagon and discharged for disability. Unable to return to duty and horrified by the endless number of wounded and sick, many dying for lack of care, he became a hospital nurse.

Judge Whittemore in 1864

The last Melatiah Bourne died in 1862, ending the Bourne presence in the saltbox on Main Street. It was purchased by Lawyer Ebenezer Stowell Whittemore who quickly became a central figure in town as speaker, lawyer, Trial Justice, politician and founder of the Board of Health. Several of his annual diaries have been preserved, the first covering 1864. He was involved in veteran's affairs, in State aid, securing pensions, reenlistments, funerals, and receptions. Deming Jarves at this time (after the death of his son John in 1863) was winding up some of his investments in Sandwich. One of Whittemore's less pleasant legal duties was the eviction of families from some of Jarves' tenements prior to sale. Other local cases he mentions recall the Seth F. Nye records:

"Sent Freeman G. Swift to jail for 2 months"

"Sent Ann Rielly to Lancaster for vagrant life"
"Jailed John F. Donnelly for assaulting Susan Landers"
"Liquor sellers of Sandwich taken to Barnstable for trial"

The death of Benjamin Burgess of Sagamore and Boston occurred this year. He owned many vessels and imported sugar from Cuba. Whittemore got the task of preparing the inventory of his Sandwich estate, and recorded with deep satisfaction that it came to $117,322.03. He spoke at the Catholic picnic at Deacon Faunce's Grove (Uplands) and reported without explanation "whenever I lose my temper with anybody or about anything I almost always afterwards have occasion to regret it." After a discussion with Reverend Chamberlain he wrote "When in an argument, close the mouth and breathe through the nose."

Other Town Events

In 1866 it was proposed to erect a central monument to Major Chipman and other deceased Civil War soldiers. A committee was appointed which delayed making its report until 1876. There must have been resistance to the design or location, as it was voted to postpone action for one year, and the monument project was not again raised.

In 1864 the town voted to establish a sinking fund of 1 mil per dollar of all expenditures, to apply against accumulated Civil War costs over what was reimbursed by the state. This soon covered the outstanding costs not previously budgeted.

In 1862 the state passed legislation regarding central town financing and control of the public school system. Sandwich accepted this in 1863 and steps were taken to rationalize the sprawling district school system that had evolved over the previous 70 years, with 23 locally operated districts and no high school. All hiring and new construction was now centralized in a Town School Board, so that districts could be combined, better buildings built and old buildings sold. Transport was allowed to a central high school at the Academy.

The number of new arrivals in Sandwich over the previous decades brought the realization that the existing neighborhood cemeteries were inadequate, especially the ancient Old Town Burying Ground that was nearly full and the B&S cemetery at Sand Hill, now Mount Hope. Two new cemeteries were opened:

Bay View on Main Street opposite Pine Street, six acres in size, was opened in 1867 and lots were taken by many leading families. There were even a few re-interrals here from Old Town Burying Ground to concentrate the family lots (Leonard, Eaton, Heald).

St. Peter's at the junction of Grove and Pine Streets was opened in 1865 as the first Catholic cemetery on Cape Cod. Dedication took place on the same day as the dedication of St. Peter's Church in Jarvesville, probably indicating that this expensive church was now completely paid off.

Another important event of this decade was a major fire in March 1869 among the crowded shops along the west side of Jarves Street. It started reportedly from an overheated stove in a barbershop in the area of the present Route 6A. It spread in both directions and consumed 13 businesses between the old section of the MacDonald's store and Willow Street. The firemen were hampered by lack of hose and distance from the Mill Creek. One businessman, John Q. Miller, promptly bought the unused Universalist Church at Main and Summer St. and moved it down to the destroyed area. Other reconstruction took place so that the area was quickly refilled.

CHAPTER 23

THE END OF THE RESERVATIONS

As most Americans began to enjoy their independence after the depression of the 1780s, the Mashpees were plunged back into the highly repressive control of guardians and overseers. In this chapter we will list the dramatic steps by which the reservation regained its district status and finally became a town, with its residents at last becoming American citizens. In the process, the present borders of Mashpee with Sandwich, Falmouth and Barnstable were finally established, a subject not before clarified to our knowledge. We will also describe the history and the end of Herring Pond Reservation.

Reverend Gideon Hawley (1726-1807)

Hawley was the Congregational minister at Mashpee from 1758. He had become deeply disturbed at the arrival and intermarriage of blacks in Mashpee after 1763. He finally pressed for the legislation of 1788 returning Mashpee to the control of white overseers, of which he was one. Many unmarried or undesired non-Indians were removed and the total population fell. Children of those in debt were bound out to service. Hawley's period, incidentally, marks the end of much Indian culture, including their own use of the Indian language, matched by the death of the last whites to use the language, Rev. Elisha Tupper in 1787, the last Mayhew minister in 1806 and Hawley's own death in 1807.

Lands Set Off to Whites

During the generous days of the Mashpee District (1763-1788), three important grants of Mashpee land were made to whites. These were:

Ten acres to Lemuel Howland in the gore in the northeast corner on Cotuit Road, in 1771. He was said to be "very helpful" to the tribe.

A large block in the northwest corner, said to be stony and poor, was sold for cash to Simeon and Nathaniel Fish, Jr. in 1777.

A grant of 200 acres to Hawley himself for his subsistence in the Revolution after English funds were cut off.

Each of these grants was properly made according to the charter of the Reservation, that is, with approval of the proprietors and with an explicit act of the legislature allowing the transfer. In addition, a large block of 400 acres of common woodland was reserved for cutting, as needed, for the support of the meetinghouse.

REVEREND PHINEAS FISH (1784-1854)-The last Congregationalist minister appointed over the Mashpee Church; he was removed after long Indian opposition. From a pastel by his son George E. Fish, courtesy of the Sandwich Historical Society.

Sandwich Supports Indian Protests

With Hawley's death in 1807 there were further Indian protests to the legislature about their total loss of self-government under their overseers and guardians who had wide powers. The Indians had a persuasive friend in Sandwich, reflected in a resolve which passed Sandwich town meeting in 1807 urging Sandwich representatives in Boston to "use their endeavors for alteration of the government of Mashpee." The reason was that the slender Indian income from wood and hay sales and land rentals was all used up in salaries and expenses of at least ten white officials, with none for the Indian poor and ill. There was no demand for return to district status, and the legislature only dropped the number of overseers from five to three.

Rev. Phineas Fish (1785-1854)

The Indians pointed out in their protests that in Hawley's presence of 50 years "not an Indian was taught to read nor a single Indian converted." With his hostile attitude to blacks, and his indifference to Indian rights, Hawley's Congregational church meetings were attended by whites and only a few Indians, and the Indians wanted no successor of his stripe. An itinerant Indian preacher had come along in 1794 with what was for them a much more welcome Baptist message. However in 1809 Harvard College, with its endowment for Indian preaching (the Williams Fund), nominated Phineas Fish to Mashpee, and through the compliant overseers, got a state law passed guaranteeing the Congregationalist minister the rights to sell wood from the parsonage lot. Fish also got a personal house lot, and when ordained got $400 per year from the Williams fund. The Indians were outraged but had no recourse under the law. At this time, by contrast, the state courts were confirming in Sandwich and many other towns that the residents of the parish controlled the parish church and its assets, the exact opposite of the situation in Mashpee.

Rev. William Apes (1798-after 1836)

Apes was a Methodist preacher, a Pequod Indian with some white blood, and a dedicated advocate of native rights. Coming to Mashpee for the first time in early 1833, he recognized the opportunity for exposing the rank injustice of the Indian position here. He encouraged and planned action with himself as cutting edge. An eloquent protest, the *Mashpee Memorial,* was sent to the governor dated May 21, stating the resolve of the tribe to govern itself and in specific terms to allow no more white woodcutting on the parsonage lot as of July 1. This was followed up by effective meetings with state officials, and the governor appointed one of his council, Josiah J. Fiske, to proceed to Mashpee by July 1 to assemble facts and report on the situation. Apes, meanwhile, believed he had received sufficient encouragement to organize the Indians, and formed a Tribal Council which wrote Fish that he would not be permitted to take wood as of July 1, and that his pastoral duties were at an end. Fish sent his friend Gideon Hawley Jr. (living comfortably on his father's broad lands) to the governor with hysterical claims that the Indians were in a state of insurrection and were armed.

THE WOODLOT RIOT - This sketch of the great woodlot riot of July 1, 1833 was drawn by Mara Booker Johnson and is reproduced from "Mashpee Land of the Wampanoags" courtesy of the author Amelia G. Bingham.

The great "Woodland Riot" occurred as scheduled on July 1 when Apes and a few friends calmly unloaded a drover's wagon on the woodlot and sent him off empty handed. Messages reaching the governor made it seem that the whites in Mashpee might be in real danger, but Fiske, although initially apprehensive, produced a clear and perceptive report of the situation. The overseers' operations, he found, produced a profit for the reservation but this was neither known nor available to the Indians. One overseer had the fatuity to claim that the discontent of the natives was news to him. Fiske stated that the Indians wanted chiefly some control of their own lives and property, although there was also a most glaring lack of schooling, acceptable religious instructions, civic facilities and employment; they felt they had a right to elevate themselves above their present state of degradation. Apes was arrested, but his $200 bail was supplied by Lemuel Ewer of South Sandwich. Fiske also reported that "Fish's usefulness is nearly at an end" and was clearly disgusted at Fish's removing "load after load" of wood with seven teams as soon as Apes was restrained.

Benjamin F. Hallett

The Mashpee people were fortunate to find as a friend at this point Mr. Hallett of Barnstable, a strong liberal who was both a lawyer and editor of the *Boston Daily Advocate.* He gave Apes and the Mashpee cause a wide hearing, and defended Apes in Court on the Riot charge. Apes and six friends spent thirty days in jail but the publicity widened to a national level, with William Lloyd Garrison calling the State's treatment of the Mashpee people a subject not of indignation but of disgust. Moved by such criticism, the Legislature passed the Mashpee District Act in early 1834. Hallett served the Mashpee cause well and asked no fee, but years later when the District was well established he was in fact paid. Apes wrote a booklet about Mashpee *(Indian Nullification... or the Pretended Riot Explained,* Boston 1835), and a more general book on Indian rights *(Eulogy for King Philip,* Boston 1836), but there was no longer a role for such a figure in Mashpee, and his career after 1836 is unknown. The new District had its own Baptist minister, a respected Mashpee named Blind Joe Amos, who did not use the meetinghouse for his services.

The Mashpee District Act of 1834

In Massachusetts an incipient town comprised of non-whites and non-citizens was a novelty and the new law did not fully reflect the complex realities of the situation. Some of the unresolved points were:

The District excluded "such parts thereof as are now annexed to the towns of Falmouth or Sandwich." The Legislature had to approve all changes of town lines, but wide stretches of Mashpee land adjoining Falmouth and Sandwich had been effectively annexed to these towns without legislative approval. Only the former Gideon Hawley homestead, an area of 200 acres within Mashpee, had been made part of the town of Sandwich by State act in 1811.

The status of the proprietors was still that of Indians, not subject to County or State tax, not voters (except locally) and not American citizens. They were not included in the Federal Census, being technically wards of the State and considered paupers.

No provision was made to assist the town to come up to a reasonable level of education, employment, or public facilities such as roads, a wharf, a town hall, a land survey.

Current contracts made by the former overseers remained in effect, and lands that had been sold or granted to non-proprietors were not invalidated. The favored position of Mr. Fish was not changed.

An appointed person was to be Commissioner, Treasurer and Moderator with much power.

The whole Act was temporary.

On the positive side, local officials could be elected: three selectmen, a clerk, constable and soon others, as fence viewers and pound keepers. This meant a start on vital records, town meeting records, and land records. Local voters were limited to males of Indian descent or males married to Indians. By-laws and regulations could be established and enforced on land use and on fisheries. Non-proprietors especially could be removed who did not follow the law. Lands could be granted to proprietors in severalty, a critically important power. The work of cutting and transporting wood was reserved exclusively for proprietors. All sales of alcohol were prohibited and fines established. The lands of Indians could not be taken for debt. Indians could be valid witnesses at trials.

THE INDIAN CHURCH IN MASHPEE - This building was built in 1757 replacing a church moved here from Bryant's Neck in 1717. It shows the architecture of the restoration work done in 1839. Sandwich Archives.

An Independent Parish

The Indian meetinghouse (built about 1758) had last been repaired at state expense in 1817. In 1838, $800 in state funds was authorized for repairs. It was at this point that the Greek Revival design features of the present Old Indian

Church were established. Efforts had been made at district meetings to dismiss Reverend Fish. There was a vote to do this in 1837, and in 1839 the selectmen were authorized (by the Indians) to sue in State Supreme Judicial Court to unseat him. The State law was finally changed, so that a Mashpee Parish was formally established in 1840, with the right to employ a missionary and to use the meetinghouse. Importantly, two thirds of the Williams Fund was made available to this Parish. The Selectmen were authorized to manage the parsonage land and its proceeds. A missionary was hired annually, but Blind Joe Amos continued as a revered figure until after 1870. Reverend Fish was bodily removed from the First Parish meeting in 1840 and became pastor of a church in Cotuit, but retained a limited following from Mashpee. He proposed to the Legislature that a second meetinghouse be allowed in Mashpee, but the selectmen opposed this vehemently. In 1844 the selectmen were authorized to "settle" with Fish when and if Harvard should give Mashpee the other third of the Williams Fund. Town records do not indicate how this was completed, but in 1845 Fish sold his house and land in Mashpee, located on what is now Route 130 at the site of the later Dare School. A parsonage home for the current missionary was obtained in 1852.

The End of the Bourne Lands

Nathan Bourne (1756-1829) of the fifth generation from Richard had reassembled much of the family lands in Mashpee by about 1788:

Two houselots totaling about 80 acres on the east of Mashpee Pond. This included a family burial ground now called the Jones Cemetery at Lakewood Drive and Maple Street in Mashpee and the eight-acre Popmonet lot.

Twelve-acre lot near the south end of the Pond.

Ten-acre mill site straddling the Mashpee River between present Route 130 and the Pond.

Monomoscoy peninsula.

Much land in Waquoit.

Rights provided in early deeds to take herring, cut wood, pasture cattle, and gather hay, still conceded to the Bournes.

The period of power of Nathan Bourne coincided with that of the overseers and guardians (1788-1834) so that he was in a favored position. In 1810 he generously, or foolishly, quitclaimed to the Mashpee Overseers all immunities and privileges of grazing, cutting wood, hay, etc. "which I hold from my ancestors." There was no price or exchange. In 1813 the Mashpee Overseers quitclaimed back to Nathan Bourne all the immunities granted in 1810. Then came the payoff: in 1816 the General Court approved two grants of land to him:

A lot of 110 acres at Great Conaumet (part of the present Lowell Reservation) extending from his homestead up to lands of Walley Goodspeed in Wakeby and over to Cotuit Road and to

South Sandwich Road.

A lot of 65 acres beside his homestead lot, running east of South Sandwich Road down to the end of his property.

The only cost to Bourne for these very valuable lands was his "Quitclaim of all the rights, easements and privileges possessed by said Nathan Bourne or derived to him from his ancestors." The fishing and grazing rights were now of the most nebulous value, and furthermore Bourne got to keep his other Mashpee real estate. The two lots above were called "The Bourne Purchase." Nathan Bourne died in 1829. The gristmill area had been sold to Hercules Weston, but the other lands were willed to Nathan's sons Richard and Mahershalalhashbaz. In 1833 these sons sold the homestead lands and Bourne Purchase to Isaac Jones, also selling the separate 12-acre lot. It is not known who bought Monomoscoy.

The extraordinary name of Nathan's son given above is found in Isaiah 8:1, and on nearby pages are the favorite Bourne names Melatiah and Shearjashub. He and Richard left Mashpee, ending the long family tradition here.

Mashpee Border Changes

Changes approved by the Legislature and recorded by the Massachusetts Secretary of State in his booklet "Historic Data on Cities and Towns" are as follows, as shown on page 346:

1. In 1841 the Waquoit area was abruptly annexed to Falmouth, obviously heavily owned by whites, but the records of which in approvals by the Proprietors and by the Legislature are almost totally lacking. The original boundary line between Mashpee and Falmouth, set in 1685 and approved in 1725, does not seem to have been perambulated since 1735. Not even mentioned was the triangle of Mashpee land at Ashumet Pond, which also suddenly became Falmouth.

2. In 1859 the large area east of both Wakeby and Mashpee Ponds, also the 12-acre lot, became Sandwich. The State Act simply listed the names of the white occupants and set them off from Mashpee to Sandwich. As with Waquoit, there was no Mashpee approval of the white occupation of the large sector from Lemuel Howland's little 10-acre corner down to the Bourne Purchase.

3. In 1860 the Fish Purchase in the Forestdale sector was annexed to Sandwich; also a mill site on Mashpee River, owned by Benajah and Virgil Collins, was set off to Sandwich.

4. In 1872 the Collins lot was returned to Mashpee.

5. In 1887 an important exchange of land between Sandwich and Mashpee occurred. The old Bourne homestead lots, down to the Jones burial ground and the lower 65-acre portion of the Bourne Purchase, were returned to Mashpee, also the discrete 12-acre lot. At the same time a triangle that had always been Mashpee in the Asa Meiggs Road area was set off to Sandwich.

Stone bounds were set all around.

6. In 1901 an official description of the Sandwich borders and cornerstones was published by the Commonwealth, but the exact bounds of the 200-acre Hawley land set off to Sandwich in 1811 were not then known. A proposal in Sandwich Town Meeting in 1901 to give up the lower 80-acre piece of this land (on Santuit River near Popponesset Bay) was tabled.

7. In 1905 a new drawing of the 124-acre upper piece of the Hawley lot (adjacent to Barnstable and extending along present Route 28) was accepted and stone bounds placed. The town voted to hold this lot and give up the rest of the Hawley land to Mashpee. This was approved by the Legislature.

8. In 1916 the above Hawley sector was the only part of Sandwich not contiguous to the main town, and it was set off to Barnstable as an abutter. The reasons for setting it off to Barnstable rather than to Mashpee were probably elicited in hearings. It is worth noting that Barnstable people respected the Mashpee line from 1658 on and left all lands adjacent to this line in Indian occupation without exception.

Progress of Mashpee District

Progressive residents of Mashpee favored private ownership of much of the District land in order to give all the adult proprietors more of a stake in the town and some personal wealth through owning a block of land. Accordingly, in 1842 each adult proprietor was allocated sixty acres. Those given land had to be twenty-year residents and had to be approved by the other proprietors. No resales to non-proprietors or to persons outside Mashpee were allowed, but sales between proprietors were permitted. This move was, in some cases, found to be premature as the new owners had little discretion or control and sold off first the wood, then the land itself and ended up poorer than before.

One of the reasons for Mashpee's progress in self-government was the skilled and devoted work of their Commissioner/Treasurer/Moderator Charles Marston. In 1853 his commissioner function was terminated but he remained as treasurer.

A State report of great value was prepared by Dr. Milton Earle and issued in 1861 entitled *The Indians of the Commonwealth.* It contained the first detailed census of persons living in Indian families or Indian neighborhoods. It reviewed the history of all the existing plantations and concentrations of Indian survivors with perception and sympathy, and recommended citizenship and an active aid program to bring them into the mainstream of civic life. As a result, concerted steps were taken in these long-overdue directions, although delayed by the Civil War. In 1862 Gay Head was made into a District on the Mashpee plan, having been set off in 1856 from Chilmark. Indians living outside the two Districts and five main Reservations were made citizens forthwith, and in 1869 the five Reservations were analyzed, with commons land either to be allocated to the residents in severalty or subdivided and sold for the benefit of the residents.

The residents then became fully enfranchised as citizens in the white town where they were located.

Last to be enfranchised were Mashpee and Gay Head, which were incorporated as fully operative Towns in 1870, with the proprietors able to vote in all elections and also liable for taxes, jury duty and other civic responsibilities. Many in Mashpee felt that more preparation and education time was needed, as in full independence, outsiders would step in and the unwary would lose all. Mashpee's remaining commons were sold in 1870 and 1871 in large auctions advertised in the newspapers. A property map was prepared in 1877 showing lands and owners. The fears of the conservatives that some families could not cope with taxes were borne out in an 1879 auction of personal lands taken by the town for non-payment. The Lowell family of Boston and Cotuit purchased property here, including the beautiful fifty-eight-acre Conaumet Neck in Mashpee and the upper 110 acre part of the Bourne Purchase in Sandwich forming Lowell Reservation.

Certain Mashpee residents were highly competent and could hold their own with anybody. Solomon Attaquin had made a stake at sea, served the town in many capacities and built a hotel which was a vital center; he knew all the important visitors from Daniel Webster through the period of Cleveland and Joseph Jefferson. Eben Quippish was highly respected, and had toured the country with Buffalo Bill Cody's troupe. Watson Hammond was the first Mashpee resident elected to the General Court.

Herring Pond Reservation

As shown in the map on page 347, this Reservation was surveyed in 1792 and found to have three distinct sectors, of which the southernmost was mainly in Sandwich. This sector included the ancient burying ground at the foot of Great Herring Pond, and the site on the hillside above it of the meetinghouse built with Judge Sewall's aid where the inscribed stone was found. Generally, the Commissioners or Overseers of Mashpee also had authority over this Reservation as its population was small (64 in 1803). The last preacher working here to use the Indian language was Ephraim Ellis, who died in 1783. Rev. Hawley and Rev. Fish occasionally preached here. The neighbors of this Reservation respected its borders so that the lands were almost entirely in Indian common ownership. Occasionally, the Acts of the General Court reflect permission to sell a lot, with proceeds to aid the community or a particular family. The large northern sector of the Reservation ran over to Cape Cod Bay, and from here Captain Solomon Webquish loaded firewood to take down to the Glass Factory. Thoreau deeply respected Indians and wrote in his 1857 walking tour from Plymouth to Sagamore of standing with a young Indian on the high bluffs here looking out over the Bay at the curve of the Cape with Sandwich in the distance. In 1850, following the Mashpee example of land issue to proprietors, each family in this Reservation was allotted a house lot and a block of woodland to own privately, where wood could be sold off at will. A new meetinghouse was built in the 1850s in the middle Pondville section. Following the state law of 1869, ending Indian

Reservations, the remaining Commons here were further allocated to proprietors and the balance was sold at public auction in 1873.

Map of Changes in Mashpee Borders (following page)

The original Mashpee outline of 1685 is shown. Later various lots were given or sold to non-proprietors which were finally annexed to Sandwich, Falmouth or Barnstable by acts of the State Legislature. These lots included:

1. *Waquoit area annexed to Falmouth in 1840; no purchase or grant found.*
2. *Ashumet triangle shown as Mashpee through 1725, then as Falmouth, but no state act found on annexation to Falmouth.*
3. *Ten acres granted to Lemuel Howland in 1772.*
4. *Purchase by Nathaniel and Simeon Fish in 1782, annexed to Sandwich 1860.*
5. *Grant of two hundred acres to Reverend Hawley in 1779 and set off to Sandwich in 1811. The lower eighty-acre piece was returned to Mashpee in 1905, the upper one hundred twenty acres was annexed to Barnstable in 1916.*
6. *House lot granted to Reverend Fish, remained in Mashpee.*
7. *Wakeby area (including Howland lot and the Bourne Great Conaumet lot) annexed to Sandwich in 1859, without evidence of purchase of the Wakeby*
8. *An "exchange" piece granted to Sandwich in 1887 when boundaries were being fixed and the Bourne lots on Mashpee Pond were returned to Mashpee.*
9. *A mill site granted the Collins brothers was transferred to Sandwich then returned to Mashpee.*

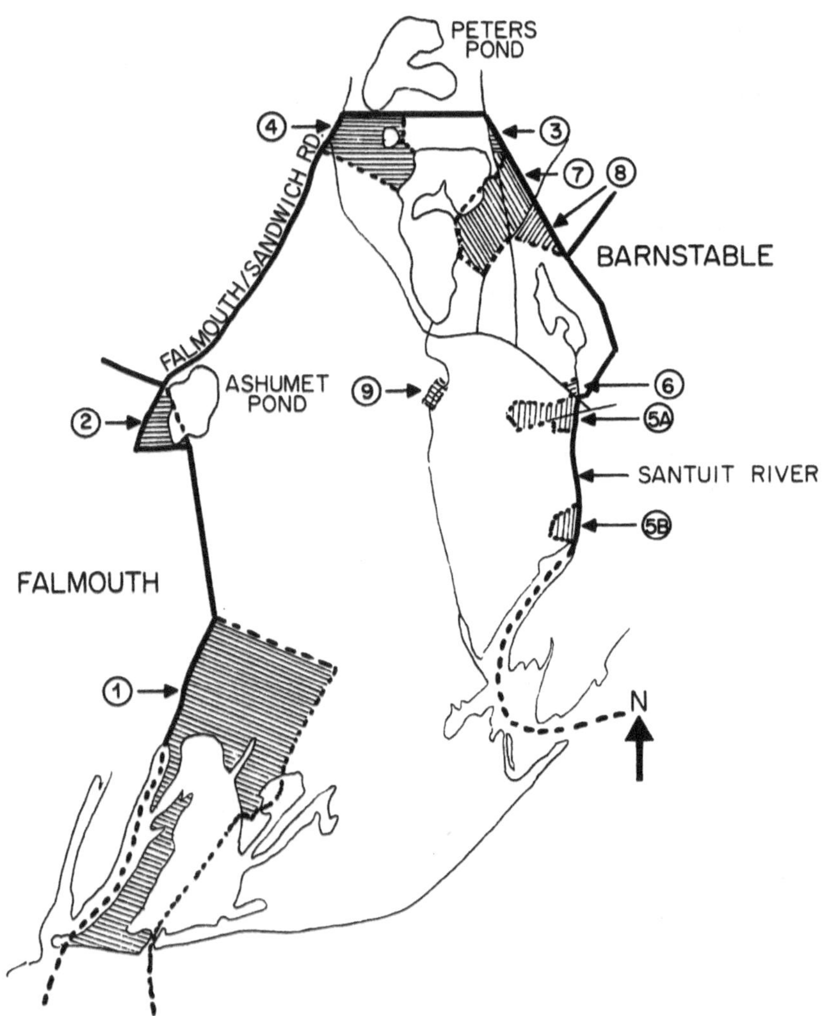
PETERS POND
FALMOUTH/SANDWICH RD.
BARNSTABLE
ASHUMET POND
SANTUIT RIVER
FALMOUTH
N
1
2
3
4
5A
5B
6
7
8
9

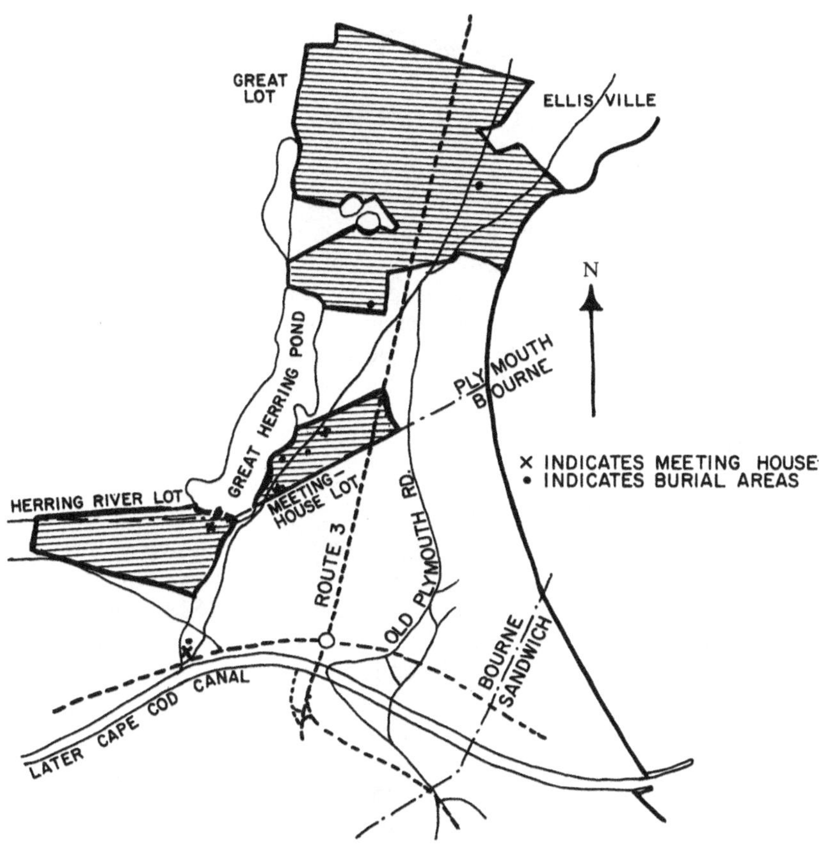

THE HERRING POND RESERVATION-This Indian settlement in North Sandwich and Plymouth was originally called Comassakumkanet. By 1700 an Indian Reservation was set up involving about 3,000 acres in three discrete pieces, the Great Lot, the Meetinghouse Lot and the Herring River Lot. The latter was mainly in Sandwich. An Indian meetinghouse at North Sandwich near present Burial Hill was approved in 1675, but was later removed to Pocasset. A second Meetinghouse was built south of Great Herring Pond in 1687. This was removed to the Meetinghouse Lot and about 1850 the present Pondville church was built on another location nearby. The lettered runestone now at Aptucxet was found at the site of the second meetinghouse.

CHAPTER 24

THE ALMSHOUSE

No photograph has been found showing the Sandwich almshouse. People had an uncomfortable feeling about the place and avoided it. Professional photographers such as Nickerson and Smith of Provincetown took excellent shots of Sandwich in the 1880s, but their handsome scenes mounted on cardboard were intended to sell, and were not made as objective documentaries. Nevertheless, a reasonable idea of the almshouse can be obtained from the perspective in the Poole view of Sandwich in 1884 and from a description in the 1873 "Paupers Register," together with references to additions in the town meeting records and newspapers.

The Almshouse Building

The main building on Charles Street was a pre-Revolutionary Colonial two-story house thirty-four feet long by twenty-eight feet deep. This had been bought by the town from Deacon Thomas Hamblin in 1823. A major extension eighteen by twenty-eight feet at the south end had been approved in 1829, with a full cellar, allowing a large clear dining room eighteen by twenty feet, with two small "warm rooms" on the ground floor for the sick. There was a one-story roofed porch on the north end. Behind were two large ells of two stories each, one added in 1868, with the privies beyond; the other was a house called the Murphy house moved here in 1878 and tied on to the south wing. This was probably the "Tramp House" approved in 1876, for overnight accommodation of the numerous vagrants that were found throughout the State at this time. The Tramp House ell was a club room for the male patients to use during the day. The whole building was heated by stoves, and the town bought coal from the B&S in addition to using wood from the town woodlots. The keeper and his family did not have a separate house so must have had a specific set of rooms in the main building. Before the Tramp House was added there were twenty-nine rooms to accommodate twenty-five people.

The Town Farm on Charles Street

The almshouse was located in an area of good farmland used since the first settlement of the town. A further lot of 15 acres had been bought in 1829 to the eastward from the Chipmans. The keeper was the chief farmer and used inmate help as far as possible to grow vegetables, crops and hay. What was not used in the establishment was sold to townsmen. A new barn was built by the town in 1846. The keeper's wife was the cook and administrator inside. One such wife, Mrs. Lawrence, in 1845 was so competent that when her husband died she herself was made the keeper, with a man hired for outside work. The almshouse was located on an ancient road crossing. Charles Street was part of the original County Road, which turned east at this corner on what is now Crowell Lane. Charles Street continued on into the woods called Cut-Hill or Poorhouse Road, and passed between two deep glacial hollows with steep sides. The eastern one was the famous Christopher's Hollow, originally a beautiful area with a spring, large trees and rocks. In the later farm-world the rocks were taken away for walls and the hollow was used as a burial place for farm animals. The other hollow, to the west, is now nearly full as the town's sanitary landfill and will probably become a waste transfer station.

From the almshouse an ancient road led west around generous springs (now the Trout Hatchery) and over past the early Wing house (now 8 Morse Road). This road connecting to Water Street was called the Upper Road, probably because the lower road (Main Street) led across the lowlands called for good reason Ford Swamp. Another ancient house on the Upper Road was occupied in the nineteenth century by a black woman called Lucy Thompson who was probably employed at the almshouse. When the glass factory needed more space for houses and for its cemetery, a bypass road was built from Charles Street over to the present Crow Farm stand, and this bypass immediately became the County Road, so that the almshouse was more isolated.

The Almshouse Burying Ground

When the almshouse was first occupied, a triangle of land in the plowed fields off Crowell Lane was set aside as a burial area. This may originally have been a boulder accumulation point when the fields were first cleared in the seventeenth century, because the overseers of the poor in 1844 found that the ground here was "too bouldery" for further burials, and the Town reserved a large area at the end of nearby Mount Hope for the burial of the town's poor. There are no markers for these burials.

Budget for the Poor

Schools, roads and the poor were the largest expense in the town's budget and were debated at most town meetings. For example for 1843:

Total almshouse expenses, including keeper	$777
Support of the poor outside the almshouse	333
Less receipts from the farm sales and contributions by relatives	(132)
Net poor cost	$978

There were fourteen inmates at this time in the almshouse, showing a cost of eighty-eight cents a person per week, not a large sum even then. We learn in 1844 that the keeper's salary was $330 per year. The budget for expenses outside the almshouse in 1844 was $400, but over one third of this covered the care of one person at the Insane Asylum in Worcester. Each year the unhappy costs and dislocation of keeping patients at Worcester or Taunton were bluntly debated and approved at town meeting. In 1848 four persons were in asylums at a cost of $457. There was a steep rise in poor costs after the Civil War, partly due to inflation, partly to numbers. Twenty-one persons were kept at the expanded almshouse in 1868 at $2.29 per week apiece, or $2,500 per year just for the almshouse. Possibly in reaction to these costs, the town voted in 1867 that all children of paupers old enough to work were to be bound out. The town had no sympathy at all for the vagrants that became a fact of life in the 1870s. When the Tramp House was approved in 1876, it was shown that the cost of giving tramps some food and a roof for the night was only twelve cents per visit. (The town of Wayland reported serving 879 meals to tramps in 1878. The overseers ordered tramps fed on crackers and water only, and reported that for 1879 only 141 had dined on crackers.) At the opposite extreme of the food spectrum, Jonathan Bourne of New Bedford, the rich whaler, for years provided everyone at the Sandwich almshouse with a free turkey dinner on Thanksgiving, up to his death in 1889.

Reverend Nathan H. Chamberlain, 1828-1901

Chamberlain was born in Monument and became an Episcopal minister in Canton, later stationed in Sandwich. He learned a great deal about Sandwich history and was the native son asked to give the principal address at the town's 250th anniversary party in 1889. His particular interest was architecture and house design as affecting the life of the people. He wrote a discourse on this subject for the New England Historic Genealogical Society. He also wrote an early novel called *Autobiography of a New England Farmhouse,* published in 1864 (see Notes on Sources, p. 615). For a few years while Nathan was growing up, his father Artemus was the keeper of the Sandwich almshouse. The novel describes a New England town called Sandowne which is clearly Sandwich, with fields running north to the sea, a fire at Great Hollow, a fisherman named John Trout, a pastor Leverick, etc. The Sandowne almshouse was a little way from the village on a lane that led to a hill-hollow. The main building was large, dark and weatherstained, and the outbuildings (barns, sheds and cornhouse) were made of saltworks timber with rusty streaks from spikes and bolts. The grounds were unkempt with weeds and broken wagons lying about. This sounds quite realistic. One incident that was not put into the novel was that in 1843 Artemus the keeper was attempting to subdue an alcoholic derelict who had somehow gotten a bottle and was making trouble. Artemus was stabbed five times, but the jackknife was small and he was not badly hurt. The attacker was sentenced to four years in prison.

Nathan and Heman

Another person well known to Chamberlain, but who did not enter the Sandowne story, was Heman Dillingham (1817-1889), a tall and strong fellow afflicted with what we would now call a severe learning disability. Heman set the record for forty-four years spent in the almshouse. He was the son of Benjamin and Polly (Tozier) Dillingham mentioned earlier, who were brought back to

Sandwich from Fairfield, Maine and aided for years by the town. Finally Heman and both parents moved to the almshouse in 1845 where all ended their lives. Rev. Nathan Chamberlain as a little boy, ten years younger than Heman, described how he went to the village school where Heman attended as a sad hulk unable to learn but so gentle and appealing that the other children even forebore teasing him. He was extremely near-sighted and kept his eyelids nearly shut. Nathan said that Heman was color-blind but had keen hearing and sense of smell. He had clear memories of many early simple events and remembered the voices of those who had been kind to him. Nathan and some friends once took him to Boston on the train but he shrank from the confusion and seemed glad to return to the peace of the almshouse where he helped the keeper with the cows, the haying, and year-round chores. When Heman died in 1889, Nathan Chamberlain wrote a moving obituary for the *Boston Evening Transcript* entitled "A Pauper Emeritus." He concluded "outmatched friendly soul, mortgaged to poverty from birth, stripped of every prize, fated to become naught...rest thou in peace!" Heman had other friends too, who buried him in Spring Hill Cemetery and provided a stone marker.

Town Aid to Others

The town aided many other persons who were infirm or destitute but had homes to live in. The town clerk kept a notebook of aid extended, with entries describing a cord of wood, a barrel of flour, medicines, etc. These entries sometimes ended in burial expenses. Some of these aided were eccentrics of whom many stories were repeated. Nancy Eldredge lived on Pine Street near Main Street and was well-known as a chicken thief but so pugnacious and quarrelsome that it was usually not worth having her arrested. She charged two men with assault and battery on her, but Judge Seth Nye let them off when they explained they were only assisting her off their property. Damey Tupper in innocent old age went around to the neighbors with a little basket asking what they had for Damey today; she would get an egg or bread or fruit. Others included Bill Freeman and the nameless whittler who carved lewd figures on locust sticks. The selectmen and overseers of the poor received stern letters from their counterparts in towns across New England saying that so-and-so of Sandwich was being supported in a hospital or jail or poorhouse and all the charges were for Sandwich account. This required a check to see whether the person really had acquired Sandwich residence, and if not, the refusal to accept charges was blunt. There was a category of state paupers for which state payments could be obtained if the person ended up here.

The End of the Almshouse

Elijah Hancock was a popular keeper here for 14 years, and when he resigned in 1890 his successor pressed for major improvements in the facility. The town debated whether to build a new modern house, but ended up voting for only certain repairs and new features including a hot water heater. The roster of inmates had begun to decline after 1884 when Bourne sent no new patients and the whole town population continued to fall. That the place was old and unfit is clear in the surviving copy of a state inspection report in 1897: Exterior of building - quite unsuitable, Fire escapes - none, Separation of sane and insane - none by day, Bathrooms - none, Stove heating -inadequate, Beds and bedding - fairly free from vermin, Bathing - women regular, men seldom, Remarks - management good but little else can be recommended.

The almshouse was closed in 1901 with the seven surviving inmates put out to private homes or sent to institutions. A buyer was sought, but failing this, the building was leased and converted for tenants. However it was empty in 1911 when it burned to the ground. The neighbors were probably not sorry to see it go. In 1912 Henry Alden Belcher of Boston bought the farm of 33 acres, rebuilt the barn and built a house for a tenant farmer on the cellar foundation for the 1829 wing. The town at this time (1915) acknowledged the presence of the early paupers' burying ground and fenced it in. There were no burial markers and since many of the deaths were not even recorded in town vital records the interrals here remain uncertain. In 1916 Belcher sold the property to David Crowell and his brother Lincoln Crowell. Lincoln later sold out to David, who built the main residence at 33 Charles Street. The farm became known as Crow Farm, for the bird, not as a contraction of Crowell. The three children of David Crowell still live on the property; Carolyn, Eleanor (Mrs. John Winslow) and Howard.

CHAPTER 25

THE TOWN DIVIDES

The first efforts at division had been more religious than political - the Scusset church formed in 1732 and the Pocasset Second Parish effort that succeeded in 1770. The first proposal for a separate **town** was **Seth Perry's** petition in 1797, to found what he wanted to call Windsor. This **created** unnecessary problems in approvals because it included parts of South Plymouth and North Falmouth as well as South Sandwich, so it foundered. The next proposal in 1860 had a north-south division line with Sandwich, leaving all Scusset with the old town as being closer to the Town Hall than to a new one in the Monument sector. This proposal was dropped by agreement.

In 1873 under the leadership of Captain Nathaniel Burgess a new proposal was made to found a town to be called "Pocasset." This proposal used the same division line as in 1860. By now the Keith Car Co. had become much larger and the expansion of the railroad to Woods Hole had made transport to Monument or Buzzards Bay as a new town center more practical. Therefore there were second thoughts that Scusset should be included, and the proposal was withdrawn.

The 1883 Petition

Captain Burgess waited ten years before trying again, but this time got wide support in his proposal to create a new town called Bourne. The petition to the Legislature dated October 29, 1883 was accompanied by nine petitions signed by a total of 329 voters, and this time included the whole area of Scusset. The proponents were determined to have this line and no other. A copy of the proposal was sent to the town government, which promptly held a special town meeting November 6. At this meeting 553 of 786 voters were present, and the vote was 386 against division to 167 for it, showing that many from the western villages did not come to the meeting. The selectmen were authorized to oppose the division, but selectman David D. Nye of Cataumet was one of the leaders for division. The activists in the western villages held organization meetings December 15 and December 29 and appointed an executive committee of six, a general committee of sixteen and a finance committee of three, Isaac N. Keith and Benjamin B. Abbe of West Sandwich, and Captain Burgess. The critical area was Scusset, where two of the wealthiest men in the town lived (Keith and Abbe, a grandson of Benjamin Burgess) and where the petition for division had included 47 names assembled by John P. Knowlton. Opposed to division however were 45 from this same West Sandwich area headed by Ebenezer B.

Nye and including Noble P. Swift, Calvin Crowell and many Swifts and Gibbses. The main petition of the remonstrants was from Sandwich village listing 145 names. The only known person from Sandwich village who favored division was Benjamin Cook, the high school teacher. The facts of the case were not disputed:

	Remnant Sandwich	Proposed *Bourne*	*Total Town*
1878 Valuation	$766,688	$531,897	$1,298,585
1883 Valuation	$786,550	$820,825	$1,607,375
Growth in Valuation	$19,862	$288,928	$308,790
Population 1883	2,156	1,388	3,544
Taxable land (acres)	26,500	23,500	50,000
Spent on Roads, Poor Schools & Police (1878/1882)	$49,488	$31,284	$80,772
Raised in Taxes "	$39,525	$41,247	$80,772

The evidence is striking that since the completion of the railroad to Woods Hole in 1872, there was a great deal of new construction in the western villages, especially on waterfront property on Buttermilk Bay and Buzzards Bay, with an accompanying rise in valuation of land, so that in five years alone the western villages had jumped from forty-one percent of the town's valuation to over fifty-one percent. The petitioners listed eighty-one new summer dwellings, many very expensive.

In population there was a slight overall decline from 1870 to 1883, masking almost certainly a larger decline in old Sandwich and an increase on the western side. Even so, over sixty percent of the population (and of the school children) lived on the eastern side. The most telling facts produced by the petitioners were the sums of the previous five years' budgets showing the eastern side expending sixty percent while only raising forty-nine percent in taxes.

Also the distances to the seat of government were telling:

	Number of Polls	*To Sandwich Town Hall*	*To a Buzzards Bay Location*	*Poll-Miles Saved*
South Pocasset	39	12½	5½	273
Pocasset	55	10½	4	357
Monument Beach	20	9	2	140
Monument	101	7½	1	656
Buzzards Bay	21	8	0	168

Head of Bay	11	7	2	55
North Sandwich	32	4	4	–
West Sandwich	68	2½	5½	(204)
Total	347			1,445

While 247 polls were saving 6½ miles per meeting, North Sandwich people broke even and West Sandwich polls had to travel an extra three miles.

The Arguments

Each side printed a simple folded page for distribution in the town and in the legislature. The remonstrants stressed that the petitioners were trying to take the lion's share; that they were taking not only twenty-five miles of Buzzards Bay but two miles of Cape Cod Bay as well; that towns decreasing in size should not be divided; that the railroad made travel to Sandwich village easy and cheap; that expenses of two small towns would be greater than one; that West Sandwich was adjacent and really an extension of the old village. The petitioners stressed their rights and the justice of their plan; that they were not resorting to tricks, aspersions or indignation meetings with brass bands; that the trains were not always convenient for return from meetings unless a special train were paid for; that no large estates were being divided by the proposed line, which a line between North and West Sandwich would do; and that the old town would benefit by an extensive dock being built on the route of the canal then already being excavated.

The Hearings

Attorneys for the petitioners were George A. King and N. Sumner Myrick; for the remonstrants, William Gaston and E. S. Whittemore. The hearing began January 31, 1884 and recounted the arguments and facts supporting both views, with both sides claiming support in West Sandwich; testimony of witnesses for division went on to February 4, including Rev. N. H. Chamberlain of Monument, Keith and Abbe of West Sandwich and Cook of Sandwich. The case against division presented Noble Swift and Calvin Crowell of West Sandwich with Charles Dillingham, H.G.O. Ellis and Frederick S. Pope all of Sandwich. The petitioners then had a great piece of luck. The senators and representatives on the committees and other parties from Boston all came down by train on February 7 to Cataumet, then boarded a long line of carriages with local hosts to go up the main road through the villages and end up at the Central House in Sandwich. The day was warm with heavy rain so that the carriages crawled slowly through the muddy roads, and there were periods of complete stop when someone bogged down. A new Minister later asked whose funeral it was, and he was told it was a town service for a former friend. When the exhausted committees got to the Central House four hours later, they were told by David Nye that that was the way he had to go at least once a week for selectmen's meetings for the past four years, and he was assured by all that there ought to be a division.

On the nineteenth, the same committees came by train to East Sandwich and were given a tour to the glass factory and then on to the canal site where the dredge was working. The committee was unanimous for division and the vote passed the House by a majority of twenty-three.

"An Act to Incorporate the Town of Bourne"

Chapter 127 of the Acts and Resolves, with this title, was signed by the Governor April 2, 1884 and the new town came into existence. Among the provisions of the Act were: State and county taxes due from Sandwich would be split between the towns in accordance with a new official set of valuations when completed. Arrears and unpaid taxes go to Sandwich. Bourne is to pay three-sevenths of the relief costs of military veterans from the town. Public funds and properties are to be divided on the basis of the May 1, 1883 valuations already tabled. A mediation system for disputes is provided. Sandwich will provide a list of voters qualified in the Bourne sector. Outstanding legal suits and liabilities are to be settled by Sandwich and the proceeds split as public funds. Bourne pays the entire cost of settling the new boundary line. Sandwich residents are to have the same rights as Bourne residents do in the Bourne fisheries.

After the Division

Both towns had meetings April 12. Bourne elected officials for the current year including–

Town Clerk		William A. Nye
Selectman and		Ezra C. Howard
	Overseers of the Poor	David D. Nye
		Albert R. Eldridge
Assessors		David D. Nye
		Moses C. Waterhouse
		John P. Knowlton
Treasurer and Collector		Nathan Nye
Supt. of Schools		Levi R. Leavitt

Sandwich held a new election, and voted to work out the fisheries agreement with Bourne, to adopt a new budget ($12,650), to allow liquor sales, to prosecute illegal sales and to petition the legislature to approve certain canal measures.

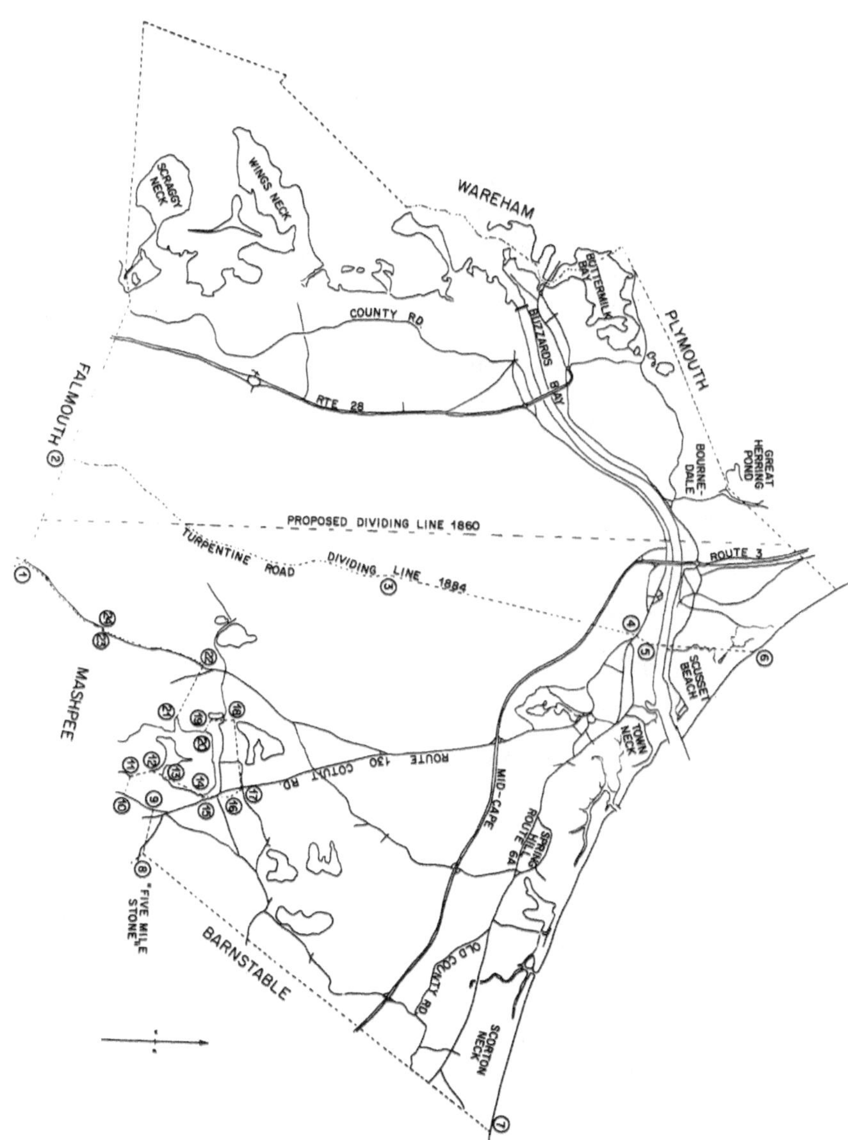

MAP OF SANDWICH & BOURNE - This map shows the dividing line of 1884, also the proposed dividing line of 1860, which would have kept West Sandwich in the old sector. There are granite markers at each of the twenty-four Sandwich border corners, except 23 & 24, which are in an Otis runway.

On April 14 the Bourne town clerk had the satisfaction of notifying his opposite number in Sandwich that the town was duly organized as of April 12. On April 23 a town meeting was held to reach official agreement on many basic procedures and authorizations — to accept a budget ($11,500), to borrow money in advance of taxes, to settle with Sandwich on the Bourne paupers in the almshouse (six of twenty), to request copies of Sandwich records, and to find an office. In May the town boundary line from Cape Cod Bay to the Falmouth line was staked out and described by Edward S. Ellis of Bourne and Charles M. Thompson of Sandwich. Bourne borrowed $4,000 from Isaac N. Keith and went into normal business. On July 23 the respective assessors and town clerks completed the new valuation of the real estate in the towns. The total, $1,622, 950. was only about 1% greater than in 1883 and produced the same percent shares by towns to use in dividing state and county tax liability and other settlements. Bourne sent out tax bills at $11.20 per $1,000. On August 6, the new bounds were formally perambulated by the selectmen and accepted. Granite marker posts cut by Daniel W. Tribou and Seth S. Maxim were later placed at the angle points. The list of Bourne voters was completed and sent from Sandwich in October. On December 24 a final accounting of public property and status of accounts as of April 12, 1884 was agreed and signed. This showed:

Liabilities	$20,308.91
Assets	21,416.01
Balance of Assets	1,107.10
Credit to Bourne	565.91
Credit to Sandwich	541.19

Bourne started town life with eight village schools, six post offices, seven telephones, four churches, two foundries, one railroad car plant, fifteen groceries, five blacksmith shops, one lumber yard, one axe factory and eight cemeteries. It had no town hall or high school. The town's first construction was a room added to the Buzzards Bay district school, for use as a high school. This opened in September 1885 with thirty pupils. Ten students from West Sandwich, now renamed Sagamore, still came to the Sandwich Academy and six went to high school in Wareham. The town was well launched with dedicated people and prospects of continued strong growth. Its particular shape however, as a long string of villages with seven railroad stations continued to be a fact of life.

Cape Cod Ship Canal Company

The deep curving valley connecting two bays was another fact of life. It was about eight miles from bay to bay, about seven of which were now in Bourne and one at the east end in Sandwich. The flood of words that accompanied the division process contained references to the prospective canal.

There had been many surveys of the canal valley since Bradford had pointed out in building Aptucxet Trading Post that a canal would save lives and avoid the dangerous distant trip around the Cape. The first company that gave promise of really digging was the Cape Cod Ship Canal Co. under Alpheus Hardy, which received a charter from the Massachusetts General Court in 1870. They were probably basing their plans on the Baldwin survey and map of 1862, which had locks and a long curving granite breakwater in the Bay parallel to the shore at the Sandwich end. The state asked the federal government to build the breakwater. The engineer assigned by the government, Col. J. G. Foster, went beyond the breakwater and proposed a bigger canal 300 feet at the surface by 23 feet deep, but without locks. His studies showed that the maximum current in the canal would be about 4 knots. Two other studies by Frizell and Clemens Herschel agreed there was no need for locks and that a much smaller canal would handle most of the prospective traffic. The charter was extended repeatedly but in 1878 the company was warned that by November 1, 1880, they must have spent $100,000 in construction and have funds of $400,000 on hand, or their charter would be invalidated and their assets on the site would go to their successor.

CAPE COD GLASS AND SPURR'S VENEER WORKS-This drawing shows the plant as of about 1884 when owned by C.P.W. Spurr, and might have been sketched from the tower of St. Peters Church as Church Street is along the right side of the view. The future canal is shown in artistic license, because the Lockwood Dredge was then already at work and interest was high. Furthermore a new freight wharf is shown on the canal which had actually been placed on dry land in anticipation of the dredging. Courtesy of Sandwich Historical Society.

The Italian Laborers

The canal scholar William J. Reid stated that there were dredges in Buzzards Bay in July 1880, but if so there is no record of any excavation. However, on September 15 at Sandwich Town Neck a work force of 112 Italian laborers started work with shovels and wheelbarrows. They lived in tents on the Neck and their excavation was parallel to the railroad to the west of Town Neck Road, at a point almost a half-mile from the likely canal route in Scusset Marsh. If long continued their trench would have connected Scusset and Shawme marshes and made an island of Town Neck. Three more gangs arrived from New York making a work force of 450 to 500 laborers. Abruptly this strange operation ceased. The contractor and the straw boss disappeared leaving the men stranded without money or food. On October 13 they marched into the town to seize the son of the contractor who was reported to be at the company's office at 4 Jarves Street. There was only one interpreter to try to calm them, and the citizens naturally thought the situation was highly dangerous. The men did return to their tents and the selectmen realized that food would have to be provided. They wired the governor for extra police and rounded up deputies to aid the local authorities. Some of the laborers went to houses looking for work but since they spoke no English, the inhabitants feared for their lives. The situation was improved with town food, and a state agency arranged with the railroad for a special car holding 60 men to be added to the end of certain trains connecting to New York. All the men were gone by November 1, when the Hardy charter expired.

500 ITALIANS—This classic view shows some of the 500 Italians hired to dig a ditch at Town Neck in 1880 in order to try to save a canal charter. Photo by Nickerson & Smith, Provincetown.

The Cape Cod Canal Company

Henry M. Whitney and Associates, the next licensees, owned a steamship line, street railways and gas companies in Boston, and had funds, but needed to study the canal project carefully before filing work plans. A new federal survey of Buzzards Bay was completed and at the eastern end of the canal, two long jetties extending out from the shore were proposed. However, Whitney lost interest and backed out when his engineers reported both hard blue clay under the eastern end and large deposits of "quicksand" elsewhere on the route.

The Ship Canal Company Again

Some of Hardy's previous partners now applied for a new charter including George H. Titcomb, William Seward, Jr., Alfred D. Fox and Samuel Fessenden, the latter of Sandwich. This group's charter of June 26, 1883 provided that they must have spent $25,000 in construction within four months, and deposit $200,000 in cash as a pledge. They contacted Frederick A. Lockwood of East Boston to do the dredging of the east end. Lockwood owned a machine shop and construction company which had East Coast rights to a new dredge designed by John A. Ball in California. When the partners failed to raise capital, Lockwood himself found the $200,000 through other investors, Quincy Adams Shaw of Boston and General Charles C. Dodge of the copper firm. Lockwood signed a contract October 9 to do the dredging but the dredge was not yet built. The answer to spending the $25,000 by October 26 was found by ordering hundreds of oak piles to be shipped to Sandwich by Railway Express. These were assembled into a large wharf on dry land built to reach the edge of the canal-to-be, probably at the site of the present fish freezer. This was successful as far as spending the money was concerned and the charter was assured for the next four years. A clear relief map of the canal area prepared by the Coast and Geodetic Survey in 1860 shows buildings, roads, and land use clearly, and reflects a peninsula of upland in this sector, with branches of Tupper Creek approaching shore in the later harbor-of-refuge area and Canal Electric area.

Lake Lockwood

Mr. Lockwood built the dredge and installed the machinery in it during the winter of 1883/1884, and had it towed to Sandwich that spring. It was an imposing structure with thirty-nine big buckets on an endless chain that raised material to a hopper 56 feet high. Here rocks were sent in a chute to barges while a jet of water forced soft soil down a 12-inch pipe to the marsh to the west. It was powered by two 75-horsepower steam engines, and had a separate steam engine that ran a dynamo producing power for four large arc lights. It was reported in awe that these were so powerful one could read a newspaper by them at 2,000 feet in total darkness. Crowds came to Town Neck to see the amazing spectacle—the canal was being dug at last. The dredge, however, was weak and broke down repeatedly, especially when it began to encounter clay and boulders. The operator was a popular local personality, Cornelius Driscoll, and Mr.

THE LOCKWOOD DREDGE—This 1884 view shows the wooden body and framework of the dredge assembled by Frederick A. Lockwood of Boston. This dredge dug a channel about 200 feet wide by 3,000 feet long from the beach up to about the present Sandwich Harbor of Refuge. It broke down repeatedly when it struck clay and boulders, and finally burned out when it was abandoned in 1889. Courtesy of Channing E. Hoxie.

Lockwood was here himself to arrange the repairs. The channel cut was large, according to the *Sandwich Observer* for March 17, 1885, 200 feet wide by 28 feet deep, although some skepticism may be permitted on the depth. This newspaper reported that Lockwood had a more powerful machine ready in Boston to bring down to speed the work, but it clearly never came. Lockwood had some $150,000 of his own funds tied up in the dredge and its operations. Fessenden and Charles M. Thompson bought up some 1,057 acres of land along the right-of-way, paying $69,000. Further capital for the work dried up when Shaw declined to raise more. There is no indication of what plans were made for the dredging at the other end into the Monument River or for dry digging in the center section. The Cape Cod Ship Canal Company got an extension of its charter in 1887 but had to promise the Town of Bourne to pay taxes on land bought up to the time digging began, also to allow contests of land claims and to establish a state agency to determine the roads and bridges to be needed. However, Lockwood was unable to raise more capital or find new partners. His machine shop suffered a fire and he himself became ill in 1889 so that he finally turned over or sold all his interests in the dredge and the Cape Cod lands to Shaw. The dredge clanked away intermittently until June 1890 when no more funds were made available. The machinery was removed and the hulk burned and sank.

Meanwhile the sea had closed the entrance to the ditch and as much as 1,500 feet of channel filled again with spoil from the banks. The remaining lake was possibly 1,500 to 2,000 feet long, ending somewhere in the region of the present Harbor of Refuge where the hulk of the dredge was later blown up when the canal was built. An article by the later Chief Engineer Parsons stated that the Lockwood dredge cut a channel 7,000 feet long, but this must be in error, since this distance from the beach would have brought the dredge up past Keith Car Works. The Lockwood ditch did not even reach the wharf that was waiting for water.

CHAPTER 26

THE END OF GLASSMAKING

Plymouth Colony towns were advised to appoint a town clerk in 1646, among Glassmaking became unprofitable on the eastern seaboard in the 1870s as energy, raw materials and markets all favored the mid-western factories. In addition, an aggressive labor union enforced new demands on management and encouraged eastern workers to strike. In the face of these and other obstacles, the Boston and Sandwich Glass Company ceased operations, and the old plant under several new owners never got back into sustained operations. Glass cutting and decorating lasted longer in small shops using blanks from other factories. The story of this ending is superbly told in the book, *The Glass Industry in Sandwich,* Volume 4, by Ray Barlow and Joan Kaiser. Our account here will be highly condensed.

The B&S After Jarves

When Deming Jarves resigned in 1858, the plant superintendent in Sandwich was the veteran glassmaker Theodore Kern. George L. Fessenden became clerk/paymaster here while his brother Sewall H. Fessenden became Agent in Boston. These brothers were sons of Captain Sewall Fessenden, born in Winchendon, Mass. and only distantly related to the Sandwich branch descended from Rev. Benjamin Fessenden. The B&S remained active during the Civil War and reached its peak employment of 520 men in this decade. After 36 years as plant superintendent Theodore Kern abruptly resigned in 1866 and George "Lafe" Fessenden became Superintendent. The Glassmakers' Protective Union had been formed in 1865, and in 1870 called a short strike at the B&S which drew a fine as illegal. Another sign of things to come was the 1870 opening of a Boston sales office for output from mid-west glassmakers. A huge fire in Boston in November 1872 destroyed the B&S office, showroom, and warehouse, and only a fraction of the loss was received in claims, due to failure of the insurance company.

In 1873 there was a financial panic and business depression, the results of which were long felt. The B&S plant had increased glassmaking capacity greatly by changing over to 1500 lb. capacity clay pots. Now in the depression came the closing of the lower glasshouse, which produced the cheaper pressed glass requiring no further decorating and cutting before shipment to market. It became increasingly clear that the B&S had to concentrate on the best grades and specialties for sales. For the 1876 Philadelphia Centennial, a brilliant collection was assembled including another pressing of the Union Bowl. At this time Joseph Bonique of the B&S also blew a huge bowl of thirty-three inches diameter, to be the base of a fountain, the gather for which weighed seventy-five pounds, supposed to be the largest such bowl ever attempted. In 1878 prices were depressed by the dumping of stocks on the market by the New England Glass Co.

PRVIOUS PAGE: THE BOSTON & SANDWICH GLASS CO. IN OPERATION- The top view shows the scene from Georges Rock Road. At left rear the roundhouse, then the stacks of the unused lower glass house; the tallest stack is on the power house, with a square stack on the pothouse; behind it the active stacks of the upper glass house; at right the three small stacks on the lead plant. Photo by Nickerson & Smith Provincetown, courtesy of Clare M. Wing.

The lower view shows the front of the plant from Jarves Street. The watch house is straight ahead, with second-floor passage over to the powerhouse and its adjacent glass cutting shop. At the left is Fountain Park with the upper glass house stacks beyond. At extreme right some of the original B&S tenements. Photo courtesy of Clare M. Wing.

Henry Francis Spurr

George L. Fessenden resigned in ill health in 1882, and the directors appointed Spurr as plant superintendent. An affable and successful salesman, Spurr saw that the past ten years had left morale low and the plant in poor shape. He proceeded vigorously to make many improvements both in the plant itself and in the range of glass being turned out. A new type of thin-walled stemware contemptuously called "bubble glass" was created which became highly profitable. A two-month vacation was taken in 1883 in all glass factories to reduce a stock glut, during which Spurr kept the staff at work painting twenty-six buildings. He insisted on inventory and procedural changes which the directors backed, causing the resignation of Sewall Fessenden, so that Spurr now became both general agent and plant superintendent. Union organizers were busy taking full advantage of the ignorance of the workmen as to the role of management and marketing in the success of the company. The B&S as well as all the eastern glassmakers were struck in October 1885 to raise wages up to the inflated level of the western companies. This was finally settled in five weeks, but caused a loss for the year. About one third of the workmen were union, and even they admitted that they were generally satisfied with the wages and working conditions. Members felt they would gain with union control and could always go west and find the same jobs. Spurr decided to save money switching back to wood and contracted to begin cutting in the old woodlots. The year 1886 was again profitable but labor was continuing to organize.

The Last Strike

The year 1887 was the last one for B&S operations. In the spring there was a huge brush fire started in Bourne which spread over 25,000 acres. This destroyed 600 cords of B&S wood already cut and stacked, and also the stands of oak and pine ready for cutting. The B&S was forced to order coal again. After the July plant vacation, the union suggested all members take another two weeks off, which they did. The representatives of all glass plants then proposed twelve rules to establish management rights in plant operations, including one providing that there be no discrimination against non-union workers. This was refused and a general strike against all manufacturers was begun after closing Friday,

December 30, 1887. The B&S lost $22,841 this year.

Afew employees stayed working on maintenance, and the decorating and cutting departments continued to work on ready stock. On February 13, 1888 the fires were put out including the steam boiler for heat and power. The cutters and decorators moved over to the workrooms at the Cape Cod Glass Works which had been used intermittently since the death of Jarves in 1869. Key workmen of the B&S were being paid up to $15 per week by the union for not working, and all union members were receiving some strike money. In April the union's strike fund was low. The mid-west manufacturers on May 1 agreed to the union conditions and went back to glassmaking at full speed, with every confidence in making a profit, leaving the eastern manufacturers with the choice of operating at a loss or not at all. The B&S saw only increasing losses and no escape from union domination. A "For Sale" sign was posted on the factory on October 16, 1888. A painful duty then followed, of evicting the families who had been living rent-free in company-owned tenements. There were thirty-three apartments in fifteen buildings. The town could never be the same.

DECORATORS AT THE BOSTON AND SANDWICH-This group of decorators at the B&S was photographed in the early 1880s. Many of these artists had great skill in painting and could work as well on canvas, wood and porcelain. Six men in back row: Edmund K. Chipman, John Brady, Edward Swann, Sylv. Chadwick, Friedman Miller, Phillip Brady; Six women at left and back row: Emma Fogarty, Mary Gregory, Niece of Mrs. Ed Chipman, Anna McKenna, Ellen Brady, Annie Nye; Five women front row: Emma Gregory, Lina Chamberlain, Annie Chamberlain, Annie O'Leary, Mary Ball; Three men at front right: Richard Murphy, William Foster, unidentified short man. Courtesy of Channing E. Hoxie.

The Last of the B&S

Directed from Boston by executors who felt none of the pain of the town or of the former employees, the dissolution of the company proceeded rapidly. Glass stocks were offered at discount; the sales offices were closed and all staff but four watchmen were eliminated. Henry Spurr had to resign as of February 1, 1889. The molds owned by the B&S were sold to Jones, McDuffie and Stratton, a wholesale glass supplier, who was then free to issue them to firms wishing to produce those patterns. Privately owned molds held by the B&S were returned to their owners. There was no wholesale scrapping of molds as had been reported. The town of Sandwich had tried twice in February and in October of 1888 to persuade the B&S management and workers to come to agreement and reopen, but did not appreciate the gravity of the economic and management crisis involved. Now the town refused to abate 1889 taxes on the B&S real estate and stocks. On October 17, 1889 the Electrical Glass Corporation bought the main property for $20,000 consisting of eight acres of land, the industrial plant, fifteen residential buildings, a store, ten acres of marsh and 1,000 acres of woodland. In 1890 and 1891 a few other properties and assets were sold off, then inactivity. On March 6, 1894 the State Supreme Court dissolved the name and title of the company.

Later Owners of the Plant

The Electrical Glass Corp. (Director James G. Pennycuick) intended to make electrical insulators and a new type of underground conduit. They converted one furnace to oil and prepared for production but were disappointed to find that many skilled workmen did not wish to work since they were receiving both union money and some town relief. Cutting and decorating space was leased to Nehemiah Packwood and Edward Swann. The company was not strong and failed on mortgage payments so that the plant and tenements were sold at auction in 1890.

George B. Jones, a glass salesman but never a manufacturer, bought the plant and was able to borrow $3,000 in Sandwich to start renovation. However, expenses were endless and he gave up and offered the plant for sale again.

Albert V. Johnston bought the B&S plant in 1892. He had leased the glass decorating and cutting premises at the Cape Cod Glass factory nearby, and also owned a lamp assembly business in Boston. Now he concentrated these activities at the decorating area and in the old pothouse of the B&S, while Packwood continued his cutting shop in the B&S cutting area. Johnston wished to restore actual glassmaking but found the expenses to be far greater than expected. He did get local and even union funds on promise to work with the union, and commenced making lamps, shades and chimneys in 1895. He restored the name Boston and Sandwich Glass Co. which had been freed by the recent dissolution. Expenses always exceeded income and he gave up manufacturing in 1897, a second blow to Sandwich families who hoped desperately to see glassmaking continue. Some lamp assembly work continued, but Packwood moved his cutting shop to new quarters. Johnston died in 1903 and his heirs sold the plant. Johnston had over his period of ownership sold off all the woodland

and marshland, the unused housing, the store, the cooper's barn, and the roundhouse, also demolished unneeded buildings in the plant area itself leaving only the big two-story buildings along Harbor and Factory Streets, the lower glasshouse and the pothouse.

INTERIOR, UPPER GLASS HOUSE, BOSTON AND SANDWICH-Tbis postcard view probably shows the interior not of the 1880s cleaned up for fresh operation under one or another of the later owners such as Alton Manufacturing Company. The pots of molten glass are in a ring inside the furnace, and an extraction is gathered through a small port for operations by a team under a foreman called the gaffer. Sandwich Archives.

George T. McLaughlin of Sandwich was a skilled businessman who had made money on most of his ventures, but his buying the B&S plant in early 1904 was not one of them. The existing lamp assembly business in the pothouse was taken over by Harry S. Dowden and continued until 1909. McLaughlin raised more local capital and established the Boston and Sandwich Glass Co. III. Again Sandwich families were invited back, and the manufacture of glass began with light globes. A new backer, B. S. Barnard of New York, was found who placed orders and lent capital. Although many repairs and improvements were made in the old plant, the business was not profitable and again was closed in March 1905.

Mr. Barnard and another backer, Lincoln Bancroft, now formed a new company called the Sandwich Glass Company which had enough capital to reopen the plant in 1906. They made electrical goods, lamp shades and blanks for cutting. Oil was being used and the higher temperatures were found to damage the old furnaces. The chimneys needed repair. Furthermore, the American Flint Glass Workers Union had observed manufacturing here and demanded union membership, rules, and wage scales. These demands finished operations and the

Sandwich Glass Company was hauled into bankruptcy court.

Now a most bizarre period began. The enterprising Mr. McLaughlin found a highly solvent businessman in Boston named Cardenio F. King, who was president of a small company called Alton Manufacturing Co. King put up capital to rescue McLaughlin and other local investors from the bankruptcy proceedings, and took over ownership of the glass factory and grounds. When King came to Sandwich in March 1907 he was treated to a parade, a banquet and a reception at Town Hall. He immediately set to work to reopen the glass plant and money seemed no object. Glass produced included gas and electric items and art glass. A new steam engine and new pots in the furnace in the upper glass house were installed. The unused lower glasshouse was demolished, as were all the old B&S housing units except the three double houses on Harbor Street and the six-apartment block on Church Street. Suddenly in March 1908 Cardenio F. King disappeared and the factory abruptly closed as no money was forthcoming. This remained a mystery for ninety days while men were unpaid and began to seek work elsewhere. King and an attorney appeared in Boston where he gave himself up. The money invested so impressively in Sandwich had apparently all been stolen. This ended the last episode of glassmaking in Sandwich. The plant was sold in 1909 to Robert A. Hammond and was adapted to other purposes.

BOSTON AND SANDWICH FACTORY—View of the B&S area before 1907 from the former town dock at the end of Harbor Street. At left the pot house, with stacks of the lower glass plant beyond. At right is the boiler house with second floor passage over to the watch house. The willow trees in the derelict plant yard had already gotten well started in the 1880s. Courtesy Laurence E. Balboni.

The Cooperative Glass Company

In early 1888 when it became apparent that the B&S would never reopen, a group of ten skilled glassmakers pooled their resources and decided to make glass by themselves. They prevailed on George McLaughlin to buy a ten-acre piece of upland in the marsh adjacent to the railroad and not far from the end of State Street. Across the rail line was Brady's Island, then occupied by Hugh Brady and his family, with an access highway over to Franklin Street (Tupper Road). There was a problem with reliance on using this causeway and crossing the railroad to get to the plant site, so the partners built a substantial wooden bridge over Mill Creek from State Street to the plant site. With more confidence than many would have had, the ten stockholders built a small furnace and an annealing oven in a long narrow wooden building on their island. Henry F. Spurr predicted failure. What was clear to him was that the small group working at the new plant, called the CRIB, had no collective management skill, very limited finances and no marketing organization. They did however want strongly to make glass and to stay in Sandwich, so that is what they did. They got some help from James D. Lloyd, the former colorist for the B&S, in both formulas and cash, but depressed Sandwich in 1888 was a poor place to raise capital. Their six-pot furnace was lit May 24 amid high hopes, but reality dogged their work in furnace problems, and in the high costs of sand, fuel, labor and molds. They simply were too small to produce enough output to meet costs let alone repay themselves. Two of the ten gave up and went to work for glass factories elsewhere, and the other eight finally had to suspend operations in early 1891. It had been a most gallant try but they never had a chance. Everyone concerned lost money, especially McLaughlin who had invested and continued to pay taxes on the land until his death. The wooden building was sold to Henry Hoxie in 1911, but before he could remove it a storm flattened it so he too lost.

Cape Cod Glass Works

For his patient research into the tangled subject of successive owners and lessees of this plant, students of Sandwich must be grateful to Ray Barlow. This is a highly condensed summary of the uses made of this building complex.

In 1864 Jarves established the Cape Cod Glass Company with several other shareholders as an existing and profitable operation. However, in these later years (he was seventy-four) he apparently let things slide so that even his greatest supporter, C.C.P. Waterman left the firm in 1866. In 1869 the other shareholders told Waterman that they declined to put more money into the operation and recommended to Jarves that he close it. Jarves did this April 15, 1869 and died on that same day. The glass stocks and ready assets were sold. Jarves' heir (his widow) paid the other shareholders $10,500 and received a clear title to the Sandwich properties, consisting of this plant, plus the old mills and water rights at Spring Hill and at Bournedale. In 1880 the plant was owned by George T. McLaughlin, but all the buildings had been stripped down to bare walls. McLaughlin must have installed a small boiler and engine in the front building, as space here was leased to William H. Schleuter who manufactured decorated wood jewelry boxes from July 1880. To this successful business he added making packing cases and cartons, but needed a better location and moved out of town in December 1881. Following him Edward Swann and Edmund K. Chipman established a private decorating shop here.

In 1882 McLaughlin sold the whole plant to Charles P. W. Spurr who owned an extensive veneer business in Boston. Spurr installed a boiler and steam engine in the 1862/1864 building and moved in the heavy lathes used to shave veneer slices off logs, and operated here from September 1882 to the end of 1892. Spurr also leased unused space to others, the first the Vasa Murrhina Art Glass Company. This was to be the last glass actually made at the plant, between May 1883 and the end of 1884. The glass was not a success and Spurr lost money restoring the furnace, liers, etc. for this short period. In 1887 Spurr installed a new larger forty-five horsepower steam engine for the veneer work and had power to spare for the installation of glass cutting operations. Some B&S decorators worked here temporarily in 1888 finishing current pieces. These teams doubtless worked in the Vasa Murrhina area in the 1858 building where there was power and heat. Although this work was profitable, the B&S finally discharged these craftsmen as the overall process of liquidating the B&S moved along. Spurr then very neatly set up Cape Cod Glass Company (II) employing these same people and had forty glassworkers at the end of 1888. However, the veneer business here and in Boston was his chief interest and in March 1891 C.P.W. Spurr sold the cutting and decorating equipment to Mr. A. V. Johnston and leased him the workspace until Johnston moved to the B&S quarters in May 1892. Spurr found his machinery aging, and rather than modernize in this big empty plant, he concentrated on his Boston operations and the old Cape Cod works fell silent.

The roof was damaged in the great Portland Gale of 1898, but was repaired. The pot house burned down in 1900. In 1911 the great expansion of the veneer business prompted Spurr to repair and reopen here which continued through 1918. Other firms that leased space here while heat and power were available were the Shawme Press in 1915 and the Elberfield Chemical and Manufacturing Company, which packaged cleaners and household products. C. P. W. Spurr died in 1919 and his heir dismantled the buildings in 1921.

Edward J. Swann, 1842-1895

Cutting and decorating glass was continuous from the closing of the B&S into the 1920s, and the work of three specialists will be traced. Swann was a gifted English artist who was brought to the B&S in 1872 as manager of the decorating department. He built a large house at 127 Main Street, at the corner of Tupper Road, in 1880. This house was later owned by Henry A. Belcher who added the stonework and porte-cochere. About 1883 Swann purchased from Schleuter an old house at 104 Tupper Road. Swann also succeeded Schleuter in leasing space at the Cape Cod Glass Co. when he and his fellow artist Edmund K. Chipman of Sandwich formed a small firm called Swann Chipman and Co. They used the old Delano furnace as a kiln here to fire special decorated pieces. One of their customers or agents was William L. Quinnell, formerly of the B&S, now a successful interior decorator in New York. Swann surrounded himself with highly gifted people, beside Chipman including Mary and Emma Gregory, the Chamberlain sisters, Will Foster and Friedman Miller. At the close of the B&S (and the departure of Chipman for New Jersey) Swann built a small decorating shop and an outside kiln in the yard of his house, where he and a few employees worked on china and pottery objects as well as glass. He ordered blanks for use here from the new and struggling CRIB group just across the marsh. In 1890 at the urgent need of many old B&S decorators for work, he leased the B&S decorating rooms from Electrical Glass, and rebuilding the heating kilns, went back into large-scale decorating at the old factory. In 1892 the new B&S owner, A. V. Johnston, needed the decorating space for his lamp business and forced Swann out. Swann died young in 1895, an artist on canvas and other media as well as glass and ceramics. His home remained in the family until the 1960s.

John B. Vodon, 1843-1919

Vodon came to Sandwich in the early 1870s to work in the cutting department of the B&S. He was a Belgian by birth, skilled in glass cutting and engraving, and was married to Clementine Gustin. In his generation, French or Belgian glasscutters named Gustin, Perrote, Burgun, and Vodon all emigrated to the United States and worked at various American glass plants, the four families being interrelated in Europe with their children continuing to intermarry here. For example, Eugene Perrote (1840-1935) came to Sandwich in 1875, worked for the B&S then for Packwood as a glasscutter. His daughter married Lucien Gustin Jr., son of Lucien Gustin and Bertha Burgun of Pittsburgh. Jules Burgun Jr. was among those who tried to revive glassmaking in Sandwich in the 1904/5 period of the B&S III.

The Spring Hill stave mill owned by Jarves and partners from the 1830s was among the assets of the Cape Cod Glass Co. acquired by George T. McLaughlin. Vodon bought the Spring Hill mill and water rights in 1894 and planned a wholly new small shop for cutting and engraving glass blanks. He tore out the old mill and wooden waterwheel, and installed a new building with power from a fifteen inch steel turbine wheel in a sluice connected to the millpond. His three sons worked here with him with one or two other skilled hands. His home was at 200 Main Street and here he kept a sales outlet for fine cut glass as well as selling in Boston. The Wing Family in 1903 for their major family reunion used souvenir table glasses engraved at this shop. The sons scattered and John Vodon closed the shop in 1916. It was rebuilt as a residence and the present owner Tom Ellis has had the Vodon sign recreated.

Nehemiah Packwood Senior and Junior

Nehemiah Senior (1836-1907) came to Sandwich by 1870 from England, with wife and two children. With them came their life-long friend John Jones (1846-1927). Packwood was superintendent of the cutting department of the B&S, and Jones one of the expert workmen. When the B&S furnaces and boiler fires were extinguished, some work was continued at the old Cape Cod plant by B&S cutters. When the B&S was sold to Electrical Glass Co., Packwood, Jones and Eugene Perrote began plans to lease the old cutting rooms.

Packwood installed a new small boiler and twenty-five horsepower engine, not a cheap undertaking. The firm of N. Packwood and Co. went into operation late in 1890. Their cut glass was deeply cut and very brilliant, and found a strong market, using blanks from Pennsylvania. The firm remained at the B&S, leasing space through the successive owners of the old buildings. Their building suffered damage in the Portland Gale of November 1898 but was repaired. In 1900 the firm removed to a separate wood building on the railroad tracks at Willow Street opposite the Cape Cod plant. This had been built in 1880 for the Bay State Tack Co. then taken over by the Sandwich Tack Co. after their fire at the Shawme Pond plant. Nehemiah Junior was also a skilled cutter and took over control of the firm from his father after 1905. This Nehemiah Junior, called MIAH, was an engaging character who never married, but who ran a store and billiard parlor, sold furniture, collected carriages and buggies, ran weekly auctions and was a part owner of the Central House. He stored his carriage collection in the unused old roundhouse, and in 1896 a heavy windstorm shook the old wood trusses of the roof badly so that it collapsed and wrecked the carriage collection. This, sadly, was the end of the roundhouse that had been such a landmark since it was built in 1847. The Central House went to new owners in 1915 and Packwood moved his auction to the cavernous old B&S furnace rooms. In 1916 the Packwood firm became Packwood-Northwood Glass Co. admitting Charles Northwood as a partner. Business in cut glass declined especially after Prohibition, and probably ceased here in 1922 with both Jones and Packwood in ill health. The building was torn down in the 1930s.

CHAPTER 27

A LOOK BACK

The *Sandwich Observer* for January 1, 1901, correctly noted that the year 1900 had been the last of the nineteenth century, and that the Cape was now embarked on the twentieth. Recalling the simple and isolated days of 1800, without railroads or turnpikes, without steam or electricity, the writer called those "the good old times," but felt sure no one would prefer them to the present. In this chapter we will look at Sandwich in what people now refer to as the good old days.

The Railroad Peak

After the Hyannis leg in 1854, the rail line went to Orleans in 1865 where there was a roundhouse. It reached Wellfleet in 1870 and Provincetown in 1873. The critical line down to Woods Hole was built in 1872, and other spurs were a short line to Onset Beach, and a line from Harwich over to Chatham in 1887. The Old Colony system became a part of the New York, New Haven and Hartford in 1893. There were daily trains from Boston and seasonal ones from New York.

Cape Population

The trains were one of the central facts of life in the Cape towns. The peak population of the Cape in 1860 had been at 36,007 persons (up from 19,192 in 1800). There was then an overall decline to 27,826 in 1900, a loss of over 10,000 in eleven towns, while in the other two towns (Falmouth and Provincetown) there had been a gain of over 1,000 each. These were two towns that benefited highly from their rail connections. A gazetteer writer of 1890 remarked of the Cape Cod population that it had retained its original Anglo-Saxon character almost intact, except for two towns, Sandwich and Provincetown.

Rail Changes in Sandwich

The turntable in the Sandwich roundhouse was probably little used, and broke down under the weight of a locomotive in 1877. Thereafter it was filled solid so that the spur simply passed through the building. In 1878 a new trackside station was built in Sandwich, south of the tracks, and the “barny” old terminal depot was torn down. A new freight station was promptly built opposite the passenger station, with car-height loading platform. The East Sandwich station had been north of the County Road (Route 6A), but in 1885 a new station was built south of the road, serving the communities between Spring Hill and

Scorton. The old station became a freight point. In 1889 the highway bridge over the railroad at Old County Road was completed by the railroad at the town's request. The highway grade crossing had been about one-quarter mile west of this point, and must have been found dangerous. The railroad even agreed to regrade Chase Road to join at this point, in return for which the town closed Great Hill Road and eliminated the grade crossing there.

On the Bourne side, a hurricane struck in 1869 and destroyed the rail bridge built in 1847 over Cohasset Narrows, the abutments of which were set on fieldstone foundations. The replacement bridge had granite block abutments and a steel truss structure. Built with a short lift span for vessels to pass into Buttermilk Bay, the lift was little used and was blocked by telegraph, telephone and other wires. Early in the twentieth century the present heavy girder bridge was installed.

A Plymouth/Sandwich railway had been a dream since 1845. So great was the railway-building fever that a route was actually laid out by Charles M. Thompson for this line in 1891, running up the Eel River Valley in Plymouth, down the east shores of the Herring Ponds then over to Old Plymouth Road and down Hunters Brook Road to Sagamore. It was not financed, but some of the route was later followed by the trolley line. The interurban trolley lines proliferated in the 1890s because they were so much cheaper to construct than the railways in weight, grades and corners. The major one built on the Cape was the New Bedford to Monument Beach line completed in 1901.

Keith Car Company

This notable plant in West Sandwich had three distinct stages of operations corresponding to three generations of the family. The first under Isaac Keith made tools, axles, ironware and probably the cars for the B&S wharf line and dump cars for railway use from 1847. In the 1860s, his sons Isaac N. and Hiram got into railway car construction but the plant was small. Under Eben S. S. Keith, a great expansion occurred in the 1890s, with the plant extending over a mile along the tracks between the rail line and Scusset Creek. The company was ultimately dominated by Pullman-Standard and national railway interests, and assigned the minor role of building and repairing wooden-body railcars. The employment here of many Sandwich people after the B&S closed was an important benefit for Sandwich.

Town Roads

There was a rapid process of grading and accepting town roads in the 1870s and 1880s, during which much of the neighborhood and intervillage road pattern, familiar now, came into existence. A writer in 1871 chided the town for not being modern enough to have easy access to Town Beach and around the major ponds. The road he said across Town Neck to the beach was the worst east of the Rocky Mountains. In 1875 the town did authorize both the Boardwalk to be built and also a town road on Town Neck alongside the ancient cow pasture area still controlled by its Proprietors' Company. In 1883 two surprising projects were considered, a causeway and bridge over Mill Creek from near State Street to Town Neck, and another causeway and bridge from near the Academy on Water Street across the millpond to the Tack Factory and around to Grove Street. Both these ambitious projects died. A town causeway and road was built from Tupper Road over to Brady's Island.

BOARDWALK TO TOWN NECK BEACH—The boardwalk was built by Gus Howland in 1875 for $500. It has been damaged by ice and other vicissitudes but is always promptly rebuilt. It is about 1350 feet long. Sandwich Historical Commission.

Mills and Farms

The Sandwich Savings Bank failed in 1874 due to the depression of that time, but still paid 80 cents on the dollar of its deposits. The town had placed its money here in 1869 and presumably lost with the others. The Sandwich Cooperative Bank was formed in 1885 and remains active today. Many small manufacturing companies were formed without much capital, and if successful moved elsewhere or otherwise folded. The Boston and Sandwich Boot and Shoe Company built a two-story building on the millstream opposite Town Hall in 1881 and employed twenty workers making fifty pairs of shoes a day. It was succeeded by the Armstrong Braiding Co. which removed to Attleboro. The brothers Levi and William L. Nye started the Sandwich Card and Tag Co. in 1879 at the Shawme milldam. The Samuel Wing cotton and woolen yarn factory at the upper milldam closed but was succeeded by the Wing and Rogers tack factory in the same area. This was taken over and enlarged by the Sandwich Tack Factory owned by Jones and Heald. The Bay State Tack Company started a new plant on the railroad at Willow Street in 1880, which was bought out by Jones and Heald when their plant was wrecked by fire. The Grove Street area became the site of the Union Braiding Company plant, the approach road to which still bears the name. Fish weirs worked in the Bay in certain seasons, with the catch salted and sent to Boston. Many of these manufacturers or owners had been to sea and accumulated a stake, or worked in a mill in a nearby city, then returned to Sandwich to buy a store, start a business or run a farm. A large number of farms were still active, and those with suitable land in these last decades of the century were going over to cranberries. This required considerable investment to prepare the flat area, the drainage ditches, the water supply and controls, and get the crop started, but once operating were usually profitable, and output increased rapidly to become one of Sandwich's money-makers. Isaiah Tobey Jones, the tack maker and selectman, was a leading figure in cranberry growing and was secretary and treasurer of the Cape Cod Cranberry Growers' Association founded in 1888.

SANDWICH ACADEMY–An early view of the new Academy on the hill with split shingles, steam heat and indoor toilets. Courtesy of Mrs. Freeman E. Crosby.

Town Buildings and Services

Town Hall downstairs remained occupied with such activities as a lumber room, furniture shop, store and newspaper plant as well as the town office. In 1871 new seats were bought and in 1880 "more seating", which refers to the balcony at the back of the room. The Town voted to start a Library in 1891 with the first room in the old Seth Nye law office. This soon moved to a room in Town Hall and its collections were enhanced by fund-raising efforts by citizens and distinguished visitors, including Joseph Jefferson, F. Edwin Elwell, Henry T. Wing, Arabella Eldred and Henry A. Belcher. A Fire Department was organized in 1869 and Fire Engineers voted in 1871, but these were for forest fires. The town voted that no one owning woodlots could be paid for fighting fires. The forest fire equipment bought was no match for the immense fires that burned the cutover woodlands in 1882 and 1887. For house fires, the town owned the ladder cart and buckets. In 1892, the town finally purchased a No. 4 Howe Chemical and Water Engine. The B&S had stopped supplying gas for street lights, so the new town street lamps of 1882 burned kerosene. New platform scales were installed near the Town Hall in 1887.

JARVESVILLE SCHOOL–Jarvesville had many children of school age. This is the two-room schoolhouse near Georges Rock Road which was replaced in 1885 by the present Clark-Haddad building on the same site. Sandwich Archives gift of Ella F. Hoxie.

The first mention of a Town Water Works appears in 1888 and in 1893, a town snow plough. The town's first set of By-Laws was adopted March 1, 1897 and published as a booklet of eight pages. Beside town finances and controls, the new regulations appear to be health-oriented in keeping filth off the streets and sidewalks, controlling dumping and regulating swimming without suitable clothing. As population declined, especially in the countryside, rural schools were combined such as Farmersville and Wakeby, or two schools relocated to serve three areas. A wholly new Jarvesville school building was built in 1885, now the Clark-Haddad building. The old Sandwich Academy was quite inadequate as a public high school, so in 1881 the academy trustees sold the Maine lands (eighteen square miles) and built the new Academy on the hill above Grove Street. It was an angular building on the bare hilltop, but it had steam heat and indoor toilets, and was much appreciated by the scholars. It was leased to the town. Reverend Burr's old Academy building was dismantled and a two-story rooming house built on the same foundation, called the Lake House. Showing typical Cape Cod economy, the school floors with the marks of the desks were relaid in the rooming house.

SCHOOL STREET SCHOOL This was the school building for District Five covering Sandwich village from the millstream to Spring Hill, excluding Jarvesville, with some 192 pupils. It was built by the local parents about 1855 replacing a smaller building on Main Street near the Methodist Church. After 1862 the town took over school operations and enlarged this building to provide grammar school (upper grade) instruction for pupils from all over the town. It was only torn down after the erection of the H. T. Wing School. Sandwich Archives, gift of Talbot Pierce.

The Unitarian Church

The church building on Main and River Streets was raised up by ten feet in 1871, allowing the installation of a steam boiler, a parlor, kitchen and large vestry room. So far no photograph has been found showing the church in the original low position. The aged two-faced clock given by Titus Winchester was still going in the tower. One memorable Sunday night in 1873, some control snapped and the clock struck off 406 bongs of the big bell before running down.

A new works was clearly needed, and the town's benefactor Jonathan Bourne of New Bedford stepped in with an offer of a new four-faced clock. A larger spire was constructed and the clock installed in 1880. The hostility between this congregation and the Calvinistic Congregational Church group, that had continued since 1808, broke forth in 1874 in a series of newspaper articles by the current ministers, Mr. Oxnard and Mr. Mulligan. Frederick Freeman and another observer contributed articles under pseudonyms, Veritas and Justicia. Their arguments now seem complex, bitter, pointless and unreadable, but were gathered together and published in a 35-page booklet by the Seaside Press. It must have been a relief to many younger persons in the two congregations when peace was established in the 1880s. The 250th anniversary of the founding of the First Parish was celebrated here on September 18 and 19, 1888.

The National Centennial

The year 1876 was celebrated by a giant exposition in Philadelphia showing the nation's progress in science and manufacturing. The B&S display was said to be breathtaking, and Edward Swann won a prize for two immense decorated glass vases. A congressional resolution urged each city and town to celebrate, and to send to the Library of Congress two copies of the address or historical paper prepared for the event.

Sandwich staged a great parade July 4, 1876, and at a public meeting that evening the selectmen called upon Frederick Freeman who promised to give two sets of his *History of Cape Cod* in answer to the resolution. Charles Dillingham, a selectman, then moved that the town prepare a memorial box of historical material, including "articles illustrative of the history and progress of the town to the present time, the same to be closed up, to be opened only after the passage of another century on the Fourth of July 1976." The committee named to fill the box was Charles Dillingham, H.G.O. Ellis the town clerk, and C.C.P. Waterman, the venerable associate of Jarves, writer and prohibitionist. This meeting and vote, although not a formal town meeting, were entered into the Town Meeting Records by Ellis with the curious marginal note "In consequence of some misunderstanding the copies of the History... from Mr. Freeman were not received; what was received will appear when the Box is opened." A notice appeared in the *Seaside Press* March 10, 1877 saying the box was about to be closed and that persons were urged to contribute something. It wasn't finally closed until August: a tin box soldered up and placed in a fitted wood box with a metal plaque saying it was to be opened July 4, 1976.

The story of opening the Box on that date will be told in due course, but we summarize what those three elderly men did put in the Box: a letter to the selectmen or mayor in 1976; an 1849 hymn book; a geography book; 1874 and 1876 Town Reports; Walling's 1857 property map; an 1876 voters' list; a railroad poster; photos of the 1876 parade, of C.C.P. Waterman and of the town from Academy Hill; a poem by D. F. Chessman; a family description by Isaac K. Chipman; an article about Pocasset by Ebenezer B. Nye; a booklet of quotations by Dr. Russell; articles by Waterman about lightning striking a barn with a bag of fused sand and nails from the site, also articles about glass and local events; and finally over 100 newspapers (of no Sandwich interest).

In sum, it was an old men's Box. There was nothing from a woman, nothing from a child, nothing from a teacher or a minister, no objects of clothing, no toy, no glass, no sewing work, no handicraft. It was a man's world, and they knew best.

VIEW FROM POPES HILL 1875 This splendid view of the town was taken in 1875 from what was then called Pope's Hill, later Academy Hill. The Unitarian Church still has the two-faced Winchester clock and the original short tower and spire. On the horizon from left to right are the stacks of the Cape Cod Works, the tower of St. Peters Church, the two stacks of the upper glass house (smoking) the two stacks on the B&S powerhouse, then the two stacks of the lower glass house. Courtesy of Sandwich Historical

The Casino

Sandwich needed a larger meeting place than the Town Hall, in which events of more than local interest could be held with a large audience, such as those of the Barnstable County Choral Union, and travelling theatrical companies. A group was formed to raise stock in such a building, including Samuel Fessenden, president, B. E. White, Secretary, William E. Boyden, Treasurer, all of Sandwich; four Boston men and Mr. A. M. Bearse of the Chatham Skating Rink Co. These stockholders engaged a Boston architect ,George M. Harding, and hired D. W. Edwards of Chatham to erect the building. The site was on School Street next to the town school, and construction began in

May 1884. The building was 130 feet by 50 feet with portico, two ante-rooms, a large gallery, toilets, a raised bandstand on the right, raised rows of seats along the walls, with a railing to separate the seats from the main floor when used for roller skating or dances. The clear 50-foot width was spanned by long wood trusses shipped down from Maine. Lighting was by gas jets in large chandeliers, plus stage footlights, and wall lights, with reflectors. The gas was produced on the spot from "gasoline" using the "Tirrell equalizing gas machine." The grand opening was Thursday, August 7, 1884. The afternoon and early evening featured roller skating by the public with shows by Miss Carrie Gilmore of Boston, "one of the finest lady skaters in the country" and music by the Sandwich Brass Band. In the evening the hall was decorated with colored lanterns and flags, and in spite of heavy rain a large crowd danced to the music of the Metropolitan Band of Boston from 9:45 P.M. to 2 A.M. It was claimed to be the largest gathering under one roof in town history, but the banquet to open the railroad service in the old depot had seated 1200.

The Town's 250th Anniversary

Planning began for the celebration in April 1887 (near the 250th birthday of settlement) but the big day was to be September 3, 1889, the anniversary of first acceptance of Sandwich Deputies to Plymouth Court. The town appointed a committee of forty, and Bourne a committee of thirty. Sandwich voters approved $600 for the event, which was forty cents per $1,000 valuation for the benefit of those who weren't enthused. The committees obtained funds from many friends, $100 each from several of the well-to-do. Mr. Isaiah T. Jones was general chairman, Dr. John Pratt secretary, Charles Dillingham president-for-the-day and William A. Nye of Bournedale grand marshal of the parade. As of July 26, the Orator had not been chosen, so Rev. Chamberlain did not have long to prepare his discourse. Also, Ambrose E. Pratt, a Sandwich newspaperman *(Observer),* was not told until October 5th that he was desired to produce a memorial volume of the event, so he had to write to all the speakers and chairmen for copies of their texts and programs, and his book although substantial, was delayed and incomplete.

The day, a Tuesday, was fine. Bells were rung at sunrise, and the decorations were completed on the streets and buildings along the parade route. There were three special trains that morning from Woods Hole, New Bedford and Boston, plus extra cars on the regular trains from Boston and Provincetown. There were bands from New Bedford, Middleboro, Plymouth (the Plymouth Rock Band), Sagamore and Bourne, as well as members of many GAR veterans' units and Masonic Lodges from the region. The town had never seen so many people in the village area. The parade began at 10 A.M. and moved out in four separate divisions to allow clearance on the two roads where countermarches were needed. The route was from the station up Jarves Street to Main, west to Uplands, counter to Grove Street, up to 24 (Cape of Ezra T. Pope) counter to Water St., then along School, Main, Liberty, Factory, Freeman, Canary, State, Church, Jarves, Main and left to School Street and the Casino, where, at 1:30 P.M., Reverend N. H. Chamberlain gave a very long oration on the history of the town with many notes on homes, social life, religion and the Cape area. While the speech went on, the bands played at various points in town and there was a ballgame. New Bedford beat the locals 6 to 3.

A clambake was then served in a huge tent behind the Casino, measuring 260 by 80 feet containing 14 long tables and seating 2,000. After dinner, a chorus of 50, accompanied by one of the bands performed the Gloria from Mozart's 12th Mass. The toastmaster was Frank H. Pope of Leominster, a witty and irreverent speaker, who teased the town for calling the millpond "Shawme Lake", and the dignified Judge Whittemore for running a judicial laundry to the tune of $10 and costs. There were toasts to New England towns, to non-resident friends, to ancestors, to soldiers, and to Sandwich First Parish, as represented by Charles E. Pope, the bell-ringer for 50 years.

1889 PARADE MARSHALS-The parade of 1889 at the town's 250th anniversary was the largest ever held here. These eight mounted marshals are looking down Jarves Street where the parade units formed up. In the background is the Benjamin Bartley store and upstairs Hum's Hall where the Charles Chipman Post 132 of the Grand Army of the Republic met. Courtesy of Sandwich Historical Society.

The parade of forty boats and barges festooned with oriental lanterns was cheered by thousands along the shore, and seems to have been the first such display held at Sandwich. It was organized by F. Edwin Elwell, the sculptor and summer resident, who based it on a Venetian boat carnival which he had witnessed.

The fireworks display was given from a raft and the shore area on Tobey's Point (now Peter Cook's, south of the Hoxie House area). This was long and elaborate with twenty-nine different set scenes, such as a giant Indian with bow and arrows, a huge sphere and eagle, a thirty-five foot column with wreath and spears, each set out in fire and color.

The last event was a ball at the Casino, which was freshly decorated with pastel muslin and fitted with the brilliant arc lights from the Lockwood Dredge. This was reported to be the first such event on the Cape held with electric lights. The Germania Band of ten pieces from Boston played for about one hundred couples, including many in military or full evening dress, with many more as spectators. Sandwich's anniversary party was given a great deal of publicity for its thorough planning and excellent effects, especially the three evening events. The Police didn't make a single arrest and the only people who complained were the Plymouth guests who had to come eighteen miles in carriages and said Sandwich hadn't fixed the road since 1637.

Storms of 1896 and 1898

Cape Cod was always a stormy place. We have mentioned the northeaster of January 1, 1896, which had intense gusty winds and heavy rain, causing the collapse of the Sandwich roundhouse. On August 19, 1896, one of those ultimate thunderstorms of tornado intensity visited this area. Instead of a twister on land, this one produced three separate waterspouts in Vineyard Sound, between Woods Hole and Oak Bluffs. The black cloud from which the successive twisters reached down was isolated with even some sunlight around, creating a remarkable effect. Even old sea captains admitted they had never seen such a sight. On shore in Bourne and Sandwich the same system produced a violent hailstorm which wrecked crops and smashed windows. Curiously there was no loss of life from this storm.

The northeaster with which all later storms are compared began Saturday November 26, 1898 with snow (all rain at Chatham). The wind from the northeast became higher and higher, reaching gusts up to 100 miles per hour. There was a full moon at this time with maximum tides, and the worst wind came at high tide between 10 and 11 Sunday morning, when terrible surges of high water came ashore, smashing everything in their path. At least 200 sailing vessels from Maine to Martha's Vineyard were wrecked, even those anchored in harbor or at docks. The loss of life from ships foundering at sea or run ashore was very great. The storm soon took the name of the largest ship to founder, the paddle-wheeler *Portland,* which went down off Truro with a crew of 68 and 108 passengers.

No lives were lost on shore although chimneys fell, trees blew over, buildings left their foundation, livestock drowned and surging sea water flooded all low-lying areas. The worst damage was to the railroad line where it hugged the north shore, and to the adjacent poles that carried the telegraph wires. There were five points where the rail line was impassable, a 1,000-foot section lost at Pamet in Truro, about 300 feet at West Barnstable near the brickyard, the section in Sandwich from Dewey Ave. to Liberty Street, the section over Shawme Marsh from Jarvesville to Town Neck, and a section along Scusset Marsh between

Town Neck and Sagamore. In all these sections the sea water came up to or over rail level, softening the ground and allowing the high waves at the peak flood to push the whole track and ties sideways off the embankments. In the words of a witness in Boyden's Block on Main Street, even the inner Town marsh was "one seething foaming sheet of sea."

STORM DAMAGE 1898 NEAR DEWEY AVENUE- This view is looking east on the rail line from near Liberty Street. Here the 1898 storm pushed flood waters over the tracks breaking railway service for several days. Courtesy of Rosanna Cullity.

Railway Repairs

Two trains stood at Hyannis on Sunday. The main train at Provincetown was unable to leave because of the break at Truro. The agent at Hyannis got the break at West Barnstable repaired, so that a train from Hyannis could get as far as the Dewey Avenue crossing. Large work crews were sent down from Boston for the Sandwich breaks on Monday and Tuesday, while passengers and mail had to be brought by carriages and wagons from Sagamore to the train east of the Sandwich station. A train got through on Wednesday but more work was needed east of Sandwich station; train service as far as Wellfleet resumed on Thursday. On that day a sad group of relatives and friends from Maine journeyed to Eastham where the bodies of the unidentified *Portland* victims had been accumulated. All but one was claimed. On Saturday the first freight trains ran again bringing needed supplies of coal and food.

In Sandwich the damages were heavy. Parts of the roof of the Cape Cod Glass Works and of the B&S at the cutting shop area were torn off. Also unroofed were the left portion of the Central House and part of Dr. Russell's house (10 Grove Street), and there were damages to Norton's cottage (7 Water Street), Dr. Robert's house (19 Water Street), and Higgins' house (8 River Street).

The latter house, with the occupants forced to the second floor, had been shifted on its foundation, cracking the chimneys and fireplaces. A gust of wind had caved in several windows in the Unitarian Church, with the unexpected result that the front doors were blown off their hinges and across the street. St. Peters brick church in Jarvesville was wrenched and the brick walls cracked, so that within a year it had to be condemned and was torn down. The Congregational church spire had rocked so badly that old Mrs. Chapouil in the Dunbar House had been evacuated, expecting the spire would fall that way. However it stood, but badly out of plumb. The only happy story told of this tremendous storm is that of a drunk who had been put in the lockup on River Street on Saturday night. By Sunday morning a boat was needed to get to the door. He might soon have drowned miserably, but was pulled out sober and thankful.

Notable People

A new history was published in 1890, Simeon L. Deyo's *History of Barnstable County, Massachusetts,* which stood the test of time and is well worth consulting. Deyo, the editor, relied on local experts for town histories and articles on specific subjects. His experts on Sandwich and Bourne were Rev. N. H. Chamberlain, Calvin Burgess, Judge E. S. Whittemore and Charles Dillingham. We present below some brief comments on certain Sandwich people who were well-known locally at the end of the nineteenth century.

Frank H. Burgess, 1843-1914 - Frank ran a general store on Jarves Street with his father Charles H. Burgess, inheriting it in 1880. He tried his hand at many other things, among them undertaker, job printer, newspaper editor (the *Weekly Register),* selectman, town clerk and town treasurer. He married a remarkable woman, Arabella Eldred, whom we will refer to again in the chapter on Thornton Burgess. They were divorced, and Frank brought up one of their adopted daughters.

Stephen Skiff Chipman, 1834-1903 - Descendant of Elder John Chipman and of James Skiff; Stephen was a retired captain, and farmer.

William C. Chipman, 1822-1900 and Isaac K. Chipman, 1826-1901 - These brothers were carpenters who ran wood-working mills in Spring Hill and Sandwich. Both were active in town affairs. Isaac's son was Edmund K., the glass decorator, and his daughter, Carrie Boyden, was a town favorite. William's son was Herbert L., the longtime newspaperman *(Independent).*

Charles Dillingham, 1821-1902 - State senator, representative, longtime selectman and school superintendent. Dillingham was a great town asset and expert on early houses and families. His son died young and this ancient name then became extinct in Sandwich. We regret that so little of his knowledge seems to have been preserved.

Edward Wing Ewer, 1818-1888 - Edward was a politician, judge and county commissioner. He married Elizabeth Gifford, a clerk of the Sandwich Quaker Meeting and their daughter, Annie Elizabeth Rose 1867-1972, became the last member of the Sandwich monthly meeting of the original lines.

John H. Foster, 1853-1935 - Born in the "Skiff House" in Spring Hill, this adventurer went to Amsterdam with a diamond buyer, and with a flair for social life founded a series of dancing schools in European capitals which became fashionable and profitable. He built an eclectic mansion on a hilltop at Spring Hill, called Masthead, where he entertained Grover Cleveland and many others.

Frederick Freeman, 1799-1883 - The closing years of Reverend Freeman's life were marked by pain and suffering. He was sued for debt in 1866 in an amount of $1,000, probably arising from his publishing the *History of Cape Cod.* Immediately after this he in turn sued the town of Sandwich for $10,000, an amount reduced to $1,000 in 1867. The suit claimed he had been injured due to bad conditions of the road between his home and West Sandwich "causing him great bodily pain and distress and unfitting him for his business and occupation." This suit was settled in 1868 for $200. The town report for 1883 did not carry any obituary notice on the passing of Reverend Freeman, one of its most distinguished citizens.

Charles B. Hal, 1830-1881- Popular and generous, he was druggist, postmaster, notary public, pension agent, insurance representative, band director and moderator at town meetings.

David Nye Holway, 1839-1902 - Distinguished Quaker teacher, a life insurance agent, became president of Boston Underwriters Association.

Gustavus Howland, 1822-1905 - Son of the Ellis Howland who built Town Hall, Gustavus was a lumber dealer and builder, specializing in moving buildings; he built the Sandwich Boardwalk in 1875.

Joseph Hoxie, 1798-1889 - Kept a shoe shop on Old County Road near the Nye Mill; postmaster, selectman, school committeeman, Quaker. He served in the State Legislature. A notable saver of letters and documents, his descendants presented a wide collection to the Sandwich Historical Society.

Dr. Jonathan Leonard, Jr. 1805-1882 - Son and successor of the first Dr. Jonathan Leonard, he was the town physician for many years. Late in life he married Mary (Waterman), the widow of John W. Jarves, and had a son Jonathan who became a teacher and writer.

William L. Nye, 1840-1936 and Levi S. Nye 1842-1914 - These brothers gained experience in the card and tag business and opened successful shops and factories in Sandwich; active in town affairs.

Ezra Tobey Pope, 1825-1907 - Longtime deputy sheriff of the county and a representative in the legislature, he was chosen as messenger and sergeant-at-arms in the State House.

Noble Parker Swift, 1830-1911- Although a native of West Sandwich, this eldest of the Swift brothers was familiar in Sandwich village where he once owned a store and came frequently selling meat and produce. An astute businessman, he nevertheless stayed in Sagamore on the farm all his life. On the death of Russell E. Tupper in 1904, Noble bought the ancient Tupper house in Sandwich, and rented it to families working at Keith Car Company. Generous and eccentric, many stories are told of Noble Swift. It was his brother Gustavus F. Swift who established the meat-packing firm in Chicago.

Asa Shove Wing, 1850-1931 - Asa was brought up in the old Foster House on Grove Street which had been part of the two-house Wing compound for generations. He was son of tack maker Stephen R. Wing and grandson of Samuel Wing of the cotton mill and furniture shop. Asa was president of Provident Mutual Life Insurance Co. in Philadelphia but came here summers and in fact died in the family house.

Henry Thomas Wing, 1842-1924 - His father, Henry Wing, was born on the early Wing farm on Route 6A in Scorton, but through marriages to daughters of Thomas Tobey of Quail Hollow, relocated there, so that the extensive lands along both millponds were inherited by his son. Henry T. Wing became a well-known and respected lawyer in the Admiralty Courts in Brooklyn and Manhattan.

Rebecca Chipman Hoxie, 1805-1865 - Not all the notable people were men. Rebecca Chipman was brought up as a Unitarian and was a teacher at the Sandwich Academy. While a student she drew a huge map of Massachusetts with town outlines and much information. This is still to be seen at the Historical Society. As a teacher she was renowned for her knowledge and ability to master new subjects. A large rock was uncovered on the almshouse farm with what appeared to be runic lettering. She made a tracing and had Reverend Goodwin take it to Harvard for study. Alas, we do not have their answer and now even the tracing cannot be found. The rock was broken up for a wall. Rebecca was attracted to Newell Hoxie, a Quaker teacher and minister, and for him became a member of the Society of Friends. They were married and had one daughter who survived, Susan F. Hoxie 1847-1921. Rebecca and Newell visited Quaker sites in England. She was a gifted sketcher and preserved the outline of the Academy and other scenes. She remained curious and questing all her life—someone found some corn kernels put away for 65 years and she had Newell sow them carefully so that she could study their growth.

Georgianna Verona Houghton Freeman, 1853-1937 - This lady was brought up in the last Freeman family living in the Ploughed Neck area, originally settled by Edmund Freeman, Jr. Her house itself is a curiosity, composed of two half-Capes joined together, but of different heights and roof pitch, so that the juncture presents an odd fit and the floors are six inches different. A diary of hers for the year 1888 has survived. She was the youngest child and was taking care of her parents. She mentions putting out the fires at the Glass Factory and describes the Blizzard of 1888. This started as rain in Sandwich, turning to snow, but the accumulation here was not great. She talks of neighborhood and family events, the sadness of giving up the horse and cows after her father died, and her work on the house and garden. In 1891 she married Daniel Lovell of Barnstable but they had no children and he died soon. She had an oil painting of herself done, and lived on in the beloved house all her long life. In her will she asked her heirs to keep her painting on the wall of this house always, and this unique provision has been continued in subsequent deeds to the property. We hope this will always be honored.

Phebe Hoxie Allen Hoxie Fuller, 1792-1880 and *Martha Hoxie, 1818-1899* - Another unique house in East Sandwich is that architect's delight, the bow-roof quarter house at Route 6A and Quaker Meetinghouse Road. Its original builder and exact age are unknown. About 1850 it was bought by Nathaniel C. Hoxie for his mother to live in, since her third husband, Joseph Fuller (1758-1846) had died. Since Joseph was a Revolutionary War veteran, we believe Phebe was the last recipient of a Revolutionary widow's pension in Sandwich. Phebe had four children by Samuel Allen, then four more by Peleg Hoxie, and then a daughter, Sarah C. Hoxie, born in 1831 to Peleg and Phebe in Sandwich Vital Records. However, Peleg died in 1827 according to the same records. Martha Hoxie, unmarried and a distant cousin of Phebe's, had sold a large piece of property and wanted a place to live. In 1868 Nathaniel, the son of Phebe, sold Martha a tiny ell and wing attached to the bow-roof house, and *leased* it to Martha at twenty-five cents a year. The land on which this building stood was about sixteen by forty feet. The two women then dwelt there together for the rest of their lives. Many stories were told of these eccentrics, Aunt Phebe and Aunt Martha, such as that Martha took the train to Boston to attend a Boston and Albany shareholders' meeting. There were so many shops to visit she didn't go to the meeting, and it developed she had never left the South Station. Both ladies kept their money in cash, but somehow nobody robbed them.

Important Newcomers - We regret we have not space to do more than mention some of the arrivals to Sandwich who contributed greatly to the life of the town in the late nineteenth century. In addition to those mentioned elsewhere, they include:

*Ambrose E. Pratt, 1*860-1942 - A newspaperman, insurance agent; married Ida Whittemore and occupied 138 Main Street, the Melatiah Bourne house.

Dr. John E. Pratt, 1850-1935 - Uncle of Ambrose, kept a drug store on Jarves Street.

Fletcher Clark, 1853-1944 - Businessman, treasurer of the Cooperative Bank, became a large property owner.

Edward C. Clark, 1869-1949 - One of the Freeman kindred who lived at the Freeman Farm year round and entertained many.

Rev. Dr. Hiram Carleton, 1811-1893 - Retired Episcopal minister, occupied the Wing farm on Route 6A in Scorton which burned in 1900. Later houses on the property are still in the family.

Rev. Bernard L. Paine, 1834-1894 - Methodist minister in Sandwich in 1856 who married a Blossom daughter owning the Wing colonial at Sandy Neck Road. He prepared a detailed map and family history of all the houses on Scorton Neck which has been of great value.

Charles H. Macy, 1844-1922 - Born in Nantucket, became a whaler, later lived in China and Japan as a purchasing agent for a curio importer. He married a Wing daughter on Scorton Neck. Much of his Orientalia was dissipated, but his collection of Indian arrowheads and certain Japanese items are at the Sandwich Library.

Sanford I. Morse, 1854-1929 - Storekeeper and businessman, owned the Stutson house at 7 Jarves Street.

Hiram H. Heald, 1828-1913 - Tack manufacturer with I. T. Jones, built the house at 15 Water Street, was a skilled musician.

The Good Old Days

The decades just before 1900 were a period of relative peace and prosperity when the railroad was at its peak, travel to resorts at the mountains or the sea or back to the old home town was popular and many later problems of cities and factories had not become perplexing. In spite of declining population, Sandwich seemed a happy and active place with much entertainment. There were two drama societies, two weekly newspapers, a choral society, two bands and two baseball clubs; sleigh racing on Jarves Street from Main Street to the tracks after a good snow; roller skating at the Casino; Camp Meetings at Onset, Martha's Vineyard, Yarmouth and down Cape; the Barnstable Fair; visits by touring theatrical troupes, circuses, lecturers and minstrel shows, local school programs that were full of life; a giant annual clambake at Cohasset Narrows; church teas and picnics, plus clubs, the Veterans Post with ladies auxiliary, and fraternal orders; the East Sandwich Grange was founded in 1887 for forty farm families. Here are a few incidents of the period.

Who Shot Isaiah T. Wright?

This Wright lived in East Sandwich near the houses of his brother Zenas and his father-in-law John Holway. One Saturday night the three talked at length at Zenas' house, after which Isaiah left to walk home. A shot was heard and Isaiah was found dying. Despite intense investigation, no solution was ever found. This occurred in 1863.

The Great Lightning Strike

On an August evening in 1874, two separate thunder heads were seen from Sandwich to merge over West Sandwich, and to produce an extraordinary display of lightning which looked like a standing column of fire, seen by many and described in the newspapers. It struck the barn of Nathan Nye just beyond the Willow Dam, and the barn exploded in flames. Later, in one corner, a vitreous mass of sand was found fused by a tremendous current. This object was broken up and a piece sent to Harvard for study, another put on display at the nearby grade school. Two aged granddaughters of Nathan Nye insisted all their lives that this was a meteorite.

President Grant in Sandwich

On August 29, 1874 President Grant took advantage of the newly expanded rail services here and stopped in Sandwich for 20 minutes on his grand tour of the Cape. He spoke briefly and shook hands with officials, and a great crowd was deeply satisfied.

1888 BASEBALL TEAM-The champions of southeastern Massachusetts in 1888 were front row left to right: Eugene Haines, Augustus R. Pope, Charles Chamberlain, Jimmy McGann; back row Ezra T. Pope Jr., Junie Dalton, Ed Kenney, Henry Dalton, George McNamee; Manager Ezra Hamlin. Ezra Pope became a professional player for Spokane in the Pacific Coast League. Photo courtesy of Eunice Dickinson and her sister Mrs. Annie Williamson, nieces of the Ezra and Gus Pope shown.

Professor Robinson's Telephone

The local writer George Burbank quotes this memorable incident but does not cite his source and we have not been able to verify it. The item reads: "1878—On this date April 11, there came to Sandwich a Professor Robinson to lecture on the telephone. A wire was strung from the Congregational Church to the Town Hall, and music played in the church was heard in the Hall. The Professor explained in detail, and offered stock at ten cents per share. Nor one single share was purchased. People were mystified. Whether this strange apparition was ventriloquism, legerdemain or hypnotism, they knew not." It was about this time that Alexander Graham Bell was doing his research on trying to aid the deaf, and visited the deaf-mutes at Chilmark. There were several deaf-mutes in Sandwich, but this Professor Robinson would seem only to be selling stock.

J.C.C. ELLIS BLACKSMITH SHOP-The shop of John Cleveland Cook Ellis was located opposite Town Hall. Courtesy of Rosanna Cullity.

The Freeman Murder

In May 1879 one Charles F. Freeman was living in Pocasset with his wife and two children. He was from the Eastham branch and not closely related to others here. He was a religious fanatic in a small group who believed that the Lord required a sacrifice of him. He accordingly killed his daughter Edith, not yet five, sure that she would be translated alive into Heaven. After eight years in a mental hospital he was released and with his wife moved to the Midwest.

"Cape Cod Folks"

Sally Pratt McLean was a 23-year-old schoolteacher from Connecticut who came to teach at the Cedarville village school in 1878. This Cedarville is in South Plymouth near the Bourne line. She stayed five months and went back home where she wrote a novel based on her life in Cedarville. This was published in 1881 as *Cape Cod Folks* and sold well. To the publisher's amazement a series of lawsuits were made against him because Sally had used the real names of people in the village. The first suit for $10,000 was settled at $1,095 and the publisher then awarded all the people named sums from $150 down to 50 cents.

The book went through many editions, with the characters renamed. It was made into a play in 1902 and into a movie, *Her Man,* in the 1920s. In his book, *Pilgrim Republic,* the Plymouth historian John A. Goodwin called the book "that consummate piece of journalistic impertinence."

Dewey Square and Manila Park

The events of the Spanish American War were received with great excitement and patriotism. On July 4, 1898 the park in front of the glass factory was the scene of a reception and speeches, and the park was formally proclaimed as Manila Park. The band and crowd moved to the road crossings in front of Town Hall, and this corner was dedicated anew as Dewey Square.

CHAPTER 28

BELMONT'S CANAL

The division line of 1884 between Sandwich and Bourne crossed the canal valley on the causeway between the Freeman Farm and Sagamore Hill, leaving about one mile of the canal in Sandwich and the rest in Bourne. For the sequence of events in planning, construction, and operation of the early canal we are particularly indebted to William J. Reid's dissertation *The Building of the Cape Cod Canal* and to Robert H. Farson's *The Cape Cod Canal.*

August Belmont 1853-1924

Without Belmont's dedication and resources the canal would not have been built when it was, and in view of the reluctance of the Congress to purchase the existing canal in the 1920s, it is possible that the canal would still not be built. Belmont himself said that his initial interest in the project arose from two sources, the chance to save lives and ships in the route outside the Cape, and the fact that his Perry ancestors came from Cape Cod. Belmont was an extraordinary example of the constructive use of great wealth. While at Harvard (1874) he introduced the spiked running shoe. He founded the American Kennel Club, aided in the defense of the America's Cup, built Belmont Park, was a horse breeder and active Democrat. He became head of August Belmont and Company on the death of his famous father in 1890. He helped in building the first segment of the Interborough Rapid Transit (IRT) in New York City, and helped to float a major sale of government bonds in 1895. He was a director of the Metropolitan Opera and of the Metropolitan Museum of Art. His descent in the Perry line was:

Edward Perry (ca. 1630-1694/5) - Married Mary Freeman, probably daughter of Edmund Freeman, founder of Sandwich.

Benjamin Perry (1677-1748) - Married Susannah Barber, 1727.

Judge Freeman Perry (1733-1813) - Married Mercy Hazard, 1755.

Capt. Christopher Raymond Perry (1760-1818) - Married Sarah Wallace Alexander, 1784.

Commodore Matthew Calbraith Perry (1794-1858) - Married Jane Slidell.

Caroline Slidell Perry - Married August Belmont Senior (1813-1890), 1849

August Belmont Junior (1853-1924) - Married Bessie Hamilton Morgan, 1881 and second Eleanor Robson (1879-1979), 1910.

Two errors are sometimes made concerning August Jr. His name was not August Perry Belmont, although he had an older brother named Perry Belmont and another brother named Oliver Hazard Perry Belmont. Also, since the descendants of Ezra Perry were more numerous than those of his brother Edward, and were especially numerous in the Monument area, the Ezra Perrys were called the ancestors of Belmont rather than those of the East Sandwich Quaker family.

The Boston Cape Cod and New York Canal Co.

An investor named DeWitt Clinton Flanagan obtained a canal charter in 1899, calling for a canal of 25 feet in depth, 100 feet width at the bottom, and 200 feet at the surface. Flanagan (who was named for the sponsor of the Erie Canal, a friend of his grandfather) paid a $200,000 deposit and looked for a financier. Flanagan prepared initial rough plans for a canal with a straight approach up Buzzards Bay into Monument River, no locks and maximum digging in the dry. In 1904 he approached Belmont, stressing that the canal, beside saving lives, would be a money-maker and would aid in the national defense. Belmont finally decided to make his own studies and in 1906 assigned his friend, William Barclay Parsons, to do the engineering study, and a marine consultant to do the freight study. (Parsons had worked on the subway, then in Panama on the canal plans there, but favored the sea level approach and left when the Corps of Engineers decided on locks.) For the survey, Parsons used Charles M. Thompson of Sandwich, the civil engineer who had bought up canal land in Lockwood's period and who had done soil and tide testing for Flanagan. Parsons recommended an approach in Buzzards Bay with two sharp bends, coming along shore at Wings Neck, then left along Monument Beach inside Mashnee and Hog Islands, then right into Monument River. This route had the deepest water. The marine freight study showed a good profit, including interest on the bonds if only half the available tonnage used the canal. Parson's plans for bridges and railroad relocation were approved by the Joint Board (Harbors and Public Lands plus Railroad Commissioners) in June 1907 and Belmont took over Flanagan's deposit, his charter and his land rights.

The Contractor Companies

Boston Cape Cod and New York Canal Co., a Massachusetts corporation, with Belmont as president, offices in New York and Boston, held the charter.

Cape Cod Construction Company, a Maine corporation, was awarded the building contract on a bid of $11,000,000; August Belmont was president, J. W. Miller, Arthur L. Devens and John B. McDonald vice-presidents, Chief Engineer Parsons, Asst. Engineer Eugene Klapp, several directors including Flanagan.

Degnon Cape Cod Canal Company (CCCCo.). This was owned by Degnon Contracting Co. of New York and Furst-Clark Contracting Co. of Baltimore and Galveston. Michael J. Degnon had been the contractor on the IRT subway work.

Degnon Contracting Co. got the contract from Degnon CCCCo. to build the two breakwaters at the east end and to riprap the banks.

Furst-Clark Contracting Co. got the contract from Degnon CCCCo. to excavate the channel.

Parsons brought on three more ex-Panama engineers, Henry Wells Durham as resident engineer, C. T. Waring in charge of work at the Sagamore end and A. S. Ackerman at the Buzzards Bay end. Charles M. Thompson used his local knowledge to acquire some 500 further parcels of land. The group had power to condemn the land but had to pay fair market value, and owners could consult the county commissioners or even go to court over their settlement. Money came from a syndicate organized by Belmont. They put up a million dollars to start, receiving Canal Company stock, then when more money was needed the syndicate bought Canal bonds of 50 years at 6%, and also received free stock in the same amount.

Thompson technically started the canal construction, which had to begin within three months of the date of approval from the Massachusetts Land and Railroad Joint Board. In August 1907 a gang of laborers dug a 350-foot trench and loaded the dirt on flat cars on a Keith Car. Co. spur track in the canal valley. The fill was used for Keith plant expansion alongside the future canal. This proven start was legally similar to the 500 Italians job of 1880 and the dry land wharf of 1884. Belmont started the real work with a little silver shovel on June 22, 1909 at Bournedale, and promised the canal would be done by the end of 1912.

The Breakwater

A granite breakwater of 3,000 feet was planned from Scusset beach out into Cape Cod Bay. The top was to be 22 feet wide and 18 feet above low water. The breakwater was to prevent drift of sediment from entering the canal from the Plymouth moraine cliffs, and to protect shipping in the wide mooring area at this end. A much smaller breakwater was to hold the other side of the canal mouth at the beach. The contract for stone moving was let by Degnon Contracting to the Gilbert Transportation Co. of Mystic Conn. under Samuel R. Rosoff. Their product came from the Stonington, Maine area where the typical stone has a coarse slow-cooled pattern of pink color, called "Deer Island" granite. In 1909 Durham noted a problem with short weight. One schooner captain questioned by Durham said that his invoice read 1,000 tons but if he had that aboard, his craft would sink. Degnon cancelled the Gilbert contract and the firm went bankrupt. In early 1909 Degnon's firm bought stone directly from the Rockport Granite Company at Pigeon Cove and brought it down in sloops and scows that could be unloaded directly onto the site. There was no problem with weight. The breakwater was finished in late 1913. Those taking the pleasant summer walk out along the top can still see the pink Maine granite and the contrasting grey Rockport granite.

BEN LOMOND GOLF COURSE AND THE BREAKWATER-This photo is of value as showing Sagamore Hill completely bare in 1915, with the new breakwater in the distance and dredged spoil on the marsh. The former course of the Scusset River was at the base of the hill on the near side. These golfers are out on Washington's Birthday. The course was formally opened in May 1915. Photo courtesy of William E. Foster.

One of the unexpected results of the canal construction was immediately noticed by Sandwich residents, who complained in 1913 that due to the breakwater work, the currents from the bay had rushed onto Town Neck shore and changed the beach beyond recognition.

Dredging Scusset Marsh

All the problems with canal construction emerged here early—inadequate heavy equipment, bad weather, and ground that was soft on top, but full of clay and boulders below. The Lockwood ditch had been about 3,000 feet long, but the sea and slumping had filled 1,500 feet at the beach. In October 1909 the suction dredge, *General MacKenzie,* started in from the beach, but was able to work only eight out of fifty-three days due to unusual bad weather. Tugs had to pull her back repeatedly to Provincetown and she finally spent the winter in Plymouth harbor. The engineers ordered two heavy excavators from Chicago, delivered in pieces by rail. These were assembled in December 1909 and January 1910 about where the fish freezer now stands. They were land-based machines with very long booms which dropped a steel scoop and dragged it back with spoil. Each weighed 110 tons, rested on a square steel base, and had to be pulled on rollers by winches. The excavators were moved from the firm upland onto the marsh at the head of the Lockwood ditch, then turned right toward Tupper Creek, a long trip over the soft marsh on rollers on a plank and corduroy road. The idea was to make a surface excavation in Scusset Marsh connecting a wide section of

Tupper Creek to the Lockwood ditch. Incredibly, this difficult work was done in winter weather, and a shallow channel was dug between Tupper Creek and the Lockwood ditch. Then a small dredge, the *Nahant,* on peak spring tides was dragged over the Scusset bar into the harbor, up Tupper Creek and through the new channel into the Lockwood ditch. The *Nahant* started to excavate the soft fill toward the beach. This was easy going but the *Nahant* was small and its "orange peel" scoop only held a small bite. Meanwhile the two excavators had to be dragged back to dry land and disassembled for shipment away. The Lockwood dredge hull was dynamited where it lay sunken at about the present fishing pier on the north bank. The *Nahant* finally cut through to the beach so that the *General MacKenzie* could enter and begin the main canal cut, 300 feet wide, at this sector. A second suction dredge was brought in and good progress was made, dumping the spoil on the marsh on the north bank, until hard clay and boulders were encountered. Then dipper dredges had to be brought in that worked during the winter of 1910/11. The worst barrier was encountered at the Sandwich/Bourne line where the causeway went over to Sagamore Hill.

LAND EXCAVATOR AT SCUSSET MARSH—When the dredge proved unable to cut into the beach near Town Neck, two land excavators were brought to Sandwich by rail and assembled. They were dragged out onto the marsh on rollers to cut a passage between Tupper Creek (tidal) and the ditch left by the Lockwood dredge. This was successful and a small dredge was able to be brought into the Lockwood ditch. Sandwich Archives. Lillian H. Tangney collection. Gift of Joan Morrow.

This causeway was low but was found to be a solid underground breakwater of clay, compacted gravel, and rocks that had to be scratched out foot by foot. By the end of 1911 the channel was up beyond the Keith Car plant. Keith had spent some $750,000 in new wharf facilities and bunding for the mile-long plant lying along the future canal, because iron, coal, lumber and other supplies could be brought in cheaply by boat as soon as the canal came. The first cargo brought in at this end was 2,000 tons of coal on the *Cassie* in December 1910, which must have been landed where the excavators had been assembled. Tourists and visitors came to see the great works. In 1911 a steamer brought 300 MIT students to the Keith wharf.

Buzzards Bay Dredging

The canal dredging was to include four miles of channel from the mouth of the Monument River to the 25-foot line off Wing's Neck Lighthouse. The work here was not quite as torturous as at the east end, but was bad enough. An old bucket dredge, the *Kennedy,* began work in the channel in 1909, also two dipper dredges and a clamshell unit. Their day and night clanking was no joy to those living along the shore. They stopped dredging in the winter; three dredges were withdrawn as inadequate. In 1910 two bigger dippers worked on the channel with the *Kennedy,* while a clamshell and a hydraulic dredge went to work in the Monument River estuary. In 1911 the dippers in the channel began to hit huge boulders of up to 100 tons. Work had to stop while divers placed dynamite to break them up. This year there were six dredges in the four-mile channel and four more in the Monument River. In spite of all this work at both ends of the canal, it was clear in the 1911 season that the plan to open the canal at the end of 1912 could not be met, and that even heavier dredges were needed.

DREDGES AT EAST END OF CANAL—Three dredges at work in the Scusset marsh portion of the early canal. Work was slowed by equipment weakness and by hard digging in clay and boulders. Sandwich Archives, Lillian H. Tangney collection, gift of Joan Morrow.

The Warfield and the Herrick

Early in 1912 two huge new dipper dredges began to be assembled, one at Sagamore and one at Buzzards Bay. These were designed by the American Locomotive Co. with all parts brought in by rail. The hulls were finished in March and launched into the channels, to be completed with boilers, engines, superstructure and machinery at dockside. The *Governor Herrick* began work at Sagamore in July and the *Governor Warfield* at Buzzards Bay in August. These powerful units had very long dipper arms, could take ten cubic yards at a bite and had steel boxes of eight yards for lifting boulders. They began to make rapid progress toward the dry digging area in the center of the cut.

Dry Land Digging

The pretty village of North Sandwich (now Bournedale) had three sets of mills on successive falls of the Herring River as it descended from Great Herring Pond down to the floor of the future canal valley. The railroad came through the village on a high embankment as the track rose to the thirty-two foot sill east of the village and then down to Sagamore. In Bournedale the canal cut was to have its cruelest impact, requiring about half the houses to be moved or destroyed. The cemetery of fifty or more burial sites had to be dug up and moved, as did an ancient Bourne family burying ground just west at the farm where Elisha Bourne had entertained the ninety-nine Acadians back in 1756. This farm was now occupied by Reuben Collins and was to be totally destroyed. The two cemeteries were excavated in 1909, with remains and markers mainly relocated at Sagamore Cemetery. Houses and barns were cleared and the rail line was relocated on the south bank. In August 1911 the excavations started as three steam shovels were brought in. Spoil was placed on narrow gauge rail dump cars and taken to fill areas near the canal. Four natural earth dams were left in place, between which were three work areas for the shovels, which took the level down to ten feet below sea level. Pumps kept ground water and rain water from accumulating in these pits. This dry digging area ran from just west of Bournedale for 7,000 feet westward or nearly to the present Bourne Bridge. The highest sill area between Bournedale and the Sagamore bridge was cut through by floating dredges. Parsons said that he would have saved time and money if he had dug all of the land cut in the dry. One by one, the three deep sections were evacuated of their shovels, tracks and spoil cars, and the dredge cut the dam allowing seawater to flood the section for final dredging to fifteen feet deep. By the spring of 1914 only one earthen dam remained, with tide water on both sides. This was located halfway between the modern highway bridges and known as Foley's Dike, for the steam shovel contractor.

Rail Line Changes

The numerous changes in rail line, bridge, and station locations were completed at the end of 1911 so that the old tracks and two rail bridges could be removed as the canal progressed. The old rail line had divided at Buzzards Bay station, the Woods Hole line going over the river on a low trestle bridge, while the main line went up the valley some distance before crossing the Monument River to the Cape side. The first work was the new railroad bridge of two tracks. This was called a Strauss bascule-type lift bridge, with a single 160-foot span pivoted on the north foundation. This was completed in September 1910. The new line to Sandwich went over the new bridge and down the south side of the valley requiring a new roadbed to a point beyond the Sagamore station. There was a large new Buzzards Bay station, and new small stations at Bourne and Bournedale, where the station was on the south side of the canal, while the remnant village was on the north. At Sagamore a new track was laid beside the old one, and a new station built south of the track with a new local freight station to the east. The New Haven Railroad put in a new heavy girder bridge at the Cohasset Narrows crossing, replacing a previous truss bridge.

EXCAVATION IN THE DRY AT BOURNEDALE-This smoky and steamy scene shows the destruction which the canal brought to the peaceful village of Bournedale. The steam shovel is consuming the embankment upon which the railroad had formerly gone through the village, and is approaching the steel girder bridge of the railroad over a village street. The narrow gauge locomotive at right is about to take the loaded spoil cars to a dumpsite. Sandwich Archives gift of William Ellis.

Bourne Highway Bridge

The old highway from Bourne Four Corners with trolley car tracks from New Bedford to Monument Beach crossed the Monument River on a bridge with stone piers, renewed in 1893. The new bridge was located downstream and was completed in May 1911. It was a Scherzer-type lift bridge, with two eighty-foot sections. By fall of 1911 both road traffic and the trolleys of the New Bedford and Onset Railway Company were running over it.

Sagamore Highway Bridge

The old road crossing the Scusset River used the Willows Dam which backed up the Swift millpond. This road went through the enlarged Keith plant at grade. The dredges came past Keith's in 1911, destroying the dam and emptying the pond. A wooden bridge with a lift section was erected here temporarily, so that tugs could pass to and from the dredges. At about the midpoint of the former millpond, the piers were sunk for the new steel lift bridge, which, like the Bourne Bridge, had two eighty-foot sections. The roadway was high enough over the canal so that the approach span was above the rail traffic in Keith's plant. A stone abutment beyond the rail tracks anchored the approach and the road went down a ramp to Bridge Street in Sagamore village. The overhead road enabled Keith's to fence in their plant completely and the temporary bridge was dismantled.

KEITH CAR MANUFACTURING COMPANY—This photo by F. C. Small of Bourne shows the Willow Dam at left and the Swift millpond in Sagamore. The canal construction of 1911 and 1912 saw dredges clear out this pond area as part of the canal route. A temporary wood bridge replaced the Willow Dam road. The Sagamore lift bridge and approach spans crossed over the Keith plant between the larger buildings on the right. Sandwich Archives.

Bournedale Bridge and Ferry

The Bournedale people had suffered the worst damages in the canal taking and their problems were not over. Rail service in 1913 was south of the open water which had been cut during 1912 by the *Governor Herrick* and other dredges. The temporary wood bridge from Sagamore with its lift span was moved here and rebuilt for the benefit of rail passengers. This bridge had to be removed in July 1914 when final widening of the canal was completed. A motor ferry was to operate here to meet all trains, with a small wharf and steps at both sides of the canal. However, the vessel provided was grossly underpowered and poorly manned, so that it was swept one way or the other by the current and often resulted in the passengers missing their train. There were repeated minor accidents so that the ferry became a stock joke. The only way to be sure of getting to the train was to drive over one of the new bridges.

THE BOURNEDALE FERRY—The 1914 canal forced the rail line to the south side of the channel, so that a ferry was needed to serve Bournedale which was on the north side. The vessel was small and proved unreliable so that many passengers missed their train and the ferry became a joke. The station was closed about 1930. Courtesy of Bourne Archives.

Starting the Flow of Water

In April 1914, the future canal was flooded from both ends to Foley's Dike. There was no flow, but for the first time the different tidal effects from each bay could be observed, a ten-foot range from Cape Cod Bay and a four-foot range from Buzzards Bay, with peak two and one half hours earlier. On April

21st Belmont staged a public event at this dike where he blended bottles of water from both sides. He had a small wooden flume built at the top of the dike where at the high tide on the eastern side a little water could be allowed to flow over to the west side. He then stated that Foley's Dike would be broken July 4th. On that date at low slack water (equal height at both sides of the dike) workmen cut a deep trench across the dike and retired to safety. Water rose on the west side and fell on the east in accordance with the tidal pattern. In about three hours the difference in heights between the two bays was about six feet, all concentrated at this dike. The first flow heading east to Cape Cod Bay was a great torrent at this point, which swept away most of the dike. The site of the dike, however, remained as a shallow point that caught heavy currents both ways until the two dredges could cut it completely down to the fifteen-foot depth, when the slosh would be uniform throughout the whole canal.

BELMONT TAKES THE FIRST SHOVELEUL—This photo was taken at Bournedale in 1909 for the ceremonial start of the Cape Cod Canal. Left to right DeWitt Clinton Flanagan original charter Holder; Belmont with silver shovel; M. J. Degnon of New York, a contractor and F. A. Furst of Baltimore, also a contractor. Courtesy of William E. Foster.

The dredges now had to work nonstop to improve the channel; other works such as navigation guides and mooring dolphins had to be readied for the grand opening which was set for July 29th. At the Sandwich end there was a substantial wharf along the canal at the point where the 1884 dry land wharf had been, but no harbor of refuge, only a floating stage for small boats. The two breakwaters had been laid about 500 feet apart, and the canal here was over 300 feet wide, with dolphins along both shores inland from the breakwaters for use of vessels seeking shelter from storms or awaiting passage in the one-way canal. The first passenger vessel in the future canal was the new excursion steamer *Dorothy Bradford* which came down on a charter run on June 9, 1914, and stopped at Sandwich wharf. She had 1,340 people to see the progress, again mostly from MIT and engineers with a professional interest.

Opening July 29, 1914

This Wednesday date was chosen by Belmont personally. Timing that summer was critical. Germany had opened the Kiel Canal in June, and in August there would be the opening of the Panama Canal. The Cape Cod Canal would be anticlimactic after that. Furthermore, the New York Yacht Club had a fleet heading for the North Shore and Maine in August, and Belmont was anxious that it should transit the new canal. He invited a host of friends and political figures. Those who did not come in their own yachts gathered at New Bedford by train on the morning of the 29th. Belmont hired the Nantasket excursion boat *Rose Standish* which sailed from Boston on the 28th, transited the canal as the first passenger vessel and proceeded to New Bedford. The following morning the parade of ships set out from New Bedford in a chorus of whistles and bells, and headed up the bay for the canal entrance. The line consisted of the *Rose Standish,* with most of the invited guests and Belmont himself, then the destroyer *McDougall,* with the Assistant Secretary of the Navy Franklin D. Roosevelt, then Belmont's yacht *Scout,* followed by six other palatial yachts, including Morgan's *Corsair,* Vanderbilt's *North Star* and Harriman's *Sultana;* then last a tugboat *Orion* carrying reporters. At the entrance to the channel at Wing's Neck doing escort duty were no less than six destroyers, two revenue cutters and two submarines. All the workboats down to the scows had flags and streamers. The procession moved slowly up the canal, and the *Scout* came forward to the *Rose Standish* and took off Belmont, Governor Walsh of Massachusetts and a few others who were going to a brief service at Sandwich. The *Scout* then stopped at the Sandwich wharf while the other vessels went on into Cape Cod Bay. When the last one had cleared the breakwater, it whistled and each vessel then wheeled and reentered the canal in reverse order.

Belmont and party would have been taken down present Freezer Road, then left on Tupper Road, where they would have passed a long parade of fifty floats stopped along the road. The parade had come from Sandwich streets to Town Neck, and was joined there by a large number of cars which had driven from Bourne after viewing the parade. A speaker's stand was set up east of Town Neck Road at the foot of the rise, which was covered with a crowd estimated at 5,000. William L. Nye represented the town on its 275th Anniversary and presented Belmont with a silver loving cup. Belmont and Governor Walsh spoke briefly, then were whisked back to the *Scout* which became the end ship in the return parade.

AUGUST BELMONT SPEAKING AT TOWN NECK 1914—During the festivities opening the canal on July 29th, Belmont and Governor Walsh of Massachusetts honored the 275th Anniversary of the founding of Sandwich by appearing at a speaker's platform set up just off Town Neck Road. A large crowd from a Sandwich parade gathered there and saw William L. Nye present Belmont with a loving cup. Sandwich Archives, gift of Elizabeth Beale.

The westward current was very strong and caused difficulties in bringing the parade vessels to their assigned docks or dolphins beyond the railroad bridge. In particular, the *Rose Standish,* with all eyes upon her was carried helplessly past her dock and had to go down to open water to turn and come back with what dignity she could muster. The reception, however, was splendid in a huge tent on Taylor's Point.

The Pageant and the Start of Business

The canal opened for business the following morning at 8 A.M. However, news of the opening party and canal prospects were pushed off the front pages by the ominous developments in Germany and Yugoslavia leading to World War I. Business was extremely slow to start up. The first day, according to Professor Farson, the tolls were only $51.00th. The first real commercial business (a tug and three coal barges) did not arrive for thirteen days. During August 1914 lights were installed and the canal opened around the clock.

A novelty of this early period was *The Pageant of Cape Cod,* a major theatrical effort held outdoors on a meadow near the Bourne Bridge. There were four free performances Saturday, August 15 and Monday through Wednesday,

August 17th-19th. Fifteen acts presented the history of Cape Cod. The master of the pageant, William Chauncy Langdon, thanked Belmont deeply for leaving the yacht *Scout* here for the period, where it had a role in the pageant by sailing past during the segment called *The Dream of the Canal.* Langdon noted that Mr. and Mrs. Belmont attended the Tuesday show.

Canal traffic was far below expectations. Apart from high the toll-rate, the main problems were the currents, the 15-foot draft, the narrow passage at the bridges (140 feet between fenders), poor visibility and the inconvenience of one-way passage. The big volume of coastal freight was in coal barges, and most of these preferred the outer route. Nevertheless, the canal operators continued work on the waterway, dredging toward 25 feet, removing boulders and adding riprap. A fleet of three tugs was kept on standby to assist those going through the canal, and a private organization, the Cape Cod Canal Pilots' Association, was available to take vessels through. Traffic increased slowly, but two sinkings in 1916 caused closures of two weeks and three months.

LIFE SAVING STATION, SANDWICH-This was the Coast Guard Station for the Sandwich end of the canal in the period 1919-1936. It was considered an adjunct boat house under the Manomet Station, Plymouth and with little staff or authority was unable to work effectively against rum runners or in emergencies. Courtesy Bernard Brady, one of the staff of this Station.

The Town of Sandwich gave a lease to Wilson Dean Fish Co. in 1914, which erected a fish freezer near the canal wharf. Keith Car and Manufacturing was operating at capacity, but what of the often-claimed new industry that would be drawn to the banks of the canal? In 1910, a flyer by the Canal Construction Company stated "A large manufacturing center will be developed at the eastern end, where mills will have the advantage of land and sea transport." The president of the New Haven Railroad predicted that where the village of

Sagamore now had 300 people, there will be 10,000 people in this area in five years. An article in *Van Norden's Magazine* predicted immense growth, and William Parsons said that a great artificial harbor at the east end was possible. This was part of the literature given by the Canal Company to reporters and visitors, but repetition did not make it happen. Apart from the fish freezer, all that was built at the east end was a station of the Life Saving Service, a branch of the main local station at Manomet Point, Plymouth. On March 2, 1914, the Town of Sandwich appointed a committee to confer with the Cape Cod Canal Company on developing the Sandwich end of the canal, but no results were announced. The only project that had been long planned and did now materialize was a portion of the proposed trolley line from Plymouth to Chatham. This had been built in 1901 as far as Raymond's Corner, Fresh Pond, then in early 1917 was pushed through to the canal. The route was along the coast touching the settlements at Vallersville and Ellisville then inland to Cedarville on Great Herring Pond. It turned left at the Cemetery there and went through the woods over to the summer colony at Sagamore Beach, then down Standish Road and old Plymouth Road to the new bridge. The tracks crossed the bridge and went down the ramp to Sagamore Village, but the startup back up the ramp seemed to cause problems and after the first few runs the line was terminated on the north bank of the canal. Passenger traffic was extremely disappointing as automobiles were coming into use and the Sagamore Beach complex did not offer the tourist the excitement of Monument Beach or Onset. After only nine months the line folded and the tracks were pulled up for scrap.

The Government Gets Involved

After the declaration of war in 1917, discussion of the government buying the canal became active. The cost of actual construction to opening day was put at $8,265,743, while with completion work and a stock bonus and operating losses the cost as of August 1917 was $12,956,718. This was still being discussed when in July 1918 a U-boat attacked a tug and barges off Chatham. The Federal Railroad Administration (FRA) promptly took over the canal operation and received the tolls while spending generously on dredging, riprap, dolphin replacement, tugboat operations and employee salaries. The FRA tried to return operations to the Canal Company as of March 1, 1920, but Belmont refused it on the grounds that condemnation and compensation proceedings were still in court. The canal was closed for four days while shipping accumulated at both ends. Finally, the Canal Company consented to go back to operating the canal on a temporary basis until the terms of government purchase and the actual appropriations could be worked out. This was thought to be imminent but it took eight years. Meanwhile the company operated the canal, and for the first time it began to show modest profits in tolls over direct operating expenses. This was due to the improvements made by the government, to better trade acceptance, to higher tolls and deferred maintenance. However, the profits did not begin to pay for costs of interest on bonds or the interest on loans made by Belmont.

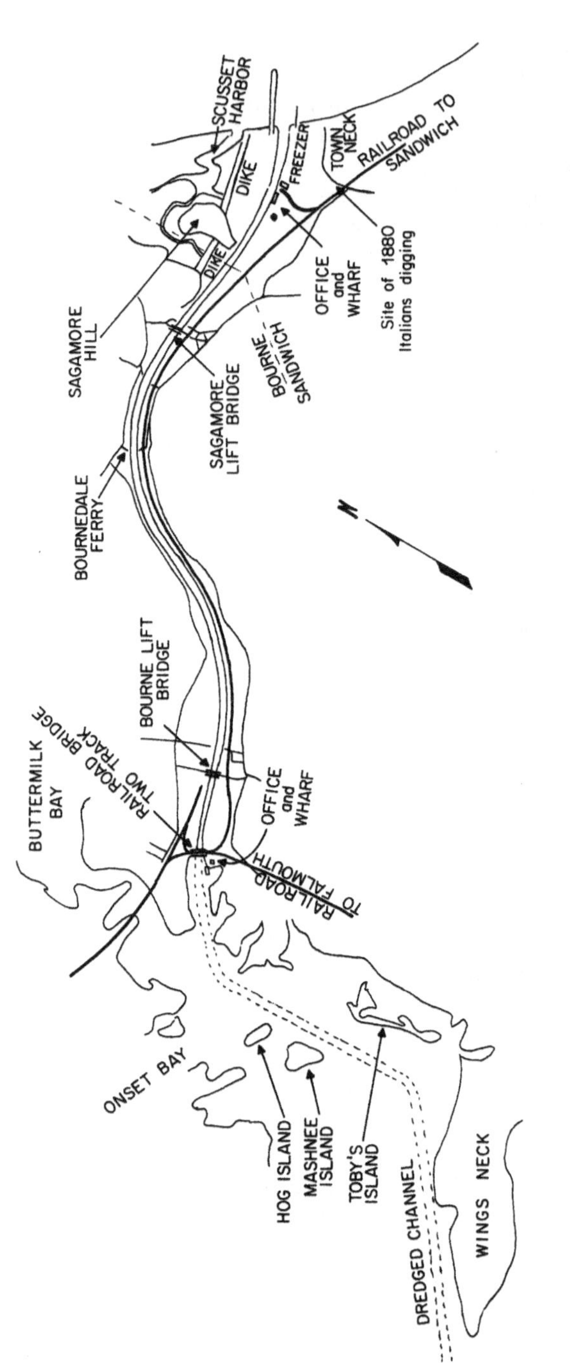
SCUSSET HARBOR
DIKE
DIKE
FREEZER
TOWN NECK
RAILROAD TO SANDWICH
OFFICE and WHARF
Site of 1880 Italians digging
SAGAMORE HILL
SAGAMORE LIFT BRIDGE
BOURNE
SANDWICH
BOURNEDALE FERRY
N
BOURNE LIFT BRIDGE
TWO TRACK RAILROAD BRIDGE
BUTTERMILK BAY
OFFICE and WHARF
RAILROAD TO FALMOUTH
ONSET BAY
HOG ISLAND
MASHNEE ISLAND
TOBY'S ISLAND
DREDGED CHANNEL
WINGS NECK

BELMONT's CANAL AS OF 1925 (see facing page)-The canal between banks was 100 feet wide at bottom with 24 feet depth at low water. It was 250 feet wide in the approach channels. The width at the bridges was 140 feet between fenders, posing a navigation problem in case of following winds or current. There was one-way traffic only. The ferry at Bournedale was erratic and often failed to meet train connections. Scusset Harbor was still open with dredged spoil from the canal being restrained by low dikes.

As to the status of negotiations, a condemnation trial had begun in 1919 in Federal District Court in Boston, with the government claiming the canal was worth $8 million, and the company $25 million. The jury set the figure at $16 million, with certain government maintenance projects to be paid by the company. This suit was contested and overturned, so that a new trial was needed if negotiations failed. However, in 1921, Belmont agreed to sell the canal for $11.5 million, of which $5.5 million was in cash to the company and $6 million repaid to bondholders, but with interest only from the date of government purchase. Bills for this purchase were introduced each year but were either rejected in committee or amended, refused and lapsed. During 1927, the money was finally approved by Congress in exactly the amounts agreed by Belmont. The Corps of Engineers took over the property and operations at the end of March 1928.

Belmont died December 10, 1924 at age seventy-one. He had lost reportedly $1 million in interest on bonds and on loans to the Canal Company. His Boston, Cape Cod and New York Canal Company was dissolved in 1931. The great private effort to build the canal had succeeded in producing a successful operation that changed the shipping charts but that had been a heavy loss to all who had put money into it. Two beautiful valleys were destroyed along with many farms and homes. There was a harvest of splendid construction photographs, as well as views of the multitude of ships that came to use the passage. Ship-watching on the canal became part of the Cape experience, the most memorable in the 1920s being the nightly transit of the passenger vessel (either the *Boston* or the *New York)* that had left Boston at 5 P.M. and reached the canal about 8 P.M. She was always brilliantly lit, and great crowds gathered on fair evenings from May to November to wave and cheer as she passed. The opposite passage of the other vessel occurred about 5 A.M. enroute to Boston, and few were up either aboard or on the banks.

CHAPTER 29

THE NEW CENTURY

The turn of the century brought a continued decline in population and in the economic base in manufacturing, in marine activities and in farming. There were, however, important new arrivals in the presence here of well-to-do summer residents, whose building and real estate taxes greatly benefited the local economy.

In Bourne, Frederick Tudor built *Tudor Haven,* later sold to President Grover Cleveland and renamed *Gray Gables.* The Tudors and the related Garland family built *Bay End Farm* at Head-of-the-Bay, now *Grazing Fields Farm.* The famous actor, Joseph Jefferson, built two successive houses called *Crowsnest* on Buttermilk Bay. Mr. W.E.C. Eustis, "the Copper King," owned Scraggy Neck; Mr. Thomas A Baxendale owned Amrita Island; Charles H. Taylor Senior and Junior, and W. O. Taylor owned Taylor's Point; Mr. Frederick E. Snow had an estate on Buttermilk Bay; George Peabody Gardner (brother of Jack Gardner) had an estate at Pocasset now known as *Briarwood.* These people are among those who brought distinguished guests and glamour to Cape Cod.

Both Jefferson and Cleveland, it is said, tried to buy land in Sandwich, but found prices raised against them. Jefferson did buy a lot at Bay View Cemetery where he was buried in 1907. His son Charles owned the house at 12 Grove Street. Frederick Tudor III came to Sandwich in 1917 and bought the former Wing Howland house at 8 Morse Road which he renamed *Wamdosa Farm.* Leonard Wesson and Henry Alden Belcher, both of Boston and both married to Nye ladies, occupied the new residences *Fairview* (now the Cape Winds Rest Home) and the adjacent house at 127 Main Street built by Edward Swann. Isaac N. Keith, and his son Eben S.S. Keith, brought many railroad associates to Cape Cod. One of these, John M. Hanson of Standard Pressed Steel Co., bought land in the John Ewer Road area and built an expensive residence facing Wakeby Pond where he entertained Diamond Jim Brady and other magnates. This house burned down in 1923.

Elwell and the Wesselhoefts

In1885, Mr. F. Edwin Elwell, a distinguished sculptor and curator of sculpture at the Metropolitan Museum of Art, bought the 100-acre Wing farm on the upper millpond which he called Shawme Farm. He converted a barn to a studio and modeled some of his famous works here, including *Little Nell.* Elwell invited Dr. Walter Wesselhoeft of Boston to attend his twin children who had scarlet fever. The doctor was greatly struck with Shawme Hill and saw it as a site for a sanitorium. He bought eleven acres of land from Elwell and sixty-two acres from Ansel Tobey in a broad wedge from the southern end of the pond up beyond the present Mid-Cape Highway. The sanatorium did not materialize, but in 1896 he and Elwell got the town to put through Shawme Road, running from Grove Street around to Water Street. Wesselhoeft built a summer home at the peak of the hill and within the next few years granted two-acre building lots to certain members of the family, or to their close friends who wished to build here and join the summer colony. In all, six houses were built, all unheated and unpretentious, but each one supplemented by outlying cottages which could be used as studios for music or writing. This was a highly intellectual and accomplished group who gathered here summers. The cottages belonged to:

Dr. Walter Wesselhoeft (1839-1920) and family of 5 girls, 2 boys. His son Robert A., an electrical engineer (1882-1967), inherited and added more land toward Water Street. His grandson, Robert A. Jr., sold this house and most of the land to a developer in 1969, except the five lots described below.

Walter's sister Emma (1842-1914) married Professor Arthur Searle, a Harvard astronomer. Their daughters Katherine and Lucy built an outdoor stage and benches, where plays and concerts were given well into the 1930s. This cottage was sold to Horace B. Davis, an author and economics professor.

Walter's daughter Ferdinanda (1869-1952) married Willard Reed, who was then principal at Sandwich Academy. Their daughter Nancy (1909-1982) married John Kykyri (1898-1981).

Walter's daughter Eleanor, a teacher and actress, married Percy Hutchison, music critic of the New York Times. This cottage was sold in 1924 to Haggott and Margaret Beckhart, he Professor of Economics at Columbia and she Economics Professor at Vassar.

John O. Powers of New York, a classmate of Willard Reed's at Harvard. His sons married Anastasia and Winifred Murphy of Sandwich, daughters of Constable Michael Murphy.

Ernest (1871-1951) and Irmgart (1877-1940) Hutcheson, friends of Mary Leavitt, second wife of Dr. Walter Wesselhoeft. He was the president of Julliard School in New York and his guests here included George Gershwin, John Erskine, Eugene Ormandy and Yehudi Menuhin. Their son Harold (born on Shawme Hill in 1904), a professor of English literature, lives in Sandwich with his wife Margaret, occupying the cottage on the hill in the summer.

This colony involved a number of highly distinguished persons and visitors, with political views ranging from left to right and with much international flavor. Many older Sandwich residents had various contacts with this summer colony, and had stories to tell. Some ultra-conservatives in Sandwich suspiciously called it "Commie Hill." The original Wesselhoeft house has now been replaced by the newest buildings of the Hilltop Condominium, but the other five cottages are still occupied summers by descendants of the above-named families.

LITTLE NELL—The sculptor F. Edwin Elwell purchased the ancient Wing estate (now Heritage Plantation) and worked in a studio on the grounds. This photograph of Little Nell was taken in his studio and presented to the Sandwich Public Library. The final sculpture won a prize at the 1892 Chicago Fair. Sandwich Archives.

The Fosters and Dodge Macknight

We have already referred to John H. Foster, the dancing master, and his unique house *Masthead* at Spring Hill. John's French wife Celeste operated a dress shop in New York. She and John traveled to Europe yearly. A nephew of John's, Chester Foster, became an assistant in operating the Foster dancing schools in Europe, and a niece, Ida Putnam of Spring Hill, worked as an accountant at the dress shop in New York during the winter. John had known the American watercolorist Dodge Macknight in Europe, and found in 1900 that Macknight had returned to this country and was visiting Cape Cod as a new subject for his watercolors. Through John Foster, Macknight bought the Spring Hill house at 260 Route 6A, formerly the Quaker school of Joseph and Mercy Wing. This he called *The Hedges* and made it his home for the rest of his life. From here he still traveled widely to paint, and entertained many famous artists in this home. His household consisted of his French wife Louise, their son John, and her sister Elise Queyrel. He became a friend of Isabella Stewart Gardner who bought many of his works. In 1911 John Foster's wife Celeste died and John became a more regular Sandwich resident. Chester Foster, and his Roumanian wife Iza (Willemot), returned to Spring Hill and occupied the house at 1 Spring Hill Road. It was just across from Vodon's glass-cutting shop, and these three French-speaking households all enjoyed talking to Vodon with his Belgian French. With Macknight's guidance, Chester became a skilled artist, and his early death in 1925 at only 51 was a great loss. Macknight's son John was a noted concert flautist, but had been injured in World War I and died in 1928. At this sorrow, Macknight, then 68, ceased all painting and devoted himself to his beautiful garden at *The Hedges.* He gave and loaned pictures to the Sandwich Public Library, and at his death in 1950 he left the bulk of his considerable estate to the Library, but with the income to go to Elise Queyrel during her life-time. The house was later purchased by the musician John Houston and his artist wife Winnie (Fitch), who renamed the house *Hedgerow.*

Marketing Cape Cod

Newcomers like Macknight, Elwell, and the Wesselhoefts sought privacy and quiet in their Sandwich neighborhoods, but many other newcomers came to Cape Cod to socialize and even to make money in real estate. Ezra G. Perry of Monument Beach was an insurance and real estate agent who had observed the greening of Onset, Buzzards Bay village, and the shore communities down to Woods Hole with great interest and satisfaction. In 1898 he published a book called *A Trip Around Buzzard's Bay Shores,* which had photographs of many of the larger new houses between New Bedford and Woods Hole, many of which were for sale by him. The book in fact was a documentary of the new tourist on Cape Cod, and recorded so much of its new appearance that the Bourne Historical Society brought out a new edition in 1975 with notes on what had happened to many of the buildings shown. Mr. Perry hastily brought out a sequel, *All Around Cape Cod Shores, Our Summer Land and Memories of My Childhood. Written by E. G. Perry, a Cape Cod Boy.* This was clearly a new breed of Cape Cod boy who was not writing for old Cape Codders. In 1903 Perry wrote a promotional booklet about the town of Bourne in which he stated that 75% of the town's taxes were paid by summer people. Deyo's history, published in 1890, stated that even as of that date:

SANDWICH RAILROAD AND FREIGHT STATIONS ABOUT 1915-Both these stations were built in 1878 when the "barny" old terminal station was torn down. The spur at left formerly led through the roundhouse to the B&S factory grounds. At right the cottage moved here from Spring Hill for Mrs. Fagan. Courtesy of Society for the Preservation of New England Antiquities.

> "That sensible practice happily increasing among city people, of checking themselves each year in the rush and hurry of business, to take a vacation at the seaside, has already modified, to a great extent, the resources and prospects of Cape Cod. Available building sites for summer cottages are rapidly being occupied by those who build more or less elaborately and spend the larger portion of the year here. This is especially true of Falmouth, where several people of large means claim their residence. *More than one-half of all the taxes of this town are paid by four such families.* These elegant residences have been erected by the summer people almost throughout the Buzzards Bay side of the county, and down the Cape on either shore; and on the higher lands as well, handsome residences beautify the landscape."

For various reasons, Sandwich did not participate in this boom of building large new summer places along the shore. The areas particularly favored were on the warm-water side from Bourne and Falmouth to Chatham and Orleans.

Old Family Associations

It was said that Cape Cod natives, no matter how scattered, cherish memories of the homeland and would return to see the places and relatives again. Those who had left before the Revolution and in the massive out-migrations just after the Revolution to Maine, Vermont, New York, and the mid-west lacked an easy route back, and after one or two generations lost touch with their home cousins. However, those numbers who left the Cape after the Civil War to go to cities or to the Midwest were in a different position, with the railroad providing rapid travel. Such families in the early 1900's would be about to retire, many in comfortable circumstances, and the inclination to see the old home town and to show it to children and grandchildren was strong, especially if encouraged by close relatives who had remained and kept attractive old Cape Cod houses to show. In Sandwich the Wings, Nyes and Tuppers found enough relatives here and away to hold large and satisfying reunions. Out of these reunions permanent organizations arose to keep the ties strong, to sponsor books and studies of genealogy, and particularly to acquire an old house to furnish as a center for the greater family. For various reasons other old families failed to do this. The Burgesses were numerous but the natural center at the Benjamin Burgess house in Sagamore had passed out of the family. The Freemans had the genealogy written and the farm center in operation here, but the occupying family, although welcoming Freeman visitors, showed no interest in sponsoring an extended family organization. The Tobeys, Dillinghams, Hoxies, Giffords, Bassetts, and others lacked the local organizing nucleus to attempt a reunion and start the process. An affectionate and efficient secretariat was indispensable.

The Wing Family of America Inc.

In 1882 the Rev. Dr. Conway P. Wing of Carlisle, Pa. and Dr. Henry Russell of Sandwich (whose mother was Content Wing) attempted a reunion in Sandwich. Only about fifteen came, but Conway Wing did get a genealogy written. A family association was formed in 1900 and a successful reunion was held in 1902 with nationwide attendance of about 100. There were frequent reunions thereafter, both in Sandwich and elsewhere. A genealogical serial publication, *OWL (Our Wing Lineage)* has continued with few breaks since 1900. In 1942 the Family purchased the house known as the Fort House in Spring Hill which had the following owners:

Stephen Wing (1621-1710) married Oseah Dillingham and Sarah
Briggs Ebenezer (1671-1738) married Elizabeth Backhouse

Joshua (1707-1790) married Mary Hoxie
Presbury (1754-1807) married Hannah L. Swift
Joshua (1781-1861) married Beulah Bowerman
Seth Bowerman (1818-1905) married Cordelia Phinney
Alvin Phinney (1846-1934) married Elizabeth C. Turner
Cora M. (1875-1964) unmarried

The house was restored and furnished with period furniture, and is open to the public during the season. The Family owns a nearby nineteenth century house for the curator/caretaker.

WING FORT HOUSE—This house has been in continual ownership of Wing family members from the 1640s. The term "fort" is not explained but may have originated in King Philip's War if this part of Spring Hill was palisaded as a community defense area. The house is now restored and furnished for use in Wing Family Reunions and for visitors. View courtesy of Wing Family.

Old Home Week 1902

The town voted to organize a week-long celebration in August 1902 in honor of sons and daughters of Sandwich and Bourne. It recognized the concurrent Wing reunion, but extended invitations to any and all from the towns who might be returning. The program included:

Sunday evening, August 24, Professor Henry N. Hoxie, Quaker teacher and student of Sandwich history; speeches and music.

Monday, parade and exercises for Grand Army Units.

Tuesday, Program by Life Savers of Monomoy with aquatic events, boat carnival and fireworks.

Wednesday, visiting friends and old homes.

Thursday, arrival of Bourne townsmen; clambake and ball game; speeches by Cleveland and Jefferson.

Friday, childrens events; Grand Ball in Casino.

Saturday, farewells and band concert

BENJAMIN NYE HOMESTEAD—This was the second home of Benjamin Nye, and may have been started in the 1660s. After occupation by the family, it was sold to the Commonwealth as part of a fish hatchery and game farm. In danger of destruction, it was bought back by the Nye Family Association and restored to its present excellent condition as a center for family reunions and interested visitors. Old County Road, East Sandwich. Sandwich Archives.

Nye Family of America Association Inc.

The Nyes of Sandwich hosted their first reunion in 1903 and formed the association. Another reunion was held in Sandwich in 1904, then one in Marietta, Ohio in 1905 where many Nyes and Tuppers were settled. George H. Nye and Frank E. Best compiled family material which was edited by David Fisher Nye and published as *A Genealogy of the Nye Family* in 1907. Later research was voluminous and resulted in the compilation of L. Bert Nye, Jr. published by the Nye Family as *American Nyes of English Origin.* Volume I (1977) covered generations 1-8 and Volume II (1980) generations 9-12. The original home of Benjamin Nye had been on Nye Road in Spring Hill, but was not large and about

1837 had been divided, with one portion moved to 10 Spring Hill Road; the original part was rebuilt to Greek Revival appearance. On Old County Road however, where Benjamin had removed in mid-life, the family home was a big colonial, still occupied by Mrs. Helen (Nye) Holway 1841-1936. The original grist mill and fulling mill were gone. In advancing age Mrs. Holway sold the house in 1910 to a distant relative, Ray Nye, who restored it but then decided in 1924 to deed the house, with much of the land, to the Commonwealth for use as a game and fish hatchery. This action removed it from Nye access for many years while the place deteriorated. Finally in 1960, the family was able to buy back the house and immediate land from the state. By 1970 their efforts resulted in a splendid restored colonial with adjoining apartment for curator/caretaker. The descent of ownership of this house was as follows:

Benjamin Nye (1620-1714) married Katherine Tupper
Jonathan (1649-1747) married Hannah __________ and Patience Burgess.
Joseph (1695-before 1749) married Mary Snow.
Deacon Sylvanus (1744-1820) married Mrs. Lydia Freeman and Rebecca Parker.
Deacon Samuel (1789-1867) married Mrs. Sarah (Rea) Tobey.
Helen Freeman (1841-1936) married Augustus Holway.

In 1907 the Nye Family placed a large boulder with plaque on a triangle of land given by the town, at the corner of Main Street and present Tupper Road.

TUPPER HOUSE—This ancient salt-box house was occupied by Tuppers from the seventeenth to early twentieth century. It was purchased by the Family Association and restored, but was burned by an arsonist in 1921. A boulder now marks the spot on Tupper Road, Sandwich. Sandwich Archives, gift of Barbara L. Gill.

Tupper Family Association of America, Inc.

Tupper family members from many cities met in Boston in 1915 and there formed the family association. This dedicated group were different from most family organizations in that at this time there were no surviving members of the family in Sandwich. Russell Ellis Tupper died in 1904, and the original family house on Franklin Street had passed out of family ownership. The association raised funds and bought the house back in 1916, holding their first reunion in Sandwich in August 1916. In honor of the family, in 1917 the Town of Sandwich changed the name of Franklin Street to Tupper Road. The house, an ancient saltbox, was restored and partly furnished when it was destroyed by an incendiary fire on April 9, 1921, a very sad loss for the family and for Sandwich.

At the Sandwich Tercentenary Event in 1939 the Tupper Family met here and dedicated a memorial plaque and boulder on the site of the original house. Then in 1959 a five-acre plot around this site was deeded to the Town of Sandwich as a memorial park with maintenance funds. Without Tupper descendants in Sandwich, and deprived of their ancestral house as well, the family in recent years has placed a number of artifacts, pictures, and documents in a Tupper memorial room at the Glass Museum of the Sandwich Historical Society for display. The Tupper artifacts were given back to Dr. Eleanor Tupper about 1980. A volume entitled *Tupper Genealogy 1578-1971* was compiled by Alexander H. Chapman and published by Dr. Eleanor Tupper, Ph.D. in 1972. The office of the Family Association is located at Dr. Tupper's home in Beverly, Mass.

The Sandwich Historical Society.

The founding spirit of the Society was Ella Frances Ellis, born in Bournedale in 1861, a teacher in the Scorton district school when she married Jerome R. Holway, son of that Augustus and Helen (Nye) Holway of the Nye family house mentioned above. The younger Holways moved to Sandwich village and lived at 117 Tupper Road. Jerome was a businessman and one of the founders of the Sandwich Cooperative Bank. Ella took a keen interest in local history, her first known project being an article about the houses built or occupied by members of the Nye family, published by the Family Association in 1904 as part of its reunion record. Next, she and Charles M. Thompson, the civil engineer, laid out a 30-foot square grid on the Old Town Burying Ground, and she recorded by location the text on each marker then surviving in the burial ground. In addition to the listing, she wrote a descriptive booklet about the background of many of those buried there. Next, she and Benjamin Denson, the town's tree warden, prepared a map of the village streets and noted the location and species of every shade tree planted along the sidewalks and borders of the town streets, including some 26 species. This was an unusual and affectionate thing to do, and we must wonder what other works she would have accomplished if her life had been prolonged. She died in 1915.

The Sandwich Historical Society was incorporated July 3, 1907, with the stated purpose of "historical research in connection with the town of

Sandwich, Mass. and the collection and preservation of its historical material." The sixteen founders were:

> William L. Nye (1839-1936) president, Arthur Braman vice-president, Charles M. Thompson, secretary; trustees Benjamin G. Bartley, Melissa M. Ellis (Mrs. John C.C. Ellis), Susan E. Silsby, Dr. Edward S. Talbot, and members Alfred E. Dillingham, Dr. Robert Faunce, Mr. and Mrs. Jerome R. Holway, Harriet A. Morse (Mrs. Sanford I. Morse), Augustus R. Pope, Mr. and Mrs. John S. Smith and Alice E. Wing.

Soon George E. Burbank joined the Society and was treasurer for many years. Other early members were Carrie B. Pope, James L. Wesson, Benjamin Webber, Charlotte Hall Chipman, Frank Chipman, Frank Ellis, Ambrose E. Pratt, Percival Hall Lombard, Harry S. Dowden, Margaret Kelleher and Martha Stevens Barry. The Society's first room for its meetings and collection was the space on the ground floor of Town Hall vacated by the Sandwich Public Library when it moved to its new building in 1911. The Society grew only slowly, but became more visible when in 1919 it acquired property at Main Street and Tupper Road through the generosity of Mr. Nye, Mr. Wesson, and Mrs. Chipman. Then in 1921, it purchased from Mr. Wesson the adjacent land toward the Mill River including two buildings. In 1922 the larger building, (formerly the barn on the Melatiah Bourne property close to the Calvinistic Society chapel), was moved to its present site on the corner and restored as a museum. The Sandwich Winter Club donated a new colonial doorway and the sons of Ella Holway donated a fireplace mantel in her honor. The Society now had a place of its own to hold exhibits.

Articles by Historical Society Members

One of the early activities of the Society was to write accounts of old houses and other historical subjects. Only a few of these papers were printed or published in the newspapers. These papers preserve much of the oral tradition of the day but are not based on research in vital statistics, town records, wills, deeds, or other documentation. Hence dates and other statements in these papers have to be treated with reservation. The papers include the following titles:

> Mrs. John S. Smith — Separate short articles describing some 20 old houses written about 1890; these were run in a newspaper in 1903 and finally typed in the 1930s by the society.
>
> Mrs. Ella Ellis Holway - *The Nye Houses in Sandwich,* 1904; *Old Houses of Sandwich,* 1907; *The Old Cemetery Sandwich Massachusetts,* 1908.
>
> William L. Nye - *Travel and Transportation,* about 1914; *Sandwich,* 1919; *Old Houses, History of Sandwich, Town Hall Surroundings,* all about 1920; *Sandwich Academy,* 1921; *Sketch of the First Church in Christ,* 1925.

George E. Burbank — booklet *Sandwich-by-the-Sea,* 14 pp. 1914; *Radio,* 1927; *My Early Life,* 1931; *Old Houses,* about 1936; list of 61 historic sites that were marked for visitors in 1939 (some of these have no description and are not now known); booklet *A Bit of Sandwich History,* 40 pp., 1939, with dated highlights from 1637; articles on Sandwich glass.

FISH FREEZER AND GLASS FACTORY BUILDINGS IN RUIN—In the upper view the fish freezer had been the old pot house building, with elevator and extensions at left and right. This closed in 1918 and was used for lumber storage until torn down in 1937. The lower view shows the deteriorating conditions around the upper glass house before these buildings were demolished in 1920. Sandwich Archives from Freeman Farm, collection of Everard Pratt, Jr.

Decline of Manufacturing

The lower glass house at the B&S factory site, with its two great furnace chimneys, was torn down in 1907. By a coincidence, the three boiler chimneys in the plant (two at the power house and one at the pot house), all fell in storms in 1909 due to lack of maintenance. A businessman named Robert A. Hammond bought the derelict plant in 1909, stripped out all the remaining machinery and fittings and began some new manufacturing there. The 1853 pot house, with heavy brick walls (Dowden's lamp business), was selected to become a fish freezer; the windows were bricked up and an elevator, tanks and compressor installed. The Sandwich Freezer Co. was an affiliate of the Boston Fish Pier Company and received bulk fish for storage. This plant enjoyed a federal subsidy during World War I, but as soon as the war was over the plant closed. Hammond had patents on belting and made industrial belts in the old power house, as well as shoes in the old cutting shop. The cavernous upper glass house was used for lumber storage, and Nehemiah Packwood, Jr. also held auctions there. Hammond had one of the Furst-Clark dredges from the canal brought over to the old harbor and it chewed its way past the old outer docks, up Dock Creek, destroying the old tide gate, and clearing the inner harbor against the plant bunding. Barges could come in with fish, coal and lumber so that the area was busy again. However, Hammond died in 1915 and his enterprises either folded or removed. The next purchaser, about 1920, was the United States Insulating Board Company, which removed all the old brick buildings along Harbor and Factory Streets, except the watch house. The two remaining glass furnace chimneys were dynamited in September 1920. A new industrial building was built beside the watch house with reinforced concrete frame and metal sheathing. Here a chemical pulp was pressed into molded shapes such as for radio cases. The freezer plant still stood, used by Tom Kelleher for lumber storage. In 1937 the *Cape Cod Standard Times* bought the freezer building and removed the bricks to Hyannis where they can be seen today in the *Cape Cod Times* office wall on Main Street. The last buildings to go from the site were the Insulating Board ones, removed in 1946, although the heavy concrete base for the press remains. A metal office shed was moved across the street and stands on the roundhouse site owned by Mrs. Melix. The only buildings remaining today that were built by the B&S are the residences at 2, 4 and 6 Harbor Street and the apartment building at 6-12 Church Street.

In 1925 the town was asked to appoint a committee to induce manufacturers to locate in Sandwich. This was voted down, probably because of the expenses involved. At the long-anticipated canal industrial site, the Cape Cod Bay Shellfish Co., established in 1914 under Wilson and Dean, became bankrupt and the buildings were seized in 1916. Later that year a new company, Canal Fish and Freezing Company, was organized and built a large plant with wharf and rail spur. However, this plant closed again in 1921. After the tack plant fire in 1883, a new plant called the Union Braiding Company was built at the small mill-site on Grove Street. It was operated by H. H. Heald and Arthur Armstrong, with a new approach road from Grove Street behind the old Wing house. In 1893, this street became a town road, Union Braiding Road, and is still in place. In 1918 this plant was sold to McCullough Mfg. Co. of Boston and was converted to make small devices for Model T engines, described as spark gaps or timers. When this plant closed, there was no work going on at this site for the first time since the cotton factory was built in 1811. The Union Braiding plant was torn down by the new owner Peter P. Cook, who had purchased the H. T. Wing estate.

U. S. INSULATING BOARD COMPANY—The last business use of the B&S buildings along Factory Street was as part of this plant, which made molded objects like radio cases. The new buildings at right were on the site of the watch house. Courtesy of Sandwich Historical Society.

Summary of Town Events 1900-1950

There was a wide array of changes and events in this period of the town's history as electricity, the telephone, modern plumbing and heating, the automobile and tourists became accepted parts of life. Here is a chronological listing of events great and small:

1900 A tennis court was built on School Street.

1901 Corpus Christi Church opened on Jarves Street, using interior fittings from the Saint Peters Church which had suffered irreparable damage in the 1898 storm.

The town adopted a Town Seal designed by Melanie Leonard, developed from the Sandwich Kent seal; the motto POST TOT NAUFRAGIA PORTUS means Haven after Storms.

1902 In the directory for all New England telephones, Sandwich had one pay phone and six subscribers: J. W. Dalton, A. V. Johnston, S. I. Morse, N.

Packwood, Jr., Charles M. Thompson, and the Cape Construction Co.

1903 Ida Putnam of Spring Hill opened the Green Briar Jam Kitchen on Discovery Hill Road; hers was the first kitchen in America to use solar cooking for strawberries and soft fruits. The Village Improvement Society was organized, sponsored work on street triangles, and helped in use of Globe Gas Lights on the streets.

GREEN BRIAR JAM KITCHEN ABOUT 1920—The ancient narrow house at left was enlarged by the kitchen ell at center about 1840. Ida Putnam inherited the house in 1902 and commenced making jam for sale in 1903. The major enlargement at right with cellar and heating plant was completed about 1916. The Jam Kitchen had this essential form up to 1979 when it was purchased by the Burgess Society. Courtesy of Rosanna Cullity.

1906 Telephone poles began to be placed on town streets. The State Fish Hatchery off present Route 6A was begun.

1907 Town paid $45 for its red granite memorial stone in the Provincetown Pilgrim Memorial Tower. Phillips Road lots were laid out as part of Sagamore Beach colony.

1908 Marconi Club founded on Jarves Street honoring achievements of Guglielmo Marconi in wireless telegraphy. Spring Hill Neighborhood Club formed with Eda Roos as a charter member.

1909 The Boston Post provided a gold-headed cane to the oldest man in each of 700 towns in New England, to be turned in on his death to his successor. Who last had the Sandwich cane?

1910 Freeman Farm family placed bronze plaques on the Saddle and Pillion burial markers. The Town Hall addition at rear for stage and stairway was installed, with half the cost paid by the Winter Club. A memorial monument to Civil War Veterans in Town Hall Square was given by William Eaton; Dewey Square became Eaton Square.

1911 Weston Memorial Library opened; the main donors were William H. H. and Sophia Weston, both born to glassmaker families. The first gasoline dealer licensed to sell in Sandwich was Joshua A. Hall; the next were Jerome Holway in 1912, Mark Ellis in 1913 and W. A. Winsor in 1915.

1912 Letters SANDWICH were placed above the entry to Town Hall. Start of the fish hatchery on Old County Road.

1913 Sandwich Agricultural Association formed which held fairs at the Casino for 15 years. Buzzards Bay Electric Co. brought electricity to Sandwich village. The Village Improvement Society paid for street lights here up to 1949 and was reimbursed by the town. Fire destroyed the Boyden block and adjacent stable with stage coaches inside; the Unitarian Church and Central House were saved, as were the horses in the stable.

1914 Plank Walk was extended over to the beach. Electricity was added to Town Hall. We believe this is also the point at which silent movie shows began at Town Hall using DC power from Bill Winsor's garage, and special fireproof booths in the balcony for the arc light projector.

1915 Opening of Ben Lomond Golf Course at Sagamore. Louis Govoni bought the Central House and changed name to Daniel Webster Inn; a big ell was built at the west end in place of the old balcony section. Town voted to discontinue the lockup on River Street and dispose of the building.

1916 Two rooms were added to the Sandwich Academy, and a fire escape. The Schumacher sisters opened Camp Cotuit, a girls' camp on Lawrence Pond.

1918 The Unitarian, Methodist and Congregational Churches agreed to hold Federated services at each church in rotation; services soon settled on the Unitarian Church; the original religious societies continued to own the properties. Michael Haddad and Alden Clark both died in Febuary 1918 of illness, the first deaths of Sandwich servicemen in World War I.

1919 Town welcoming event for returning service people. The Town voted to employ a district nurse.

1921 A giant historical pageant was organized and written by poetess Bangs Burgess (Mrs. Joseph A. Mahoney); given at Pope's pasture off Grove Street with two hundred in the cast.

1922 State threatened to close Town Hall if the toilets were not repaired. Another giant pageant was put on for the Sandwich Winter Club by Bangs Burgess, entitled *Contrasting Cameos The Evolution of Womanhood.* Methodist Society sold its church to the Masonic Lodge, first selling off the bell and communion set.

1923 A huge forest fire burned from Pocasset to East Sandwich. Formation of the Sandwich Woman's Club with annual projects of social value.

1925 A fire engine was bought for $4,000 and the department reorganized. The Cooperative Bank built a new brick building on Main Street. There were tea rooms at Mrs. Harvey's on Shawme Pond, at the Dunbar House, at Green Briar and elsewhere, popular with automobile visitors to the town.

1926 Feb. 28, a strong earthquake at 7 P.M.

1927 The ladder wagon with leather fire buckets (formerly kept at the rear of Town Hall) was sold to the Ford Museum at Dearborn, Michigan. The town was advised not to enlarge roads for automobiles, as this would only increase speeds.

1928 The town accepted Jarves Street from the railroad to the factory, and Factory Street from Harbor Street to Liberty Street as town roads, previously private. Also, the town purchased the Fountain Lot (Manila Park) from Keith Car to be a town park. Start of Camp Burgess by Quincy YMCA on Triangle Pond; the area grew to 550 acres, connecting to Lawrence and Spectacle Ponds. Dedication of H. T. Wing School, built largely through bequests from Henry T. Wing and his wife Clementine (Swain) Wing.

1930 A new State Road (now Route 6A) was completed from the Bourne line to Charles Street with lights at the Jarves Street crossing, diverting through traffic out of the town center.

1931 Former Jarvesville school leased to American Legion Post.

1932 In deepening depression, the State asked if Sandwich was prepared to annex part of Mashpee if the latter failed as a town; response negative. Many houses were offered for sale at depressed prices, for example the Henry T. Wing colonial house, 24 Water Street with barn and 20 acres for $15,000. September 10 a total eclipse of the sun.

1934 Great minstrel show and dance at Casino, a fund-raiser for Jimmy Alvezi under treatment at Warm Springs Georgia for polio. Start of Camp Good News under Rev. Wyeth Willard on Snake Pond, now 211 acres.

1935 The town voted to favor a National Guard camp, previously opposed. A Planning Board was established to study zoning and development.

1936 Sandwich Academy sold; the Trustees gave proceeds to the town and disbanded.

1937 Deep cuts in rail service to Cape points and closure of the Chatham line. Sandwich Community Center started on Jarves Street with WPA funds, director Mary Morrow. A forest fire killed three firemen off Route 130, Forestdale.

1938 The town bought a forest fire truck. The New England Hurricane did some damage, chiefly to the Casino which was later torn down. A town park along the millstream again was proposed with lawn, flowers, and bridges.

1939 A modern fire station was built. Town offices were remodeled with matching funds; the John H. Stone paintings were accepted for the ground floor. A Youth Hostel was opened at the Skiff House, Spring Hill.

1941 A Police Department with a cruiser was authorized. The Town Dump area was leased from the Shawme-Crowell State Reservation. A Civil Defense Department was set up. Total of 201 persons from Sandwich served in Armed Forces; three were killed: Robert E. Johnson, Floyd H. Lewis and Theodore A. Gagner.

1942 Building at 14 Jarves Street used as United Service Organization (USO) center for uniformed people and social activities. The Town established a Rationing Board and a Military Procurement Board. First aerial photo survey voted.

1943 The Sandwich/Falmouth road was closed to allow Otis AFB runway construction; a new way in to the Military Base was accepted; Mid-Cape highway from Sagamore Bridge to Exit 2 (one lane only) was reserved for military use.

1944 Town voted $5,000 to repair hurricane damages, mostly in tree removal.

1946 The return of service men and women was honored at July 4th events. The town accepted Lombard Park at Snake Pond from Percival Hall Lombard.

1947 New Assessors' maps of the whole town were begun by Newell Snow, requiring six years to complete. The Village Improvement Society sponsored the first Christmas street lights.

1948 A second officer was added to the Police force. A program began to mark the graves of veterans of all wars. A World War II memorial plaque was dedicated at the library.

1950 A World War II memorial plaque was dedicated at the library. Honor Rolls for World Wars I and II were lettered and hung in Town Hall.

CHAPTER 30

GLASS BECOMES COLLECTIBLE

A glass rolling pin was received by the Sandwich Historical Society in 1919, and was described as the first piece of Sandwich glass in its collections. There may have been earlier gifts of glass, but this illustrates the late and casual start of the Society in the field in which it was to become famous. However, the decade after World War I became one of strong interest in American antiques, with much collecting and with a new freedom of the public to travel by automobile to remote corners. Newspapers and magazines ran regular antiques and art features which both utilized and spurred research in these subjects. Prices on good pieces rose keeping interest high. An article, "Glass Making in Sandwich", appeared in the *Boston Transcript* in August 1920, one of the earliest articles on Sandwich glass for the general public.

The 1925 Centennial Exhibit

The Sandwich Historical Society altered its building from a dwelling to a small museum with the special purpose of holding an exhibit to commemorate the first making of Sandwich glass in 1825. The exhibit of glass, borrowed from local families ,ran for three weeks from late July to mid-August, 1925, and attracted about 6,000 visitors, at 300 persons per day, an unheard of number. Visitors came from several foreign countries and from 46 states. The *Boston Transcript* ran a full page description of the show, which must be considered a seminal event. Photographs of the interior of the small building show long tables, some with extended drop-leaves, covered with glass, all completely open. However, nothing was lost or broken. A state policeman was on duty each day.

After the glass was returned, work on the building continued. In 1926, the Society moved its spinning wheels and other historical items over from Town Hall and opened to the public at twenty-five cents. In spite of the obvious high popular interest in glass, it was not until 1931 that another loan exhibit was held, and these then became annual events. Large collections of glass were being formed by dealers and well-to-do persons, so there was a ready market for the books of Ruth Webb Lee. Her *Early American Pressed Glass* appeared in 1936 with much attention to Sandwich, and her *Sandwich Glass, the History of the Boston and Sandwich Glass Company* appeared in 1939 with important new historical information. These books helped to make the name Sandwich important nationally. The venerable William L. Nye, the Society's president since 1907, died in 1936 at ninety-six and the next president, James W. Freeman, may have initiated a more systematic effort to acquire glass for the Society through gifts and regular purchases. It was in his period that the Museum became known as the Glass Museum. (James Freeman was the son of the Society's curator Caroline W. Freeman and grandson of its benefactor James L. Wesson.)

SANDWICH HISTORICAL SOCIETY GLASS CENTENNIAL—The Society's display of Sandwich glass in 1925 honoring the centennial of opening the drew national attention. Most of the pieces shown were borrowed from residents. Here a lady in a cloche hat brings in her epergne for display. Courtesy of Society for the Preservation of New England Antiquities.

Other Glass Writings

Caroline Freeman assembled clippings about Sandwich glass and about the Museum from 1925, by such writers as Charles Messer Stowe *(N.Y. Sun* antiques editor), Lura Woodside Watkins (author of *Cambridge Glass* 1930), Mary Elizabeth Prim, and William Germain Dooley *(Boston Transcript* antiques editor). Dorothea Setzer of Dennis wrote a leaflet about Sandwich glass for the Society in 1936, which was reissued in 1951. George Burbank of the Society wrote an article "History of the Sandwich Glass Works" in 1925, published in the *Cape Codder* in 1926 and used in the town's tricentennial booklet in 1939. He also wrote a highly anecdotal paper, "Glass House." An article appeared in *Antiques* in 1938, "Deming Jarves and his Glass Factory Village" by Mabel M. Swan. A different sort of study of Sandwich glass was conducted by Professor Frederick H. Norton of MIT, who with his students analyzed glass composition from fragments and also built a model or diorama of the glass-making process including clay-treading, pot-making, the furnace, the glory-hole and the annealing oven, with miniature tools and glass objects. This diorama was given to the Society in 1940.

An article appeared in *Life Magazine* in 1943 entitled "The Puritan Spirit," featuring Sandwich and its glass, contributing to the power of the legend. Another milestone was the appearance in 1948 of *Sandwich, the Town that Glass Built* by Harriot Buxton Barbour, again appealing to a national readership. With each such stimulus, there was a rise in attendance at the museum and further prestige encouraging loans and gifts.

Expansion of the Museum

The Society's property obtained from James L. Wesson in 1922 included an ancient shop building at the corner of the millstream and Main Street. This was occupied by Fred Bunker selling glass and antiques, and he continued sales here, paying rent to the Society and living upstairs, while his sign proclaimed his shop was the "Old Glass Museum." He owned the land on Tupper Road east of the Society's premises, and on his death in 1940 his daughter, Minnie Bunker Wimmer, sold the Society the land for a parking lot (badly needed) and vacated the old shop which the Society promptly removed. This helped for outside space. The Society's great expansion occurred later under the presidency of Everard Stowell Pratt. The son of Ambrose Pratt and grandson of Judge Whittemore, Pratt was a college-educated businessman working in New Jersey. His own Sandwich roots were reinforced by his marriage in 1914 to Evelyn Fessenden Carpenter of the Freeman Farm family. Evelyn was a cousin of former president James W. Freeman. The Pratts came to Sandwich on vacations and holidays, and became interested in the affairs of the Society. The museum was now heavily overcrowded in its single building of ancient and rather rickety wood construction. Pratt's great contribution was his success at fund raising through college and business friends, particularly in the Corning Glass Company. In 1957 the Jarves Wing on the south side of the central building was built. This was dedicated by Mrs. Charlotte Hall Chipman, through whose generosity the original lot of land had been acquired in 1920. The matching Craftsman's Wing on the north side was dedicated in 1959 by Mrs. James H. Tangney of Spring Hill, daughter of Gaffer Edward Haines and niece of Reverend (and glassmaker) Benjamin Haines. The third addition, a central ell at the rear, was named in honor of Pratt himself and dedicated by Mrs. Charles S. Lloyd, whose father-in-law was James Lloyd, the color expert at the and Cape Cod plants, son-in-law of the legendary mold-maker Hiram Dilloway. These modern additions and the publicity they generated enhanced the Society's prestige, and allowed increased attendance. Another successful effort of the Society was the inauguration of a series of Glass Forums with expert speakers, which attracted wide attendance. The first two Forums, in 1961 and 1962, were organized by Dorothea Setzer. Under Robert Paul Ashley the Society began, in 1965, to publish a newsletter called the *Acorn* (acorns and oak clusters were Jarves family motifs) and Ashley himself wrote a booklet on the history of the Society published in 1967. With ever-increasing attendance and administrative work, Doris Kershaw, the curator was named director in 1967 and Mrs. Ruth Wakefield became curator.

BUNKER'S GLASS MUSEUM—This building was opposite Town Hall and adjacent to the millstream. Fred Bunker lived upstairs and called his shop "Bunker's Old Glass Museum and Antique Exchange Gifts." The Historical Society owned the building and land, and on Bunker's death in 1940 tore the building down. Sandwich Archives, gift of Minnie Bunker Wimmer.

The Society's Growth

By the late 1960s the Glass Museum was attracting 70,000 persons per year, and became a fixture on the tourist bus schedules and a "must" for visitors to Cape Cod. It represented national fame for the old town and its glass. The Society had been in the right place at the right time in reaping this harvest of national interest in glass collecting, with its promise of ever-increasing values and the chance of finding a rare piece in a closet or an antique shop anywhere in the country.

Left, WILLIAM L. NYE (1840-1936—The grand old man of Sandwich in the early twentieth century, Mr. Nye represented the town in many causes and was the first president of the Historical Society. Courtesy of Nye Family of America. Right, ELLA FRANCES (ELLIS) HOLWAY—The leading spirit in the creation of the Historical Society and its first curator. Her studies of houses and of the Old Town Cemetery were of great value to later scholars. Courtesy of Sandwich Historical Society.

The Society had benefited immeasurably from the research into glass identification that had been done by many experts, and the abundant free publicity for Sandwich, its glass, and its museum in the sustained series of newspaper columns, magazine articles and books on glass. The resources of the Society itself, as generated by membership and attendance, were only enough to pay for operating expenses and a modest budget of glass purchases, but not to build endowment funds or new wings. The bulk of the collections had to come from gifts. As attendance and interest in the museum rose, so did the expenses of better cases, security, insurance, maintenance, sophisticated record-keeping and identification. A separate but related problem had faced the museum since its emergence, namely the temptation to accept loan collections over extended periods to enrich the displays. These were deeply gratifying to the lender, but carried a museum responsibility for record-keeping, protection and identification. In an atmosphere of prestige and success there could be problems and misunderstandings, so that growth was not without strain.

The chief officers of the Sandwich Historical Society have been as follows:

Presidents		*Curators*	
William L. Nye	1907–1935	Ella Frances Holway	1907–1915
James W. Freeman	1935–1948	Susan E. Silsby	1915–1919
Theodore Horton	1949	Melissa M. Ellis	1919–1928
Eugene S. Clark, Jr.	1950–1954	Caroline W. Freeman	1928–1944
Everard S. Pratt	1954–1964	Ruth T. Bartley	1945–1954
Robert P. Ashley	1964–1968	Faith Cook	1954–1960
William A. Walker	1969–1970	Doris Kershaw	1961–1967
Dr. Sanford Limouze	1970–1971	Ruth Wakefield	1967–1971
John A. Coe	1971–1973	George Anderjack	1971–1972
W. Gordon Swan	1973–1979	Nancy O. Merrill	1973–1977
Robert L. Gerling	1979–1984	Kauko E. Kahila	1977–1983
Blanche E. Robinson	1984–1985	(Glass Curator)	
John E. Flagg	1986–	Dorothy Hogan	1980–1983
Directors		*(Assistant Glass Curator)*	
Doris Kershaw	1967–1971	Russell A. Lovell Jr.	1977–1979
George Anderjack	1971–1972	(Historical Curator)	
Nancy O. Merrill	1973–1977	Martha Hassell	1979–1984
Dr. Albert C. Cook	1977–1981	(Historical Curator)	
Barbara Bishop	1981–1984	Dorothy Hogan	1984–2000
Barbara Rockefeller	1984–1986	(Glass Curator)	
Barbara Bishop	1986–	Lynne Horton	1984–2001
		(Historical Curator)	

The Town Outside the Historical Society

The explosion of interest in glass that began in the 1920s affected many families in Sandwich, many of whom never had any connection with the Sandwich Historical Society. Long before the main buildings were torn down in

1920, children and souvenir-hunters had prowled the industrial area picking up fragments. These were spread on tables by the roadside for tourists to pick over. Glass and ashes had been used to raise the factory yard level, toward the waterfront, and also spread on two large dump areas north and south of the plant. The old railway line across the marsh was built on glass and ashes, and this mix had been used for decades in the town to fill cellar holes and ditches. The first discriminating fragment hunter was Mrs. Hazel Blake French, who had been trained in jewelry design, and who found that colored glass fragments could be made into splendid jewelry. She continued to craft jewelry until her death in 1972. Another craftsman whose name has become synonymous with Sandwich glass jewelry is Nina Sutton, who with her mother Nina Baer, became expert in identifying glass. The critical importance of fragments to the study of Sandwich glass became clear to scholars and dealers, in that the fragments showed what patterns had been used in Sandwich, what range of objects had been made in each pattern, and which colors had been used here and which not. Even this analysis was not unfailing because pieces from other factories could have been brought in for study, and because glass not made at Sandwich (such as flat glass, blanks for cutting or marbles) was brought here for decoration or sale. To knowledgeable collectors, the removal of the brick floors around the upper glass house furnaces in 1920 was a unique opportunity for digging because these floors were laid in 1841 and 1850 and had protected the earliest fragments of blown-molded and of lacy glass. A *Boston Globe* article in 1923 called the Sandwich glass works excavators "an army." One of the active diggers was Francis "Bill" Wynn who gave information and fragments generously, usually without compensation. He provided Professor Norton's collection (later removed to the Smithsonian) and was highly praised by Ruth Webb Lee for his knowledge and help. Wynn was even retained by the Sandwich Historical Society briefly in a research capacity. Other early diggers were Lou Grady and Lee Flournoy.

The brick store had been a residence for many years in the Hamblin family when representatives of the Ford collections attempted to buy it for disassembly and removal to Dearborn, Michigan. However, the arrangement failed, and the building was torn down about 1959 by later owners, the Carons. Excavation in this lot and in the yards of other homes in Jarvesville showed how much historical evidence was underground.

Other Sandwich Writers on Glass

Bangs Burgess (Mrs. Joseph A. Mahoney) wrote a pleasant and informed article, "History of Sandwich Glass, " appearing in the *Boston Herald* in June 1925. She used this male pen name in honor of her Revolutionary War ancestor of that name; she was Helena Heffernan (1871-1952), niece of Thomas Heffernan, a glassmaker, and she wrote of her visits to the factory as a child and young woman. A book, *Story of Sandwich Glass and Glassware* was published in 1926, written by Frederick T. Irwin of Sandwich, son of glasscutter Benjamin Irwin. The ancient gaffer William F. Kern, living in New Bedford in his nineties, wrote some reminiscences.

SANDWICH GLASS—Pieces of Sandwich glass of different periods. At upper left, early blown and molded pieces; left a dolphin candlestick and right a pineapple epergne. Courtesy of Sandwich Glass Museum, Sandwich Historical Society.

In 1926 a series of seven highly informative articles on Sandwich glass began to appear in *Cape Cod Magazine,* written by Lavinia Donovan Walsh of Sandwich. These articles were said to be part of her forthcoming book to be entitled *The Romance of Sandwich Glass.* They caused so much interest that the magazine reprinted them in 1927/1928, followed by the concluding chapters of the promised book. Lavinia (1880-1951) was daughter of glassmaker John Donovan and his wife Mary (Maley), and had many roots in the B&S. She also studied original papers on the B&S found in the attic of C.C.P. Waterman at this time. Her sister Grace was married to Frank W. Chipman (1872-1935) a newspaper stringer and political aide. Frank's brother, Sands C. Chipman of Boston, was part owner of the *Cape Cod Magazine,* which ran not only Lavinia

Walsh's excellent articles but, beginning in 1927, full page ads for sales of Sandwich glass at the Chipman shop in Sandwich, manager Frank W. Chipman. Next, Frank conducted a Question and Answer Dept. on glass in this magazine, and by late 1927 the Chipman shop had become the "Old Sandwich Glass Museum," and Frank ("son and grandson of Old Sandwich Glassmakers") was showing pictures of glass he had sold to the famous and the rich. Chipman was not a scholar himself but was a gifted entrepreneur who found the eager public appetite for Sandwich glass to be profitable, and his sister-in-law's timely research to be very useful. His sales "Museum" was in the Donovan house opposite the Daniel Webster Inn, on what is now the library lawn. In 1932 he and his brother published a book, *The Romance of Old Sandwich Glass* by Frank W. Chipman, containing much of Lavinia's work word-for-word, but nowhere mentioning her name or that of the Donovans or the *Cape Cod Magazine.* Some errors were noticed in his text and captions, but these were not Lavinia's. Chipman's well-advertised Museum was closed after his death in 1935, and the title moved along Main Street to the Historical Society's emerging Museum and Fred Bunker's rather down-at-heel "Old Glass Museum."

The National Early American Glass Club

Frank Chipman's real contribution was in introducing glass to many who became dedicated and informed collectors. In January 1933 a meeting of collectors was held at the Boston winter home of Caroline Freeman, the Historical Society's Curator, resulting in the formation of The National Early American Glass Club. Frank Chipman became the first president and Mrs. Freeman treasurer. The Club held a show in the vestry of the First Parish Church in Sandwich in August 1933, giving visitors to the town the privilege of seeing both this and the Historical Society's annual loan exhibition. The writer Charles Messer Stow had the highest praise for the quality and breadth of the Glass Club's show. The Club and the Sandwich Society have enjoyed cordial and supportive relations ever since, for example recently from the museum Nancy O. Merrill, Kauko Kahila and Blanche E. Robinson have also each served as Glass Club presidents.

The Town's Glass Memorial Committee

In 1950 the town accepted from George Mooney the gift of a small plot of land on Factory Street opposite Jarves Street where the watch house of the B&S had stood. A Glass Memorial Committee was formed to prepare a suitable marker to honor the contribution of the Boston and Sandwich Glass Company to the town. The memorial chosen was a large bronze map of the 1849 layout of the factory, mounted on a concrete plinth. The plaque therefore does not show the plant as it was in the 1880s, which was the way people remembered it and the way it appeared in photographs, quite different from the layout of 1849.

In 1953 the Glassware Institute of America bought a lot in Jarvesville once owned by the B&S with the intent of making a "suitable building...which would be a memorial to the Boston and Sandwich Glass Co. and its founder

Demming Jarvis (sic)." This idea was supported in Sandwich Town Meetings, which asked the town's Glass Memorial Committee to assist in the design. Nothing further was reported in town meeting on this project, and nothing was built.

TOWN MARKER FOR BOSTON & SANDWICH GLASS CO.—A small lot near the former watch house was given to the town by George Mooney, and a committee under Col. Seymour Clark designed the bronze marker. At the dedication in 1951 are Colonel Clark (speaking), Patrick Russell, an unidentified man. Charles Montague, Thomas Kelleher, Colonel Roy Brown, George Wing and George Mooney. Sandwich Archives, gift of Clarence H. Haines.

The Glass-Making Memory

Among the gifts to the Historical Society after the 1925 Centennial Exhibition were George McLaughlin's gift of the big watch-house bell and John Kelleher's gift of a set of glass maker's tools. The glass that was given by Sandwich people seems to have come mainly from the Main Street houses of Lloyds, Leonards, Fessendens, Spurrs, Watermans and other families associated with the plant management. However, elsewhere in the town was a great store of memories and artifacts—pieces of glass made for special occasions, tools, photographs, documents, odd bits and the stories that went with them. This intimate knowledge of the B&S and of the Cape Cod and Crib factories was a slowly dissipating treasure, available in some measure to those who sought it out but never exhausted. Writers and reporters, fragment hunters and serious collectors all might go to one or another house to talk to some persons and come away with some gleanings to be written about, or some purchases showing the family share of the legend. Much left Sandwich in this way. However, no one did massive or even systematic research—it would have required a degree of resources, techniques, access, skilled people and coordination that simply did not exist in the decades after 1925, although the value of such knowledge was obvious. Much research was done as shown by all the books and articles but much was lost through death, scatter, shyness, uncertainty or simply because no one asked. In 1959 at the dedication of the Craftsman's Wing of the Glass Museum, one of the items on the program was the solemn reading of a list of relatives of glass makers known to be still living. This was impressive but no one took it as a call to go and talk to each one.

THE B&S SITE IN 1946—This desolate scene is all that remained of the B&S industrial area after the final removal of the US Insulating Company buildings. A number of modern homes were soon built on the six-acre site. Courtesy of Leona Melix Koslowski.

CHAPTER 31

USING THE LAND

In this chapter we will outline some remarkable events having a common thread of relations to the land. These include the formation of Shawme-Crowell State Forest, the evolution of Camp Edwards and the Otis Air Force Base, the extraordinary career of Samuel Dudley Hannah, the way in which Town Neck was lost to the Town, and lastly the story of the Faunce Demonstration Farm and of the decline of farming here.

Coonamesset Ranch and Bear Hollow Farm

In 1916, a corporation of New York investors started to buy up land in southern parts of Sandwich and Bourne, and adjacent Falmouth, paying as little as $2.00 per acre for the poorer land. Many of the Sheep Pasture Lots and Woodlots had lain untaxed for years as owners were absent and unaware even of their inheritance. This corporation, the Coonamesset Land Co., hoped to develop the largest ranch east of the Mississippi, and in 1921 had 14,000 acres, although there were many gaps with unknown owners or those who refused to sell. The ranch headquarters was in Hatchville, and initially 500 acres were cleared for market gardens and for cattle. Although it claimed to be making a profit, the ranch sold out to the Crane family in 1930.

Percival Hall Lombard (1872-1932) owned a ranch in Colorado, but sold this just before World War I and bought the property known as Bear Hollow Farm in Forestdale and Bourne near Coonamesset. Mr. Lombard is wellremembered in Bourne as founder of the Bourne Historical Society and a leading spirit in the project to recreate the Aptucxet Trading Post. He made certain gifts to the Sandwich Historical Society as well, and gave the Town of Sandwich land at Snake Pond for a town park and bathing beach. Both he and the Coonamesset Ranch people were sure that the land could some day be farmed intensively and profitably.

State Forests

In 1914, the Commonwealth created a Forestry Commission of three members and appropriated $90,000 to buy land for reforestation. With later appropriations, the state owned 610,000 acres and by 1922 had started to buy burnt-over woodland in Bourne and Sandwich. To set a good example, James L. Wesson, a summer resident of Sandwich, and Hon. Eben S.S. Keith of Sagamore, donated many acres of woodland to the state to help in forming large blocks for reforestation. The Cape Cod Chamber of Commerce and the Massachusetts

Forestry Association formed a joint Cape-wide committee to promote planning for reservation of appropriate lands in every town. The Massachusetts Forestry Association had a standing offer to provide and plant 5,000 trees for any town that would establish a forest of 100 acres or more. The towns were to provide fire lanes, fire fighting men and equipment, and to clear areas in advance of the intended plantings. In spite of all preparations, early in 1923 a fire started in Bourne, got quickly out of control and in seven days, burned over 25,000 acres extending to Route 6A, Sagamore, Old Main Street, Sandwich and down to Spring Hill. Many houses were saved only with the greatest effort. The State Commissioner of Conservation stated flatly "that something is radically wrong in those towns. It was not a 'fire day.' There was no reason why the fire could not have been stopped. It could have been confined to less than 1,000 acres if it had been properly handled." Since he could decide against further reforestation on the Cape in favor of areas with less risk, there were hasty protests that all possible had been done. Lincoln Crowell of Sandwich, a Cape official of the State Forestry Division under the Commissioner of Conservation, urged continuance of the state program and declared the fire a blessing in clearing away brush, but pointed out that planting and firebreaks should be done before brush grew back. (It took only five years to grow enough brush for a big fire.) Later, in 1923, the state legislature passed an act creating the Shawme State Forest of about 8300 acres from land in Sandwich and Bourne, north of Forestdale, and extending up to Sagamore and Route 130 in Sandwich. This act allowed the taking of all lots at fair market value. In 1924, the town of Sandwich made a gift of two town lots to be included in this area.

The name of this State Forest was changed to Shawme-Crowell State Forest in 1938, honoring the long and devoted service of Lincoln A. Crowell to Cape Cod forestry. Mr. Crowell, of the Sandwich Crow Farm family, was killed in a car-train accident in Brewster in 1938 while on forestry duty.

A Massachusetts National Guard Camp

Early in 1934 word got out that the state and/or federal government was planning to purchase the former Coonamesset Ranch area to establish a military base. The Crane owners were represented by Hon. Charles R. Crane, a Woods Hole summer resident and former Ambassador to China. The Chamber of Commerce and tourist interests protested loudly, calling the plan a blight on the landscape. It developed that the state planned to buy the land in order to have a big enough area to gather the whole Twenty-Sixth Division Massachusetts National Guard for training, replacing Camp Devens near Fitchburg which was small and could not be enlarged. The federal government would aid by putting up 400 buildings to house 8,000 men. Opponents organized and petitioned to stop it, stating that the loss of 20 square miles in Bourne alone would deprive the town of land for development and expansion, that it would stop the proposed Mid-Cape highway from the new Bourne Bridge then being built, and that the size of guns and garrison would increase, with more noise and danger. The town of Bourne voted against it 170 to 11, and the town of Sandwich voted likewise. The state arguments were that the Cape site was the best in the state, that the area of the camp was not fit for development, that thousands of extra visitors would arrive, that construction work would be a bonanza and that the troops would spend locally as well. The bill to create the camp failed in the legislature, but Representative William A. Jones of Hyannis voted for it and wrote in favor of it believing that overall the Cape would benefit.

In 1935 the project was revived by the new Governor James M. Curley, and possibly in the Depression atmosphere, the prospect of all that construction money and all that extra local spending began to sink in. In February 1935 Bourne switched and voted for the Camp 223 to 32. The voters of Sandwich also switched, and the measure quickly passed the legislature to purchase the Crane land and other areas up to the borders of the Shawme Forest, which would be partly in the firing range. The Bourne vote asked that the Camp proper be one mile east of Route 28, although the land taking ran close to the highway. The former Coonamesset Ranch land, taken at this time for $50,000, consisted of 4,307 acres in Bourne, 3,841 in Sandwich and 597 in Falmouth. Much of the Bear Hollow Farm land and much more to the north was also taken, so that the total, including Shawme Forest, was about 25,000 acres as compared to 2,280 acres at Fort Devens.

Camp Edwards

By February 1936 four hundred men were at work on the underbrush and had roughed out 40 miles of road. At this time the plans were for 300 permanent buildings but no barracks, since army regulations were that National Guard units on intensive field training should sleep under canvas. The first 1200 men and 50 horses came down from Fort Devens in June 1936. The tent area was flooded by a cloudburst but soon raised board floors were installed. Hundreds of tourists came to see the sights. The Camp improved rapidly. By 1938 it had an outdoor amphitheatre seating 5,000, eight baseball diamonds, a boxing ring, running track, rifle range and a level parade ground of almost a square mile. The associated camp airport for light training planes had a pair of grassed strips, one of 3,850 feet, one of 4200 feet. The camp had a 200,000 gallon water tank and a sewage treatment plant. There was a shortage of men available from local towns to fill all the jobs that were funded. The camp was named Camp Edwards for Major General Clarence R. Edwards, commander of the Twenty-Sixth Division in World War I. The dedication of the camp in July 1938 was a memorable event. The entire Yankee Division assembled for the first time since 1919, forming a parade twelve miles long. The reviewing stand contained the governor and many state dignitaries, and a crowd of about 50,000 came to witness the show.

Federal Government Operations

The government took over control of Camp Edwards on September 4, 1940, and promptly began a vast enlargement of the base so as to enable it to house, train, and feed over 30,000 men. The architect-engineer firm was Charles T. Main, Inc. of Boston, and the Walsh Construction Co. of Davenport, Iowa was in charge of building. The speed and mechanization with which some 1500 new buildings were built remain amazing even now. Blocks of new barracks surrounded the central drill field. Concrete foundations were built just ahead of an army of carpenters, followed rapidly by plumbers, electricians, sheet metal workers, etc. There were some 18,000 men working at peak with a payroll of nearly a million dollars a week, and the workmen had to commute daily to the site. The movement of construction supplies was by the trainload, and the first had to be unloaded at Buzzards Bay. However, by November 1, a new siding was laid from Falmouth into a network of lines in the base so that supplies could come direct by rail to the quartermaster's warehouse, to the coal depot and the cold storage building. New draftees for a year's training started coming in December. The building contractor's last men vacated in March 1941 and the huge base was then fully operational and self-contained. Beside training some 100,000 men for overseas duty, the camp later had other functions, including a convalescent hospital for wounded veterans, a processing center for returning AWOL and deserters from overseas, and a prisoner-of-war work center. The prisoners even did seasonal work for cranberry and strawberry growers.

SAMUEL D. HANNAH (1867-1945)-This view was taken in his latter home in the ancient Wing house on Scorton Neck. The fireplace is noted for its great size. Courtesy of heirs of Junia Hannah Curtin.

Otis Air Force Base was named in honor of Lieutenant Frank Jesse Otis, Jr. MD, of the Massachusetts National Guard who had been killed on flying duty in 1937. After the start of the war in December 1941, the first concrete runways were laid in 1942 and were lengthened and widened in 1943, with necessary airfield facilities. First an anti-submarine patrol was based here, then in 1944, the Navy Air Arm controlled the base. At the end of the war, both the camp and the air base were deactivated, and the barracks were later removed. In 1948 the air base was reopened for a Fighter/Interceptor Wing, and remained open until the recent return of the base to Massachusetts Air National Guard and Coast Guard use..

Samuel Dudley Hannah, 1867-1945

Mr. Hannah is a unique figure in Cape Cod history, and with his residence and large landholdings in Sandwich in his latter years, he invites our interest and attention. Junia Hannah Curtin (1898-1980) made available many of her father's papers to the Archives, some of which were highly unorthodox. He is particularly of value to us now for his clear warning and blunt summary of the Town Neck land case. Hannah was born in Ohio, studied real estate law at Ohio University, went into real estate in Boston in 1893, and formed a marketing company called Homestead Trust. He did well in Revere Beach developments and in 1902 bought 18 acres on Buttermilk Bay in Buzzards Bay. In 1905 the Homestead Trust attempted to sell lots in a 1500-acre site on Turpentine Road, partly in Sandwich, partly in Bourne where 500 acres had been laid out by Charles M. Thompson in five-acre home-sites with roads and water supply. This remote "Farm Village" development, in spite of heavy promotion, did not sell well and probably went into Shawme Forest. Hannah moved to New York in 1906 and engaged in residential and commercial development, retiring to Buzzards Bay to live in 1920 at age fifty-three.

The Homestead Trust had remained alive and had even acquired property for Coonamesset Ranch in 1919. Hannah was active on this and other Cape Cod investments. The largest was a 745-acre tract in North Truro along the outer beach at Pilgrim Heights, purchased for about $90,000 in 1921. This parcel eventually became a part of the National Seashore. Because of the complex and torturous uncertainties of tracing the title of Cape Cod real estate in these important cases, Hannah came to study the history of Plymouth Colony and of the original Cape towns in great detail. Curiously enough, at this exact time a scholarly book was published, "The Town Proprietors of the New England Colonies, a Study of their Development, Organization, Activities, and Controversies, 1620-1770" by Roy H. Akagi. This mass of detail on land transactions and proprietors' companies seems to have fired Hannah's imagination, possibly because, in spite of its title, the Akagi book contained nothing at all on Cape Cod. So he set out to record a number of early land transactions and legal findings on land suits in Barnstable County. He accumulated many notebooks of references and wrote a number of articles on land titles, concentrating on the acts of early proprietor companies. While he was doing this research in the late 1920s, his Homestead Trust acquired a large tract formerly in the Wing family on Scorton Neck. Here he laid out Sandwich Downs lots in 1926. His ads in Boston newspapers at this time refer to a "wide range of Cape Cod acreage for investment or development, from one to one thousand acres, none with doubtful titles." He would have been safe sticking to land investment and sales, but a statement in Akagi's work remained in his mind that an original proprietorship must remain in legal existence if all its land had not been allotted, even if it had no meetings and even if the descendants of the proprietors were unknown. Grasping this as a valid principle, he attempted to revive ancient and hypothetical proprietorships by finding a few descendants and forming a new corporation which claimed power to inherit, own, and sell land. This effort was viewed with great alarm wherever it was attempted, in both the legal and the real estate community, and each time was contested and defeated in court. It is especially curious, and even sad, that after all his hard and detailed study Hannah should come up with an unfounded and completely unworkable thesis, making many doubt his judgment in other matters.

He moved to the former Edward Wing colonial house on Scorton by 1931 purchased from the Blakes, and sold his Buzzards Bay property. His wife died in 1933. His correspondence with Sandwich Town Clerk Frank Howland indicates a cash flow problem in the Depression, as many lots in Sandwich Downs were taken for taxes. One of his last notable appearances in public was in 1937 in a successful protest against certain poll tax practices. The town of Bourne, and possibly others, fined delinquents (particularly immigrants) for not paying their poll taxes (two dollars per year), and added costs of the town collector to go to their homes to collect. Although it knew of his change of address to Sandwich, the town of Bourne kept trying to collect Hannah's last poll tax at the old Bourne address until it had escalated to twenty-eight dollars with fines and costs. Hannah refused to pay and went to jail (like Thoreau) in a gesture of protest at the system. The Boston newspapers had a field day at a famous landowner jailed over a two-dollar item. The charges were dropped, and soon the whole poll tax system as well. Mrs. Curtin commissioned a memorial biography of Mr. Hannah, together with some of his most cogent writings and research findings. "The Proprietary Lands of Plymouth Colony and Cape Cod" by Samuel D. Hannah (1867-1945), edited by Stephen Connolly, was published in 1980 just after her death.

Town Neck Background

As discussed in chapter 7, in 1689 Town Neck was placed under control of a group of proprietors representing nearby families on both sides of the millstream who wished to use the Neck for pasturage. Many nearby families (Dillingham, Bassett, Dexter, Skiff, Chipman, Smith, Prince for example) did not join the proprietors to use Town Neck at first, but were admitted later. The area was 132 acres, considered suitable for 66 cows, and the phrase "cow right" is found in later wills and deeds as an inheritable and saleable right to use the Town Neck land for pasturage in common.

Town Neck—Changing Perceptions

An article in the *Seaside Press* in June 1874 reflected the new interest in summer visitors and land development, doubtless based on what was going on in

Bourne, Falmouth, and other shoreside towns. It read:

> "Proprietor's Neck or what is better known by the name of Town Neck affords good pasturage this season for 45 cows and 14 young cattle...This is another locality well suited for summer residences, being situated on high ground. It affords a fine view of the ocean, the town and its surroundings. Many sites with far less attractiveness have been purchased by Land Companies in many towns on the Cape and laid out for building lots. With a good roadway to the beach and other improvements which might be made by the town, not only in connection with this particular location, but in others that we have spoken of in the PRESS, and would be an investment in the right direction to make Sandwich more attractive and an investment which the town would never have cause to regret."

The writer here assumed clearly that the Neck was the town's to develop as it wished. Without any town vote to make a layout, a road around the outside of the pasturage area suddenly appeared, and in February 1875 the Town approved accepting the new road from the railroad crossing to the beach, over the land of William Fessenden and the lands of the Town Neck proprietors. This may have been an effort to deflect the town from taking the whole neck for development through guaranteeing town access to the beach. The town seems to have liked the beach access idea, because it accepted a plan in June 1875 to build the plank walk over to the beach from Jarvesville. Meanwhile the proprietors held a meeting to see if they would vote to organize themselves into a corporation under the laws of the Commonwealth. In 1888 the proprietors applied for incorporation as the Town Neck Land Company of Sandwich. Samuel Fessenden testified that since 1690 the land had been owned by 66 persons in common, and that he now owned 38 of the rights. He did not say "cow rights" but stressed that as principal owner he had had to go to expense to fence the common area because of interest in the prospective canal (i.e., crowds watching the Lockwood Dredge) and was having trouble sharing the expense of the fence.

In 1908 the Town accepted a large block of marsh and dune land just east of Town Neck offered by Dr. L. C. Jones, and voted to take by eminent domain land for a public playground from Town Neck Road to the Plank Walk along the upland and down to the edge of the beach. A sum of $500 was approved for expenses of the taking and the selectmen were directed to file a certificate of this taking with plan by Charles M. Thompson dated November 30, 1908. There were questions as to whether a taking for this purpose was legal but it was allowed. In 1912, by petition, a town way was laid out from the northerly end of Town Neck Road easterly to where the Humane House once stood, near the harbor.

Town Neck Land Court Proceedings

Much involving Town Neck from 1919 on is not clear from available records, but obviously the proprietors were determined to obtain full ownership in place of their ancient pasturage rights. The progress of the case was as follows:

1919 - The town voted that the selectmen oppose any sale of rights the town may have in Town Neck.

1920 - A committee under William L. Nye reported to the town that the town had lost all rights in Town Neck and that the proprietors were the owners. The proprietors had voted to allow Charles H. Taylor to petition for possession. Mr. E. B. Howland very swiftly moved to accept the report and for the selectmen to give a quitclaim deed for any claim the town may have in the property.

1920 - Charles H. Taylor initiated Land Court proceeding #19252 to determine the owners of Town Neck. After hearings a report was accepted and confirmed in 1921.

1923 - Frederick Tudor petitioned for a physical partition of the land. He had bought 46 of the cow rights from the estate of Charles H. Taylor. This proceeding #20458 listed the 66 rights holders.

1924 - The Court appointed Allen Beale and Bertrand C. French of Sandwich and Arthur P. Crosby of Brookline to make the plan of partition. Their plan showed Hamilton Garland now the holder of 59 shares, the others held by Michael J. Murphy and Jonathan Clark (two each) and George Burbank, F. Tudor, and Fletcher Clark (one each).

1932 - The report on the above case was not filed until the end of 1931, with the detailed plan showing the location of all the rights. The area was then 124 acres, probably due to the town taking in 1909. The hearing in Barnstable was held February 23, with a number of persons from Sandwich in attendance including the selectmen. Judge Campbell very pointedly put off a decision until the town of Sandwich had an opportunity to take some action if the voters at the annual town meeting so desired.

Town Neck—The Town's Rights

Judge Campbell doubtless knew of legal precedents establishing town rights in ancient commons no matter who claimed them. One such precedent had been published in the *Sandwich Independent* in 1914 describing an Ipswich case exactly parallel to the Sandwich case. Jeffrey's Neck Pasture in Ipswich of 400 acres had been a town common, then assigned to proprietors in 1713. Recently the proprietors had deeded rights to an individual who planned to make sale. The town brought suit against both the proprietors and the individual, and the full Supreme Court found the town still the right holder, and voided the proprietor's deed of sale.

Only two months previous to the Barnstable hearing, Samuel D. Hannah had discussed the Town Neck case in a long interview in the *New Bedford*

Sunday Times. He said:

> "One of the outstanding examples in Massachusetts of this type of use (cow rights) of a common area is Town Neck in Sandwich...During the past several years by various "loop the loop" legal procedures they (the present proprietors) are endeavoring to translate a permissive use into a property right of title to the land as tenants in common...this area is without doubt the property of the present town, which is subject to use as a common pasture until such time as the town sees fit to cancel the pasturing use and devote the area to other purposes...In the town of Sandwich...there is a divided opinion as to the necessity of protecting so-called town rights in such areas, the reason being that in many instances town voters or some of them claim the rights of pasture, tillage, etc. setting up ownerships as tenants in common in themselves and defeat town action either through wire pulling at town meetings or by continued propaganda to frighten the town because of prolonged litigation with its high cost, expensive lawyers, etc. Thus towns are forced into a corner and permit others, usually few in number, to walk away with the spoils...It is stated that some years ago the town of Sandwich voted to grant to the proprietors of the Town Neck all its title and interests if any, etc. But if the real proprietor of the Neck is the Town, then such conveyance is to itself."

Hannah clearly knew what was going on in Sandwich and his words were prophetic. At the town meeting on March 7, 1932, the town voted to take no legal action on its interest in Town Neck but the selectmen were instructed to take such steps as might be necessary to protect the interests of the town in the public playground, as though that were threatened. The proprietors had done their work well, and as Hannah forecasted, walked away with the spoils.

The Faunce Demonstration Farm

Doctor Robert H. Faunce (1859-1908) was a popular physician in Sandwich who lived in the family home *Uplands* (111 Main St.) with his widowed mother Harriet T. Faunce (1830-1909). He was unmarried and an only child. The Faunces had come to South Sandwich from Plymouth in the 18th century, and had acquired *Uplands* through the marriage of William Faunce to Mary Bourne in 1804. *(Uplands* had been built by Timothy Bourne about 1740.) Dr. Robert Faunce was only 49 when he died unexpectedly in 1908. His mother, with no close relatives, decided to make the place into a memorial for her son, and in her own will provided for the whole property to be administered by four trustees and to be used at their discretion for some educational or charitable purpose for the whole county. On her death in 1909 the trustees had a difficult choice how to carry out their mandate, and decided to try to convert part of the land into a farm to demonstrate what could be done with determination and the new scientific knowledge. The aims of the Demonstration Farm were established as:

1. To demonstrate the possibility of raising certain crops on Cape Cod at a profit, including poultry, fruit, and vegetables.
2. To encourage existing farmers to change to better methods and crops on their land.
3. To interest young people to consider agriculture as a vocation.
4. In view of the general benefit clause in the Trust, to assist the spreading concern for community betterment on Cape Cod.

THE BOURNE-FAUNCE HOUSE: "UPLANDS"-Tbis beautiful colonial house at 111 Main St. was built by Timothy Bourne and passed by marriage to the Faunce family. Doctor Robert Faunce and bis mother established a trusteeship by which the land above this residence (now Dale Terrace) became the Faunce Demonstration Farm and was operated as a profitable farm in the period 1911-1916. Sandwich Historical Commission.

What made this plan difficult was that the endowment funds were not overly large, and that the property was not and never had been a fruit and vegetable farm. The main house and land near the street were only about two acres, and then there were steep slopes of heavy clay up to the upper level (Dale Terrace area) where there were about eight acres of fairly level land. The rest of the property was in woodlands. The Trustees felt that if a new farm could be created here, one could be made or improved anywhere, and the lesson would be valuable. The property included another house at 110 Main St. which would be the superintendent's house while the main colonial house would be rented for estate income. The first superintendent was Mr. Albert W. Doolittle, who had to draw down the endowment to build farm buildings, clear land, make terraces, buy equipment and build up supplies. Later, a well and water supply system were added. The interest from only $20,000 remaining was to provide Doolittle's salary and working capital, with future income from produce and house rental to cover salary of an assistant and other expenses. This was a desperately tight budget requiring extraordinary work to make it operate. Doolittle however, employing casual labor in 1911 and 1912, managed somehow to plant an orchard of 150 apple, peach and plum trees, set 3,000 strawberry plants, 600 raspberry bushes, 1,000 asparagus roots and eight varieties of grapes. The latter were grown on terraces facing south after the soil had been lightened. There was a poultry plant with 200 birds in two laying houses, plus an incubator and place for 500 chicks. Haw, straw and field corn were grown for the chickens, plus mangel beets. Doolittle decided on potatoes as a cash crop. He had only one horse, and hired heavy horses for plowing. There was a greenhouse. As a demonstration farm, it showed technical aspects of pruning, spraying, land use, cultivation, soil treatment, and so on, but did not have modern equipment or showy grounds, as there was neither money nor time for anything but basics.

An assistant, Bert Tomlinson, started work early in 1913 and had to room and board out on a salary of $600 per year. Doolittle left for a teaching job in 1913 and Laurence B. Boston became the new superintendent. In addition to running the farm and doing some of the work, Boston had to serve for two days a week as the County Agent for the Extension Service in Barnstable County, traveling to various farms for demonstrations plus giving talks to groups, writing reports on county agriculture and keeping up with the literature. He also wrote a monthly column for the *Cape Cod Magazine,* arranged displays and showed visitors around. Somehow the farm showed a profit in a great variety of goods sold through local stores and stands. Marketing without interfering with the other local farms required careful planning.

Experience proved that demonstration farms were not effective routes for reaching the farmers who needed technical help. The Faunce Farm, the similar Calvin Paige Farm in Hardwick, a demonstration orchard and a mobile unit were phased out by the Extension Service. In 1916 Boston became full time Extension Service Agent in Hyannis while Tomlinson moved to Maine. The Faunce Farm trustees had to find other routes to use their funds in their idealistic goals. The Faunce house and lands were sold to build a Trust Fund from which the interest went to various causes.

Cranberries on Cape Cod

Cape Cod did not have the broad acres needed for efficient production of food grains, but certain crops did grow well here and commanded a ready market. Cranberries were a special case, which their growers regarded as an art and science distinct from all other agricultural production. Bogs had been built from about 1850, requiring an expensive process of preparing a wide flat surface, water supply, drainage ditches, water run-off and exact soil preparation. It was found that Finnish immigrants had a natural understanding of this construction and the annual cycle of growth. By 1921 there were 3500 acres of bogs in this county, and the first power-assisted devices for gathering the crop were first tried. It was early recognized that unlike other fruit and vegetables, a cooperative marketing organization was a necessity to process, pack and release cranberries to the national consumer. Mr. Isaiah Tobey Jones of Sandwich was an early leader in establishing this approach. Through the efforts of the Cape Cod Cranberry Growers Association, the State established an experimental station at East Wareham as part of the Agricultural College, later the University of Massachusetts. The director was Dr. H. J. Franklin, then Dr. Chester Cross of Sandwich. Cranberry production has continued to increase and is one of the Cape's only remaining exports.

Decline of Farms

Dairies were common on Cape Cod in the nineteenth century. A gazetteer reports that in 1870 Sandwich (including Bourne), had 242 farms from which 16,580 gallons of milk were produced for market plus 7,632 pounds of butter. Dairy production remained substantial into the 1920s, but declined when strict state standards and pasteurization became law. Mr. J. Louis Roberti of Sandwich recalls that at this time there were 20 farms producing milk in Sandwich, and 200 Cape-wide.

The Barnstable County Agricultural Agents, like Mr. Boston and his successors, found it hard to convince old Yankee farmers (and even some recent European ones) of the need for changes from old ways. The more a farmer needed help the less he was inclined to make basic changes in his operations, such as in land allocation, crop rotation, new varieties and especially in growing crops that were plowed in to replenish the soil. Farmers tended to be conservative and to continue to do things that had been profitable in their fathers' time. Changes of lot sizes meant moving fences, trees and walls. New equipment or livestock or buildings meant loans with risk of failure. For example, it is hard for us now to visualize the revolution that tractors represented when they were introduced about 1915.

One of the first on the Cape was at Bay End Farm at Head-of-the-Bay in Bourne (now Grazing Fields Farm) where the tractor was used to pull stumps and do deep plowing. Many Cape farmers resented the necessity to join in cooperative arrangements for purchasing and marketing because it reduced their options and lessened their independence—even though it was the only route to profits.

Nevertheless, just as State aid and technical advice was becoming freely available to Cape Cod farmers, there was a steady decline in the number of farms. A State publication tells this record of farm owners on Cape Cod:

	1910	*1920*
Native whites	734	548
Immigrant whites	113	115
Indians & Blacks	17	12
	864	675

As the old owners died or retired, the farms stopped. Sons preferred other ways of making a living, especially when the land could be sold for development. One of the exceptions here in Sandwich was the Veg-Acre Farm of 440 acres in Forestdale, located on very deep fertile soil near Weeks Pond, once part of Bear Hollow Farm. This was established about 1941 and was operated successfully for many years by Mr. William Richards. The production was so great that crops from here were brought to as many as 38 farm stand outlets in eastern Massachusetts for sale. This farm closed in 1972 and about half the area has since been developed for housing. However, some 220 acres is now protected under the State Farmland Preservation Act and can only be used and taxed as farmland. Crow Farm in Sandwich, on the old almshouse farm site, has been in operation since 1916 under David Crowell and his son Howard Crowell and continues to grow and sell fruits and vegetables through its own popular farm stand and other outlets. Quail Hollow Farm is owned and operated by Peter Cook at the ancient Tobey and Wing property on Water Street.

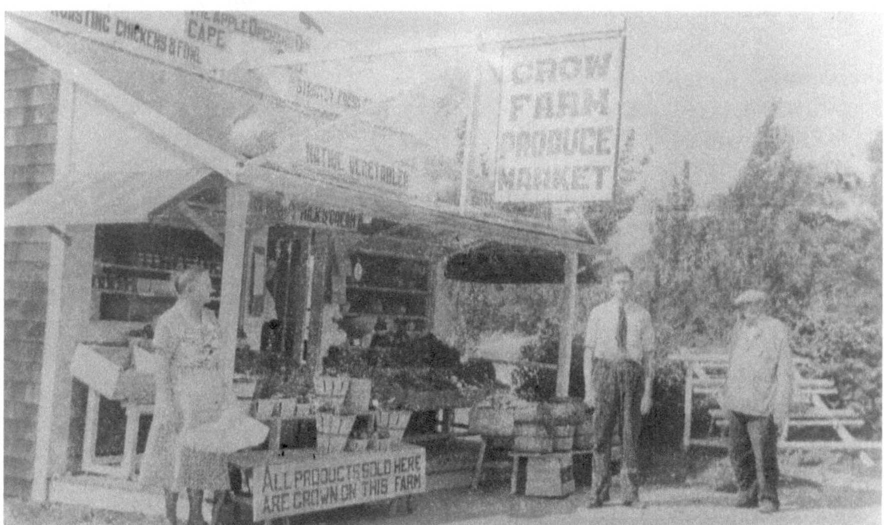

CROW FARM STAND—This view of about 1935 shows the earlier stand with Gertrude Pierce, David Crowell and Joe Fish. Credit Carolyn Crowell.

CHAPTER 32

THE CORPS OF ENGINEERS' CANAL

When the Corps of Engineers took over the Cape Cod Canal in March 1928, studies were begun immediately to correct major defects, particularly to enlarge the channel to two-way shipping and to widen the slots between the abutments of the three bridges. Another poor feature of the Belmont Canal was the dog-leg approach in Buzzards Bay with its two sharp turns. A detailed hydraulic model of the Belmont canal and various enlargements was commissioned to be built at MIT to study the currents and the effect of a proposed change in the Buzzards Bay channel. The federal government received the deed to the canal land area, removing some $100,000 worth of real estate from the tax rolls of Bourne and Sandwich, and started a fresh land survey to replace the description of the outer lines of the property which, in many cases, were still described in the simple terms of colonial period deeds with their trees, stumps, boulders and approximate directions. During the study period from 1928 to 1932, dredging was continued to maintain the channel as received. As the plans for the new canal began to become firm, dredging was increased to widen the channel from 100 feet to 170 feet on the bottom, with a 25-foot depth. This preliminary enlargement was particularly along the south bank. A number of new lots of adjacent land were taken to enlarge the corridor, of which the largest was the Keith Car Works which had been in decline since the end of World War I and which was bought for $325,000. The contents of all the buildings were auctioned off, after which the buildings were torn down, except for the office south of the tracks. Another area grievously affected was the village of Bournedale where the widening had to take several more streets and all the houses on them. When these were relocated or demolished, only a handful of houses of the once thriving village remained. The Herring River ran through a concrete holding tank into a concrete channel and pipe to the canal.

The New Highway Bridges

By 1932 the plans for enlargement of the canal were complete, and the first elements could be designed for contracts. These were the Bourne and Sagamore highway bridges, conceived as identical main arches of 616 feet, allowing a 135-foot clearance over a 500-foot width at mean high water. The Sagamore Bridge was located between high banks so that only one approach span was needed on both sides, whereas the Bourne Bridge was on lower ground requiring three approach spans on each side. Hence, the overall length of the Sagamore Bridge is 1,408 feet and the Bourne Bridge 2,384 feet. Both bridges were begun in Dec. 1933 and completed in early 1935. The field construction engineer was Allan Beale of Sandwich, and he recalled how he had to run back and forth between the two bridges as the superstructures went up. Because of expansion in these long steel structures, he said that only one steel foundation support was fastened to the concrete abutment by anchor bolts, the other resting on rollers. Mr. Edgar Caron of Sandwich put up the construction lights for round-the-clock work on the bridges.

BRIDGES AT SAGAMORE-The Sagamore bridge in early 1935 not yet open for traffic. The old bridge in Sagamore village is still in operation. Buildings in the Keith Car plant are not yet razed and much widening remained to be done on the channel when the old bridge could be removed. Approach roads to the new bridge are not yet in place. Courtesy of Donald R. Small.

The Town of Bourne staged a civic event over the weekend of June 22 and 23, 1935 to celebrate opening the two bridges. A number of marching units with bands set out from Bourne Trading Post Corner, moved to the south rotary (not then yet connected to the Falmouth road), over the bridge to the north side, around the loop and under the bridge, to Hunters Brook Road, then up the hill to the Sagamore Rotary, over the bridge and disbanded in Sagamore Village, a solid seven-mile hike. From the Sagamore Bridge south there was no Mid-Cape highway at first, only the approach road over to Sandwich Road. To the north, the connection from the rotary was to Route 3A.

The Bourne Bridge won a national prize in 1935 for "Most Beautiful Steel Bridge" from the American Institute of Steel Construction. The ribbon-cutting on the Sagamore Bridge was done by Mrs. Eleanor Robson Belmont, widow of August Belmont.

The Railway Lift Bridge

It was out of the question to raise the rail line to 135 feet to cross the canal on a fixed bridge. Hence a lift or drawbridge had to be devised to cross the clear 500-foot width. The firm of Parsons, Klapp, Brinkerhoff and Douglass of New York were chosen as consulting engineers for the vertical lift design. Parsons had been chief engineer on the Belmont Canal, and Klapp was his assistant. (Klapp owned *The Lindens* on Water St. up to his death in 1938.) The square towers are 260 feet high, and the steel span truss 544 feet long, 27 feet wide and 70 feet high at the center. The truss at the low position for train crossing allowed seven feet clearance over mean high water, but when raised allowed over 135 feet clearance (this clearance incidentally, for the railroad and the two highway bridges, is said to have been suggested by the 135-foot clearance of the Brooklyn Bridge). The contractor for the steelwork was Phoenix Bridge Company. The truss is 2,050 tons and is connected by cables to counterweights of 1,000 tons each inside the two towers. There are two electric motors of 150 horsepower each in each tower, which are able to raise or lower the span in *2½* minutes. The bridge is not lowered when a large vessel is approaching. When the bridge is down, it is locked and power to the bridge is disconnected by the signal tower operator, so that the bridge cannot move until the train clears. The bridge rests on roller bearings. This allows for expansion and contraction with temperature, and gives the towers resilience from stresses due to wind and to the movement of trains. When built this was the longest such lift span bridge in the world. The clear channel between fenders at the new bridge is 466 feet..

New Rail Line

The new rail bridge was sixty feet east of the old bascule bridge, requiring a new single line crossing with a switch to Falmouth or the down-Cape line. From about the Bourne station east to Sagamore, four miles of new track had to be laid in 1935 to allow for widening the canal. The Bourne station, relocated in 1911, now was discontinued; the Bournedale station and its luckless ferry had been closed since about 1930. The fixed point in Sagamore was the underpass where the rail line went under the former raised highway, going over the Keith Car yard and onto the Sagamore lift bridge. Late in 1935 this bridge and the Keith plant were dismantled, but the abutment and causeway in Sagamore remained. At this point the rail line, the service road and the new edge of the canal were close together. Rail service across the new bridge began in January 1936, after which the former rail line and old bascule bridge steelwork could be dismantled. The old constricting foundations of the railway bridge and the two highway bridges were dynamited in 1936 to allow widening of the whole canal.

THE RAILROAD BRIDGES-Looking west through the new single-track lift-span bridge at the old double track bascule-type bridge. The improvement in width of channel at the bridges was one of the great attractions of the new canal. Courtesy of Howard C. Goodwin

New Excavation and Dredging

The new canal was to be 540 feet wide at the surface by 32 feet deep at the 480-foot bottom width in the land cut. Work began in late 1935 but reached full speed in 1936 with dredging in the channel, dry steam-shoveling in the Bournedale area and massive new work in the revised Buzzards Bay channel. The canal stayed open during this work except for very short periods. The south bank was finished first to its final line with riprap protection, because of the revised location of the railroad and the automobile road on this side. The dredge *Governor Herrick,* built at Sagamore in 1912, was part of the dredge fleet assembled for work here. Colonel Henry P. Dunbar of Sandwich was the assistant resident engineer on the widening work. The old canal had involved some 15 million cubic yards of spoil to be excavated and moved, but the new canal at more than twice the width and more than four miles longer required some 39 million cubic yards excavated. The two breakwaters at Sandwich had fortunately been over 500 feet apart when built, so required no change. At the east end, north side, a new mooring basin 350 feet wide by 2500 feet long by 25 feet deep was excavated, and the old Sandwich wharf was pulled out to allow widening by 75 feet on this side. The old Keith plant area was completely dredged away. At the west end a new mooring basin, 350 feet by 3300 feet by 32 feet, was made, and at Taylor's Point a new canal administrative office with docks for tugs and service work, plus workshops and storage area.

New Buzzards Bay Channel

The shallows opposite the mouth of the old Manomet, River plus the bulk of Hog Island lying in the center of the Bay, had deterred the first canal builders. Howeve, now the builders cut off about half of Hog Island and moved the spoil so as to connect Hog Island to Mashnee Island. Other spoil was brought to connect Hog Island to the Bourne shore, so that a new protective dike was formed on this side of the channel. On the Wareham side, a new two-mile dike was built called the Stony Point Dike, ending opposite Wings Neck. From here the new dredged channel proceeded for 4.1 miles down to Cleveland Ledge. A side channel was dredged into Onset Bay so that smaller craft could use this bay as a refuge if necessary.

Sandwich Harbor of Refuge

The Life Saving Service became the U.S. Coast Guard in 1916, but the Sandwich station had little prestige or equipment because it was considered an adjunct boatyard to the Manomet Point Station in Plymouth. However, in 1935 by act of Congress, the Manomet station was closed and Sandwich became a main station. With the canal being widened seventy-five feet in this sector, a new Coast Guard Station and barracks was built further inland, with a boathouse in the future canal line. A steel bulkhead was driven along the waterfront here, with a break into the bank for an East Boat Basin near the fish freezer. This boat basin was completed in 1938 with an initial area of eight acres and a thirteen-foot depth.

The Loss of Scusset Harbor

The Belmont Canal did not close Scusset Harbor, which was protected from the spread of dredging spoil by a dike from the mainland to Sagamore Hill, and again from Sagamore Hill to the beach. However this east end of the canal was subject to buildup of sediment, both from the banks and from the intake from Cape Cod Bay, so that dredging and accumulation of spoils on the north bank continued. It was during the period of enlarged dredging after 1932 that the accumulation of wet spoil on the north bank overran the inadequate dike near the beach and slumped over to spill into the mouth of Scusset Harbor. Never very deep here, Scusset Harbor mouth became choked, and with the addition from the sea of sediment from the Plymouth moraine, and rapidly closed over forming a smooth beach. The outflow of fresh water from Bass Creek (Sagamore Beach), plus rainfall and seepage, filled up the marsh with fresh water so that a lake appeared with no outlet. This was a boon to ducks, geese and herons, but it threatened to break through to the canal at the narrow section between Sagamore Hill and the mainland (where the Scusset Creek had once flowed). Hence, just at the Sandwich/Bourne line a large drainage pipe was placed in the canal bank, and a trench was cut from the pipe to the marsh. This drained the lake (which never seems to have been named) and permitted reestablishment of a tidal salt marsh.

The Belmont Memorial Boulder

During the relocation of the automobile highway on the south bank in 1935, at a point opposite Bournedale, a large feldspar boulder was uncovered. Fortunately this remarkable find was recognized and saved instead of being dumped with other spoil. The Corps of Engineers decided to use the unique boulder as a memorial to Belmont, and the location chosen was on the north bank where an overlook near Bournedale provides a splendid vista of the canal. The bronze plaque reads as follows:

IN MEMORY OF
AUGUST BELMONT
FEBRUARY 18, 1853 DECEMBER 10, 1924
WHOSE VISION, INITIATIVE AND INDOMITABLE
COURAGE MADE POSSIBLE THE FIRST COMPLETE
CONSTRUCTION OF
THE CAPE COD CANAL
CONNECTING BUZZARDS BAY AND CAPE COD BAY
WHICH WAS OFFICIALLY OPENED FOR TRAFFIC
JULY 29, 1914
FROM HIS MATERNAL GRANDFATHER
COMMODORE MATTHEW CALBRAITH PERRY
HE INHERITED A WARM ALLEGIANCE TO THE INTERESTS
OF NEW ENGLAND AND HIS DEEP CONCERN FOR
THOSE WHO GO DOWN TO THE SEA IN SHIPS

U. S. COAST GUARD STATION—With the new canal, the Coast Guard station here became the main unit and the Manomet Plymouth station was closed. These are the new buildings set well back from the shore, with new boat house. The S.S. Matra is in transit. Courtesy of Benjamin S. Harrison,

Use in World War II

Even before the Government's enlargement of the canal was finished in 1940, the canal was being used for movement of warships and supplies to Europe. Convoys of tankers and supply vessels gathered in Buzzards Bay and then proceeded in column through the canal for Halifax. There was a Port Director's Office for Buzzards Bay in Woods Hole. With the entry of the United States into the war, the Coast Guard was assigned the duty from July 1, 1942 of operating the traffic in the canal, with headquarters at Sandwich but, of course, observers at Buzzards Bay. The army was given aircraft spotting, coastal defense and anti-aircraft assignments. A coastal defense camp was established on Sagamore Hill, 74 feet high, with a staff of 240 Massachusetts National Guardsmen. Their chief weapons were two 155 millimeter long guns (called GPF or Model 1918) mounted on circular tracks, which were capable of hurling a shell as far as Provincetown. This camp had an excellent view of Cape Cod Bay. Another army camp was located on Scorton Neck on the Carleton land, with anti-aircraft batteries. This unit practiced on drone aircraft towed over the Bay. It is reported that one or more planes crashed in the bay in accidents and one amphibious duck vehicle sank offshore here. These camps were torn down after the war, but the two steel tracks and concrete gun bases still remain on Sagamore Hill with the remains of underground passages and storage vaults. There was a regular beach patrol as part of the coastal defense work in this area, extending from Plymouth to Sandy Neck. To allow a continuous path, wooden swing bridges were built over the mouth of Sandwich Harbor and of Scorton Harbor. These bridges were removed in 1946. The first portion of the Mid-Cape Highway was extended from the Sagamore Bridge to Route 130 with the activation of Camp Edwards as a military training base, but this road sector remained only for military use until the end of the war.

The canal was a military asset of high value, so identity checks were made of possible security risks in this area. Attention was immediately focused on Friedrich W. Schumacher who, in 1938, had purchased fourteen acres at Spring Hill around Masthead, the mansion built by John H. Foster, the dancing master. Schumacher had moved here from Jamaica Plain to establish his tree farm and his F. W. Schumacher Seed Company, growing and selling seeds from hundreds of kinds of trees. Masthead had a glorious view of the ships leaving the canal for Europe, and Schumacher admitted that he had fought in the German army in World War I. The tree farm and seed company could have been a perfect cover for a spy operation, so that Schumacher was watched intensively for months by American agents for signs of radio broadcasts or information-gathering, but he was found to be completely innocent and devoted to his botany.

The Tidal Slosh in the Canal

In the early 1920s when the government was studying the canal, and Belmont's company was still reluctantly operating it, another lock plan was seriously presented. The currents generated by the tidal differences, particularly the west-flowing currents, made navigation difficult, and threading the passages through the lift bridges was especially tricky. The solution proposed was a single lock of about 1,000 feet long in the Sagamore area, with two slots for two-way passage, so that no currents would flow between the bays. One of the persisting objections to this plan was the difficulty of ice-breaking in narrow channels. The sea-level plan was adopted for the enlarged canal with reliance on width of channel, lights and navigation aids for safe passage.

A diagram shows the four-foot range of tide at the railroad bridge near Buzzards Bay, and the larger 9½-foot range at the eastern end of the canal at Cape Cod Bay. The time of high tide at the railroad bridge is taken as hour zero, and the hours are marked for the twelve hour, twenty-five minute period to the next high. At the Sandwich end, hour zero finds the tide about 2½ hours short of high. This is the point called "high slack, " where the equal level at both ends of the canal produces a period of fifteen to twenty minutes of no current. As the tide falls in Buzzards Bay and continues to rise at Sandwich, a differential is produced which soon sets canal water into a westward flow. This continues for six hours until the point of "low slack" is reached, where low tide at Buzzards Bay is at the same level as the falling tide at Sandwich. The west current then slows to a stop, and after a pause the reverse process begins, a slow rising tide at the railroad bridge with a falling tide at Sandwich, inducing an eastward flow into the deeps of Cape Cod Bay. By connecting the hourly numbers, the direction and intensity of the current can be perceived directly throughout the cycle. The greater heights and depths of water in Cape Cod Bay act to power the flow, while the level at Buzzards Bay, always intermediate in height, provides the regulator that sets the time of stop and reversal.

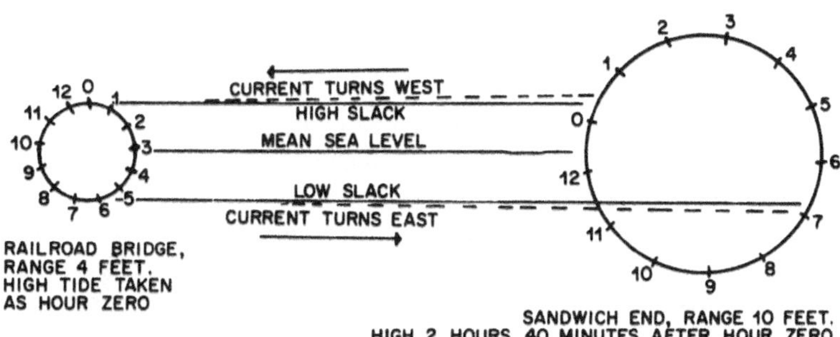

SKETCH OF TIDAL CURRENTS IN THE CANAL—With its greater range of height and depth, Cape Cod Bay water forces the currents to flow back and forth in the canal, while Buzzards Bay tide height provides the regulator. In the above diagram, connecting the same number in both circles shows the direction of current flow as well as its intensity. A full tidal cycle is completed in 12 hours 53 minutes.

This slosh of current back and forth is of great interest on many counts, first to administrators of the ship traffic in the canal. The depth of water at low tide is thirty-two feet, and for large vessels may be a factor in timing their passage. The best time for entry is one hour before high tide at the railroad bridge, so that in case of grounding the rising water will help to free the vessel. The Army Corps of Engineers publishes a booklet annually giving times of high and low tides at Sandwich, at the railroad bridge and at Wings Neck, and also the times when the current turns at the railroad bridge. This exact information is computer-generated based on historical and forecast tidal performance, and on actual canal behavior. However, specific present conditions can affect the times of slack and reversal. Strong winds from the northeast or southwest raise the level of the respective bays and alter the normal current turns. Cape Cod Bay is so large that the volume of water entering from or flowing into the canal has no effect on its local level. The upper reaches of Buzzards Bay, however, are affected by the canal volumes and there are shallow water effects which cause odd changes in the timing of low tide at the railroad bridge.

At the Canal Electric power plant in Sandwich, deep tankers arrive with fuel oil so that the canal has been deepened to forty feet from the Bay to the tanker dock. These large vessels both arrive and depart from the Cape Cod Bay entrance. Careful studies have been made of the water temperature here around the tidal cycle so that cooling water can be withdrawn and the warmer water put back into the canal with minimal effects on sea life. So regular is the tidal slosh that (given the temperatures of Cape Cod Bay water well offshore and Buzzards Bay water) the temperature of water at the plant intake and outlet points can be accurately predicted around the clock, and this temperature is an exact measure of the relative proportion of water present in the canal from both sources.

Another prospective use of the canal waters is as an outlet for treated effluent from sewage gathering plants. An analysis of the volumes and rates of flow in the canal waters was made for a possible Sandwich treatment plant to be located near the Canal Electric plant. This was not built when proposed, but the study remains valid for the future and shows how thoroughly the canal is swept by each tidal reversal. Yet another study of canal flow concerned the buildup of sediment at Scusset Beach, estimated at seventeen thousand cubic yards per year, and the erosion of material from Town Beach and lower shoreline of about sixty thousand cubic yards per year. There is a steady counterclockwise motion of all the water in Cape Cod Bay, resulting in a change of water every two weeks. Sediments, particularly from the Plymouth moraine, are swept around but are intercepted by the three thousand foot long canal breakwater which causes accumulation on the upper side and scouring on the lower side.

Volume of Water in the Canal

The volume of water involved in each complete tidal cycle in the canal have been studied. The flow that runs west from Cape Cod Bay to Buzzards Bay starting at high slack and ending at low slack is 21.9 billion gallons. The flow from Buzzards Bay to Cape Cod Bay starting at low slack is 18.4 billion gallons. Water entering Cape Cod Bay turns east with the general circulation and most of it is gone out of the area when the reverse flow begins, whereas in Buzzards Bay much of the canal water is held between the dikes or in Onset Bay, and is available to be drawn back into the canal on reversal. There is a net flow of 3.5 billion gallons into Buzzards Bay. However, this net flow conceals the fact that water from Buzzards Bay carried away by the circulation in Cape Cod Bay escapes permanently so that there is opportunity for sea life to move in either direction through the canal.

Rates of Flow in the Canal

The flow west, as reflected in the above figures, is of much greater volume, even though it takes place over a shorter period on average than the east flow, six hours versus six hours twenty-five minutes. The reason seems to be the greater depth of Cape Cod Bay and the straight run into the canal from deep water, as opposed to the shallower Buzzards Bay and the baffles from side effects. The average flow west is 670,000 gallons per second with a peak of 960,000 gal/sec, with a peak speed of 5.4 knots or 7.6 feet per second. The east flow averages 440,000 gal/sec with a peak of 760,000 gallons per second, with peak speed of 4 knots or 6.76 feet per second.

Post War Changes

The Cape Cod Canal remains a marvel of man-made nature in operation. A few changes have occurred along its banks—Scusset State Park and Beach were put into operation by the Massachusetts Department of Public Works and have been popular for camping, fishing in the canal and swimming. The Sandwich Boat Basin was enlarged in 1963 and soon became crowded again, with Sandwich becoming second only to Provincetown in fish landed. A further expansion is being planned. Canal Electric plant Unit I went on-stream in 1968 and Unit II in 1974, with their stacks in a single concrete column 500 feet high, visible from great distances. Unit I is in steady base-load operation and has proven to be one of the most efficient producers of electricity in the whole world. At the other end of the canal, the Massachusetts Maritime Academy, in 1948, opened its large campus on Taylor's Point adjacent to the canal. Its library has assembled a considerable collection on the history of the canal. The Army Corps of Engineers has attractive lectures, hikes and story programs about the canal area for summer visitors, given by its well-trained Ranger group.

CHAPTER 33

THORTON W. BURGESS

Thornton Waldo Burgess is easily Sandwich's best known native son. Leaving here at 18 in 1892, he was living in Springfield when he began the series of writings on nature and conservation that brought him world-wide fame. He returned to Sandwich frequently throughout his life, for as he wrote:

> "Peter Rabbit, having become a national, even an international, character, it is perhaps of some interest that the dear Old Briar Patch, as first described, was located in Sandwich. When the author of the *Bedtime Stories,* in which Peter and his friends of the Green Forests and the Green Meadows are the chief characters, began writing of these little people, he had in mind a certain big briar patch located at Spring Hill, where, as a boy, he had many times seen Peter and Mrs. Peter." (Quoted in *About Cape Cod* by Stanley Kelley, Boston 1936)

Descended from the original settler Thomas Burgess of West Sandwich, Thornton's ancestral line lived in Harwich for several generations, then returned to West Sandwich in 1791. Thornton's grandfather, Charles H. Burgess (1815-1905), moved his family to Sandwich village about 1858 and opened a general store at Jarves Street and Cross Street. Charles' son, Thornton Senior (1850-1874), married Caroline F. Hayward in 1872 and Thornton Jr. was born on January 14, 1874. Caroline Hayward and her sister Lucy Emma had been born in Cambridge, but were orphaned by 1854 and brought up in Sandwich by their aunts, Caroline in the home of glassmaker C.C.P. Waterman and Lucy in the home of glassmaker Henry V. Spurr. Lucy married William R. Tobey and had a son Willie just older then Thornton. The husbands of these sisters both died, leaving each with a young son and continued dependency on relatives in Sandwich.

Some of Thornton's earliest memories were of adventures with this cousin Willie, going over the boardwalk to the beach to see a stranded whale, and trying to transport fingerling fish in a sloshing bucket in a wheelbarrow. Willie's mother remarried in 1884 and removed to Springfield. Thornton's mother had to economize, and many of his activities as a small boy were in earning money—selling candy to the men at the B&S, gathering blueberries and arbutus, tending cows at Town Neck, selling magazine subscriptions, trapping muskrats at cranberry bogs. By the time he was twelve he was able to buy all his own clothes. One very special memory was walking to Spring Hill where Mr. William C. Chipman had a row of pools where he grew a rarity, pink pond lilies. These could be shipped off as roots, or as cut flowers packed in damp moss, and young Thornton took the packages to the post office. Near Chipman's, off Discovery Hill Road, was a woodsey path around the boiling spring pond where there was a profusion of wildlife, and this place, together with some other favorite haunts in Sandwich, remained in his mind as wonderful places to see nature close at hand. After the death of his great-uncle C.C.P. Waterman in 1884, Thornton and his mother lived in various houses in the village on a rental basis.

TOWN NECK PASTURE—This peaceful scene existed for nearly 300 years as generations of youngsters, among them young Thornton Burgess, brought cows from nearby farms to Town Neck for seasonal pasture. Present Town Neck Road, after crossing the railroad track, bears left at the point shown in this postcard, where bars admitted into the pasture area. Courtesy of William E. Foster.

ARABELLA ELDRED BURGESS (1843-193l)-Thomton Burgess' real aunt Arabella communicated vocally and publicly with animals, birds, fish and plants all her long life. Here she is in old age with a puppy (Laddy Boy) and a favorite hen who clucked on command at a glass egg. Sandwich Archives, gift of Nellie.S. Atwood.

Aunt Arabella Eldred Burgess (1843-1931)

Thornton's uncle, Frank Burgess, was a town official, cranberry grower and storekeeper, and doubtless employed young Thornton for odd jobs. Frank's wife was Arabella Eldred, and their home must have held a fascination for children for it was a unique place, called the Deacon Eldred house at 4 Water Street, inherited by Arabella herself on the death of the Deacon in 1884. Arabella raised plants in bay windows, and bred canaries; she had dogs, ducks and chickens who had the run of the house; her most remarkable pets were two carp, a horned pout, and an eel in the millpond which would come to her wharf when she signaled, eat bits of smoked herring and even permit themselves to be lifted out of the water. To all these pets and plants Arabella addressed a spate of communications. She was regarded as somewhat odd by the townspeople but was no recluse. She taught Sunday School, organized picnics, gave nature lessons to groups of school children and even presented a fund-raising show for the new library. Frank moved out and lived apart, but here if anywhere in Sandwich, young Thornton Burgess would have seen, heard, and experienced a knowing person communicating with animals, birds, fish and plants as a vibrant two-way process.

His Early Life

Thornton's grandparents, Charles and Ann Burgess, moved to Colorado in 1880 with their youngest son Willard who had tuberculosis. The young man was cured and became a successful merchant there. The senior Burgesses, remaining in Colorado, offered each of their grandchildren a year's trip to the west or a year's tuition at a training school. Thornton chose school and went to Boston in 1892 to study business accounting. He was unhappy at it and at the clerical jobs he held, trying also to write poems and slogans for extra money. His mother had come to Boston with him but due to ill health had joined Lucy in Springfield. Finally in 1895 she and Lucy got him a job as office boy at Phelps Publishing Co. in Springfield. Here, among supporters, he found work that was congenial and began to get on his feet. He became a reporter and learned to study subjects of interest and write factual articles. Among his projects were farm machinery, early automobiles, household work, the Gloucester fishing fleet, the cycle of nature around the year and railroad work. His first book in 1905 was on homemaking and bore the unexpected title *The Bride's Primer* and was based partly on real experience as he married Nina Osborne in 1905. She died the following year at the birth of Thornton III. He bought a home in Springfield and here his mother helped to bring up the baby. In 1910, Thornton had read all the available Beatrix Potter stories to his four-year-old, and wrote out some further nature stories in the Peter Rabbit vein to be read to the boy while at his Osborne grandparents' home. These stories were published by Little, Brown & Co. as a new book, *Old Mother West Wind,* in 1910, with illustrations by George Kerr. Thornton became sub-editor of *Good Housekeeping* and confidently married again, this time to a widow with two children, Mrs. Fannie Phillips Johnson. He wrote two further Mother West Wind books in 1911 and 1912 but suddenly was out of a job as the magazine was sold. He had to decide whether to remain working as an editor elsewhere, or to make his living writing on his own. His daily newspaper column, *Bedtime Stories,* began on February 17, 1912, six columns a week for thirty five dollars per week. Among other early ventures were writing advertising copy, land promotion copy, and a Boy Scout book. His mother died and he was now fully on his own. He produced a fourth Mother West Wind book in 1913 with Kerr illustrations, and another Boy Scout book.

Walter Harrison Cady (1877-1970)

In 1913 Burgess sent three stories to the *Peoples Home Journal,* which had an artist named Harrison Cady illustrate them. He was struck with the results and wrote Cady a grateful letter, later meeting him in New York. Walter Harrison Cady was born in 1877 in Gardner, Massachusetts and had come to New York in 1896 to try to sell some drawings. He caught on quickly and by 1912 was an established illustrator for the *Brooklyn Eagle, Harpers, St. Nicholas* and the old *Life.* Hence, although three years younger than Burgess, Cady was a well-known artist when they commenced collaboration on the daily stories and on book illustrations. Cady had a summer home in East Gloucester, later settling on Atlantic Avenue, Rockport. The two men became good friends. Their collaboration over the next 52 years became a standard and happy pattern which was satisfying to generations of Americans. Cady illustrated the next four Mother West Wind books, and then the twenty books, *Adventures of Reddy Fox,* etc., that formed the Bedtime Story book series. Cady created everyone's picture of life in the Briar Patch and around the Smiling Pool, but he had a career of his own as well. He had a comic strip in the *New York Herald Tribune,* and did serious painting. The Salmagundi Club held a one-man show of his work in 1950 in New York, and much of Cady's work is in Rockport, at Laughing Brook, Hampden, and at the Burgess Museum, Sandwich.

Burgess' Chief Contributions

It was at Cady's suggestion that Burgess saw the editor of *Peoples Home Journal* and worked out a plan that became "The Green Meadows Club, " with competitions and prizes for land conservation projects. This popular project ran for twelve years, resulted in setting aside several million acres for conservation, and brought Burgess to the attention of Dr. William T. Hornaday of the New York Zoological Society. Among the Bedtime Story books, *The Adventures of Poor Mrs. Quack* in 1917, was written with a serious intention of helping Dr. Hornaday to get laws passed protecting migrant wildfowl. Similarly, a group of teachers helped organize *The Bedtime Stories Club,* featuring a red button bearing Peter Rabbit's picture. These buttons were prized and were used in schools to reward local wildlife protection programs. Burgess was awarded a medal by the Wildlife Protection Fund at the Waldorf-Astoria in 1914 before a distinguished audience. With this kind of publicity he quickly became a well-known figure and was invited widely to speak. He had a continued series of these early successes, using his familiar motifs and characters for national purposes. His proposal for a Happy Jack Squirrel Savings Club started in 1917, based on the squirrel saving up nuts, and became immensely popular; even President

Wilson was photographed wearing a Happy Jack pin. This resulted in wide sales of Victory Bonds and savings stamps. Some complained that his characters were unnatural in going on and on, talking and clothed, always escaping death, capture or the trap, but behind this familiar pattern with its ready acceptance, especially with the young, Burgess went beyond simple entertainment and tried to convey behavior toward wild life. Children could be taught from the animals more easily than by direct talk from humans what was right and wrong, what was needed for a creature's survival, what caused suffering, and many other lessons. The Society for the Prevention of Cruelty to Animals gratefully noted Burgess' great help in better understanding the life cycle and problems of animals.

Burgess' greatest contribution to conveying factual information to a wide audience was unquestionably his series of four natural history books beginning with *The Burgess Bird Book for Children* in 1919. He concluded that "there is no method of approach to the child mind equal to the story." These four books accordingly use the Peter Rabbit and Jenny Wren or Danny Meadowmouse format to carry the material along, but the text is fully factual and descriptive with wonderful illustrations. The distinguished artist Louis Agassiz Fuertes did the bird illustrations, and also those in the *Burgess Animal Book for Children,* while the Flower Book and Seashore Book used colored photographs. The only other Burgess book illustrated by Fuertes was *Birds You Should Know,* in 1933, which had no plot or usual Burgess Briar Patch characters.

Burgess considered himself a serious seeker after truth in nature, and wrote an important summary of his principles in an article "Nature as a Universal Teacher", appearing in *Natural History Magazine* in 1922. He participated with Dr. Alfred O. Gross of Bowdoin College in observing and banding the last heath hens on Martha's Vineyard, and also went with Dr. Gross to study bird life in Labrador. He did not wish his name to be confused with glib writers who he said were hucksters using nature as a vehicle. Former President Theodore Roosevelt called them "nature-fakers."

One of Burgess' most famous contributions to the national scene was his Wednesday evening "Radio Nature League," a program which originated from WBZA Springfield from 1924 through 1934. The nasal voice of Neighbor Burgess became familiar to a wide audience discussing natural events, reading letters sent in by readers, quoting unusual items such as problems that certain species were having according to experts, and similar material. The announcer for this series was W. Gordon Swan who, by coincidence, came to retire in Sandwich years later and recalled many funny events in those early unrehearsed programs when live snakes escaped from their boxes, and very dead specimens were mailed in. This popular program was finally terminated by Burgess, citing his busy schedule of writing and speaking, and the increasing work involved in organizing the show. He never received a salary for this very demanding and valuable effort. Only after the radio program ended was he able to take his first tour to Europe, where his work had been translated into several languages.

"Aunt Sally"

Burgess got a glimpse of talking to animals, birds and fish from his aunt Arabella Burgess in Sandwich early in life, but he did not correspond with anyone about it later. However, another mentor in Sandwich is much better documented, Alice Rebecca Cooke (1861-1956). Alice was not a relative, but came to be known better as "Aunt Sally" than by her own name.

Alice's early life had two parallels with Thornton's. Her grandfather (Rufus Conant) came to Sandwich in 1857 as a storekeeper, and her mother Abigail (1822-1922) lost her husband to tuberculosis and had to return to Sandwich with her children to the grandparents' home. Alice was a slight fair girl. She graduated from Sandwich Academy in 1876, attended Miss Cobb's private school on River Street and then entered a nursing school. In about 1884 she was retained by Quincy Adams Shaw of Boston to care for his daughter who had tuberculosis. We have mentioned Mr. Shaw in Chapter 25 as one of the financial backers of the Lockwood Dredge operation in Sandwich. Alice cared for the girl in Spring Hill, and apparently sent messages by telegraph to Shaw in Boston, not only about the girl but about the dredging. There certainly was a telegraph office here on Main Street near the Central House, and it is possible that Alice even learned Morse code. Her canal connection at this time was well known, but at the end of her life, people got it out of date and said that she had worked for August Belmont as a telegrapher.

Alice became an assistant matron at the State Mental Hospital at Tewksbury, but preferring to live at home with her mother and sister, she entered into a formal agreement in 1886 with the State Board of Lunacy and Charity to care for three mildly deranged women from Tewksbury at her home in Sandwich, for the sum of $3.25 per person per week, plus the cost of clothing and medical attendance. A State inspector later mistakenly tried to remove the women, but Alice was ably defended by the selectmen and overseers of the poor, of both Sandwich and Bourne plus a number of leading citizens. In 1895 the governor and council formally licensed her to keep a private house for the reception and treatment of insane female patients, provided that a physician be named as medical director. She was said to be the first such licensee in the state. She and her medical collaborator, Dr. G. E. White, thought of establishing a larger mental care facility such as in the empty school of the late Frederick Freeman, but there was opposition. So Alice kept Locust Grove Asylum in the house at 238 Route 6A, Spring Hill, with as many as five women under her care.

The Woodshed Nightclub

Alice's household included her mother Abigail and her sister Minnie. The three lived in a consciously archaic fashion, in complete harmony, sharing a common purse. They were abstemious, prohibitionist, and vegetarian. Alice's eyesight was poor so Minnie read aloud to the others. Minnie was small but very quick and handy. She early became an expert photographer and kept a studio in Sandwich village. Her stereoptican views of Sandwich scenes were popular in the town, taken with two separate cameras and viewed in a special frame to give a three-dimensional effect. Minnie was the carpenter and handyman in the manless household. These ladies had a profound respect for the sacredness of all life, and found it impossible to kill even the rats and mice that came into the house. They kept no pets but fed the birds and wild animals of the neighborhood in their yard. They even moved the horse stalls in the barn and cut windows in the barn wall so that the two horses could look out into the yard. They had a horror of hunting and especially of steel traps. A skunk was injured by a car in front of their house in 1915 and they nursed it back to health. Then a litter of five baby skunks were found at the kitchen door, orphaned and starving. These were all fed, survived hibernation and came back the next year. The sisters found that these skunks, night feeders, would enter the woodshed by an ancient catport and would feed happily among observers, even climbing up into a person's lap if the bowl were there. They spoke gently to the animals and knew most of them by name, either from markings or humorous likeness to a townsperson. Minnie took their mother's picture every year on her birthday, sitting at the same table with the same ancient dress. The sisters were desolated when she died in 1922 at just over 100. One of the patients at this time, from a wealthy Boston family, had suffered a nervous breakdown after a love affair. Alice found that this girl greatly enjoyed and benefited from buying antiques, china and glass when the two took the light buggy and drove around. They would then resell things to visitors, taking no profit.

It was to this unique household, then, that Thornton and Mrs. Burgess came in 1925. They had just bought an ancient (1742) house in Hampden, outside Springfield, as a summer home, and were interested in buying antiques. As soon as she learned his name, Alice immediately recalled that when she was a library trustee she had written Thornton asking for copies of his books for the library, and she knew of his career. He on his part recalled passing her house on the way to Chipman's as a boy, and had a special fondness for Gully Lane near her house. She mentioned her evening feeding of skunks, and either then or soon after he came with camera and flash to record the scene. He loved the skunk, which he said would make a better national symbol than the eagle. To his delight the skunks did not bolt with the flash, and he was able to get some novel photos and amusing stories. Alice did not want her name used, so the term "Aunt Sally" was invented, and soon through the Radio Nature League and his articles the story of the woodshed and Aunt Sally was introduced to thousands.

They corresponded after this, and Alice sent him word of new events. If a man with a cigar entered the woodshed, no animal would enter. He sent her autographed books and called himself "Your nephew Waldo." The first raccoon found its way into the woodshed, in unusual proximity to the skunks. In 1932 her sister Minnie died at seventy-eight, and Alice was grief-stricken at the loss of this companion who had been such a support.

Distraught, Alice took all Minnie's papers, photos and personal things to their dump-site in the woods, and burned them in a tragic farewell. Her neighbors now rallied around and insisted that the house be wired for electricity. When Burgess learned of this he brought moving picture equipment and floodlights so that he could take extended movies of the scene in the nightclub, which now included a mix of raccoons and skunks. He photographed Alice with a favorite three-legged raccoon, Crip, on her knees, victim of a steel trap. The skunks and raccoons kept apart, but only on one or two occasions did a skunk feel sufficiently threatened to fire its scent. These movies and stories of the woodshed nightclub became an indispensable part of the lectures and programs that Burgess gave, of such value to him that he refused to lend the film or allow it to be copied.

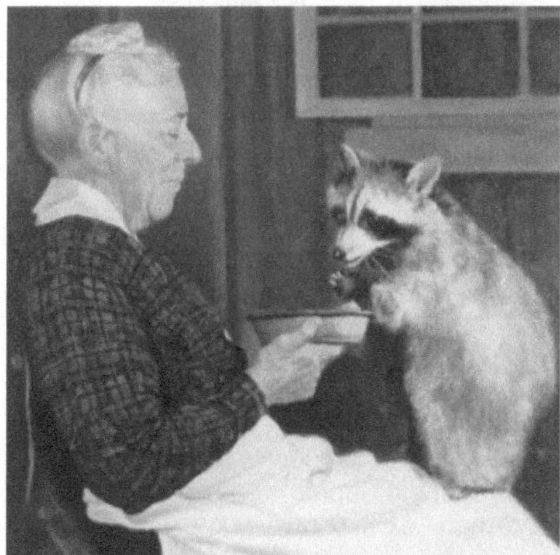

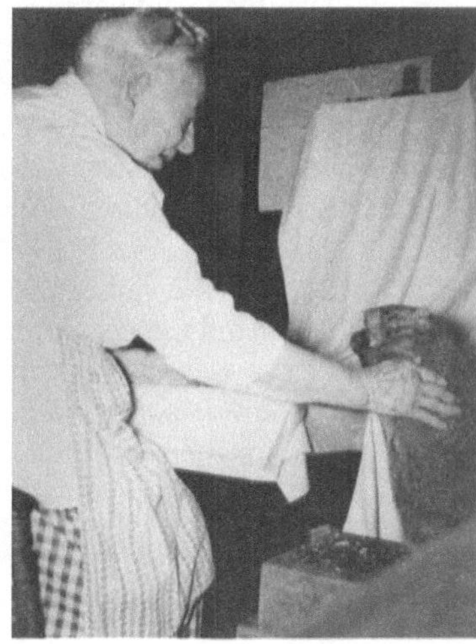

AUNT SALLY—Left, Burgess's Aunt Sally (Alice R. Cooke) with a three-legged raccoon which she called Crip. Courtesy of Sandwich Historical Society. Right, Burgess and several friends visited Aunt Sally in August 1951 on her 90th birthday. She had discontinued the nightly feeding but made a pet of Polly Chuck who is here seen at the kitchen table. Photograph by Irving B. Freeman.

The Legend of Aunt Sally

Without Minnie to help, Alice took no new patients, and in 1938 she transferred the last one to the Gould Nursing Home in Sandwich village, by coincidence located in the Arabella Eldred Burgess house. (Arabella had died in 1931 and the new facility was operated by her granddaughter May Doten Gould.) Alice was then seventy-seven and needed some help herself. She had devoted neighbors, Mr. and Mrs. Ralph Freeman and Mrs. Harriet Cheney who looked in and who supported the animal feeding with gifts. Clarence Cahoon delivered groceries to her from about 1935, and learning of the animal nightclub with its heavy demand for animal food, Clarence found the stocks of stale bread, pastry and cheap supplies to keep it going. Alice had been desperately honest all her life, but now had little savings or income. Whenever one of her patients had died, she had returned any funds remaining for their care to their families, or had turned it in to the state treasury as a gift. She had buried two of her patients without family in her own family plot in Cedarville Cemetery.

The end of the woodshed nightclub came in November 1947. The raccoons had displaced all the skunks and had become numerous in the neighborhood, and their presence was now well known. A group of men with hunting dogs and flashlights appeared, and the raccoons were treed and shot. When the barking and firing and shouting was over, in the woods just up the hill, her membership was decimated. She could not begin any new feeding with that scene to be repeated and her own health precarious. No one wanted to hear about or talk about the slaughter of Alice's pets. A lady reporter came down from the *Boston Sunday Globe,* and her piece printed March 16, 1952 describes "Thornton Burgess' lovable Aunt Sally, a real 90-year-old Cape Codder," and the charming scenes as the skunks and raccoons, bringing their babies, crowded around her. Only at the very end of the article was there a brief mention of the hunters and dogs, where few would absorb it. Burgess had always said he would put the Aunt Sally story and pictures into a book, but somehow did not get around to it until 1954. His book, *Aunt Sally's Friends in Fur,* appeared in 1955 and in it there was no reference at all to the end of the Friends in Fur. By this time Alice herself was in a nursing home and the skunk pictures were thirty years old. She was delighted at his joke that she was such a stubborn old woman to wait so long to see herself in a book, and she was surprised to receive a small check from Little, Brown and Co. as a royalty for the use of her name. Burgess wrote the Cahoons that he was pleased at the publisher's generosity.

Alice Cooke died in January 1956, leaving much of her property to the Cahoons who had been so helpful in her failing health from 1948.

Burgess' Visits to Sandwich

Thornton renewed his contacts with Sandwich scenes, friends and relatives often. There was a big family picnic at Onset Beach in 1896 to honor the return from Colorado of the grandparents Charles and Ann Burgess. Thornton and his mother, Lucy and her Quinnell daughter all came down from Springfield. Frank Chipman, the newsman and glass expert, had been Thornton's classmate in 1891 at Sandwich Academy, and organized an active alumni group of Sandwich High School graduates. Thornton came to a number of these reunions. He subscribed to the *Sandwich Independent,* published here to 1932, then the succeeding *Cape Cod News,* and his careful reading is attested by many letters to the editor. In 1919 he and Mrs. Burgess had an extended summer visit to friends in Cotuit. The *Independent* reported that in 1922 Burgess gave a talk at Tremont Temple, Boston, at which for the first time in Boston he showed moving pictures of wild animals. The previous year he had showed lantern slides here. In 1939 the town had a big civic event for its 300th anniversary, and asked Burgess to give a talk after the clambake. The text of his message has survived, laughingly recalling his previous "oration" at this spot in 1891 as high school class orator. The talk was affectionate and sincere, and included, possibly for the first time, his poem *Gully Lane.* His particular friends here included his classmate Lillian Haynes Tangney, Ida Putnam of the Green Briar Jam Kitchen, Carrie Chipman Boyden, George and Nina Sutton, Colonel Eugene Clark and the Leonard, Donovan, and Jones families of his early days. Burgess loved the Green Briar Jam Kitchen which was located on his favorite Smiling Pool, and in 1939 dedicated a book "To Ida—it is a wonderful thing to sweeten the world which is in a jam and needs preserving." In 1951 there was a Thornton W. Burgess day at the Sandwich elementary school, where he was escorted from room to room in the morning for class programs, had lunch with a huge decorated Rabbit cake, then in the afternoon gave an illustrated talk to all the students plus many from Bourne.

THORNTON W. BURGESS (1874-1965)-The author aged over seventy autographing a reprint of one of his most successful books, The Burgess Bird Book for Children. Courtesy of Sandwich Historical Society.

In 1950 it had been proposed by the Sandwich Board of Trade that a Thornton W. Burgess Memorial Park be created in honor of Sandwich's world-famous son. A prestigious committee was formed including Edith Deering, Robert Kershaw, Philip Granger, John Coe, Nina Sutton, William Campbell, Charles Papazoni, Caesar Alvezi, Ben Fleet, J. Foxcroft Carleton and Camilla Williams. At first the park was to be at the beach on Route 130, with a landscaped trail along the waterfront near the Hoxie House (then owned by Caroline Thomas). Burgess and Cady were contacted and approved the idea of a park in general, if large enough and arranged to be effective and appropriate. Then the shores of the mill stream behind the Historical Society were proposed, and also an acre or so of the original Briar Patch area off Discovery Hill Road. Nina Sutton made some ceramic model figures for a possible trail, but the whole project foundered in 1952 when substantial costs were found to be required for landscaping, buildings, parking, staffing and other aspects of a permanent memorial. The bandstand area was named Thornton W. Burgess Park, but no other memorial was completed and the committee dissolved in embarrassment.

In 1955 Burgess came to Sandwich to be best man at the wedding of his second cousin Ted Waterman, a widower, to Jane Bradford Jones, an artist and Sandwich native. In 1959 Burgess gave another talk to school classes here and toured the new wings of the Glass Museum. He gave the society several items, including some Aunt Sally pictures and the manuscript to *Aunt Sally's Friends in Fur.* In 1962 he toured the new Hoxie House restoration and the new Dexter Mill; he wrote a poem, *The Honest Miller,* which was framed and hung on the wall of the mill. His last visit to Sandwich was in September 1963 when he also accompanied a reporter to Martha's Vineyard to record his early studies of the heath hen there.

Burgess' Later Years

The year 1950 was a critical one for Thornton. At 76 he was still healthy and active, but was pained by arthritis in his knees. He had a mild heart attack while shoveling snow, and had to restrict his activities. Then in the summer his wife, whom he called Lady, suffered a stroke and died. He hired a couple named Kathy and Frank Jones to look after him, Kathy a nurse to type and cook, Frank to drive, run errands and garden. Before this, he had done all his own typing. He kept well ahead in his daily Bedtime Stories, then at the 12,000 mark, but decided to spend the winter of 1950/1951 not in Springfield but on the island of Tobago near Trinidad off the South American coast. We do not know who suggested this particular Caribbean retreat to him, but he loved it and spent eleven winters there. Kathy and Frank saw him off in New York for Miami and Trinidad, and kept the Springfield house and opened the mail. He stayed in a guest cottage on the Bacolet Coconut Plantation, where his daily routine was to answer letters and type stories and articles all morning, then to join other guests and plantation people at lunch, the main meal of the day. In the afternoon he either took a walk or hired a car for a drive, and took a swim. In the late afternoon there was tea, then a long happy hour for rum drinks, and light supper. He enjoyed the chat and made some very faithful new friends including Art and Belle Saltford, but did not drink the rum. His friends here called him Doc or Spiffy, because conservative that he was, he dressed for the public in white shirt, bow tie, neatly creased trousers and leather shoes, just what he would have worn in Sandwich, but not what anyone else on Tobago wore.

Every January 14 he hosted a cocktail and dinner party to mark his birthday, an event he called getting over another stile. This was his toast on his eightieth in 1954:

"Here is to YOUTH! How we all hate to lose it.
Try as we may, no one ever renews it.
Here is to AGE! 'Tis all as we take it.

Here is LIFE! 'Tis just what we make it."

One of his most faithful correspondents was his schoolmate "Tiger Lil" Tangney. She sent him obituaries, newspaper clippings, articles and Sandwich news, and saved his postcards and letters that tell of increasing affliction. They agreed it was awful to get old. He said he was hanging on to a shaky ladder, and that his wiring was getting the shakes; he was tripped by a dog, and had to make his walks shorter; maybe he was too old to be so far from home. Each spring he would get back to New York about May first, and would stay in the city for a few days seeing his publishers, appearing in radio and TV talk shows, and meeting friends. Then it was off to Hampden with Kathy and Frank to plan the summer's visits, trips and activities. In 1957 he added more utilities at Hampden and sold the Springfield house, making his year-round address at Hampden. After completing the Aunt Sally book in 1954, he increasingly turned his attention to organizing his own affairs and sorting over his vast files of letters, clippings, and articles. He also began to list his Sandwich background events and career highlights in anticipation of the autobiography which his publishers had been urging on him for years.

Before he left for Tobago in October 1959 he had finished writing the daily stories through the 15,000th and finished the text for the autobiography to be called *Now I Remember.* Hence, he felt he was free to concentrate on letters and plans, and to do the re-editing of some twenty-five-year old stories which were going to appear in the daily newspaper space. The day of the 15,000th column was January 19, 1960 just after his eighty-sixth birthday. There was a great deal of publicity about his career, and lots of correspondence to be answered. In September 1960 Little, Brown brought out both *Now I Remember* and a golden anniversary issue of *Old Mother West Wind,* this time with illustrations by Cady. The year passed in a constant blaze of publicity and receptions, including a lengthy TV show taped at Hampden by a Canadian broadcaster. He went to Tobago for the winter of 1960/1961, but with worsening arthritis the Joneses drove him to Arizona for the winters of 1961/2 and 1962/3. Here he found a quick welcome and appeared on many radio and talk shows, and was taken on tours and to fund-raisers for good causes. In 1963 he replaced the Jones couple with a devoted neighbor, Mrs. Ernestine Johnson, who helped with editing the daily stories and with arranging his letters, manuscripts and articles for disposition. He hoped at this time to leave most of his archives to the Springfield Public Library. Somehow it had been made clear to him that his first choices (the Sandwich Historical Society and, the Sandwich Public Library) did not have room for his collection or felt it would be a burden. He regretted this and it was a great loss to Sandwich.

In December 1963 Burgess had a mild stroke and had to enter a nursing home. However, he fought back and each day was taken to Laughing Brook to continue working on papers. Now, a very touching thing occurred. His son Thornton III came to Hampden for the first time in many years, and the two were reconciled and talked at great length. This son, his only child, had never gotten along with his stepmother and had left home at an early age. His life had been bitter and stormy. He had worked for a number of years with ARAMCO in Saudi Arabia. Shortly after this visit to his father, he died in California. Burgess made his own funeral arrangements through Ernestine Johnson (no relative of his former wife) and kept up his correspondence. Ernestine read to him and waited for the end, hastened for him by late cancer. He died June 5, 1965, and was buried in Springfield Cemetery. A couple came to live at Laughing Brook while the estate was being settled, and a few effects were put into a ten-year trust to be held while income from copyrights and current license agreements accumulated. In 1966 the Massachusetts Audubon Society bought the property and later enlarged the land holding to form the present Laughing Brook Nature Center and Wildlife Sanctuary.

CHAPTER 34

ON BECOMING HISTORIC

Sandwich was not much affected by the building booms of the late nineteenth or the early twentieth century. With a declining population, new people could occupy old houses, and only a few new houses were built anywhere in the town. The 1930 construction of Route 6A from the Bourne line to Charles St. was of critical importance in keeping through traffic out of the narrow and curving streets of the village center; and when these older streets were finally paved their shape was still relatively narrow and curving. An appreciation of the value of these complexes of old houses in their street-scapes with nearby ponds, streams and old trees came only slowly. In this chapter we will trace, in abridged chronological order, some of the highlights of the process by which Sandwich became consciously historic, building on its heritage. This process was a gradual one and there were setbacks in losses of valuable old buildings. The town remained deeply conservative and there was a prolonged resistance to many modern features such as moving picture houses, bowling alleys, hotels, dance halls, new restaurants, apartment houses, automobile sales lots and light industry. It is probably fair to say that much of historic Sandwich was saved by the absence of exploiting and developing interests, rather than by a conscious civic action to preserve it.

THE HOXIE HOUSE BEFORE AND AFTER—The photo at the left shows the angular old saltbox with stove chimney and modern windows as last occupied by descendants of Captain Abraham Hoxie. At left is the Lake House built on the foundation of the Sandwich Academy. Courtesy of Sandwich Historical Society. The view on the right shows the house restored to its 1675/1680 construction period with massive fireplaces and chimney, and small leaded casement windows. Sandwich Historical Commission.

1939

Town Anniversary. The town held a three-day celebration of its tricentennial with the usual Grand Ball at the Casino, clambake, baseball game, parade, band concerts, fireworks and boat carnival. This time there were three specific historical elements not seen in previous celebrations:

a. The Historical Society rooms were open free to the public.

b. Sixty one buildings or sites were marked with wooden signs, and a list was available so that these places could all be found.

c. A booklet, "A Bit of Sandwich History, A Few Historical News Items Pertaining to the Old Town of Sandwich", by George E. Burbank was printed for use during the Tercentenary Celebration.

1948

Veterans' Graves. The town voted to identify the graves of the veterans of all wars, and to mark them for Memorial Day.

1951

Burgess. The town voted to name the beach and landing area on Water Street the Thornton W. Burgess Memorial Park, and later placed a wooden bandstand platform here.

1954

Pageant. A new program, the Sandwich Sheep Washing Festival and Historical Pageant, was organized by John Coe and held June 20, with parade, speeches and awards at the Burgess Park. The pageant involved real Indians from Mashpee, many costumed settlers, a ducking stool and some sheep. This was well attended but was not repeated.

1957

Hoxie House. A committee was named to investigate the restoration of the Hoxie House on Water Street. Tax title had been taken as the descendants of the last owners were widely scattered.

Artesian Well. At the suggestion of the Woman's Club, a committee was named to report on beautifying the artesian well near Town Hall where water was spouting from a short pipe protruding from the bare ground.

1958

Hoxie House and Mill. The report on the Hoxie House was accepted, and the town voted to purchase the Dexter Mill building and adjacent nineteenth century building with a view to restoring the Mill. A special legislative act was required to allow the town to spend money on these novel projects.

1959

Hoxie House. Restoration of the Hoxie House began. A study of how to restore the Mill was authorized.

Artesian Well. The artesian well project, under Winnifred Coe, was funded and completed with attractive masonry and a wooden surround for the fountain. This fountain is used constantly and is one of Sandwich's unique features. Many believe the water has a special quality.

Wren Church. The restoration and addition of modern facilities at the unused Congregational Church were begun, with the aid of an interest-free loan from Mr. and Mrs. G. Melville Hill.

1960

Hoxie House. The Hoxie House was opened to the public May 28.

Wren Church. The First Church of Christ in Sandwich was dedicated, with Unitarian and United Church of Christ accreditation, while Federated services were discontinued at the older Unitarian Church.

Yesteryears. Colonel and Mrs. Ronald Thomas leased the Unitarian Church and took out the pews, making exhibit cases for their doll collection.

Rip Van Winkle. An outdoor version of the play *Rip Van Winkle,* starring Frederick A. Morey, was held at the bandstand in Burgess Park; nine performances were given each Wednesday evening from July 6 through August 31.

THE GRIST MILL AS A TEA ROOM—The two mill buildings at the end of Shawme Pond were no longer in any industrial use by the twentieth century. The building at left formerly housed the grist mill closed in 1881, and that at right had been the Sandwich Card and Tag Co. Mrs. Alice Harvey operated a tea room here in the 1920s. Sandwich Archives, Lillian H. Tangney collection, gift of Joan Morrow.

DEXTER GRIST MILL AND TOWN WELL—The two dilapidated mills here were bought up by the town in 1958 and after careful study a new gristmill was built with European stones, and a wooden breast wheel. This was opened in 1962 as a popular historical attraction. The stonework and wooden holder for the artesian well were installed in 1959 after plans by a town committee under Winnifred Coe. This free-flowing water is widely held to be the best on Cape Cod and is in year-round use. Sandwich Archives.

1961

Grist Mill. After two years of planning, the new Dexter Grist Mill was built with undershot wooden wheel; the mill stones came from France. A complete photographic record of this restoration work was preserved.

1963

Adolph Bell. The Captain Peter Adolph bell of 1675 was returned to Sandwich from the Barnstable Courthouse where it had remained since being given or sold to the Court about 1760. This town relic, with its stand and turntable, was placed in the Wren church.

Historic District. The Town voted to establish a committee to administer its historic tourist attractions, but this was shifted over to a study committee to form an Historic District under State Law Chapter 40C, with control of the Hoxie House and Grist Mill remaining under the control of the Selectmen.

1964

Library. A major enlargement of the Weston Memorial Library added two new wings in honor of Mary C. Baker and Dodge Macknight. The library also purchased three adjacent lots.

Anniversary. The Town celebrated its 325th anniversary on August 8th with open house at historic buildings, a parade, and a concert at Burgess Park. Also, in honor of the 50th anniversary of the Cape Cod Canal, a boat flotilla, band concert and fireworks were given at the East Boat Basin. Bourne made the canal the subject of a twelve-day series of events.

Yesteryears. Colonel and Mrs. Ronald Thomas became the owners of the First Parish Church building and land, the first time this lot had been in private hands since the town took it in 1639 to build the meetinghouse.

1965

Historic District. The town accepted protective zoning establishing the first Historic District. The bounds of the district were the Town Hall environs: on Main Street from Uplands to Liberty Street; on Tupper Road to Helen French's house; on Water Street to Quail Hollow; on Grove Street to Lewis Weil's; on Jarves Street through the Morse house and all River Street. A commission of seven members reviewed proposed changes against standards of appropriateness.

SANDWICH PUBLIC LIBRAR Y-1969-The building of 1910 is at right, and the Mary C. Baker wing of 1964 at left. Beyond the original buildings is the Dodge Macknight Room also of 1964. Courtesy of Horace C. Pearsons.

HERITAGE PLANTATION OFFICE-This colonial home started in the Wing family about 1687 and remained as a Wing residence until 1865. Located on Grove Street on the upper mill pond, it had attractive grounds rendered highly important by the rhododendrons later cultivated here by Charles O. Dexter. The property was purchased by Josiah K. Lilly in 1967 and opened as Heritage Plantation of Sandwich, Inc. The old house remains in active use as office and caretaker's residence. Sandwich Historical Commission.

1967

Heritage. The 76-acre Charles O. Dexter Estate was sold by Stanley Berns to Josiah K. Lilly III of Falmouth.

1969

Heritage. The Heritage Plantation of Sandwich opened to the public with two museum buildings, the Round Barn and the Military Museum, under the direction of Nelson O. Price.

1971

Research. The town voted to establish an Historical Commission under State Law, Chapter 40C, charged with conducting research into historical assets found in the town: buildings, structures, sites, memorials and grave markers. This accurate knowledge is then the basis for recommending appropriate action by the town as to preservation, creation of historic districts, marker programs, tourist literature, school programs and other purposes utilizing detailed historical knowledge.

Glass Museum. The Glass Museum was enlarged by adding ells to the Jarves and Craftman's Wings, permitting circulation around the building and chronological sequence of displays. The Tupper collection was taken back by the family.

The Saddle & Pillion graves on one half acre of land on Tupper Road were given to the town by Mrs. Evelyn Carpenter Pratt of the Freeman Farm.

Losses. Two serious losses were suffered in the town's historic assets by the burning of the Daniel Webster Inn and the abrupt demolition of the ancient (1696) Asa Wing house on Grove Street. The loss of the Asa Wing House on Grove Street was without public notice or due process of law.

1972

High School. The town voted for the land and architectural design of a new Junior/Senior High School on Quaker Meetinghouse Road.

Sandwich Academy. The Historical Society placed a boulder and marker near the Hoxie House honoring the 1804 Sandwich Academy built in 1797 by Rev. Burr.

East Sandwich. The Historical Commission completed its inventory of historic assets in Spring Hill and East Sandwich. At the petition of residents in this sector, the town voted to establish an East Sandwich Historic District Study Committee under Donald Bourne, chairman; this Committee decided to enlarge its study area to a strip along Route 6A from Bourne to Barnstable, including Tupper Road, Spring Hill Road, Old County Road and connector roads to the existing Town Hall Historic District.

Heritage. The Plantation was enlarged by the popular Arts and Crafts Building with its restored carousel.

THE DANIEL WEBSTER INN—The Central House was purchased by the Govoni family in 1915, enlarged and renamed the Daniel Webster Inn. The former west end portion with balconies was replaced by a large modern ell with dining room, kitchen and guest rooms. The original Fessenden home of 1729 in the center had its roof raised four feet and the shed dormer installed is visible in this view. Courtesy of Robert H. Ellis.

NEW DAN'L WEBSTER INN–Following the fire in April 1971 that destroyed the ancient tavern and inn, a modern hotel and restaurant was built in 1973 by Carl Schmeltzer. This was purchased in 1980 by Vincent J. Catania and was enlarged, also including the adjacent Federal house of Capt. Ezra Nye.

T. W. Burgess. A committee was formed under Nancy Titcomb to plan honors to Thornton W. Burgess, whose centennial was approaching.

Annie Rose. A living historical treasure in the person of Annie Ewer Rose was lost with her death February 3 in her 105th year.

1973

Daniel Webster Inn. A new Dan'l Webster Inn was opened by Carl H. Schmeltzer.

Eldred House, Briar Patch, Rider Property. The town voted to purchase three properties: the Deacon Eldred House from Mary Crockett Peebles, the Old Briar Patch conservation area from Robert S. Swain, and a large conservation area on Wakeby Pond from the Rider family.

Glass Museum. The Glass Museum was further expanded and improved by new wiring, lighting, foundation and enlargement of the meeting hall, under the direction of Dr. Albert C. Cook.

Old King's Highway. A Planning Committee was established by the state legislature to explore formation of a Nine-Town Regional Historic District from Bourne to Eastham.

1974

T. W. Burgess. The Burgess Centennial Committee held a number of events, including a proclamation honoring his birth, publication of a book, *The Cape Cod Story of Thornton W. Burgess,* a parade by the Junior Woman's Club, dedication of the Briar Patch, a musical at Burgess Park by John Houston, *The Briar Patch,* a pet show, speakers and displays at the Eldred House. The Sandwich Woman's Club adopted the Eldred House restoration as its Community Improvement Program for the Bicentennial period, and under the guidance of Mrs. Shirley Cross organized work parties, fund-raising through house tours, and docent services in this year and over the next several years.

Dunbar House. The town purchased the 1740 Dunbar House to control the land and for possible civic use of the residence.

Historic District. The East Sandwich and Route 6A Historic District Study Committee completed its report, which was approved by the Massachusetts Historical Commission.

Bicentennial. National Bicentennial events got underway with a staging of the historic 1774 "Body of the People" event which stopped Barnstable County Courts and Militia from serving in the King's name. Mr. Eugene Freeman of Sandwich acted the role of Nathaniel Freeman and many Sandwich residents participated. Movies were made of the later attack by Tories on Doctor Freeman and of their punishment under the Sandwich Liberty Pole.

Old King's Highway. The Old King's Highway Regional Historic District came into existence through a State referendum in November, making the area north of the Mid-Cape a controlled District. This eliminated the previous Sandwich Town Hall Historic District and also the newly approved Route 6A Historic District. Donald Bourne was named chairman of the Sandwich Historic District Committee.

1975

Glass Museum. The Glass Museum honored the 150th anniversary of the first making of glass in Sandwich. In October the Empress of Japan paid a visit to Sandwich and to the Museum.

TOWN HALL—Throughout much of its life, there were various occupants in portions of the ground floor of Town Hall such as stores, carpenter shops, newspaper printing office, library and early Historical Society. In this postcard view, there were two doors in the western wall of the building. The rear extension for stage upstairs and town offices was added in 1914. Originally the upstairs public room was reached by stairways in the front corners of the building with direct access from the front porch. Public use of the hall continued until after the construction of the Henry T. Wing School in 1928. Sandwich Archives from Lillian Tangney collection, gift of Joan Morrow.

Eldred House. The Eldred House restoration commenced in a town-approved project removing an ell, wing, bay window and portico, and renewing the siding and windows. The Woman's Club sponsored extensive cleanup and repainting within. The seasonal displays honored both the Bicentennial and Burgess.

National Register. The National Park Service announced the approval of the Town Hall Square National Register District in Sandwich, and also the approval of the Wing Fort House in Spring Hill as a separate National Register building. These designations carry no local obligation but confer prestige and assure national review before they are affected by nationally or state-funded projects.

THORNTON W. BURGESS MUSEUM—The Deacon Eldred House at 4 Water Street with its memories of Arabella Eldred Burgess was bought by the town in 1973. Displays of Burgess material were held here from his centennial year 1974 forward, and the building has been greatly improved by restoration work contributed by the Sandwich Woman's Club, by the town itself and by the Burgess Committee and Society. The Museum has been highly successful with many nature-related events held around the year. Courtesy of Thornton W. Burgess Society.

1976

Bicentennial. The Town's July Fourth events included a ceremonial opening of the "mystery box" laid down in 1876, a parade, and the dedication of a plaque honoring the Revolution. The Town's Bicentennial Committee, under Carl Leino, organized a new Centennial Box to be opened in 2076. This Box, a 30-inch cube, was placed upstairs in Town Hall. The contents of the 1876 Box were displayed at the Eldred House.

T. W. Burgess. The Burgess Centennial Committee members and others received state incorporation as the Thornton W. Burgess Society, Inc., a non-profit educational corporation. The papers of Thornton Burgess (which had been put aside in a trust for ten years after his death as discussed in the previous chapter) were now opened in Hampden, Massachusetts. His three grandchildren received a number of manuscripts of his books, but the vast collection of his letters, articles, pictures, clippings and papers on which he had been working up to his very death was not found, and neither was his motion picture film. These had not been accepted by Springfield Public Library and we sadly conclude they were destroyed.

Town Hall. A detailed study of Town Hall was begun for possible interior rebuilding to enable it to cope with enlarged town functions and space demands.

1977

Opera of Cape Cod. The first opera staged in the auditorium of the Junior/Senior High School was "Rigoletto" in April 1977. Since then operas have been presented twice a year, drawing audiences from all over the county.

State Meeting. State-wide historical representatives assembled in Sandwich under the Bay State Historical League and held meetings at the Glass Museum, Heritage and Dan'l Webster Inn.

Historical Society. At the Glass museum the addition of a shed dormer provided new office space and access to storage space for glass and other collections. A new post of Historical Curator was established to extend the interpretation and display of objects in the collections outside of glass. With these and other basic organizational improvements, the Glass Museum received accreditation by the American Association of Museums.

Town Hall Annex. The town purchased the former Cooperative Bank building to house the Town Clerk, Treasurer and Tax Collector functions, also the Building Inspector's Office, thereby relieving pressure to rebuild the interior of the old Town Hall.

Town Archives. The town accepted a new department of Sandwich Archives and Historical Center under a committee headed by Channing E. Hoxie, Town Clerk.

Railroad Station. The unused railroad station was heavily damaged by fire.

SANDWICH GLASS MUSEUM—The Sandwich Historical Society's central building was moved here from its earlier position nearer the millstream, and rebuilt as a museum. Its main wings are the Jarves Wing (right), Craftsmen Wing (left), and Pratt Room (center rear). The whole has been connected for circular chronological flow and is being enlarged again in 1984. It was accredited by the Association of American Museums in 1979, and attracts world-wide visitors. Courtesy of Sandwich Historical Society.

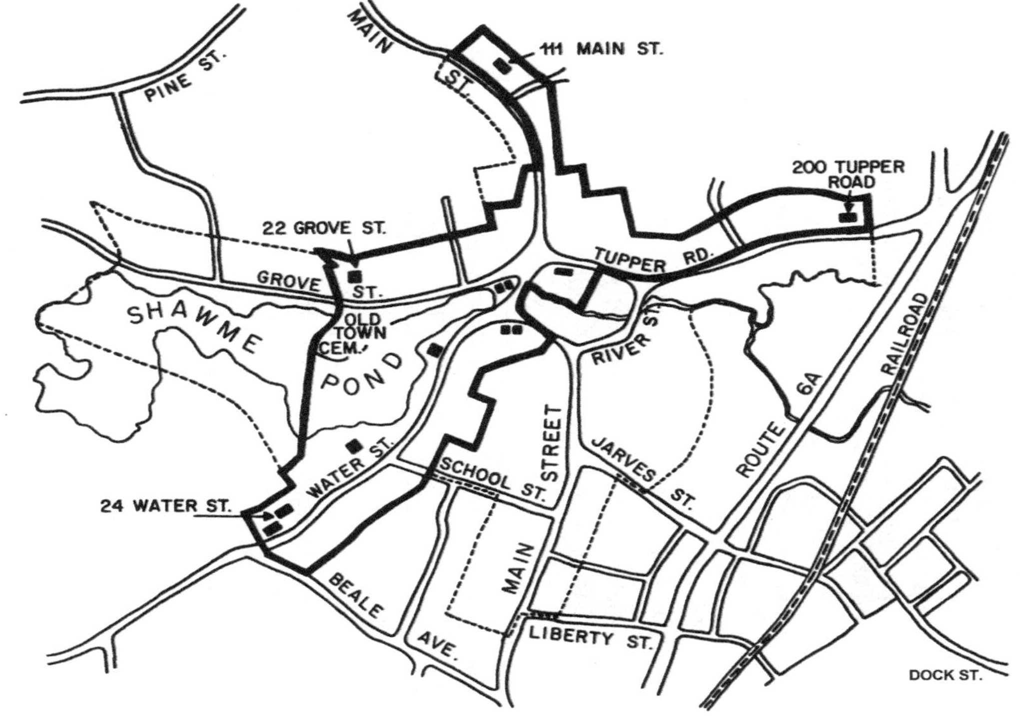

HISTORIC DISTRICTS SANDWICH VILLAGE—The heavy outline shows the limits of the Town Hall Square National Register Historic District approved in 1975. About fifty buildings are enclosed. Listing conveys prestige and ensures hearing before damage from federally or state-funded projects. The larger area enclosed by dotted lines is the former Sandwich Historic District approved in 1964. This was superceded by the Old Kings Highway Regional Historic District in 1974, covering the entire area north of Route 6. The seven unmarked buildings are the Hoxie House, Eldred House, Grist Mill, Town Hall, Glass Museum, Dunbar House and First Church.

1979

Eldred House. The Deacon Eldred House was improved by a completely new chimney and five new fireplaces, funded by the Woman's Club and by the Burgess Society, followed by a new roof paid for by the town.

Glass Factory Site. Mr. David Barnet, an archaeologist from Cornell, worked here for twelve weeks under an intern program sponsored by the National Trust for Historic Preservation and by the Town of Sandwich. His studies concerned the layout of the Boston and Sandwich Glass Factory and the conditions under which controlled excavations might be conducted in open areas now privately owned. The response of residents was strongly favorable, but no such excavations were actually anticipated. The Glass Factory area is an historic asset of National Register caliber.

Green Briar. The Burgess Society purchased Green Briar Jam Kitchen at 6 Discovery Hill Road, Spring Hill, from its former owner Martha Blake, who wished to retire. The Society reopened the jam kitchen under Mae Foster and commenced restoration work on the buildings and grounds to make an office, residence apartment, and nature center.

Freeman Farm. The Freeman Farm buildings and land were sold by Everard S. Pratt, Jr. of Cincinnati to Canal Electric Co. which owned adjacent land.

Railroad Station. The shell of the railroad station was demolished and the site cleared to the platform level.

1980

Dan'l Webster Inn. The Dan'l Webster Inn was purchased by Vincent J. Catania and associates who planned expansion as a major tourist facility.

Freeman Farm. The Historic District Committee under George Sutton was unable to get permission for interim use of the Freeman Farm residence from Canal Electric, which wanted the buildings removed in order to use the area for a coal conveyor, if, as expected, they were forced to convert to coal. The Historic District Committee in turn refused to permit the removal or demolition of the buildings. The Archives staff was allowed to remove a quantity of family documents subject to approval of disposition by Mr. Pratt.

1981

Scenic Railway. The Hyannis and Cape Cod Railway commenced operating a daily tourist train between Sandwich and Hyannis, with buses bringing passengers to the Sandwich attractions of Heritage, Yesteryears, Glass Museum, Burgess Museum, Hoxie House, Grist Mill and Dan'l Webster Inn.

Historical Society. The Historical Society published a new booklet on the history of the Society, by W. Gordon Swan.

1982

Freeman Farm. The Freeman Farm residence was destroyed in December after damage from a brush fire and repeated vandalism of the interior.

Town History. The town voted funds for the Archives to prepare a new town history book.

1984

Sandwich Glass. The first of a definitive series of books on Sandwich Glass by Raymond Barlow and Joan Kaiser was published entitled *The Glass Industry in Sandwich Volume 4* covering the period 1882-1920.

Green Briar. The Burgess Society dedicated its Nature Center and Jam Kitchen in July ceremonies, especially honoring Mrs. Nancy Titcomb, founder and leader of the Burgess Society since its start.

Library, First Church, Glass Museum. All three Sandwich institutions broke ground for new adjoining buildings to increase their capacity.

CHAPTER 35

SANDWICH POPULATION AND FAMILIES

Sandwich goes on not only in its historic landscapes and its buildings but also in its stock of people. The mix has changed greatly over the life of the town, even before the great influx of newcomers in the industrial period. In this last chapter we will look at overall population changes, at our records of vital statistics and the published records of Sandwich families; we will also review some of the families arriving here in the nineteenth and early twentieth centuries, and note a few facts about our last resting places.

Early Population

In earlier chapters we showed the number of families here at key dates from the first settlement period up to the Federal Census in 1790. The heads of these families at each date are all known by name. The following list shows our estimates of population in the sectors that finally arose in the division of the town:

	Total Families	*Persons per Family*	*Total Population*		
			Sandwich	*Bourne*	*Town*
1640	61	4	240	10	250
1650	60	5	260	40	300
1700	100	6	440	160	600
1730	162	6	630	340	970
1750	209	6	794	456	1,250
1790	326	6.11	1,247	744	1,991

The 1730 Census of households was recorded by Reverend Fessenden, and the heads of household in it are consistent with the charts of descent of the various town families which have been built up by the Archives from town records and genealogies.

The 1790 heads of household are from the Federal Census which shows the number of individuals in each family. Using the later Federal Census schedules, the following population changes are found to the year of division of the town:

	Average	*Total Population*		
	Family	*Sandwich*	*Bourne*	*Town*
1790	6.11	1,247	744	1,991
1800				2024
1820	5.50	1,467	1,017	2,484
1830				3,361
1850	5.0	2,569	1,612	4,181
1860	4.7	2,920	1,559	4,479
1870				3,694
1880	4.06	2,096	1,447	3,543
1884		1,966	1,489	3,455

This table shows the peak population in 1860. At this time Bourne had grown about 53% over 1820, while Sandwich, with its glass factory had grown 99%. Bourne's population actually had peaked in 1850 and declined to 1870 when it was about 1300, then began to grow again with the railroad and tourism, while Sandwich continued to decline. There seems to be no census of the two towns at division (except in polls and voters) so the above 1884 figures were simply interpolated between the 1880 and 1900 Federal figures. The 1890 Federal Census was lost.

The twentieth century has seen growth in Bourne in all decades, while Sandwich only began to grow after 1940. The following are year-round residents:

	Sandwich	*Bourne*	*Total*
1900	1,448	1,657	3105
1910	1,688?	2,474	4,162
1920	1,458	2,530	3,988
1930	1,437	2,895	4,332
1940	1,360	3,315	4,675
1950	1,418	4,720	6,138
1960	2,082	7,426	9,508
1970	3,634	8,772	12,406
1980	8,727	8,910	17,637

The previous figures from the Federal Census exclude Otis Air Force Base, population of 1,411 in 1950, 6,585 in 1960, 5,596 in 1970 and 4,964 in 1980. All or most of this group was usually counted in Bourne in County-wide lists. The average family size in 1980 in the Sandwich/Bourne area was down to 2.59 persons per family.

Sandwich Vital Records—The Town Books

The town meeting records and our town's statistics of births, deaths and marriages began to be recorded permanently by the town clerk by 1651. Before this the town clerk was supposed to send vital statistics to Plymouth to be preserved among colony records, but only a small portion of this record has survived. There are six volumes of the older Sandwich vital records preserved in the town clerk's vault which bring our statistics of births, deaths and marriages up to 1900. These six volumes are as follows:

1. General Records - 1651-1691. These pages were loose, torn, worn and incomplete when they were encapsulated in thin wax paper and rebound in 1901. This book also includes town meeting records and other entries. The vital records on certain families have been extended to earlier dates than the period of the book by information supplied by the family such as the birth of spouses and children born in England. The earliest is the birth of Thomas Tupper in 1578.

2. Births, Marriages, Death, Earmarks - 1658-1809. This second early volume also had the pages treated and was rebound in 1901. This volume is commonly called the *Earmarks* book. Extensive entries begin in 1682. Some pages are missing and lost. An index survives which shows the nature of the entries on each original page.

3. *Births and Deaths - 1803-1842, Marriages - 1813-1837.* This volume has original entries for these periods; also, in 1869 the Town Clerk, H.G.O. Ellis, copied in what he could read of the *General Records.* A number of errors were made in this process.

4. Births and Deaths - 1836-1842. This contains further original entries plus a number of past marriages of Sandwich persons in the period 1700-1857 which occurred in other towns. Town clerks were required by law in 1857 to search their records of marriages and report those involving persons from other towns to the town clerk of that town.

5. Births - 1682-1842, Marriages - 1720-1812, Deaths - 1701-1841. This book is entirely a copy of previous records, namely the *Earmarks* and the *Births and Deaths 1836-1842.* The copying was done by Thomas Newcomb in 1893 and contains many errors of reading.

6. Births, Marriages, Deaths - 1843-1900. These are all original entries, on standard forms. Vital Records of Bourne residents are here to the division date in 1884, after which they were kept by the Bourne town clerk.

These six volumes are an irreplaceable record, in which the original entries are the sources from which formal certificates are copied for family records and legal purposes. To save search in the original volumes (which are not indexed) 3 x 5 inch cards were prepared by persons employed by the Works Progress Administration (WPA) in the 1930s, and have been available to the public in the town clerk's office ever since. These are arranged alphabetically, white for births, pink for marriages, blue for deaths. Unfortunately, this work was done from the recopied not the earliest records because of ease of reading, so that errors were perpetuated, but the cards remain a great convenience.

Town Vital Records to 1850

The state required that all vital records from 1840 be reported to a central statistical office in Boston. This made access there relatively easy, and in order to cover the period from the founding of each town to 1850, the state launched a program to publish each town's vital records to 1850 without expense to the towns. This program went on for several decades from about 1900, and resulted in new published books of records from about two thirds of the towns in the state. On the Cape only Truro and Brewster bothered to comply, and most of Plymouth and Bristol County towns failed as well. Each town library received a full set of all the volumes so printed. The Sandwich failure to allow publication of its own vital records was then followed by the decision of the librarian here to sell our set of other town vital records, a lamentable decision for research in Sandwich. Due to the recent surge of interest nationally in family history and in town history, some of these early books of vital records are being republished and other towns are at last preparing their vital records to 1850 for printing. On the Cape, Falmouth, Yarmouth and Harwich records have been printed. Sponsoring agencies have included the Massachusetts Society of Mayflower Descendants, town committees, dedicated individuals and the New England Historic Genealogical Society.

Sandwich Vital Records in Print

While many people are deeply involved in searching vital records, still the great majority are probably little interested. Hence, we will list our information on Sandwich vital records in print only very briefly, as those who want more details can readily find them. There are four present sources of Sandwich records, each of limited scope:

1. Plymouth Colony Records Volumes 1, 2 & 8 contain the scraps of records of the period 1637-1651. A single volume of these collected vital records for the whole colony was published by Genealogical Publishing Company in 1976. This is the source, for example, of the marriage of Benjamin Nye and Katherine Tupper in 1640.

2. A quarterly periodica,l *Genealogical Advertiser,* edited by Lucy Hall Greenlaw was published in Cambridge 1898-1901. Four issues contained Sandwich records but only covered the *General Records* entries and the start of the *Earmarks* volume, and used the recopied books as sources.

3. *The Mayflower Descendant,* a quarterly of the Massachusetts Society of Mayflower Descendants, contains a careful reading by the editor George Ernest Bowman from the original volumes, but only covers the *General Records* and about one-sixth of the *Earmarks*. An index of the names in these six articles was published by Col. Leonard H. Smith, Jr. of Clearwater, Florida.

4. During the 1960s a team of devoted researchers, including Lydia Brownson, Grace Held and Doris Norton, visited Sandwich and other Barnstable County towns and abstracted vital records to about 1850. These were hand written in alphabetical order by family in 29 large notebooks, which were deposited with the Sturgis Library, Barnstable. Microfilm copies have been made which are in reference libraries. This film record is in the Sandwich Archives, as are all the above references.

Other Vital Records of Sandwich

The town vital record books were never totally complete, due to failure of families to report to the town clerk. At a rough estimate, 5% of the marriages, 20% of the births and 50% of the deaths are not in the present official record before 1800. Supplemental information is contained in records of marriages, baptisms and deaths kept by various churches in the town and on burial markers, and much of this information has been copied out by the Archives and placed on record cards. Other vital records are found in Bible entries, in letters, diaries, and in wills and deeds.

Genealogies of Sandwich Families

Devoted members of families have assembled family records in organized form, and many have been published in books and journals. There are two general types, one taking an immigrant ancestor and tracing all his descendants in the male lines; the other type starts with a particular living person or couple and identifies the parents, grandparents, and so on back to the immigration point of all the antecedents. Some of the Sandwich genealogies that have been particularly useful are a Burgess genealogy by Rev. Ebenezer Burgess (1865), the *Freeman Genealogy* by Rev. Frederick Freeman (1875), the *Swift Genealogy* by George H. Swift (1900) and the *Genealogical Notes of Barnstable Families* by Amos Otis (1888). Other genealogies of town families are listed in the Bibliography of this book. Special notice should be given to the remarkable series of five-generation studies of many Sandwich founders written chiefly by Maclean W. McLean, most of which were published in the *Register* of the New England Historic Genealogical Society. These studies are enriched through a wide search in wills and deeds in courts of Barnstable, Plymouth and Bristol County, as well as in church records and other sources.

Since its inception in 1977, the Archives office has prepared charts of descent of persons in Sandwich, especially of the older families, for use in studying family formation, house ownership, removal to other areas and other uses. These charts are of great convenience and value to persons studying family descent in Sandwich, and draw on all available sources of knowledge. The charts generally stop at the point of removal of individuals from Sandwich.

Survival of Early Families

By the year 1700 a number of families had put down strong roots here, and certain members in each generation became influential in town government and as land owners. The dominance of these old families was probably highest about 1790, when some 38 family surnames accounted for 82% of all the families in the town. With the spread of population to cities and to the west after 1790, and especially after the arrival of industrial workers (in our case the glass factory), the pattern of names of residents changed drastically. Certain of the old families disappeared entirely, while others shrank greatly in numbers as the opportunities for making a living within the town became limited. There are three aspects or measures of this social composition over the whole history of the town (Sandwich & Bourne combined), which we wish to summarize here, although partly covered in earlier chapters as well:

	Percentage of the whole town represented by families of 38 early surnames.	*Number of families of ten earliest surnames.*	*Number of families of ten other surnames (Marine Interest)*
1640	23%	12	1
1650	53%	21	8
1700	79%	37	24
1790	82%	111	83
1820	72%	132	99
1850	43%	111	15 1
1880	38%	88	14 1
1900		83	16 6
1983		43?	13 5

The "ten earliest surnames" are those of Allen, Bourne, Dillingham, Fish, Freeman, Holway, Landers, Nye, Tupper and Wing. As a group these families peaked in absolute numbers in 1820 and then declined. The number 43 in 1983 in Sandwich and Bourne is from the Cape Cod telephone book, and probably is too high, as persons (such as eleven Allen families) who may not be descended from the original Sandwich stock are included.

In the nineteenth century most families here had a few men at sea. However some Sandwich families (see Chapter 20) had a strong association with marine activities, and the third column above profiles ten of these families: Barlow, Blackwell, Burgess, Ellis, Gibbs, Handy, Hoxie, Perry, Phinney and Swift. These ten showed a growth in size that was parallel to the other ten named above through 1820, then because of their marine livelihood continued to expand through 1850, then to decline slightly by 1880. However, this set of ten somehow remained firmly rooted here in various employment, and increased in size in 1900. They remain even today, an active and substantial block of families in Sandwich and Bourne. In 1983 most are clearly of continuous descent from the original lines, and are the only such families of all the original stock still present in strength.

The 38 families mentioned above as the core of the town's population in the eighteenth century include, beside the above 20 named families, the following other early families: Atkins, Bassett, Chipman, Ewer, Fessenden, Gifford, Goodspeed, Hall, Hamblin, Howland, Jones, Lawrence, Meiggs, Percival, Pope, Smith, Tobey and Weeks.

Later Arrivals

The glassmaking arrivals were a highly varied lot both in nationality and in skills. Many left to work elsewhere when the glass industry here closed. However, by the second or third generation in Sandwich certain of these arrivals had put down firm roots, as shown by this list of Selectmen from their ranks:

James Shevlin	1884-1886
John McCann	1899-1900
George T. McLaughlin	1907-1912
James M. McArdle	1914-1926, 1933-1934
Charles E. Brady	1916-1919
James H. Kelleher	1925
Thomas F. Kelleher	1935-1937, 1941-1947

Later immigration is best viewed from a county-wide perspective. In the decades after 1890, a number of immigrants came to Barnstable County, especially from Portuguese areas, from Italy, and from Finland. In his perceptive book, *Cape Cod and the Old Colony,* Professor Albert Brigham reviews the foreign-born population here as of 1910. He found that 13.6% of the Cape population, or 3,769 persons were then foreign-born. Of these some 40% or over 1,500 were Portuguese, centered first in Provincetown in fishing, then in other towns, especially East Falmouth in vegetable and fruit-growing. A few families came to Sandwich, including Almeida and Alves. By 1910 there were 400 Italians on the Cape, nearly all connected with the Keith Car Co. and living in Sagamore and Sandwich. The empty homes in the Jarvesville area were an attraction to this group. Italian family names included those of three later Selectmen, Joseph F. Bazzinotti, John L. Roberti and Carlo A. Pola. Also among the foreign-born in 1910 were some 250 Finnish people who centered initially in West Barnstable.

Many of these families later came to Sandwich and worked on farms and cranberry bogs where they showed natural skill. Among the arrivals were families of Ahonen, Elvander, Hendrickson, Luksanen, Maki, Parssinen, Toolas and Wirtanen.

In addition to these new arrivals, many families settled here about the turn of the century and contributed significantly to town activities. These include families of Armstrong, Bartley, Beale, Burke, van Buskirk, Carleton, Caron, Fleet, French, Magnusson, Mooney, Morrow, Morse, Paine, Roos, Russell and Torrey.

Cemeteries

The burial places of most of the early settlers were on their own lands, and were not marked by inscribed stones due to the absence of slate and marble in this region. It is regrettable that the descendants of those families with private burial areas did not fence the areas permanently or indicate locations by later central markers or in a deed description. Among the surviving known private areas are:

Saddle and Pillion, on the original Freeman Farm, burials of Edmund and Elizabeth Freeman in 1682 and 1676 respectively. Sites were marked by boulders, with plaques placed in 1910. This area was given to the town in 1971.

Tobey family cemetery off Quaker Meeting House Road, north of Peters Pond. Burials date from early eighteenth century, but the first inscribed slate marker is 1788. Last interrals were in the1850s. The land is owned by The Town of Sandwich. The stones were heavily damaged by a vandal in 1878 but have been partly restored.

James Percival graves, Farmersville Road, South Sandwich. Four stones, 1831-1848.

Joe Wilson graves off Quaker Meetinghouse Road, Forestdale. One marker, fenced. Wilson was a Civil War veteran who died in 1886.

Freeman family cemetery, Route 130 at Pine St. Started in 1806, with a formal Society in 1889, accepted by the Town in 1966.

The Town itself set aside land for three cemeteries:

Old Town Burying Ground, off Grove Street. Land was set aside in 1663. The oldest surviving stone is 1685, and the most recent burial was in 1939.

Almshouse Cemetery, Crowell Lane. This was part of the almshouse farm, and was used for interment of the town poor between 1823 and 1845. There are no markers.

New Town Cemetery, Route 130 Forestdale. Land was set aside and landscaped in 1979.

There are three cemeteries which were set up by religious societies:

The Old Quaker burial area on Quaker Road in Spring Hill. This is about one-half acre and is fenced. There are no markers. Burials date probably from the 1640s.

The main Quaker burial area behind the Quaker Meetinghouse in Spring Hill. This is 3.5 acres, and is fenced with granite posts and wrought iron rails.

St. Peters Cemetery at Grove and Pine Streets was dedicated in 1865. The area is about six acres.

There are seven neighborhood cemeteries laid out originally by groups of citizens for the convenience of the families in the district. By age of earliest marker they are:

The Wakeby area cemetery on Cotuit Road. Interrals from 1803. Presently inactive.

Cedarville Cemetery on Route 6A at Ploughed Neck Road. Earliest marker 1805. The town took control in 1976.

South Sandwich Cemetery on Boardley Road. Earliest marker 1811.

Spring Hill Cemetery on Route 6A west of Spring Hill. Earliest marker 1812.

Mount Hope Cemetery on Route 6A near Charles St. This cemetery was initiated by the Boston and Sandwich Glass Co. for employees but soon came into more general use. It was accepted by the town in 1964. Earliest interral 1826.

Forestdale Cemetery, Route 130. Earliest marker 1826. Taken over by the town in 1980.

Bay View Cemetery, Main Street opposite Pine Street. The Association was incorporated in 1868 and is still active.

The Present Town

Sandwich is one of the fastest growing communities in the Commonwealth, a fact which continues to strain the town's resources and agencies. There is a sense of great vitality and action in the town, but rapid growth brings specific problems such as in lot size and in zoning, changes of property valuation, waste accumulation and disorientation. The tax rate remains low due partly to the presence of the Canal Electric plant with its high valuation with little cost to the town. The attraction of light industry is often said to be a goal to create more local jobs, but objections are raised against many proposals. Some new arrivals are retired but many are willing to live on the Cape and commute daily to Boston. Whether young or older, the arrivals bring a wealth of skills and talent which are of great service to the churches, clubs, museums and town committees in volunteer services. The townspeople are strongly supportive of conservation of land and of protection of natural resources, and do not want to see the ponds abused, the wetlands encroached on, and all streets endlessly widened. Nevertheless the pressure to build on all available land is strong and some conflict or loss is inevitable. Eventually the town must dispose of its wastes more efficiently, and some areas of the town will probably have to be sewered. The town's historic character and appearance will continue to be one of its chief resources, and it is hoped that in this recognition and understanding this book will have made some contribution.

WING FAMILIES OF THE HERITAGE MUSEUMS & GARDENS AREA

Children of Daniel Senior, 8 Morse Road

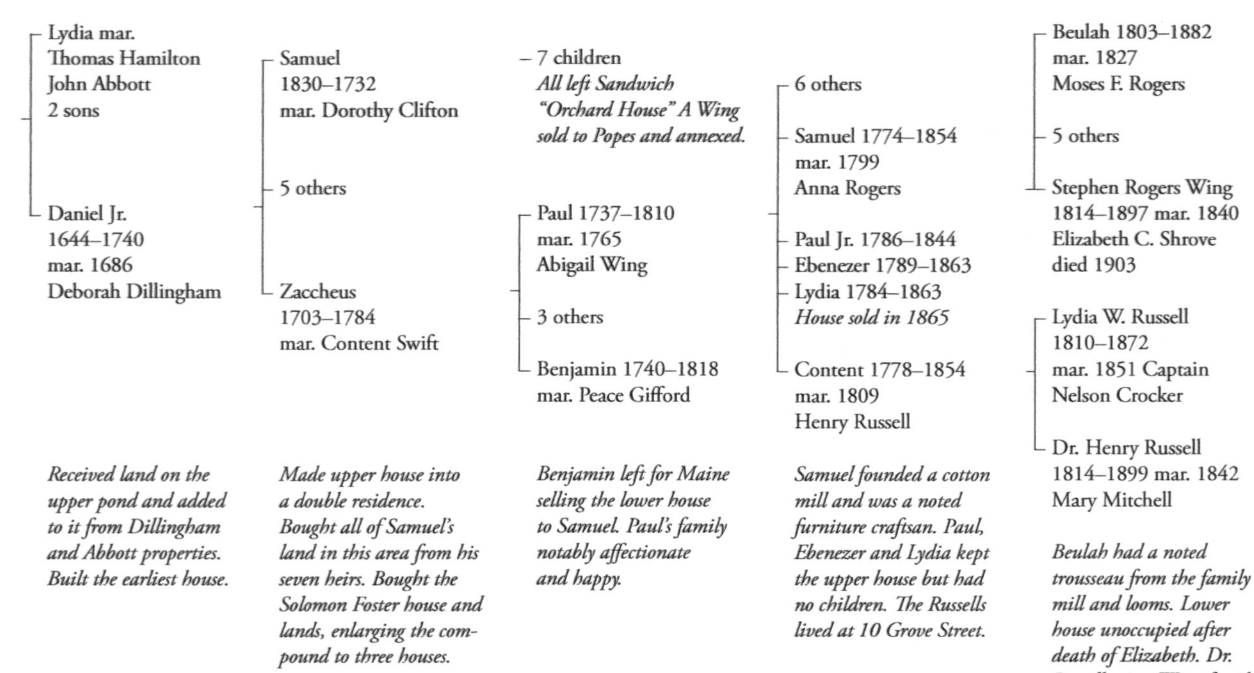

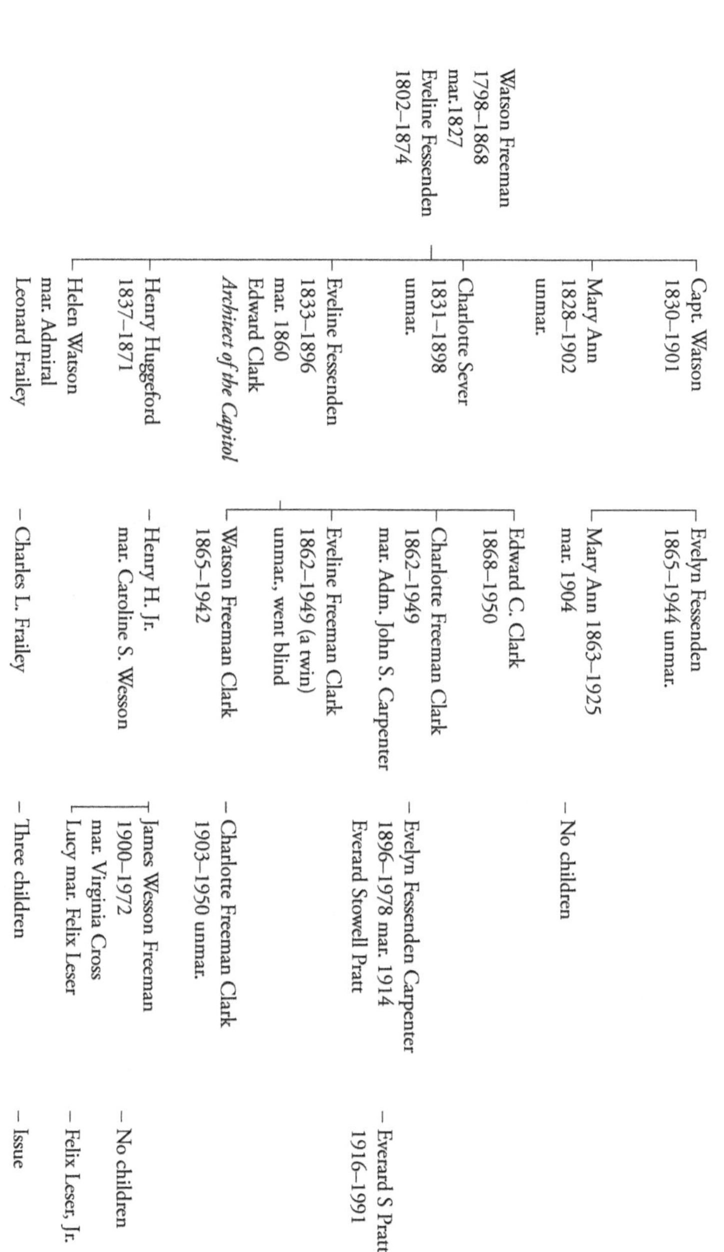
FREEMAN FARM PEOPLE
Watson Freeman
1798–1868
mar.1827
Eveline Fessenden
1802–1874
Capt. Watson
1830–1901
Evelyn Fessenden
1865–1944 unmar.
Mary Ann
1828–1902
unmar.
Mary Ann 1863–1925
mar. 1904
– No children
Charlotte Sever
1831–1898
unmar.
Edward C. Clark
1868–1950
Charlotte Freeman Clark
1862–1949
mar. Adm. John S. Carpenter
– Evelyn Fessenden Carpenter
1896–1978 mar. 1914
Everard Stowell Pratt
– Everard S Pratt, Jr.
1916–1991
Eveline Fessenden
1833–1896
mar. 1860
Edward Clark
Architect of the Capitol
Eveline Freeman Clark
1862–1949 (a twin)
unmar., went blind
Watson Freeman Clark
1865–1942
– Charlotte Freeman Clark
1903–1950 unmar.
Henry Huggeford
1837–1871
– Henry H. Jr.
mar. Caroline S. Wesson
James Wesson Freeman
1900–1972
mar. Virginia Cross
– No children
Lucy mar. Felix Leser
– Felix Leser, Jr.
Helen Watson
mar. Admiral
Leonard Frailey
– Charles L. Frailey
– Three children
– Issue

BIBLIOGRAPHY

BOOKS

Akagi, Roy H. *The Town Proprietors of the New England Colonies.* Reprint. Gloucester, MA: Peter Smith, 1963.

Anthony, Katherine. *First Lady of the Revolution: The Life of Mercy Otis Warren.* Garden City, NY Doubleday & Co. Inc., 1958.

Arsenault, Bona. *History of the Acadians.* Ottawa, Ontario, Canada: Editions Leméac, Inc., 1978. 6 Vols, in French. 1 Vol. in English.

Ashley, Robert Paul, *The Sandwich Historical Society.* Plymouth, MA: Leyden Press Inc., 1967.

Atkins, Gaius G. and Frederick L. Fagley. *History of American Congregationalism.* Boston, MA: Pilgrim Press, 1942.

Bacon, John. *The Town Officer's Guide.* Haverhill, MA: 1825.

Banks, Charles Edward. *The History of Martha's Vineyard, Duke's County, Mass.* Edgartown, MA: Duke's County Historical Society, 1966.

Banks, Charles Edward. *The Planters of the Commonwealth 1620-1640.* Reprint. Baltimore, MD: Genealogical Publ. Co., 1975.

Banks, Charles Edward. *Topographical Dictionary of 2,885 English Emigrants to New England 1620-1650.* Reprint. Baltimore, MD: Genealogical Publ. Co., 1976.

Barbour, Harriot B. *Sandwich The Town That Glass Built.* Boston, MA: Houghton Mifflin Co., 1948.

Barlow, Raymond E. and Joan E. Kaiser. *The Glass Industry in Sandwich.* Vol. 4. Windham, NH: Barlow-Kaiser Publishing Co., Inc., 1983.

Belliveau, Pierre. *French Neutrals in Mass.* Boston, MA: Kirk S. Giffen, 1972.

Benes, Peter. *The Masks of Orthodoxy.* Amherst, MA: University of Massachusetts Press, 1977.

Bentwich, Helen C. *History of Sandwich in Kent.* Deal, Kent, England: T. F. Pain & Sons Ltd., 1975.

Berkhofer, Robert F., Jr. *The White Man's Indian.* New York, NY: Alfred A. Knopf, 1978.

Billias, George Ethan, Ed. *Law & Authority in Colonial America.* New York, NY: Dover Publications, 1970.

Bingham, Amelia G. *Mashpee Land of the Wampanoags.* Mashpee, MA: Mashpee Historical Commission, 1970.

Blair Associates. *Cape Cod 1980. A Sector of the Massachusetts State Plan.* Plus supplement. College Hill Press, 1963.

Blake, Francis Everett. *History of Princeton Mass.* Princeton, MA: Publ. by the Town, 1915.

Blunt, E. and G. W. Blunt. *American Coast Pilot.* 11th edition. New York, NY: E. & G. W. Blunt, 1827.

Bodfish, David Lewis, comp. *First Congregational Church of Wareham, Massachusetts, 1739-1939.* Wareham, MA: 1939.

Bolton, Charles Knowles. *The Real Founders of New England.* Boston, MA: F. W. Faxon, Co., 1929.

Bourgoin, Rev. Raymond B. *The Catholic Church in Sandwich 1830-1930.* Boston, MA: E. L. Grimes Printing Co., 1930.

Bradford, William. *Of Plymouth Plantation. 1620-1647.* Samuel Eliot Morison, Ed. New York, NY: Alfred A. Knopf, 1952.

Brigham, Albert Perry. *Cape Cod and the Old Colony.* New York, NY: Grosset & Dunlap, 1920.

Brown, Oliver B., Ed. *Vital Records of Falmouth Massachusetts to the Year 1850.* Warwick, R.I.: Society of Mayflower Descendants in the State of Rhode Island, 1976.

Brown, Wallace. *The Kings Friends, the Composition and Motives of the American Loyalist Claimants.* Providence, R.I.: Brown University Press, 1965.

Bunker, Mary Powell. *Long Island Genealogies.* Reprint. Baltimore, MD: Genealogical Publishing Co., 1976.

Burbank, George E., Ed. *A Bit of Sandwich History.* Sandwich, MA: 1939. Reissued as *Highlights of Sandwich History,* 1946.

Bureau of the Census. *Heads of Families at the First Census of the United States Taken in the Year 1790—Massachusetts.* Reprint. Spartanburg, S.C.: Reprint Co., 1964.

Burgess, Rev. Dr. Ebenezer. *Memorial of the Family of Thomas and Dorothy Burgess.* Boston, MA: Press of T. R. Marvin & Son, 1865.

Burgess, Thornton W. *Aunt Sally's Friends in Fur.* Boston, MA: Little Brown & Co., 1955.

Burgess, Thornton W. *Now I Remember.* Boston, MA: Little, Brown & Company, 1960.

Burrows, Fredrika A. *Cannonballs and Cranberries.* Taunton, MA: William S. Sullwold Publ., Inc., 1978.

Burrows, Fredrika A. *Windmills on Cape Cod & the Islands.* Taunton, MA: William S. Sullwold Publ., Inc., 1978.

Calnek, W. A. *History of the County of Annapolis, Nova Scotia.* Reprint. Belleville, Ont.: Bonanza Books, 1954.

Carse, Robert. *The Seafarers—A History of Maritime America 1620-1820.* New York, NY: Bonanza Books, 1954.

Cataldo, Louis and Dorothy Worrell. *Pictorial Tales of Cape Cod.* Hyannis, MA: Tales of Cape Cod, Inc., Vol. I 1956, Vol. II 1961.

Centennial Committee. *The Old United Empire Loyalists List.* Toronto, Canada: Rose Publ. Co., 1885.

Chamberlain, Barbara Blau. *These Fragile Outposts.* Garden City, NY: The Natural History Press, 1964.

Chamberlain, N. H. *Autobiography of a New England Farmhouse.* New York: Carleton, 1865.

Chamberlain, N. H. *Samuel Sewall and The World He Lived In.* Boston, MA: DeWolfe, Fiske & Co., 1897.

Chipman, Frank W. *The Romance of Old Sandwich Glass.* Boston: Sands C. and Frank W. Chipman, 1932.

Chipman, John Hale III. *A Chipman Genealogy.* Norwell, MA: Chipman Histories, 1970.

Chipman, Rev. Richard Manning. *Chipman Family.* Lisbon, CT.: 1872.

Confession of Faith and Covenant Adopted by the Calvinistic Congregational Church in Sandwich June 29, 1820 Also A Brief History of the Church. Revised and ReprintEd. Boston, MA: 1855.

Crapo, Henry Howland. *Certain Comeoverers. 2* Vols. New Bedford, MA: E. Anthony & Sons, Inc., 1912.

Crocker, Dr. Benton P. *The Percivals of Cape Cod.* Ms. Foxboro, MA: 1938

Dalton, J. W. *The Lifesavers of Cape Cod.* Old Greenwich, CT.: The Chatham Press, 1902.

Dartmouth, Mass. Vital Records to the Year 1850. 3 Vols. Boston MA: New England Historic Genealogical Society, 1929-30.

Davis, William T. *Ancient Landmarks of Plymouth.* Boston, MA: Damrell & Upham, 1899.

Demos, John. *A Little Commonwealth.* New York, NY: Oxford Univ. Press, 1970.

Deyo, Simeon L., Ed. *History of Barnstable County, Massachusetts.* New York, NY: H. W. Blake & Co., 1890.

Digges, Jeremiah. *Cape Cod Pilot.* Poor Richard Associates Modern Pilgrim Press & The Viking Press, 1937.

Doane, Doris. *A Book of Cape Cod Houses.* Old Greenwich, CT.: The Chatham Press, Inc., 1970.

Dudley, Dean. *Historical Sketches of Plymouth and Barnstable County.* Wakefield, MA: 1873.

Durant, John and Alice Durant. *Pictorial History of American Ships.* New York, NY: A. S. Barnes and Co., 1953.

Dwight, Rev. Timothy. *Travels in New England and New York.* 4 Vols. New Haven, NH Published by the author, 1822.

Dykes, Hannah S. B. *History of Richard Bourne and Some of his Descendants.* Cleveland, OH: Benjamin F. Bourne, 1919

Earle, Alice Morse. *Curious Punishments of Bygone Days.* Rutland, VT: Charles E. Tuttle Co., 1972.

Earle, Alice Morse. *Customs & Fashions in Old New England.* New York: Charles Scribner's Sons, 1894.

Earle, John Milton. *Report to the Governor and Council Concerning the Indians of the Commonwealth.* Boston, MA: William White, Printer to the State, 1861.

Farmer, John. *A Genealogical Register of the First Settlers of New England.* Reprint with additions and corrections. Baltimore, MD: Genealogical Publ. Co., 1976.

Farson, Robert H. *The Cape Cod Canal.* Middletown, NH Wesleyan Univ. Press, 1977.

Faunce, James Freer. *The Faunce Family.* Akron, OH: Privately printed, 1967, 1973.

Fawsett, Marise. *Sandwich—the Oldest Town on Cape Cod.* East Sandwich, MA: Marise Fawsett, 1969.

Finney, Howard Sr. *Finney/Phinney Families in America.* Richmond, VA: The

William Byrd Press, Inc., 1957.

Freeman, Frederick, *Freeman Genealogy.* Boston, MA: Franklin Press — Rand, Avery, and Co., 1875.

Freeman, Frederick. *The History of Cape Cod.* Vol. I, The Annals of Barnstable County and of its Several Towns. Vol. II, The Annals of the Thirteen Towns of Barnstable County. Reprint. Yarmouthport, MA: Parnassus Imprints, 1965.

Goodwin, John A. *Pilgrim Republic.* Boston, MA: Tichnor and Company, 1879.

Hallowed, Richard P. *The Quaker Invasion of Massachusetts.* Boston, MA: Houghton, Mifflin Co., 1883.

Hannah, Samuel D. *The Proprietary Lands of Plymouth Colony & Cape Cod.* Edited by Stephen Connolly. Hyannis, MA: Patriot Press, 1980.

Hannibal, Edna Anne with Claude W. Barlow. *John Briggs of Sandwich, Mass., and His Descendants.* Ms. Palo Alto, CA.: 1962.

Harlow, Alvin F. *Steelways of New England.* New York: Creative Age Press, Inc., 1946.

Hartley, E. N. *Hammersmith.* New York, NY: American Iron and Steel Institute, 1955.

Hayward, John, comp. *Gazetteer of Massachusetts.* Boston: John P. Jewett & Co., 1849.

Hersey, Alan F. *The Old Colony Story.* Privately printEd. 1959. Rev. 1962, 1969.

Historical Data Relating to Counties, Cities and Towns in Massachusetts. Boston, MA: Commonwealth of Mass., 1975.

A History, Sixty Years of Cooperative Extension Service in Massachusetts. Amherst: University of Massachusetts, AB. 1965.

Holbrook, Stewart H. *The Yankee Exodus.* Seattle, WA: University of Washington Press, 1950.

Holway, Mrs. Jerome R. *The Old Cemetery Sandwich, Mass.* Hyannis, MA: F. B. & F. P. Goss, 1908.

Hoxie, Leslie R. *The Hoxie Family.* Ukiah, OR: 1950.

Hutchins, Francis G. *Mashpee, the Story of Cape Cod's Indian Town.* West Franklin, NH: Amarta Press, 1979.

Irwin, Frederick T. *The Art of Glassmaking as Practiced at Sandwich Mass.* Manchester, NH: 1926.

Ivers, Harry B., Ed. *The Official Old Home Week and Canal Bridge Dedication Book.* Boston, MA: George D. Hill, Inc., 1935.

James; Sidney V., Jr. *Three Visitors to Early Plymouth.* Plymouth, MA: Plimoth Plantation, Inc., 1963.

Jehn, Janet. *Acadian Descendants.* Covington, KY: Janet Jehn, 1972.

Jennings, Francis. *The Invasion of America, Indians, Colonialism, and the Cant of Conquest.* Chapel Hill, NC: University of North Carolina Press, 1975.

Jennings, Herman A. *Provincetown, or Odds and Ends from the Tip End.* Yarmouthport, MA: FrEd. Hallett, 1890.

Jordan, David Starr & Sarah Louise Kimball. *Your Family Tree.* New York, NY: D. Appleton Co., 1929.

Journals of the House of Representatives of Massachusetts. 1715-1775. Boston, MA: Massachusetts Historical Society, 1919-to present.

Keene, Betsy D. *History of Bourne 1622-1937.* Yarmouthport, MA: Charles W. Swift, 1937. Reprint 1975 with index.

Kelley, Stanley. *About Cape Cod.* Boston, MA: Thomas Dodd Printers, 1936.

Kittredge, Henry C. *Cape Cod-Its People and Their History.* 2nd Ed. Boston MA: Houghton, Mifflin Co., 1968.

Kittredge, Henry C. *Shipmasters of Cape Cod.* Hampden, CT: Arch on Books, 1971.

Langdon, William Chauncy. *Everyday Things in American Life.* New York, NY: Charles Scribners Sons, 1937.

Lawrence, Harry V., Chairman. *Ships Logs and Captains' Diaries of Old Cape Cod.* Hyannis, MA: Cape Cod Chamber of Commerce, 1937.

Lee, Helen Bourne Joy. *The Bourne Genealogy.* Chester, CT: The Pequot Press, Inc., 1972.

Lee, Ruth Webb. *Early American Pressed Glass.* Wellesley Hills, MA: Lee Publications 1936.

Lee, Ruth Webb. *Sandwich Glass.* Wellesley Hills, MA: Lee Publications, 1939. Reprint 1966.

Lewis, Alonzo. *History of Lynn.* Lynn, MA: Samuel N. Dickinson, Boston, 2nd edition, 1844.

Lewis, Alonzo and J. R. Newhall. *Annals of Lynn.* 1865.

Lombard; Percival Hall. *The Aptucxet Trading Post.* Bourne, MA: Bourne Historical Society, 1968.

Lovell, Daisy Washburn. *Glimpses of Early Wareham.* Taunton, MA: Wareham Historical Society and William S. Sullwold Publ. Inc., 1970.

Lovell, Russell A., Jr. *The Cape Cod Story of Thornton W. Burgess.* Taunton,

MA: Town of Sandwich in conjunction with William S. Sullwold Publ., Inc., 1974. Reprint 1979.

Ludlum, David M. *Early American Hurricanes 1492-1870.* American Meterological Society, Boston, 1963.

Maine, The Revised Statutes of the State of. 4th revision. Including a lengthy historical note by C. W. Goddard, Commissioner, on the sources of land titles in New England. Portland, ME: Loring, Short & Harmon, 1884.

Massachusetts Soldiers and Sailors of the Revolutionary War. 17 Vols. Boston, MA: Wright & Potter Printing Co., 1913.

Massachusetts Soldiers, Sailors, and Marines in the Civil War. 7 Vols. Norwood, MA: The Norwood Press, 1931.

Mather, Cotton, Diary of Vol. I, 1681-1708. Vol. II, 1709-1724. New York, NY: Frederick Ungar Publishing Co., Third printing.

Mattapoisett, Committee of the Town of, *Mattapoisett and Old Rochester Massachusetts.* New York, NY: The Grafton Press, 1907.

Miller, John C. *Origins of the American Revolution.* Boston, MA: Little, Brown & Co., 1943. Reprint. Stanford University Press, 1959.

Mitchell & Davis, Compilers. *The Fairfield Register.* Kent's Hill, ME: H. E. Mitchell Publishing Co., 1904.

Morgan, Edmund S. *Birth of the Republic 1763-1789.* Reprint Chicago: University of Chicago Press, 1973.

Morgan, Edmund S., Ed. *Stamp Act Congress Declarations and Petitions, Oct. 1765.* Boston, MA: Old South Association, 1948.

Morison, Samuel Eliot. *The Maritime History of Massachusetts 1783-1860.* Boston, MA: Houghton Mifflin Co., 1941.

Nason, Rev. Elias. *A Gazetteer of the State of Massachusetts.* Boston, MA: B. B. Russell, 1874.

Nason, Rev. Elias. *A Gazetteer of the State of Massachusetts.* Enlarged by George J. Varner. Boston, MA: B. B. Russell, 1890.

National Archives Project, W.P.A. *Ship Registers, District of Barnstable, Massachusetts 1814-1913.* The National Archives. Boston, MA, 1938.

Nickerson Family Association. *The Nickerson Family.* Chatham, MA: Nickerson Family Association, 1973.

Nye, L. Bert, Jr. *American Nyes of English Origin.* 2 Vols. Vol. I, Generations 1-8. Charlotte, N.C.: Nye Family of America Assoc., 1977. Vol. II, Generations 9-12. Charlotte, N.C.: Nye Family of America Assoc., 1980.

Oldpath, Obadiah (James R. Newhall). *Lin: Her Jewels.* Lynn, MA: Bookstore of

George C. Herbert, Reprint 1890.

Otis, Amos. *Genealogical Notes of Barnstable Families. 2* Vols. Barnstable, MA: The Patriot Press, 1888.

Paige, Lucius R. *History of Hardwick, Mass.* New York, NY: Houghton Mifflin & Co., 1883.

Paine, Josiah. *A History of Harwich, Barnstable County, Massachusetts, 1620-1800.* Yarmouthport, MA: Parnassus Imprints, and Taunton, MA: William S. Sullwold Publ., Inc., Reprint, 1971.

Peckham, Howard H. *The Colonial Wars 1689-1762.* Chicago, IL: University of Chicago Press, 1964.

Perry, E. G. *A Trip Around Buzzards Bay Shores.* Reprint. Bourne Historic Commission. 1976.

Perry, E. G. *A Trip Around Cape Cod.* Boston, MA: Chas. S. Binner Co., 1898.

Pierce, Frederick Clifton. *Batchelder, Batcheller Genealogy.* Chicago, IL: Pub. by author, 1898.

Poor, Alfred Easton. *Colonial Architecture of Cape Cod, Nantucket, and Martha's Vineyard.* New York, NY: Dover Publications, 1932.

Pratt, Ambrose E. *Two Hundred and Fiftieth Anniversary Celebration of Sandwich and Bourne at Sandwich, Massachusetts, Sept. 3, 1889.* Falmouth, MA: Local Publishing and Printing Co., 1890.

Pratt, Rev. Enoch. *A Comprehensive History, Ecclesiastical and Civil, of Eastham, Wellfleet, and Orleans, County of Barnstable, Mass.* Yarmouth, MA: W. S. Fisher and Co., 1844.

Pratt, Harvey Hunter. *The Early Planters of Scituate.* Scituate, MA: Scituate Historical Society, 1929

Preston, Belle. *Bassett-Preston Ancestors.* New Haven, CT: Turtle, Moorehouse & Raylor Co., 1930.

Randall, Eunice K. *Kelley Genealogy.* Privately printed: 1962.

Raymond, Rev. W. O., Ed. *The Winslow Papers 1776-1826.* St. John, N.B: The Sun Printing Company, LTD., 1901.

Reid, William James. *The Building of The Cape Cod Canal.* New York, NY: Privately printed, 1961.

Reynard, Elizabeth. *The Narrow Land.* Boston, MA: Houghton Mifflin Co., 1934.

Rochester, Mass., Vital Records of, to the Year 1850. 2 Vols. Boston, MA: New England Historic Genealogical Society, 1914.

Ruggles, Henry Stoddard. *General Timothy Ruggles 1711-1795.* Privately printed, 1897.

Ruggles, Henry Stoddard. *Ruggles Genealogy.* Privately printed, 1892.

Ryder, John J., *Reminiscences of Three Years Service in the Civil War,* Reynolds, New Bedford, 1928.

Sandwich Historical Society. *Sandwich-By-The-Sea.* Sandwich, MA: Sandwich Historical Society, 1914.

Savage, James. *A Genealogical Dictionary of the First Settlers of New England.* 4 Vols., Reprint. Baltimore, MD: Genealogical Publ. Co., 1977.

Setzer, Dorothea. *The Sandwich Historical Society and its Glass.* Sandwich, MA: 1936. Reprint. 1951.

Sherwood, George. *American Colonists in English Records.* First series. London, Eng.: 1932.

Shurtleff, Nathaniel B. and Pulsifer, David, eds. *Records of the Colony of New Plymouth in New England.* 12 Vols. Boston, MA: Press of William White, 1855-1861. (Vol. 1-8 Shurtleff, Vol. 9-12 Pulsifer).

Shurtleff, Nathaniel B., Ed. *Records of the Governor and Company of the Massachusetts Bay in New England.* 5 Vols. Boston, MA: Press of William White, 1853-1854.

Small, Isaac M. *Shipwrecks on Cape Cod.* North Truro, MA: 1928.

Smith, Leonard H., Jr., Ed. *Records of the First Church of Wareham, Mass. 1739-1891.* Clearwater, FL: 1974.

Stark, James H. *The Loyalists of Massachusetts and the Other Side of the American Revolution.* Boston, MA: privately owned, 1910.

State Street Trust. *Town and City Seals in Massachusetts.* 2 vols. Boston, MA: State Street Trust, 1950.

State Street Trust. *Towns of New England and Old England, Ireland and Scotland.* Boston, MA: State Street Trust, 1920.

Steegmuller, Francis. *The Two Lives of James Jackson Jarves.* New Haven, CT: Yale University Press, 1951.

Strahler, Arthur N. *A Geologists' View of Cape Cod.* Garden City, NY: The Natural History Press, 1966.

Sutherland, Amelia Pope. *Pioneer Popes.* Waupaca, WI: 1938.

Swift, Charles F. *Cape Cod the Right Arm of Massachusetts, an Historical Narrative.* Yarmouth, MA: the Yarmouth Publishing Co., 1894.

Swift, George H. *Descendants of William Swift of Sandwich, Mass.* Amenia, NY: 1900.

Thomas, M. Halsey, Ed. *The Diary of Samuel Sewall 1674-1729.* 2 Vols. New York, NY: Farrar, Straus and Girous, 1973.

Thompson, David Allen. *George Allen Ralph Allen.* Albany, NY, 1910, 66 pages

Thoreau, Henry D. *Cape Cod.* Edited by Dudley C. Lunt. New York, NY: Bramhall House, 1951 edition.

Tobey, Rufus Babcock and Charles Henry Pope. *Tobey (Tobie) Genealogy.* Boston, MA: Charles H. Pope, 1905.

Travers, Milton A. *The Wampanoag Indian Federation.* Rev. Boston, MA: The Christopher Publ. House, 1957.

Trayser, Donald G. *Barnstable, Three Centuries of a Cape Cod Town.* Yarmouthport, MA: Parnassus Imprints, and Taunton, MA: William S. Sullwold Publ., Inc., Reprint, 1971.

Tudor, William. *The Life of James Otis of Massachusetts.* Boston, MA: Wells & Libby, 1823.

Tupper, Dr. Eleanor, Ed. *Tupper Genealogy.* Compiled by Alexander H. Chapman. Beverly, MA: Tupper Family Association, 1972.

Tupper, Franklin Whittlesey. *Thomas Tupper and his Descendants.* Boston, MA: Tupper Family Association, 1945.

Vaughan, Alden T. *American Genesis.* Boston, MA: Little, Brown & Co., 1975.

Vaughan, Alden T. *The New England Frontier, Puritans and Indians 1620-1675.* Boston, MA: Little, Brown & Co., 1965.

Wakefield, Robert S. *Plymouth Colony Marriages to 1650.* & Charles T. Libby, *Mary Chilton's Title to Celebrity.* Two vols. in one. Warwick, RI: Society of Mayflower Descendants in the State of Rhode Island, 1978.

Warden, William A. and Robert L. Dexter. *Genealogy of the Dexter Family in America.* Worcester, MA: The Blanchard Press, 1905.

Waters, John F., Jr. *The Otis Family in Provincial and Revolutionary Massachusetts.* Chapel Hill NC: University of North Carolina Press, 1968.

Weeks, Alvin G. *Massassoit of the Wampanoags.* Norwood, MA: The Plimpton Press, 1920.

Weis, Frederick Lewis. *The Colonial Clergy and the Colonial Churches of New England.* Reprint. Baltimore, M.D.: Genealogical Publ. Co., 1977.

Willison, George F. *Saints and Strangers.* New York, NY: Reynal and Hitchcock, 1945.

Wilson, Fred A. *Some Annals of Nahant, Mass.* Nahant, MA: Nahant Historical Society, 1977.

Wing, Rev. Conway P. *John Wing of Sandwich, Mass. and his Descendants*

1662-1881. Carlisle, PA: 1881.

Winsor, Justin. *History of the Town of Duxbury, Ma.* Boston, MA: Crosby & Nichols, 1849.

Winthrop, John. *The History of New England.* Edited by James Savage. 1st edition. Boston, MA: Phelps & Farnham, 1825. 2nd edition. Boston, MA: Phelps & Farnham, 1853.

Wood, Virginia Steele. *Live Oaking.* Boston, MA: North Eastern University Press, 1981.

Wood, William. *New England's Prospect.* Edited by Alden T. Vaughan. Amherst, MA: University of Massachusetts Press, 1977.

Worrall, Arthur J. *Quakers in the Colonial Northeast.* Hanover, NH: University Press of New England, 1980.

Wright, John K. Editor. *New England's Prospect: 1933.* Special Publication No. 16. New York, NY: American Geographical Society, 1933.

Wright, Wayne W. *Thornton W. Burgess, A Descriptive Book Bibliography.* Sandwich, Mass. The Thornton W. Burgess Society, Inc., 1979.

JOURNALS AND MAGAZINES

"An Abstract of the Laws of New England, as they were Established in the Last Century." *Collections of the Massachusetts Historical Society,* V (1798), 173-187.

Alexander, H. B. "Notes: Humfrey." *New England Historical and Genealogical Register,* 65(1911), 86-87.

Anderson, F. W. "Why Did Colonial New Englanders Make Bad Soldiers? Contractual Principles and Military Conduct During the Seven Years War." *William & Mary Quarterly,* July, 1981.

Badger, Rev. Stephen. "Letter Containing Historical and Characteristic Traits of the Indians." *Collections of the Massachusetts Historical Society,* V (1798), 32-45.

Boston, L. B. "Replanning a Farm for Profit." *Cape Cod Magazine,* July 1915.

Bowman, George Ernest, Ed. "Bourne Deeds." *The Mayflower Descendant,* 25 (1923), 50-60.

Bowman, George Ernest, Ed. "Sandwich Records from the Benjamin Percival Diary." *Mayflower Descendant,* Pilgrim Notes and Queries, Vol. I No. 5, 6, 7, 8 (1913); Vol. II No. 2, 3 (1914)

Bowman, George Ernest, Ed. "Sandwich Vital Records." *The Mayflower Descendant,* 14 (1912), 106-112, 166-174. 29 (1931), 21-33, 68-75. 30 (1932), 58-68, 99-104.

Bullock, Chandler. "Bathsheba Spooner." *Worcester Historical Society,* V. 2 No. 4 (1939).

Burgess, Thornton W. "The Gold Mine I Discovered When I was 35." *American Magazine,* May 1919.

Cahoon, R. H. "Agricultural Possibilities on Cape Cod." *Cape Cod Magazine,* Jan. 1916.

Clarkson, Paul S. "Bathsheba Spooner." *Monthly Newsletter of the Worcester Bicentennial Commission,* No. 9, June 1976.

Cotton, John. "An Account of the Church of Christ in Plymouth." *Collections of the Massachusetts Historical Society,* IV (1795), 107-141.

Crane, Priscilla C. "The Boston and Sandwich Glass Co." *Antiques Magazine,* April, 1925.

Davis, Wendell. "Description of Sandwich in the County of Barnstable." *Collections of the Massachusetts Historical Society,* VIII (1802), 119-126.

"Dedications to the Rev. John Eliot's Indian Version of the Old and New Testament." *Collections of the Massachusetts Historical Society,* VII (1800), 222-228.

"Ecclesiastical History of Massachusetts and the Old Colony of Plymouth." *Collections of the Massachusetts Historical Society,* VII (1800), 262-279.

Engstrom, Victoria B. "Eel River Valley." *Pilgrim Society Notes* No. 23 Plymouth, Mass. March 1976.

"The Faunce Demonstration Farm." *Cape Cod Magazine,* May 1915.

Frost, John Eldridge. "Maine Genealogy." *New England Historical and Genealogical Register,* 131 (1977) 243-266.

Furman, Lucy. "The Woodhouse Night Club." *Nature Magazine,* Oct. 1948.

Gifford, Stephen W. "Rebecca Hatch of Sandwich, Mass, and Her Daughter Lucianna." *New England Historical and Genealogical Register,* 128 (1974) 10-17.

Gookin, Daniel. "Historical Collections of the Indians of New England." *Collections of the Massachusetts Historical Society,* I (1792), 141-227.

Green, Samuel Swett. "The Case of Bathsheba Spooner." *Proceedings of the American Antiquarian Society.* New series. Worcester, MA: Vol. 5 (1888) 430.

Greenlaw, Lucy Hall. "Sandwich Vital Records." *The Genealogical Advertiser,* Vol. III No. 2 (1900), 33-36, No. 3 (1900), 73-77. Vol. IV No. 1 (1901), 9-14, No. 4 (1901), 99-103.

Griffiths, Naomi E. S. "The Acadians of Belle-Isle-en-Mer." *Natural History*

Magazine, Jan. (1981).

Harding, Anne Borden "The New Englander of Nova Scotia." *New England Historical and Genealogical Register,* 116 (1962) 3-12.

Hawley, Rev. Gideon. "Biographical and Topographical Anecdotes Respecting Sandwich and Marshpee, Jan. 1794." *Collections of the Massachusetts Historical Society,* III (1794), 188-193.

"Historical Account of John Eliot, the First Minister of the Church in Roxbury." *Collections of the Massachusetts Historical Society,* VIII (1802), 5-35.

Horner, Dr. George R. "The Pilgrims and the Wampanoags: a Survey of Attitudes and Behavior in the Early Years." *Pilgrim Society Notes* No. 29 Plymouth, Mass. May 1981.

Jacobs, W. "The Railroad on the Cape." *Cape Cod Magazine,* Nov., 1916.

Jones, C. R. "Settlers of Fairfield, Maine." *The Chedwato Dispatch,* Winter 1979/80 issue.

Kittredge, Henry C. "The Boston Packets." *The American Neptune,* 1972.

Library of Cape Cod History and Genealogy C. F. Swift publisher Yarmouthport, Mass. (over one hundred pamphlets on Cape Cod subjects).

Locke, J. G., Ed. "Records of Marriages, Baptisms and Deaths, Copied from the Diary of Rev. Benjamin Fessenden." *New England Historical and Genealogical Register,* 12 (1858)311-12.

Longley, Dr. R. S. "An Annapolis County Loyalist." *Collections of the Nova Scotia Historical Society,* Vol. 31, 1957.

McLean, Maclean W. and Almon E. Daniels. "William Gifford of Sandwich, Mass." *New England Historical and Genealogical Register,* 128 (1974) 241-261; 129 (1975) 30-44, 221-237, 335-346; 130 (1976) 40-45, 130-141, 284-291; 131 (1977) 51-57, 133-141, 214-220, 294-298; 132 (1978) 211-217, 293-301; 133 (1979) 49-56, 134-140, 211-215, 294-298; 134 (1980) 59-64, 121-134, 237-241, 310-315; 135 (1981) 45-56, 138-147, 307-321; 137 (1983) 147-162; 138 (1984) 203-222.

McLean, Maclean W. and Lydia (Phinney) Brownson. "Ezra Perry of Sandwich Mass." *New England Historical and Genealogical Register,* 115 (1961) 86-99, 181-198, 268-289; 116 (1962) 27-44, 100-109, 191-204.

McLean, Maclean W. and Lydia (Phinney) Brownson. "Henry Sanders, alias Sanderson, of Sandwich, Mass." *New England Historical and Genealogical Register,* 127 (1973) 250-257.

McLean, Maclean W. and Lydia (Phinney) Brownson. "Lt. John Ellis of Sandwich, Mass." *New England Historical and Genealogical Register,* 119 (1965) 161-173, 260-275; 120 (1966) 26-38, 97-122, 187-202, 272-292; 121 (1967) 37-45, 127-141, 224-229, 260-268; 122 (1968) 51-62, 131-143,

196-207, 254-264.

McLean, Maclean W. and Lydia (Phinney) Brownson. "Michael Blackwell of Sandwich, Mass." *New England Historical and Genealogical Register,* 117 (1963) 180-194, 295-310.

McLean, Maclean W. and Lydia (Phinney) Brownson. "Richard Handy of Sandwich, Mass." *New England Historical and Genealogical Register,* 125 (1971) 124-137, 184-194, 246-256; 126 (1972) 50-63, 103-112, 191-200.

McLean, Maclean W. and Lydia (Phinney) Brownson. "The Rev. Richard Bourne of Sandwich, Mass." *New England Historical and Genealogical Register,* 118 (1964) 83-89, 197-214, 275-290; 119 (1965) 26-42.

McLean, Maclean W. and Lydia (Phinney) Brownson. "Thomas Butler of Sandwich, Mass." *New England Historical and Genealogical Register,* 127 (1973) 18-26, 108-113, 193-198.

McLean, Maclean W. and Lydia (Phinney) Brownson. "Thomas Gibbs of Sandwich, Mass." *New England Historical and Genealogical Register,* 123 (1969) 54-67, 129-144, 205-219, 266-277.

McLean, Mclean W. and Lydia (Phinney) Brownson. "Thomas Landers of Sandwich, Mass." *New England Historical and Genealogical Register,* 124 (1970) 42-60, 209-224, 266-284.

McQuaid, Kim. "William Apes, Pequot." *New England Quarterly,* (1980).

Merrick, Dorothy D. "A Framework for 17th Century Plymouth." *Pilgrim Society Notes,* No. 11. May, 1963.

O'Neil, Paul. "Fifty Years in the Green Meadows." *Life Magazine,* Nov. 14, 1960.

Russell, Francis. "Apostle to the Indians." *American Heritage,* Vol. IX No. 1. (1957).

Saltford, Herb. "A Man, His Dream and a Happy Ending." *Yankee Magazine,* June, 1973.

Sandroff, Ivan. "Forgotten Giant of the American Revolution." *Worcester Historical Society Publications,* new series, Vol. III, No. 6, 1952.

Smith, David C. "Coastal Shipping Trade on the Eve of the Railroad: Gardner, ME." *Maine Historical Society Quarterly,* v. 13 no. 3, winter 1974.

Swan, Mabel M. "Deming Jarves and his Glass Factory Village." *Antiques Magazine,* 1938.

Tenney, Dr. Samuel. "Letter on the Dark Day, May 19th, 1780." *Collections of the Massachusetts Historical Society,* I (1792), 95-98.

"The Triumph of the Puritan Spirit." *Life Magazine,* Aug. 28, 1944.

Walsh, Lavinia D. "Million Children Would Choose Him for President at Bed-time." *Cape Cod Magazine,* Aug. 15, 1927.

Walsh, Lavinia D. "Sandwich Glass." *Cape Cod Magazine,* 1926, Reprint, 1927-8.

Waters, Henry F. Ed., "Genealogical Gleanings." Geere Will. *New England Historical and Genealogical Register,* 37 (1883) 239.

Wetz, Jon. H. "The Horse Railroad." *Acorn,* Sandwich Historical Society, Aug. 1977.

Wing Family of America. *The OWL (Our Wing Lineage)* beginning 1900. Complete sets at Sandwich Public Library; Newberry Library, Chicago; New Bedford Public Library and New England Historic Genealogical Society, Boston.

NEWSPAPERS, SANDWICH INTEREST

The Barnstable Patriot. 1830-1968. Pub. Barnstable, MA.

The Cape Cod Advocate and Nautical Intelligencer, Pub. Sandwich 1852-1864

The Cape Cod Gazette. 1870-1872. Pub. Sandwich, MA.

The Cape Cod News. 1933-1938. Pub. Sandwich, MA.

The Falmouth Enterprise. 1896-present. Pub. Falmouth, MA.

The Independent. 1895-1908. Pub. Sandwich, MA.

The Sandwich Independent. 1908-1938. Pub. Sandwich, MA.

The Sandwich Mechanic. 1851. Pub. Sandwich, MA.

The Sandwich Observer. 1846-1851. Pub. Sandwich, MA.

The Sandwich Observer. 1884-1899. Pub. Sandwich, MA.

The Seaside Press. 1873-1880. Pub. Sandwich, MA.

The Yarmouth Register. 1836-1878. Pub. Yarmouth, MA.

NEWSPAPERS - Specific References.

Blake, Fran "Meet Thornton Burgess' Lovable Aunt Sally." *Boston Sunday Globe.* Mar. 16, 1952.

"Cape Cod Branch Railroad." *Yarmouth Register,* Apr. 9, 1846.

Cooley, John L. "Harrison Cady-Lively Artist." *Gloucester Times.* Dec. 1970.

Freeman, Frederick. "History of the Original Congregational Church in Sandwich." *Yarmouth Register,* May 12 to Aug. 11, 1877. (14 articles).

Freeman, Russell. "Nathaniel Freeman." *Sandwich Observer.* Oct. 31, 1846.

Headley, Rev. P. C. "Extracts from An Historic Discourse..." *Cape Cod Advocate.* Feb. 7, 1857.

"Jarvesville." *The Seaside Press.* July 26, 1879.

Kendall, Edward Augustus. "Trip to Cape Cod, 1807-8." *Yarmouth Register.* Apr. 23, 1869.

"Marine Intelligence." *Sandwich Observer 1846-1851.*

"Marine Intelligence." *Yarmouth Register. 1846-51.*

Methodist Church Articles. *Sandwich Observer,* May 29, 1894. *The Independent.* Feb. 15, 1898. *Sandwich Independent.* Mar 14, 1914. Aug. 1, Aug. 8, 1928. *Seaside Press.* June 26, 1875. Sept. 28, 1878. June 10, 1876.

Railroad Construction Articles. *Sandwich Observer.* Oct. 17, 1846. Jan. 28, 1847. Mar. 27, 1847. Apr. 3, Apr. 17, 1847. July 3, 10, 1847. Sept. 4, 1847, Oct. 21, 1847, Dec. 4, 1847. May 6, 13, 20, 27, 1848.

Sandroff, Ivan. "Stormy Giant of a Man." *Worcester Sunday Telegram.* Jan. 13, 1952.

"Sandwich Catholic Church." *Cape Cod Advocate.* Dec. 22, 1855.

(Spooner Murder) *The Worcester Spy* Mar. 5, 1778; July 6, 1778.

"Stave Mill at Spring Hill." *Yarmouth Register.* Nov. 29, 1838.

"Thornton Burgess." *Worcester Telegram.* Jan. 15, 1961.

Waterman, C.C.P. "The Sandwich Glass Works." *Yarmouth Register* Apr. 15, 1876.

Wixon, Clarence M. (Chief Red Shell) "History and Legends of the Cape Cod Indians" *Sandwich Independent,* at least eighteen chapters beginning with issue of May 16, 1928. Typescript at Sandwich Archives.

MANUSCRIPTS

Allen, John Kermott. *George Allen of Weymouth, Lynn, and Sandwich, Mass.* Ms. Brookline, MA: 1924. Typescript at Library of Congress, New England Historic Genealogical Society, New Bedford Public Library, and Sandwich Town Archives.

Boyden, Jesse. *Map of Sandwich.* Mass. Archives Series 1830. vol. II p. 12, no. 1844.

Burbank, George E. *Glass House.* Sandwich Historical Society. 1940.

Burgess, Hannah Rebecca, *Journals,* Sandwich Historical Society.

Calvinistic Congregational Society Records. First Church of Christ, Sandwich, MA.

Cedarville Gem. 1849-1860. Unpublished. Sandwich Town Archives.

Collins, Mary E. *The Life and Not-so-hard Times of Irish Factory Workers in Sandwich Mass. 1825-1890.* Boston University, 1972.

Dodge, Raymond, *Swift Genealogy.* Unpublished. Dorothea Dodge, Barnstable Mass. 1970.

Doubleday, Elwyn J. Jr. *The Post Offices of Massachusetts.* North Amherst, Mass. 01059. 1976.

First Parish Church Records. First Church of Christ, Sandwich, MA.

Forbes, Esther and Harriet Merrifield Forbes. *Notes on Bathsheba Spooner.* Unpublished. Possession of Mrs. Margaret Erskine, Worcester, MA.

Freeman, Georgiana V. H. *Diary 1888.* Unpublished. Copy at Sandwich Town Archives.

Freeman, Nathaniel. Collection of MSS. Clements Library, University of Michigan, Ann Arbor, MI.

Goodwin, Rev. Ezra Shaw *Diary 1815.* American Antiquarian Society, Worcester, MA.

Gould, James Warren *A New Account of the History of the Society of Friends on Cape Cod.* Cotuit, Mass., 1978.

Haines, Rev. Benjamin. *Letters.* Unpublished. Sandwich Town Archives.

Haines, George L. *Civil War Letters.* Unpublished. Sandwich Town Archives.

Harlow, John *J. Journal 1850-63.* Unpublished. Sandwich Town Archives.

Holway, Mrs. J. R. *Methodist Church in Sandwich.* MS. AB. 1912.

Hudson, Abigail Smith. *Journals 1821.* Unpublished. Copy at Sandwich Town Archives, Sandwich, MA.

Marsh, Rev. Joseph. *Methodist Church Record Book 1864 with a History Account.* First Church of Christ, Sandwich, MA.

Martin, Dennis. *"Sandwich, Mass. 1760-1789."* Wheaton College, Indiana.

Massachusetts State Archives. *French Neutrals.* State House, Boston, MA: Vol. 23 (1755-1758), vol. 24 (1758-1769).

Massachusetts State Archives. *Marine References* Vol. 7: 108, 1696; 191, 1701; 262, 1705; 409, 1711; 511, 1714; State House, Boston, MA.

Massachusetts State Archives. *Mashpee Papers 1788-1865.* Includes Mashpee Memorial and Fiske Commission Report. 3 boxes, State House Boston. Copy at Sandwich Town Archives, Sandwich, MA.

Methodist Church Records. First Church of Christ, Sandwich, MA.

Nye, Seth F. *Business Records.* Notebook at Sandwich Historical Society.

Nye, Seth F. *Law Cases.* Two notebooks at Sandwich Historical Society.

Nye, William L. *Sandwich Academy.* Sandwich Historical Society 1921.

Nye, William L. *Sketch of the First Church in Christ, Sandwich, Mass. 1638-1925.* Sandwich Historical Society, Sandwich, MA.

Percival, Benjamin. *Diaries, 1777-1817* Original at Sandwich Archives.

Perry, Elwell Herbert. *Perry Genealogy.* Edited and typed by Rita Pliskin. New Bedford, MA: revised 1979. (spiral bound 277 pages).

Pratt, Ambrose *Diaries: 1900, 1912, 1919, 1921, 1922, 1924, 1926, 1930, 1932, 1935, 1938, 1939.* Sandwich Town Archives.

Robie, Thomas, *Diary 1710.* American Antiquarian Society. Worcester, MA.

Robinson, Philip. *Diary 1851.* Sandwich Town Archives.

Rogers, Alice. *Letterbook.* Possession of Wing Family of America. Sandwich, MA.

Sandwich Quakers, vital records and meeting minutes. Originals at Rhode Island Historical Society, Providence. Microfilm and typescript at Sandwich Archives.

Sandwich Town Meeting Records. Volumes 1-18 Town Clerk, Sandwich, MA. Typescripts Vol. 1-5 (1651-1835) Sandwich Archives.

Sandwich Vital Records. Vols. 1-6 (to 1900) Town Clerk, Sandwich, MA.

Sandwich Records: Cemeteries, Voters, Military Records, Tax Records, Poor Relief, etc. Town Clerk, Sandwich, MA.

Trayser, Donald G. *The Acadians on Cape Cod.* Meeting, Barnstable Historical Society, 1944.

Whittemore, Ebenezer S. *Case Book 1862-1892* and *Diaries 1864, 1874* Sandwich Town Archives.

Wing, Mary Howland. *History of the Unitarian Church.* 1911. Copy at Sandwich Town Archives, Sandwich, MA.

INDEX OF NAMES

SHIPS' NAMES

INDEX OF NAMES

INDEX OF SUBJECTS AND PLACES

NOTES ON SOURCES

As stated on page X of the Introduction, we dropped from the first edition of this book the lengthy footnotes and source references for each chapter, because of delays in completing the text and the unexpected length of the text itself. This decision to omit the footnotes has been much regretted ever since, and has been remarked on unfavorably in serious reviews, since the book as printed lacked scholarly credentials. We therefore warmly welcome this opportunity to add the notes on the sources used in each chapter. Admittedly, the Sandwich Town Meeting references and the early newspapers are not available to most researchers, but can be consulted on application to the Sandwich Archives and Historical Center, Sandwich Public Library, 142 Main St., Sandwich MA 02563.

It has been said by reviewers that our Sandwich book is like the detailed town histories written a century ago. As we wrote in the Introduction, this book was written to fill a gap, to tell the townsmen and those whose families came from Sandwich what happened in this town over its long 350-year history. Other Sandwich histories with such detail simply did not exist. With the addition of these notes on sources, those who wish now to prepare scholarly studies on one or another aspect of Sandwich history will at last have the references they need.

R.A. Lovell, Jr. May 18, 1987

Key to Abbreviations

Authors & Editors fully cited in the Bibliography, pp. 526-538.

Records of the Colony of New Plymouth by Shurtleff and Pulsifer, will be called PCR.

Records of the Governor and Company of the Massachusetts Bay by Shurtleff will be called MBR.

The New England Historical & Genealogical Register will be called Register.

Sandwich: Town Meeting Records will be called TM.
Vital Records will be called SVR.

References to TM I (1651-1692), are to typescript at Sandwich Archives.

Chapter 1: Settling Sandwich

Early voyages: Bolton 26, 33; Davis 1:33-37; Vaughan, American Genesis, 97, 174; Bradford 81-84; Goodwin 78, 118, 122, 152

Gosnold: *The Gosnold Discoveries,* Ed. by Lincoln A. Dexter, Brookfield, Mass., 1982; Old Dartmouth Historical Society. *Historical Sketches,* No. 1, June 1903 & No. 4 Sept. 1903; Banks' Martha's Vineyard II, Annals of Gosnold.

John Smith: Vaughan, American Genesis, 174

French Ship 1616: Goodwin 79

Dermer: Bolton 26, 33; Goodwin 78-9

Manomet 1622/3: Davis 29; Goodwin 213; Freeman I: 109; Willison 213

Aptucxet: Goodwin 230, 303-9; James 74-5; Bradford 111, 192, 195, 202, 279, 378

Garrett Wreck: Goodwin 341

Hurricane 1635: Bradford 279

Ten Men of Saugus: PCR, 1:57; Lewis 101

Saugus Plantation: Lewis 60; Wilson 20-23

The Plantation now Eight Towns: Historical Data on Cities & Towns, Massachusetts Secretary of State 1966

Winthrop: Freeman, 1:123

Spread from Saugus: Lewis 106, 109, 113-4

Freeman Origins; PCR, 1:53; Dawes-Gates Genealogy, 11:349-356; Lewis 90; Savage 203

Abigail 1635: Banks 161-7; Hanks 61

Elizabeth Raymen: Shipley, Sussex Church Register, August 10, 1632; Second Boat, V. 5 No. 1, May 1984; Register, 49:136 (1895)

Mary Freeman: Freeman Genealogy 23, 30

Geere Will: Sherwood 22; Register 124:42 (1970) and 37:239 (1883)

Almy: MBR, 1:88, 163

Chadwell: PCR, XII: 172

Dexter: MBR, 1:86 et seq.; 11:59 et seq.; Warden 5-9; Lewis 64, 80, 87, 120, 159;

Oldpath 187-216; Hartley 21

Dillingham: MBR, 1:177

Carman: MBR, 1:92

Wood: MBR, 1:164; Lewis 61; Banks' Planters 24, 27, 174; Freeman, 1:164, 11:15; Oldpath 62

Feake: Lewis 64

Leveridge: MBR, 1:148; PCR, 1:53; PCR, XII:25; Winsor 275

Bachiler/Wing: Lewis 78, 93-7; Wing (OWL) 1428-1430, March 1915; Freeman,

1:135-6; Pierce 82-94

Duxbury People: PCR, 1:43, 53, 64, 101, 107; Winsor 226 et seq.; Freeman, 11:16 et seq

Winthrop on Sandwich: Winthrop History, 1:253

Lin for Saugus: MBR, 1:211

Manomet for Sandwich: Goodwin 214

Scusset for Sandwich 1635: Bradford 290; Goodwin 393

Turner vs. Davis: PCR, VII:7

1648 Transfer: PCR, XII:210

1685 Deposition: Town Meeting Records III: 1; Freeman, II:77

Humphrey: MBR, I & II; Lewis 114-119; Winthrop, I:40, 90, 160, 399; II:31, etc.

Sandwich, Kent: Bentwich; Jordan 246; Lewis 147, 149, 152, 187, 196-202; Savage 495; Register, 65:86 (1911)

List of Settlers: TM I; Freeman I:163-5; II:15-17, 64

Thomas Bowerman & Thomas Boardman: Bowerman Family Newsletter, Issue 9, June 1985, Los Angeles, California

Chapter 2 - The Old Colony

Plymouth Population: Goodwin 288-291; Willison 318

Town Formation: Goodwin 362, 440, 525; Willison 316, 331; Bradford 253

Price Collapse 1641: Bradford 253; Willison 325-7, 331; Goodwin 415

Indian Areas: Goodwin 193, 363, 524; Davis 81-2

Plymouth Lack of Ministers: Goodwin 422, 467; Willison 316; Benes 17-19

Tolerance Effort 1645: Willison 360-7

Adventurers & Finance Problems: Goodwin 288-91; Bradford 185-8

Purchasers and Undertakers: Bradford 185-8; PCR, XI: 12-18; Willison 261-3

Allerton & Sherley: Willison 260-3, 306; Bradford 211, 250; Goodwin 333

Winslow Jailed: Goodwin 385, 397

Payments to Adventurers: Willison 306-8; Bradford 288; Goodwin 410-12

Final Debt Clearance: Willison 309-11, 325; Bradford 414-20; PCR, XII: 127-133; Debts Hopeful and Desperate: Financing the Plymouth Colony, Ruth A. Mclntyre, 1963

Colony in 1623: Bradford 120, 133; Willison 177; PCR XII: 3

Constable: Davis 75

New Regulations 1636: PCR, XI: 6-7, Davis 75; Willison 317

Oath of Fidelity: Davis 78-80; PCR, XI: 9, 191

Freeman's Oath: PCR, XI: 8

Colony Messenger: PCR, XI: 18-19

Town Constables: Davis 75-6; PCR, XI: 10, 64 10, 164

Town Deputies: Goodwin 397-408

Town Functions: PCR, XI:18, 32, 36; Bradford 319

Town Clerk: Davis 83; PCR, XI: 190

Towns Not Incorporated: Town Government in Massachusetts, by John F. Sly, Reprint 1967, pp. 22-26; A Framework for 17th Century Plymouth, 6, Pilgrim Society, No. 11, May 1963; Bradford 1629-30; Goodwin 362-3

Laws of 1636: Willison 317; PCR, XI:6, 12, 46, etc.; Freeman, I:131; Goodwin 339, 342, 406, 601; Bradford 320

Chapter 3: Early Days in Sandwich

Maps of Sandwich Marshes: U.S. Coast Survey, A.D. Bache, Supt., 1860, *Route of the Proposed Cape Cod Canal,* and *Part of Cape Cod, Mass. from Sandy Neck to West Sandwich; The Walling Property Map, 1857,* is notably defective in showing wrong location of Sagamore Hill.

Meaning of Shawme: Otis, 483 (footnote)

Counterclockwise motion of the Bay: Chamberlain, 225-6; Draft Environmental Statement, Addition of Unit No. 2, Cape Cod Canal Plant, U.S. Army Engineers, Waltham, 1973 p. 2.2-5

Glacial background: Chamberlain, B., 25, 36, etc.

Canal valley: Chamberlain, B., 108-9; Brigham, 56.

Comassakumkanet: Chief Red Shell (Clarence Wixon), Sandwich Independent series, 1928, p. 5; PCR, XII:226-7; Keene, 192, 214; Freeman, I:101, 686, 697

Original land grants: PCR, I:57, 80.

Leveridge questions: PCR, I:88; Freeman, II:38-9

Redivision of meadowlands: PCR, I:117

Andrew Hallett lands: PCR, I:117, 121

Failures of the Committees: PCR, I:131, 134

New Controls on Lands: PCR, I:133, 148

New Meadowlands Authority: PCR, I;147

Meadowlands list: TM, I:1; Freeman, I:163-165; PCR, I:149-150; (all three lists differ in names and amounts).

Leveridge: Savage, 84; Weis, 126-7; Goodwin, 422, 532, 608; PCR, I:53, 134. 149; Freeman, I:204, 222; II:16, 44, 47, etc.

Sandwich Meetinghouse: PCR, I:133.

Hartford Meetinghouse: Connecticut Historical Collections, p. 42, John Warner Barber, New Haven, 1836; Barnstable Patriot, Aug. 28, 1930; Drawing, June 15, 1884, E.K. Chipman, at Sandwich Hist. Soc.

John Vincent: PCR, I:54, 80; Freeman, II:17, 44, etc.; PCR, VIII: 175, 206.

George Allen: PCR, I:117, 155; MD, 9:224-5 (1907).

Deputies 1639: PCR, I:126.

Warnings to Sandwich: PCR, I:98, 106, 107, 117, 131-4; II:8; Freeman, I:133.

Confederation of Four Colonies: PCR, IX & X; Bradford, 330-343, etc.

John Ellis: PCR, II:75-6, 85, 140; XII:188; Register, 119:161 et seq (1965).

John Blakemore: PCR, I:130; Freeman, II:16.

Eel River Bridge: PCR, I:156; Pilgrim Soc. Notes, No. 23, 1976.

Edmund Freeman: PCR, I:53, 54; XII: 127-133, 143.

Hutchinson on Freeman: Freeman, I:128.

Freeman's Trip to England: PCR, XII: 120-125.

Assistant Governor: PCR, I:140, 154-157, 161; II:8, 15-19, 24, 27-8, 38-40; VII: 16, 18-20, 24, etc; XI: 34.

Freeman a liberal: Freeman, II:49; PCR, II:173; III:46, 47, 52; Willison, 362.

Deputies 1646: PCR, II:104, 106.

Bradford's transfer to Freeman: PCR, XII: 210

Freeman's transfer to Sandwich: PCR, XII: 211-212.

Extinction of Rights of the "Ten Men": PCR, XII: 84, 106, 118-9, 211-12.

William Almy: PCR, XII:84; Bunker, 117.

John Carman: PCR, I:157; Bunker, 164-6; Freeman, II: 15.

Richard Chadwell: PCR, XII; 118-9; Pope's Pioneers, 91.

Thomas Dexter: PCR, II:8, 135; Dexter & Wardwell Genealogy.

Edward Dillingham: Archambault, 10-26; MD, 16:161-2 (1914).

Henry Feake: Bunker, 202-3; Flint, 166.

Edmund Freeman, Sr.: Freeman Genealogy, 12-22; PCR, II:106; IV:40-5; XII: 143, 210-2.

George Knott: PCR, VIII:6; Freeman, II:46; MD, 9:157 (1907).

Thomas Tupper, Sr.: PCR, I:57, 149, 155; II:28, 36-7, etc.: Mass. Hist. Coll. III:188-193, Hawley, (1794); Tupper Gen., 1-2.

William Wood: PCR, II:75-6, 117; VIII: 6, 9; Freeman, II:169.

Chapter 4: The 1667 Property Survey

Note: Sandwich Proprietor's Records, Vol. 1, an original volume in Sandwich Town Clerk's vault; references are to copied typescript pages in Sandwich Archives.

Town Clerks from 1646: PCR, XI: 52-3.

Early Sandwich VR: PCR, I:134, 153; II:98, etc.; VIII:3, 5, 6, 8, 9, etc.

Perry Family: Register, 115:86-99, et seq (1961); Perry Gen., 72-3, Elwell H. Perry, New Bedford, 1979.

Perry-Freeman marriage: Freeman Gen., 30; PCR, III:46, 47, 52.

Tupper marriage authority: PCR, II:155 (bestowed); III:47 (removed).

Edward Perry: Well-known desc., Oliver H. Perry, Matthew C. Perry, August Belmont, Jr.

Religious toleration: Goodwin, 443-4; Willison, 361-3; Freeman, I:192-4

Qualifications for freeman: Bradford, 185-8; PCR, XI:8, 80, 156, etc.; Goodwin, 290

Presentments: Ralph Allen, *St.,* etc 1651, PCR, II:173-4; III:96.

Leveridge departure: Freeman, II:56, 173; PCR, X:91; Goodwin, 532.

Divisions in Colony Churches: Freeman, I:203; II: 173; PCR, III;80-3; Willison, 363-6, 530-6.

Colony Ministers:

Plymouth - Raynor: Weis, 172; Willison, 363, 458.
Cotton: Weis, 62; Goodwin, 531; Willison, 366-7, 459.

Barnstable - Lothrop: Freeman, I:208-9; II:243-6; Weis, 129.
Walley: Freeman, I:248-9; II:268; Weis, 213.

Yarmouth - Miller: Freeman, I:249-50; II:186; Weis, 141.
Thornton: Freeman, I:248-9, 261; II:199, 200; Weis, 203.

Scituate— Chauncey: Freeman, II:244; Goodwin, 421-9; Weis, 53.

Taunton - Street: Weis, 196-7.
Shove: Weis, 187.

Eastham - Mayo: Freeman, I:156, 248, 339; II:246-7, 358; Weis, 139.
Crosby: Freeman, I:299, 339; II:358, 365; Weis, 64.
Treat: Freeman, I:339, 350; II:380; Weis, 208.

Sandwich - Smith: Freeman, I:248, 338; II:55; The American Genealogist, 61:2-6(1985).

Leveridge Indian work: PCR, IX: 196, 204; Felt's Ecclesiastical Hist., 2:72, 114, Boston, 1862; Mass. Hist. Soc. Coll., III:188-93, Hawley, 1794; Weis, 126-7.

Meetinghouse subscription: TM, I:6, 9, 10, 12, 14, 18.

Thomas Dexter, Jr.: PCR, II: 96, 115, 135, etc.; TM, I:22, 33, 47, 247-8; Dexter & Wardwell Gen., 9-11; Freeman, II:45, 55, 67 etc.

Rebuilding the mill: TM, I:4-6, 22; PCR, IV:84-5.

Nye Gristmill: TM, I:22, 25, 37, 57

Herring Run: TM, I:1A, 25, 51, 68, 74

Goody Bodfish: TM, I:2, 9, 27.

Militia: TM, I:3, 6, 9, 11, 33, 253.

Population changes 1640-1650: Sandwich Archives worksheets based on references in PCR, TM I, and published genealogies.

Jane Powell & David O'Kelley: PCR, III:91; Kelley Gen., 14-21, Randall.

George Allen lands: PCR, II:76; Freeman, II:162.

Leveridge land: TM, I:5; PCR, III:194.

Bourne Old Field: PCR, I:57, 150.

Manomet Purchase: PCR, II: 162; TM, I:5.

Aptucxet History: Bradford, 193; "Old Time New England," Soc. for the Preservation of New England Antiquities, Oct. 1927 & Apr. 1933.

Burgess Herring Right: PCR, III:76.

Skiff grant: PCR, III:52, 68, 84; TM, I:20.

Bourne grant: PCR, IV: 3; V:140.

Bassett purchase from Indians: TM, I:9, 12.

Scorton purchase: Freeman, II:57; TM, I:11, 15, 18, 20.

Saconesset purchase: PCR, III:164, 208, 216.

Hallett-Wing deed: Proprietor's Records, I:48.

Carman property: PCR, I:157.

Town Land Records: TM, I:12; PCR, 2:106.

New Land Regulations: Freeman, I:212-3; II:59;TM, I:15.

Order to complete land records: TM, I:23; Freeman, II:66.

"The Lots" planting area: TM, Ml, 21.

George Burbank: "Old Houses," manuscript, pp. 4, 14, 15 at Sandwich Historical Society.

Old Town Burying Ground: TM, I:21.

Tupper land for dock: TM, I:16, 20, 42, 52, 53, 58.

Chadwell vs. Allen: PCR, IV:48, 82, 117, 183.

George Slawson: PCR, I:107; Prop. Rec, I:27, 48; Slawson Gen., pp. 1-4, Waverly, NY. 1946.

Wing & Tobey grants in Heritage area: Prop. Rec, I:42.

Besse Home: PCR, IV: 70.

Ezra Perry: Keene, 54.

Robert Lawrence: PCR, VI: 16.

Grants on the Plains: Prop. Rec, I:18, 20, 24, 25, 39.

John Tobey at Peters Pond: Prop. Rec, II:9, 10.

Chapter 5 - Indians

Note: "Red Shell" below is a reference to Clarence Wixon articles in Sandwich Independent beginning May 16, 1928. The references below are to the typescript at the Sandwich Archives.
The "Vaughan" references below are to his book entitled "New England Frontier".

Indian Background: Red Shell, 2-5; Amos Otis, 75-89; Goodwin, 117-120; 129-137; Weeks, 68-90.

Land sale concepts: Vaughan, 104-9, 305-6, 323-6; Jennings 242; Goodwin, 216-34.

Winslow & Massasoit: Freeman, I:99, 106; Weeks, 120; Bonfanti, 43-4; Travers, 71-90; PCR, I:133.

Fight at Wessagusset: Freeman, I:106, II:110; Weeks, 120; Red Shell, 15, 18.

Death of Cape Sachems: Freeman, II:110; Red Shell, 18.

Squanto: Weeks, 118, 120, 151; Travers, 155-160.

Hobamock: Goodwin, 2-8; Weeks, 110, 124, 151; Bonfanti, 45.

Sowamet Trading Post: Goodwin, 357.

First Settlements in Indian areas: Willison, 390; PCR, I:33; PCR, II:49; Travers, 87; TM, I:5.

Mayhews: Goodwin, 538-9; Banks' Martha's Vineyard, I:117-130, 213-257; PCR, III:84; Red Shell, 19.

John Eliot: Willison, 388; Vaughan, 20 etc.; Russell in American Heritage No. 9, Dec. 1957.

Leveridge: PCR, IX: 196, 204; PCR, X:34, 183, 189.

Swansea grant: Willison, 390.

Bay Colony: Jennings, 242; Vaughan, 103, 263.

Massacre of Pequods: Bradford, 398.

Narraganset relations: Freeman, I:173-6; Red Shell, 20; Weeks, 163.

Praying towns: Freeman, I:678; Hutchins, 38-41.

Treatment of Indians: Freeman, I:678; Hutchins, 35-41; PCR, II:99, 103; PCR, IX: 70-1; Bingham, 31.

Roger Williams: PCR, X:441-2; Vaughan, 118-121.

Winslow in England: Jennings, 244; Willison, 388-9; Goodwin, 444; Freeman, I:201.

Activities of the Society: Jennings, 250; Vaughan, 270-276, 282-288.

Costs of Indian work: PCR, X:34, 183, 189, 218-9, 246, 263, 296, 330, 358; Vaughan, 282-8.

Indian Bible: Russell in American Heritage No. 9, Dec. 1957; PCR, X: 310-317; Keene, 212.

Richard Bourne: Reynard, 78-85; Vaughan, 288, 295; PCR, X:384; TM, I:28; Swift, 332-3.

Bourne purchases: PCR, III:84-5, 200, 208; PCR, IV:3-4; Freeman, I:242-3; Hutchins, 46-50.

Grants in Mashpee blocked: Freeman, I:211; PCR, III:68, 193-4, 208; Hutchins, 35.

Barnstable purchases: PCR, II:22, 130, 164; PCR, III:143; PCR, X:202, 205; Trayser, 438-441; Freeman, I:677; II:187, 258-9, 264-5; Hutchins, 19, 24-8, 49, 49.

Bourne Mashpee lands & rights: PCR, III:84-5; IV: 3-4; Hutchins, 47-8; MD, 33:50-52(1935).

Massasoit events: Goodwin, 473-4; TM, I:16; Bonfanti, 43-4; Weeks,

"Massasoit"; Red Shell, 23.

Wamsutta events: PCR, IV:8; Goodwin, 542-3; Red Shell, 25; Willison, 393-4; Travers, 93-97; TM, I:16.

Sassamon: PCR, X:384-5; Freeman, I:278-9; Willison, 395; PCR, V:159, 167-8.

First Mashpee Document: PCR, IV:80; Freeman, I:252-3; Hutchins, 41.

Second Mashpee Document: Deed Dec. 11, 1665 (original at Mass. Historical Soc); Hutchins, 46-50; Freeman, I:242, 309, 345; PCR, VI:159.

Third Mashpee Document: Deed Nov. 20, 1666; PCR, VI: 159; Mass. Archives, 33:149-50; Freeman, I:677; Hutchins, 50.

Convocation in 1666: Freeman, I:257, 310, 679.

Inauguration in 1670: Freeman, II:678-9; Bingham, 34; Vaughan, 295, 298; Dykes, 4-5; Keene, 215.

Report to Gookin: Mass. Hist. Soc. Coll., I:196-9; Freeman, I:686; Willison, 395.

Quachetisset: PCR, IV:8; Goodwin, 290; TM, I:28; Red Shell, 23.

Bournedale Meetinghouse: TM, I:30; Deyo, 333, 339; Keene, 213.

Thomas Tupper, Jr.: Freeman, I:686; Tupper Genealogy, 2-3.

Testament of Fealty 1671: PCR, V:66, 70; Vaughan, 295, 298; Freeman, I:266-7; Hutchins, 50.

Indian Courts on Cape Cod: PCR, XI: 239; TM, I:28.

Renewal of Fidelity 1675: PCR, V: 177-8; Freeman, I:278.

Population 1675: Goodwin, 415, 563; PCR, V:183.

Philip & Plymouth positions: Willison, 393-5; Goodwin, 547-51; Freeman, I:279-281; PCR, X:151, 164-5.

Death of Sassamon: Willison, 395; Freeman, I:278-9, 686; Goodwin, 536-7; PCR, X: 384-5.

War in 1675: Goodwin, 550-555; Hitchins, 55; PCR, V:159, 167-8; Willison, 396-8; Jennings, 300, 309.

Great Swamp Fight: Jennings, 304-12; Goodwin, 553-7; Willison, 397; Freeman, I:283; Christenson in Howland Quarterly, July 1980.

Early 1676: Jennings, 313-20; Goodwin, 552-8; Willison, 398; Hutchins, 55.

Benjamin Church: Freeman, I:281; PCR, V:174, 201-3; Goodwin, 558-9.

War Captives: Freeman, I:286-95, 680; PCR, V: 173-5; Willison, 400; Hutchins, 57-8; PCR, X:451-3; Goodwin, 563.

Cape Watch Line: Hutchins, 57; TM, I:33-5; PCR, V:183; Freeman, I: 290; II:70-

1; Sewall Diary, I:27. (cited under Thomas, editor).

Garrison: TM, I:34; Freeman, I:281, 285; PCR, V:185-6, 201-3.

Amy Tuspaquin: Red Shell, 28-35; Travers, 110-11; Weeks, 129-145.

Joseph Burgess: PCR, X:366; Freeman, II:72, 278, 296.

Royal Regalia: Goodwin, 563; Travers, 213-5.

Chapter 6: Quakers

Bradford humility: Bradford 171-2 (said by Morison to be a quote from Rev. John Robinson).

Enforced religion: Goodwin 443-4; Willison 361-3; Freeman 1:192-4.

Sarah & Jane Kerby: PCR II:173-4; PCR III:4, 96, 111; Freeman I:221; II:56, 173.

Peter Gaunt: PCR III:74, 130, 200, 213; Freeman II:57.

Bradford statement 1655: PCR III:80.

Prence: MD 6:4 (1904); MD 3:203 (1901).

George Fox: see Worrall, 1-25.

Swallow and *Speedwell* in Boston: Winthrop 326; Hallowell 34-42; PCR X: 155-6; Bishop, George, "New England Judged, etc.," London, 1661, p. 12.

Boston laws: MBR III:415-8; PCR X: 155-6; Hallowell 133-36.

Upsall: MBR III:417-8; PCR III:96, 111, 113; Register 34:21-31 (1880).

Plymouth laws 1656: PCR III:224; PCR X:155-158.

Woodhouse 1657: Newman, Daisy, "A Procession of Friends, Quakers in America," Garden City, NY 1972, pp. 27-31; Hazard, Caroline, "The Narragansett Friends' Meeting in the XVIII Century," Cambridge, 1899, pp. 10-12.

Rhode Island: PCR X: 180-1, 212; Hazard 7-10.

Holder & Copeland I 1657: Bishop 123; PCR III:123-4, 130; Gookin in Mass. Hist. Soc. Collection I:203.

Dyer & Burden: Hallowell 111; Bishop 38.

Norton & Hodgson: PCR III:123-5, 130; Freeman I:220.

Boston laws 1657: Hallowell 136-7.

Plymouth laws 1657: PCR XI:68, 100; Amos Otis 270-1.

Copeland & Brend: PCR III: 127; Worrall 17.

Plymouth reaction: PCR III:83, 138; Deyo 169-70.

Norton & Rouse: PCR III: 139-40, 149; Hallowell 56; Amos Otis 267; Swift 91-2; Worrall 22; Freeman I:220, 235.

Marshall Barlow: PCR XI:137, 140-1; Amos Otis 258-9; MBR I:203.

Sandwich Meetings from 1658: PCR III:147; Deyo 157; Swift 93; Bishop 171; Amos Otis 268-9.

Holder & Copeland II: PCR III:213.

Report of brutality: Bishop 135; Swift 196; Freeman I:223, II:60; Deyo 165; Amos Otis 260-1; Crapo 389.

Court in Sandwich: PCR III:153-4; Otis 103; Swift 96-7.

Rose (Holway) Newland: PCR III:150, 154, 155, 158; PCR VIII:95-6.

Day of Humiliation: PCR III: 151.

Plymouth laws 1658: PCR XI: 101, 120; PCR III: 137, 153-5; Hallowell 162-72.

Copeland & Cole: Newman 35; PCR VIII:95.

Cudworth letter: PCR III: 130, 134; Amos Otis 252-275; Swift 91-2.

Boston 1658: MBR IV pt I:349; Hallowell 137-141.

Rouse letter: Deyo 165; Freeman II:60-1.

Holder friends: Crapo 371-9; Worrall 11; Hallowell 172-7.

Death sentences encouraged: PCR X:212; Mass Archives X:246; Hallowell 153-6.

Pearson & Leddra: PCR VIII:96; Freeman II:62; PCR III:178-9, 184.

Plymouth laws 1659: PCR XI: 121-2; PCR III:158, 165-9.

Boston persecutions: MBR IV pt 1:383-4, 391, 410-1, 450; Newman 35-6; Freeman I:232; Worrall 19; Goodwin 486.

Dyer & Greenfield: PCR III:178; Goodwin 484; PCR VIII:95.

Robinson & Cudworth: PCR XI:124; Freeman II:265; PCR III:183, 189.

Wenlock in Sandwich: PCR III:185-6, 197, 199, 200, 206, 213.

Mary Dyer death: MBR IV:419; Hazard 32-38: Winthrop 261, etc.

Plymouth edicts: PCR III:173-177, 180-183, 190-1, 197-200.

Sandwich fines: Freeman II:61; PCR VIII: 93-105; Amos Otis 263, 272; PCR III:138, 153, 168, 173-5, 181, 191, 200, 209, 224; Worksheet at Sandwich Archives of 6/3/83.

Reap & Pearson: PCR III:203-4.

New Plymouth laws 1660: Amos Otis 263; PCR XI: 124, 129, 130.

Boston 1661: MBR IV pt 2:2, 3, 20, 34; Amos Otis 263; Goodwin 489-90; Hallowell 141-3.

Newport Yearly Meeting: Hazard 38.

Barlow in Sandwich: TM I:23; PCR III:190-191, 206; PCR IV:7, 10; Amos Otis 104-5, 256-8; Bishop 388 (Prence Remark), 143.

Besse Trial: PCR IV: 7, 10.

Chapter 7: Events to 1692

Note: Minutes of Sandwich Mens' Monthly Meeting 1672-1693 were placed on microfilm by Rhode Island Historical Society; a 47-page typescript is at Sandwich Archives, cited below as "Mens' Minutes."

Barlow: TM I:19, 23.

Newland gift: TM I:18.

Quakers in town records: TM I:16, 17, 21, 23, 32, 44; Freeman II:68, 73; Mens' Minutes 8, 44; PCR V:94, 158.

Old Town Burying Ground: TM I:21; Holway inventory of stones (1907), cited.

Town boundaries: PCR V:41; PCR VI:71, 147; Freeman II:84-5.

Herring: PCR III:76; IV: 3; V:140; TM I:1A, etc.

Selectmen & officials: PCR XI:143, 217; PCR IV:159; Town Meeting Records.

Dock: TM I:13, 20, 42, 52, 58, 70.

Dexter Mill: TM I:1, 4, 5, 6, 22; PCR IV:84-5, II:135.

Nye Mill: TM I:22, 25, 37.

Dexter Causeway: PCR III:108.

Town Neck use: TM MA, 5, 8, 16, 21, 23, 27, 31, 32, 42, 68, 69; TM II:17.

Scorton Neck use: TM MA, 11, 15, 18, 20, 29, 36, 42, 50, 55, 68, 69.

Schools: PCR V:107; TM 1:36, 45, 48, 65.

Wiswall & Walley: PCR IV: 194; TMI:26.

John Smith: PCR V: 171-2; TMI:29, 32, 48; Freeman I:263, II:69-70; Mens' Minutes 6, Sewall Diary I:26-7, cited as Thomas, Ed.

Sandwich Town Meetinghouse 1677: Mens' Minutes 12.

Meetinghouse repair: TM I:6, 7, 10, 12, 14, 19, 40, 48 (Subscription in TM: I:48 is dated 1677 not 1644 as reported and widely repeated by genealogists as evidence of the presence of subscribers here in 1644).

Taxes & Commodities 1666: PCR VIII:117-18.

Colony organization: Merrick, Pilgrim Society Notes 11 (1963), cited.

Colony charter efforts: Willison 286-7, 334-5, 402-3, 406-7, 455. PCR IV:62; XI: 186.

Colony changes 1685-92: PCR VI:246-7; Freeman I:306-7, 309, 311-4, 317, 319, 327, Freeman II:77, 82; Willison 402-408.

Sandwich charter 1685: TM III: 1-2; Freeman II:77-8; also see manuscript volume of deeds at Plymouth County Commissioners' Office for this and other towns' charters.

Tax collections from 1675: Goodwin 561-2; Jennings 324, PCR X:392; TM I:34, 35, 46, 49, 60; Freeman II:71.

Indian Lands: PCR VI:16, 19, 51; TM I:47, 60.

Indians enslaved: PCR V: 270.

Perry writings: Deyo 174; Mens' Minutes 4, 25, 30, 36, 42, 52, 58.

Mary Mills: Sewall Diary I:44, cited as Thomas, Ed; Hallowell 193-202; Mens' Minutes 10, 23, 42, 44.

Chapter 8: Family Sketches

General references: Sandwich Archives files on each family contain references from VR, Town Meetings, wills, deeds, church records, correspondence with descendants and other materials.

Allen: Clark, Bertha W., "Allen Line, " Ms at NEHGS Library, Boston, Jan. 1956. Allen, J.K., "George Allen of Weymouth, Lynn and Sandwich, Mass.," Ms cited.

Barlow: This family still awaits a thorough genealogy, and the recent death of Dr. Claude W. Barlow, a careful scholar, is deeply regretted. The account of the death of the Marshal in Reynard's "The Narrow Land," pp. 99-123 (in the snow at Christopher's Hollow) is evocative, but totally unfounded.

Bassett: Preston, Belle, "Bassett-Preston Ancestors," cited; Freeman I:333-5; Register 125:7-21 (1971); 139:299 (1985).

Besse: Will, MD 14:152 (1912); TAG XXVI: 193-5 (Oct. 1950); Freeman II:16, 44, 54; PCR IV: 7, 10, 36, 41, 70.

Blackwell: McLean & Brownson, Register 117:180 et seq (1963).

Bourne: Lee, "The Bourne Genealogy," cited; Dykes, "History of Richard Bourne," Cleveland, 1919; McLean & Brownson, Register 118:83 et seq (1964).

Burgess: Burgess, Rev. Ebenezer, "Memorial of the Family of Thomas & Dorothy Burgess," cited; Freeman II:91.

Chipman: Will, MD 3:181-6; Chipman, John H., Chipman Genealogy, 1-9, cited;

TM I:32, 61, 68; Freeman II:73, 81, 164; Otis, Amos pp. 153-165; Lovell, R.A., Jr., TAG 61:2-6. Prince quotation, Dykes, "History of Richard Bourne," 10-11, cited.

Dexter: Warden & Dexter, "Dexter Genealogy," 1-15, cited; Freeman II: 78-9, Lewis, "History of Lynn," 64, cited.

Dillingham: Archambault, Phyllis D., "Genealogy of the Dillingham Family of New England," Lynn, Mass., n.d.; Freeman II:66; Paine, "History of Harwich, " 97-8, 116-7, cited.

Ellis: McLean & Brownson, Register 119:161 et seq (1965); Ellis, Ernest C, "Reminiscences of Ellisville," Plymouth, 1973; Freeman II:72, 133.

Fish: Gill, Barbara L., unpublished Fish Genealogy, 386 Quaker Meetinghouse Road, East Sandwich, MA 02537.

Freeman: Freeman, Frederick, "Freeman Genealogy," cited; McLean, TAG (1964):103-110; Perry, Henry J. & Canfield, Rosemary, "The Second Boat," 5:1:15-18; Freeman, Dr. Stephen A., "My Branch of the Descendants of Edmond Freeman," Middlebury, VT, 1984.

Gibbs: McLean & Brownson, Register 123:54et seq (1969).

Gifford: McLean & Daniels, Register 128:241 et seq (1974).

Handy: McLean & Brownson, Register 125:124 et seq (1971).

Holway: PCR IV: 88; Freeman II:161; Holway, Thomas E., "Holway & Eldred Records," Sandwich, 1913; Holway, William Rea & Holway, Frances (Kerr), "The Holway-Kerr Family Book," 1956.

Hoxie: Hoxie, "The Hoxie Family," Ukiah, Oregon, 1950.

Landers: McLean & Brownson, Register 124:42 et seq (1970).

Lawrence: Sturgis Library, Barnstable, Genealogical Notebooks; Brown, Falmouth Vital Records, cited.

Newland: Will, Sandwich Quaker Records. Rhode Island Historical Society, typescript copy at Sandwich Archives.

Nye: Nye, L. Bert, Jr., "American Nyes of English Origin," cited.

Percival: Crocker, Benton P., "The Percivals of Cape Cod," cited; MD 14:118-9; Connecticut Society of Genealogists 4:2: Sept. 1971.

Perry: Perry, Elwell, "Perry Genealogy," Ms, cited; McLean & Brownson, Register 115:86 et seq (1961); Perry, Rev. C.B., "The Perrys of Rhode Island and Tales of Silver Creek," NY 1913; MD 24:59-61; Black, David, "The King of Fifth Avenue, The Fortunes of August Belmont," NY, 1981.

Pope: Freeman II: 152-3; Sutherland, Amelia P., "Pioneer Popes," cited; Lee, Helen B.J., "Bourne Genealogy," pp. 15, 21, 23 cited.

Skiff: Banks, C.E., "History of Martha's Vineyard, " II West Tisbury 71-3, II Chilmark 36-9, III:432-441; Freeman II:86; Preston, Belle, "Bassett-Preston Ancestors, " pp. 255-6.

Smith: Lovell, R.A., Jr., TAG 61:2-6; Smith, John S. (1851-1930), unpublished article, 15 pp., at Sandwich Historical Society; Freeman II:80, 83-4.

Swift: Swift, "Descendants of William Swyft," cited; Dodge, Raymond, "Swift Genealogy," unpublished manuscript, Barnstable, MA 1970, copy at Sandwich Archives.

Tobey: Tobey, R.B. & Pope, C.H., "Tobey Genealogy, " cited; Freeman II:156-7.

Tupper: Tupper, Dr. Eleanor & Chapman, Alexander H., "Tupper Genealogy," cited; Freeman II:71, 103.

Wing: Wing Family of America, The OWL (quarterly publication), beginning 1900, set at Sandwich Public Library; Freeman II:100-1; Pierce, F.C., "Batchelder, Batcheller Genealogy," pp. 30, 82-94, cited.

Chapter 9 New Faces

Note: Town Meeting Records, Volume II (cited as TMII) covers the period 1692-1767. A typescript has been prepared which follows the original paging.

Rowland Cotton: Freeman I:361-2; II:70, 80-85, 92; Sewall Diary (cited) 176, 305-6, 377-9, 388-9, 415, 627, 635, 639, 726, 746-55, 853-5, 936, 993, 1009, 1040, 1047, 1055; Cotton Mather Diary I:319-20, 551, II:403-5, 470, 474, 813-5; cited; Locke, Register 12:311-2 (1858); Cotton, John, Mass. Hist. Soc. Coll. IV: 107-141 (1795); Davis III Register, cited (on Denison); TM I:72, II:11-2, 17, 31-2, 46-7, 50-1, 72-3; (Cotton was the first minister ordained in Sandwich and the first licensed to solemnize marriages.); Old Town Cemetery, see Holway Ms, cited; Weis, Colonial Clergy 63, cited.

Samuel Prince: TM I:70, II:12-13; Robie Diary, 1710, at American Antiquarian Society, Worcester; Freeman I:357-9, II:69, 75, 77, 86, 87; James Mills record, cited below.

James Mills: Mercier, Jane, Mayflower Quarterly, May 1980, 70-2; Savage 214; Ship register, Mass. Archives, 7:108, 191, 238, 262, 409, 511; Copy of 1699-1704 shipping log at Sandwich Archives.

Peter Newcomb: Newcomb, Bethuel M., "Andrew Newcomb and His Descendants," New Haven 1923, pp. 28-9; Banks, Martha's Vineyard II Edgar-town 84; III:338; Sewall Diary 747-8, 754-5, cited; Freeman II:98.

Peter Adolph: Benes, Peter, "Masks of Orthodoxy," cited. Benes identified the carver of the gravestone at Old Town Cemetery as Lamson, in personal communication; Will, NY Hist. Soc. Coll. Vol. 25 1892 (Abstracts of wills 1696-1704, I:388); Family information from The New York Genealogical and Biographical Society, 112 East 58th Street, NY 10022, in a letter to the Sandwich Archives Jan. 3, 1979.

Thomas Robie: Diary, 1710, at American Antiquarian Society, Worcester; TM II:51-2; Sewall Diary 1081-2, cited; Sibley's Harvard Graduates V:450-4.

Nathaniel Otis: Freeman I:273, II:99; TM II:52-3, 62-3; Waters, "Otis Family," pp. 58-9, cited, confuses a Nathaniel Otis born in Scituate Jan. 30, 1689/90 son of Joseph, with the above Nathaniel born in Barnstable May 28, 1690, son of John.

Melatiah Bourne: Lee, "Bourne Genealogy," pp. 15-6, 23-8, cited: Freeman II:92, 101, 437, 488.

Benjamin Fessenden: Fessenden, Edwin A., "Fessenden Family in America," 1971 pp. 675-687; Locke, Register 12:311-2 (1858), 13: 30-33 (1859); Freeman I:651-3; II:69, 70, 93, 95-7; TM II:73-4, 90, 98, 98-100, 110-1; Will, MD 20:59-61; Weis, Colonial Clergy 83, cited; Keene, cited, 34, 62, 92; Sandwich Observer, Apr. 17, 1847 (typescript at Sandwich Archives).

School Teachers: TM I:36, 45, 46, 48, 65, 71; II:15, 27, 45, 51-66, etc.; Freeman II:78, 84, 87, 89, 92.

Woodlots: TM II:22-3, 26-7, 30-35, 52-5; Freeman II:87; PCR XI:257; Proprietors Record Book II, an original volume in Sandwich Town Clerk's vault (typescript and index at Archives), Jesse Boyden Woodlot Map, Nov. 12, 1847, Barnstable Registry of Deeds (copy at Sandwich Archives).

Shops: TM II:12, 18, 19, 45, 52.

Mills: TM II:16, 18, 63; Freeman II:83, 90, 91.

Canal: Sewall Diary p. 27, cited; Freeman I:333.

Meetinghouse: TM II:26, 34, 36-9, 48, 56, etc.; Freeman II:83, 85, 86, 90.

New Roads: TM II: 23, 64.

Dike Meadow: Freeman II:91.

Health: TM II:41, 53, 67; Freeman II:91.

Lebaron: Mass. Archives 30:330a; Freeman I:333; Goodwin 380.

Town Poor: TM II:44, 56, 81; Freeman II:93.

Chapter 10: Ruggles Period

Edmund Freeman V: Freeman Genealogy 45-6, 72-4; Freeman II:99.

Ruggles: Ruggles, H.S., Genealogy (cited) 78-9; Freeman II:99-100; TM II:109, 120, 125, 126, 128, 131, 138; Lee, "Bourne Genealogy," cited, 28-33; Sandroff, (cited in Journals) 16-28; Paine, "Harwich" (cited), 362; Paige, "Hardwick, " 1883, many references; Ruggles, H.S., "General Timothy Ruggles," cited; Sibley's Harvard Graduates VII: 199-223; Stark, "Loyalists," cited, 133, 136-7, 142, 225-9, 380; Old woman story: Ruggles, James L. in "The Offering," Hardwick, 1848, p. 27 quoting Abraham

Holmes' address before the Bar of Bristol County, New Bedford 1834; Tudor, William, "Life of James Otis," cited, pp. 224-236; Hardwick Fair: Journal of the House of Representatives, Vol. 38 pt 2: 252, 285.

Judah Swift: Dodge, "Swift Genealogy," Ms cited, 173.

Melatiah Bourne Will: MD 19:36-40 (1917).

Abraham Williams: TM II:138-142.

Meetinghouse: TM II:37, 53; Freeman II:24, 138, 157, 163, 183, 203; Wing, "Unitarian Church," Ms cited.

Grist Mill: TM II: 116-7, 177, 213.

Herring: TM II:95, 193, 198, 208, etc.

Docks: TM II:156, 193, 213, 220, etc.

Census: Archives Worksheets; Freeman II:94; Register 13:30-33 (1859).

Money: Freeman I:345, 347, 352, 360, 364, 371, 383-6, etc; TM II: 68, 78, 138.

Chapter 11: Acadians

Background: Calnek, "History," cited, 132-144; Arsenault, "History of the Acadians," cited; Griffiths, "The Acadians," (cited, magazine); "Historic Acadia," pamphlet by Parks Canada, 1979, cited.

Dispersion: Belliveau, "French Neutrals," cited, pp. 23-27, 245; Journals of the House of Representatives V. 32 1755 pt. I:150, 218, 219, 224, 233, 248, 263-6; V.32 1756 pt 2: IX-XI; V. 33-44 numerous references.

Barnstable: Trayser, "The Acadians on Cape Cod," Ms cited; Trayser, "Barnstable," cited, p. 466.

Records of Acadians in Mass.: Mass. Archives, Vols. 23 & 24, index of items related to Cape Cod and other references made by Sandwich Archives; Vols. 13 & 14, Council Records; Governor Lawrence correspondence, V. 23:158-9, 162; Sandwich group references, V. 23:163, 166-7, 175-6, 181-4, 198-9, etc.

Elisha Bourne: Lee, "Bourne Genealogy," cited, p. 40; Davis, "Ancient Landmarks," cited, I:179; Freeman I:392-5, 399; Belliveau, "French Neutrals," cited, pp. 23-27, 245.

Removals to Nova Scotia: Harding, "The New Englanders in Nova Scotia," Register 116:3-13, cited; Freeman II: 770-1; McLean, "Landers," Register, cited; Smith, W.C., "History of Chatham," cited, pp. 323-5.

Pubnico group: d'Entremont, H. Leander, "The Baronie de Pombcoup and the Acadians," Yarmouth, N.S. 1931, p. 55.

Resettlement of Trahans in Canada: Letter from Conrad Trahan, Sept. 6, 1980.

Longfellow: "Evangeline A Tale of Acadie," Boston 1881, pp. 95-121.

Grand Pre: "Grand Pre National Historic Park Nova Scotia," pamphlet by Parks Canada 1976.

Chapter 12: Indian Reservations

Plymouth Colony law 1682: Hutchins 61-3; PCR XI:252-5; Freeman I:300-6

Simon Popmonnet: Freeman I:679-80.

Shearjashub Bourne: Archives 31:70-1, 33:246-7; PCR VI:153; Freeman I:681, 703; Holway, Old Town Burying Ground (cited); Keene 215-6; Hutchins 60.

Richard Bourne: Lee, "Bourne Genealogy," 1-13; Amos Otis 104-111.

Sh. Bourne lands: MD 25:50-60 (1923); Hutchins 60; PCR VI:153, 159.

Mashpee Title 1685: PCR VI: 159-60; Freeman I:309-10, 679-80.

Sh. Bourne further lands: General Laws 1694-5, Ch. 47; Freeman I:332, II:83; Deed from William Bradford, March 4, 1688/9, original owned by Donald Bourne, Esq., Sandwich, typescript at Sandwich Archives.

Mashpee borders: TM II:20, 150, 204-7; Freeman I:345, 675, II:83, 85-7, 443-4.

Indian population 1692: Freeman I:556, 687, II:372-3.

Mass. Bay Province Act 1693/4. Province Laws 1693/4 Ch. 17.

Popmonnet petition 1700: Mass. Archives 30:456; Prov. Laws 1700/1 Ch. 10; Hutchins 63-4.

Laws of 1718 and 1726: Province Laws 1718/9 Ch. 9, 1725/6 Ch. 10; Freeman I:687.

Meetinghouse removal 1717: Pamphlet, "Mashpee Old Indian Meetinghouse," Mashpee 1961.

Ezra Bourne: Lee, "Bourne Genealogy," 16, 33-5; MD 30:38, 62 (1928), MD 33: 124(1931).

Rev. Joseph Bourne: Weis, "Colonial Clergy," cited, 36; Mass. Hist. Soc. Coll V:206 (1798); Freeman I:680-2; Hutchins 64, 66-7; Journal of House of Representatives 1730 p. 258.

Act of 1746: Province Laws 1746/7 Ch. 12; Protests, Mass. Archives 31: 102-3, 576; 32:245, 248, 277, 288, 415, 424-6, 445-7, 452; Hutchins 71-73.

Meetinghouse rebuilt: Mass. Archives 32:616; Freeman I:703; Hutchins 90; Lowell, A. Lawrence, address quoted in *Sandwich Independent* Sept. 12, 1923.

Bryant & Hawley: Mass. Hist. Soc. Coll. II:188-193 (1794); Freeman I:378, 682-5, 689, 692-3; Hutchins 79, 88, 91.

Reuben Cognehew: Freeman I:687; Hutchins 73-80.

Mashpee District 1763: Province Laws 1763/4 Ch. 3; Mass. Archives 33: 146-8.

Mashpee population changes: Hutchins 68, 77-9, 82-7; Freeman I:687-8.

Blacks in Sandwich: TM II:162-3; Sandwich Archives files & genealogy; Davis, "Ancient Landmarks" III.

Changes in Mashpee: Freeman I:689, 696, 703; Hutchins 66-8, 82-88; Province Laws 1779/80 Ch. 207; Archives 33: 537.

Mashpee in the Revolution: Hutchins 87-91; Meetinghouse land deed 1783 in Mass. Resolves 1809 Ch. 47; Freeman I:688, 692; Acts & Res. 1777 Append. 15; TM III:98; Typescript at Sandwich Archives: list of Mashpee veterans from "Mass. Soldiers & Sailors of the Rev. War."

Acts of 1788, 1789, & 1790: Acts 1788 Ch. 2, Ch. 38; Acts 1789 Ch. 53; TM III:171-3, 176; Hutchins 88, 92-3, 96-7.

Bourne lands in Mashpee: See Sandwich Archives array: wills, deeds, and references, including 13 deeds in MD 25:50-60 (1923); 31 Bourne family documents owned by Donald Bourne, Esq., of Sandwich, with copies at the Archives; also copies of deeds from PCR and Mass. Archives, including Bourne and Mashpee; McLean article on Richard Bourne, cited.

Herring Pond: Freeman I:558, 559, 686, 687; Freeman II:87, 90, 98; General Laws 1695/6 Ch. 3.

Herring Pond Meetinghouse: Sewall Letterbook, Coll. of the Mass. Hist. Soc. V.I, 6th Series, Boston 1886 pp. 62, 85; Sewall Diary (Ed. Thomas) I: 165; Keene, cited, 213-4; Notes at Archives on visit to site with Mr. Warner Eldredge 1982.

Inscribed stone: Dr. Barry Fell in *Cape Cod Times,* Apr. 16, 1975; Dr. James W. Mavor, Jr. talk at Bourne Historical Society 1984; Edmund Delabarre, "The Indian Petroglyph at the Aptucxet Trading Post in Bourne Mass." in *Old Time New England,* Jan. 1936, pp. 110-2, Society for the Preservation of New England Antiquities.

Plymouth line and Indian lands: TM I:30, 47; TM II:.45-6; Freeman I:87, 382, 559; Bingham 39; Acts & Res. 1777 Append. 15; 1782/3 pp 676-7; 1792/3 pp 299, 601; Map p. 363 prepared by Mr. Charming Howard and presented to the Bourne Historical Society in 1942; Mass. Archives 33: 558-561, 186; 32:228.

Josiah Cotton: Davis, "Ancient Landmarks," cited, I:110-1.

Elisha Tupper: Freeman II: 110-1, 121, II:697-9; Tupper Genealogy; Mass. Archives 33:442.

Pocasset: Freeman I:703; II:110-1; Mass. Archives 14:545-551; Sandwich comments: TM III:10-12; Mass. Archives 118: 406, 409.

Chapter 13: Dr. Freeman

Stamp Act Congress and background: Morgan, "Birth of the Republic" and "Stamp Act Congress," cited; Freeman I:400-429.

Ruggles departure from Hardwick: Lee, "Bourne Genealogy," cited, p. 32.

Flour shipment & Machin survey of Canal: Goodwin 291; Freeman I:493; Mass. Archives 819, series 3, Vol 15 p. 5.

Freeman chart: Freeman Genealogy, cited, 6 generations.

Biography of Dr. Freeman: Freeman Genealogy 122-5; Freeman History I:461-5; Russell Freeman in *Sandwich Observer,* Oct. 31, 1846.

Otis dynasty in Barnstable: Waters, "The Otis Family," cited, pp 58-110. (Mr. Waters, on pages 58 & 59, confused two Nathaniel Otises and has missed entirely the return of Dr. Freeman to Sandwich at the behest of James Otis, Sr. Nathaniel Otis, born in Scituate Jan. 30, 1689/90, was the son of Joseph of Scituate, and is the shipwright, Nathaniel who was briefly Town Clerk of Barnstable and died intestate 18 Feb. 1729/30. Nathaniel Otis, born May 28, 1690, son of Col. John of Barnstable, Harvard 1710, married Abigail Russell and was a merchant and lawyer at Sandwich, as well as Register of Probate; he died Dec. 1739.)

Dr. Freeman in Sandwich: TM III:4, 13-31, 56-64.

Committee of Correspondence: TM III:21, 31-56.

Import ban: Freeman II:110; TM II:222-4; TM III:13.

Body of the People: Freeman I:424-454.

Nabby Freeman event: Freeman I:452-3; II:305-6; Amos Otis 232-5, 387; Trayser 124; Waters, "Otis Family," cited, 187-8.

Plymouth event: Freeman I:455-6, 460-1.

Attack on Freeman: Freeman I:453-465; TM III:29; Amos Otis 231-235, 385-7.

Provincial Congress and Ruggles Circular: Freeman I:467-8.

Town actions 1774-1776: TM III:29-31, 56-8, 60-62, 64; Freeman I: 482, 485; II:116-120.

Pocasset Precinct Petition: Freeman I:412-3. II:112; TM III:8-13; Mass. Archives 14:545-551; Vol. 118, 406, 409.

Scraggy Neck: PCR IV: 155, 161.

Quaker Petition: TM III:3.

Grist Mills: Dexter & Nye Mills; see Chapter 8 notes.

Bourne Mill: TM II:16.

Perry Mill; Keene 99, 180.

Wing Mill; TM II:116-7.

Barlow Mill; TM III:62, 64.

Boyden Map 1831; Mass. Archives 1844 Series 1830 V. 2:12.

Map of 1825; Perault Survey of a Proposed Canal, copy at Sandwich Historical Society.

Salt: TM III:25, 26, 60, 62; Freeman I:493, 505-6.

Wood Exports & forest fire: TM III: 11-12, 18; Freeman I:416-7.

Prayers at meetings: TM III:20, 22, 23, 28, 29, 56, 68.

Slaves: TM III:24; references in wills & deeds at Sandwich Archives; Sandwich VR; see also, Strick, "The Black Presence in the Era of the American Revolution 1770-1800," Smithsonian, Washington, D.C., 1973, pp. 15-17.

Chapter 14: Life in Wartime

Note: Rev. Frederick Freeman (1799-1883) inherited from his father, Dr. Nathaniel Freeman (1741-1827,) a large collection regarding the Revolutionary War period, which gives the "History of Cape Cod" unusual authority for this period. This collection seems to have been broken up and sold in Sale 2019 Feb. 21-22, 1961 and Sale 2098 Mar. 27, 1962. Parke-Bernet Galleries auctioned a number of historical documents related to Nathaniel Freeman as described in the catalogues. The University of Michigan Clements Library at Ann Arbor has a set of Nathaniel Freeman papers, including some that were in the 1961-2 sales, plus others, ref. letter May 19, 1983 from Dr. John Shy, University of Michigan.

Background: Morgan, "Birth of the Republic," cited; Deyo 70-75; Freeman I:478-545; Trayser 121-140.

State Constitution: TM III:71, 74, 75, 84, 91, 211.

Dr. Freeman roles: Freeman I:468, 487, 490, 501-8, 518-9, 523-4, 530-8; TM III:21-2, 26-7, 29-56, 174, 182; Amos Otis 231-5, 387; Trayser 133.

South Carolina appeal: Freeman I:486.

Militia activities: Freeman I:487, 504-8, 517, 523, 536-7; Shipton, *New England Quarterly,* Dec. 1966, 498-512; Deyo 71, 73.

Benjamin Percival Diary: Original diary 1777-1817 at Sandwich Archives.

Continental Army: TM III:65, 70; Freeman I:500-502; Deyo 72; List of Sandwich men in Militia & Continental Service at Sandwich Archives from "Soldiers & Sailors of the Rev. War,"

Sandwich Memorial 1777: Manuscript page at Sandwich Historical Society. A copy was shown to the Mass. Archivist, Mr. Leo Flaherty in 1978, but he was unable to locate the original in available files in the State House or

Archives.

Levies and Supply Requisitions: TM III:75-6, 82-4, 88-106, 109-110, 112-4; Freeman I:514-8, 533-40, 543, 545.

Sandwich Tories: Stark, "Loyalists," cited, p. 139; List of 38 names compiled by Sandwich Archives; TM III:79, 80, 120, 121; Freeman I:501, 513, 521-2, 541.

Smallpox: *American Heritage* VIII:5, 40-43, 109, Aug. 1957; Freeman I:360, 510; II:122, 298, 639; TM II:70, 71, 189.

Inflation & Tax Collections: TM III:59-70, 81, 84, 89, 95, 99, 105, 109, 114, 117-136; Freeman I:486, 495, 536-7.

Prices: "Mattapoisett," cited, p. 363-6; Trayser 136; Deyo 73; TM III: 84-6.

School Teachers: TM III:77, 112, 117, 133.

Herring Run: TM III:77-9, 90, 130.

Tax abatements: TM III:82, 89, 103.

Elisha Bourne: TM III: 129, etc.

Ellisville petition: TM III:125.

Dark Day: L. Hussey in Letterbook of Alice Rogers, Wing Family of America, Sandwich; Mass. Hist. Soc. Coll. 1792, I:95.

Magee Storm: Deyo 73; Trayser 135; Amos Otis 349-358; also Potter in *Yankee,* Dec. 1964.

Removals from Cape Cod: Freeman I:535; TM III:113.

Hartwood, Lee, Lenox: Secretary of State, "Historical Data on Cities & Towns," cited.

Bathsheba Spooner Case: Isaiah Thomas in *Worcester Spy,* Mar. 5, May 7, July 6, 1778, (papers at Amer. Ant. Soc, Worcester); article, "A Souvenir of Old South Meetinghouse," Worcester, 1887; Bullock in Worcester Hist. Soc. Vol. 2, No. 4, Sept. 1939; Sandroff in *Worcester Sunday Telegram,* Jan. 13, 1952; Green, "Case of Bathsheba Spooner," American Antiquarian Society Proceedings, Vol. 5, p. 430, Oct. 1888; Clarkson, "Bathsheba Spooner," in Worcester Bicentennial Commission Newsletter 9, June 1976.

Chapter 15: Federal Census

"Heads of Families at the First Census of the United States Taken in the Year 1790 - Massachusetts," Washington D.C., 1908, Reprint, Spartanburg, SC, 1964.

Archives Office has analysis sheets by family and neighborhood in Sandwich, also of the non-Indian families in Mashpee (Indians were not included in the Census).

1820 Federal Census - National Archives Microcopy 33, Roll 47, with analysis by families, both Sandwich and non-Indians in Mashpee, at Sandwich Archives.

Sandwich Highway District Annual Schedules - about 57 handwritten booklets covering the period 1805-1827, issued by Sandwich Selectmen to Road Surveyors in 15 road districts, specifying names of residents, amounts of road tax due, and the roads in that district to be maintained.

Chapter 16: A New Start

Dr. Freeman: Deyo 200, 203, 205, 208, 227; TM III:174, 182; *Sandwich Observer,* Oct. 31, 1846; Amos Otis 387; Freeman Genealogy 120-5, 197-8, 202; Dudley, "Historical Sketches," cited, p. 150; Major John Freeman letter to Gov. Elbridge Gerry, Feb. 23, 1811, copy at Sandwich Archives.

General Ruggles: Ruggles, H.S., "General Timothy Ruggles," cited, 19-24; "The Winslow Papers 1776-1826," Raymond edit, St. John, N.B,, 1901, pp.42-3, 70, 106-8, 164; Calnek, "History," cited, pp. 227, 231-2, 407-9, 583-594; Longley, "Annapolis County Loyalist," cited, pp. 73-95; Obituary, *Royal Gazette,* Halifax, 11 Aug. 1795.

Benjamin Percival; Kittredge, "Cape Cod," cited, p. 120; Bowman, "Pilgrim Notes & Queries," (journal cited), V. I No. 5-8 (1913), V. II No. 2-3 (1914); TM IV:138-9; Tobey Cemetery, Sandwich Historical Commission inventory of markers, on file at Sandwich Archives, 6 Percival interrals.

Town situation 1785-1789: TM III: 135-168.

Riot ANH Bacon, "TownOfficer's Guide," cited, pp. 29-31.

Resumption of Spending: TM III:139, 142, 160-6, 173, 177, 179-81, 189, etc.

Voters from parts of Mashpee: TM III:146-8; Freeman II:134-5.

Newcomb Tavern: TM III:154, 165, 178.

New State Laws: TM III: 145, 180, 192, 210.

Town Division: TM IV:8-9.

Improvement Association: TM IV:72-3.

Town Poor: TM III:135, 141, 149, 154, 164, 178, 192, 205; TM IV:2, 10, etc.

Warning our 1790: TM III:175.

John Freeman letters: Originals at Sandwich Historical Society, quoted in Burbank, "A Bit of Sandwich History," cited, pp. 16, 17.

Poor House: TM IV: 12, 142, 198, 203.

Travel: Deyo 124; TM IV:24, 209, etc.; Percival Diary, June 1795.

Manomet bridge: TM III:168, 185, 188, 192; TM IV:22, 26, 155, 167, 171, 205;

Keene, cited, pp. 106-7.

Marine events: Deyo 55-6, 110, 112; Keene 67-8, 140; TM III:136, 197; TM IV: 193, 196, 203-4.

Wreck in 1825: Freeman I:625.

Live Oak: Wood, "Live-Oaking," cited; Swift, Katharine W., "The Swift Family," Whitinsville, Mass. 1955, pp. 2-3; "Mattapoisett," cited, pp. 295-6; Harris, John, "Old Ironsides," in *Boston Globe,* Oct. 16, 1977.

Whaling: Deyo 131-5; Guba, Frederick, "Nantucket Odyssey," 27-31, 251-63.

Canal Proposals: TM IV:27 (1801), 161 (1818), 212 (1825); Davis, Wendell, in Mass. Hist. Soc. Coll. VIII:119-126 (1802).

Postal Service: Deyo 123; Doubleday, "Post Offices of Massachusetts," (ms cited).

Schools: TM III:133, 140, 145, 154, 188, 192, 198, 205, 214; TM IV:3-129, (annual entries 1796-1813); Peters Pond area, TM IV:3, 193.

Sandwich Academy: Dwight, "Travels in New England," cited; Vol. 3, pp. 74-6, 385 (Visit of 1800 showing the Academy already in existence); Pratt, Ambrose, "Celebration," cited, pp. 76-7 (quotations from Rev. Chamberlain); *Sandwich Observer,* Apr. 24 and May 29, 1884; Nye, William L., "Sandwich Academy" (ms cited); Freeman II: 138-142; TM IV: 36-7.

Brickyard: Freeman II:24-5; Burbank, "A Bit of Sandwich History," cited, and letter to Editor, *Cape Cod Standard Times* Nov. 22, 1937; TM IV: 175; Barbour, "Sandwich," cited, 93; Lee, Ruth Webb, "Sandwich Glass," cited, p. 107; "Map of the Town of Sandwich" by H. F. Walling, Boston, 1857.

Saltworks: Percival Diary 1777; Keene 83, 103; Deyo 142-5; TM IV: 86; Map of Sandwich, 1831, at Archives.

Cotton Mill: TM IV: 105-6; *Sandwich Observer,* May 17, 1851; Freeman II:143; Beulah Wing (1803-1882), daughter of Samuel Wing, received a long list of textile items in her trousseau; list, found in the family house, now at the Sandwich Archives.

Pocasset Iron: Deyo 337; Keene 128; Maps 1831, 1857, 1880; Sandwich Tax lists from 1822, owner Hercules Weston.

Herring River Mills: TM II:62-3; TM III:131, 169-70; TM IV:189, 198; Deyo 328, 339, 340; Freeman II:136; Map 1831; Keene 128.

War of 1812: TM IV: 138-9; Deyo 76-82; Burbank, "A Bit of Sandwich History," cited, p. 13; "Records of the Mass. Volunteer Militia 1812-14," Boston, 1913, pp. 71-76; Bliss, "Colonial Times of Buzzards Bay," cited, pp. 210-17.

Levi Gifford's ship: Notes on Sandwich Quakers by Annie Ewer Rose (1867-

1971), Sandwich Quaker, now at Sandwich Archives.

Maine: Frost, "Maine Genealogy" in Register, cited, 243-266; Federal Census 1790; "The Fairfield Register," Mitchell Publishing Co., Rents Hill, Me. 1904; Jones, "Settlers of Fiarfield, Maine," (journal, cited); TM IV: 186; Freeman I:767-9; Burgess, "Genealogy," cited, 43-4; Fairfield letter, June 4, 1834, original at Sandwich Historical Society.

Visitors: Dwight, "Travels in New England," cited, (Sandwich references in *Yarmouth Register,* Aug. 12, Sept. 23, 1852); Deyo 208, 276; TM IV: 173; Davis Wendell, "Description of Sandwich," in Mass. Hist. Soc. Coll. VIII:119-126 (1802); Freeman I:630-1; II:149, 570; Kendall, Edward A., "Trip to Cape Cod 1807-8," quoted in *Yarmouth Register,* Apr. 23, 1869; Rich, Shebnah, "Truro," Boston 1883, references to Rev. Dr. James Freeman 16, 110, 114, etc.

Hurricane: Freeman I:606-8; Keene 104-5; Diary of Ezra S. Goodwin, cited; Ludlum, "Early American Hurricanes," cited; "Mattapoisett and Old Rochester," cited, pp. 155-158.

Freeman Farm: Deyo 199-200; Sandwich Tax Records Shadrach Freeman 1790-1854 and Watson Freeman 1855-1868; TM IV:115; Freeman II: 159-160; McLean, Ellis Genealogy in Register, (cited journal), es pec. 120: 291-2 (1966) and 121:37-8 (1967); Deeds, Tupper Family, at Sandwich Archives; Maps, letters, photos, etc. from the Farm, at Sandwich Archives.

Sandwich Map 1831: Mass. Archives Series 1830, Vol. II p. 12 No. 1844.

Taxpayers: Books of Records 1790-1860, at Sandwich Archives.

Chapter 17: Drama in the Churches

Rev. Jonathan Burr: Freeman II: 134, 141; *Yarmouth Register,* Aug. 11, 1842; Deyo 293; First Parish Church record books, now at First Church of Christ, Sandwich; Collection of Burr letters at Sandwich Historical Soc., Freeman, Frederick, "History of the Original Congregational Church in Sandwich," *Yarmouth Register,* May 5 to Aug. 11, 1877 (14 articles), Scrapbook at Sandwich Historical Society.

Enlargement of Meetinghouse 1804: Freeman II: 104-7; Church Record Book G 175-189.

Sketches of Meetinghouse: Sandwich Historical Society.

Titus Winchester: Freeman II:123-4; Rev. Williams, Freeman I:575-6; Will, Barnstable Probate 3:57 (1807); Williams/Tobey house, Sandwich Historical Commission Asset Inventory No. 130, 133 Route 6A at Jarves Street; Holway, Old Town Cemetery, cited, Tablestone; Chamberlain quotation, Pratt, Ambrose, "256th Anniversary," cited, p. 67.

Conservative-liberal background: Goodwin, cited, pp. 605-7; Atkins & Fagley, "History of Congregationalism," cited.

First Parish situation 1808-1811: Freeman II:144-6; Deyo 293; Scraggy Neck Partition, TM IV: 106; Nye, William L., "Sketch of the First Church of Christ in Sandwich, Mass.,": a paper at the Sandwich Historical Society.

Calvinistic Congregational Society: View of chapel from John Warner Barber, "Historical Collections of Massachusetts," Worcester, 1839, pp. 51-4; Broadside, Feb. 23, 1813, soliciting building funds, Sandwich Archives; "Confession of Faith and Covenant Adopted by the Calvinistic Congregational Church in Sandwich June 29, 1820 also a Brief History of the Church," Booklet, 17 pp., Boston, 1855; "An Historical Discourse," by Rev. P. C. Headley, *Cape Cod Advocate,* Feb. 7, 1857.

Town Records of Church Membership: TM IV: 110, 113, 114, 116, 119-24; Freeman II:144-5.

Rev. Ezra Shaw Goodwin: Harvard 1807; Holway, Old Burying Ground, cited; Diary 1815, at American Antiquarian Society, Worcester, 46 leaves, (analysis at Sandwich Archives).

Methodists: Perry Genealogy, cited, 171-5; *The Independent* (Sandwich), Feb. 15, 1898, quoting from *Zion's Herald,* Jan. 7, 1848; *Sandwich Observer,* Dec. 18, 1847; Deyo 294-5, 331-3; Paper, "Methodist Church in Sandwich," by Mrs. J. R. Holway, Sandwich Hist. Soc; *The Seaside Press,* June 26, 1875; *Sandwich Independent,* Mar. 14, 1914; Record Book P, at First Church of Christ, Sandwich.

Dr. Hersey: Freeman I:554, 609-10; Deyo 231; Amos Otis 7-18; Pratt, "Eastham" cited, 140.

Sale of Parish lands: TM IV: 172.

Chapter 18: A Glass Factory

Tudor quotation: Freeman II:35 (quoted from the Monthly Anthology for 1821).

John Trout: Freeman II:34-5; Barbour, "Sandwich," cited, 4-7.

Deming Jarves: Barbour 1-7, 21; Lee, "Sandwich Glass," cited, 3-49; "Your Obd't Serv't, Deming Jarves," Bishop & Hassell, edit., Sandwich, 1984, 1-7.

Nathan Smith: Sandwich Vital Records 1800-1882; Smith family documents at Sandwich Archives.

Melatiah Tobey: Sandwich Vital Records 1766-1851; Property records and house history, Sandwich Archives.

Sandwich Tax Records: Original Assessor's records 1790-1860 at Sandwich Archives.

Sandwich Town Meeting Records! Vol. IV 1798-1825, Vol. V 1826-1844, Originals in Sandwich Town Clerk's Vault, typescripts at Sandwich Archives.

Rev. John Smith House: Article by Mrs. John S. Smith, in a series, "Old Houses of Sandwich," written about 1903, at the Sandwich Historical Society; Deed of April 1, 1694, from John Smith to his son Thomas Smith, refers to the house, original at Sandwich Archives.

Beach sand: Barbour, cited, 22, 33-36; Keene 40.

Company store: Record books at Sandwich Historical Society.

Town Dock: TM II:51-2 (1710), 156-7 (1755); TM IV:193 (1822); TM V:32 (1831), 107-9 (1839) including drawing of the dock.

Old Harbor Landing: TM II:220-1 (1767); TM IV:203-4 (1824); TM V:102 (1838).

New B&S Wharf & Railway: Plan by Newell Snow, Registered Land Surveyor, dated Aug. 6, 1963, Barnstable Plan Book 179 p. 45; Dr. Jon H. Wetz, "The Horse Railroad," in Sandwich Historical Society magazine "The Acorn," Vol. 11 No. 3 (1977).

Brickyard at Town Neck: Article, "Glass House," by George Burbank, Sandwich Hist. Society; Freeman II:24-5; *Cape Cod News,* Dec. 8, 1937.

Cohasset Narrows on Buzzards Bay: Lee, "Sandwich Glass," 76; Boyden, Map of Sandwich 1831; Keene 43.

Jarvesville School: TM V:17; Amos Binney map 1849; Dr. John Harper reports, Sandwich Archives.

Spring Hill mill: *Yarmouth Register,* Nov. 29, 1838; deed, Aug. 29, 1836, Clark Hoxie to Deming Jarves, et al., Barnstable Registry, Book 16 p. 157.

Manomet Iron Co.: Deyo 340; Keene 128; Waiting's Property May 1857.

H. H. Thayer: Waiting's Property May 1857.

Chipman brothers: Sandwich Vital Records, census records, and property records, William C. Chipman 1822-1900, Isaac K. Chipman 1826-1901.

Mt. Hope Cemetery: Sandwich Historical Commission inventory of markers, earliest 1826; Deyo 301-2.

Old Town Burying Ground: Holway, cited; Irish interrals are Fagan, Swansey, Walsh, Rocks, Quinn, McKenna, & Montague.

St. Peter's Chapel: Bourgoin, "Catholic Church," cited; *Cape Cod Advocate,* Dec. 22, 1855; Deyo 295-7; Freeman II:161-2.

Town Income: TM V:90, 134, 152; Freeman II:153.

Nathaniel Nye: Article, "Nye Homes of Sandwich," by Mrs. E. E. Holway, in booklet, "The Nye Family of America," Second Reunion, Sandwich, 1904, pp. 78-86.

Glassmaking: See chronological display at Sandwich Glass Museum; description in Ruth Webb Lee, cited, and current publication, "The Glass Industry in Sandwich," by Raymond E. Barlow and Joan E. Kaiser, Windham, NH

First Parish Church: Article by C.C.P. Waterman in *Seaside Press,* May 29, 1875; Deyo 293-4; Freeman 150-2; Original books of church records at First Church of Christ in Sandwich, pp. 309-322, on construction of the new building in 1833; *Cape Cod Gazette,* June 17, 1871, on new ground floor.

Town Hall: TM V:55, 80, 86; Article, "Town Hall Surroundings," by William L. Nye, Sandwich Historical Society, 1920, Unpublished.

Universalists: Freeman II: 154; *Sandwich Independent,* May 18, 1927; Deyo 278, 294, 304.

Puritan Church: Freeman II:154; *Sandwich Observer,* Nov 27, 1847; copy of original book of records of the church from 1847, 65 pp. at Sandwich Archives.

"Wren" Church: *Sandwich Observer,* Nov. 18, 1848; correspondence with the Cambridge Historical Commission on career of Isaac Melvin.

Methodist Church: *Sandwich Observer,* Dec. 18, 1847; Deyo 295; *The Independent,* Feb. 15, 1898 and Mar. 14, 1914.

Benjamin Haines: Xerox of letters & notes by Rev. Haines (1798-1888) from 1807 at Sandwich Archives, copied from originals held by Mary Haines Morrow; Methodist Church, Forestdale records.

Joseph Marsh: (1796-1887); autobiography at Sandwich Archives.

Gazetteer: Hayward, cited, pp. 264-5, 348, 401-8.

Public Schools: TM V: 169-173 (1844 report); *Sandwich Observer,* April 8, 1848 (year 1847/8 report), etc.

Freeman's Institute: *Yarmouth Register,* Feb. 6 and July 10, 1845; Hayward's Gazetteer, 1849, p. 265; *Sandwich Independent,* March 30, 1927.

Three Wing Schools: "Catalogue of the Teachers and Students of the Spring Hill Boarding School," Barnstable, 1840 & 1841; "A Quaker School," by John A. Preston, in Cape Cod Magazine, Jan. 1917; *Yarmouth Register,* Mar. 10 and Aug. 4, 1842, Mar. 16, 1843; The OWL, Wing Family of America, pp. 1683-6, Fall, 1927; *The Advocate & Intelligencer,* May 10, 1862; *Sandwich Observer,* April 26, 1851.

Fessenden Tavern: *Yarmouth Register,* Sept. 2, 1841 and May 4, 1866; folder, "History of the Central House of Sandwich," by P. P. Cooney, 1910 Sandwich; *Sandwich Observer,* May 16, 1847 and Sept. 16, 1848.

Newcomb Tavern: *Seaside Press,* May 29, 1875, article by C.C.P. Waterman; "Andrew Newcomb and His Descendants," Comp. by Bethuel M. Newcomb, New Haven, 1923; *Sandwich Observer,* Oct. 5, 1850; *Yarmouth Register,* Dec. 12, 1903

Scorton River Bridge: *Sandwich Observer,* July 8, 1848; *Yarmouth Register,* Dec. 29, *1854; Advocate & Intelligencer,* Apr. 14, 1860; TM VI: 38, 50, 53, 97; Freeman I:653.

Early Newspapers: Freeman I:770-1; *Seaside Press,* Jan. 3, 1874; Deyo 259-263; *Sandwich Observer,* Apr. 24, 1884; *Sandwich Independent,* June 17, 1915.

Barnstable County Records Building Fire: Trayser, "Barnstable," cited, pp. 360-2; Freeman I:627; NEHG Register 4:192 (1850).

Chapter 19: The Railroad

Start of Railroads: Brigham, "Cape Cod & the Old Colony," cited, pp. 205-232; Harlow, "Steelways of New England," cited; "History of the Old Colony Railroad," Hager & Handy, Boston, 1893; Hayward's Gazetteer, cited, pp. 421-434.

Cape Cod Branch Railroad: Freeman I:779-80; Keene 42-3; Deyo 124-8; *Sandwich Observer,* Sept. 26, Oct. 3, Oct. 17, Nov. 14, Dec. 12, Dec. 19, 1846; Jan. 2, 23, 30, Mar. 27, Apr. 3, 17, July 3, 10, Sept. 4, Oct. 21, Dec. 4, 1847; Jan. 1, May 6, 13, 20, 1848; *Yarmouth Register,* Jan. 22, 29, Feb. 5, 12, May 24, Apr. 9, 1846; TM VI:72 (encroachment at Town Neck); Perry, E.G., "A Trip Around Buzzards Bay Shores," cited, pp. 182-3.

Grand Opening: *Sandwich Observer,* May 27, 1848.

Regular Service Opening: *Sandwich Observer,* June 3, 1848.

Subscribers: List of names at Sandwich Historical Society, with analysis by Sandwich Archives.

Effect of the Railroad: Hayward's Gazetteer, cited, p. 265.

Freight Contracts: Notebook at Sandwich Historical Society, pp. 16-18, Boston & Sandwich Glass Co., pp. 19, 59, Express service, p. 8 Cohasset Narrows & North Sandwich.

Keith Spur Track: TM VI:136.

Railroad profits: Freeman II:779-80.

Barnstable County manufacturing: Hayward's Gazetteer, cited, 31, 344, 347-9, 382-8.

The Acorn and Harbor Works: Burbank, "Glass House," ms. cited, pp. 7, 12, 18-19; Lee, "Sandwich Glass," cited, 29-30, etc; Sylvanus Bourne (1797-1861): Lee, "Bourne Genealogy," cited, pp. 68-71; TM VM93; *Yarmouth Register,* June 23, Oct. 6, Nov. 10, 1854.

Old Boardwalk: *Seaside Press,* Dec. 21, 1874; Burbank, "Glass House," ms. cited, p. 7; Sandwich Historical Commission, study & photographs of remains, Sept. 8, 1979 (asset No. 137A).

Chapter 20: Marine Matters

Increase in tonnage: Morison, "Maritime History," cited, pp. 300-1.

Ezra Nye: Kittredge, "Shipmasters," cited, pp. 122-7, 141, 180, etc.

William & Hannah Burgess: Kittredge 160, 172-4; Collection of articles & documents at Sandwich Historical Society.

Benjamin F. Bourne: Dykes, "History," cited, 88-100; Lee, "Genealogy," cited, 164-6; Deyo 345-6.

Jonathan Bourne, Jr.: Lee, "Genealogy," cited, 102-4; Keene 106, 124, 150.

Zenas W. Wright (1815-1894): Deyo 322; *Sandwich Observer,* Mar. 29, 1851.

John J. Harlow (1833-after 1920): Author of a lengthy manuscript about his adventures at sea, typescript at Sandwich Archives.

John Hoxie (1811-1898): *Sandwich Observer,* April 13, Oct. 5, 19, 1850;

Hoxie, L.R., "The Hoxie Family," cited, pp. 78, 138; Harlow stories pp. 18-9.

Abraham Hoxie (1808-1887): Hoxie, L.R., "The Hoxie Family," cited, 44, 87; *Cape Cod Advocate,* May 5, 1860.

Ebenezer F. Nye: Nye, L.B., "Nye Genealogy, " cited, pp. 340, 484.

Sandwich Harbor: Hayward's Gazetteer, cited, p. 265; detailed analysis of Marine Intelligence columns in the *Sandwich Observer* from Sept. 26, 1846 thru June 30, 1849, including all arrivals, departures, cargoes (worksheets at Sandwich Archives.)

Gardiner, Maine: Maine Historical Society Quarterly, V. 13, No. 3 (1974) pp. 148-177.

Ezra B. Freeman: "Freeman Genealogy, " cited, 311; *Yarmouth Register,* Aug. 3, 1860; Aug. 2, 30, Sept. 13, 1861; Sept. 14, 1872.

Seth Burgess & other Bourne captains: Deyo 342-365.

Sandwich Packets: Deyo 110-2; Hassell, Martha, "Deming Jarves and His Ships," in Sandwich Hist. Soc, "The Acorn," Mar. 1985.

Sandwich-built: Deyo 112, 327-8; Alphabetical List of Ship Registration, District of Barnstable, Mass, 1814-1913, National Archives Project, WPA, Boston, 1930 (13 vessels listed as built in Sandwich); Kittredge, "Cape Cod," cited, p. 148; records at Sandwich Archives.

Family Effects: Worksheets of number of families in Sandwich, by surnames, at Sandwich Archives.

Chapter 21: The 1850s Peak

California: Federal Census 1850, typescript of Sandwich persons, at Archives;

The Independent, Nov. 7, 1902, May 30, 1913, Jan. 31, 1902; *Observer,* Nov. 10, 1849, Apr. 13, 1850, Oct. 5, 1850, Jan. 4, 1851, Mar. 15, 1851.

Walling Property Maps: TM VI:235 (1,000 ordered).

Town Reports: TM VI:113 (1850); earliest report at Archives, 1857.

School Districts: TM VI: 45, 177-182, 214, 246.

Town Hall: TM VI: 162, 212, 219, 341, 352, 373.

Street System: TM VI: 16, 88, 102, 134, 142-5, 169, etc.

Sidewalks: TM VI: 323, 349, 363.

Railroad extensions: Deyo 128, 129; booklet, "A History of Railroads in Yarmouth Mass.," by William C. Sokolosky, Cape Cod Community College, West Barnstable, Mass. Feb. 1975; Harlow, "Steelways," cited.

Fire Department: TM VI: 16; *Register,* July 6, 1860; *Observer,* June 16, 1849.

Proposed Division 1860: TM VI: 341, 350-352, 369.

Moving Houses: Files of the Sandwich Historical Commission on houses in Sandwich village.

Boyden Block: *Register:* Oct. 24, 1854.

Gas Supply: *Advocate,* Oct. 20, 1855.

Masonic Lodge: Deyo 300; *Advocate,* Mar. 21, 1863; DeWitt Clinton Lodge pamphlet Mar. 15, 1980.

Old Town Burying Ground: Burbank, "A Bit of Sandwich History," cited.

John W. Jarves: Sandwich Vital Records; Ruth Webb Lee, cited, 40, 146; Barbour 99, 194-6, 219, 235, etc.

Episcopal Church: Freeman II:160-1; Deyo 294; *Independent,* Oct. 16, 1900; St. John's Church Folder June 23, 1974.

Saint Peter's Church: Deyo 295-7; Freeman IM61-2; *Register,* May 15, 1865; Bourgoin, "Catholic Church," cited; *Advocate,* Dec. 22, 1855.

Picnic for the bell: *Register,* Aug. 26, 1859.

Removal of the Chapel: *Cape Cod Advocate,* Dec. 22, 1855.

B&S Buildings: Ruth Webb Lee, 115-136.

Union Bowl: Freeman II:24.

Power Plant: *Register,* Mar. 25, 1859.

New Schoolhouse: School Committee report 1852, Archives files.

Cape Cod Glass Factory: *Register,* Aug. 6, Nov. 12, Dex. 4, 1858, April 8, May 20, May 27, 1859, etc., Oct. 26, 1860; Freeman I:672; C.C.P. Waterman article, "Cape Cod Glass Manufactory," undated (about 1875).

Previous boardwalk: Burbank, "Glass House," p. 7; Sandwich Historical Commission survey & photographs.

Bridge to Town Neck: TM VI: 193; Bertrand French interview, Dec. 2, 1982.

Taxpayers 1855: Sandwich Assessors list of real estate & personal property taxes, Sandwich Archives.

Sandwich Savings Bank: Freeman I:654; *Register,* Sept. 12, 1856; *Independent,* Apr. 20, 1927.

Isaac Keith Co.: Deyo 341; Thesis, William C. Sokolosky, "The Keith Car & Manufacturing Co., An Historical Survey," Cape Cod Community College, 1976.

Railroad Spur: TM VI:136.

Seth F. Nye Records: Three notebooks at Sandwich Historical Society; analysis and index at Sandwich Archives.

Joshua Arcy: Sandwich Vital Records; Seth Nye business records at Sandwich Historical Society; Keene 174-5; *Sandwich Observer,* Oct. 13, 1891.

Sal-N-Pry Carvings: Freeman II:140; Keene 180-1; *Cape Cod Independent,* Mar. 19 & Apr. 25, 1975.

1859 Celebration: *Register,* July 8, 1859.

1860 Celebration: *Register,* July 6, 1860.

Two Phebe Fullers: *Advocate,* May 17, 1860; Phebe Hoxie Allen Hoxie Fuller in Leslie Hoxie Genealogy, cited, p. 40; Sandwich Vital Records.

Temperance: TM VI:76, 83, 108, 227, 452; *Register,* Mar. 17, 1854, Jan. 26, 1855, Aug. 8, 1856, Dec. 4, 1858; *Advocate,* Aug. 28, 1858.

Town Liquor Agency: Town Annual Report 1857.

Shooting Death: *Register,* Jan. 1, 1858.

Know-Nothing Party: Bourgoin, "Catholic Church," cited.

Frederick Freeman career: Freeman Genealogy 204-6; *Sandwich Independent,* Mar. 30, 1927; Deyo 250-1; *Register,* June 19, *1857; Advocate,* May 10, 1862; Davis, "Ancient Landmarks," cited, 102-3, 173; *NEHG Register,* 13:84, 180 (1859); Swift, "History of Cape Cod," 341-2.

J. Wingate Thornton: Freeman II:80, 172; Freeman Genealogy 118; *NEHG Register,* 30:135-6 (1876).

Philip Robinson Diary 1851: Pocket Memorandum Almanac found in the Wing-Blossom house, Sandy Neck Road, Sandwich, typescript at the Sandwich Archives.

Rev. Benjamin Haines letters: Copies at Archives, originals owned by Mary Haines Morrow of Sandwich.

Cedarville Gem: Many originals at Sandwich Archives 1848-1860, all retyped from handwritten pages.

Thoreau Trips: Lunt, cited, 13-14, 28-31, 245-150. Wendell Davis quotation: Mass. Hist. Soc. Coll. VIII: 119-126 (1802); Local references: *Yarmouth Register,* Aug. 3, 1855, Mar. 24, 1865.

Cape Cod Reporting: Hayward Gazetteer 30; *Register,* Sept. 9, 1853; Cape Cod Association of Boston: Freeman I:780; Cape Cod Association of New York: Freeman I:784; Freeman I:744, 748, 760; Central House: *Advocate, Nov.* 24, 1855; Oyster harvest: TM VI:119, 140, 317-18; Freeman II:22-33; *Register,* Dec. 4, 1857; Dwight, "Travels," cited: Cape Cod portions of main text Reprinted in *Yarmouth Register,* Aug. 12, 19, 26, Sept 23, 30, 1852.

Chapter 22: The Civil War Period

Capt. John Pope: *Register,* Feb. 15, Aug. 2, 1861.

Events April/May 1861; Deyo 84-5; TM VI: 382-4; *Register,* Apr. 26, May 3, 10, 17, 31, 1861; *Independent,* May 20, 1925.

Northern vessels: *Register,* June 7, Aug. 30, Sept. 13, 1861.

Raising quotas: TM VI: 387, 391-2, 397, 401-2, 415, etc.; Record book in Town Clerk's vault, "Enrollment of Citizens 18-45, dated Aug. 4, 1862," also Military Book, June 7, 1863.

George L. Haines: *Register,* Aug. 1, 1862; file of letters at Archives copied from originals of Mary Haines Morrow of Sandwich.

Twenty-Ninth Reg't: Deyo 84-5; *Register,* Dec. 20, 1861, Jan. 10, 31, 1862, June 27, 1862, June 3, 1864; *Cape Cod News,* Dec. 20, 1933; Mass. Soldiers & Sailors, cited, III:275-332.

Other veterans: Deyo 90-107, 275; *Register,* Jan. 24, 1862; *Independent,* Feb. 29, 1912; Mass. Soldiers & Sailors, cited, by Regiments.

Major Charles Chipman: Deyo 306; *Register,* Dec. 19, 1862, Aug. 12, 19, 1864, Dec. 27, 1867; Post 132 GAR documents at Sandwich Historical Society.

Lt. Ephraim B. Nye: *Register,* Mar. 31, Apr. 7, 1865, June 26, 1875; *Independent,* Jan. 23, 1914, Apr. 26, 1917.

John J. Ryder: Co. G., 33rd MVI; booklet, "Reminiscences of Three Years Service, etc.", Bourne Archives.

Casualties: TM VII: 10; *Independent,* May 25, 1895; Federal Census, 1890 - list of surviving veterans & widows.

Stillman Ellis: *Independent,* Feb. 9, 16, 1927.

Patrick McGirr: *Register,* Sept. 19, 1862.

Judge Whittemore: Deyo 219-20; diary of 1864 at Sandwich Archives, with analysis; *Register,* May 3, 1867.

Proposed Monument: TM VI:518, 524; TM VII: 156, 176; *Independent,* Mar. 12, 1874.

Town School Board: TM VI:442-8, 455-6, 468-9, 487-9, 501, 526-7, etc.; *Register*, Nov. 13, 1863.

Bay View Cemetery: *Seaside Press,* June 19, 26, July 3, 1875; *Register,* July 24, 1857, May 11, 1866, May 17, 1867.

Saint Peters Cemetery: *Register,* June 16, 1865; Sandwich Historical Commission inventory of markers; Whelan, Harold A., "Catholicism on Cape Cod," Center Rutland, VT 1984, pp. 6-7.

Jarves St. Fire: TM VII: 35-6, 38-41, 66; *Register,* Mar. 5, 1869; *Independent,* Oct. 20, 1926.

Chapter 23: End of the Reservations

Notes: Two reels of microfilms at Mashpee Town Clerk's Office include Parish Records, District Records, and Vital Records. Typescript at Sandwich Archives, identified as "Mashpee Records" below.
Volume, "Atlas of the Boundaries of Town of Sandwich, Barnstable County 1901," issued by the Commissioners of the Harbor and Land Commission (Sheets A-D text, Sheets 1-12, maps), referred to below as Sandwich Bounds.

Gideon Hawley: Dwight, "Travels in New England," cited, III:103-7, 387; Freeman I:692, 697-701; Hutchins 99-100.

Grants to whites: Acts & Resolves of the House of Representatives, Ch. 148 p. 299 (1792/3), Ch. 47 p. 350 (1809), Ch. 87 (1811), Ch. 21 p. 39 (1812); Hutchins 100-1; TM IV:28, 115-6, 193; Freeman II:144.

Petition for Self-Government: Freeman I:589, 690, 701-2, 708; TM IV: 75-6, Acts & Resolves, Ch. 89 p. 486 (1818).

Phincas Fish: Freeman I:695-6, 712; Hutchins 101; Amelia Bingham, "Mashpee," 1970, p. 41-2; *Yarmouth Register,* Feb. 13, 1837; Mashpee Records, 1842-5.

William Apes: Hutchins, cited, 98, 102-4; Freeman I:703-5, 709; Mashpee Memorial: Freeman I:706, 709-10; Woodlot Riot & Fiske Report: Hutchins 105-110; Freeman I:685; Mashpee Papers at Mass. Archives.

Benjamin F. Hallett: Freeman I:706; Hutchins 108-110, 114, 118.

Blind Joe Amos: Hutchins 102; Freeman I:711; Bingham, "Mashpee," pp. 43-5.

Mashpee District Acts & Resolves Ch. 166 (1834), Ch. 14 (1839); Freeman

I:634, 711, 712; "Historical Data Relating to Towns, etc.," cited, P. 43; Bingham, "Mashpee," pp. 46-7.

Sectors alienated: Mashpee TM Records 1834 as to 1705 line; TM VI:130.

Parish status: Freeman I:642, 646, 702, 711; Acts & Resolves (1840); Hutchins 110-111; Mashpee Parish Records.

Nathan Bourne lands: MD 33: 55, 59, 60 (1935); Deed Sept. 19, 1816 from Mashpee Commissioners, copy & typescript at Archives.

Border changes: "Sandwich Bounds," Sheets A, B, D and 6-12; TM VI: 130;

Waquoit & Ashumet: Freeman I:642; Acts & Resolves Ch. 102 (1841).
Wakeby/Mashpee Pond area: Acts & Resolves Ch. 150 (1859); TM VI: 318; TM VII: 301-3.
Fish Purchase: TM VI: 177.
Collins site: Acts & Resolves Ch. 67 (1860), Ch. 109 (1872).
1887 changes: Acts & Resolved May 27 (1887).
1901 bounds: TM VIII: 99-100, 270-1, 415-7, 472-3.
1905 change: Acts & Resolves Ch. 306 (1905); TM IX:77-8.
1916 change: Acts & Resolves Ch. 266 (1916).

Land Grants 1842: Freeman I:645, 713; Acts & Resolves, Ch. 72 (1842).

Earle Report: "Indians of the Commonwealth," by John Milton Earle, Boston, 1861 (copy at Archives), Mashpee pp. 46-67, and xx-xxxvii.

Land Sales: *Yarmouth Register,* Dec. 2, 1871; Bounds: TM VII:81-2, 301-3; Acts & Resolves June 18 (1885).

Town Incorporation: Acts & Resolves Ch. 293 p. 213 (1870); TM VII:30; Census: Hutchins, Table 142.

Solomon Attaquin: Hutchins 115-120, 126-131; Bingham, "Mashpee," p. 16.

Eben Quippish: Hutchins 137-8, 187.

Watson Hammond: *Independent,* Dec. 21, 1916; Bingham, "Mashpee," p. 22.

Herring Pond: Census: Freeman I:584.

Map: presented to Bourne Historical Society 1942, by Channing Howard of Whitman & Howard Co.

Meetinghouses: Deyo 333; Keene 42, 213-4.

Land sales: Acts & Resolves Ch. 463 p. 780 (1869); *Sandwich Observer,* Feb. 13, 1847, Mar. 24, 1849; *Cape Cod Gazette,* Sept. 26, 1872, *Seaside Press,* Nov. 15, 1873; *Observer,* June 5, 1894; *Bourne Courier,* Jan. 13, 1982.

Solomon Webquish: "Reminiscenses of Ellisville," Ernest C. Ellis,

Plymouth, 1973, p. 35-6; *Seaside Press,* May 29, 1875.

Thoreau: Lunt edition 248-9.

Earle Report: cited above, 67-71 and xxxviii-xli.

Interviews with Mr. Warner Eldredge of Sagamore, Oct. 18, 1982 and June 10, 1983.

Chapter 24: Almshouse

Establishment: TM IV: 142, 152, 179, 193, 198, 203, 208.

Extensions: TM V:23, 43, 64; TM VI:29, 162, 539.

Murphy house 1878: *Seaside Press,* April 6, 1878.

Tramps: TM VII: 174; *Seaside Press,* Feb. 22, Oct. 7, 1876.

Chipman lot: TM V:23.

Operation of the house: TM VI:8, 23, 59, 83, 162, 539, etc.

Mrs. Lawrence: TM VI:8-9, 59.

Charles Street: Named for Charles W. Lapham, a long-time resident.

Christopher's Hollow: Sandwich Historical Commission, Inventory of Sites, No. 372. Named for Christopher Holder, English Quaker.

Upper Road: Shown on Walling's Map of 1857 & early Quadrangle maps.

Lucy Thompson: Sandwich Vital Records; Federal Census 1850, 1860, 1880; Wallings Map 1857.

By-pass Road: Shown on Boyden Map 1831, privately built by B&S Glass Co.

Cemetery: TM V:158-9; TM VI:7; TM VIII:214.

Budget for the Poor: TM V:119, 152, 158, 166, etc; TM VI: 10, 23, 59, 89, 247, 311, 411, 539; TM VII: 398, 423.

Wayland Tramps: "The Puritan Village Evolves," H.F. Emery, Canaan, NH, 1981, pp. 178-180.

Jonathan Bourne, Jr.: TM VII:399; Deyo 330; Lee, "Bourne Genealogy," pp. 103-4; *Yarmouth Register,* June 10, 1852, Mar. 29, 1861.

Rev. Nathan H. Chamberlain (1828-1901):

1889 oration: Pratt, Ambrose, "250th," cited, pp. 21-88.

Almshouse design: A.F. Poole, Sandwich Village Map 1884.

"Autobiography of a New England Farmhouse," Boston, 1888 (copy at Cape Cod Community College.)

Artemus Chamberlain: TM V:153; *Yarmouth Register,* Apr. 6, 1843.

Heman Dillingham (1817-1889):

Tupper Genealogy p. 46-7 (Benjamin & Polly).

Almshouse occupant 1845-1889: Town & Federal Census.

Letter, June 4, 1824: From town of Fairfield, Maine to Sandwich Selcectmen on destitute Dillingham family, original at Historical Society.

"A Pauper Emeritus," *Boston Evening Transcript,* Nov. 29, 1889; *Sandwich Observer,* Dec. 10, 1889.

Spring Hill Cemetery: TM VIII: 28; Sandwich Historical Commission, Census of Markers.

Town Aid: *Yarmouth Register,* Mar. 1, 1838, Jan. 13, 1842; Booklet, "Pauper Account," 1876-1883, by Town Clerk, HGO Ellis.

Nancy Eldridge: Sandwich Vital Records (1804-1879); *Independent,* Apr. 20, 1927; Burbank, "Old Houses," cited, pp. 3-4.

Damey Tupper: Sandwich Vital Records (Diadama 1783-1856); Burbank, "Old Houses," cited, pp. 9-10.

Bill Freeman: Keene, cited, pp. 182-3; *Sandwich Observer,* Jan. 3, 1888.

Whittler: *Observer,* July 24, 1847; examples at Sandwich Historical Society; Notes at Archives by Benjamin S. Harrison.

Selectmen correspondence on paupers in other towns: Many originals at Sandwich Archives.

1890 status: TM VIII:27, 28, 32-4; *Observer,* Apr. 15, Aug. 19, Sept. 9, 1890.

1897 report: An original report at Sandwich Archives, Nov. 16, by Charles E. Woodbury, Inspector of Institutions.

1901 closing: TM VIII: 429; TM IX: 78.

1911 fire & sale 1912: TM X:222, 307, 373; *Independent,* Sept. 7, 1911.

Henry A. Belcher & David Crowell: Detailed article by Carolyn Crowell, appearing in the *Village Broadsider,* June 6, 1979.

Chapter 25: The Town Divides

1732 Scusset protests: Deyo 327; Chapter 9 Notes, Fessenden ministry.

1770 Second Parish Pocasset: Deyo 327; Chapters 12 & 13, Pocasset Notes.

1797 Windsor plan: Deyo 327; Keene 124, Chapter 16, Windsor Notes.

1860 Proposed division: Deyo 329; TM VI: 341, 350-2, 369; Keene 324.

1873 Pocasset plan: Deyo 329; Petition of John A. Beckerman, Dec. 2, 1872, copy at Archives; *Yarmouth Register,* Dec. 7, 1872.

1883 petition: Deyo 329; petition of William A. Nye Oct. 29, 1883 (copy at Archives.)

Background & Statistics: *The Acorn,* (Sandwich Historical Society), Feb. 1974, article, "The Division of Sandwich to Form Bourne," by R. A. Lovell, Jr.

Sandwich plans: Broadside, "Reasons Why Sandwich Should Not Be Divided, etc." original at Sandwich Historical Society; TM VII: 333-4; Petition of remonstrance by Frederick S. Pope, Jan. 17, 1884 & of Ebenezer Nye, Feb. 2, 1884 (copies at Archives).

The Hearings: "Division of the Town of Sandwich, Arguments by Mr. George A. King, etc.", Boston, 1884.

The Carriage Tours: *Independent,* May 6, 1910, article by David D. Nye.

Sandwich Town Meeting Apr. 12: TM VII: 340.

Bourne Town Meeting Apr. 12 & Apr. 23: Ezra G. Perry, "Buzzards Bay, Mass," cited, pp. 172-179; Deyo 329-331; TM VII:341, 355, etc.

Town Boundaries: TM VII: 354-5; Mass. Gen'l Law 1884, Ch. 127, p. 105-9.

Bourne voters, fisheries, etc.: Opinion, Attorney Darwin E. Ware, Boston, Sept. 22, 1885, 10 pages, original at Sandwich Archives; Keene 124-7; Town of Bourne 1884 Report.

Cape Cod Ship Canal Co.: Farson, cited, 18-21; Reid, cited, 12-14; *Yarmouth Register,* Mar. 6, 1875.

The Italian Laborers Incident: Farson, cited, 21-2; Reid, cited, 14; *Independent,* Apr. 27, 1927; Town Reports 1880//1, 83/4

Whitney Associates: Farson, cited, 21-3; Reid, cited, 15-16; TM VII:259; *Register,* May 20, 1886.

Lockwood arrangement: Farson, cited, 23-5; Reid, cited, 16-18; TM VII: 319, 339: *Observer,* Mar. 17, 1885.

Relief Map: "Map of the Route of the Proposed Cape Cod Ship Canal, U.S. Coastal Survey," A. D. Bache, Supt., 1860, Register No. 1530.

"Lake Lockwood": Notes by Mr. Warner Eldredge of Sagamore, Oct. 15, 1892 & May 5, 1983; Reid, cited, 18; Farson, cited, 24, 39; *Observer,* Mar. 17, 1885.

Chapter 26: The End of Glassmaking

B&S after Jarves: Lee, cited, 551-5; *Observer,* May 17, 1887; *Seaside Press,* May 13 & June 10, 1876; Barlow-Kaiser, "Glass Industry," Vol. 4, cited, pp. 1-11; Record book of glass production by each gaffer, June-Dec. 1887, presented to Archives by Clarence Haines of Sandwich.

Henry F. Spurr: Barlow-Kaiser, cited, 23-30; *Observer,* Apr. 21, 1885.

The Last Strike: *Observer,* Dec. 10, 1887; Barlow-Kaiser, cited, pp. 11-17; TM VII:418-9, 457; Barbour, cited, pp. 280-305.

Closing the B&S: Barlow-Kaiser, cited, 17-20; *Antiques,* Dec. 1941, "The Closing of the Boston & Sandwich Glass Factory," by Mabel M. Swan, pp. 372-4; Lee, cited, 556-564.

Electrical Glass Corp.: Barlow-Kaiser, cited, 73-6.

George B. Jones: Barlow-Kaiser, cited, 76.

Albert V. Johnston: Barlow-Kaiser, cited, 76-83.

The Roundhouse destroyed: *Independent,* Jan. 7, 1896.

George T. McLaughlin: Barlow-Kaiser, cited, 83-5.

Sandwich Glass Co.: Barlow-Kaiser, cited, 85-7.

Alton Mfg. Co.: Barlow-Kaiser, cited, 87-9.

Robert A. Hammond: Barlow-Kaiser, cited, 89-91; TM X:352, 443, 447.

Co-operative Glass Co.: Jon & Jacqueline Wetz, "The Co-Operative Glass Co., Sandwich, Mass. 1888-1891," Sandwich, 1976; Barlow-Kaiser, cited, 323-335.

Cape Cod Glass Co.: B&S Director's Meeting Minutes, Aug. 30, 1858, on old boardwalk use by Jarves; *Register,* Nov. 12, Dec. 4, 1858, Feb. 4, Apr. 8, May 20, May 27, July 1, Sept. 23, 1859, Oct. 26, 1860; Barlow-Kaiser, cited, 123-5; Whittemore Diary, Mar. 31, 1864; *Seaside Press,* Nov. 22, 1873; Freeman I:672; Article, "Cape Cod Glass Manufactory," by C. C. P. Waterman, undated (after 1875).

William H. Schleuter: Barlow-Kaiser, cited, 125-6.

Swann, Chipman & Co.: Barlow-Kaiser, cited, 126.

Charles P. W. Spurr: Barlow-Kaiser, cited, 31-4, 126-133.

Vasa Murrhina Art Glass: Barlow-Kaiser, cited, 127, 135-8.

Cape Cod Glass Co. II: Barlow-Kiaser, cited, 128-131.

Reopening Veneer Works: Barlow-Kaiser, cited, 132-3.

Shawme Press 1913: Interview with Benjamin S. Harrison, Feb. 9, 1979.

Elberfeld Chemical & Mfg. Co. 1915: Stock Certificates at Archives, showing Treasurer Sanford E. Morse.

Salisbury Mfg. Co.: *Independent,* Sept. 19, 1923.

Buildings dismantled: Barlow-Kaiser, cited, 133.

Edward J. Swann: Barlow-Kaiser, cited, 241-245.

John B. Vodon: Barlow-Kaiser, cited, 175-182.

Nehemiah Packwood Sr. & Jr.: Barlow-Kaiser, cited, 151-160.

Chapter 27: A Look Back

Railroad Peak

Woods Hole 1872: *The Caper,* Hyannis, June 2, 1977, pp. 12-13; *Independent,* Sept. 19, 1918.

Provincetown 1873: "A Gazetteer etc,", Nason, cited, p. 423.

Onset Beach: *Yarmouth Register,* May 1885.

Chatham 1887: *Cape Cod Times,* Mar. 29, 1987.

NY, NH & H: *Boston Sunday Globe,* Mar. 7, 1943; "The Trains We Rode," by Lucius Beebe & Charles Clegg, Berkeley, Cal. 1965, pp. 297-329; Booklet "Quaint Cape Cod and the Summer Delights," NY, NH & H, Old Colony Division, Boston, 1895.

Population: Gazeteers: Hayward (1849) and Nason (1874, 1890) cited: Federal Census with analysis at Archives; Brigham, "Cape Cod," cited, 235-240; *Seaside Press,* Mar. 6, 1875.

Rail & Trolley Items

Roundhouse: *Seaside Press,* April 7, 1877.

Sandwich Stations: *Seaside Press,* July 31, 1875, Aug. 3, Aug. 21, Sept. 14, 1878.

East Sandwich: Sandwich Historical Commission Inventory, Asset No. 377. Bridge - Old County Rd. 1889: TM VII:457, 471; TM VIII:97.

Chase Road 1889: TM VII:426, 457; TM VIII:28.

Cohasset Narrows: *Yarmouth Register,* Sept. 10, 1869; *Independent,* Dec. 28, 1900; Keene, cited, 156-7.

Plymouth/Bourne Rail Line: *Observer,* Sept. 21, 1891.

Buzzards Bay/Sandwich Trolley: *Independent,* July 11, Oct. 17, Oct. 24, Oct. 31, 1902, etc.

Plymouth/Sandwich Trolley: *Observer, Nov.* 7, 1899; *Independent,* Sept. 26, 1904.

New Bedford/Monument Beach Trolley: *Independent,* June 27, Aug. 1, 1902.

Keith Car Co.: Deyo, cited, 341; William Sokolosky papers, "Keith Car & Mfg. Co., 1826-1910," Williams College, June 1978 and Cape Cod Community College, June 1976; *Bourne Courier,* Sept. 7, 14, 1977; extensive files and photographs at Archives.

Town Roads: Town Beach, TM VII:155; Mill Creek Crossing, TM VII:333; Lower Millpond Crossing, TM VII:317; Brady's Island, TM VIII:386; State Highway 1894, TM VIII:172, 275, 294, 387; Snowplow, TM VIII: 124.

New Boardwalk: TM VII: 161, 317, 333; opened July 3, 1875 per *Seaside Press.*

Sandwich Savings Bank: TM VII: 30; Broadside 1865, at Sandwich Hist. Soc.; Freeman I:654; *Register,* Sept. 12, 1856; *Seaside Press,* Sept. 8, 1877.

Sandwich Co-operative Bank: *Observer,* Dec. 22, 1885; *Independent,* Dec. 22, 1926.

Boston & Sandwich Boot & Shoe Co.: *Seaside Press,* Sept. 15, 1877.

Armstrong Braiding Co.: *Independent,* Sept. 30, 1931.

Sandwich Card & Tag Co.: *Seaside Press,* Feb. 8, 1879; paper, "Old Houses," W. L. Nye, at Sandwich Historical Society.

Samuel Wing factory: TM IV: 105. 106; *Observer,* May 17, 1851.

Sandwich Tack Co.: Original Record Book 1861-4, at Archives; display panel of products at Sandwich Historical Society.

Union Braiding Co.: TM VIII: 121; *Independent,* Mar. 5, 1904.

Fish weirs: TM VII:436, 473, etc.

Cranberries: TM VIII: 3-5; documents of I. T. Jones, Secretary of Cape Cod Growers' Assoc. 1886-1893, at Archives; booklet, "The Cranberry Industry in Mass.," Dept. of Agriculture Bulletin 201, June 1968; Freeman I:663.

Town Hall: TM VII:78, 197, 259, 363, 399, 404, etc.

Library: TM VIII:60, 63, 89, 182, 214, 382; *Independent,* Oct. 13, 1895; booklet, "History of the Free Public Library," by Eva H. Clark, Sandwich, 1911.

Fire Dept.: TM VII:35-6, 38-41, 66, 157, 260, 308, 478; TM VIII:89, 98, 385; *Observer,* June 16, 1849; *Register,* Apr. 29, 1870, Feb. 11, 1871; *Independent,* Dec. 6, 1912.

Street Lights: TM VII: 293, 300; *Seaside Press,* Oct. 31, Nov. 21, 1874, etc.

Platfrom scale: Seth F. Nye business records to 1856 at Sandwich Historical Soc; TM VII: 399, 404 (1887).

Town Water Works: TM VII:417 (1888); *Observer,* Dec. 20, 1887.

Town By-laws: TM VIII:252-262; Judge Whittemore case record 1862-1892, at Archives, pp. 24, 151, 162, etc.

School buildings: TM VII:74, 78, 127, 199, 210, 220, 243, 295, 482.

Jarvesville: TM VII:309, 318, 323; TM VIII:120, 150, etc.

New Academy: Deyo 299; School paper, *Academy Breezes,* from 1884, originals at Sandwich Historical Soc; newspaper, *The Weekly Review,* Feb. 18, 1882; paper, "Sandwich Academy," by W. L. Nye, 1921, at Sandwich Historical Soc; *Observer,* Apr. 24, 1884 and Feb. 15, 1886.

Unitarian Church: Deyo 294; paper, "Sketch of the First Church, Sandwich, Mass. 1638-1925," by W. L. Nye, Sandwich Historical Soc.

Clocks 1871-80: *Independent,* Aug. 24, 1927; *Register,* June 17, July 22, 1871; *Seaside Press,* Nov. 15, 22, 29, 1873, Mar. 21, 1876, Oct. 25, 1877, Dec. 16, 1879, Apr. 1880.

Seaside Press booklet; Sandwich, March 1874, original at Sandwich Historical Soc; Whittemore Diary, Feb. 14, 1874.

Anniversary 1888; *Observer,* Sept. 22, 1888.

Centennial Events: Burbank, "A Bit of Sandwich History," cited, 19-222 *Seaside Press,* July 1-8, 1876.

Centennial Box: TM VII: 179-80; *Seaside Press,* July 15, 1876, Mar. 10, 1877; original box & contents at Sandwich Archives.

The Casino: *Observer,* May 15, 22, 29, June 5, 12, July 3, 10, 17, 24, 31, Aug. 14, 1884, June 27, 1893.

Town 250th: Pratt, "250th Celebration," cited; TM VII: 394, 425, 457; TM VIII:25; Broadside, Aug. 30, 1889, at Sandwich Historical Soc; Invitation Program Folder at Archives; *Boston Sunday Herald,* Sept. 1, 1889.

Storms 1896: *Independent,* Jan. 7, 1896; *Yankee,* Aug. 1967. "The Vineyard Waterspout," by David M. Ludlum, (Aug. 19, 1896).

Storm 1898: Burbank, "Highlights," cited, 29; Letter from Benjamin Haines, Jr. to Ambrose Pratt, Nov. 30, 1898, at Archives; *Observer,* Nov. 21, 1899; *Independent,* Nov. 29, Dec. 6, 13, 20, 1898, Feb. 6, 1900.

Notable People: The descent of all Sandwich persons listed is known from the founding of the town, and their careers may be studied in the family files at the Archives; Diary of Georgianna V. H. Freeman for 1888 at Archives; also much on these persons in the Sandwich Historical Society collections.

The Good Old Days 1870-1900: Files at Sandwich Archives of newspaper clippings and typescripts of town news and related subject files.

Women's Suffrage: TM VII:278; TM VIII: 120, 201, etc.

Isaiah T. Wright: "And This is Cape Cod," by Eleanor Early, Boston 1936, p. 27; *Register,* Jan. 16, 1863; Swift, "Cape Cod," cited, p. 279.

Lightning Strike: Note in Centennial Box, with a bag of fragments from the fire.

President Grant: *Seaside Press,* Aug. 29, 1874.

Professor Robinson: Burbank, "A Bit of Sandwich History," cited, 23; *Seaside Press,* April 11, 1878.

Telephone line in Sandwich: TM VIII:227 (1896).

Charles F. Freeman: *Seaside Press,* June 26, 1875; TM VII:269, 293, 309.

"Cape Cod Folks": Article, "First Fiction Libel Suit," by Helen J. Estes, *Yankee,* Oct. 1971; Goodwin, "Pilgrim Republic," cited, 290; *New York Times,* Feb. 15, 1884, "Verdict for Cradlebow"; *Boston Sunday Globe,* Dec. 6, 1953; index of names in first edition 1881, by Sandwich Archives and analysis of Sandwich & Plymouth families involved (Swift, Fish, Ellis, Norris, Nightingale, etc.).

Chapter 28: Belmont's Canal

Sandwich/Bourne line: Boundary stones 4, 5 & 6, Atlas of the Town of Sandwich, Barnstable Co., Commissioners of Mass. Harbor & Land Commission, 1901.

August Belmont Jr: Black, David, "The King of Fifth Avenue, The Fortunes of August Belmont," New York 1981, pp. 95, 186 etc., on the life and career of August, Jr.

Perry Descent: Rev. Calbraith B. Perry, "The Perrys of Rhode Island and Tales of Silver Creek," New York, 1913.

Canal Company: Reid, "The Building of the Cape Cod Canal," cited, pp. 19-30; Farson, "The Cape Cod Canal," cited, pp. 31-34.

Contractors & Engineers: Reid 30-32, 34; Farson 30-35; *Cape Cod News,* May 18, 1938; *Columbia Engineering Quarterly,* May 1954, pp. 18-20 (Durham).

Legally proven start: Photo at Sandwich Historical Society; Keith gravel spur, TM VI: 136; Reid 33; Farson 34-5.

Breakwater: Reid 33, 34, 37; Farson 35, 36, 38, 40, 41, 44, 46, plates 32-35; *Independent,* Mar. 19, July 30, Sept. 24, Nov. 12, Dec. 3, 1909, May 20, June 3, 10, 1910, etc., Nov. 1913.

Scusset Dredging: Reid 35-39; Farson 36-40, 42, 43, plate 29; *Independent,* Apr. 15, 1910.

Buzzards Bay Dredging: Reid 37-39; Farson 40-46; *Independent,* Aug. 17, 1911.

New dredges: Reid 40; Farson 43, 45-48; *Independent,* Aug. 3, 1911.

Dry digging: Reid 39, 41-2; Farson 43, 46, 47, plates 63-7.

Rail Line Changes: Reid 38, 40, 43; Farson 40, 44, plates 44-46; *Independent,* Oct. 19, 1911.

Bourne Bridge: Reid 38, 42; Farson 40-41, plates 53, 54.

Sagamore Bridge: Reid 40, 41; Farson 41, plates 51, 52.

Bournedale Crossing: Reid 46; Farson 40, plate 89; *Falmouth Enterprise,* June 15, 1984; *Independent,* July 24, 31, Aug. 14, 28, 1914, May 14, 1915.

Foley's Dike: Reid 42; Farson 47, plates 74-77;

Tidal effects: analysis by Sandwich Archives based on published tide schedules.

Opening Scene: Reid 48-56; Farson 49-51, plates 78-86; Belmont, Eleanor Robson, "The Fabric of Memory," New York, 1957, pp. 121-126; *Independent,* July 31, 1914; TM X:490.

Pageant: *Cape Cod Independent,* Summer 1980, p. 14; Farson, plate 90; Booklet by William Chauncy Langdon, 1914, copy at Archives; Letter from Wm. C, Langdon to August Belmont, Aug. 25, 1914, copy at Archives.

Operating Problems: Reid 56-62; Farson 51-56.

Town Dock on Canal: TM X:352, 425, 443, 447, (1914); TM XI:101, 130, 347; *Independent,* Aug. 24, 1916, Mar. 22, 1917.

Expected new industry: Wendell Davis in Mass. Hist. Soc. Collections VIII: 119-126 (1802); Booklet, 1910, by Cape Cod Construction Co., at Archives, "The Cape Cod Canal;" *Washington Star,* Aug. 6, 1911; Reed Carradine, "The Cape Cod Canal," in VanNorden Magazine, 1909, pp. 113-128; Parson's address, May 25, 1910, "Cape Cod Canal," New York, 1910.

Plymouth Trolley: Ellis, E.C., "Reminescences of Ellisville," Plymouth, 1973, pp. 42-3; *Independent,* Aug. 3, 1917, Aug. 4, 1920; Notes on the trolley and the former right of way, from talks with Warner Eldredge, Oct. 15, 1982, May 23, and June 10, 1983; Trolley timetable 1917, at Archives.

Government operation: Reid 63-83; Farson 56-58.

Negotiations for sale: Reid 84-103; Farson 55-64; *Independent,* Dec. 22, 1926, Feb. 29, Mar. 21, Apr. 4, 1928.

Chapter 29: The New Century

Frederick Tudor: Notes on discussion with Mrs. Hope Ingersol Apr. 20, 1979; Perry, E.G., "Around Buzzards Bay Shores," cited; Keene, cited, 145; Mass. license plate No. 1, at Sandwich Hist. Soc.

Joseph Jefferson: *Register,* Apr. 29, 1905; Bay View Cemetery, Sandwich Inventory of Markers; *Munsey's Magazine,* June 1906; *Independent,* Jan. 5, 1891, Oct. 31, 1893, Oct. 13, 1895; memorabilia at Sandwich Hist. Society.

Grover Cleveland: Allan Nevins, "Grover Cleveland, A Study in Courage," New York, 1933, esp. pp. 451-9, 739-42; Cleveland, G., "Fishing and Shooting Sketches," New York, 1906; Lynch, Denis T., "Grover Cleveland, A Man Four-Square," New York, 1932; *Cape Cod Independent,* Dec. 19, 1973; *Cape Cod Magazine,* June 1915; memorabilia at Bourne Historical Society.

F. Edwin Elwell: *Boston Gazette,* Sept. 6, 1885; *Observer,* Sept. 23, 1890, Dec. 8, 1891, Mar. 8, 1892; Dict. of American Biography, New York, 1959, III:120-22; *Independent,* May 30. 1901, Oct. 14, 1910.

Dr. Walter Wesselhoeft: Typescript, "The Wesselhoeft Family," by Walter Hoffman, Cambridge, 1969, 77pp.; family file, at Archives.

Shawme Road accepted: TM VIII:249 (1897), TM IX: 150 (1907).

John H. Foster: Sandwich Vital Records; notes on interviews with relatives, Lombard Jones, Martha Blake, William E. Foster; programs of Dancing Schools from Martha Foster McEachern.

Dodge Macknight: Fitzgerald, Desmond, "Dodge Macknight, Water Color Painter," Brookline, 1917; "Fenway Court," publication of the Isabella Stewart Gardner Museum, Boston, 1982, pp. 36-47; Display at Heritage Plantation of Sandwich, Nov. 15-Dec. 21, 1980, with catalogue and lectures by Lombard C. Jones and Russell A. Lovell, Jr.

Ezra G. Perry: "Buzzards Bay Shores," cited, new edition by Bourne Hist. Society, Taunton, 1976; "All Around Cape Cod Shores," cited, Bourne 6-10, 110-158, Sandwich 10-14; *Cape Cod Times,* May 11, 1980, article by Peter Hartley on marketing Cape Cod.

Falmouth Taxes: Deyo, cited, 153; Cape Cod's attraction to tourists and investors, Deyo 152-156.

Wing Family of America: TM VIII:476-480 (1902); The OWL, June 1924, p. 2392, on the 1902 reunion; current newspaper coverage at Archives.

Old Home Week: TM VIII:475-476, TM IX: 7, 8, 41; original program folders at Archives.

Nye Family of America: TM IX: 110, 145, TM XI: 335; *Independent,* Feb. 6, 1903, and subsequent coverage of the 1903 event at Archives.

Tupper Family Association: *Cape Cod Magazine,* Aug., Oct. 1916; *Independent,* Aug. 10, 1916; statement of organization of the Association, Dec. 3, 1915, 9 Ashburton Place, Boston.

Sandwich Historical Society: Charter, July 3, 1907, by Secretary of the Commonwealth; Ashley, "The Sandwich Historical Society," cited; articles by early members of the Society, with copies at the Archives.

B&S plant area: Dated series of photographs at Sandwich Historical Society; files of Sandwich Historical Commission, including Sanborn Insurance maps of the B&S area 1915 & 1931.

Canal area plants: Files of Sandwich Historical Commission on the Fish Freezer and Marina area.

Grove Street plants: TM VIII:121, 419, 430, TM X:71; files at Archives and Historical Commission, with photographs and clippings.

Town events 1900-1950: see detailed subject and chronological files at Archives office, and property files of Sandwich Historical Commission.

Chapter 30: Glass Becomes Collectible

First exhibit of Historical Society: *Independent,* Aug. 16, 1912.

Centennial Exhibit: *New Bedford Times,* July 25, 1925; *Boston Transcript,* August 1925, copy at Sandwich Historical Society.

1931 Exhibit: *Independent,* July 15, 1931 through Sept. 2, 1931.

Ruth Webb Lee: "Early American Pressed Glass," and "Sandwich Glass," both cited.

James W. Freeman: Chart, p. 521.

Glass Writings: scrapbook of early articles, at Sandwich Hist. Soc.

Dorothea Setzer: booklet, "The Sandwich Historical Society and Its Glass," Sandwich, 1951.

Life Magazine: Aug. 28, 1944, "The Triumph of the Puritan Spirit."

Harriot Buxton Barbour: "Sandwich, the Town That Glass Built," cited.

Fred Bunker: Notes on interview with Minnie Bunker Wimmer, Apr. 3, 1984.

Everard Stowell Pratt: Chart, p. 521; Ambrose Pratt diaries, ms, cited.

Paul Ashley: "The Sandwich Historical Society," cited; "The Acorn," the Society's publication, Mar. 1965-Dec. 1968.

Francis "Bill" Wynn: *Boston Evening Transcript,* Mar. 8, 1941.

Brick store: Photographs of 1920's from the Hamlin owners, and discussions with Mrs. Anna Caron, the last owner.

Bangs Burgess: "The Acorn," Nov. 1978; *Independent,* Aug. 30, 1922, Jan. 2, Apr. 30, 1924.

Frederick T. Irwin: "Story of Sandwich Glass & Glassware," cited.

William F. Kern: *Boston Evening Transcipt,* Sept. 27, 1924.

Lavinia Donovan Walsh: *Cape Cod Magazine,* June 15, 1927; other writings on Sandwich at Historical Society.

Frank W. Chapman: Sandwich Vital Records; "The Romance of Old Sandwich Glass," cited.

National Early American Glass Club: Extensive references at Sandwich Historical Society.

Town Glass Memorial: TM XIII:233.

Glassware Institute project: TM XIII:294.

Chapter 31: Using the Land

Coonamesset Ranch: TM XII:215; Information from Bourne Historical Commission, Oct. 2, 1978; Allison Blake in *Cape Cod Times* - Summer Preview-1985.

Percival Hall Lombard: TM XI:164, 237; TM XII:215, 255; Letter from Bourne Historical Commission, Oct. 4, 1978; references at Bourne Hist. Soc. & Sandwich Hist. Soc.

State Forests: TM X:123, 127, 171, 352; TM XI:405; *Yarmouth Register,* Sept. 7, 1927.

Forest Fire: *Independent,* May 30, June 13, 1923; State Report 120, "Preventing Forest Fires in Certain Towns," Nov. 22, 1926.

Lincoln Crowell: *Boston Globe,* Apr. 5, Apr. 24, 1938.

Shawme-Crowell State Forest: *Independent,* Jan. 11, 1922, Feb. 13, 1924; Barnstable County Registry Plan Book 58, page 135 (1938).

National Guard Camp: TM XI:410, 418; TM XII:274 (against) 327 (for); *Cape Cod News,* Jan. 31, Feb. 7, June 20, 1934, Apr. 17, 24, Aug. 14, Oct. 9, 1935, Feb. 19, June 17, 1936; *Boston Traveler,* Apr. 12, 1934; *Boston Herald,* Feb. 15, 1935.

Camp Edwards: *Cape Cod News,* Feb. 9, May 4, July 20, 1938; *Boston Post,* Jan. 10, 1939.

Federal Enlargement: Typescript, "Camp Edwards is Completed," by Fred E. Blake, Capt. QMC, early 1941.

Otis Air Force Base: Letter from Bourne Historical Commission, Oct. 4, 1978; Booklet, "Welcome to Otis AFB," Summer 1957, Tribune Publ. Co. of Boston; *Boston Post,* Apr. 1, 1946.

Samuel D. Hannah: Connolly, Stephen, edit., "The Proprietary Lands of Plymouth Colony & Cape Cod, by Samuel D. Hannah 1867-1945 - Research and Writings," Hyannis, 1980, pp. 11-22.

Homestead Trust: Agreement and Declaration of Trust dated Dec. 15, 1904, recorded with Barnstable County, Mass., Registry of Deeds, Book 267, page 413.

Farm Village: *Yarmouth Register,* Apr. 8, 15, 22, 1905; map at Archives.

Pamet Tract: *Provincetown Advocate,* Mar. 5, 1925; Plan of land in Truro, by Arthur L. Sparrow, August 1917, No. 11032A, sheet 1; *The Cape Codder,* Orleans, Nov. 1, 1956.

Akagi book: "The Town Proprietors, etc." cited.

Hannah land title studies: *Yarmouth Register,* May 5, 1928; Library of Cape Cod History and Genealogy, No. 6, 7, 8, Register Press, 1927.

Sandwich Downs: Map by Allan Beale, May 1926, filed with Barnstable Co. Deeds, Plan Book 19, page 125.

Reviving old proprietorships: Connolly, cited above, 22-28; *Cape Cod Times,* Feb. 17, 1981.

Edward Wing House: Sandwich Historical Commission Inventory No. 29.

Poll Tax, Bourne: Connolly, cited above, pp. 28-9.

Hannah Papers: Sturgis Library from January 1981, gift of Mrs. Curtin's heirs; parts quoted in Connolly, cited above; parts copied by Sandwich Archives, with notes on meetings with Mrs. Curtin in 1979.

Town Neck: See Chapter 7 (page 108) and source notes; letter June 4, 1925 from George Burbank to Mrs. Richard S. Bourne of Brooklyn, original at Archives; Keene, cited, 20; Proprietors of Town Neck Meeting records from 1690 example, May 6, 1925 and Mar. 7, 1928.

Developing Town Neck: *Seaside Press,* June 13, 1874; TM VII: 155; TM IX:48, 49; TM XI: 271, 287.

Town Neck Land Company: *Seaside Press,* Apr. 24, 1875; *Observer,* Jan 24, 1888.

Dr. Jones' gift: TM X:47, 69, 128.

Beach taking: TMX:71, 131, 171; TM XI:391.

Road to harbor: TM X:299.

Town Votes: TM XI: 271 (1919), 287 (1920).

Land Court 1920: *Independent,* Aug. 25, 1920; Court Record No. 19252, copy at Archives.

Tudor Petition 1923: Court Record No. 20458, copy at Archives.

Plan of Partition: Dec. 24, 1931, by Allan Beale, No. 9003.F, print at Archives.

Hearing, Feb. 1932: *Independent,* Nov. 11, 1931, Feb. 24, 1932.

The Ipswich Case: *Independent,* Sept. 18, 1914.

Hannah Warning: *New Bedford Sunday Times,* Dec. 13, 1931.

Town collapse: TM XII:209, 216.

Uplands property: 110 & 111 Main Street, Sandwich Historical Commission files of assets No. 215 & No. 188 resp.

Farm Operation: Sandwich Town Report 1910, pp. 53-5, 58; *Cape Cod Magazine,* May 1915; *Independent,* May 4, 1911.

Bert Tomlinson: Notes at Archives on his visit to Sandwich, May 25, 1978; Letters from him Apr. 8, June 5, 12, July 13, 1978 to Archives.

Lawrence B. Boston: *Cape Cod Magazine,* June-Nov. 1915.

Closing out the Farm: Letter from Trustee Fletcher Clark to David Crowell of Dennis, Jan. 1916, copy at Archives; Booklet, "A History of Sixty Years of Cooperative Extension Service in Massachusetts," Amherst, 1971, p. 15.

Cranberries: TM VIII: 3-5 (1889); *Observer,* May 8, 1884; Keene, cited, 87; Burrows, "Cannonballs & Cranberries," cited, 55-91; Collection of documents on Cape Cod Cranberry Growers' Association, at Archives, 1886-1893, collected by I. T. Jones, Secretary; *Cape Cod Times,* May 22, 1977; Bulletin No. 201, "The Cranberry Industry in Massachusetts," Dept. of Agriculture, Boston, June 1968.

Dairies 1870: *Nason Gazeteer,* cited, p. 72.

Cape Cod Farm Bureau: TM XI: 183, 242, 293, 350; *Cape Cod Times,* May 25, 1981; packet of original records of 1916-1966, at Sandwich Archives.

Tractors: *Cape Cod Magazine,* May 1915.

Farms in 1910 & 1920: Booklet, "Population and Resources of Cape Cod, " Dept. of Labor & Industry, Boston, 1922.

Veg.-Acres: *Cape Cod Business Journal,* May 1984; *The Village Broadsider,* Aug. 11, 1982, Jan. 12, 1983; *Cape Cod Times,* Feb. 6, 1983.

Crow Farm: *Cape Cod Business Journal,* June 1983.

Chapter 32: The U.S. Army Corps of Engineers' Canal

Federal Plans: Reid, cited, 104-112; Final Environmental Statement, Cape Cod Canal, Bourne and Sandwich, Mass., U.S. Army Corps of Engineers, Waltham, Mass., Apr. 1977.

Property taking: *Cape Cod News,* Nov. 27, 1935, March 25, 1936.

Dredging south bank: Photo p. 8, "Cape Cod in the Sun," Samuel Chamberlain, New York 1937; *Cape Cod News,* September 8, 1937.

Keith Car: *Cape Cod News,* Nov. 27, 1935; *Independent,* Sept. 18, 1929 on dissolution; Notes on talk with Warner Eldredge May 5 & June 10, 1983, about gravel fill for the Keith expansion before the first canal was built.

Bournedale: *Cape Cod News,* Nov. 18, 1936; *The Morning Mercury,* New Bedford, June 22, 1935.

Highway bridges: *Boston Globe Magazine,* June 16, 1985.

Allan S. Beale 1887-1980: MIT 1913; resident 8 Summer St., Sandwich; *Broadsider,* July 2, 1980; *Cape Cod Times,* Oct. 9, 1976; see large sheet of 32 early construction photos, copyright 1934, Allan Beale, printed by Spaulding Moss Co., Boston.

Edgar Caron: resident 9 Harbor St., Sandwich; founder Caron Electric Co.

Opening events June 22, 1935: Official Program, Opening Cape Cod Canal Bridges, 26 pp.; Book, "The Official Old Home Week and Canal Bridge Dedication Book, Cape Cod," Ed. by Harry B. Ivers, Boston, 1935, 72 pp.

Railway Bridge: *Cape Cod News,* Sept. 2, 1936, Jan. 1, 1936; *The Morning Mercury,* New Bedford, June 22, 1935; Folder, "Bridges of the Cape Cod Canal," by the U.S. Army Corps of Engineers.

Eugene Klapp: resident 23 Water St., Sandwich; *Cape Cod News,* May 18, 1938.

New rail line: *Cape Cod News,* Jan. 15, 1936.

Colonel Henry P. Dunbar: owner of colonial house at 1 Water St., Sandwich; Associate Engineer, Cape Cod Canal widening.

Buzzards Bay channel work: Reid, cited, 110-111; Farson, cited, plate 160.

Sandwich Coast Guard Station: notes and photos, Donald R. Small, Mar. 29, 1980; talk with Bernard Brady, May 12, *1981; Cape Cod News,* Mar. 4, Nov. 4, 1936, Sept. 22, 1937.

Harbor of Refuge: *Cape Cod News,* Apr. 17, Aug. 21, 1935, Sept. 8, 1937, July 27, 1938; Harbor of Refuge was not part of the original widening plans of the Corps, but was added in 1935. In 1979 the consultants for revising the bunding and harbor design, Tibbetts Engineering Corp., 210 Deane St., New Bedford, 02746, contacted the Sandwich Historical Commission to see if early plans in this sector were preserved in Sandwich, as they could not be located in the original Corps of Engineers records available to Tibbets describing the 1935 plans in this sector.

Scusset Marsh Dikes and Harbor: *Cape Cod News,* Sept. 8, 1937; notes on talk with Warner Eldredge of Sagamore, Oct. 15, 1982, May 5, June 11, 1983; Mr. Eldredge stated that the coast from the Sandwich breakwater up to Ellisville, was freely used 1920-1932 by rum-runners, who could enter Scusset Harbor and off-load on Sagamore hill; Scusset Harbor was open through 1932, at least.

Belmont Feldspar Boulder: Belmont, Eleanor R., "Fabric of Memory," cited, 125-6; notes on talks with Benjamin S. Harrison on the discovery and preservation of the boulder; Reid, cited, 120.

World War II Traffic: Notes on talks with Donald R. Small of Sagamore, a pilot; *Cape Cod Standard Times,* Mar. 30, 1969; U.S. Coast Guard undertook wartime control of traffic July 1, 1942; Reid, cited, 113-117; Farson, cited, 68-70.

Sagamore Hill Camp & Two Gun Mounts: Original camp photographs provided by Rangers; Notes by Archives July 24, 1981; Notes on talks with Bill Norman, Chief Ranger, June 29, Aug. 3, 1983; Talk with Donald R. Small, Sept. 16, 1981; Farson, cited, plates 141, 142.

Scorton Neck Camp and wood swing bridges: Barbara L. Gill, Sandwich, from personal recollections; no photographs have yet been located.

Mid-Cape Highway to Route 130: A Soil Conservation Office Hyannis map dated Fall 1938, shows one lane of the Mid-Cape completed from the Bridge to Route 130.

F. W. Schumacher: Notes on talk by Mr. Schumacher Feb. 8, 1973; *Cape Cod Times,* Mar. 20, 1986, *Cape Cod Independent,* Feb. 28, 1973; *Masthead,* 36 Spring Hill Rd., in Sandwich Historical Commission Inventory of assets, No. 59.

Sagamore lock plan: Reid, cited, pp. 105-6, 108-9; Farson, cited, 65-7.

Tidal slosh: Design by Sandwich Archives, based on published tide schedules for the canal, with times of current change.

Buzzards Bay Tides: Annual tide schedule booklets published by the U.S. Army Corps of Engineers warn of wide variation in the time of low tide with respect to successive highs, and in the pattern of the fall of the water level to and from low, caused by shallow water and baffle effects of surrounding bays with wind and other factors.

Canal Electric water use: Draft Environmental Statement, addition of Unit No. 2, Cape Cod Canal Plant, U.S. Army Corps of Engineers, Waltham, Mass. 1973, including a Dept. of Natural Resources Report of March 13, 1971, "An Assessment of the Effects of Electrical Generation on Marine Resources in The Cape Cod Canal," by Fairbanks, Collings, and Sides.

Sewage Study: Draft Environmental Impact Statement, Environmental Protective Agency, Boston, 02203, "Waste Water Collection and Treatment Facilities, Sandwich, Mass.," Sept. 1981; includes water volumes in the Canal and in each tidal cycle.

Sediment study: "Shoreline Processes in the Vicinity of the Eastern Entrance to the Cape Cod Canal," by Provincetown Center for Coastal Studies, Sept. 1980.

Sandwich Marina: Historical Commission Asset file No. 578, showing successive enlargements and plans.

Mass. Maritime Academy: *Cape Cod Independent,* Mar. 27, June 26, 1974, Nov. 25, 1980; letter from MMA to Archives 17 July 1981; historical references to naval school for Mass. boys from *Yarmouth Register,* May 5, 1854, May 29, 1857, Feb. 28, Aug. 1, 1862, Sept. 22, 1871; *Sandwich Observer,* Dec. 6, 1892, Apr. 9, 1895, etc.

Chapter 33: Thornton W. Burgess

Peter Rabbit quote: Kelley, Stanley, "About Cape Cod," cited, 62.

Genealogy: Burgess, Rev. Ebenezer, "Thomas & Dorothy Burgess," cited; Lovell, "Cape Cod Story," cited, pp. 33-4, 44-5, 50-1; Obituary, *New York*

Times, June 7, 1965; *Independent,* Mar. 14, 1902 (Quinnell-Tobey).

Arabella Eldred Burgess: Deyo, cited, 305; Crosby, Katherine, "Blue-Water Men and Other Cape Codders," New York, 1946, 25-31; interviews with Miss Kathryn Bourne, Miss Nellie Atwood, Willard E. Boyden, and Miss Ella Hoxie, old residents of Sandwich.

Early Life: School records in Town Report, 1891; Class of 1891 graduation program; Burgess, "Now I Remember, " cited, 13-48; *Boston Gazette,* Sept. 6, 1885 on William Chipman's Pond Lillies; the 10 houses he & his mother lived in 1874-1892 were listed by Mrs. Carrie Boyden for Mrs. Mildred Cahoon.

Boston Period: "Now I Remember," cited, 48-70.

Early Career: *Independent,* Aug. 19, 1915, May 28, Nov. 12, 1919, July 21, 1920, Oct. 19, 1921, Nov. 29, 1922, May 2, 9, 1923, Sept. 12, 19, 1923, June 11, 1924, Nov. 27, 1929, Oct. 15, 1930, Apr. 8, 1931; *Cape Cod Magazine,* Aug. 15, 1927, article by Lavinia D. Walsh; Burgess, T.W. in *American Magazine,* May 1919, "The Gold Mine I Discovered When I was 35"; "Now I Remember," pp. 71-139.

Harrison Cady: *Gloucester Times,* Dec. 1970, John L. Cooley of Rockport.

Natural History Magazine: Copy of 1922 article, "Nature as a Universal Teacher," at T.W. Burgess Museum, Sandwich.

Radio Nature League: Description by W. Gordon Swan, announcer for the programs, resident of Sandwich from 1960; *Independent,* Jan. 28, 1925; "Now I Remember," 141-148.

Bibliography: Wright, Wayne D., "Burgess Bibliography," cited.

Alice Rebecca Cooke: "Now I Remember," cited, 242-250; home at 238 Route 6A, Spring Hill, Sandwich, Sandwich Historical Commission inventory.

Q.A. Shaw connection: Mrs. Eleanor Conant Yaeger of Falmouth, a cousin of Alice and life-long friend.

Woodshed Nightclub: *Nature Magazine,* Oct. 1948, article by Lucy Furman, "The Woodhouse Night Club."

Photographs of Abigail Cooke: several at Sandwich Historical Society.

Sandwich Library: "A History of The Sandwich Public Library," by Nancy Elizabeth Steves, Sandwich, 1969, showing service by Alice Cooke, and gifts of Burgess books.

Minnie Cooke: Newspaper references in 1870's & 1880's to her studio in Sandwich; several stereoptican views survive; photographs of the Cookes held by Mrs. John Little of Sandwich, a relative.

Mrs. Charles Cheney, Mrs. Ralph Freeman, Mr. & Mrs. Clarence Cahoon, neighbors and friends of Alice and of Burgess: interviews in 1973 for

Lovell book, "Cape Cod Story of Thornton W. Burgess," cited.

Cedarville Cemetery: Inventory Conant-Cooke lot, Sandwich Historical Commission.

End of the night club: Fran Blake article, *Boston Sunday Globe,* Mar. 16, 1952, "Meet Thornton Burgess' Lovable Aunt Sally."

Onset Picnic: Lovell, cited, p. 40, photo from Miriam I. Walsh.

High School reunions: *Cape Cod Standard Times,* Nov. 20, 1949.

1939 town event: Files and program at Archives, including text of Burgess remarks; set of 45 town photographs of events.

Lillian Haynes Tangney 1873-1970: classmate and lifetime friend; a collection of her TWB memorabilia given to the TWB Society through her niece Mrs. Joan Morrow.

1951 School Celebration: Photographs, *Broadsider,* June 4, 1980; interview with Miss Vema Consolini, a teacher.

Burgess Memorial Park Project: Discussion with participants, 1973: plan of Thornton W. Burgess Park, Town of Sandwich, Feb. 19, 1951; file of correspondence and clippings, Board of Trade, 1950 & 1951; letter from Harrison Cady to Mrs. Edith Deering, April 21, 1951 on a memorial design.

Glass Museum: Photographs and gifts from TWB, including manuscript of "Aunt Sally's Friends in Fur," and painting of Aunt Sally and Crip.

1950 events and Tobago Trips: "Now I Remember"; correspondence between TWB & Lillian H. Tangney, Miriam Walsh, and Herb Saltford preserved at TWB Society, Sandwich.

Art & Belle Saltford: article in *Yankee Magazine,* June 1973 by Herb Saltford, "A Man, His Dream and a Happy Ending"; extensive correspondence between TWB and the Saltfords, copies at Archives.

15,000th story: *Cape Cod Standard Times,* Feb. 27, 1960; *Life Magazine,* Nov. 14, 1960, Paul O'Neil, "Fifty Years in the Green Meadows."

"Now I Remember" and anniversary edition of "Old Mother West Wind": Reception by Little Brown, *Boston Globe,* Oct. 2, 1960.

Lifetime Collection of Papers: "Now I Remember," cited, and Mrs. Ernestine Johnson; see page 510 - collection and film destroyed shortly after his death.

Thornton W. Burgess III: Discussions with W. Gordon Swan and Miriam Walsh; letter from TWB to Cahoons, May 7, 1964.

Ernestine Johnson: Discussions in letters and talks; article by Louis Levine, *Reader's Digest,* Oct. 1967, "Unforgettable TWB."

Ten Year Trust: Correspondence by TWB Society with Bank officers and TWB grandchildren on material held in trust.

Hampden home & Mass. Audubon Society: Dorothy M. Fox article, "A Ninety Year Romance with Nature," in *Audubon Magazine,* Sept. 1964; the Society acquired 18 acres at Laughing Brook in 1966; article in *Worcester Sunday Telegram,* May 12, 1985; article in *Life Magazine,* Aug. 28, 1944, "Life Visits the Bed Time Story Man"; *Boston Sunday Globe,* Nov. 9, 1975.

Chapter 34: On Becoming Historic

Conservative vote: TM XI:452, 460 (1925) against a committee to solicit new business enterprises in Sandwich; resistance to commercial development is said to have been strong in Mr. Fletcher Clark, Mr. E. B. Howland, and other officers of the Sandwich Cooperative Bank.

Events described: files at the Archives and the Sandwich Historical Commission describe successive celebrations, enlargements, and changes in the 1939-1984 period.

Chapter 35: Sandwich Population and Families

Town Census, Sandwich and Bourne: Contained on worksheets listing individual families, at the Archives office, based on Federal Census from 1790 on, and consistent with the genealogy of the various families from Sandwich Vital Records, town meeting records, and published genealogies.

Town Vital Records: Since the completion of the manuscript for "Sandwich A Cape Cod Town," in 1984, the author and Mrs. Caroline L. Kardell of the Massachusetts Society of Mayflower Descendants have prepared a manuscript of the Sandwich Vital Records to 1885. The typescript, before indexing, is about 1,550 pages. Beside the contents of the Town Vital Records books, this manuscript also includes vital records from Plymouth Colony Records, from diaries, Bibles, church records, Quaker meeting records, newspapers and cemetery markers. Publication of this text is expected through the New England Historic Genealogical Society.

Cemeteries: Inventory of marker information in 18 burial areas is contained in the files and index cards of the Historical Commission.

www.ingramcontent.com/pod-product-compliance
Lightning Source LLC
Chambersburg PA
CBHW020415010526
44118CB00010B/256

* 9 7 8 0 9 9 6 7 0 2 3 0 0 *